JEWISH LEARNING IN
AMERICAN UNIVERSITIES

The Modern Jewish Experience

Paula Hyman and Deborah Dash Moore, editors

JEWISH LEARNING IN AMERICAN UNIVERSITIES

The First Century

PAUL RITTERBAND

AND HAROLD S. WECHSLER

INDIANA UNIVERSITY PRESS

Bloomington and Indianapolis

The authors and the publisher gratefully
acknowledge the generous financial support
of the Lucius N. Littauer Foundation.

© 1994 by Paul Ritterband and Harold S. Wechsler

The paper used in this publication meets the minimum requirements of
American National Standard for Information Sciences—Permanence of
Paper for Printed Library Materials, ANSI Z39.48-1984.
Manufactured in the United States of America

Library of Congress Cataloging-in-Publication Data
Ritterband, Paul.
Jewish learning in American universities : the first century /
Paul Ritterband and Harold S. Wechsler.
p.   cm.—(Modern Jewish experience)
Includes bibliographical references and index.
ISBN 0-253-35039-5
1. Judaism—Study and teaching (Higher)—United States—History.
2. Jews—History—Study and teaching (Higher)—United States.
3. Universities and colleges—United States—Departments—History.
4. Jews—United States—Intellectual life.   I. Wechsler, Harold S.,
date / . II. Title.   III. Series: Modern Jewish experience
(Bloomington, Ind.)
BM75.R57   1994
909'.04924'0071173—dc20   93-48233
1 2 3 4 5 00 99 98 97 96 95 94

Paul Ritterband dedicates this book to
Oren S. Ritterband.

Harold Wechsler dedicates this book to
Lynn D. Gordon.

CONTENTS

PREFACE

The scholarly field of Jewish learning examines a people, its history and way of life, and its religious, esoteric, and popular literature. This book examines the nineteenth-century incorporation of Jewish learning into American universities and the field's growth in the twentieth century.

Jews continually cherished and studied the texts that guided their lives, but traditional European Judaism looked askance at secular studies, save perhaps for medicine. Medieval and early modern European universities usually suppressed Jewish learning; even when university scholars elicited Judaic information or concepts from learned Jews, they did not invite Jews within ivy walls. Jews who contemplated university attendance, despite the prohibitions, faced nearly insurmountable restrictions until the late eighteenth century, when access accompanied political emancipation. Even then, informal barriers—especially the conduct of student social life—remained widespread, and faculty appointments were rare.

Wissenschaft des Judentums, the post-emancipation movement among European Jews to promote the rational, scientific, and critical study of Jewish experience and beliefs, made Jewish learning congruent with university-based moves toward the scientific study of religion and with the norms of those institutions. But the Christian belief that Jewish learning became anachronistic after Christ combined with pervasive academic anti-Semitism to deny the field a place in the university pantheon. Traditional Jewish learning remained confined to *yeshivot*; *Wissenschaft des Judentums* was institutionalized, if at all, at rabbinical seminaries founded in the nineteenth century.

Apart from the *yeshivot* and seminaries, Jewish learning found its first academic home not in Europe but in nineteenth-century America, a nation with relatively small Jewish communities and fledgling universities. Colonial and antebellum American colleges accommodated an occasional Jewish student, but denominational identification—most colleges compelled chapel attendance and New Testament studies, for example—made these colleges unattractive to Jews even when, occasionally, they offered Hebrew instruction. Toward the end of the nineteenth century, in contrast, Jewish economic and political integration accompanied heightened interest in American higher education. Reform Jews, especially, viewed "secularizing" universities, which included growing graduate and professional divisions, as vehicles for educational, cultural, and social advancement, acceptance, and recognition, not as hostile, Gentile-dominated bastions.

Six American universities—California, Chicago, Columbia, Harvard, Johns Hopkins, and Pennsylvania—reciprocated Jewish communal interest by including Jewish learning among their offerings. Weakened ties between these universities and Protestant denominations provided latitude for Judaica appointments; the changing social, intellectual, and institutional scene provided the occasion. Key university presidents—William Rainey Harper at the University of Chicago, Daniel Coit Gilman at Johns Hopkins, and Charles William Eliot at Harvard— believed that Jewish learning could significantly help counter the threat posed by European higher criticism to Biblical scholarship and reconcile seemingly an- tithetical scientific and religious outlooks. Jewish learning, these presidents also believed, might bring added recognition to their institutions and permit them to tap into the increased prosperity of American Jewry for financial, moral, and political support.[1]

The appearance of Jewish learning at the university brought attention and recognition to practitioners and to American Jews. But incorporation also sub- jected Jewish learning to potentially hazardous academic norms, including ex- ternal validation, that is, critical scrutiny of Judaism by Jewish and non-Jewish peers. Traditionalists asked whether Gentiles, usually Christocentric if not preju- diced, could render fair academic judgments on Jewish learning and even whether *Jewish* scholars could, or should, exercise the same objectivity about Ju- daica exhibited by, say, chemists about chemistry. Did not the closeness of Jew- ish learning to the Jewish essence make universities, as opposed to seminaries or *yeshivot*, inappropriate scholarly settings?

Supporters of university-based Jewish learning considered these "problems" remote, the benefits immediate. Some proponents offered to underwrite appro- priate chairs; others responded to institutional invitations. Late nineteenth- century American justifications for these initiatives exhibited a universalist—an outward, inclusionist, even assimilationist—orientation associated with Reform Judaism. Reform Jews, by then, viewed America as their permanent home—the majority repudiated the nascent Zionist movement—and urged maximum Jewish-Gentile personal, religious, and intellectual commingling to assure comity. Universalism, traditionalists argued, might lead to abandonment of Ju- daism, but Reform Jews emphasized prophetic, as opposed to *halakhic* (law- based) Judaism and noted that apostasy seldom occurred. Recognition of the centrality of Jewish knowledge and scholarship for Western thought, Reform Jews added, might hasten Gentile acceptance of American Jewry.[2]

American Reform Jews, contrasting the failure of *Wissenschaft des Judentums* to produce a Jewish presence on continental university faculties with the recep- tivity of American college presidents, hastened to subsidize the Hebraic aspects of Jewish learning within graduate-level Semitics departments—at least 16 Jews taught Semitics in universities at the turn of the century.[3] This subfield—Hebrew was the propaedeutic language for the Semitic language family—resonated with contemporary Gentile intellectual concerns, including philology, archaeology, and textual translation and interpretation.[4] Semitics thus helped legitimize the Jewish and Judaic presence—a smattering of Jews had also appeared in other uni- versity departments—when religion could still disqualify a candidate for an aca- demic post.[5]

Heightened American anti-Semitism followed the mass of Jewish migrations at century's end, thereby threatening the tentative embrace of Jews and higher education. Administrators, reasserting collegiate life and social criteria for leadership, often considered Jews an "undesirable" constituency and implemented covert admissions restrictions at colleges hitherto viewed as open to all meritorious candidates, a practice that deeply scarred American Jewry. Segregation of Jewish and Gentile campus life led Jewish students to establish their own fraternities and sororities, a recognition of second-class status. Jewish academics, faring little better than the students, experienced singular difficulty in obtaining humanities appointments. Semitics posts were no exception—campus anti-Semitism, coming on the heels of waning communal and institutional interest in philological scholarship, doomed any chance for a replacement generation.[6]

As anti-Semitism increased in the 1920s and 1930s, cultural pluralism—advocacy of full participation in the political, social, economic, and educational institutions of the dominant culture, balanced by maintaining the integrity of Judaism when cultural differences existed—replaced Reform's universalism, assimilation, and anti-Zionism as the dominant Jewish response to the majority culture. Advocates of university-based Jewish learning adapted this pluralism by arguing that other aspects of that field surpassed the ability of Semitics to contribute simultaneously to Jewish learning and to disciplinary and other external agendas. Between the wars, universities added Jewish history, a field that spoke to multiple agendas, and modern Hebrew language and literature—the vernacular of Palestinian Jews— a field that shared problems confronted by other modern languages.[7]

Restrictions on Jewish student admissions and faculty appointments persisted in some colleges until the 1970s, but a strengthened public higher education system, renewed emphasis on scholarship, enactment of anti-discrimination legislation in the 1940s, and increased competition for competent faculty offset much remaining prejudice. Waning Greek society influence in the 1960s reduced concern with fraternity and sorority discrimination. By the 1980s, Columbia and Princeton, two institutions that earlier exhibited anti-Semitism, had their first Jewish presidents; Yale would have joined the pantheon, but its invitee declined the honor.

The considerable growth in Jewish collegiate enrollment during the 1950s and 1960s, foreshadowed in New York and other cities before World War II, led to the expansion of Jewish learning into enrollment-driven regional universities. Enrollment expansion implied a shift from a graduate to an undergraduate orientation, a viable alternative to growth based upon philanthropy or presidential largesse. But this strategy raised new issues for the field. Practitioners, for example, debated whether university-based Jewish learning could or should maintain the Jewish identity of undergraduate students as well as the efficacy of the social sciences and other areas of Jewish learning in maintaining identity. Bible study, Yiddish, and religion attained supporting curricular roles, the last of these fields gaining prominence especially after the 1963 Schempp Supreme Court decision, which permitted public institutions to teach *about* religion.

Earlier advocates of university-based Jewish learning sought university recognition of commonality, but successors increasingly sought legitimation of difference. Post-war practitioners, more often Conservative and Orthodox Jews, gravitated from pluralism toward particularism, a predominant concern with Jewish learning over disciplinary agendas, and said little about "recognition." The 1967 Six Day War and the rise of ethnic studies movements at American colleges and universities assured a hearing, and faculty appointments, for particularists. Particularism, indeed, may dominate Jewish learning and other academic fields in the (post-)modern university, but the continued presence of universalists and pluralists assures continued debate on the field's aims.[8]

Throughout the nineteenth and twentieth centuries, Jewish practitioners and interested community members often united to urge the field's presence in universities, but tension between academy and community distinguished university-based Jewish scholarship from seminaries, Hebrew teachers colleges, and *yeshivot*. Community members might urge a student of Jewish crime, for example, to choose another topic, lest the results provide anti-Semites with ammunition—the "What will the Gentiles say?" syndrome. Scholars might, in turn, criticize communal critics for trying to orchestrate a self-serving portrait.

Adherence to different norms meant that conflicts could appear even when academics and community members shared a universalist, pluralist, or particularist outlook. Scholars, for example, might emphasize generating new knowledge over disseminating extant knowledge. Jewish learning subsumed both possibilities, but the community often questioned the time invested in a marginal scholarly discovery—especially if the discovery primarily benefited a parent discipline—when the world, including many Jews, knew little about essentials.

University-based practitioners of Jewish learning offered varied solutions to conflicting academic and communal demands. Pennsylvania's Morris Jastrow (appointed 1886), finding that allegiance to philology took him outside the pale of Jewish learning, had the term "rabbinics" deleted from the title of his professorship, and he and other practitioners lost communal support by emphasizing disciplinary agendas. Max Margolis, a prolific scholar, reversed this priority by leaving the University of California (where he had been from 1898 to 1905) for an identifiably Jewish institution. Prominent rabbis who also held part-time university appointments—first-generation examples included Max Heller (Tulane), Emil G. Hirsch (the University of Chicago), Abram Isaacs (New York University), William Rosenau (Johns Hopkins), Jacob Voorsanger (the University of California)—emphasized knowledge dissemination over generation, partly out of volition, and partly because their rabbinical duties precluded the major investment of time required by original scholarship. Some Judaica practitioners sacrificed their teaching and scholarship to direct communal service. Many Judaica scholars, caught between conflicting academic and communal demands, faced a conundrum: Those, like Jastrow, who *could* produce Jewish scholarship often *would* not; those, like Hirsch, who *would*, often *could* not.

In writing the history of Jewish learning in American universities, we undertook archival research, analyzed polemical literature about Jewish learning and its subfields, and conducted statistical studies. The archival record, primarily examined in the first seven chapters, allowed us to delineate the field's inclusion and early development, the relationship of practitioners to concerned constituencies, and patterns of resolution when academy and community exerted conflicting demands. Since these pulls endure, archival materials speak to practitioners and community members concerned with understanding the field's current status.

Practitioners of Jewish learning gained academic entrance by defining academic relationships with potentially hospitable parent disciplines, themselves at times seeking a departmental niche, since stand-alone "Jewish studies" departments appeared only at the end of a century of university inclusion (1870–1970). Chapters 1 through 3 detail the history of Judaica in Semitics departments, the field's first home. Later chapters show how the process was repeated, successfully or not, in other fields. "Success" required a Judaica field to contribute to a parent discipline while maintaining internal coherence. Differential success resulted in part from congruence with changing rationales for inclusion, from a universalism characterizing the late nineteenth century, through a pluralism straddling World War II, and finally to a particularism congruent with the dominant post-1968 academic outlook.

Chapter 1 discusses the effects of European and American academic history on the late nineteenth-century appearance of Jewish learning in American universities. The second chapter examines the motives of university presidents and the interested Jewish community, especially the theme of "recognition," for establishing Judaica positions. The chapter also demonstrates that Judaica appeared in relation to Semitics, rather than Bible or Talmud studies, because of congruence between the agendas of practitioners and the "parent" discipline. Chapter 3 discusses the early practitioners, their adopted and mandated agendas, and their strategies for resolving conflicting academic and communal expectations. Chapter 4 examines the "price of admission" that the field and its practitioners might pay for academic inclusion. A loss of Judaic focus within a weakened parent discipline helps to explain why Judaic Semitics failed to institutionalize itself permanently despite the enthusiasm of the 1880s and 1890s. On the other hand, the field's advocates subsequently contended with the precedents set by the encounter between Jewish learning and Semitics.

The 1910s and 1920s were decades of much discussion, dominated by the Intercollegiate Menorah Association founded at Harvard in 1906, but there was little action. Harvard's Harry Wolfson was the exception, a second generation Judaica scholar who taught in a marginalized Semitics department at a university whose president was hostile to everything Jewish. Chapter 5 describes how Wolfson agonized over his academic fate and over Jewish philosophy, the field he wished to introduce into the university curriculum. Communal intervention, not Harvard's recognition of the significance of Jewish philosophy, saved Wolfson's career at Harvard—an indicator of the subject's failure to become a key component of the Judaica curriculum at universities.

Chapter 6 examines alternatives for Judaica scholars who would not, or could not, opt for universities, and asks why universities failed to nurture key pre-1950 Judaica projects. We note the criticism of seminaries—Hebrew Union College and the Jewish Institute of Religion (Reform), the Jewish Theological Seminary of America (Conservative), and Yeshiva University (Orthodox)—as centers of scholarship. Their profession of Judaism, critics believed, compromised their *study* of Judaism. The growth of Jewish learning, university advocates argued, had to await renewed academic receptivity.

Between the world wars, a single scholar could personify each Judaica subfield in American universities. Salo Baron's 1929 appointment to the Columbia history department marked his identification with Jewish history in American universities. The appointment, detailed in chapter 7, marked the successful incorporation of a new field into the university-based Jewish learning pantheon, but it occurred only after a lengthy search, a unique circumstance among early Judaica appointments. Columbia, brokering between academic and communal forces and candidates, took nearly two years to make an appointment that in retrospect appeared "propitious." In placing the academic introduction of another Judaica subfield ahead of the donor's request that the chair help "reach" the spiritual side of undergraduate students, the university helped to determine the future direction of Jewish learning.

Chapters 8 and 9 note the changing rationales for Jewish learning, especially the implications of reliance on an undergraduate constituency. The number and distribution of practitioners, and the uneven availability of archival materials, led us to change research strategies.[9] Chapter 8, which analyzes the subfields of Jewish learning that were considered for academic incorporation between the 1940s and the 1960s, is based on the "self-assessment" literature produced by practitioners and concerned observers and on course descriptions in catalogues. Articles summarizing the field's status, or assessing the strength of the subfields, often appeared at major turning points, and they varied in tone from the eulogistic and laudatory to the trenchantly critical. Some assessments reflected a scholarly consensus, others attempted to affect the course of events. Chapter 8 examines Bible studies, modern Hebrew, Yiddish, religion, and history, fields that gained an academic niche, as well as philosophy and social sciences, which failed to attract many undergraduates before 1970. Successful incorporation continued to require congruence with a parent field, but the "pluralist" rationales employed had to balance deftly the needs of both parent discipline and Judaica under the changing conditions experienced by American higher education after World War II.

Chapter 9, based upon college catalogues, university and disciplinary association reports, and government publications, documents changes in the field and assesses its status at the time of the founding of the Association for Jewish Studies (1969). The late 1960s, not coincidentally, mark the first time that university-based Jewish learning was found in separate departments, where the need to relate, even integrate, Judaica subfields outweighed the need to establish a relationship to a parent discipline.

A note on terminology: Jacob Neusner, a major contributor to the current discussion about the problematics of Jewish learning in university settings, defined the field as "the systematic study of the beliefs, actions, and literary and cultural products of all persons who have been called, or have called themselves 'Jews.'"He subdivided Jewish learning into Torah (traditional, religiously motivated study based on Talmud and cognate studies, less frequently found in the university setting), Hebraica (the study of the Hebrew language), and Judaica (the study of Jews as a group and of the history and theology, law and practices of Judaism). Within "Judaica," he differentiated between Judaism and Judaic, that is, pertaining to Judaism as a religion, and the Jew and Jewish, the culture and social organization of a distinct historical group.[10] We employ these categories in our narrative, but we also note variations in the terminology used by earlier practitioners.[11]

Jewish Learning in American Universities thus describes the effect of Judaica scholars, their subjects, and the concerned community on American universities, and the effect of American academic life on practitioners and on American Jewry. The field tempered the Christian orientation of universities, especially the Christological focus of humanities departments, while strengthening the Jewish role in American higher education. Judaica academics and concerned Jewish community members tried to force host Gentile university authorities to adhere to professed norms of merit and objectivity, even when they were inconvenient or conflicted with other goals. Indeed, forcing adherence to professed norms by Americans and their institutions became a key strategy for Jewish accommodation to American academic life.

American universities, by using the same criteria to judge the work of Judaica practitioners and other subjects and by legitimating the field for Gentiles as well as Jews, attempted to separate devotion from scholarship (a movement contemplated only later at the seminaries), and to shape a research and curricular agenda congruent with "parent" disciplines, not around Jewish books or modes of internal organization. Judaica's universal-plural-particular trajectory resembles Peter Novick's delineation of the evolution of the historical profession. Chapter 8 notes similarities between Jewish learning and other fields of knowledge that might benefit a constituency while making an academic contribution, older and rival fields, new constituencies, and research-teaching conflicts.[12]

To what extent can we generalize from this study about the Jewish encounter with American higher education and perhaps even with America itself? The academic experiences of Jews and Jewish learning are synergistic. From the outset, the presence of Jewish faculty members and students facilitated the growth of Jewish learning, while practitioners of Jewish learning became involved in general issues of academic and social policy involving Jews. Harry Wolfson served, for example, on a Harvard committee that debated restricting admission of Jewish students. As American higher education became an arena where majorities and minorities competed for status and rewards, a broader spectrum of the Jewish community took an interest in university-based Jewish learning.

"Survival" became the most urgent, and nearly inescapable, postwar communal concern as Jewish learning came to depend more on undergraduate enrollments and as a broader spectrum of Jewish students and faculty members entered Jewish learning programs. The enlarged constituency included many traditional Jews as well as others who viewed their Jewishness primarily as an ethnic identity—not as a "religion" that resembled other American creeds. Reduced anti-Semitism, commentators noted, accelerated an alarming assimilation—manifested in apostasy, intermarriage, or indifference—into a more benign American environment. Many post-1968 advocates of Jewish learning said little about recognition or acceptance, except insofar as it promoted Jewish survival.

We have tried to maintain the conceptual independence of the "universal-plural-particular," and "academy-community" themes. Just as some early universalists had extensive communal agendas, some contemporary particularists adhered to academic norms and participated in few communal activities. But Jewish learning also displayed a characteristic that can blur these thematic distinctions. University-based Judaica scholars, as traditionalists note, scrutinized material that was also an essential part of their belief systems. Some practitioners who inextricably associated scholarship with belief replaced the synagogue with the library as the primary setting for expressing their Judaism.[13] In exalting human reason over the supernatural and over worldly withdrawal, many Judaica scholars endorsed a major tenet of Judaism. But this association of faith and intellect militates against conceptual clarity. With these caveats, we begin our history of university-based Jewish learning in America.

ACKNOWLEDGMENTS

The collaboration on this book began when Walter Metzger arranged a meeting between the future authors, who quickly discovered a fortuitous match of interests and abilities. Ritterband, an ordained rabbi, holds a doctorate in, and teaches, sociology. Wechsler's doctorate and scholarship are in American history, especially the history of American higher education. Collaborations, especially those that span more than a few years, become difficult to disentangle when it comes time to attribute responsibility for a finished book. Suffice it to say that the authors extensively discussed the book's thematics and that the book is the result of an egalitarian collaboration.

Walter Metzger remained the project's guardian angel throughout its history. Without his intellectual and personal support, the manuscript would never have seen the light of day.

This manuscript relies on materials provided by the archivists at the American Jewish Archives (Jacob Rader Marcus, Stanley Chyet, and Abraham Peck), the American Jewish Historical Society (Nathan Kaganof and Bernard Wax), Brandeis University, the University of California (J. R. K. Kantor), the Central Zionist Archives, Jerusalem, Columbia University (Marion E. Jemmott and Sara Vos), Harvard University (Clark Eliot and Harley Holden), the Jewish Theological Seminary of America (Menachem Smelser), Johns Hopkins University, the Museum Archives of the University of Pennsylvania, New York University (Bayard Still), Stanford University (Peggy Cosfeld), Temple University (Marian Crawford), the University of Chicago (Michael Ryan, Albert Tannler, and Richard Popp), the University of Pennsylvania (Francis James Dallett), the Western Jewish History Center of the Judah Magnes Memorial Museum (Ruth Rafael), Yale University (Judith Schiff), and the Zionist Archives, New York City. During his many visits to the American Jewish Archives in Cincinnati, Wechsler received extraordinary assistance from Fannie Zelcer.

We received financial support from the American Council of Learned Societies, the Bernard Rapoport Fellowship Program of the American Jewish Archives, the National Foundation for Jewish Culture, the Spencer Fellowship Program of the National Academy of Education, the Fellowship Division of the National Endowment for the Humanities, the Ossabaw Island Project, the City University of New York Professional Staff Congress Faculty Awards Program, and the Social Science Research Committee of The University of Chicago.

Many friends and colleagues, including Emanuel Goldsmith, Edward Greenstein, Marvin Herzog, Abraham Karp, Alan Mintz, Yochanan Muffs, Jacob Neusner, the late Marshall Sklare, and Bernard Sohmer, offered helpful suggestions after reading parts of the manuscript or after hearing our presentations. Jack Wertheimer extensively critiqued an earlier draft. Lynn D. Gordon uncovered relevant material and offered several comprehensive assessments of the manuscript. Her suggestions improved virtually every page. Jenna W. Joselit, Alfred Jospe, Benny Kraut, and Jacob Neusner shared their unpublished work with us. Elinor J. Grumet's important manuscript on the history of the Intercollegiate Menorah Association, "The Menorah Idea and the Apprenticeship of Lionel Trilling," informed our work. The Association for Jewish Studies accorded us many courtesies, including a forum for the presentation of our material and a list of association members. E. C. Ladd of the University of Connecticut permitted us to examine data from his biennial survey of American faculty members.

Statements of the book's major arguments have appeared elsewhere, and we acknowledge the permission of the original publishers to incorporate revised versions into this manuscript. Therese Chappell, Yvette Courtade, Dolores Ford, Margaret Halisy, and Martha Harris typed drafts of the manuscript; their silent editing prevented many errors. Sandra R. Ingram carefully checked many citations.

The breadth of knowledge and the enthusiasm of Deborah Dash Moore and Paula Hyman, our series editors, were crucial to the completion of the book. So was the faith and interest of Janet Rabinowitch of Indiana University Press. Melanie Richter-Bernburg's editing strengthened the book's content and style. Sheila Cummins's careful proofreading helped assure the integrity of the typeset text, and Catherine Fox brought intelligence and skill to the unenviable task of preparing the index.

Finally, we owe our greatest debts to our families, whose personal and intellectual advice, support, and caring made this book possible. The dedications reflect our love for—and the inspiration we received from—Lynn and Oren. Special thanks also to Abigail Wechsler, truly a father's joy, and to Samuel Wechsler, an all-star in any league.

JEWISH LEARNING IN
AMERICAN UNIVERSITIES

I

EUROPEAN BACKGROUND AND THE AMERICAN SETTING

European Background

"How does it happen . . . that at a time when magnificent, all-encompassing vistas have opened up, allowing all sciences and man's every endeavor to be illuminated by bright rays of light," asked Leopold Zunz, a young German Jewish intellectual, " . . . that our scholarship alone must languish?"[1] "Our scholarship" meant Jewish scholarship, which was absent from the flourishing German research universities.

Wissenschaft des Judentums—the movement for the scholarly study of Judaism and Jews, their history, and their literary manifestations—was "a new creation, representing a break with the old learning and demanding a fundamentally different method," argued Judaica scholar Ismar Elbogen in the early twentieth century. For two millennia, Jews had defined study as the supreme religious act, and those who studied were accorded the highest honors. "An ignoramus cannot be pious," declared the venerable Hillel.[2] But this traditional, *yeshivah*-based Jewish learning required, for the most part, no contextual studies, frequently considered secular knowledge inimical, and concentrated on understanding the details of Talmudic tractates in an ahistorical and noncritical manner. *Wissenschaft des Judentums*, in contrast, addressed the range of Jewish beliefs and behavior critically and historically. Attempts to juxtapose Torah and *wissenschaft*, Elbogen added, reflected an unjustified sentimentality.[3]

Zunz's "On Rabbinic Literature" (1818) was considered the manifesto of *Wissenschaft des Judentums*. The polemic identified objective impediments to the field's development—poor career opportunities, the greater attractiveness of other fields of study and other occupations, the need for extensive linguistic, literary, and historical education, and the unavailability of scholarly apparatus, including dictionaries and concordances. Zunz then added a subjective obstacle: "But it is due also to a coldness toward religion in general and to one's ancestral literature in particular; to the irrational fear that occupation with that literature might be considered disgraceful; and to a good-natured lack of thoroughness." Indifference and laxity, he added, also retarded the field. Some researchers failed

1

"to enter into the Hebrew spirit and to develop a sense of empathy with the author" of the texts they studied. Carelessness "led not infrequently to the destruction of some of the most significant works and robbed otherwise sober minds of the ability to judge the material under consideration without bias."[4]

Without sympathetic practitioners of *Wissenschaft des Judentums,* anti-Semites could exploit the resultant intellectual vacuum to their own ends. "Scholars would pick out some half-understood passages from this or that source so as to expose their age-old opponents to public scorn," Zunz noted. "And until about one hundred years ago, one could not find a single case of a learned doctor who might have culled from the writings of the Hebrews the beautiful and good they contain in order to present the Jews in a positive light."[5]

To overcome the damage, Zunz concluded, *Wissenschaft des Judentums* required empathetic, educated researchers—not enemies, dilettantes, or even rabbis preoccupied with practical concerns. He expected the *Verein für Kultur und Wissenschaft der Juden*—The Society for Culture and Scientific Study of the Jews—to fill this scholarly vacuum. The *Verein,* though it lasted only five years past its 1819 founding in Berlin by Zunz's group of young Jewish intellectuals, permanently expanded the definition of Jewish scholarship.

A thorough knowledge of traditional Judaism guarded *Verein* members against dilettantism. But Zunz and his colleagues would primarily contribute to, and benefit from, research in linguistics, history, and literary studies, and would conduct investigations with the same spirit and methods as other scholars—hopefully in the same university setting. The rise of German universities struck Zunz, no less than other Germans, as a singular cultural development. He emphasized literary studies as the "entrance gate" to understanding cultural development—how external and internal forces mold character: "how fate, climate, customs, religion, and chance interact in a friendly or hostile manner; and how, finally, the present emerges as the necessary result of all those phenomena interacting in the past."[6] But literary studies were only the entrance point: "Our scholarly efforts," Zunz added, "have to deal with many areas, each of which must be cultivated lest the whole be distorted due to fundamental errors."

Advocates thus perceived university inclusion of *Wissenschaft des Judentums* as an opportunity to end centuries of Judaic scholarly retrenchment and to replicate earlier intellectual exchanges between Jews and non-Jews. Beginning with Muslim rule in the tenth century, *Wissenschaft des Judentums* advocates knew, Jews simultaneously codified Jewish law and participated in the intellectual life of the Iberian peninsula.[7] Maimonides, for example, wrote the *Mishneh Torah,* his codification of the Talmud, while attempting to reconcile Aristotelian thought with Judaism in his *Guide for the Perplexed*. Maimonides precipitated a schism within the Jewish community on the relationship of Judaic to general knowledge, but the Jewish withdrawal from more universal discourse was more closely related to the Church's intensified anti-Jewish activities, which crested when the Christian reconquest of Iberia resulted in Jewish expulsion in 1492.

Dominicans, beginning in the thirteenth century, helped to suppress the Talmud—confiscated and burned in Paris (1244), Spain (1413–1414), and Germany

(1509–1520)—while simultaneously exhorting, even directing, universities to offer Hebrew, Aramaic, Arabic, and other Oriental languages. Dominican Raymond Lull's lobbying led to a decision from the Council of Vienna (1312) to promote instruction in languages "which the infidels chiefly use" so that missionaries "may come to know the infidels themselves, and be able to instruct them in sacred institutions, and add them to the company of worshipers of Christ by knowledge of the Christian faith and reception of baptism." Dominicans continued to study Hebrew in the following centuries, but Church persecution, expulsion, and forced conversion undermined efforts at obtaining voluntary conversion. For three centuries after 1492, Jewish scholarship continued its retreat from western intellectual life in favor of Talmudic and Kabbalistic studies in the southern and eastern European areas that still permitted Jewish settlement.[8]

Advocates of *Wissenschaft des Judentums* noted some exceptions to Jewish—and Judaic—withdrawal from European intellectual life.[9] In England and elsewhere, university towns housed separate but contiguous Jewish academies. David ben Abraham Provinciale, rabbi of Mantua, fearing a decline in Jewish religious studies in sixteenth-century Italy, proposed a Jewish university that included Jewish and secular subjects.[10]

Verein members recounted persistent Jewish interest in general scholarship to buttress their claims for university posts when restrictions on Jewish life in Europe diminished in the eighteenth and nineteenth centuries.[11] But they drew mixed lessons from the most notable instance of Judaic-Christian interaction between the Spanish expulsion and Jewish emancipation—when the need to understand the Bible and relevant commentaries led to a rise in Hebraism among sixteenth-century Protestants and to the introduction of Hebrew into many universities. Historian Jerome Friedman included Jewish scholarly cooperation among the prerequisites for the growth of Christian Hebraica, a list that also included the legitimation of the subject in the university curriculum, external subsidy, and availability of a Hebrew printing press under Christian auspices.[12]

The appearance of Greek in Renaissance universities, Friedman suggests, paved the way for Hebrew by expanding curricula beyond the trivium and quadrivium. Johannes Reuchlin's confrontation with the Jewish apostate Johannes Pfefferkorn called attention to the language. In 1509, Pfefferkorn obtained from the German emperor an order to confiscate and destroy all Hebrew books owned by the Jews of Frankfort and Cologne. Reuchlin (a non-Jew) delayed confiscation by arguing that most Hebrew books were irrelevant or indifferent to Christianity. The debate called attention to Reuchlin, his Hebraic scholarship, and its potential uses by the Church's supporters and foes—Martin Luther issued his ninety-five theses two years before Pope Leo ended 11 years of controversy by ruling for Pfefferkorn's Dominican supporters.[13] Royal supporters of the Reformation thereupon subsidized trilingual colleges, while the Venice printing house of Daniel Bomberg, a Christian, published over 200 Jewish books, including Hebrew grammatical works, a rabbinic Bible (1517–1518), and, with Pope Leo's permission, the Babylonian and Jerusalem Talmuds (1520–1523).

Jewish cooperation, Friedman concludes, was essential, since the few early six-teenth-century Christian Hebraists could neither fill the growing need of the universities for Hebrew scholars nor supply needed grammars or dictionaries.[14] Sympathetic Gentiles befriended Jews, who reciprocated by offering Hebraic in-struction. Obadiah Sforno and Elias del Medigo taught Hebrew and Kabbalah to Reuchlin and Pico, respectively. Elias Levita taught Sebastian Munster and Paul Fagius, who introduced Hebrew studies to Germany. Collaborations often led to friendships—Basel authorities, for example, investigated Johannes Bux-torf, Professor of Hebrew at the University of Basel, for socializing with Jews in the late sixteenth century. Learned Jews, respecting Buxtorf's Judaic knowledge, consulted with him on ceremonial law.

The Christian Hebraica movement, Zunz and his colleagues concluded, may have helped individual Jews but neither helped the Jewish community nor changed the underlying religious agenda. Renaissance and Reformation He-braists used scholarship for Christological ends; both celebrators and denigrators of pre-Christian Judaism considered the religion and its people insignificant af-ter Christ. Buxtorf's insistence that Hebrew vowel points originated with the creation of the language—not, as Levita claimed, in the seventh or eighth cen-tury—arose from his embrace of the Bible's, not the Pope's, authority. Christ-ian Hebraists sympathized with the Jewish refusal to convert to Christianity as long as conversion implied accepting the papacy, but they often evinced ani-mosity when Jews later refused to accept their improved version of the religion. Reuchlin, for example, opposed forced conversions but believed that Jews would voluntarily accept Christianity. Martin Luther's increasing hostility to the Jews is a bellwether of Protestant attitudes that came to vary between bare toleration and suppression.

Reuchlin and Buxtorf were not the last "sympathetic Gentiles" to accord per-sonal or scholarly aid and comfort to Jews or to Jewish learning. But not all He-braic scholars were equally congenial, nor did Hebraic scholarship advance Jewish interests. Sixteenth-century Hebraists—as well as nineteenth-century Semitists—evinced anti-Semitism, noted Zunz. The growth of Christian He-braism, in any case, soon obviated the need for Jewish collaboration. Christian Hebraists, Zunz concluded, may have demonstrated the potential contribution of "rabbinic" studies—the study of post-Biblical Jewish literature—to general scholarship; but Jews who had no conversionist motives, and who had a better understanding of the texts should now pursue this scholarship, thereby reenter-ing general intellectual discourse.

Jewish emancipation, which arose out of the eighteenth-century Enlighten-ment and proceeded fitfully throughout the nineteenth century, provided the opportunity. Enlightenment thinkers, wrote historian Jacob Katz, posited a neutral—non-religious—intellectual sphere where individuals could interact re-gardless of creed. The *Haskala,* the Enlightenment movement of *maskilim*— Jewish intellectuals who sought social integration—helped to reduce academic isolation. The *maskilim,* finding the attractions of the broader society irresistible, exploited the gradual lifting of formal restrictions on Jews to reconcile themselves, if not their communities, with the majority culture.

The Enlightenment also fostered new educational practices. Naftali Herz Wessely, an eighteenth-century scholar, responded to the promulgation of Austria's 1781 Edict of Toleration by calling for major changes in Jewish education. Jewish schools were to de-emphasize Talmud and invest more time in *Torat haAdam*, secular studies, and in the Hebrew language and the Bible—aspects of Jewish learning that linked them with general high culture. First a trickle and then significant numbers of Jews opted for advanced *secular* studies, especially at German universities.[15]

European Jewish responses to *Haskala* ranged from opposition ("The new is forbidden by the Torah," declared The Hatam Sofer, a traditionalist) to social rapprochement through assimilation, to conversion and intermarriage. Cultural integration, indifference, tolerance, or courtship, concluded some contemporary Jews and some historians, could destroy the Jewish community, a result that Christian coercion had failed to accomplish.

Wissenschaft des Judentums, which arose a generation later, allowed young Jewish intellectuals to seize the middle ground—to study their history and culture critically, without rejecting their heritage. Practitioners applied the "scientific" techniques, developed in universities, "critically and objectively, yet with sympathy," in order to assess the social evolution and situation of European Jewry.[16] Zunz and other practitioners disagreed on emphasis: Zunz considered literary studies the "entrance gate"; Abraham Geiger gave primacy to theology. But a scientific approach to the study of Jews and Judaism would demonstrate the vitality of contemporary Judaism to enlightened Christians, while providing Jews with perspectives.

Zunz edited, and contributed to, the *Zeitschrift für die Wissenschaft des Judentums* and wrote *The Sermons of the Jews,* which gained recognition among German academics. But the *Zeitschrift* made up only one volume, and initial hopes for *Wissenschaft des Judentums* soon faded, wrote Zunz, because Christians—and especially their universities—evinced little interest in embracing Judaism—or Jews—on any terms. The conversion to Christianity of *Verein* member Edward Gans immediately followed the denial of his application for an academic post. A generation later, the Prussian education ministry and the University of Berlin rejected Zunz's petition for an academic post for *Wissenschaft des Judentums* and his candidacy for that post.[17]

Nineteenth-century German scholarship, despite some exceptions, no more acknowledged the contributions of *Wissenschaft des Judentums* than Christian Hebraists acknowledged the integrity of prior Jewish scholarship. A clarification of essential Judaism would not overcome generations of anti-Semitism at this late—less than fully enlightened—date. When the *Verein* failed, some practitioners rejected the concept of neutrality and converted to Christianity. But *Wissenschaft des Judentums* remained essential for others who viewed the movement as a way to retain a rationale for the continued existence of a Judaism caught between a hostile environment and a traditional community. Some still hoped for cultural recognition. Yet others, including Zunz, found solace in scholarship. "I must confess that, next to submission to the judgment of God, occupation with this science is my support and consolation," wrote Zunz. "Nothing remains for the members but to work within their limited circles, remaining true to themselves and leaving the rest to God."[18] The *Verein* promoted neither apologetic nor condemnatory scholarship. It showed German—and later American—practitioners how to doubt, yet remain a Jew; to scrutinize from the outside, yet be inside; to be au courant, yet remain part of the Jewish tradition. It moored Jews who felt conflicting cultural pulls but were willing to acquire, or rely upon an already acquired, erudition to complement or supplement belief.

The Jewish community shared the blame, argued Zunz, for the movement's failure. German Jews, by ignoring *Wissenschaft des Judentums,* proved themselves unreformable, parochial, and materialistic. "The Judaism which we wanted to rebuild," Zunz wrote after the *Verein* collapsed:

> is torn apart, the prey of barbarians, fools, money changers, idiots and *Parnassim* [community leaders]. Many years will yet roll over this race and find it as it is today; torn asunder; out of desperation flowing over into Christianity; vacillating, without principles. . . . Their own science died among the German Jews and they have no understanding for the European, because, disloyal to themselves, they were estranged from ideas and became the slaves of mere self-interest. . . . Everything is a pap of praying, bank notes and *Rachmones* [charity], with *Aufklärung* and *Chilluk* [Talmudic dialectics]![19]

The contributions of *Wissenschaft des Judentums* to the intellectual rationale for modernizing Judaism may help to explain its failure to gain subsidies from community leaders that perceived change, including pursuit of secular knowledge and interaction with universities, as a threat. Reform Jews, in particular, claimed that many rituals were inauthentic or irrelevant to contemporary Jewry since they arose only in the post-Biblical period, and they appropriated the claim of *Wissenschaft des Judentums* to distinguish essential from vestigial practices. The organization of Jewish life into communities that had legal status—as opposed to voluntaristic congregational polities—meant that traditionalists who dominated communal life could often thwart the aspirations of insurgent Reform Jews. Many Jews who desired modernization of Judaism found American conditions more to their liking, since congregational organization allowed them to exercise greater latitude, including cooperation with secularizing universities, without communal sanctions.[20]

Some mid-nineteenth-century liberal Protestants responded to Reform Judaism by trying to expand the "neutral area" where German Jews and Gentiles could interact. But other liberals continued to demand Jewish assimilation into a supposedly benign society. *Maskilim* sought to straddle the two worlds, enriching the larger society while bringing traditional Judaism in line with it.[21] In any case, the divided efforts of liberals to bring Jews into German intellectual life soon faded before a romantic emotionalism that emphasized the native German "*volk*" culture—the primitive, enduring bonding of a people, *blut und erde*. Some proponents of the *volk* would tolerate other cultures within the state, but many advocates contended that Jewish physical and cultural separateness precluded assimilation. Attempts at assimilating a people whose religion had been superseded by nineteen centuries of history, they added, could only dilute indigenous culture. In Germany, the Reformation had won only a partial victory, and enduring divisions between Catholics and Protestants precluded the use of religion for maintaining and enhancing group identity and unity. "Culture," therefore, became a secular rationale for group cohesion.[22]

Cultural characteristics soon became identified as racial traits—inherited directly from the earliest progenitors and threatened, perhaps fatally, by inheritance (through interbreeding) of traits that characterized other races. Count Arthur de Gobineau's *Essai sur l'inégalité des races humaines* (1853) posited the independent emergence of the major races and attributed variant mental, emotional, and physical characteristics to each race. Emerging biological evidence challenged traditional religious accounts of creation and progeneration. But in Europe, especially Germany, racial theorists relied more heavily on philological than on biological evidence to justify racial theories.

Discovery of the Rosetta stone in the late eighteenth century led to the efflorescence of philology throughout European universities, and by the time the Gentile philologist Ernest Renan (1823–1892) assumed a professorship, his subject had attained substantive and methodological centrality. Scholars recognized the Semitic group as a distinct family of languages of which Hebrew was neither the oldest member, nor of divine origin. Renan helped turn philology into a science that identified linguistic categories—Indo-European and Semitic, for example—with the racial characteristics of the people who spoke them. Renan—regarding history as a progressive force rather than as a chronicle of degeneration, and reversing the Babel myth—argued that certain languages and civilizations gained superiority over time. Hebrew, like traditional Judaism, was vestigial, and cultural differences increased as the Semitic and the Indo-European language families diverged. Semites and their tongues remained static and antiquarian, while European languages and culture were dynamic and progressive.[23]

While his initial publications may have influenced Gobineau, Renan explicitly incorporated Gobineau's ideas in later editions of his book. He was more friendly to Reform Judaism, which rejected *halakha* or traditional Jewish law, and concurred in the opinion that, through self-selection of universalistic traits, Judaism "will contribute to the social progress of humanity."[24] But anti-Semitic polemicists, notably Houston S. Chamberlain, subsequently utilized Renan's scholarship to buttress their intuitive arguments of racial superiority.[25]

Linguistic theories supposedly related to biological differences thus justified the continued omission of Judaica—and of Jewish academics—from nineteenth-century German universities. Non-Jewish German scholars who favored adding Jewish theology or literature to university offerings because they illuminated other topics did not tie these subjects to the appointment of Jewish specialists. Nor could Jews rely on Gentiles to make sympathetic contributions, since many Gentile scholars, in addition to Renan, portrayed Rabbinic Judaism in terms of "the unbearable yoke of the Law, the transcendence of God, the abandonment of prophetic religion, national particularism and soulless piety."[26] The scholarship of orientalist Paul Lagarde, for example, combined traditional religious stereotyping with an attack on contemporary Jews as the main impediment to the emergence of a new German *übermensch* or superman.[27] *Babel und Bibel*, assyriologist Friedrich Delitsch's unfavorable comparison of Biblical to Babylonian religion (1902), followed several decades of criticism and attacks by Protestant higher critics such as Adolph Harnack and Julius Wellhausen.[28]

University restrictions, some advocates of *Wissenschaft des Judentums* argued, inhibited the ability of Jews to respond effectively to a rapidly diffusing rationale for segregation, attack, and ultimately destruction. "The state must complete the benefits of emancipation," wrote Jewish philosopher Hermann Cohen, who taught at the University of Marburg, "by including the Jewish religion in the orbit of its cultural tasks." This inclusion, many German Jewish intellectuals agreed, could only occur at the university since "German scholarship has been developed primarily in the universities."[29] But Cohen himself left Marburg for the *Hochschule für die Wissenschaft des Judentums* (founded 1869, opened 1872 in Berlin) in 1912, and few Jews believed that *Wissenschaft des Judentums* would improve their social condition by the time Martin Buber was appointed to a Judaica chair at Frankfurt in 1923. Confined to specialized institutions—such as the *Hochschule* and the Breslau seminary, the intellectual home of historical, later Conservative, Judaism—*Wissenschaft des Judentums* could at best somewhat mitigate the effects of a university-based scholarship with detrimental implications for the Jewish community.

Zunz hoped that universities would absorb the entirety of *Wissenschaft des Judentums;* instead, the field's linguistic aspects were thus appropriated for hostile purposes. Jewish learning, if it were to enter the continental university, would enter piecemeal and subject to the fortunes of parent disciplines such as linguistics. How, then, would *Wissenschaft des Judentums* relate to these disciplines? Could the field retain its own integrity and serve a social purpose beyond "recognition?" Ismar Elbogen, a historian and the long-time mainstay of the *Hochschule,* acknowledged the dependence of *Wissenschaft des Judentums* on cognate fields of scholarship for problem formulation and for methodology. Indeed, most subfields of Jewish learning were also parts of university-based disciplines. "History of the Jews in the dispersion," he wrote, "forms a part of the history of each particular country, and . . . it is the task of sociology to explore their life as a community and in the community." Elbogen added:

> The philosophy and theology of Judaism certainly can become objects of scientific research only as special divisions of general philosophy and theology. Hebrew and Aramaic linguistics are subdivisions in the sphere of Semitic philology, and Hebrew or Aramaic literature belongs precisely there, even though the study of the Bible, because of its special significance, has become a main subject of theology. Biblical scholarship . . . today has deeper roots in Christian (particularly Protestant) theology than

in the Wissenschaft des Judentums. The Talmud, if we disregard its language and consider only its content, belongs to the history of law, religion, and culture.[30]

But, Elbogen contended, *Wissenschaft des Judentums* had its own integrity; it was not just the amalgamated residue of excluded university subjects. *Wissenschaft des Judentums* was a separate "purpose-directed science"—closer to an ameliorative profession than a discipline—whose components were connected by their use in solving a practical task. The field, he wrote, "must be guided by an awareness of its obligation to serve living Judaism, to comprehend it as an entity in the totality of its spatial and temporal phenomena, and to contribute to its understanding, preservation, and continuous development."[31]

Elbogen described a meeting between Zunz and the historian Heinrich Graetz, the author of a multi-volume *History of the Jews* (1853–1876), to illustrate his concept of purposefulness. Told that Graetz had completed this history, Zunz said, "What, another Jewish history?" Graetz replied, "Indeed, but this time a *Jewish* one." "Graetz did not want to excavate dead bones or accumulate scholarly notes as a learned explorer of the past," Elbogen contended, "he wanted to describe the historic development of Judaism as a member of a living organism, as a feeling Jew for whom the Judaism of all ages and countries formed an entity."[32] Heinrich Treitschke, the nationalistic historian of Germany, considered the work ethnocentric and parochial, and the ensuing Treitschke-Graetz controversy may have further hindered university inclusion of *Wissenschaft des Judentums*.[33] But rather than assert that the study of Jewish history in a university would curb nationalistic excess in favor of a more contextual and non-partisan approach, Elbogen saw its exclusion as the price of espousing a different social vision.

University inclusion of *Wissenschaft des Judentums*, Elbogen feared, would come at the price of purpose. "Every purpose-directed science," Elbogen warned, "is threatened by the danger that individual subdivisions strive for expansion and autonomy without consideration for the ultimate goal." He added: "A phenomenon like Judaism, of such long historical duration, so widely dispersed, and of such strong cultural interests, frequently offers the temptation to scientific research to lose itself in other fields."[34] *Wissenschaft des Judentums* depended on the scholarly fields, but the whole was greater than the sum of the parts. The rabbinical seminaries could employ academic methods to a Jewish end. Could advocates of *Wissenschaft des Judentums* say the same for universities?

In Germany there could be no answer; in America the question recurred throughout the history of Jewish learning in secular institutions.[35] American higher education offered more opportunities for Jewish learning, but the location of practitioners within disciplinary departments implied compromises, at least from Elbogen's point of view. Would Jewish learning, by emphasizing contributions to general scholarship, start and remain communally aloof? Would it follow the path of sociology, which, failing to combine scholarship and ameliorationism, separated from social work and other instrumental studies? Or would the field become "purpose-directed," as Elbogen hoped, and gravitate outward from the nurturing parent disciplines? Jewish learning practitioners usually remained associated with parent disciplines and adhered to the scholarly straight and narrow until the late 1960s, when scholars in newly established Jewish studies departments echoed Elbogen's call for a "science of living Judaism, standing in the stream of development as a sociological and historical entity."

The American Setting for Jewish Learning

American Jews also saw university recognition as a route to social and cultural inclusion. American higher education may have had less centrality, and concomitantly less certifying power, than German universities, but American Jews felt compelled to demonstrate that the nation's colleges respected and appreciated their culture and contributions to American civilization. Indeed, the failed attempts to incorporate *Wissenschaft des Judentums* into European universities may have impelled Jews to explore America's potentially more receptive academic atmosphere. These explorations bore fruit: at least 16 Jews occupied positions in university Semitics departments, the most common location for Jewish learning for the next half century. Rapid academic incorporation gave American Jews hope that, contra Elbogen, university-based Jewish learning could serve both a parent discipline and the Jewish community in this friendlier culture. Perhaps practitioners might not reject a Judaic emphasis for topics at the discipline's cutting edge. Perhaps Judaic contributions to general scholarship would result in scholarly and communal recognition.

Most celebrants and scholars therefore accepted—even promoted—a historical framework for the field that emphasized compatibility, even continuity, with 250 years of American higher education. This framework defined a line of academic inclusion of Jewish learning from Hebrew instruction at seventeenth-century Harvard to late nineteenth-century Semitics departments. Renditions often justified an innovation as part of the lengthy tradition or rationalized a departure by juxtaposing the innovation with all that came before.

The litany proposed by these Jewish celebrants began with the Puritan emphasis on the Old Testament, progressed to Harvard's 1674 establishment of the Hancock Chair in Hebrew and 1722 appointment of Judah Monis, a converted Jew, to a Hebrew professorship, and thence to eighteenth-century Hebrew courses at Yale, the University of Pennsylvania, and Kings College (later Columbia).[36] Kings College president Samuel Johnson, these accounts noted, "tried to persuade both governors and students that familiarity with Hebrew is a fashionable study and even a gentlemen's accomplishment." The accounts then detailed the discourses between Yale President Ezra Stiles and learned members of the local Jewish community, the 1836 appointment of Isaac Nordheimer to an Arabic professorship at the University of the City of New York (later New York University), and perhaps critical Biblical scholarship at Harvard and Andover during the first two-thirds of the nineteenth century.[37]

"Semitic Studies in American Colleges" (1896), by Baltimore rabbi William Rosenau, then pursuing graduate work at Johns Hopkins, documented continuity and progress by enumerating institutions that gave Semitics instruction by year of first offering, and by listing chairholders chronologically by institution, starting with Harvard's founding in 1636.[38] Cyrus Adler, the first American to receive a Semitics Ph.D. from an American university (Johns Hopkins, 1887), also emphasized continuity. Adler, while president of Dropsie College for Hebrew and Cognate Learning, argued that "the beginnings of Hebrew and Semitic studies in America . . . furnish the background for what we are attempting to do in this College."[39] Articles that noted lengthy hiatuses between Hebrew's colonial and twentieth-century curricular inclusion often suggested that American colleges were now back on track, or had superseded the commitment of their colonial predecessors to the subject.[40]

Twentieth-century assessments added late nineteenth-century chair foundings in Semitics or rabbinics to the great tradition. New York University Hebrew professor David Rudavsky distinguished New York University's 1930s venture into modern Hebrew from "The Classical Approach," a term that included all prior developments.[41] Post-World War II development office materials often tried to catch the eyes—and wallets—of potential benefactors by emphasizing a "long tradition" of Jewish studies.[42] But the "continuity approach" was not confined to celebrants. The rendition of Salo Baron, Columbia's eminent historian of the Jews, resembled the schemas of progressive historians. Hebraic studies, after initial entry, encountered and overcame obstacles—including indifference and hostility—and finally triumphed during the post-World War II period of growth in American higher education.[43]

But did early ventures in Hebraica at a given institution, or at American institutions in general, somehow pave the way for later Judaica initiatives? Was there a continuous line of development? Celebrants say yes; we believe that the links between successive Judaica innovations, even at the same institution, were often weak and that discontinuities were more the norm. But one can go too far, and we balance the evidence for discontinuity by showing that antebellum Yale, though it did not subsequently enter the early Judaica pantheon, affected the history of Jewish learning in late nineteenth-century universities.[44]

At the Harvard of Henry Dunster (president, 1640–1654), freshmen studied Hebrew grammar, juniors read the Aramaic books of the Old Testament, and seniors studied the Syriac New Testament.[45] These additions to a curriculum that otherwise resembled seventeenth-century Cambridge came about, Harvard historian Samuel Eliot Morison suggested, not from humanist urgings or Puritan interest in the Bible but because Dunster and Henry Chauncey, his successor, were themselves Hebraists.[46] Hebrew encountered immediate, frequent, and substantial student resistance. Michael Wigglesworth, a seventeenth-century Harvard tutor, noted that Harvard students petitioned for its discontinuance. "I withstood it with all the reason I could, yet all will not satisfy them," he wrote, " . . . thus am I requited for my love; and thus little fruit of all my prayers and tears for their good."[47]

The Monis appointment failed to improve the subject's attractiveness. Reappointed annually for almost 40 years, Monis met four times a week with sophomores, juniors, and seniors, and instructed them, after 1735, from his own published Hebrew grammar.[48] The Harvard Corporation, after years of student dissatisfaction, asked Monis to reexamine his instructional methods, which were "thought so tedious as to be discouraging." The corporation made Hebrew an elective subject in 1755. Enrollments fell immediately, and Monis resigned his professorship five years later.[49]

The circumstances surrounding the Monis appointment illustrate the problem with positing a linear connection between colonial Harvard and contemporary university-based Jewish learning. American Puritans, like continental Reformationists, believed they had inherited the "Chosen People" designation. Rejecting the overlay of "Popish" commentary and distortion, they studied the Hebrew Bible (Old Testament) for evidence of the divine nature and messianic mission of Jesus. Colonial Puritans, like the Europeans, believed that Jewish rejection of Christ's messianism rendered them a "fossilized" people of antiquarian interest.[50] And, like Europeans, American Puritans believed that each Jewish convert demonstrated the correctness of their theology, especially given the fact that Judaism had survived despite Catholicism's centuries-long campaign for its degradation or control. Each believing Jew, in contrast, was a rejection, and therefore a threat. This background casts doubt on claims that Judah Monis was a key figure in the history of Jewish learning. Monis converted to Christianity in 1722, two years after his arrival at Cambridge. He took communion at the First Church of Cambridge and eventually joined that church. His background—sometime Rabbi of the Synagogue in Jamaica, and afterwards in New York—and his custom of celebrating the Sabbath on Saturday led some observers to question his sincerity. But his conversion address suggested that he would defend and proselytize for Christianity. He entitled the address: "The Truth, Being a Discourse which the Author delivered at his Baptism, Containing Nine Principal Arguments the Modern Jewish Rabbins do make to prove the Messiah is yet to Come: With the answers to each . . . not only according to the Orthodox Opinion, but even with the Authority of their own Authentick Rabbins of Old, and Likewise, with the Confession of his Faith, at the Latter End. Dedicated to the Jewish Nation and Prefac'd by the Reverend Increase Mather, D.D."[51] The appointment of Monis left Harvard traditions—especially its Christian orientation—intact.

Anglican-supported Kings College (1754) included Hebrew in its curriculum from the outset, and Johann Christoff Kunze, a non-Jew, became professor of Oriental languages when the institution reopened as Columbia College after the American Revolution.[52] Kunze served two brief terms but lost his appointment permanently in 1799 when New York State discontinued a subvention for chairs in Oriental, French, and legal studies. Columbia suspended Hebrew instruction until 1830 when, perhaps responding to a movement to establish the rival University of the City of New York, it appointed the Rev. Samuel Turner, D.D.—professor of Biblical learning and interpretation of the Holy Scriptures at General Theological Seminary—to a professorship of Hebrew language and literature.

The University of the City of New York, aspiring to offer instruction in many areas covered in continental universities, soon appointed George Bush and Isaac Nordheimer to Hebrew and Arabic chairs, respectively. Nordheimer, one of America's first Jewish college professors, is oft-noted for his Hebrew grammar.[53] The work of Bush and Nordheimer allowed Turner to cease instruction at Columbia, though Nordheimer died within three years of his appointment.[54] Unfulfilled announcements signified Columbia's good intentions, but instruction in Hebrew awaited Columbia's venture into Semitic philology—part of its move towards university status in the 1880s.

Hebrew fell by the wayside, in institutions that included it at all, because other subjects made more compelling claims to inclusion in the antebellum college curriculum. Latin held undisputed curricular primacy. In the battle for second place among languages, lack of faculty and resources made Hebrew a more likely candidate for exclusion than Greek, the language of the New Testament and of much secular literature.[55]

Curricular traditionalists justified Latin and Greek for their ability to discipline or strengthen the mind—which in turn facilitated study of other, more practical, subjects—but partisans of Hebrew rarely offered this argument. The defense of the faith and the strengthening of belief in the divine authority of Scripture—the arguments usually advanced—convinced few college presidents to include the subject. "Isaiah is in all respects, in simplicity, in fire, in originality, in sublimity, as worthy of study as Homer," added Harvard professor B. B. Edwards; "the Lamentations of Jeremiah will not yield to the Elegies of Tyrtaeus." But claims for the influence of Hebrew on imagination and taste fell upon deaf ears, as did the desire for Jewish conversion—the traditional rationale for the study of Hebrew.[56] Hebrew was largely confined to occasional, ill-comprehended antebellum commencement orations.[57]

The inadequacy of nineteenth-century grammars also hindered the subject's development. Existing grammars, which usually aimed at Bible comprehension, often contained erroneous material and lacked pronunciation rules.[58] Accuracy and standardization awaited the late nineteenth century, when university-educated scholars published grammars that viewed philological analysis of Hebrew as a branch of Semitics.[59] In any case, colleges were unlikely to adopt the grammars published by Jewish authors, including Nordheimer.[60] Clergy and secondary school teachers could help students prepare for collegiate studies in Latin and Greek, but the marginal curricular role of Hebrew, abetted by the absence of grammars, perpetuated the dearth of qualified tutors.

Endowment of the Hancock Chair of Hebrew (1674), the Hollis Chair of Divinity (1721), and the Dexter Lectureship (later professorship) of Sacred Literature (1811) permitted Harvard to shift from Old Testament apologetics to Biblical criticism after 1819, when it located the chairs in the Unitarian-dominated divinity school. Orthodox Congregationalists relied on the new Andover Seminary—specifically upon Moses Stuart's Biblical scholarship—for conservative responses. Stuart, an important mentor, translator, and scholar, advocated a "grammatic historical interpretation" of Scripture and greatly admired German Biblical criticism. In 1826, Harvard engaged a German language instructor to help its divinity students keep up with German scholarship (and thereby with Stuart). Unitarians and Trinitarians battled over Biblical scholarship for several decades, but philosophical attacks from the transcendentalist Unitarian left eventually overshadowed these controversies.[61]

Biblical criticism, unstable in a divinity school environment where practitioners could not accord it primary attention, collapsed by the onset of the Civil War.[62] Its demise, historian Jerry W. Brown added, also resulted from the predominantly social-religious orientation of a no longer particularly learned ministry, denominational strife that diverted attention to subsidiary issues, the decline of bibliocentric theology, the deaths of major practitioners, and social indifference. "American biblical studies had never been firmly established as an independent intellectual tradition," Brown concluded. Only later in the century, as Scripture gained freedom from the need to serve as the cornerstone of faith, could scholars study and interpret the Bible without a central concern for its religious and denominational consequences.[63]

Neither colonial Hebrew instruction nor antebellum Biblical criticism led *directly* to late nineteenth-century university-based Jewish learning. But is the case overstated—were there no links between antebellum higher education and the appearance of Jewish learning? Biblical criticism, we note below, re-emerged at Harvard's divinity school with the 1880 appointment of Crawford Howell Toy; contra Brown, perhaps the *absence* of Biblical criticism during the 1860s and 1870s was the abnormality. In any case, a group of "New Haven scholars," Yale academics who had studied in Europe, helped pave the way for the graduate division Semitics departments that nurtured most late nineteenth-century university-based Judaica. These scholars, historian Louise Stevenson suggested, bridged old and new by enlisting scholarship "as a means for securing the intellectual conviction of godly men to an evangelical future." Scholarship was a primary activity for these intellectuals. "The college had replaced the church, books and articles replaced itinerant preachers, and intellectual conviction gained from study replaced the emotional experience of the revival," Stevenson argued. Disseminating purposeful scholarship to specialists *and* to educated citizens, they hoped, would result in thought and action consistent with religious teaching.[64]

Two New Haven scholars, Edward Elbridge Salisbury and William Dwight Whitney, secured a key place for philological studies within their circle. Yale appointed Salisbury, who twice journeyed to Europe for advanced study in Sanskrit, to a professorship of Arabic and Sanskrit in 1841. A founder of the American Oriental Society (1843) and an editor of its journal, Salisbury fulfilled his vow to interest others in linguistic scholarship by helping to endow a Sanskrit professorship for Whitney at Yale (1854). Whitney, who studied with Salisbury before journeying to Berlin and Tübingen to study Egyptology and Sanskrit (1850–1853), later published *Language and the Study of Language* (1867), which helped legitimate philology as a university-based discipline in America.[65] Under Whitney's leadership, a New Haven-based philological club that he co-founded with Salisbury and other New Haven scholars (ca. 1850) evolved into the American Philological Society (1869).

Philological studies at Yale included Indo-European, especially Sanskrit—Whitney's specialty—and Semitics.[66] Semitics, as organized in continental universities, included four major language groups: Northeast, including Assyrio-Babylonian or Akkadian; Northwest, including Aramaic and its Syriac dialect, Ugaritic, and Canaanite, which in turn included Hebrew in its language family; Southwest, including Arabic, and Southeast, including Ethiopic and Amharic.[67] Hebrew's presence in a language family that had a high philological priority for scholars became an important opening for Jewish learning in American higher education.

Yale, for reasons explored below, did not become a nineteenth-century home for Jewish learning. But Daniel Coit Gilman, president of the University of California and later of Johns Hopkins University, and William Rainey Harper, president of the University of Chicago, studied under the New Haven scholars. Both scholars also taught at Yale early in their careers and became strong promoters of Semitics departments that made room for Judaica.[68] Gilman, indeed, belonged to "The Group," an intellectual inner sanctum of community members and New Haven scholars. Familiarity with using "scholarly means for evangelical ends" enabled Gilman and Harper to cooperate with late nineteenth-century Jews, often migrants from Germany and central Europe, who hoped for a warmer American reception of *Wissenschaft des Judentums.*

Jewish learning found its niche in late nineteenth-century universities—not colleges—that emulated European universities by creating Semitics departments. Save for George Foot Moore's work on Judaica as part of the history of religions at Harvard, we found little evidence of consistent Judaica offerings in other contemporary departments—the fate of university-based Jewish learning depended on the strength and direction of Semitics. Motives for the incorporation of Jewish learning, chapter 2 notes, included complex communal and institutional agendas involving both symbol and substance. But the incorporation of Semitics by late nineteenth-century universities established two precedents—Judaica subfields obtained academic access primarily on the graduate level and only when the rationales for their inclusion were congruent with the needs of relevant parent disciplines. To anticipate: university presidents and Jewish communities expected this congruence to continue—that disciplinary representatives would continue to see Jewish learning as an integral component of their subject, and that scholars appointed to Judaica positions within that discipline would retain an emphasis on this subfield. But when, as Ismar Elbogen feared, the parent field made independent demands, the failure of some Jewish Semitists to meet presidential and communal expectations became a matter of concern.

Which universities were most likely to offer Semitics and Judaica instruction? William Rosenau's 1896 survey uncovered 40 to 50 Semitics instructors at 15 colleges and universities. From Rosenau's list, we sought institutions where faculty research and the curriculum included identifiably "Judaic" work.[69] Since even religiously liberal universities reserved Bible chairs for Protestants—Bible studies was in any case, as we will show, a problematic subject for university-based Jewish scholars—we distinguished Judaic and non-Judaic Semitics campuses by the presence of scholarship and courses in the post-Biblical language, literature, or history of the Jews: rabbinic Aramaic, Talmud, *mishnah,* medieval poetry, or philosophy.

Four of Rosenau's 15 Semitics colleges and universities—Chicago, Columbia, Johns Hopkins, and Pennsylvania—included "Judaica" offerings. A fifth institution, Harvard, joined the Judaica ranks in the same year that Rosenau published his survey (1896) when Crawford H. Toy, a non-Jew, offered a Talmudic text course. Harvard appointed Andover's George Foot Moore, another Gentile, to a theology professorship in 1902 and to its Frothingham professorship of the history of religions in 1904. Moore, who taught a course on Talmud and the history of Jewish literature to 200 C.E., later published *Judaism in the First Centuries of the Christian Era: The Age of the Tannaim* (1927–1930) a three-volume study that "legitimated" the study of rabbinic Judaism in America. His view of religion as a universal activity, of which Christianity and Judaism were manifestations, led him to argue that religion had a place in graduate study as well as in theological schools, and that post-Biblical Judaism played a key role within the study of religion.

Rosenau overlooked the Semitics program begun (1894) at the University of California, a public university, which emphasized Jewish learning for more than a decade after its inception. Elsewhere, status as a public institution inhibited the appearance of Judaica. Public institutions were more susceptible to church-state issues and to utilitarian appeals.[70] Private, secularizing universities often provided a better sanctuary for controversial and esoteric studies.[71] In all, nearly half of the self-proclaimed research universities offered Jewish learning by 1902.

The role played by institutions with Semitics programs, especially Judaica, in the creation in 1900 of the Association of American Universities (AAU) illustrates their prominence in the university movement. Five of the six universities that offered, or would soon offer, Judaica signed the invitation to the AAU organizing session, which aimed to advance the interests and academic culture of the American research university. The University of Pennsylvania, the sixth Judaica university, *received* an invitation to the meeting.[72] Historians of education may now find considerable continuity between the antebellum college and late nineteenth-century universities, but Semitics professors usually belonged to the "university parties" that emphasized professional scholarship and graduate education at the expense of undergraduate, liberal education that championed the inculcation of mental discipline. Between 1876 and 1905, universities with Semitics hosted 15 new scholarly societies and many new disciplinary journals—and moved toward a value neutrality that distinguished them from the "New Haven scholars."[73] Changes in academic governance paralleled changes in the organization of knowledge. Protestant identity replaced denominational affiliation as either a formal or an informal prerequisite of appointment to a presidency or trusteeship, although liberalization rarely went further.[74]

What happened to Yale, another AAU founder, after the departures of Salisbury, Whitney, and Harper? The scholarly consensus, reported George Foot Moore, still at Andover, was that Yale "has been something like a South American revolution—the proclamations out of all proportion to the fighting men."[75] The 1900 appointment of Andover's Charles C. Torrey helped fill the Semitics vacuum created by Harper's departure, and the Yale catalogues for 1898–1899 and 1902–1903 even listed courses in modern Hebrew conversation and in rabbinic and Talmudic literature, offered by a graduate student. But Yale neither sustained these Judaica courses nor continued to emphasize graduate work and research in Semitics.[76]

Arthur T. Hadley, Yale's first nonclerical president, gave the highest priority to finding "a man who can build up widespread public interest in Scriptural study among the undergraduates," not to Semitic studies, and therefore rejected Torrey's recommendation to add Moore (A. B. Yale, 1872) to the faculty for Judaica in 1900. "Professor Moore, when in college here," Hadley told Torrey, "was distinctly a man who influenced a few men only. He rather held himself aloof from the bulk of the class, and did nothing to enter into college spirit and college life." Hadley added, "If such was the case thirty years ago, is there not added danger that, at the age of fifty he will find himself unable to take part in our life here?"[77] Yale instead hired Brown professor Charles Foster Kent who taught undergraduates and became a national advocate for the study of religion, especially after World War I.[78]

Comparing divinity school–graduate division relationships further clarifies the demarcation. All six Judaica institutions—including publicly controlled California and private, secular Johns Hopkins—established, or attempted to establish, relationships with local divinity schools. Integration with the respective graduate schools enabled the functionally nonsectarian Harvard and Chicago divinity schools—President Charles Eliot declared the Harvard divinity school "unsectarian" in 1878—to help develop Semitics and Judaica.[79] Harvard and Chicago cross-listed graduate and divinity school courses, maintained the same calendar for both divisions, and equalized tuition charges for divinity and graduate students. The divinity school's prior policy of reduced tuition policy, Eliot argued, continued "to disparage its own instruction and discipline." He added: "This indiscriminate eleemosynary system in theological education should be done away with."[80] Chicago initially charged no tuition fee to divinity students, but Chicago president William R. Harper noted that equalization "has contributed largely to the position of respect and eminence enjoyed by the Divinity School in relation to other divisions of the work."[81] "Only two institutions, it is believed, have taken this step," Harper later added, "which marks a distinct advance in the history of theological education."[82]

Protestant divinity schools faced the same decision that Jewish seminaries would confront a half century later: whether to approve the methods of the secular disciplines for the study of sacred subject matter, and whether to emphasize the education of scholars of religion or that of pastoral ministers. Integration of the Harvard graduate and divinity schools, Dean Francis Peabody noted, establishes the position of the divinity school "as a university school; it fixes in it the same standards of work which prevail in other departments; it sets Divinity Students in immediate competition with other advanced students of the university; and it encourages in other students appreciation and respect for theological studies."[83] Seminaries, Peabody wrote, offered "the straightest and easiest course for the average student to enter the denominational ministries." Harvard, instead, offered "exceptional opportunity for scientific and advanced theological study. It has the peculiar advantage of a University School, and of liberty of thought and utterance."[84]

Yale, in contrast, desired to produce *pulpit ministers* who were "self-directive personalities, capable of independent thought." Yale's denominational character limited its catholicity. Non-Congregational Protestants attended the divinity school, but Yale authorities asserted, "by heritage, preference and custom it remains a Congregational institution" that produced an orthodox, Trinitarian ministry.[85] Scholarship, Yale officials added, "is not encouraged at the expense of other kinds of development. No student can avoid contact with a carefully planned scheme of social, religious, and missionary as well as intellectual activity."[86] Yale used its tuition policy to attract students to the ministry. "No charge is at present made," Yale announced, "for tuition or the use of the libraries [for Divinity School students]."[87] The divinity school did coordinate its calendar with the rest of the university and did allow students to "take electives in other Departments of the University," *but,* the catalogue added, "under suitable conditions."[88] The school did not go unaffected by the forces that produced dramatic change elsewhere, but its denominational ethos limited innovation.[89]

Yale's location in a city with a small Jewish population—the entire state of Connecticut had only 15,000 Jews in 1900—also helps to explain its failure to advance Jewish learning. The six Judaica universities were located at or near important Jewish population centers. New York's estimated 674,000 Jews (1900) were a natural constituency for Jewish learning. The 1900 Jewish population of the other five cities ranged from San Francisco's 20,000 to Philadelphia's 75,000 and Chicago's 80,000—not in New York's league, but enough to generate instructors, benefactors, libraries and students.

Yale, along with Princeton, remained "very agreeable and charming country clubs for young men and boys," in the eyes of Columbia president Nicholas Murray Butler (1902–1945).[90] Its undergraduate orientation, religious ethos—Yale retained compulsory chapel for years after Harvard discontinued the practice—broad commitment to curricular prescription, relative indifference to research, ambivalence towards integrating its divinity and graduate schools, and location away from a significant Jewish community resulted in a limited commitment to the legacy of New England scholars.[91] Permanent appointments in Judaica awaited the mid-twentieth century.[92]

Judaica's inclusion in a Semitics department required substantial institutional resources, a research orientation, a contiguous Jewish community, and available practitioners. Save for communal contiguity, these factors also sustained other fields. Jewish learning—to use Laurence Veysey's formulation—was most likely found in schools with numerous, deep, and elective course offerings. The field remained nonexistent at colleges that did not transform themselves into universities until modern Hebrew appeared at New York City's municipal colleges in the 1930s.[93] When Felix Frankfurter, then a Harvard law professor, was asked to support a student petition for Hebrew instruction at the College of the City of New York, he replied that a college, unlike a university, could not offer all subjects; other subjects had a greater claim to inclusion.[94] Colonial educators considered Hebrew an important liberal study for undergraduates who needed to learn the Bible, but the late nineteenth-century appearance of Semitics in some of the same institutions resulted from its potential contribution to a field of advanced scholarship.

Semitic philologists found their initial niche on the graduate level but made common cause with colleagues in other "newer" disciplines to secure adoption of the elective system on the undergraduate level. This innovation permitted the entry of philology, science, and social science into a curriculum heretofore largely reserved for Latin, Greek, and mathematics, thereby freeing the graduate strata from elementary instruction and creating a constituency for advanced work. No logical reason existed, wrote a practitioner, for awaiting the junior year or later to begin the study of Semitics "beyond the fact of the insistent demand of studies that are seemingly more urgent and the fact that Orientalism will attract only a chosen few."[95]

Colleges and universities, advocates of Semitic studies added, should include Hebrew, the propaedeutic language upon which advanced Semitic scholarship depended, on the list of subjects accepted for undergraduate admission. Secondary school instruction in history and science, these advocates noted, aided these subjects in their battle for acceptance as college entrance requirements, which in turn strengthened the case for undergraduate instruction. But the implied invitation to the secondary schools, as well as the foray into the undergraduate domain, sputtered until the 1920s and 1930s, when some New York City high schools and colleges offered Hebrew—and then, mainly modern Hebrew.[96]

The six universities that offered Judaic Semitics—California, Chicago, Columbia, Harvard, Johns Hopkins, and Pennsylvania—viewed themselves as part of a community of research institutions that presented a common front to the rest of academe and to America. But these universities competed among themselves for funding, faculty members, students, and recognition.[97] Were there ample resources for all? Could Judaica grow from its Semitics base into a "purposeful" science? If not, could the field at least maintain its academic foothold? We now examine the motives, actions, and interactions of concerned constituencies, and the place of Jewish learning within the field of Semitic studies.

II

REFORMING THE UNIVERSITIES: PRESIDENTS, PROVIDERS, AND PHILOLOGY

The attractiveness of Semitic studies explains the great attention lately paid to them. The world's remaining problems in the history of nations and of religions are to be answered by the students of Semitic languages. . . . What is the beginning of art? Greek history takes you back to Asia Minor, and from thence you must go back to a Semitic origin. What is the beginning of civilization? You must go back of Greece to Semitic Phenicia, and back of that, again, either to Egypt or to Semitic Babylonia. What is the beginning of religion? Already the classical religions, and those of India and China as well, are proved to be but eddies in the current. The real stream is nothing but Semitic; and it is Semitic studies that must answer the Mosaic problem, and that must explain the source and authority of those beliefs about the creation of the world, the deluge and the dispersion of man which we have inherited from those wonderful chapters of Genesis. I repeat my confidence that our new, young, enthusiastic school of Semitic scholars, which this last ten years has seen arising among us, will have the ambition and patience to contribute much to the solution of these problems.

—William H. Ward, 1888[1]

The appearance of Semitics in late nineteenth-century American higher education is associated with the aspirations of some institutions for university status, the availability of resources, and with proximity to a significant Jewish community. In all, only six institutions—California, Chicago, Columbia, Harvard, Johns Hopkins, and Pennsylvania—fulfilled the criteria of resolve, support, and location.

Semitic studies facilitated institutional transformation at a time when governing boards gradually shifted from ecclesiastical to lay control, presidents sported business suits instead of clerical robes, and faculty members espoused research over creed. Semitics coursework allowed university authorities, charged with "Godlessness" by clergy and colleges left behind by the academic revolution, to cite continued connection with religion. "Non-theological" Semitics differed from Christian Hebraica in its "scientific," rather than devotional, approach to subjects fraught with religious implications. A modern linguistic field, Semitics suffered neither the "advantage" of sacred association nor the disadvantage of Hebrew's third rank among the classical languages. Students and faculty members might study Semitics for religious purposes, but defenders also noted the subject's philological value and importance for the reconstruction of Semitic culture.[2]

Semitics also appealed to some devotionalists. Darwinism and the higher criticism placed religion on the defensive, and faith became an inadequate defense of the key tenets of Christianity. "Rational evidence" became the exclusive criterion for academic acceptability of religious knowledge—the study of religion would remain in universities by paralleling the spirit and method of other subjects. "Science is organic," wrote Reform Rabbi Emil G. Hirsch of Chicago's Temple Sinai congregation; "Truth has the same methods for him who studies Blackstone as it has for him who reads his Moses or his Jesus."[3] Semitics departments enrolled adherents to many varieties of religious truth, which in turn further spurred acceptance of the criterion of rational evidence.

"Secularizing" universities helped develop an American response to evolution and to the higher criticism. Many late nineteenth-century clerical and lay college authorities confronted the implications of the new knowledge with either optimism over the likelihood of an early peace treaty[4] or pessimism about the consequences of a failure to secure a prompt truce.[5] Missionary work, for example, was difficult to justify when higher critics attacked the basis of Christianity. Some institutions offered a shrill response. In the 1870s, Amherst dismissed an empiricist biology professor and directed his replacement to teach his subject "as an absolutely dependent product of an absolutely independent and spiritual Creator."[6]

Religious centrists and liberals, in contrast, often enlisted Semitists to help reconcile new scientific and inherited religious knowledge. Semitic scholarship cast new light on—and often confirmed—events recounted in the Bible and related texts. Princeton president James McCosh demonstrated the parallels between Darwin's evolutionary theory and the first chapter of Genesis and opened a School of Science. But he also interrogated faculty candidates for evidence of religiousness.[7]

Other mediators reaffirmed the Bible's narrative validity. "If American scholars are to be prepared to take their part in deciding the vital questions that have arisen concerning the Old Testament," wrote William Rainey Harper, soon to be president of the University of Chicago, "surely Oriental Studies, and particularly Semitic studies, must be introduced into the curriculum of non-professional schools."[8] "We have thus far been," echoed Charles Augustus Briggs of Union Theological Seminary, "at the best, spectators of the battle that has raged on the continent of Europe over the biblical books. The Providence of God now calls us to take part in the conflict. Our Anglo-American scholars are but poorly equipped for the struggle. We should prepare ourselves at once."[9]

Assuming the middle ground made Semitists the targets for both fundamentalists and extreme critics. Missionary zeal, and the belief that Darwinism and continental scholarship challenged religion more seriously than fundamentalism, allowed Semitists to absorb denominational attacks. Conducting "scientific" research on topics that touched deep beliefs and emotions, presidents and scholars agreed, was a risk worth taking. The lack of guarantees legitimated and strengthened results that supported religion. Semitic scholarship required a special kind of faith: that research would confirm and not challenge beliefs that scholars and the community held sacred.

Liberal American religion, in the late nineteenth and early twentieth centuries, emphasized ethical precepts, usually based upon the Bible's prophetic books, rather than dogmatic elements. Protestant and Jewish social gospelers, frequently citing the prophets, helped justify higher education's shift from a pietistic to a service orientation. Indeed, in some early professional schools and academic departments, it was difficult to show where the social gospel left off and where social science began.[10] The location of Semitics departments in graduate faculties permitted a similar, salutary ambiguity: Semitic scholarship might help to nurture ethical, universalistic religious formulations.

Nor did a demand for contributions to the ideological underpinning of anti-Semitism—a key role of continental Semitics departments—hinder the field's development in America. Physical characteristics often failed to provide a distinction between Gentiles and Jews, so Europeans based demands for "racial" separation upon the hypothesized existence of proto-Aryan languages that antedated, or were contemporaneous with, Semitic languages. European Jewish advocates of *Wissenschaft des Judentums,* eager for inclusion, if not assimilation, agreed that Indo-European and Semitic were different language families. But, they argued, neither this difference nor the ultimate scholarly determination of the existence or non-existence of proto-languages bore on the racial or ethnic status of contemporary groups. European Jewish intellectuals were caught between liberal demands to abandon distinctiveness in return for social as well as political emancipation and racist insistence upon the unassimilability of the Jews. The resulting balancing acts failed to yield the desired university appointments, much less social acceptance.

But the arguments of Gobineau, Renan, and Max Müller for early racial differentiation based on language found little favor among American linguists, or even among American racist thinkers. William Dwight Whitney devoted many pages to refuting simplistic past or present associations of race and language.[11] Americans thought in racial categories, but color, not language, played the decisive role in racial ascriptions. American racists rarely argued, for example, that black use of the English language threatened white racial purity. Nineteenth-century American racists directed most salvos at blacks and formulated few doctrines with Jews specifically in mind. Americans, whatever their degree of racism, rarely viewed linguistic evolution as anything more than analogous to biological evolution.[12]

Semitics thus found a home in universities that regarded a broad-based Protestantism, an ethical definition of religion, and acceptance of nondenominationalism as the price of growth, if not as a virtue. Universities were neither to be Godless nor God-centered. Among their many missions, they defended themselves against both denominational opponents and those who would eliminate their Christian orientation in the name of science.

This climate was conducive to a limited Jewish presence. Appointment of Jews to Semitics chairs often indicated philo-Semitism, an aura of tolerance—the "neutrality" rarely achieved in Europe, and complementary interests in defending middle ground positions. Reform Jews, like their Protestant counterparts, accepted the outlines of evolutionary theory and the higher criticism without accepting all conclusions. An attack on the People of the Book, some Gentiles believed, might also affect Christianity. European linguistic studies were often turned against contemporary Jewry, but Jewish insight might help Americans turn back European and especially German attempts to Nordicize Jesus, to attack the Old Testament, and to subordinate ancient Israelite culture and accomplishments to other Semitic cultures, as in the scholarship of Friedrich Delitzsch. The group of Gentiles who believed that the fruits of Jewish learning might force a retreat from continental extremism included key presidents of American universities.

Presidential Power

The six universities that welcomed Jewish learning met one other decisive condition: the personal interest and commitment of the chief executive. "The president in the multiversity," stated Clark Kerr in *The Uses of the University,* "is leader, educator, creator, initiator, wielder of power, pump; he is *also* office-holder, caretaker, inheritor, consensus-seeker, persuader, bottleneck. But he is mostly a mediator."[13] Kerr characterized the late nineteenth and early twentieth-century "giants" as "innovators during a wave of innovation" and distinguished these presidents from the "gentler hands" needed in a more complex late twentieth-century environment.[14]

The Kerr dichotomy suffers from exaggeration. Trustees who ignored the now commonplace distinction between policy-making and implementation, denominational representatives in a far from secularized world who kept perpetual vigil lest the specter of Godlessness rear its head, legislators who might turn any presidential failing to political advantage, and journalists who understood that the more an academic institution's norms deviated from community standards the better the copy, forced many "giants" into mediative postures.

Presidential interest in Semitics—especially Judaic Semitics—permitted the simultaneous exercise of leadership and mediation between constituencies. Semitic studies could advance institutional aspirations, address important intellectual problems, and improve relations with interested communities, including Protestant denominations and a growing Jewish constituency.

A successful Semitics program required a politically astute president who understood the functions of the subject and who shared the universalist liberalism of the age. Ideally, he also had a personal—religious, academic, or both—interest in the field. Presidents expected that successful Semitics programs would encourage the munificence of the local Jewish community for other projects, but presidents justified the field's presence by the role it could play in resolving the intellectual debates of the time and in advancing the fortunes of nascent universities.

Institutional prestige in the late nineteenth century could derive from growing enrollments—universities took pride in demonstrating student enthusiasm for the proliferating array of graduate and undergraduate majors and professional courses—*and* from creating chairs in ornamental subjects—high prestige, high quality, but not necessarily high demand—that were present in European universities, such as Semitics. The importance of orientalism in continental universities, sympathetic presidents concluded, outweighed possible low student interest. America might soon boast an indigenously educated Semitics professorate worthy of foreign recognition and domestic support. Other students of Semitics might begin a ministerial career after exposure to universities that separated true faith from dogma, thus reversing the perceived decline in a learned ministry in the face of evangelical excess and offering weapons for the inevitable battles over interpretation. Seedling Semitics departments required careful nurture.

Fortunately for the field of Semitics, two university presidents, William Rainey Harper of the University of Chicago and Daniel Coit Gilman of Johns Hopkins, had a professional interest in the subject. They also maintained close relationships with individual Jews and the local Jewish communities. Before ascending to the Chicago presidency (1892), Harper had already attained recognition as "the person who has done more than anyone else towards furthering Semitic studies in this country."[15] Harper began his study of Hebrew as an undergraduate under Muskingham College president Dr. David Paul. Paul also gave the precocious youth the opportunity to teach a small class in that subject in 1872–1873. Accounts of Harper's Yale graduate years under William Dwight Whitney's tutelage are scanty.[16] Harper subsequently taught at Masonic College, Denison University, and the Baptist Theological Seminary in Morgan Park, Illinois, a Chicago suburb. Biographers more frequently note the influence of E. Benjamin Andrews, the Denison president who became a lifelong friend, and of George W. Northrup, president of the Morgan Park seminary.

Pedagogy initially attracted Harper to Hebrew studies; his attempts to master the language challenged him to devise an interesting method of instruction.[17] He first tried his method on his Muskingham class, then, lacking a Hebrew class after graduating from Yale, he instructed his wife. Andrews later wrote of his protégé's zest for teaching:

> Teaching did not weary or cloy him. Before his class his mind and his body also were all activity. . . . It was model teaching. Bright pupils shot forward phenomenally; dull ones made good progress. All worked to the best of their ability, made to share what seemed to be their teacher's conviction that, unless they became efficient classicists, some terrible fate certainly awaited them—in this world at any rate, and possibly hereafter.[18]

But Andrews considered Harper "non-contemplative" during his tenure at Granville, not betraying "any special interest in theology, in biblical study, or in any of the great themes of religious philosophy."[19]

A Morgan Park colleague suggested that the scope of Harper's activities—not his "non-contemplative" outlook—changed at the seminary.[20] Harper immersed himself in Chautauqua activities, published four textbooks, offered Hebrew instruction by correspondence, and edited two journals, *The Hebrew Student* (later

The Old Testament Student, The Old and New Testament Student, and finally *The Biblical World*), and the more technical *Hebraica* (later *The American Journal of Semitic Languages and Literatures*).[21] He taught at Yale for five years (1886–1890), simultaneously holding three academic appointments.

Harper's Baptist belief was not of a narrow, dogmatic sort. He opposed the strengthening of denominationalism by preaching that in an enlightened age, doctrinal belief paled before the greater import of ethical behavior.[22]

> The present is an age of toleration, with which no past age of history may be compared. Though at first it may seem paradoxical, it is true that in proportion as less emphasis is placed upon a particular form of belief, greater emphasis is laid upon conduct. In proportion as larger liberty of thought, within reasonable limits, prevails, ethical standards are elevated.[23]

During his years at Yale, Harper convinced himself of the correctness of liberal Biblical criticism through a published dialogue, "The Pentateuchal Question," conducted with orthodox professor William Henry Green of Princeton Theological Seminary.[24] His stance jeopardized his chances to become president of a proposed Baptist university in Chicago, underwritten by John D. Rockefeller. Augustus Strong, who hoped that Rockefeller would endow a university in New York City with himself at the helm, challenged Harper's orthodoxy, but influential Baptists came to his defense. Northrup wrote that Harper was "the most remarkable young man in the religious history of our country in this century."[25] George Edgar Vincent, the chancellor of Chautauqua, stated: "A rationalist who denies all inspiration is a very different person in faith and works from the Christian Scholars who are quite sure Moses did not write the account of his own death and are willing to inquire diligently into all matters pertaining to the authorship of the books of Moses."[26] Discerning his denomination's favorable consensus with regard to Harper's devotion and beliefs, Rockefeller began negotiations toward endowing a university in Chicago with Harper at its head.

With his own integrity under attack, Harper allowed others to defend him, but he regularly editorialized on behalf of constructive, critical Semitic scholarship:

> Has it ever occurred to those who have written these polemic statements, and to those who have read them, that perhaps the great duty of the church is to train higher critics rather than to fight them? . . .

> Shall Christian men come forward to give themselves to the fullest training in the philology, archaeology, history, chronology, and literature of the Semitic peoples and thus to fit themselves for the highest contributions to biblical science? Will the churches encourage them to do this? or is it to be left to those who are not in sympathy with evangelical Christianity?[27]

Once in Chicago, Harper found a strong ally in Temple Sinai's prominent leader, Rabbi Emil G. Hirsch, whose universalism—the doctrine that God will ultimately save all souls—reflected his studies with Abraham Geiger, the German liberal rabbi. Hirsch's brand of Reform emphasized prophetic ethicalism, rejected *halakha,* and asserted that the higher criticism posed no threat to Judaism's fundamental tenets. Harper pointed to the prophets as achieving an advance over religions that emphasized worship and often identified commonalities and consistencies between Judaism and Christianity.

Hirsch helped to nurture a working relationship between reformed Judaism and reformed Protestantism in Chicago during the initial funding campaign for the new university. Jewish community leaders associated with Temple Sinai, the city's wealthiest Reform congregation, and with the Standard Club—a social club whose membership included most wealthy German Jewish families—pledged $25,000. The first list of trustees of the University of Chicago included E. B. Felsenthal, a Jewish lawyer, Sinai congregant, graduate of the antecedent University of Chicago, and strong backer of the financial canvass.[28] The first list of faculty members included Emil G. Hirsch as instructor of rabbinical literature and philosophy.

Harper and Hirsch created a mutually beneficial alliance. Chicago, officially a "Christian university," welcomed Jewish students and faculty members.[29] Jewish munificence toward the university continued, and Chicago generally avoided the official confrontation with its Jewish constituency, especially over admission to college, that many eastern peer institutions experienced after World War I.[30] And Emil Hirsch acknowledged Harper's encouragement of Judaica scholars, as well as his scholarly contributions:

> Jews certainly had not ceased cultivating acquaintance with the idioms of their sacred writings; but somewhat impatient of the slower step of the grammarians, they had attempted to fly when they should have walked. Grammar was not to their taste. Though in mediaeval times the pathfinders in Hebrew grammar were of their faith, the modern Jewish scholars relied upon their *Sprachgefühl*—their linguistic intuition—too boldly. The result was that many of the niceties of Hebrew expression escaped their quick eye. Even in Jewish circles the work of Dr. Harper, in his textbooks in Hebrew, has brought about a better understanding.[31]

William Rainey Harper shared the enthusiasm of a Congregationalist minister who wrote that Semitics was "the biggest and newest movement of the time" and that "the liberal-conservative school of scholarship . . . will soon have answered the skepticism of Germany by utilizing the best and only permanent results of German scholarship."[32] His energetic defences of Semitic scholarship while still at Yale led Johns Hopkins Semitist Paul Haupt to write: "If Harper is appointed President of the Baptist University, it will greatly promote Semitic study in America."[33] Harper recounted that he would have refused the call to Chicago if he had thought he could accomplish more for Semitics at New Haven than he could on the Midway.[34] At Chicago, he chaired the Semitics department while serving as president. This arrangement, though not administratively ideal, symbolized the importance he accorded the subject.

Daniel Coit Gilman presided over two of the six institutions that eventually offered Judaic Semitics programs: California and Johns Hopkins. An ordained minister and a Yale graduate, Gilman became professor of physical and political geography at Yale's Sheffield Scientific School in 1863. As professor, Yale librarian, and then secretary of Sheffield, he supported the school against an antagonistic faculty still dominated by the classical assumptions of the 1828 Yale Report. His advocacy of Sheffield led Yale trustees to pass over his candidacy for the presidency in favor of theologian Noah Porter in 1870. The next year, Gilman accepted California's second presidential overture.[35]

Abraham Flexner, a Gilman biographer, traced his subject's spirit of tolerance and catholicity to childhood attendance at Jewish and Catholic, as well as Protestant, religious services.[36] Gilman, like Harper, exhibited an intellectual affinity with modern Judaism. Reform's belief in the ultimate reconcilability of its "enthusiasm for new knowledge and our devotion withal to the old faith" closely paralleled a key concern of Gilman, just as Reform's universalism and mediative stance concerning the higher criticism appealed to Harper.[37] Gilman's optimism about the reconcilability of science and religion dated from his membership in "The Club" at Yale, where he, Whitney, and others regularly debated this issue. Gilman tried to effect institutional reforms consistent with this optimism and his general "liberal orthodoxy in religious matters."[38] While Yale librarian, he built up scientific holdings at the expense of theology. Gilman viewed the breakdown of Yale's senior course in moral philosophy into its disciplinary components as an opportunity, not a misfortune, for religion. He emphasized scientific subjects at California and Hopkins and recommended a prominent role for modern languages and for history—including the history of Christian civilization—in his California inaugural.

Gilman did not initiate the drive for Hebrew and Semitic instruction at California, but he responded positively to the movement. Several months before Gilman's arrival in 1872, Reform Jews in San Francisco and Los Angeles petitioned the university for Hebrew instruction. "The undersigned . . . would esteem it as a great favor if you would provide, even though in a moderate way, for instruction in Hebrew in your institution," stated the Los Angeles petition, signed by parents with children at the university. "The number of Israelites on this coast is numerous, and among all of our faith there is a strong predilection for this ancient tongue, whenever any of us seek to acquire a liberal education."[39] The university soon engaged James M. Philips, an aging Russian Jew who had studied Oriental languages while residing in England. Contemporary accounts state that Philips had come to San Francisco to seek a position as a Hebrew teacher.

Gilman attempted to capitalize on this momentum. His inaugural address noted that the university was a religiously and ethnically heterogeneous constituency that included "many among us . . . who look for a Messiah yet to come."[40] Gilman envisioned that professorships in Hebrew and Semitic languages, "which, perhaps, some other citizen will be glad to establish," and in Sanskrit and the comparative philology of Indo-European tongues, would someday complement the already endowed chair of Chinese and Japanese, itself a rarity in American universities.[41]

Gilman hoped that California's Jewish community might endow the chair to garner recognition, but no one stepped forward for a generation. When an untenable political situation confronted Gilman at California during the mid-1870s, he accepted an offer to preside over the creation of Johns Hopkins University. Philips left the university in 1881 after financial exigency led the Regents to declare the Hebrew, chemistry, mathematics, physics, and Spanish professorships vacant. He subsequently lived, some say as a recluse, in Oakland until his death in 1888.[42]

At Hopkins, religious affiliations of potential faculty members underwent scrutiny, but Gilman appointed Joseph Sylvester to one of the first professorships. Sylvester was a Jewish mathematician who failed to receive his degree from Cambridge after refusing to subscribe to the Articles of Faith of the Anglican church.[43] By century's end, at least eight other Jews had taught at Hopkins, including three junior Semitics instructors—Cyrus Adler, Casper Levias, and William Rosenau.[44] For Gilman, no less than for Harper, catholicity became an article of faith, and the university's Semitics department, in which he took special interest, exemplified this spirit.[45]

Gilman urged that scholars study all languages comparatively, historically, and scientifically.[46] When Thomas Chalmers Murray applied for a post at Johns Hopkins and offered Semitics as his specialty, Gilman acted with alacrity. Murray studied at Union and Princeton Seminaries after graduating from Williams in 1869. He then spent nearly three years in linguistic study at Halle and Göttingen, working under Paul Lagarde.[47] He noted that "the pursuit of branches so important for the proper solution of many of our most vital historical and linguistic problems has been barred to all not connected with our theological schools"—an early example of many similar laments. Even in theological schools, he added, study of Eastern religion and literature languished. Gilman appointed the young scholar to the faculty with the title of associate. Murray offered instruction in Hebrew, Arabic, Assyrian, and Egyptian, and assisted in the university library—as did other Semitics scholars who experienced low demand for their courses.[48]

Gilman failed to lure William Dwight Whitney to Hopkins permanently, but a visiting professorship for the Yale scholar coincided with Murray's appointment, as did Charles Lanman's appointment as associate in Sanskrit.[49] After Murray's sudden death in 1879 and Lanman's departure for a Harvard professorship in 1880, Gilman secured continuity in Hebrew instruction by enlisting faculty members John W. Gross, whose principal interest was Greek, and then Maurice Bloomfield, who became associate in Sanskrit. Jews such as Bloomfield and Harvard's Leo Wiener obtained positions in philological departments that would have been denied to them in many continental universities.[50] In 1883, Gilman appointed Paul Haupt to a permanent Semitics professorship. Haupt remained at Hopkins until his death in 1926. Gilman's interest in Semitics and Oriental languages also led him to serve a lengthy term as president of the American Oriental Society.

Harvard president Charles W. Eliot (1869–1909) realized early in his presidency that Semitics had a legitimate role to play in a nascent university. Unlike

Harper and Gilman, Eliot was a chemist, and did not view Semitics as a curricular solution to an intellectual issue of personal importance. His devout Unitarianism may help explain his interest and his philo-Semitism, but corporate considerations were probably decisive in winning his support for Semitics.

A nephew of Biblical critic Andrews Norton, Eliot combined a deep devoutness with an equally deep mistrust of ritual and dogma. His father taught him that "God had chosen the Hebrew people as instruments through which to teach men, and that the authors of the Bible were therefore essentially though not literally inspired."[51] His Unitarianism led him to agree with Jewish denial of the Trinity and of the doctrine of original sin.

Eliot announced a policy of non-sectarianism upon becoming Harvard's president. "Yale represents Congregationalism," he wrote in 1872, "Harvard . . . is truly liberal and catholic in religion." At Eliot's Harvard, stated Joseph H. Choate, a prominent New York attorney and a Harvard graduate, "the American and the foreigner, the Christian and the Jew, the Papist and the Protestant, the white man and the black man and the yellow man, can study side by side with equal right and learn alike whatever is worth learning."[52] Eliot did not permit discrimination against Jewish students. He enthusiastically supported the 1906 founding of the Harvard Menorah Society, which promoted the non-partisan study of Jewish literature and philosophy. "There is not one particle of anti-Semitic feeling in the University," he told Menorah members. "Some of the most distinguished of our staff are Jewish, either by descent or practice. . . . Some of my best friends are of Jewish descent." This famous remark has come down to us as an exemplar of Gentile hypocrisy, but the comment actually reflected Eliot's pride.[53]

Eliot kept abreast of European philological developments, especially the scholarly excitement attendant upon the discovery and deciphering of languages within the Semitic family. Nor did Gilman's interest in Oriental languages go unnoticed. Eliot hoped that American higher education and Harvard in particular would assume an important role in that field. But financial restrictions and the subject's continued unpopularity among undergraduates made its growth difficult at a university built around a college.[54] In 1879, shortly after receiving permission to begin graduate instruction, Eliot enticed Charles Lanman to Cambridge.[55] Authorities at Johns Hopkins consoled themselves with the knowledge that Lanman's hiring implied recognition for their institution and for a new field of study.[56] Lanman became a Harvard fixture for half a century and left the famous Harvard Oriental Series, a series of edited volumes, as his legacy.[57]

The following year, Divinity School professor Rev. Edward J. Young resigned the Hancock professorship, which he had held since 1869. According to a knowledgeable source, Eliot decided to offer the chair to a member of the "newer" school when, lacking a competent faculty member to read a student's thesis on an Arabic subject, he had to send it to Yale's professor Salisbury. He thereupon resolved that a similar incident would never recur.[58] Eliot first offered the post to William Hayes Ward, an ordained preacher, superintending editor of *The New York Independent,* and an authority on Assyrian and Babylonian seals.

Ward, whose ability to read Assyrian made him one of very few possibilities, declined the offer because he lacked proficiency in classical Arabic and because he
wished to continue his editorial duties.[59]

Eliot turned next to Crawford H. Toy (A. M. Virginia, 1856), a European-
trained Semitist who had recently resigned under pressure from the Southern Baptist Theological Seminary because he accepted the theory of evolution and
sympathized with the higher criticism.[60] Toy accepted Eliot's offer and continued
Young's work in the Divinity School. But, with Eliot's encouragement, he also established the rudiments of a Semitics department by offering courses in Hebrew,
Aramaic, and Old Testament criticism. Harvard historian Samuel Eliot Morison
later wrote that "Eliot's mind was Roman rather than Greek or Hebraic," but his
interest in and sympathy for Semitics grew. After retirement, he chaired the visiting committee to the Semitic Museum, established during his presidency.[61]

Eliot, Gilman, and Harper demonstrated their personal leadership and commitment—Kerr's first set of characteristics—to the place of Semitics in the university. Gilman and Eliot did not await external (Jewish) initiatives before
establishing a Semitics department. None of these presidents chose a Jew as department head, but all recognized the role of the Judaic aspects of Semitics in a
fully staffed department. The three schools included Judaic Semitics early on—
taught by Jews at Chicago and Hopkins, by Gentiles at Harvard—and welcomed
interested Jewish students and benefactors.

At California, Columbia and Pennsylvania, communal and corporate considerations compensated for lack of presidential intellectual engagement. Presidential receptiveness and responsiveness—Kerr's second set of characteristics—to
Reform Jewish initiatives at the University of California led to a Semitics department with strong Jewish communal identification.

After Gilman's departure from California, his successors reiterated his Jewish
outreach and plea for communal support for Semitics. The appointment of Jewish regents Isaias W. Hellman and Jacob B. Reinstein during the 1880s—a time
when east coast colleges often excluded Jews from their boards—manifested the
university's receptive attitude toward its Jewish constituency. Reinstein, a former
chair of the California alumni association and a lawyer, helped to obtain a leg-
islative appropriation for a building to house the university's Professional Colleges in San Francisco. University historian William C. Jones recognized him as
"foremost in organizing and encouraging this movement, as in every other question of large interest to the University during several years past."[62]

Rabbi Jacob Voorsanger of San Francisco's Reform Temple Emanu-El rewarded
the university in 1894 during the presidency of Martin Kellogg (1893–1899), the
son of a minister who came to the state as a missionary. Voorsanger organized Jewish communal support for a Semitics department, which he chaired for over a
decade.[63] Kellogg's successor, Benjamin Ide Wheeler (1899–1919) appointed
William Popper, a Jew and the Semitics department mainstay for several decades, in
1905. Wheeler was also a minister's son and a student of the Bible who spent four
years in Europe studying comparative philology and general linguistics.[64]

A generation older than Gilman, Columbia president Frederick A. P. Barnard was influenced by similar intellectual currents. A member of Yale's Class of 1828, Barnard gradually migrated from formal observance of Congregationalism to a more enthusiastic participation in the Episcopal church. Barnard, like Gilman, studied for the ministry, but his biographer writes that he intended to consecrate his teaching, that is, infuse his teaching with piety, rather than enter upon ministerial work.[65] And also like Gilman, his interest in the sciences changed and developed. Originally a Yale mathematics tutor, Barnard became professor of mathematics and natural philosophy at the University of Alabama in 1837. He later moved to the University of Mississippi, where he served as president (1856–1858) and chancellor (1858–1861).

Barnard, whose beliefs resembled Gilman's, later brought his science–religion reconciliationism to the Columbia presidency. He entitled his 1864 inaugural address "The Relation of Physical Science to Revealed Religion." "I believe," he wrote, "indeed, that in spreading out His wonderful works before us, and clothing them with so many attractions, it has been the manifest purpose of the Creator to make them the means of drawing men to Himself."[66] But Barnard did not share Gilman's faith that study of Semitic languages would help achieve the reconciliation. He attributed the omission of Oriental languages—and other subjects—to the absence of an elective system at Columbia.[67] An 1880 announcement of intent to conduct graduate work omitted any reference to Semitics, but Barnard and the trustees accepted a Jewish communal gift for the support of a professorship for Richard Gottheil in 1887.[68] Barnard thus neither advocated nor opposed the field's appearance at Columbia.

Seth Low and Nicholas Murray Butler, Barnard's successors, displayed no personal interest in Oriental languages. But Low's philo-Semitism, his desire for cordial relations with New York's Jewish community, and perhaps his political progressivism—he left Columbia after his election as New York City mayor in 1901—led him to regularize Richard Gottheil's appointment in 1892. "It is the glory of Columbia," Low wrote, "that it makes no discrimination against the Jews either in its faculty or in its student body."[69] Chapter 4 shows that Gottheil's personal relationship to President Butler, a Columbia College classmate (A. B. 1882), did little to enhance his department's status. Semitics at Columbia remained closely identified with Gottheil.

Stronger presidential leadership, Cyrus Adler's memoirs imply, might have impelled the University of Pennsylvania to begin Semitics work under Adler's direction several years before it became committed to the subject. Adler, the first American Semitics doctorate recipient (under Paul Haupt at Johns Hopkins) delivered his Pennsylvania master's oration on the relationship of Near Eastern archaeological work to the Bible and the history of civilization. Provost—the title assigned the university's highest administrative officer—William Pepper attended and told Adler that the address aroused his interest in Semitics. A desire for university expansion, rather than a thoughtful conception of the role of Semitics in resolving contemporary intellectual debates, probably motivated Pepper, a physician by training.[70] Adler reported that two trustees supported his appointment to a regular post but that Pepper opted for externally subsidized professorships with designated incumbents.[71]

Pepper later enthusiastically chaired a committee of contributors to a university-sponsored Babylonian expedition.[72] John Peters, the chief organizer, recalled Pepper's entrepreneurship. The expedition "could be made to appeal mightily to men's imaginations" and could lead to further growth. A museum could house the treasures unearthed, for example. "He would reach out into this field and that, and build a real University on great lines," Peters wrote. "It was the vision of a prophet alike in breadth and scope and fervor. It fairly swept me off my feet, and from that day onward I became a warm admirer of the genius of William Pepper."[73]

The University of Pennsylvania had exhibited the most consistently philo-Semitic attitude among the six institutions. In 1802, the trustees invited Moses Levy, class of 1772, a prominent attorney and the first Jewish graduate, to board membership.[74] The university produced a steady stream of Jewish graduates throughout the nineteenth century, and it awarded Sabato Morais, rabbi of Philadelphia's Congregation Mikveh Israel and founder of the Jewish Theological Seminary in New York City, an honorary Doctor of Laws in 1887.[75] The Jewish community viewed the award as a recognition of Jewish learning and of their community, since Morais was the first Jew so honored by the university.[76]

Late nineteenth-century academic growth involved a widening of intellectual scope and constituency. Success required presidents able to initiate action without compromising prior accomplishments. The influence of philo-Semitic presidents assured at least a conditional welcome for the Judaic aspects of Semitics—the appointments were not calculating, despite instances of anti-Semitism at these institutions.

Each president also knew that Semitic studies elicited Jewish communal interest. Jewish communal willingness to bestow intellect and wealth on these universities demonstrates a belief in the authenticity of presidential gestures, and in the complementarity of agendas.

The Jewish Community

Academic, entrepreneurial, and empathetic motives help to explain university interest in Semitics in late nineteenth-century America. Expansion permitted, and sometimes required, allocation of resources to ornamental subjects. Ample intellectual justification, a growing number of trained practitioners, and sympathetic presidents were all present. The decline of denominationalism facilitated intellectual tolerance within the field. Few officials worried, as did the succeeding generation of university presidents, that a Jewish intellectual or social presence would drive away non-Jewish practitioners or students. Presidential philo-Semitism assured the representation of Judaic Semitics within a Semitics department.

Prior Jewish interest in American colleges—such as the connections of Gershom Mendes Seixas with Columbia and Moses Levy with Pennsylvania—had been sporadic, associated with post-Revolutionary, cosmopolitan institutions, and with an earlier period of Jewish migration. Some prominent nineteenth-century Jews, such as Mordechai M. Noah and Isaac Leeser, had objected to Jewish attendance at colleges sponsored by Christian denominations. In any case, few Jews were interested in the small rural colleges typical of the nineteenth century.

As Jewish community-building proceeded, access to American cultural institutions appeared both desirable and more feasible than in Europe. What prompted a local Jewish community to respond to an academic courtship or to initiate a relationship? The universalism at the heart of Reform Judaism helps to explain the interest of that branch.

American Reform Jews rejected Jewish social distinctiveness—no *kashrut,* for example—and welcomed the modern era "of universal culture of heart and intellect." They defined the mission of Judaism as "the realization of Israel's great Messianic hope for the establishment of the Kingdom of truth, justice and peace among all men."[77] University-based Jewish scholars could help Protestants devise a "new theology" that would evolve into a "universal faith grounded in universal evolution," develop the study of orientalism, and debate "the finality of the Christian religion."[78] If Reform Judaism was not *the* universal religion— many advocates considered it the strongest candidate—the universal religion that liberals developed would necessarily incorporate its outlook. This outlook included a theological (monotheistic) and ethical emphasis, a rationalist approach, and a rejection—some dissented on this point—of Biblical law and peoplehood: "America is our Zion," repeated Reform Jews. The academic search for truth and disregard of dogma would confirm liberal tenets and thereby facilitate theological convergence between prophetic Judaism, the Protestant social gospel, and liberal Catholicism. Never before nor thereafter did theologians presume such affinity between Jews and Christians.

A university base would also strengthen the Reform movement against Jewish opponents. Traditional Judaism considered evolutionary thinking and the higher criticism blasphemous, but Reform Jews contended that modern thought did not necessarily lead to rejection of religion or to indifference. Instead, evolutionary theory demonstrated the validity of Reform's innovations. Semitics and other university studies would advance liberal Judaism by identifying "foreign" elements incorporated as a result of historical circumstances.

"Beliefs and ceremonies and rites of the Acadians [sic] and of the Egyptians, of the Assyrians and Persians, of the Greeks and Romans, of Christian and Mohammedan borrowed heathenism," wrote Reform Rabbi Joseph Krauskopf, "all these had sent their quota into the *Talmud,* into the *Caballah,* into the *Schulchan Aruch,* into the Ghetto synagogue, and this fantastic make-up received the name of Orthodox Judaism." Krauskopf identified nationalist particularism as "that peculiarly Oriental notion."[79] Traditional Jewish practices and the Bible's legal aspects, Reform Jews maintained, were of historical rather than contemporary significance. And if the Bible itself amalgamated the thinking of different times and places, then Reform had simply continued the process of recreating Judaism for a specific time and place. University-based scholars could study evolution and the higher criticism to develop rationales for liberal religion, and could apply to the Talmud the critical methods used to study other texts.

University recognition of Jewish learning, many American and European Jews agreed, pointed toward social, religious, and intellectual acceptance. Parallel interests and outlooks would lead to social recognition from religious liberals. The scholarly documentation of the Jewish contribution to civilization would also counter the subjectivism and intuitionism of European and American opponents of cultural and social assimilation. A Jewish presence in Semitics departments would grant a full hearing to Jewish contributions, dispel stereotypes and myths about Jews, and reduce anti-Semitism inside and outside American universities.[80]

Recognition that Jerusalem contributed as much to western life as Athens and Rome, and that Judaism remained a vital, legitimate religion despite centuries of persecution and discrimination, advocates suggested, would increase the stature and status of contemporary Jews. Joseph Jacobs, in his prolegomenon to the *Jewish Encyclopedia* (1901–1905), edited by American Judaica scholars, wrote:

> The impression that Jews are a mysterious sect like the Gipsies [sic] and that their conduct is inspired by unsocial motives, must disappear before the evidence presented in the *Encyclopedia,* that they are men like other men, with their prejudices and their failings indeed, but also with their ideals, which latter are seen to be in most cases the foundations of the ideals of humanity.[81]

Few advocates thought that university inclusion of Jewish learning would by itself result in full social and economic acceptance. Members of the Reform community could themselves cite extensive evidence of social anti-Semitism. But academic inclusion would help to offset Jewish exclusion from other cultural institutions, businesses, clubs, and resorts.

Jews also adopted a comparative perspective. Not even one German university had established a chair in Jewish theology "in an organic and harmonious relationship with all other departments" (Abraham Geiger's phrase), so it would not require many faculty appointments for the Jewish community to fare better with American than German universities.[82] And even if communal social recognition did not result from these appointments, acceptance would at least come to Jewish benefactors and scholars who associated themselves with the university movement.

Nineteenth-century rabbis and lay leaders took note of the demise of Hebrew in post-colonial American colleges and perceived the need for higher Jewish education. These observers viewed the creation of a Jewish institution of higher learning in America as a viable alternative but differed on whether the institution should be aimed primarily at the preparation of rabbis, teachers, or simply knowledgeable Jews. Moses Levy proposed a Jewish college in 1821 in connection with his attempt to found a major Jewish settlement in Florida.[83] In the 1840s, Isaac Leeser promoted a seminary with a Jewish and secular curriculum to remedy the shortage of American rabbis and teachers. The Pennsylvania legislature chartered such a seminary in 1849, but Leeser's attempt failed for lack of funds. So did a similar New York effort in 1852, Isaac Mayer Wise's Zion Collegiate Association in the mid-1850s, an 1864 attempt by younger Jews to establish a National Hebrew College based upon existing Hebrew literary societies, an 1866 endeavor by Benjamin Franklin Pexiotto of the Order of B'nai B'rith to establish an American Jewish university, an initiative by New York's Temple Emanu-El congregation to establish a seminary for Reform rabbis, and Maimonides College in Philadelphia in the early 1870s.[84]

American traditionalists, agreeing with their European counterparts that even partial instruction at a university rendered a student ineligible for the rabbinate, initiated some of these projects.[85] Some members of the historical school—the progenitor of Conservative Judaism—promoted Maimonides College, which had close academic ties to the University of Pennsylvania, but few counterparts outside of Philadelphia converted favorable attitudes into action.[86]

A lack of funding, scholars, or enthusiasm thwarted all efforts until Isaac Mayer Wise successfully established Hebrew Union College in Cincinnati (1875), a rabbinical seminary that became associated with the Reform movement.[87] East coast laymen and congregations concluded that H.U.C., added to the presence of the Berlin and Breslau seminaries and Jews College in England, would siphon off most resources aimed at distinctively Jewish institutions.

Financial reality thus combined with Reform Jewish intellectual and social predispositions to dictate a turn to universities. "Seminaries," wrote Emil G. Hirsch, "are survivals of the unfittest," even though H.U.C. had by then become identified with Reform Judaism.[88] Reform Rabbi Bernhard Felsenthal of Chicago envisioned that with an appointment in Talmudic and Midrashic literature, the newly opened University of Chicago "might render service even as a Jewish-theological Seminary."[89] In practice, H.U.C. and the under-financed Conservative Jewish Theological Seminary in New York City (1886) were located near universities, and seminarians also studied at the neighboring institutions.

The congregational nature of American Jewish life facilitated support of university positions when the resources, including scholars, became available. The need for communal unanimity had inhibited the growth of Reform Judaism in Germany. Abraham Geiger, for example, considered his position as Breslau rabbi "above party" and followed many practices that he personally questioned or opposed for the sake of the community.[90] But the American synagogue or temple was the essential unit of religious authority—no central force, such as a synod, checked centrifugal tendencies in American Judaism. Individual congregations—such as Temple Emanu-El in New York City—and congregants could help integrate Jewish and secular higher learning within the university without a veto from local orthodox elements.

American Jewish communal subventions could advance the fortunes of the field in the absence of university expenditures or non-Jewish philanthropy. Conversely, after a promising start, inadequate communal and institutional support contributed to the field's failure to grow. Jewish scholars who taught Semitics also contributed to this failure. These scholars, as we will see, had their own agenda for personal recognition that required either a commitment to academic norms of scholarship and concomitant abandonment of substantial communal identification, or an affirmation of Jewish identification that resulted in inattention to scholarship. Reduced communal support allowed some scholars to intensify their academic commitments. The resulting communal disappointment led to further disequilibrium.

At the outset, personal relationships between Semitists and the Jewish community—practitioners were often rabbis or their sons—blunted potentially divergent communal and professorial goals. Nor did these goals appear mutually exclusive. Social and intellectual recognition did not necessarily preclude each other. The tendency of Jewish Semitists to venture beyond the Judaic aspects of Semitics into other branches of the language family did not initially concern a community with a strong universalist orientation. Communal interest in Jewish contributions to western civilization implied an emphasis upon subjects not considered traditional Jewish literature. Reform Judaism, in fact, considered Talmudic study irrelevant to the present. But the divergence between scholars and community increased as scholars produced highly technical monographs and as the academic welcome for American Jews became less enthusiastic in the twentieth century.

The Jewish quest for recognition—avidly sought from social and cultural arbiters such as American universities—occurred at a specific time, place, and among a specific constituency. Thirty years before Judaic Semitics appeared among the offerings of American universities, the Jewish community had neither a sufficient critical mass nor the interest to involve itself with denominationally oriented American higher education, while 30 years later, the Jewish community was frequently snubbed. Coming at a time of heightened presidential interest, the quest for recognition permitted the field to attain an academic foothold by the turn of the century.

Semitic Philology

Presidents and benefactors helped Jewish scholarship find a home in late nineteenth-century American university Semitics departments. Rebutting extreme higher critical statements required study of the Bible. Reconciling science and religion required attention to culture, history, and society—the domain of philology as originally conceived. But would practitioners fulfill external expectations? Communal recognition required attention to "Jewish contributions." Academic recognition required emulation of continental scholarship. How, precisely, would practitioners define the new field?

In Europe, advanced instruction in Hebrew or Aramaic Talmud—the core of the traditional, advanced Jewish curriculum—occurred in *yeshivot* and rabbinical seminaries such as Berlin and Breslau, not in universities.[91] Traditional and modern Jewish institutions retained the preeminence of the Talmud by emphasizing tractates relevant to their constituencies. The Lithuanian *yeshivot* trained *talmidey chachamim*—learned Jews who upheld tradition without becoming communal functionaries—and emphasized the orders of *Torts* and *Women* that most clearly expressed the logical structure and form of rabbinic thinking. The Breslau seminary, which trained pulpit rabbis, pastors, and teachers, stressed the "practical" tractates—the laws of marriage, divorce, personal status, *kashrut* (keeping kosher homes), Sabbath, and holy days—that rabbis needed in their work.[92] But continental universities contained no constituency for Talmud, and a late nineteenth-century survey of Semitics courses in German universities found only two Talmud courses.[93]

Late nineteenth-century American Semitics departments occasionally offered "rabbinics" instruction that included Talmud.[94] But no one—presidents, providers, or practitioners—considered Talmud a central text. Talmud appeared to separate Jewish and Gentile intellectual life at a time when supporters of university-based Jewish scholarship desired academic convergence. American Semitists trained no Talmudic adepts, and the content and pedagogy of Talmud instruction thwarted the dreams of Felsenthal and Hirsch for rabbinical training at American universities. American instructors taught religious tractates from the Talmud, including *B'rakhot,* which dealt with liturgy, and *Yoma* (The Day of Atonement), from a Protestant—not a traditional Jewish—religious orientation.[95] The Johns Hopkins course announcement for *Avot D'Rabbi Natan,* a pietistic, aphoristic text contemporaneous with the *Mishna,* noted: "Special attention was paid to the New Testament as well as to Rabbinical Ethics."[96] Nor did the pedagogy appear modern. Academic instructors, like *roshey yeshivah,* covered folio pages of Talmud, thus also echoing the pedagogy of the classical curriculum. Paul Haupt, for example, annually reported the number of pages of text covered in his seminars.

Talmudists in *yeshivot* dismissed Christian scholars, including Harvard's George Foot Moore, who had not grown up within the *beit-ha-midrash,* the Jewish house of study, but university Judaica scholars decried the "absorption in the Talmudic atmosphere" that led to "excessive narrowness and provincialism" in the traditional Jewish scholar.[97] During the twentieth century, university instructors who taught this infrequently offered subject were, more often than not, part-time, Jewish—often the local rabbi—and of junior rank.[98] Colleagues usually viewed these Talmudists as parochial Jewish insiders, not university scholars.

Would university-based Jewish learning emphasize Biblical scholarship? "During the second half of the last century," wrote G. Ernest Wright, "... a great change occurred, in which the scholarly study of the Old Testament was shaken loose, very largely, from its churchly mooring ... [and] it was carried on as a neutral science."[99] If Wright's characterization was correct, Biblical scholarship would be a prime candidate for field definition within universities. Some prominent non-Jewish Semitists testified that their interest in the Bible motivated their scholarship.[100] Their Jewish colleagues were presumed to have an even greater interest. The Hebrew Bible was, after all, at the heart of all Jewish learning. Rabbinic literature was largely exegesis of Biblical texts; medieval Hebrew poetry resonated with Biblical vocabulary, metaphor, and linguistic structure; and modern Hebrew included locutions, images, and turns of phrase that Bible readers

can recognize and place. The place of the Jews in western history is in large measure the response of Christendom and Islam to divine revelation as recorded in
the Biblical text.

Jewish Biblical scholarship began in the tenth century, flowered in the
eleventh to early thirteenth centuries, and lingered into the sixteenth.[101] But traditional Judaism, assuming the divine origin, accuracy, and unity of the text under scrutiny, derived interpretations from the received text. Biblical critics, in
contrast, assumed that all texts had histories that included revisions and emendations, and suggested that failure in interpretation might result from defects in
the text, not errors by the interpreter. Many Americans believed that nineteenth-
century Protestant Biblical scholarship ignored, perhaps purposely, the earlier
Jewish Biblical scholars and the sixteenth-century Christian scholars who collab-
orated with Jews.[102] The resultant speculative scholarship, critics of the critics
charged, was guilty of gross interpretive excesses in emending and reinterpret-
ing sacred texts.

Semitists in American universities were neither unaware of, nor indifferent to,
the implications of their research for Biblical scholarship, in part because of continued presidential and communal interest. Higher critics, and scholars who refuted their claims, frequently used the work of Semitists to place Biblical study
on the same "scientific" basis employed in the study of other ancient texts.[103] But
presidential hopes that Jewish Semitists would help refute the more extreme arguments of higher critics ran afoul of Jewish hesitation to study the Bible.

Solomon Schechter, later president of the Conservative Jewish Theological
Seminary, called contemporary Biblical criticism "the higher anti-Semitism."
"We must save the Bible from the goyim if Judaism is still worth anything to us,"
he exclaimed. "Mysticism and history are very nice in their way but without a
Bible they are worthless."[104] But Judaic scholars, wherever based, rarely took up
the implied challenge. Traditionalists found it hard to accept any emendations,
and scholars who applied critical methods to rabbinical literature often refused
to apply them to the Pentateuch. For traditionalists, Talmudic scholarship had
long since eclipsed pietistic and scientific Bible study. Some traditionalists later
took "excessive" knowledge of the Bible as a sign of heterodoxy and Zionist sec-
ularity. Programmatic documents of *Wissenschaft des Judentums* likewise paid
little attention to biblical scholarship. Early practitioners of *Wissenschaft des Judentums* avoided Pentateuchal criticism, in part, to avoid friction with Christian
scholarship.[105] Nor were either European or American Jewish seminaries hospitable to Biblical scholarship. Hostility to Protestant Biblical criticism led the
Jewish Theological Seminary under Schechter, Hebrew Union College under
founder Isaac Mayer Wise, and the Breslau Jewish Theological Seminary to avoid
study of the Pentateuch.[106]

Jewish Semitists in American universities likewise saw little reason to venture
into this thorny field. The few university-based Bible specialists felt uncomfortable in the "neutral" university environment.[107] "Only a Jew who knows himself
at one with the Bible religion," wrote Bible scholar Max Margolis, "can adequately interpret the Scriptures. . . . it requires a religious mind to understand

psalmist and prophet."[108] Margolis taught at the University of California for eight years before opting for sectarian institutions where he could be "at one with the Biblical religion." University-based Jewish Semitists, contending with Christian supremacists and their own inhibitions, mainly viewed Bible instruction as chrestomathies, sets of Hebrew and Semitics exercises, entitling their courses: "Rapid Reading of the Bible" or "Philological Study of the Bible" or "Cursory Reading of the Bible."[109]

Philology—not Talmud, nor Bible as religion—dominated the agenda of Semitic scholarship in American universities, especially the work of Jewish Semitists. These Semitists engaged in a delicate balancing act by offering courses that appeared to address presidential and communal concerns but were more congruent with "philology." To understand scholarly motivations, we must place this emphasis on philology in the context of curricular developments in the late nineteenth century. Language and literature departments debated curricular issues around four polarities: philology-literature, ancient-modern, specialization-liberal education, and graduate-undergraduate. This led to certain clusters: the graduate curriculum stressed specialized philological study of premodern texts, when available, and the undergraduate curriculum emphasized liberal study of recent literature. Contemporaries considered scientific scholarship appropriate for serious graduate students; a literary curriculum best suited undergraduates.[110]

Placing a specialist graduate school on top of the generalist American college created opportunities and dilemmas. The curriculum and the academic staff at universities that became members of the Association of American Universities grew more rapidly than the student body in the late nineteenth century.[111] Rapid staff growth at universities that also enrolled large numbers of students permitted inclusion of arcane and esoteric subjects, such as Semitics, that required a low faculty-student ratio.[112] But intellectual and structural separation of the graduate and undergraduate divisions could lead to substantive and methodological differences. In Judaic Semitics, this bifurcation had important implications for enrollments, isolation from religious controversy, and the ability of Jews to participate as faculty members.

The Semitists who took positions with regard to the four polarities understood these implications. Hebrew was optional and peripheral, if it existed at all, in the nineteenth-century American college. During the nineteenth century, modern languages—first French, then German—entered the undergraduate curriculum, first marginally and then as an occasional substitute for a classical tongue. A niche for modern languages was not secure at century's end, but their presence—whether for disciplinary or utilitarian reasons—precluded the reemergence of classical Hebrew as an undergraduate subject.[113]

Changes in scholarly preference complemented this curricular reality. At its inception, philology studied culture, history, and society through literary remains. A historian described the aspirations for nineteenth-century philology as "Janus-faced . . . [looking] in two directions at once: toward the study of language and toward the study of history."[114] Another historian boasted that philology "had recognized its calling, to be the transmitter of eternity, thus affording us the enjoyment of unbroken identity, across thousands of years, with the noblest and greatest peoples of antiquity; to make us as familiar with their spiritual creations and their history as if no gulf separated us."[115]

But by century's end the unitary science of philology broke into autonomous disciplines, including history, archaeology, and linguistics. The field retained its name, but its content became identified with linguistic analysis, the predominant discipline. "Scientific," linguistic, and textual philological studies, especially of ancient tongues, became a measure of institutional commitment to graduate study and to scholarship. Specialization overtook philology, the romantic vision was lost.[116] Basil Gildersleeve of Johns Hopkins brooded: "There is no Science of Antiquity, there is nothing but a cycle of studies; there is no unity, there is only diversity."[117] William Dwight Whitney "rebuked scholars who used their disciplines to confirm or deny religious and scientific theories, such as Darwin's explanations of the origin of the species or Adam and Eve as parents of the entire human race."[118] Scholars in other humanistic disciplines similarly noted that specialization meant fewer attempts to write "without fear and without footnotes."

Ismar Elbogen, however, refused to give up. *Wissenschaft des Judentums,* he contended, must extend beyond philology, as Leopold Zunz had envisioned. Zunz adopted this vision from his mentors, F. A. Wolf and August Boeckh, who saw philology as "a rediscovery and exposition of the totality of human knowledge."[119] Semitic philology, Elbogen believed, could not only contribute to a grand science, it could improve "living Judaism." "Even though it counts the most careful historical-philosophical investigation of the sources and discovery of facts among its tasks," he wrote, "it pursues this research not as a purpose in itself, not to resurrect past eras and dead monuments of literature, but in order to uncover the foundations on which the present time was built."[120]

Elbogen cited Arabic as a precedent for the creation of a living science. Political and economic contacts between the Muslim and western worlds, Elbogen wrote, led scholars to expand the study of Arabic language and literature from a branch of Semitic philology to include contemporary studies of life and culture. "These investigations," he added, "broke through the framework of philology and acquired the dignity of a separate discipline as Islamic studies."[121] Elbogen's characterization of the evolution of Arabic into Islamic studies did not accurately describe American conditions, as the battle over succession to Richard Gottheil's chair at Columbia shows (see chapter 4). And Elbogen's belief in "living Judaism" as the beneficiary of Jewish scholarship no more became the basis of American graduate study than the nineteenth-century vision of a grand philological science.

Ironically, the field's truncation was salutary for Jewish Semitists, whose academic status appeared more precarious to themselves than it did to presidents or providers. Problems of grammar, syntax, morphology—*the* problems of philology—did not impinge on faith or culture, so Jewish Semitists could comfortably profess philology at nominally Christian universities. Through philology, one could study Biblical and cognate civilizations without alluding to religious values. Technical questions required technical answers, and the accuracy and quality of a translation—not the brilliance of a literary interpretation—determined achievement in an American graduate seminar.[122] Even when the "so-called study of Literature" is offered, noted a late nineteenth-century scholar, it tends to be "grammar and philology run to seed."[123] Philological studies so dominated Johns Hopkins that in the English Department it was not unusual to find a dissertation that examined the comparative grammar of great writers.[124] A Semitics department thesis used sophisticated statistics to describe the distribution of linguistic forms in the Biblical text.[125]

Exceptions to this technical orientation existed within the humanities. Scholars, some observers believed, could straddle the fissures between graduate and undergraduate studies and between language and literature. "They taught graduate students bibliography and sources, 'Shakespeare on the graduate level' (that is, the distinctions of quartos and folios, sources, stage conditions)," wrote a historian of literary scholarship, "and meanwhile they read poetry to undergraduates in a trembling or unctuous voice." He added: "Sentimentalism and antiquarianism are not incompatible, even philosophically."[126] But this was a minority opinion; most administrators and many faculty members believed that literary and linguistic approaches were contradictory. "The characteristics which lead a man to take deep interest in philological questions," noted Columbia president Seth Low, "are distinctly unfriendly to what may be called the natural and spontaneous enjoyment of the literary productions of the languages."[127]

Exceptions, in any case, rarely occurred in Semitics. Judaic Semitics rejected the historic, romantic, and literary potential within its subject domain for a scientific, positivistic, and graduate orientation. Columbia guarded against an imbalance by appointing literary specialists and philologists in each language department except Semitics and Indo-Iranian, where it conceded the predominance of philology.[128] Johns Hopkins also exempted Semitics when it moved toward literary analysis.[129] The University of Pennsylvania ruled out its Semitics scholars as instructors of a proposed undergraduate course in the English Bible: "A man who has specialized in any Semitic study has done much to unfit himself for such work as should be done in this department . . . the method of the Specialist in a limited department tends to that pedantry which is the bane of all true literary study."[130]

Semitics instructors did not object to these limitations. Undergraduate student interests may have been primarily literary, but prudence dictated that Semitists, particularly Judaic Semitists, remain circumspect about exposing undergraduates to the higher criticism. These scholars also preferred the discovery and decoding of new languages and the editing and interpreting of extant documents to elementary instruction.[131] Semitists, for example, deciphered Hittite after a 1906 discovery of a library of Hittite tablets in Boghaz-Koi, Turkey.

The sizable proportion of undergraduates enrolled in Harvard's Semitics department still represented a smaller fraction of undergraduates than the proportion enrolled by any other language department. These enrollments resulted largely from Crawford Toy's "History of Israel" course. With this course removed, Semitics enrollments declined by one-fourth. President Abbott L. Lowell later referred to the course as one of which "it was said to have been very easy, and . . . attracted a class of men not very serious in their intentions." Lowell did not view its disappearance from the curriculum after Toy's retirement as a serious intellectual loss.[132] William Popper, the California Semitics mainstay after 1905, reported that his department confined itself "largely to the use of advanced students."[133] At the University of Chicago, undergraduates comprised three percent of the Semitics enrollment and at least fifty percent in classical, Germanic, and Romance languages in 1895–1896.[134]

Semitics professors attained short-term security but paid a high long-term price for neglecting undergraduates. The cost per student of Semitics departments reduced their competitiveness within universities. A 1905 committee that reviewed Harvard's Arts and Science courses "in respect to their cost and the propriety of diminishing or increasing their number" found that only six undergraduate courses enrolled fewer than 10 students. But 70 courses open to both undergraduates and graduates and 103 courses exclusively for graduate students enrolled fewer than 10. The Harvard Overseers then asked the faculty to "undertake a comprehensive revision of the present scheme of instruction with a view to securing more concentration of effort, increased educational efficiency, and if practicable, diminished expenditure." The faculty overwhelmingly rejected a proposal to charge tuition by the course rather than by the year on the grounds that it "would operate eventually to the disadvantage of the small expensive courses."[135]

The Harvard faculty won that battle, but the trend toward efficiency harmed the long-term interests of graduate-oriented departments, such as Semitics. Undergraduate enrollments, noted a University of Chicago dean, could subsidize the more expensive graduate courses. "A great advantage to the costly graduate school," he wrote, "is the presence of a large body of college students who can, by entering the less advanced of the graduate courses, share the costs of instruction." Undergraduate alumni, the dean added, could continue these subsidies. "The men who are appreciative of the achievements of their alma mater in both research and instruction and are in a position to contribute to the institution's financial security and growth are usually alumni of the college."[136] The dean expected few financial contributions from the scholarly doctoral alumni.

By concentrating on specialized education, Semitists not only increased the cost of instruction, which scarcely endeared them to cost-conscious administrators, they also failed to recruit a graduate constituency. "A department which does not maintain thoroughly good elementary courses," Charles Eliot warned, "will have difficulty in recruiting adequately its advanced courses; and . . . a teacher who does not prove his value year after year to large elementary classes may find himself without a suitable audience in the advanced courses he especially likes to give."[137] Yale president Arthur Hadley, who was more uncomfortable with the stress on graduate and specialized education, suggested that the continued prosperity of the intellectual producer required an audience of intellectual consumers. Hadley granted the significance of creativity and original research but argued that "the appreciation of science and letters by the many made possible their successful pursuit by the few." Academization, he feared, would result in the loss of the lay constituency.[138]

Ideally, lay courses would lead some students to prepare for graduate instruction. Johns Hopkins Semitics professor Paul Haupt early on called for "a more general course . . . otherwise the attendance on the Semitics courses would fall off." Haupt's candidates for liberal arts courses included "lectures on cuneiform inscriptions, the O.T. or History of Israel."[139] But most Semitists, when they offered undergraduate courses at all, eschewed elementary courses for upper division courses in the text of the Hebrew Bible. These courses directly prepared "students who intended to pursue theological studies for advanced work [while] serving at the same time as an introduction to the graduate work in Semitic Languages."[140] Greek and Latin departments, in contrast, offered instruction for all four years of the undergraduate curriculum.

Graduate instruction contributed to scholarly productivity and research university growth and shielded scholars from religious controversy. But this emphasis not only removed Semitics departments from large enrollments, it reduced the interest of lay constituencies. The history of the American Oriental Society further illustrates the triumph of a philological research ethos. John Pickering, a prominent Boston attorney, and William Jenks, a Boston clergyman, founded the American Oriental Society in 1843 to advance "the cultivation of learning in the Asiatic, African and Polynesian languages."[141] Membership was unrestricted, and the society heard many reports from overseas missionaries. But the AOS included scholars from the outset, for instance Andover's Moses Stuart and Edward Robinson, and Society officers explicitly encouraged philological studies.[142]

Within a decade, scholars held the upper hand, and academic papers replaced missionary accounts at meetings. In 1849, the Society designated Yale's E. E. Salisbury as corresponding secretary and adopted research and the cultivation of a taste for oriental studies as society goals, thereby assuring scholarly primacy. William Dwight Whitney succeeded his Yale mentor as corresponding secretary and filled many issues of the *Journal of the American Oriental Society* (*JAOS*) with his own scholarship. Whitney dominated the Society until his 1890 resignation from the presidency after a six-year tenure that followed 27 years as corresponding secretary and 18 years as librarian. The society's academic emphasis led it to discontinue the special category of corresponding member—foreign missionaries—in 1896, though the Society formally remained open to all. The American Oriental Society emphasized Semitics and Sanskrit scholarship, while serious attention to the Far East awaited the twentieth century. Semitics and Sanskrit representatives divided positions and influence—*JAOS* editorship in the 1890s, for example—though Semitics recruited more practitioners.[143]

A philological bent permitted Semitists to derive short-term gains from reduced opposition from Jews and Gentiles with apprehensions about research that had no preordained results. But this indifference was offset by reduced moral and tangible support from sympathetic community members who also absented themselves from AOS affairs. Opting for a constricted definition of philology threatened the long-term security of Semitic studies. Low external subsidies, accompanied by small enrollments, led twentieth-century administrators to conclude that the costs of maintaining Semitics programs outweighed their attractiveness.[144] Jewish learning, its fate still largely tied to Semitics, entered a period of stasis after World War I, when heightened academic anti-Semitism reinforced these factors. But advocates of university-based Jewish studies learned a lesson, and the field took undergraduate education and communal concerns more seriously when it regrouped in the interwar and postwar years—in Near Eastern and Middle Eastern language and literature departments and elsewhere.

III

SCHOLARS: COMMUNAL AND ACADEMIC NORMS

Community and Academy

On October 11, 1873, Felix Adler, son of Rabbi Samuel Adler, delivered a sermon to the congregation of New York City's liberal Temple Emanu-El. Felix, heir apparent to his father's Emanu-El pulpit, had just returned to America after extended study at Germany's universities and Jewish seminaries. Profoundly influenced by Abraham Geiger, Adler spoke in a universalistic, humanitarian vein: "Judaism was not given to the Jews alone," he claimed. "Its destiny is to embrace in one great moral state the whole family of man."[1]

Critical contemporaries, such as Emanu-El's newly recruited associate rabbi Gustav Gottheil, noted Adler's failure to refer to God in his talk. Some Emanu-El members asked if the speech's universalist tendencies left any room for Jewish particularism. Other congregants were uneasy with the sermon's progressive social views. Still others noted Adler's critique of European Reform Judaism. "The Old has been torn down, but the New has not been reared in its stead," Adler said. "Looking to Europe, where the movement of Reform took its origin, what a spectacle meets the eye! Stagnation everywhere; hopes that were once so high, changed into hopeless indifference."[2] These members asked if the critique also applied to American Reform Jewry, and perhaps to the Emanu-El congregation. Gottheil threatened to resign in protest, and the Emanu-El board of trustees asked Adler for clarification. Adler concluded that he could not conscientiously succeed his father, and he eventually broke with Judaism.

Unemployed, and seeking an intellectual forum, Adler accepted Cornell University President Andrew Dixon White's offer of a professorship of indeterminate duration in Hebrew and Oriental literature and history. White acted at the behest of Emanu-El congregant Joseph Seligman, who nominated Adler and funded the professorship. Adler, initially, was to offer classes in Hebrew and other Semitic languages. "It is to be hoped," the 1874 university *Register* stated, "that in time sufficient interest in this direction will be developed to warrant the establishment of classes for the Arabic, Syriac, and other cognate languages to the Hebrew, and that Semitic philology in the term's best and widest sense will find a home at the University."[3] Benny Kraut, Adler's biographer, suggests that he might have thereby enlightened the Cornell community on Judaism, helped to fulfill Cornell's ideal of nonsectarian faculty appointments, and attracted Jewish students to an institution concerned about finances and enrollment.[4]

But Adler accomplished few of these goals. He lectured on comparative religion and its consequences for contemporary belief—not on Semitic literature and history—and his comments offended key sectors of the Cornell community. Some Cornellians objected to the appointment of a Jewish faculty member, while others expressed disappointment, perhaps disingenuously, at Adler's failure to uphold a more traditional Jewish perspective.[5]

In May, 1877, Cornell's trustees decided not to renew Adler's contract. Henceforth, they announced, no benefactors would have the right of nomination to an academic post, as Seligman had. President White inferred that Adler's "new work in our great metropolis [he referred to the beginnings of the Ethical Culture movement], which will doubtless require all his energies and cause him to turn from the field of literature to that of a public teacher," led to his termination. The increased importance of Semitics, White added, required full-time attention to instructional duties "uninterrupted by engrossing duties elsewhere."[6] Despite these fine words, the trustees—not Adler—initiated the move.[7]

Adler's brief Cornell tenure established several precedents. The appointment indicated the willingness of an American university to hire an individual identified as a Jew to offer instruction in Semitics—especially "Judaic Semitics," which included such topics of concern to Judaism and Jews as Hebrew and rabbinics. Only James M. Philips had obtained a similar appointment since Isaac Nordheimer's brief tenure at the University of the City of New York in the 1830s, but the appointment of Jews to Semitics professorships thereafter occurred frequently.[8] "As I look back upon that period," wrote Cyrus Adler (no relation to Felix) during the 1930s, "I feel sure that our America was much broader, much more liberal, much freer from prejudice than it is today."[9] While not necessarily a universally valid generalization, Cyrus Adler's comments reflect the willingness of some late nineteenth-century American universities to receive Jewish contributions to Semitic, Biblical, and post-Biblical research.[10]

But under what circumstances? Late nineteenth-century academics developed a set of norms governing "scholarship." "Even if the role is performed by an individual who happens to be also a priest, this fact is supposed to be irrelevant to his status as a scholar," wrote Florian Znaniecki in his classic work on knowledge and the individuals who acquire it.[11] Znaniecki posited a straightforward distinction: A priest may invoke divine authority as the source of knowledge, but the secular scholar could rely only upon "rational evidence," a criterion not peculiar to the idiosyncratic beliefs of the members of a sect. In late nineteenth-century America, the formidable challenges to knowledge heretofore justified by recourse to divine authority—the Bible as God's word—led traditionalists and reconciliationists in universities to accept the same rational criterion of evidence as their challengers. Prestige, recognition, and acceptance increasingly went to scholars who conformed to this criterion, at the expense of colleagues who refused to renounce explanations based on divine authority. A struggle was underway as the growth of a "neutral arena" permitted the "advancement of knowl-edge" to replace faith and piety as goals for higher education.

This neutral arena directly benefited Jewish Semitists who accepted the ratio-nal evidence criterion. These scholars sought cooperation with their Gentile col-leagues and recognized their dependence on Gentile goodwill for scholarly legitimacy and personal advancement. The Jewish and Judaic presence was greater in Semitics than in most other academic fields, although university-based Semitics was neither a large nor a completely "Jewish" field, either by intellec-tual orientation or personal affiliation. Judaic aspects of Semitics rarely predom-inated even when a university included work in this subject, and Jews dominated Semitics departments only at California and Columbia. Still, the environment within Semitics departments was largely benign, and presidential and communal backing led even recalcitrant Gentile Semitists to adopt a *modus vivendi* with Jewish colleagues.

Writing in the 1930s, Florian Znaniecki readily distinguished between the priest's performance of sacred duties and secular scholarship, but a half-century earlier, the norms were still evolving. Neither philo-Semitic Protestant presidents nor members of the Jewish community consistently distinguished between two possible roles for Jewish Semitists—as representatives of a constituency that wished university recognition and whose support the university desired, or as practitioners of a discipline or field who happened to be Jewish. The ambiguity appeared in Semitics in the late nineteenth century and recurred when other as-pects of Jewish learning—history, religion, social science, and literary studies—entered the university.

Felix Adler's appointment at Cornell led many Jewish and Gentile observers to view Jewish Semitists as communal representatives. In 1874, before the full extent of Adler's apostasy became known, the *Jewish Messenger* editorialized:

> It is significant of the progress of culture in this country, when a thriving educa-tional institution—such as Cornell University—adds to its faculty a young and tal-ented Israelite to fill the professorship of Hebrew and Oriental Literature. . . . We hail the appointment of a Hebrew professor as a grand concession to the liberal-ity of the age, and congratulate the faculty of Cornell University in having thus demonstrated their freedom from prejudice. . . . [Adler's supporters who financed the position] have the satisfaction of having not only placed their friend-protege in an honorable position, but elevated the Jewish name and Jewish interests in the opinion of the world, again demonstrating that the Jew has higher ideas than mere moneymaking.[12]

Adler's Jewishness meant as much as the subject matter, and his apostasy led most concerned members of the Jewish community to restrict financial and moral support to faculty members with a positive Jewish identity. Some univer-sities assured orthodoxy—albeit of the Reform variety—by choosing the rabbi of a prominent local congregation.[13] But the different conceptions of the Semitist's role held by practitioners, presidents, concerned community, and practitioners resulted in ambiguities for nearly all appointees—full-time scholars or part-time rabbis. Did the university retain a scholar because of group membership or academic accomplishment? Why did the scholar accept the appointment? Did the scholar consistently adhere to academic norms? Did the Jewish community reward the university's gesture and the scholar's academic contributions? Ambiguity increased along with the strength of conflicting conceptions.

Communal expectations for Jewish scholarship, though ever present, varied in intensity and changed along with American Judaism and the American Jewish community. The dominant communal expectation in the late nineteenth century was the attainment of recognition and social acceptance through scholarship. Jewish participation in academic life would illustrate the benefits of removing barriers to Jews in political, economic, and social life, while Jewish learning would show prior contributions to the general polity. After World War II, Judaism gained greater acceptance as one of three American creeds, and communal preoccupation shifted from tolerance and acceptance to preservation within a benign environment.[14] Thus, the community now emphasizes survival of American Judaism—universities should teach Judaism since religious institutions do not reach all young Jews. Communal interests then gravitated from the late nineteenth-century emphasis upon the universalistic aspects of Judaism—aspects that Judaism shares with other religions and peoples—to an emphasis upon what is relatively unique yet desirable.

The Jewish community was never blind to the uses of the university, nor did practitioners fail to perceive the dominant communal interest, whether or not they personally agreed with it. Each practitioner also had personal intellectual and social goals that might or might not coincide with communal expectations. At the time of Felix Adler's appointment, Semitics scholars and the Jewish community were optimistic about obtaining recognition and acceptance of American Jewry. Some Semitists agreed that recognition of the field would accelerate social recognition. Others viewed recognition of the field mainly as a prerequisite for personal scholarly acceptance. Still other academics extolled the pursuit of scholarship for its own sake. It was not ordinarily necessary to declare oneself on this issue. Indeed, scholars whose views diverged from communal expectations usually kept discreetly silent. In any case, both scholars and community members could unite behind William Rosenau's insistence that "An institution to be worthy of the title 'University,' should have a chair in Semitics":

> It is recognized as one of the principal disciplines at all European universities. A European university would as little think of being without a Semitic chair as being without a chair in the Greek and Latin classics. The European University has always been the model of the American College. . . . The university which does not look to the establishment of a Semitic professorship falls behind in the race to perfection, recognition and influence.[15]

Cyrus Adler hoped, contra Elbogen, that Semitic studies at Johns Hopkins would obtain "an ever-increasing recognition in the world of learning at large" while proving salutary for the Jewish community.[16]

Jewish Semitists were not the only practitioners of the "newer" scholarly fields who came from religious backgrounds and who had personal doubts. The university environment—where one could go no further than allowed by rational evidence—permitted these practitioners to elevate hesitation and questioning to positive virtues. But if questions did not necessarily have to be definitively answered, practitioners found that presidents and providers expected them to be addressed. Self-imposed communal and academic agendas, added to these external expectations, produced a high degree of ambiguity among these Semitists.

The strategies that scholars employed to reduce ambiguity varied within and across generations. Two patterns of conflict resolution that emerged in the late nineteenth century became end points of a continuum that defined the behavior of subsequent Judaica scholars—Semitists, historians, scholars of religion, or representatives of other academic disciplines. Rabbis who did not claim competence in comparative Semitic scholarship taught Biblical Hebrew and Rabbinics, often without remuneration and usually on a part-time basis. These rabbis, often viewed as communal representatives, conducted few scholarly investigations and therefore often felt set apart from their colleagues who emphasized research.

Other practitioners, often armed with European doctorates in Semitics, opted for conformity to the norms of academic life. Several scholars were sons of prominent American rabbis who, like Felix Adler, had expected to assume their fathers' pulpits. Richard Gottheil and Morris Jastrow, two notable cases, returned to America from Germany in the mid-1880s after studying Darwin, the higher criticism, *Wissenschaft des Judentums,* and philology. Gottheil and Jastrow forsook rabbinical careers for scholarship, although Gottheil continued to express his stronger Jewish identification through religious, communal, and scholarly activity. Gottheil and Jastrow conformed to academic norms, but university authorities and concerned communities sometimes viewed them as rabbis, not scholars. Throughout the nineteenth century, college instructors were often seen as young men awaiting a pulpit. Even at century's end, Gentile and Jewish communities were slow to recognize that some young Jewish intellectuals had opted for academic—not ministerial—careers.

Jewish Semitists who became strongly socialized to academic norms usually declined to engage in teaching and research aimed primarily at meeting communal expectations. Felix Adler's ill-fated appointment illustrated the need for circumspection and probably discouraged other Semitists from entering into contemporary religious debates.[17] For other Semitists, academic life appeared a viable alternative *after* a decision to reject a rabbinical career. Morris Jastrow despaired of ministering in materialistic German and American cultures in which religion, indeed any transcendent ideal, appeared irrelevant. "I know how many doubts I have had," he wrote while a student in Germany,

> since devoting myself more seriously to the preparation for life and to performing the duties that will devolve upon me and I know that the greatest doubt has been whether I will be able to remain firm in the right path. It is not so much personal

failure that I fear but the fear that I may through a false course, false steps, do harm
to American Judaism. Judaism in America is to me like a young and tender plant
that needs careful nursing. The unskilled gardener may with the best of intentions
kill the plant. Have I made myself clear?[18]

Felix Adler later compared Jastrow to Ernest Renan. "Both had discovered
their inability to expound the teachings of the religion in which they were
raised"; he noted, "both, being religious-minded men, were mastered by the desire to understand that mighty force in human nature called Religion, which had
exercised its spell over so many generations and to which they, too, confessed."[19]
Morris Jastrow, like Ernest Renan, had to come to terms with religion, rather
than represent it. Both opted for the professorate, not the pulpit. In Jastrow's
case, this choice meant communal and familial disappointment and a difficult
personal redefinition.

This group of academically oriented Jewish Semitists "compartmentalized"—
adopted or suspended modes of thinking and belief in specific settings—a
method by which intellectuals often confronted a changing world.[20] Jewish Semitists found compartmentalizing more difficult than, say, economists, who could
divorce theological beliefs from their academic discipline while employing the
discipline to advance an ethical and reformist agenda. Semitists, as chapter 2
noted, therefore often opted for working at the philological frontiers of their
field, at the expense of demonstrating the relevance of Jewish learning to general knowledge. This option, Jewish Semitists hoped, would permit them to resemble "the idealized product of the *Haskalah*, the Jewish Enlightenment, . . .
a Jew at home and an ordinary man on the street."[21] This resolution also placed
the doubters out of the range of forces earlier brought to bear on Felix Adler.

Disciplinary recognition, Semitists knew, resulted from discovering and decoding new languages, not from incremental advances in knowledge about a
language whose structure was already well known, or from exegetical commentaries. They therefore offered Hebrew only as a propaedeutic study and specialized in another Semitic language or in comparative linguistic analysis.[22]
Theological interest in Hebrew, noted Richard Gottheil, by then a Columbia Semitics professor, "has made, and in many institutions it still does make, all the
other Semitic tongues mere handmaids of the Hebrew of the Bible." But by
World War I, Semitists sufficiently separated themselves from "theological interest" to reverse the traditional relationship between Hebrew and the "cognate" languages.[23] Avoidance of Biblical criticism and rabbinics combined with
the lure of philology to give their work a non-Judaic cast.

Thus historians later asked if Jewish learning really entered American universities in the late nineteenth century. "At best," wrote Leon Jick, "the number of
positions remained small and the treatment of the totality of the Jewish tradition
as an area of study of intrinsic worth without regard to its relationship to the predominant culture was negligible."[24] Hebraica, one might respond, was present
in a form more Jewish than Christian. Some Jewish Semitists, mainly the rabbis
who held part-time academic posts, undertook "Judaica," and even Johns Hop-

kins offered Talmud courses. The *Jewish Encyclopedia* (1901–1905), in addition, relied heavily on university-affiliated Jewish Semitists. Other scholars showed their concern and commitments in their teaching and service.

More important, most late nineteenth-century Semitists and many current practitioners rejected Jick's "intrinsic worth" criterion. The "relationship to the predominant culture," these scholars argued, defined the proper role for Jewish learning within universities. William Rosenau's survey of Semitics, Jick added, failed to mention any benefits of Semitic study for Jews or Judaism. Yet, Rosenau, writing in the journal of the Central Conference of American Rabbis, may have assumed his audience took these benefits for granted. Finally, Jick presupposed the existence of mature disciplines rather than subjects still in gestation or infancy.

The indeterminate status of the field—Semitic studies entered universities simultaneously with many competing disciplines and professional schools—complicated the adjustments made by academically-oriented scholars. Morris Jastrow opted for a scholarly career within a year of his return from Europe. "During my last year abroad," he wrote, "I devoted myself almost exclusively to Assyrian and shall very likely make that with Arabic the special object of my life's works." But the young scholar had few academic alternatives. "Cannot something be done to arouse a greater interest in Philological studies in this country?" he wrote to Harvard Semitist David Gordon Lyon. "The great defect of our American civilization is its one sidedness," he added. "All the talent and power of the country is being turned in the direction of the applied sciences and the value of the abstract sciences—owing to the vicious principle of utilitarianism so general in this country—is underrated, or rather, almost entirely ignored. Oh, for a little German idealism." The unsalaried lectureship in Semitics that Jastrow obtained from the University of Pennsylvania in 1885 evolved into a professorship, but Jastrow took a risk in opting for a professorship rather than the pulpit. "The outlook for Semitics and other Philology in this country is not encouraging," he wrote before receiving his professorship. "The University of Pennsylvania is not yet prepared to add a real university wing in the German sense of the word to its already numerous departments."[25]

Jastrow's experiences in Germany, his reintroduction to Gilded Age America, and the utilitarian and professional slant of the University of Pennsylvania affected his personal perceptions, but few other aspirants to Semitics professorships overestimated the prospects of their discipline.[26] Semitic scholarship addressed important contemporary issues, but the relative scarcity of faculty positions, competition from other disciplines, and the subject's formidability dissuaded potential graduate students. Practitioners contended that difficulties in mastering the languages were overrated but could not dismiss the other factors.[27]

Nor would Semitics department budgets stand up to a rigorous cost-benefit analysis. American Semitists, lacking libraries, manuscripts, and artifacts, required research trips to Europe and the Near East. Presidents of aspirant universities understood that the archaeological discoveries that brought international recognition required costly expeditions to remote sites. High costs and low revenues made universities reluctant to enter Semitics work without outside support, but reliance upon external constituencies often increased practitioner anxiety about their own, and their field's, future.

The identification of Semitics with Jews and Judaism proved both a liability and an asset. In Europe and America, race, religion, ethnicity, and gender often excluded individuals from universities and their ideas from objective evaluation. The subordinate social status of Jews, despite political emancipation, and fear that Jewish learning might challenge Christianity led German universities to refuse admission to *Wissenschaft des Judentums* and to Jewish students and faculty members.[28] A religious quarrel became transmuted into a hierarchy of civilizations based upon racial characteristics.

In 1877, the year that Cornell's trustees failed to renew Felix Adler's appointment, Joseph Seligman, who underwrote Adler's salary, was refused accommodations at the fashionable Grand Union Hotel in Saratoga Springs, New York, because "no Israelites shall be permitted in the future to stop at this Hotel."[29] Thus, the growth of Semitics in the late nineteenth-century American university also took place against a backdrop of heightened anti-Semitism, intensified by mass Jewish migrations, from which even well-established Jews received few immunities. It was usually up to the president to overcome any unfriendly social currents.

Appointment of a Jewish faculty member could arouse consternation, ire, or outright opposition. Some Cornellians saw Felix Adler's appointment as a threat to Cornell's Christian nature. One critic said Adler offered the "cheapest sort of infidelity. . . . Cornell cannot afford to have such a teacher on its faculty. . . . I do not know whether this young *Rabbi* is with you still."[30] A candidate's Jewishness helped or hurt, but always influenced, his employment opportunities. Once aboard, a Judaic scholar had to deal with his colleagues, demonstrate that his scholarship would not threaten the fundamental tenets of Christianity, and remember the expectations of the Jewish community.

Particulars of Universalists

A successful Judaic Semitics program required the cooperation of presidents, community, and practitioners with different agendas. Optimism about American universities and about the ability of Semitics to contribute to academic, communal, and personal aspirations helped to mitigate latent tensions. The following discussion of the intrainstitutional mechanics of program establishment emphasizes practitioner appointment and promotion; subject growth, specialization, and differentiation; and knowledge creation and dissemination. The next chapter discusses interinstitutional activities affecting the entire field—the quest for international professional recognition, standard setting, creation of research dissemination arenas, and the conflicting pressures of practitioner cooperation and competition.

The process of program creation reflected the opportunism generally evident at the late nineteenth-century universities concerning subjects taught, staff hired, and methods of finance. Contemporary practice reflects a rationalized process: a faculty vacancy results (in good times, at least) in an administrative authorization to fill a slot. A search ensues, and the department, division, administration, and trustees confirm the recommended appointee. In the late nineteenth century, however, carts often preceded horses. Academic specialization, for example, did not preclude shifts between chairs, and the availability of an endowment or a scholar might occasion creation of an entire department.[31]

Presidents, providers, and practitioners each initiated two Judaic Semitics positions or departments, and permanence usually depended on the sustained interest of the initiator. At Columbia and Pennsylvania, the initiatives of (Jewish) scholars received communal support, mainly salary subsidies for stated terms. Presidents exhibited more corporate than intellectual interest in the field, and both institutions soon regularized the appointed scholar's status. But field continuance depended upon the practitioner's ability to defend his department's interests.

At Chicago and California, prominent rabbis offered their services as Semitics instructors. These universities accepted the offers, aroused tensions by exempting rabbi-practitioners from the academic norms that governed their colleagues, and thereby raised questions about the purpose of their appointments.

Our third institutional pair—Harvard and Johns Hopkins—featured strong presidential interest. This interest assured the field's academic position, but did not assure that Jews would obtain the available Semitics appointments. A non-Jew chaired the Johns Hopkins Semitics program, although several Jewish faculty members taught in the program. At Harvard, appointment of a Jewish faculty member had to wait until after 1910. In both cases, the succession of presidents with little interest in the field and the simultaneous diminution of communal interest led to program weakening after the turn of the century.

Despite the presence and strong interest of William Rainey Harper, Chicago does not belong in this third group because presidential support translated into different results. At Johns Hopkins, the Semitics seminary featured Gilman-authorized salaried Judaic assistants, Talmud courses, and projects, such as the Polychrome Bible, with a Judaic bent. Harvard's Semitics department, with Charles Eliot's assent and assistance, had a strong Judaic presence in Crawford Toy, David Gordon Lyon, George Foot Moore, the Semitics Museum, and the Palestine archaeological expedition. At Chicago, in contrast, Judaic representation under Harper was confined to one rabbi, and the field's development involved the Jewish community in a manner more closely resembling California. Harper helped assure the presence of Semitics at American universities. At Chicago, he may have decided that Hirsch, in combination with his own interests in Biblical Hebrew, adequately covered the Judaic flank.

Analysis of Jewish learning at the six founding institutions identifies recurrent patterns of institutional growth and of practitioner conflict resolution. The field thrived when all three parties retained their enthusiasm, responsibility for which usually lay in the hands of practitioners. When one or more parties became disenchanted, continued sustenance from the initiating party maximized chances for survival.

Columbia and Pennsylvania: Practitioner Initiatives

Morris Jastrow and Richard Gottheil—our two scholarly initiators—opted for the academy instead of the rabbinate and then defined their professional agendas. Both scholars enlisted communal and institutional support but ultimately depended on themselves.

Declaring one's candidacy for a position yet to be created frequently occurred in Semitics and other fields at late nineteenth-century universities. James McKeen Cattell and Morris Jastrow, both just returned from European study, offered their services in psychology and Semitics, respectively, to the University of Pennsylvania. The trustees appointed Cattell—whose father was a socially prominent University of Pennsylvania trustee—because he met a perceived need, held solid academic credentials, and would not initially encumber the university's budget.[32] Jastrow's appointment took longer because other candidates vied for a professorship in Semitics. But the factors that led to Cattell's appointment also resulted in a position for Jastrow.

Richard Gottheil did not intend to became a Semitist. His father, Gustav Gottheil, had attained prominence as a rabbi, first as an assistant at the Berlin Reform Temple, then as rabbi to the Jewish congregation in Manchester, England, and finally as associate and then successor to Rabbi Samuel Adler (Felix's father) at Temple Emanu-El in 1874. After receiving a Bachelor of Arts degree from Columbia in 1882, Richard studied at German rabbinical seminaries and universities. By the time he was awarded his doctorate at Leipzig in 1886, Gottheil's ardor for Semitic studies had increased, and his interest in succeeding to his father's pulpit diminished. Two years later, the senior Gottheil still insisted that Richard had only temporarily set aside a rabbinical career, but the young scholar had by then opted for scholarship.[33]

Columbia received Gottheil warmly when he returned to the United States in 1886. Gottheil's appointment allowed the institution to fulfill, at no expense, its long-standing commitment to offer instruction in Oriental languages and Hebrew since Gottheil asked "to lecture at the College on the Syriac Language and Literature 'without any expectation of remuneration.'" The time was also auspicious for Columbia to extend a hand of friendship to New York's Jewish community. Gustav Gottheil was rabbi of the city's most prominent Jewish congregation, many of whose members might enhance Columbia's endowment.[34] Columbia's commitment to graduate education—a School of Political Science opened in 1880 and advanced humanistic and scientific instruction soon followed—amid stirrings at similar institutions also prompted the move.

In 1887, a year after Gottheil's appointment as instructor in Syriac language and literature, Columbia's trustees accepted a five-year endowment of a Rabbinics chair from some Temple Emanu-El congregants in association with Gustav Gottheil. The donors requested that the chair's occupant teach in areas of Jewish concern, including the Aramaic version of the Scriptures, the Talmud, the history of Jewish exegesis and Hebrew grammar, post-Biblical poetry and philosophy, and the secular history of the Jews since their dispersion after the fall of the Second Temple.[35] The chair's backers requested the right of "presentation," or nomination, and asked that instruction be free of religious bias and that the occupant hold the same rights and privileges as other chair holders.[36] Columbia accepted these conditions and appointed Richard Gottheil, the congregants' nominee. In return, the donors promised to consider a permanent endowment after the initial term.[37]

Morris Jastrow's biography and tenure at the University of Pennsylvania closely resemble those of Gottheil, his friend and colleague. The similarities begin with family background. Jastrow's father, Marcus, born in Poland, occupied the pulpit of the progressive German synagogue in Warsaw and advocated Polish independence from Russia (1861–1863). Briefly imprisoned, Jastrow was expelled from Poland and, after several brief intermediate moves, accepted the call of Philadelphia's Rodef Shalom synagogue in 1866. A leader of the historical school that, opposing Isaac Mayer Wise's anti-*halakhic* orientation, evolved into Conservative Judaism, Jastrow attempted to balance tradition and innovation as Rodef Shalom's rabbi, as a founder and teacher of religious philosophy, Jewish history, and Biblical exegesis at Philadelphia's Maimonides College, and as a founder of the Young Men's Hebrew Association and the Jewish Publication Society.[38] A holder of a doctorate from Halle, the elder Jastrow devoted much of his later life to scholarship after illness curtailed his ability to perform rabbinical functions. His magnum opus was a *Dictionary of the Targumim, the Talmud Babli* [Babylonian] *and Yerushalmi* [Jerusalem] *and the Midrashic Literature* (1886–1903).

His son, Morris, born in Warsaw in 1861, attended private schools in Philadelphia before entering the arts department of his future employer in 1877. After graduation in 1881, he studied for the rabbinate at the Jewish theological seminary at Breslau, and studied Oriental languages at the universities of Breslau, Leipzig, Strasbourg, and Paris, receiving his doctorate at Leipzig in July, 1884. His thesis translated a partial text by Judah Ben Davud Hayyuj, a tenth-century Hebrew grammarian.[39]

Jastrow's doubts about the rabbinate increased each year, as did the seriousness with which he considered the academic calling, and his decision to remain in Europe for another year of advanced Semitic study permitted him to continue the weighing process. Jastrow did not extoll the attractions of Semitics in his early correspondence, but scholarship was clearly an attractive alternative if his doubts prevailed.[40]

Jastrow foreclosed no options upon his return to Philadelphia in September, 1885. He worked for a year both as assistant rabbi in his father's synagogue and teacher in the congregational school, and as lecturer in Semitics at the University of Pennsylvania. He taught Arabic and Hebrew at the university and considered himself a specialist in Arabic, Assyrian, and Rabbinical literature in connection with Hebrew and Biblical exegesis. By December, 1886, he opted for an academic career after closely observing American Jewry—"the pulpit exercises but little influence today"—and American Judaism—conceived by Reform so widely "to be vague and indeterminate."

Jastrow declined the renewal of his rabbinical appointment and offered a parting sermon on Jews and Judaism to Rodef Shalom congregants. Some newspapers sensationalized the talk, while others defended it as a synthesis of Jastrow's remarks during his year's tenure. Jastrow did not discuss his own religious convictions, but he noted that a minister's example and words are equally important: "He must not be expected to do anything merely for the sake of appearances, and, if expected, must refuse."[41]

Gottheil and Jastrow faced different academic hierarchies at the beginning of their careers. Gottheil began as a very junior man at an institution where several colleagues had established beachheads. But the field was rapidly left to him. The death of a Latin professor, for example, allowed Harry T. Peck, tutor in Latin and Semitics, to devote his full energies to Latin.[42] Gottheil (Semitics) and A. V. W. Jackson (Indo-Iranian) eventually divided Oriental studies at Columbia.

Gottheil had several assistants during his 50-year tenure, notably the incumbent of the Gustav Gottheil lectureship.[43] But Columbia added only one more Semitics professor during Gottheil's tenure—John D. Prince, who came from New York University in 1902. Prince's multifarious political activities—speaker of the New Jersey House of Representatives, later ambassador to Denmark and Yugoslavia—limited his academic usefulness, and in 1915, he shifted his specialization from Semitic to Slavonic languages.[44] University authorities did not fill the vacancy, so the shift resulted in a net loss for the Semitics department. Richard Gottheil thus determined the direction of Semitics at Columbia.

At Pennsylvania, in contrast, the field became more crowded.[45] In summer, 1886, Pennsylvania's trustees considered creating one or more Semitics chairs, but two other available candidates also exhibited impressive qualifications: Reverend John P. Peters, professor of Hebrew at the Episcopal Divinity School, and Herman V. Hilprecht, who migrated to Philadelphia as Oriental editor of the *Sunday School Times* shortly after obtaining his doctorate at Leipzig. The trustees, cognizant that none of the candidates required a university salary, elected Peters, who retained his divinity school appointment, to a Hebrew professorship; Jastrow to a lectureship in Arabic and Assyrian for a year; and Hilprecht to a lectureship in Egyptology for the same period.[46] Jastrow, learning that Hilprecht had the inside track for a contemplated professorship of Assyrian, wavered between entering the lists ("for my standing"), or resigning his lectureship.[47] He ultimately declared his candidacy after an apparent arrangement between himself and Provost Pepper but suggested that if the trustees appointed a rival, they should also create a chair in Arabic and rabbinical literature, "branches no less worthy of finding a place at an institution which has lately made such a decided advance towards the ideal of a University."[48]

The trustees realized that both candidates still requested no compensation and assented to Jastrow's later proposal.[49] In 1888, Jastrow became head of the library, in part, claimed a historian of the university, because his academic services "did not make much claim upon his time," and in part because the library served as a temporary repository for the artifacts acquired by the university's expedition to Babylonia.[50]

Gottheil suffered from the lack of colleagues, but Jastrow found himself with one colleague too many. Chapter 4 shows how tension between Jastrow and Hilprecht divided the Pennsylvania Semitics program and eventually involved most American Semitists. Here, we note only that neither the Jewish nor the Gentile community imposed these tensions. At Pennsylvania and Columbia, practitioners had substantial discretion, despite local Jewish communal or institutional financial support of their professorships. At the outset, conditions did not appear that way to Jastrow, who was impatient with an academic system that inadequately recognized his field. He doubted his personal prospects until Pennsylvania regularized his externally funded appointment.

But inclusion in regular budget lines did not end the problems for either Jastrow or Gottheil. Neither scholar ever commanded a premium salary. Their supposed replaceability by clergy who, having another source of income, needed little or no remuneration, compromised their bargaining ability. Nor did enrollments bode well for future growth. John Hopkins, which had the largest Semitics enrollments, averaged 35 students during the 1890s, and many students went no further than the elementary courses, with others more likely to become clergymen than Semitists.

Communal support waned as academic identification increased and as Jastrow, like Felix Adler, abandoned his religious commitments. Only scholars who completed undergraduate theological work, warned Johns Hopkins Semitics professor Paul Haupt, should study Semitics. Richard Gottheil retained his strong personal commitment to Judaism, but communal pressures affected even committed scholars if their conclusions contradicted revealed religion. Early in his Columbia tenure, Gottheil congratulated Solomon Schechter, his former tutor, on his fight in England to advance Biblical scholarship. He enviously contrasted Schechter's ability to work with impunity with his own need for circumspection:[51]

> I am not in such a position and have to keep my mouth severely closed. Poor Professor [William Rainey] Harper [then at Yale] is now being hauled over the coals in orthodox America for his article in the last *Hebraica*. It has already cost him one Summer School and will cost him the support of most of his most moneyed backers. Poor fellow—he beareth our pains and for us he is stricken. But the fight has to come sooner or later in America. *Nolens volens* [whether willing or not], we shall all have to take 'flattery' one way or the other. But many heads will fall and many hearts ache before the victory is won.[52]

Schechter retained his emphasis on the scientific study of specifically Jewish questions first at Cambridge and then at New York's Jewish Theological Seminary. At J.T.S., he drew upon significant communal resources to assemble a strong group of scholars—including Israel Davidson, Israel Friedlander, Louis Ginzberg, and Alexander Marx—who were committed to Jewish learning. Gottheil reflected the general tendency of university-affiliated American Semitists to carve out a broad philological mandate that was not restricted to Jewish topics. He knew he had parted company with his erstwhile mentor. "I have just received another MS of my Bar Ali from Linden," he wrote Schechter in 1889:

> That makes No. 15 . . . I ought to get a good text out of so much material. But I see my Schechter shrug his shoulders. He would so gladly see my work of a different kind. Perhaps at one time I would have agreed with him but now I have developed into a full-fledged philological worm; who, at best, can creep from one root to another, and nibble a little here and there![53]

Gottheil justified his philological emphasis: "It is quite impossible to be a student of Oriental literature or of Oriental history," he explained, "without having the ability to handle readily the texts in which this literature and this history have found their expression." He continued:

> The documents in question are all difficult to understand, and often fragmentary in character. They can never be used as a basis for historical presentations, or for a study even of their purely literary form, without first undergoing a rigid textual criticism. And a large amount of the material—perhaps, in point of actual amount, the largest part is still stored up as manuscripts in museums and libraries. The scholar is thus compelled first to edit the texts before he is able to use them for his investigations.[54]

Richard Gottheil's course offerings, in keeping with his research interests, gravitated from rabbinics to a general philological program that included Hebrew, Syriac, Arabic, and Babylonian cuneiform, a general linguistics course, and an advanced philological seminar.[55] By 1898, several years after the Emanu-El subsidy ended, Gottheil relegated rabbinics instruction to two half-year courses. When the Jewish Theological Seminary called Solomon Schechter to its presidency and moved its plant to Morningside Heights, both in 1902/03, Gottheil discontinued rabbinic and Biblical Hebrew coursework.[56]

Columbia authorities may have unwittingly helped Gottheil's intellectual shift. In 1889, Columbia accepted Gottheil's offer to teach Semitic languages and changed his title to "Professor of Rabbinical Literature and Instructor in the Semitic Languages." Seth Low, Columbia's new president, added $1,000 to Gottheil's salary to recognize this additional service. "It seemed to me," he wrote, "that his friends would be much more likely to provide permanently for the endowment of his professorship, if Columbia showed some appreciation of the zeal and excellent service in the department where he was serving without pay."[57]

The gesture, however, had the opposite effect on the Temple Emanu-El trustees who, discerning the divergence between Gottheil's intellectual direction and their own interests, identified other, more pressing, needs. Tightened restrictions on Russian Jews and a series of pogroms increased Jewish migration into the United States, and Jewish philanthropists gave highest priority to the welfare of the newcomers.[58] Columbia's support of Gottheil led the Emanu-El trustees to let the 1887 gift expire.[59]

Morris Jastrow's intellectual history closely resembles Gottheil's. His title—Arabic and Rabbinics professor—reflected his early scholarly interests, especially with respect to Hayyuj's grammatical treatises. An evolving interest in the history of religion, and a desire to participate in the mainstream of American Semitic research, led Jastrow to study Babylonian and Assyrian religion, and the university changed his title to professor of Semitics in 1891 to recognize his breadth.[60] The recognition of his colleagues followed: "In this field no American scholar has done so much as he to stimulate an intelligent interest," wrote one colleague about Jastrow's scholarship in the history of religions.[61]

"During the nineteenth century," wrote twentieth-century Semitist William F. Albright, "the languages of the ancient Near East were deciphered and the main principles of comparative philology were discovered; this was the heroic age of philology."[62] Richard Gottheil and Morris Jastrow wanted to advance these discoveries. Gottheil's promotion to professor of Semitics in 1892 and Columbia's assumption of his salary at the expiration of the Emanu-El endowment gave him that opportunity. Morris Jastrow's initial interest in Semitics arose from his rejection of the rabbinate, but he did not look back. Institutional interest waxed just as communal interest waned, and both scholars paid less heed to communal aspirations. "I am turning more and more exclusively to Arabic," Gottheil wrote in 1906.[63] But the next chapter shows that the conflict between academic and communal goals did not disappear.

In 1888, Provost Pepper, on behalf of the University of Pennsylvania, held a reception for the members of the American Oriental Society at its first meeting in Philadelphia. The meeting marked a recognition of the university and the city as centers of Oriental scholarship. Jastrow detected a hopeful tone in the addresses made at the reception. "The outlook for the future of Semitic studies," wrote this recent denouncer of American philistinism, "is indeed promising." The field now most needed "*original* material in the shape of Hebrew, Arabic and Syriac manuscripts, cuneiform tablets and all manner of Oriental antiquities," he added. "Until we have *original* material we need look in vain for *original* scholarship," he asserted.

Jastrow's comments reflected a belief that led to the mounting of archaeological expeditions to the Near East by Pennsylvania and then by California, Harvard, and Chicago. His own position secure—he remained at Pennsylvania until his death in 1922—and the fortunes of his field improved, Jastrow confidently concluded: "But all will come in time."[64]

California and Chicago: Communal Representation

In the 1890s, prominent rabbis taught Hebrew and Judaica courses at the University of California and the University of Chicago. Jacob Voorsanger at California and Emil G. Hirsch at Chicago integrated their teaching duties into their rabbinical functions by spending one day a week at their respective universities. Voorsanger and Hirsch relied on communal subsidies—an indirect contribution of the rabbi's substantial salary, in contrast, for example, to the Emanu-El contribution to Columbia for Gottheil's salary. Voorsanger and Hirsch differed from Gottheil and Jastrow in their course offerings, the nature of their commitments, and their objectives. Fifty years earlier, faculty members often represented both a denomination and a subject, but at late nineteenth-century universities, the relevance of denominational affiliation to institutional mission diminished. Service rendered as a communal representative—no matter how distinguished the community, the service, or the representative—set the practitioner apart from his colleagues. Practitioners, if not always the communities they represented, strongly perceived the changed environment.

In 1894, about a decade after the departure of James M. Philips, Jacob Voorsanger offered to organize a Semitics department at the University of California and to teach there gratis. Voorsanger was rabbi of San Francisco's Reform Temple Emanu-El, the city's most prominent Jewish congregation. Born in Amsterdam, Holland, in 1852, Voorsanger obtained his early education at an Amsterdam Jewish parochial school. He broke with orthodoxy during his youth, and his belief that "the world's salvation lies in the hands of those who devote themselves to the cause of research and education no less than of those who work through the Church" may have germinated at the same time.[65] His opportunities in Holland limited, Voorsanger migrated to the United States in 1873 and cast his lot with the Reform movement. After cantorial service in Philadelphia, Washington, D.C., and Providence, he obtained his first pulpit in Houston. Voorsanger came to San Francisco in 1886 as Emanu-El's junior rabbi, succeeded to the senior position three years later upon his predecessor's death, and presented his plan for Semitic studies to the California Regents five years later.

Voorsanger's curriculum emphasized Biblical Hebrew and Aramaic. Advanced students would study Arabic, Assyrian, and the comparative grammar of the Semitic languages. But Voorsanger, unlike Gottheil and Jastrow, had no "special knowledge" of Semitics and he declined to offer the announced advanced courses.[66] Voorsanger offered a religious rationale for Semitics instruction—especially the need for a learned ministry. He also appealed to institutional and regional pride. California would be the only university west of the Mississippi to offer work recognized as of great importance.[67] The Regents accepted Voorsanger's offer to teach and his proposed curriculum. For more than a decade he journeyed weekly from San Francisco to Berkeley to teach Hebrew, Aramaic, and Talmud—the original proposal included "Outlines of Rabbinical Literature."

Voorsanger had to organize a department that had no books, students, or research materials. Only five students appeared for the first class, "more from curiosity than from anything else," he wrote.[68] Recruiting produced some undergraduates but no theological students.[69] However, when San Francisco Jewry donated several important Judaic libraries, university authorities responded positively.[70] President Wheeler wrote that the gifts would "aid in keeping alive the sacred fires of highest scholarship, of preserving and glorifying the national traditions of your people and of bringing the material of Semitic learning, literature and thought into its proper place in the great body of thought and learning with which this university deals, and which makes our civilization vital."[71]

In 1897, the Regents authorized an assistant for Voorsanger, who chose university-educated Max Leopold Margolis.[72] Born in 1866 and educated primarily by his father in traditional and secular subjects, Margolis graduated from the Leibnitz Gymnasium in Berlin in 1889, just before coming to America. Biographers of Margolis agree that his Berlin years and his Columbia studies under Richard Gottheil were intellectually crucial.[73] He excelled in Greek and Latin at Berlin and wrote his dissertation in Latin because he felt more comfortable in that language than in English. He originally hoped to produce a critical edition of the Talmud, and his dissertation explored the value of Rashi's commentary for the proposed text. However, he later wrote, "not only did America prove to be the wrong place for such an undertaking, but the circumstances were not lacking to lead me away from my proposed plan into entirely different work."[74] These circumstances probably included his 1892 appointment as instructor and then assistant professor of Hebrew and Biblical exegesis at Hebrew Union College, where his scholarship largely addressed grammatical and philological questions.[75] Margolis was the more proficient Talmud scholar at California, but Voorsanger continued to teach the Talmud courses.

The hiring permitted curricular expansion into Arabic, Assyrian, Ethiopian, and Syriac, "besides the idioms, and the literatures and histories of the nations represented in these tongues."[76] But Voorsanger also articulated strong communal expectations for Margolis. "We expect much from Professor Margolis' presence in our midst," he wrote. "Aside from his acknowledged scholarship, he has become a strong educational factor, and so far as his duty will permit, he will doubtless make his influence felt in the progress of our university life and in the development of our religious institutions."[77] Margolis promptly assumed the superintendency of Emanu-El's newly created Free Religious School. During his California years, Margolis adopted a "radical position" on the theology of Reform Judaism in a controversial monograph, *The Theological Aspect of Reform Judaism* (1903). He testified that he became an ardent Zionist while in California.[78]

Margolis returned to Cincinnati in 1905 to assume the chair of Biblical exegesis at Hebrew Union College. Voorsanger was satisfied with his communal participation. "Always interested in Jewish affairs," he wrote, "he has been a force in our educational interests and a warm friend and advisor of the rabbinical body which rarely failed to seek the support of his keen, logical mind and his vast experience."[79] A lucrative salary offer helped occasion Margolis' departure,[80] but less tangible factors also affected his decision.[81] California lacked the manu-script materials necessary for Margolis to undertake the textual reconciliations at the heart of his research. Environment also played a key role. Cyrus Adler, head of Dropsie College, where Margolis taught beginning in 1909, wrote that Berlin and Columbia "gave him a broader field of knowledge, but so impressed was he with the primary importance of the Bible and Jewish studies that he absorbed all the new knowledge, brought it back and utilized it for that which was nearest to the Jewish soul."[82] While contemplating a second tenure in Cincinnati, Margo-lis wrote, "I feel that I belong there rather than in a secular institution where my Jewish knowledge lies idle."[83] Many contemporary Jewish Semitists concentrated their research on non-Judaic aspects of Semitics or on topics with at best indi-rect implications for Jewish history and thought. But exposure to the university led Margolis to reaffirm his scholarly interest in Judaism. His California tenure was his only employment in a secular university.[84]

Margolis may have resigned in part from concern about the university's treat-ment of Semitics. Voorsanger served the university for a decade and secured stu-dents, libraries, and fellowships.[85] Verbal recognition came with each gift, but more tangible rewards only infrequently. "I feel that I have been very loyal to Berkeley," Voorsanger wrote, "but Berkeley is not doing very much for my de-partment. . . . Loyalty should not be conditional, but it needs an occasional stim-ulus."[86] Wheeler's reliance upon a communal donation to match Hebrew Union College's offer to Margolis may have been a case in point. Margolis might have remained in California if there had been any indication of the personal and ide-ological controversies that would surround his Cincinnati tenure.[87] Lacking such foresight, he resigned in the summer of 1905. His departure prompted a hasty search for a successor.

Word of Margolis's resignation spread, and Wheeler made the usual inquiries for a successor.[88] William Popper, the successful candidate, strengthened his chances by journeying to the campus from the east coast.[89] His availability, cre-dentials, and willingness to work for a $1,400 annual salary led Wheeler to en-gage him immediately.[90] Born in St. Louis in 1874, Popper and his family moved to Brooklyn, New York, where a young rabbi introduced him to Hebrew. After undergraduate work at the College of the City of New York and Columbia, Pop-per began graduate study under Richard Gottheil. He intended to concentrate in Hebrew, but became "entranced" by Arabic. After completing his dissertation on "The Censorship of Hebrew Books" in 1899, he studied abroad for three years. Popper worked for two years as the Gustav Gottheil lecturer at Columbia upon his return in 1902.[91] He was assistant (1906), associate (1916), and full (1922) professor of Semitic languages at California until his retirement in 1945.

Popper shared certain traits with the man he replaced, but important differ-ences affected his communal and institutional relationships. Popper was more at home in the California environment. Margolis had engaged in at least two sets of negotiations to leave the university, but Popper later said that he "was happy here from the first [I wouldn't even consider having my name offered at any other place] and all through the various administrations."[92] Margolis played a significant role in the Bay area Jewish community, but Popper's participation was minimal. Instead, he devoted much of his time to university administrative and committee work. Margolis's California years cemented his commitment to Jewish scholarship, while Popper's experience reinforced his emphasis on Arabic studies. After his studies of parallelism in Isaiah met with indifference or adverse criticism, Popper devoted most of his energies to preparing a critical edition of Egyptian historian Ibn Taghri Birdi's manuscripts.[93] Margolis and Popper also differed outwardly. Popper learned from Gottheil "that Wheeler had said that I don't look like a Semite. My predecessor here had an accent."[94]

Voorsanger consciously attempted to increase student enrollments, but Popper counselled students who did not adamantly insist upon rigorous Semitic training to study in another department or institution. Voorsanger painstakingly put together a basic lecture course on the history of the Bible and its peoples. But Popper wrote, "The Department . . . is compelled to choose between training adequately through recitation the small number of qualified students in several Semitic languages and lecturing in English to several larger classes of those who know no Semitic language. Believing that in this field comparatively little is accomplished by the lecture method, the Department continues to devote itself to teaching a large number of small classes and to research."[95] The department retained this orientation throughout Popper's tenure.

The Bay area Jewish community and university authorities initially viewed the Semitics department as the communal representative to the university or as the university's offering to the community. Presidents Kellogg and Wheeler granted the department considerable autonomy as long as it did not become a financial burden to the university. All believed that a representative Jew should chair the department. Wheeler, added Popper, believed that "no one who doesn't have a supreme belief in the Semitic spirit should be head of the Semitic department."[96]

Popper's arrival changed communal and institutional relations. He established a friendship with Martin A. Meyer, Voorsanger's successor at Emanu-El, and had him appointed lecturer in Semitic language and history.[97] But Popper's next full-time colleague was Assyriologist and Egyptologist H. F. Lutz.[98] Thus Semitics at California originated with a communally oriented rabbi, grew with a scholar who experienced conflicting communal and institutional agendas, and took final form under a scholar who accepted the norms that governed his colleagues. The regularization, propelled by growing Jewish communal indifference, occurred with minimal university intervention.

The University of Chicago similarly obtained the gratis services of Chicago Sinai congregation's Rabbi Emil G. Hirsch. Hirsch taught rabbinic literature and philosophy, but his institutional position was more constricted. Jacob Voorsanger defined his department's intellectual and communal agenda and had substantial influence in selecting an assistant, while Hirsch was the only Jewish Seminist in a Protestant, academically oriented department.

Emil Gustav Hirsch was born in 1852 in Luxembourg, where his father Samuel Hirsch, who held a doctorate from Leipzig and vigorously advocated radical Reform, was Grand Rabbi. He brought Emil to Philadelphia in 1866

when he accepted a call to Keneseth Israel Congregation. After study in Luxembourg's primary schools, Philadelphia's Episcopal Academy, and the University of Pennsylvania (from which he graduated in 1872), Emil Hirsch attended
the universities of Berlin (1872–1876) and Leipzig (doctorate 1876) and the
Hochschule für die Wissenschaft des Judentums under Abraham Geiger. Hirsch
generally agreed with *Hochschule* classmate Felix Adler's reasoning on the nature
of God and the benign nature of progress. But for intellectual or emotional reasons—or both—he refrained from a similar break with organized Jewish life.[99]

Instead, Hirsch opted for a career in the Reform Jewish ministry that emphasized "the changeless moral mandate of Sinai, that unwithstandable imperative
of the Jewish ethical law."[100] He preached briefly at Philadelphia's Rodef Shalom
Congregation upon his return from Europe and then accepted calls from congregations in Baltimore and Louisville. In 1880, he succeeded Kaufmann
Kohler, his brother-in-law, at Sinai. The temple wanted someone learned, ideologically sound, and able to work effectively with the larger Chicago community.
It found in Hirsch all these qualities, plus an intense interest in social reform.[101]

During his more than 40 years at Sinai, Hirsch participated in a prodigious
number of Jewish, multisect, and secular humanitarian activities.[102] His universalistic outlook predisposed him to enter into a personal relationship with the
new, Baptist-dominated University of Chicago and to advocate a central place
for universities in ministerial education. Seminaries lacked the resources that major universities commanded, Hirsch contended. Non-Jews and Jews could both
offer a (desirable) scientific approach to their subjects. "There is no Orthodox
science and there is no liberal science," Hirsch stated:

> The facts of the Hebrew grammar are the same whether taught by [an] Orthodox
> Jewish rabbi or by Professor Harper here at our noble university. The application
> of the great laws to the reorganization of human society on the basis of justice and
> equal fellowship is the same for the one who is a Baptist as for him who claims to
> be the prophet of a new dispensation on the ethical platform. There is but one sci-
> ence, and we who wish to found one universal religion ought not to place a little
> bit of an attempt of a school in some way-off corner, when we have the larger uni-
> versities willing to give us room and space and scope, extending their hands and
> asking us merely to come.[103]

Other Jews derided Hirsch's proposal. "It will be [Dr. Harper's] duty to con-
fer the diplomas and exhort the young Rabbis to go forth and preach Judaism
undefiled to the world," wrote one critic. "Just exactly what a Baptist preacher's
conception of pure Judaism may be is hard to conceive, and I, for one wait
with impatience Dr. Harper's first baccalaureate address."[104] But Hirsch
only stated publicly what his fellow rabbi, Bernhard Felsenthal, suggested in
private. The significance of the suggestion lies in the university's reception of
Hirsch's overtures.

President Harper knew that Bible study at Chicago's divinity school had to
ward off both fundamentalists and extreme higher critics. He placed Hebrew

Bible courses in the graduate divisions—rather than in the divinity school—and supplemented them with work in ancient Near East specialities, literatures, and cultures.[105] Divinity students confronted the larger academic culture and attended classes with non-divinity students, including Jews. These students were exposed to scholarship that Harper believed was crucial for a modern ministry. The fixed curriculum of the traditional theological school "made scholarly work impossible," but Harper's divinity school placed scientific scholarship at the center: "Never in the history of Christendom," Harper asserted, "has the demand been greater for scholarship of the highest character."[106] Hirsch's vision of a neutral, scientific setting—envisioned by many nineteenth-century liberals—was not far-fetched. Before 1910, nearly half the divinity school enrollment was non-Baptist. In 1905/06 three Jewish students enrolled, and by 1914/15 there were 19 Jews. The first Jew graduated in 1911.[107]

Hirsch's universalism, visible commitment to Judaism, knowledge, and influence in the Jewish community account for the University of Chicago's interest in him. Correspondence between Harper and Hirsch reveals affection, concern, and respect.[108] Hirsch offered courses in rabbinics, Old Testament criticism, cognate Semitic tongues, and Arabic civilization.[109] His studies were "mainly those of his own people." He helped edit *The American Journal of Semitic Languages and Literatures,* published by the university press, and spoke at many university functions, including the Haskell Oriental Museum dedication and President Harper's 1906 memorial service. Hirsch's presence assured that Chicago Sinai members would offer additional gifts to the university. He facilitated the contribution of a Semitic library, the Hirsch–Birnays modern language collection in 1904, and the construction of Leon Mandel Assembly Hall and Julius Rosenwald Hall.[110] Contemporaries noted Hirsch's scrupulous attention to his academic commitments.[111]

Hirsch's undertakings on behalf of the university were substantial, the university's gratitude genuine, but during his early years at Chicago he evinced an unease over his academic status. This unease emerged in his distress over apparently inconsequential matters. A university announcement omitted the title "professor" from his name, and Hirsch doubted "whether the election of which I have been officially notified was bona-fide."[112] Several years later, he asked the trustees to grant him the title "head professor" since it would "gratify my vanity and would look better."[113] Hirsch expressed concern in 1895 that "the Assyriologists would make . . . trouble [for him]."[114] Later that year he asked "whether the Board had established a custom *not* to thank its convocation orator for his services."[115]

That Hirsch dwelled on such slights, imagined or real, belied his professed indifference to "titles or etiquette."[116] The Germanic preoccupation with rank and protocol affected many academics. The squabble with the Assyriologists probably reflected the difficulties many colleagues experienced with Robert Francis Harper, the president's brother, a faculty member in the Semitics department. Eventually, the president nominated his sibling for Semitics positions in other universities.[117]

But Hirsch's sensitivity arose from a more fundamental source. Hirsch was seen as someone apart—not because of his Jewishness, but because his appointment arose from communal rather than academic considerations. Thomas Goodspeed wrote that trustee Eli B. Felsenthal was the "Jewish representative" to the board, and Hirsch was perceived as the Jewish representative to the faculty, even though the faculty contained other Jews.[118]

Hirsch's oft-assumed communal role as "ambassador to the Gentiles" compounded the problem. He maintained "that Jesus was not a Christian, but a Jew; that the New Testament was largely a Jewish document, with the old Midrashic and Talmudic literary gems reset and repolished . . . that Judaism did not end with the Old Testament but began with it, that Jews wrote the Bible, that it was a product of their religious genius."[119] These pronouncements bore the stamp of an advocate, not a scholar—an image further compounded by Hirsch's vigorous social activism.

Questions of salary and scholarship illustrated the gulf between Hirsch and his colleagues. Hirsch received no university salary. Membership in the Chicago Sinai congregation rapidly increased from 40 to over 900 during Hirsch's tenure, and many congregants experienced rapid increases in wealth. Hirsch's rabbinical salary grew commensurately, from $3,600 in 1881 to $7,000 in 1886 and then rapidly to $12,000. Thus Hirsch, the highest paid rabbi in the world, could volunteer his services to the university at a time when annual professorial salaries typically ranged from $2,000 to $5,000 and while James Breasted, Hirsch's junior colleague, lived on a yearly academic salary of $800. Other independently wealthy faculty members understood the importance of receiving a salary so as not to be set apart from their colleagues.[120] But Hirsch continued without a university salary throughout his university affiliation.

Hirsch's scholarship, or rather the lack of it, also set him apart. He edited and contributed to the *Jewish Encyclopedia* and Chicago's Semitics journal, but our main evidence of his academic knowledge comes from his collected speeches and sermons. Hirsch's thought demonstrated a desire to reconcile contemporary intellectual trends and Judaism. "Evolution is to be dreaded as little by us as was Platonism by Philo, Aristotelianism by Maimonides," he wrote.[121] He viewed the higher criticism as helpful for an appreciation of Judaism: "Israel may have appropriated foreign terms, but it filled them with a new meaning. . . . Israel's originality is the one point that more than any other comes into sharp prominence under the searchlight of the 'Higher Criticism.'"[122] Hirsch emphasized the meliorative and humanitarian aspects of Judaism: "Israel's great men are named Prophets—not soothsayers but truthsayers—souls aflame with the passion for righteousness and social justice, heroes impressed with the certainty that justice is central in the all, and therefore heralds of the Messianic destiny of mankind, martyr and priest of which Israel was called to be."[123] He claimed for Judaic Semitics a legitimate place in the secular university:

> To have given rabbinics and Jewish history a place in its temple is one of the distinctive services rendered to the cause of Semitic studies and broad religious tol-

erance grounded on an intelligent appreciation of differences, and respect for honest convictions, by our own university; and this welcome and hospitality is all the more signal when it is born in mind how indifferent and apathetic, not to say hostile, most universities, even in Europe, have been to this great field.[124]

Cyrus Adler later wrote that Hirsch "secured through the contributions of wealthy Jews of Chicago, the title of Professor of Rabbinical Literature in the University of Chicago."[125] Hirsch himself believed that his claim to his professorship rested on grounds other than scholarship: "I know full well that I have no title to [scholarly] recognition," he wrote Stephen Wise. "I have never done anything along the lines of original research. People in their goodness have given me credit for honors which are not my due."[126] Throughout his lengthy tenure on the Chicago faculty, Hirsch tried to reduce the ambiguity of his role through teaching, academic citizenship, and fund-raising.

Columbia and Pennsylvania soon budgeted for positions initially established without institutional outlay, but California and Chicago authorities accorded prominent communal representatives indefinite tenure in return for their service as instructors. Both rabbis were similarly distanced from their academic colleagues, but after Voorsanger left the scene, the Semitics department regularized its relationship to the University of California. Hirsch's position remained a Sinai rabbi sinecure for another generation, after which the University of Chicago conspicuously omitted permanent posts in Jewish learning from its Oriental Institute.[127]

Other universities also appointed local rabbis to Semitics posts. Reform Rabbi Abram S. Isaacs[128] became professor of Hebrew Languages and Literature at New York University in 1886.[129] Temple College in Philadelphia appointed Reform Rabbi Joseph Levy to a Hebrew professorship in 1894.[130] Reform Rabbi Max Heller assumed a similar position at Tulane in 1912.[131] Isaacs, Levy, Heller and many successors rarely institutionalized the university posts they held by virtue of their local prominence and their general knowledge of Judaism and Hebrew. Some observers criticized these rabbis for accepting university posts that might have gone to scholars, for exhibiting general knowledge in universities increasingly characterized by specialization, and for acting as clerics at institutions that rejected devotionalism and piety as conscious goals. The frequent rabbinical appointments to modern Jewish studies programs elicit a similar debate—the stress between communal and academic norms endures.

Harvard and Johns Hopkins: Institutional Impetus

Strong presidential and institutional interest characterized the Semitics departments at Harvard and Johns Hopkins. Appointments to these departments followed the standard pattern: university officials identified an important area of scholarship, created and filled a "position," and funded it from university resources. Semitics appointments garnered Jewish communal support, but departmental health depended upon continued internal support. Communal expectations only marginally affected scholarly agendas, but Semitics professors demonstrated interest in the Jewish aspects of Semitics as a way of attaining subject growth. Only Gentiles taught at Harvard before 1915, but four Jews taught at Hopkins by that date. A difference in program origins may explain this variation in Jewish participation: Harvard's Semitics program gradually evolved out of a base in its divinity school, while Johns Hopkins started with a clean slate.

The debates over Biblical criticism that had engaged the Harvard and Andover divinity faculties abated in the 1870s.[132] During that transitional decade, most of the Harvard divinity faculty still served in pulpits prior to their academic appointments. Only Ezra Abbott, a New Testament specialist, produced distinguished scholarship, but retirements and resignations soon permitted a redirection of the school. Crawford Howell Toy thus replaced Edward James Young, who failed to fulfill expectations for Biblical scholarship and resigned under pressure in 1880.

By the turn of the century, the divinity school accepted the methods of scholarly inquiry employed in secular subjects and developed a close relationship with the arts and science faculties. Acceptance of academic norms was so complete that divinity school authorities contemplated "a possible absorption of the School into the Graduate Department of the . . . [College]; a return that is to the original relation of Theological instruction to the University."[133] Dean Francis Greenwood Peabody wrote that the divinity school's increased integration into the university "establishes its position as a university school, it fixes in it the same standards of work which prevail in other departments; it sets Divinity students in immediate competition with other advanced students of the university; and it encourages in other students appreciation and respect for theological studies."[134]

Peabody attributed the closer relationship to natural causes. It "came about without deliberate agreement on their part," he wrote. "It simply happened that the courses of the School have seemed adapted to general culture, and being announced in the general pamphlet of elective courses, have proved attractive."[135] But Eliot believed that the relationship was cemented by Toy's 1880 appointment and the 1882 appointment of David Gordon Lyon, Toy's former student at Southern Baptist Theological Seminary, to the Hollis divinity professorship. Toy and Lyon, Eliot believed, brought with them the ability to speak to a broader audience through their Semitic scholarship.

Several overseers, fearing the outcome that Eliot desired, objected to Lyon's appointment to the long vacant Hollis professorship, stating that Semitic instruction—Lyon had earned a doctorate in Assyriology at Leipzig—lay beyond the scope of terms of the Thomas Hollis bequest. Eliot agreed that Hollis may never have heard of Assyriology or Semitic languages, but "Hebrew was a subject long taught by the Hollis Professor, Assyrian was a closely related tongue, Assyriology was germane to Biblical study and, under existing conditions, so different from those of 1721, all the terms of the Hollis requirement could not possibly be carried out."[136] Lyon provided additional evidence of eligibility. "I must confess," he wrote, "that my interest in the Hebrews is a large part of my interest in the Assyrians." The overseers eventually ratified the appointment.[137]

Throughout the 1880s Lyon lived on the small Hollis income, and wondered about the extent of Harvard's commitment to Semitics.[138]

Over a decade lapsed before Harvard ventured further into the field. In 1896, Eliot appointed George Reisner to a Semitic languages instructorship. An Egyptologist, Reisner founded a separate Egyptology department in 1910.[139] In 1902, Harvard appointed Andover Seminary's George Foot Moore to a theology professorship.[140] Moore was noted at Andover for his Biblical scholarship (especially on the Book of Judges), but in Cambridge, he concentrated on the history of religions and comparative religion.[141] Scholars elsewhere used the comparative method to study "pagan" and "primitive" religions that were expected to dissolve in the face of Christian missionary activity.[142] But Moore's course, "History of Religion in Outline," extended comparative and historical methods to include Judaism, Islam, and Christianity.

In 1904/05, Moore taught Hebrew 179, which involved traditional Jewish work: "Genesis with the Aramaic version of Onkelos and a Hebrew commentary (Rashi)." He also revived the Talmud course that Toy had previously offered.[143] In 1905/06, he offered "Judaism from 198 B.C. to Modern Times." Moore was one of the first non-Jewish Semitists to go beyond the philological aspects of his subject and emphasize its identifiably Jewish components. He was not above *ad hominem* comments about his Jewish coworkers, but when a colleague described him as able to read "the *Misna* and the *Gemara* with the same fluency as an old time Yeshiva Bochar [student]," Moore correctly interpreted the comment as a compliment.[144] Moore and to some extent Toy were less circumspect in their scholarship than their Jewish colleagues.[145] Indeed, Moore gave the field social and intellectual legitimacy. Exposure to Moore, Toy, and Lyon may explain why Harry Wolfson, who became Nathan Littauer professor of Jewish literature and philosophy, ventured beyond the philological realm into substantive analysis and criticism.

Harvard eliminated another lacuna by appointing University of Chicago professor James R. Jewett to an Arabic post in 1911.[146] Harvard appeared to have a substantial Semitics roster, but Reisner's lengthy absences and eventual dissociation and Lyon's shorter leaves to supervise the Harvard Samaria expedition after 1906 constrained the department. Toy's retirement cost the Semitics department a position since Harvard thereupon transferred Lyon from the Hollis to the Hancock professorship, transferred the Hollis chair back to the divinity school, and appointed New Testament scholar James H. Ropes to the Hollis chair.[147] Semitics at Harvard did profit from two fortuitous circumstances: the philanthropy of Jacob H. Schiff, discussed in chapter 5, and the 1908 affiliation of Andover Seminary.

Johns Hopkins, like Harvard, built its Semitics program around a noted scholar. Paul Haupt's 1883 appointment was an example of successful American importation of a recognized young European academic. Haupt's presence helped to legitimate the entire American Semitic enterprise. His name in an American scholarly journal meant that European Semitists would take note. As coeditor, with Friedrich Delitzsch, of *Assyriologische Bibliothek* and *Beiträge zur*

Assyriologie und Semitischen Sprachwissenschaft, he encouraged and facilitated access to European publications by his American colleagues and brought European recognition to Johns Hopkins.[148]

In 1880, shortly after Thomas Murray's death, the Johns Hopkins trustees designated Semitic studies as one of ten fields in which Gilman might identify a candidate for appointment.[149] Gilman asked Francis Brown of Union Theological Seminary to consider an appointment.[150] Brown declined but suggested Haupt's name. Brown, one of the first Americans to teach Assyriology, probably met Haupt—who obtained his doctorate under Delitzsch at Leipzig in 1878—in Berlin, where he moved for post-doctoral study. Haupt wrote that he had "long entertained the idea of making America my home," despite its scarce scholarly resources, scarcity of colleagues and lack of provision for elementary Semitic instruction, and despite his difficulties with English. His primary hesitation—concern that others would interpret his move as a failure to succeed in Germany—evaporated when Göttingen promoted him to a professorship in 1883.[151] Haupt soon accepted a Johns Hopkins professorship, the first created since 1876. He was the only German-born, German-trained scholar that Gilman could attract at that time.[152]

In 1887, Haupt chose Cyrus Adler to fill an assistantship promised by Gilman—the first of several Jews to teach in the Johns Hopkins Semitics seminary during his tenure. Adler had received basic Jewish education from several prominent Philadelphia rabbis, including Marcus Jastrow and Samuel Hirsch, obtained a bachelor's degree from the University of Pennsylvania, and briefly read law in the office of his cousin, Mayer Sulzberger. He then opted for graduate study in Semitics. Apprised of Haupt's impending arrival, Adler moved to Baltimore and became one of his first students. When Haupt returned to America in the fall of 1884 after his wife's sudden death, he asked Adler, who was a year younger, to room with him. Their colleagueship grew,[153] and personal sentiment along with political and academic considerations prompted Adler's nomination to the assistantship.[154] "With his help," Haupt told Gilman, "it would be possible for me to establish courses in Oriental history, especially in the history of Israel and the Mesopotamian empire—a subject heretofore almost entirely neglected at this university."[155]

Adler taught the introductory language courses and Biblical history and archaeology from 1887 until his resignation in 1893. But he considered a heavy emphasis on Jewish learning inappropriate in a university. When a member of the Baltimore Jewish community proposed an expansion of the university's Talmudic offerings, Adler noted that "instruction is now given in Mishnaic Hebrew and that one course in this branch will probably be given each year, that it would hardly come within the scope of the Semitic Department, which makes comparative philology its end, to dwell especially on Rabbinical studies."[156] When Adler left Johns Hopkins, Haupt proposed that he continue to teach "the History of Israel, Jewish Antiquities, and Post-Biblical Hebrew. I should be sorry if these courses could not be continued. It is true that there are not many students desirous of studying the Talmud, but I think it important to provide instruction in these branches."[157] Adler declined the offer.

While at Hopkins, Adler simultaneously worked for the Smithsonian Institution—nominally as Haupt's deputy—on the participation of Near Eastern nations in the 1893 Columbian Exposition in Chicago. William R. Harper offered him the directorship of a museum at the University of Chicago in 1893. Gilman advised his acceptance, stating that Johns Hopkins could not soon offer him a full professorship; he had become an associate professor in 1890. Adler did forsake a scholarly career in favor of "establishment of institutions that would create many scholars," but he opted for the Smithsonian librarianship to launch his administrative career.[158]

Adler suggested the motivations for his departure when he wrote that he "never became an entire convert to the Hopkins idea of a University which, while it called for students and required teaching, made that secondary to research."[159] He left the Smithsonian in 1906 to assume the presidency of the new Dropsie College of Hebrew and Cognate Learning in Philadelphia. He then succeeded Solomon Schechter as president of the Jewish Theological Seminary in 1915—he taught there as early as 1887—while retaining his Dropsie post.

Adler's career is difficult to compare to that of any other Jewish Semitist. He turned down opportunities to make the Hopkins Semitics program more Judaic, but, like Max Margolis, he eventually abandoned the university for Jewish—Ismar Elbogen would say "purposeful"—environments. But Margolis sought a more congenial environment for his research, whereas Adler increased his communal commitments, including extensive work for the American Jewish Committee, while remaining in, but not quite of, the scholarly world.

With Adler and then Christopher Johnson, a physician turned Semitist, as assistants, Haupt reduced his instructional burden and initiated several schemes designed to enhance the international reputation of Johns Hopkins and of American Semitics. He continued to coedit the *Beiträge,* and began an Assyrian lexicon[160] and a Polychrome Bible, indicating variant authorships of the Scriptures by type of different colors.[161] He also attempted to organize, or to participate in, an archaeological expedition to Babylonia.[162]

These plans met with mixed success, but Haupt's own Semitic scholarship and his continued European contacts—he spent his summers in Europe until the onset of World War I—facilitated European recognition. Contemporary critics were more divided over Haupt's Biblical scholarship, to which he devoted increased attention.[163] After 1901, he emphasized the study of Hebrew metrics and reconstructed and emended the books of Biblical poetry. This research—whatever its scholarly value—attracted Jewish students, including Aaron Ember, Casper Levias, and Rabbi William Rosenau.[164] Ember, Rosenau, and Rabbi Samuel Rosenblatt succeeded Adler as faculty members in Semitics.

Haupt, a Quaker, understood the need for prudence in a field where communal and scholarly interests did not always coincide. His philo-Semitism and his career choice may be traced to his childhood when a friend's father, a rabbi, introduced him to Hebrew. Haupt's close association with several members of the Baltimore Jewish community led them to underwrite the costs of the Polychrome Bible.[165] Two prominent rabbis, Rosenau and Adolf Guttmacher, received doctorates in Semitics from Hopkins. The presence of identifiably Jewish faculty members assured a Jewish constituency for Semitics at Hopkins and al-layed fears generated by Haupt's acceptance of the higher criticism.[166] Haupt urged that students finish a theological course before they began advanced Semitic studies and that John Hopkins establish a theological seminary. That plan came to naught.[167]

William Rosenau, a student and then an instructor in Haupt's department, was born in Wollstein, Germany, in 1865. Brought to the United States at age 11, he attended the University of Cincinnati (A.B. 1888) and Hebrew Union College (ordained 1889). After three years in an Omaha, Nebraska, pulpit, Rosenau came to Baltimore's Oheb Shalom Congregation, where he remained for over half a century. His tenure at Johns Hopkins began with an instructorship in rab-binics. Thus here, as elsewhere, a local rabbi taught the Talmud courses. Rose-nau attained communal prominence as a member of the Central Conference of American Rabbis (president 1916–1918), the Jewish Welfare Board, and the Jewish Chautauqua. The Board of Governors of Hebrew Union College con-sidered Rosenau (himself a governor) for the college presidency upon Kaufmann Kohler's retirement in 1921.

Rosenau's vita, like Emil Hirsch's, lacked scholarly publications, and his com-munal base created ambiguity. When called to "one of the largest pulpits in the country" in 1909, a position that would "lead to my association with a very prominent American university," Rosenau asked the Johns Hopkins authorities to promote him to associate professor—he held the title of associate—and re-quested a nominal salary. As with Hirsch, Rosenau's Oheb Shalom salary well outdistanced professorial salaries at Hopkins, although Hirsch held a professor-ial title from the outset. The university's academic council withheld the recog-nition these concessions implied: "We have uniformly refused to give the title of Associate Professor to anyone not devoting all his time to the work of the Uni-versity."[168] But he remained on the Johns Hopkins faculty until 1932, though other commitments prompted him to offer his resignation at least once.[169]

A physically imposing man with a strong personality, Paul Haupt welcomed Jewish scholars, encouraged Biblical and rabbinic studies, and assured the su-premacy of institutional over communal norms. William Foxwell Albright, who succeeded Haupt after his death in 1926, continued these precedents. Albright's more conservative Biblical scholarship led to even closer ties to the American and Israeli Jewish communities.[170]

Haupt's constant quest for European recognition was his most significant con-tribution to Jewish scholars and scholarship. Despite his frequent European trips, Haupt knew that his European colleagues would increasingly perceive him as an American scholar of high stature. His encouragement of Jewish students to engage in Biblical scholarship forced German and other European scholars to deal with a constituency they consciously excluded from their own faculties. The Hopkins and Harvard appointments—some of the field's earliest—thus sig-nalled the perceived importance of Semitic scholarship for international and do-mestic academic recognition while allowing the field to define itself independent of theology.

Conclusion

The long-term health of Judaic Semitics, our analysis suggests, depended more upon the sustained commitment of the initiating constituency than the source of initiation. At Harvard, the *institutional support* that nurtured the growth of Semitics atrophied soon after Abbott Lawrence Lowell replaced Eliot as president in 1909. The Johns Hopkins program declined after Gilman's departure and hit bottom after Haupt's death in 1926. But the retirement of the Columbia and Pennsylvania presidents who oversaw establishment of Semitics had no adverse programmatic effects because presidents had not initiated these programs.

Waning *communal interest* at California and Chicago adversely affected departmental growth and orientation. William Popper essentially replaced both Margolis and Voorsanger, who died soon after the Margolis resignation. Popper obtained little of the communal support that Voorsanger successfully cultivated and remained alone in his department for 15 years. At Chicago, the lack of communal support deterred further Judaica appointments, but reduced communal interest at Columbia, where Jewish learning was scholar-initiated, did not bode ill. Columbia assumed Richard Gottheil's salary and soon hired a second Semitics professor.

Diminished *scholarly interest* in the Jewish aspects of Semitics damaged the field's prospects at Columbia and Pennsylvania. At Harvard and Johns Hopkins, Judaica remained independent of any one scholar's continued interest, as the Toy, Moore, Wolfson, Adler, Ember, Levias, and Rosenau appointments indicate. At Chicago, scholarly interest remained constant—Emil Hirsch made no intellectual migration during his 30-year tenure. At California, a negative communal reception led Popper to abandon Judaic lines of research—not the other way around.

Did peer pressure lead Jewish Semitists who worked in larger departments to abandon the Jewish aspects of Semitics—Morris Jastrow at Pennsylvania, for example? Contemporary scholars frequently contrast the collegial American department, where scholars employed the same disciplinary techniques on different topics or periods, with the ordinarian's prerogatives to explain differing patterns of university development. But departmental size explains few variations in behavior among Semitists, partly, perhaps, because all American Semitics departments were relatively small, and partly because practitioner behavior arose from the same complex circumstances that first led them to the field. Not only Jastrow but William Popper and Richard Gottheil, neither of whom had many colleagues, studied non-Jewish aspects of Semitics.

Conversely, at Harvard, where somewhat larger size permitted greater heterogeneity, Gentile Semitists helped to legitimate the substance of Judaica as well as the critical method. "[George Foot] Moore . . . greatly altered the tone of Christian scholarship on Judaism," wrote Samuel Sandmel, "this, one can see by comparing a book in English on New Testament written before and after the publication of Moore's *Judaism* (1924)."[171] Moore led Gentile colleagues to reinterpret Judaism as a living force rather than as an anticipation of Christianity or as a derivative sect, as the pan-Babylonians would have it. Gentile American Semitists worked to assure that the field would not dismiss the work of Jewish colleagues as inevitably apologetic and that Jewish scholarship exhibited breadth, not parochialism. Gentile and Jewish Semitists generally received students of all backgrounds.

Gentile Semitists also sided with Jewish academics—Semitists or otherwise—as academic anti-Semitism increased in the early twentieth century. David Gordon Lyon, for example, took a strong anti-quota stance during the Harvard debates over restriction of Jewish students in the early 1920s. Indeed, without Harper, Haupt, Moore, and Toy, there would have been fewer Jewish Semitists and less interest in the Judaic aspects of Semitics. The group of six Judaica universities—not the departments—is the proper unit of analysis, and the story of the maturation of the first generation of American Semitists is related in the next chapter.

Unfortunately, Gentile scholars could not resolve all the difficulties faced by their Jewish colleagues—especially the problems caused when Jewish communal expectations conflicted with the direction of their scholarship. Judaic Semitists such as Emil G. Hirsch, who adhered to communal norms in a scholarly department, experienced stress. Conversely, chapter 6 demonstrates that "scholars" who worked in seminaries did also. Richard Gottheil attempted the most complex resolution of conflicting academic and communal expectations, chapter 4 reveals, by maintaining different personae at Columbia and in the Jewish community, but every Jewish Semitist had to decide how to address communal expectations, and even Harvard's Gentile Semitists were much influenced by Jacob Schiff's gifts.

Judaic Semitics required not only a special type of scholar, one who could live with ambiguity, but also a special type of benefactor, and the field only partly succeeded in attracting needed external financial support. At the outset, the university-based Semitics endeavor appealed mainly to Reform Jewry anxious to promote Judaism as a universalistic faith; gifts from orthodox philanthropists awaited the twentieth century. Even among Reform Jews, however, financial support had a low priority. Benefactors preferred gifts for specified terms or projects and often ended their subsidies when emergencies, such as those attendant upon the Russian migration to America, demanded their attention.

The prototypic benefactor of Judaic Semitics—apart from the rabbis who donated their time and effort—is not easily characterized. A secularized donor in this largely Jewish group would probably lack interest in Jewish scholarship, but an orthodox benefactor might hold university-based scholarship, which differed from the work of the *yeshivah,* inherently suspect. Reform and Conservative donors often had to decide between university work and the conflicting claims of the new Jewish seminaries. The benefactor of a rabbinical seminary soon saw the fruits of investment in an educated rabbinate and did not have to be concerned with scholarship.

Yet the education of professionals, and other communal considerations, took second place to scholarship in Semitics departments. The abstruseness of Semitics rendered most benefactors incapable of fully appreciating the fruits of the gift. These benefactors had to believe that these fruits would render Judaism more recognized and accepted, and that Judaism's tenets would stand up to critical inquiry—a difficult balancing act. Once the university trustees accepted a gift, benefactors had little or no say over a recipient's research agenda even if, as in Richard Gottheil's case, the donor had the right of "nomination." Occupants of subsidized positions, as Ismar Elbogen feared, often gravitated toward non-Judaic Semitics in response to the institutional, not the communal, norm for the field.

The importance of communal ties and financial support may help explain the widespread immobility of first generation Semitists. Dependence upon gifts for libraries, texts, and perhaps an archaeological expedition led most Semitists to cultivate the communities where they had roots and benefactors. After obtaining their university appointments, Salo Baron, Breasted, Ember, Gottheil, Haupt, Heller, Hilprecht, Hirsch, Husik, Isaacs, Jastrow, Lyon, Moore, Philips, Popper, Rosenau, Torrey, Toy, Voorsanger, and Harry Wolfson remained where they were.[172] Growing anti-Semitism in twentieth-century America also helps to explain this immobility. Non-Jews were more likely to fill vacancies in Semitics departments, and many members of university communities, as we shall see, did not carefully distinguish between Semite and Semitics.

The six institutions that housed Judaic Semitics did so on a modest but significant scale. These institutions disregarded low or moderate student demand for the subject in anticipation of scholarly recognition or of Jewish communal support. Five of the six institutions absorbed the costs of a Judaic Semitics professorship either from the outset or when the initial arrangements ended, but, further growth proceeded slowly, if at all, in the early twentieth century, and retrenchment sometimes occurred. Columbia, California, and Johns Hopkins became departments with one allotted professorship and several assistants, while Hirsch's part-time appointment in rabbinics remained Chicago's only Judaic appointment. Semitics at Pennsylvania grew in a non-Judaic direction, while the field's fortunes at Harvard declined during Lowell's presidency.

After World War I, save for Chicago's Oriental Institute, nearly all American Semitics departments experienced stasis or decline. The six universities no longer overlooked the failure of either elementary (undergraduate and theological student) courses or advanced philological seminars to generate large enrollments. At Johns Hopkins, for example, the trustees contemplated diverting funds from philology to place an intended institute of law upon firmer footing.[173] Some professors discouraged potential students from entering the field since they knew that years of diligent preparation would probably result in unemployment. The next wave of growth in university-based Jewish learning would occur after World War II; by then the field had found hospitality in other departments and in other institutions.[174]

But during its first 50 years—the last quarter of the nineteenth century and the first quarter of the twentieth—Semitic studies gave Jewish learning its first university entré, and offered practitioners the opportunity to decipher and analyze the languages and literatures of the people who stood at the headwaters of the western world's three major civilizations.

IV

THE PRICE OF ADMISSION

Jewish learning found a home in those late nineteenth-century Semitics depart-ments that profited from communal, scholarly, and presidential aspirations. Jews gained faculty posts in Semitics and other departments as a research ethos re-placed college devotionalism and as the norms of theological neutrality—albeit with a Protestant cast—replaced partisanship. Rapid enrollment growth at uni-versities housing Judaic Semitics—Columbia was the nation's largest university for a time—permitted subject growth and differentiation. University-based Jew-ish Semitists gained status from their academic association and made important academic contributions to their field.

But some rabbis, philanthropists, students, and even practitioners soon asked whether Jewish learning paid too high a price for admission to the academic pan-theon. No one failed to notice the intense competition among university-based Semitists. Had this competition undercut the field's academic viability? There was also dissatisfaction among observers with the quantity of Judaica publica-tions, or courses, offered by university-based Semitists. Was Ismar Elbogen cor-rect—had the parent discipline's agendas superseded Judaic approaches? These questions assumed added importance as elements hostile to Jews and Judaism filled the vacuum left by philo-Semitic supporters in the early twentieth century.

Competition appeared the greater threat during the early years of presiden-tial and provider support. Concurrent establishment of marginal Semitics de-partments resulted in debilitating contests for recognition, security, and scarce resources among institutions, even among colleagues at the same university. The extent of competition may appear surprising since other disciplines engaged Se-mitics in curricular and financial clashes, while clergy, excluded amateurs, and lay elements remained vigilant lest research threaten a cherished tenet or value. Many projects, in addition, required practitioner cooperation—texts needed editing, grammars and dictionaries required compilation, and entire languages awaited deciphering. But competition persisted despite its disabling conse-quences.[1] Some observers blamed German scholars and/or Gilded Age America for instilling this trait, others noted intense rivalries among researchers in fields with more resources and a longer history. "Academic Darwinism" in Semitics peaked in the late 1880s and 1890s, when American Semitists undertook few interinstitutional projects, such as archaeological expeditions, and could not even unite behind a plan to host an international congress of orientalists.

Most Semitists purported to understand the importance of cooperation for the field's success. Paul Haupt, a competitive practitioner, remarked that William R. Harper's ascendency to the Chicago presidency created another strong rival for his program at Johns Hopkins but worked to the entire field's benefit. Yet some Semitists sacrificed cooperative efforts that might have helped the field's long-term growth in favor of an institutional foothold and for a chance to compete for external rewards and for the few academic vacancies to which no local candidate laid claim.[2] By the early twentieth century, the emergence of a Semitics "oligopoly"—and exhaustion from competition—led many practitioners to cooperate, especially in minimizing the damage wrought by Herman Hilprecht, an ambitious, competitive practitioner. The lengthy Hilprecht affair marred the first important American archaeological expedition to the Near East but also taught practitioners to emphasize academic affinity over destructive competition.

Some observers then suggested that the elimination of competition revealed more fundamental problems: did practitioner emphasis on knowledge advancement and on scholarly publication debilitate the field by increasing the distance between scholars and the communal constituency and between the parent discipline and Judaica? Academic-communal distancing long antedated Jewish participation. In mid-nineteenth-century America, Semitics practitioners slowly ridded themselves of the amateurs: the American clerics and lay persons who established it and the polyglots—such as Cornell's Frederick Roehrig and Columbia's Abraham Yohannan—whose extensive travels and verbal facility enabled them to learn new tongues almost at will but who lacked "scientific" philological training. By the late nineteenth century, Semitists accorded primacy to languages with philological rather than religious-communal significance and the Ph.D., as in other academic fields, became *the* entrance credential. A shift in source of pedigree symbolized the strength of this trend: the first generation acquired European degrees; successors increasingly opted for domestic certification.

Jewish Semitists, especially Pennsylvania's Morris Jastrow, played key roles in the Hilprecht controversy. But the controversy neither involved Jewish learning nor the Jewish community. Instead, it confirmed Ismar Elbogen's fear that Jewish practitioners would opt for the non-Judaic aspects of their discipline over Jewish learning, and thus also illustrates the unraveling of the practitioner-communal-institutional coalition that sustained Judaic Semitics. University-based Judaica scholars, Elbogen would have been pleased to learn, did not *inevitably* opt for the parent discipline—the field flourished in the more benign post-World War II academic world. But, the story of Columbia's Richard Gottheil and the succession to the Semitics professorship he held for half a century illustrates the price of university admission for Semitics and Jewish learning in the changed conditions of early twentieth-century academic life.

Competition

When Jewish Semitists entered the universities in the 1880s and 1890s, the decades of scholarly triumph, the American Oriental Society became an arena of academic competition. These scholars played a key role in the 1890 "crisis" that challenged the distribution of rewards among the elect—Yale and Harvard faculty members. Cyrus Adler of Johns Hopkins proposed that the Society seek federal chartering and move its library away from Yale, and the University of Pennsylvania, through Morris Jastrow, offered to assume responsibility for the library.[3] Adler argued that the Society's charter provision that called for the annual meeting to take place in Boston placed an unjustified travel burden on many orientalists. The financial inability of the *Journal of the American Oriental Society* to publish all significant submissions, Adler added, retarded scholarship. Federal chartering, he claimed, might allow the Government Printing Office to publish the journal without charge. Removal of the Society's library to, say, Washington's Smithsonian Institution, where he worked, would permit use of the government frank for sending books to borrowers.[4]

The AOS added Paul Haupt, Adler's mentor, to its board of directors in 1891 and held the 1892 annual meeting in Washington, D.C., after amending its charter to permit annual meetings outside Massachusetts. Daniel Coit Gilman, still president of Johns Hopkins, became the Society's president in 1893, but the organization declined to solicit a federal charter, ignored Adler's library proposal, and declined Jastrow's offer. By adding the principles of institutional and geographical parity to scholarly primacy and language parity, the AOS became a more neutral arena for scholarship.[5]

The 1890 American Oriental Society compromise did not end personal and academic rivalries among Semitists. Assyriologist Robert Harper reported to his brother, William R. Harper, that Paul Haupt had called the Chicago president "no scholar" and claimed to have him "under his thumb." "He is a disgrace and people should know it," Robert Harper wrote. "He has talked a good deal about you, but to no effect, as he is not taken seriously here [among Semitics scholars at the British Museum] or anywhere else, except by Ward, G. F. Moore, etc."[6] Jastrow also endured Robert Harper's barbs. "Jastrow cannot translate," he wrote on one occasion. "Neither one of these men [Jastrow or Gottheil] is a *careful* philologist or a writer of decent English," he added on another.[7] Robert Harper maintained many grudges. His relationship with James Breasted, his junior colleague at Chicago, bore the stamp of jealousy from the outset, while his insistence that "the field [of Assyriology at Chicago] is mine" reflected personal insecurity as much as full professorial privileges.[8]

Paul Haupt, in turn, did not spare his Pennsylvania colleagues. "Hilprecht ordained?" he mused. "Well, well! Perhaps Jastrow will follow his example. They certainly have better chances as ministers than in the field of shemitic philology. *Asur likrub sunuti!* [May Ashur bless you!]"[9] These judgments circumscribed cooperation among practitioners, but even when mutual admiration characterized personal and professional relations, the field's dependence upon local, external support made cooperation difficult.

Magnanimous rhetoric did come from Harvard Sanskritist Charles Lanman, because Harvard could draw upon relatively strong resources in building its Oriental studies program. Lanman urged that universities establish a "series" of Oriental monographs, thereby emulating Harvard's sponsorship of America's one endowed series, the *Harvard Oriental Studies*. "The success of each helps all the rest," he wrote William R. Harper, who contemplated such an endeavor. "We are all *at one work*. It is absolutely petty and mole-eyed to let the slightest shadow of a shade of jealousy ever cross our field of ambition. (Pardon the mixedness of the metaphor.)"[10] Lanman encouraged Richard Gottheil to seek an endowment for a Columbia Oriental Series and called for "classical and Semitic and Sanskrit publication funds established not only here but at Johns Hopkins and Columbia, Clark, Cornell, etc."

Lanman adopted a different tone when it came to the publication of scholarly articles, where Harvard was more vulnerable, and advised Gottheil, who contemplated the publication of a journal to be called *Oriental Notes*, to refrain from journal submissions or editorial work. He argued against "the mania . . . for contributing to as many different publications as possible" and against Gottheil's "temptation to *Flüchtigkeit:* doing too many things to do any of them well." Lanman accused himself of the same failings: "I'm getting too often into the slough of despond by reason of the ever-growing conviction that I am an unmitigated humbug in 'professing' Sanskrit at all, for I never seem able to accomplish anything like what it is my duty to do."

Should Gottheil be faulted for questioning the motives behind the words of his successful senior colleague? Did Lanman, Gottheil wondered, discourage Columbia Sanskritist A. V. Williams Jackson from coediting *Oriental Notes* in part to protect the *JAOS*, with its close ties to Harvard?[11] "I don't think it [*Oriental Notes*] would make any serious withdrawal of good matter from its Journal perhaps," Lanman wrote, "and yet, why not give what good matter we can produce, to *it,* since it is an established and well-known medium of publication of really first-rate repute?"[12] Lanman also attempted to convince William R. Harper, editor of *Hebraica,* that the *JAOS* should take precedence over the establishment of rival journals.

Lanman and his colleagues agreed that the *JAOS* needed resuscitation—it had published only 14 volumes in 49 years—to keep up with the increasing number of productive Semitics scholars. Yet he opposed an 1893 proposal to make the journal a quarterly, arguing that "the quality of material offered for publication should be the sole determinant of the question whether any given paper should be printed; that the needlessly created necessity of issuing a number upon each quarter-day might make quality a co-determinant, a result for which parallels are not far to seek, and which would be most sincerely to be deprecated."[13]

Rhetorical magnanimity was possible for a scholar who implicitly identified the profession's best interests with Harvard's, but others enunciated a more parochial viewpoint. "I do think that we men *at* Chicago should stick together *for* Chicago," Robert Harper wrote after learning that two Chicago colleagues were approached to edit volumes in a competing series. "We have our own work, and we can organize more. . . . This year has made me more loyal to Chicago than ever. We should not scatter our efforts but work to a plan. While I have absolutely no objection to Arnolt's or Smith's working for Jastrow, I think it would be better for *them* and *us all* to do our own Series and volumes and articles, etc., etc."[14]

Parochialism may have been necessary to secure the field's position within each university, but it entailed domestic and international costs. "I have more and more reached the conclusion," Paul Haupt wrote, "that all Assyriologists are a pretty bad set. There are all sorts of intrigues everywhere."[15] Charles Lanman, writing from an American academic mecca, contended that "the success of one could [not] possibly block the success of another. That would be as doltish in me as to suppose of two men trading that one man loses because the other gains."[16] But Semitists located on less hallowed ground disagreed.

Presidential and communal support for Semitics arose from the field's supposed ability to address questions that concerned the larger public. "The growth of research at the American universities," noted sociologist Joseph Ben-David, "was not only a result of imminent scientific progress in the various fields, but, at times, was also a result of the desire to provide research to meet practical demands."[17] But Semitics practitioners failed to follow this path to success.

Might practitioner cooperation compensate for diminished communal support as the field proved unable to address "practical demands?" Yes, but the realization came perhaps too late. Competition, Semitists recognized in retrospect, led to rifts over early projects of supposed universal benefit, such as the American hosting of the 1893 International Congress of Orientalists. The AOS arrangements committee, Gottheil, Haupt, and Jastrow, strived for unanimity, since most orientalists were Europeans still skeptical of American scholarship. But plans came to naught, and postmortem assessments blamed New England demurrers to the proposed Washington, D.C. site, intradisciplinary intrigues, and fear of exposing the quantity and quality of American scholarship to foreign judgment.[18] Intense competition, combined with loss of external support, weakened the field at the outset. By the time the field united a generation later in the Hilprecht affair, renewed growth was almost impossible.

The Hilprecht affair arose from the University of Pennsylvania's Babylonian expedition (1888–1900). John P. Peters, who studied Semitics in Germany for four years after graduate work at Yale, conceived the idea and secured funds for the expedition even before he began his Hebrew professorship at Pennsylvania. Parity with Europe in Semitic studies, Peters told the American Oriental Society, required unearthing, cataloguing, and translating unknown antiquities, not merely processing extant pieces. "England and France have done a noble work of exploration in Assyria and Babylonia," Peters added. "It is time for America to do her part. Let us send out an American expedition."[19]

After returning to America in 1883, Peters convinced philanthropist Catherine Lorilard Wolfe to underwrite W. H. Ward's exploratory venture to Babylonia. Benefactors such as Wolfe emphasized more material—and more lofty—goals than scholarly parity with Europe. These philanthropists expected the discovery of valuable artifacts that would uphold traditional accounts of Biblical events, especially against the higher criticism.[20] So did Peters. "Its special importance to me," he wrote, "is the light it throws on the Bible but it is also important for the understanding of the origin and history of Greek civilization."[21] But among Gentiles, as among Jews, only an occasional benefactor wanted to fund expeditions of such uncertain expense and result. Wolfe failed to donate funds for excavation in the area scouted by Ward, and several years passed before E. W. Clark, a prominent Philadelphia banker, stepped forward. With Clark on board, the University of Pennsylvania agreed to sponsor the expedition.

To excavate in Babylonia, Peters had to secure a *firman* or permit from the Turkish government. Johns Hopkins authorities protested the Pennsylvania application to the American State Department, because Paul Haupt wished to lead a similar expedition, and the Turks were likely to grant only one *firman*. The prize went to Pennsylvania, and in 1888, Peters set out on the first of four expeditions to Babylonia.[22]

The contentiousness surrounding the expedition resulted from Pennsylvania's simultaneous recruitment of Peters, Hilprecht, and Jastrow—three marginal, unsalaried Semitic scholars, each of whom hoped the project would secure for himself a stronger position within a university slanted towards professional education. Peters left the university in 1893 to assume the pulpit of St. Michael's Church in New York City, which his father and grandfather had previously occupied, but each of the two academics who cast their lot permanently with the university concluded that they could only gain at the other's expense.

The rivalry between Herman Hilprecht and Morris Jastrow manifested itself over large and small issues: the location of reference books, the right to offer Assyriological courses, and their relationship to the university museum. But the discovery of a large cache of antiquities at Nippur during the fourth expedition (1899–1900) precipitated a bitter, full-scale dispute that eventually engulfed most American Semitists. Peters and Jastrow questioned whether the evidence Hilprecht offered in *Explorations in Bible Lands* (1903), his account of the four expeditions, justified his claims of major discoveries.[23] Hilprecht, his accusers suggested, specifically failed to support his claim to have discovered a temple library at Nippur on the fourth expedition. They charged that the antiquities Hilprecht offered as evidence of a library were purchased, not excavated, as many as eleven years before that expedition and might not even have come from Nippur. Both accusers reserved judgment as to whether Hilprecht actually discovered a temple library.[24]

Jastrow and other colleagues added charges concerning Hilprecht's role in the discovery of the purported library and his ownership of antiquities. University of Pennsylvania authorities agreed with other American orientalists about the need for adjudication but not about the method. A 1905 university panel including the provost (president) and university trustees exonerated Hilprecht, but Semitists charged that this lay panel was unqualified to render judgments on the use of scholarly evidence. The panel's failure to publish the proceedings exacerbated matters. Hilprecht cited the committee's report in response to scholarly requests for a "full and frank statement."

The Semitists imposed academic quarantine on Hilprecht, but it took five years for the Pennsylvania trustees to pay heed.[25] In the summer of 1910, Hilprecht offered his resignation to protest Jastrow's unauthorized entry into his office. Hilprecht apparently hoped to act as prosecutor in a new tribunal, this time with Jastrow and other enemies as defendants. But the heretofore supportive administration and trustees surprised Hilprecht by accepting the resignation. University museum authorities, stated the Pennsylvania trustees, properly entered his offices out of concern about deterioration of the tablets that Hilprecht kept in the museum's damp basement. The entry, the trustees added, caused no destruction or damage. Hilprecht pressed his case, but the trustees remained steadfast. The scholarly world subsequently heard little from Hilprecht, save for two additional volumes of inscriptions.

How could Hilprecht have miscalculated so badly in 1910? Hilprecht's competitiveness and egocentrism—he helped choose the contributors to a 1909 *festschrift* that celebrated two "milestones": his 50th birthday and the 25th anniversary of his doctorate—typified the field in 1890, when most practitioners were insecure about their positions. But by 1910, these characteristics were out of place. "If in the business world efforts are now being made to get rid of dishonorable methods," wrote Morris Jastrow, "we scholars ought not, by our silence, to countenance them."[26] "Scientific dishonesty is worse than business dishonesty," Gottheil observed, "because scientists are supposed to have renounced the world for the purpose of living up to their ideals."[27] The Hilprecht affair denotes the emergence of a "progressive" impulse among Semitists, manifested in their greater willingness to regulate academic conduct; cutthroat competition was a feature of the past.

Hilprecht also failed to note the changed relationship between American and European Semitists. Jastrow testified in 1905 that Carl Bezold, a German Assyriologist, first suggested that the fourth Babylonian expedition may have discovered an archive, not a library. Other European scholars accepted Hilprecht's account as proving the existence of the library. Hilprecht, Jastrow argued, threatened the considerable recognition accorded to American scholarship over the previous two decades. Hilprecht understood the terms of battle, and frequently cited European testimonials to his work's veracity. Contributors to his 1909 *festschrift* included only one American—Hilprecht's Pennsylvania assistant—but nearly 30 European academics.[28]

By 1910, however, Hilprecht had to answer to American orientalists. "I cannot well see," Charles Lanman wrote to Hilprecht, "how anything short of that [a statement that Hilprecht laid himself 'open to just criticism'] will reinstate you in the good opinion of men whose opinion, for my part, I should value the most if I were in your place."[29] During the controversy, and perhaps as a result of it, American orientalists stopped referring their disputes to European arbitration. Hilprecht, in contrast, increased his reliance on foreign support. Several months after the trustees accepted his resignation, Hilprecht mounted a campaign among European scholars while shunning aid from American colleagues. Some American scholars viewed the resulting European remonstrance as an unwarranted intrusion into domestic affairs. "There are, as you know," responded Pennsylvania's provost Edgar Smith to the formal communication from the Europeans, "certain situations in which an institution of learning must be content to forego the services of even its most eminent scholar."[30] By 1911, the competition for European "recognition and cooperation" diminished; even a unified denunciation of Jastrow by Hilprecht's American colleagues would not have saved Hilprecht, but it was his only chance.[31]

To be fair, the field's European orientation did not completely disappear. An Indo-Europeanist colleague, though recognizing the changed relationship, articulated an ambivalence shared by most orientalists. This scholar praised two series of oriental texts: the Harvard series, edited by Lanman, which actively enlisted the support of European Sanskritists, and the Columbia series, edited by Jackson, which relied on New York talent. "We may, as Americans," he wrote, "well be proud of both series, in one case because we have been enabled to secure for an American enterprise so many distinguished foreigners, and in the other because we have been able to do without them."[32] World War I provoked anti-German attitudes that decisively broke the umbilical cord in Semitics, as in other fields. In arriving at their definition of permissible academic conduct, and in distancing themselves from European scholarship, American Semitists recognized the virtues of self-reliance.

Nor could Hilprecht turn to the community. Just before the laboratory incident, Hilprecht published a translation of a tablet from the Nippur collection that, he claimed, went beyond standard Babylonian accounts of the Flood to confirm the Biblical rendering—an event designed to stir Philadelphia's religious circles. Scholars soon cried foul. Columbia's John D. Prince charged that Hilprecht obtained the parallel by interpolating a Biblical phrase unsupported by the extant language of the mutilated tablet. In thus violating scholarly protocol, Prince added, "Hilprecht has largely injured the interest and value of his discovery from a scientific point of view."[33] But Philadelphia's pietistic circles neither defended Hilprecht's translation nor saved his academic position.

The playing field, though, was level; by 1910, Morris Jastrow had distanced himself from the Philadelphia Jewish community, and Jewish and Gentile communal support were equally extraneous to this academic dispute. Neither Jastrow's Jewishness nor the Judaic aspects of Semitic scholarship were at issue during the Hilprecht affair. That Jastrow could become so heavily involved in a controversy that did not involve Jewish learning shows the extent of his intellectual gravitation. The irrelevance of Philadelphia Jewry during a visible, passionate dispute that involved the son of an illustrious rabbi illustrates the fissure between Semitics and communal hopes for university-based Jewish scholarship.

Jastrow, during the controversy, nudged his orientalist colleagues to internalize Biblical values and invoked his father's righteousness and his tradition in comparing his actions with Hilprecht's "moral degeneracy and dishonesty." Gottheil, who mobilized American Semitists during the controversy, saw himself as their conscience.[34] "Most of our colleagues," he wrote Jastrow, "while being exceedingly righteous themselves, do not possess enough of the spirit of the old Hebrew enthusiasm for righteousness with which we are familiar from the old testament."[35]

Gottheil's judgment was harsh, for American orientalists frequently viewed their scholarship as a corrective to German practice. "When we were discovering the antiquities of Sargon, his actual inscriptions, in Babylonia," recalled Peters, "a distinguished Berlin Assyriologist was publishing a work in which he proved Sargon to be a myth, and in which Babylonian chronology was reduced to the same sorry pass as that of the Bible in the hands of its critics."[36] Restraint exercised in judgment, wrote a colleague, is "as essential to progress as direct contributions to knowledge, the guiding hand that does not permit the steed of progress to leap the fence but keeps it to the road!"[37] The Judaic outlook, Gottheil implied, might affect the ethos and ethics of university-based Semitic studies—if not their substance—by elevating restraint from an academic obligation to a righteous act. But this role was a far cry from the agenda articulated by presidents, providers, and practitioners only a generation before.

"More as a Rabbi than a Professor": The Two Careers of Richard Gottheil

Semitic scholarship in American universities lost its Judaic bent, and much Jewish communal support, in the early twentieth century. A Jewish community that sought recognition through scholarship would find little encouragement in Morris Jastrow's emphasis on Assyriology or William Popper's critical edition of the writings of an Egyptian historian. Communal estrangement compounded familial disappointment—Jastrow and Gottheil failed to ascend to their fathers' pulpits, for example. Jastrow viewed Semitic scholarship not as a "calling" but as a viable occupation after he rejected the rabbinate. His commitment to his field, his institution, and to the pursuit of disinterested scholarship deepened over time, and Hilprecht's perceived failure to play by academic rules unsettled him. The verdict of the Pennsylvania provost and trustees after Hilprecht's 1905 hearing was probably a harsher blow since Jewish Semitists hoped that the mutuality of interests between presidents and practitioners, especially a presumed shared belief in the disinterested pursuit of knowledge, would compensate for lost communal support.

We do not know all the reasons for the 1905 verdict, but it was a rare lay board that ignored personalities, and personal characteristics, such as a scholar's religion. In general, this worked both ways: Adherence to Judaism contributed both to acceptance of first generation Semitists and to rejection of their successors. During the early twentieth century, institutional agendas and academic norms diverged as universities, succumbing to anti-Semitism, discriminated in faculty hiring.[38]

Anti-Semitism, chapter 5 notes, strongly affected Jewish learning at Harvard after World War I. But fear of a growing Jewish constituency also influenced admissions decisions, student life, campus governance, and academic careers at Columbia.[39] Harvard and Columbia sacrificed quality of scholarship and teaching because they failed to live up to meritocratic principles. But Jewish academics, who may already have made difficult decisions when defining their relationship to community and academy, confronted a diminished academic opportunity structure. These scholars, when hired at all, often found themselves working in a hostile institution where intellect guaranteed neither recognition nor retention. Ironically, as the fissure between presidents, providers, and practitioners widened, members of the Jewish community learned to benefit from invoking and upholding academic norms subverted by Gentile trustees, administrators, and scholars.

The career of Richard Gottheil illustrates the difficulties faced by Jewish Semitists in American universities during the early twentieth century. Gottheil, as much as any Jewish Semitist, lived a double professional life. His philological orientation, which arose from a commitment to scholarship and from constraints imposed by a suspicious, prejudiced world, led him to create a Semitics department that lacked a distinct Judaic orientation. Outside the university, Gottheil, a founder of American Zionism, visibly and effectively participated in myriad Jewish social, educational, and political activities.

Gottheil compartmentalized these agendas, but the Columbia administration and concerned observers confounded them. Confusion was probably inevitable since Gottheil's prominence in Jewish causes stemmed from his position at Columbia, as well as his abilities and his parentage, and since he remained committed to Jewish learning in settings other than Columbia. Cognizant that his external activities might cast suspicions on his academic conduct, he remained ever-prudent within the university. But his precautions did not allay the perceptions and prejudices that came to the fore when Columbia chose his successor.

Gottheil spent the first years after his 1886 appointment creating a full-fledged Semitics department from limited resources. Columbia, after assuming Gottheil's salary, did little more than help to secure outside endowments. Salary increases were few and far between; so were additional appointments.[40] Gottheil had some teaching assistance from Reverend Abraham Yohannan, who learned Arabic and vernacular Syriac when growing up in the Near East. When Columbia made a budgetary provision for Yohannan, who was supported by outside funds, Gottheil objected that he was a poor teacher and did no administrative work. He added that his salary "could be put to much better use either in strengthening our present position or in adding to it the services of some man trained in our modern methods of research and of teaching and able to be of solid service to the department."[41]

In 1903, on the occasion of Gustav Gottheil's 75th birthday, the Temple Emanu-El trustees allocated $10,000 for a Gustav Gottheil Lectureship in Semitic Languages at Columbia.[42] The lectureship, intended as a springboard, launched several early holders on prominent academic careers and later subsidized the salary of department assistant Abraham Halkin for almost 20 years. Columbia received no other instructional endowments for Semitics before Gottheil's death.[43]

Gottheil failed to get external backing for additional professorships, but he obtained a steady flow of donations for books, manuscripts, and artifacts. He did not purchase Hebrew and Judaic materials exclusively. Instead, when a collection became available, he requested funds from whomever he thought might be forthcoming—personal acquaintances, college classmates, or fellow congregants whose interest Gottheil took special pains to cultivate.[44] He usually approached Jews when he wished to acquire Hebrew materials and non-Jews for other purchases. He thus built up a good collection, emphasizing Hebrew manuscripts, Arabic and Hebrew books, and Babylonian inscriptions.[45]

Gottheil's scholarship reflected evenhandedness and circumspection. He began his Columbia service as an instructor in Syriac, and conducted research in Hebrew and Aramaic texts. By 1906 he had shifted his focus sufficiently to say that his research was mostly in Arabic. His major scholarly publications included *Selections from the Syriac Romance of Julian the Apostate, The Syriac-Arabic Glosses of Isha bar Ali, A Treatise on Syriac Grammar,* and *Genizah Fragments* (written with William H. Worrell). Gottheil did not discriminate in selecting students or offering fellowships. He insisted on a broad foundation for all his students and discouraged no specializations. His students included Judaic scholars Max Margolis and Abraham Halkin, as well as Arabists William Popper and Philip Hitti.[46] Stephen S. Wise, founder of the Free Synagogue of New York and president of the Jewish Institute of Religion, also took his doctorate under Gottheil.

Gottheil's academic comportment resulted from external conditions—even during Seth Low's benign presidency—and from internalized beliefs. The original Temple Emanu-El endowment and Gottheil's appointment encountered no formal resistance.[47] Columbia trustees, whose ranks included several high-ranking Episcopalian clergymen, saw its value "to students that are preparing for the Sacred Ministry"—and mentioned no danger to Christianity—when accepting the endowment.[48] But Richard Gottheil understood that certain research was likely to elicit criticism. Gentile fear of Jewish control of economic, social, and cultural institutions also dictated circumspection. Seth Low discouraged official anti-Semitism, but Nicholas Murray Butler, his successor, did not.[49] Gottheil personally confronted anti-Semitism in 1898 when he attempted to register his son at the Horace Mann School, a preparatory school with close ties to Columbia. Virgil Prettyman, the Horace Mann headmaster, combined an admission offer with a statement that he desired to restrict the number of Jews. Gottheil instead registered the boy at Julius Sachs' non-denominational, but predominantly Jewish, preparatory school.[50]

The need for circumspection may have increased after the 1904 merger of the three graduate faculties—Philosophy (including the Semitics department), Political Science, and Pure Science—under Dean John Burgess, a man with pronounced anti-Semitic tendencies.[51] Several years later, when Horace Kallen, then at the University of Wisconsin, inquired about teaching prospects at Columbia, Gottheil replied, "Columbia—entre nous—is not a good berth for a Jew."[52]

Gottheil relied upon Seth Low to adjudicate in difficult situations. He decided in 1896 to offer a course on the bearing of recent archaeological research in Egypt, Babylonia, and Palestine on the elucidation of the Bible. He had heretofore confined himself "strictly to the philological study of the Bible," he told Low, and requested reassurance "for reasons which I am sure you well understand—that my action will not be mistaken."[53] If Low would authorize the course, Gottheil promised "to keep as strictly to the archaeological as I have hitherto to the philology." If the Columbia president objected to the title, but not the content, "it could be veiled and changed to 'Recent archaeological research in the orient.'" "Our College and University men," Gottheil maintained, "should be given a chance to know what light the investigations of scholars have thrown upon the Bible." But, he added diplomatically, "Semitic research can never forget that the interest the intelligent layman class shows in the East, is in the largest part due to his interest in the Bible and in all that concerns it."[54] Low approved the class under the more oblique title.[55]

Several years later, Gottheil suggested a broader mandate. "Hebraics," he wrote, "ought not to confine itself altogether to philology. History and Kultur-Geschichte are in its province as much as is philology."[56] At the same time, he published *Jewish History in the Nineteenth Century,* and secured a minor in "comparative study of religions" for higher degree candidates in the Faculty of Philosophy.[57] Despite these initiatives, scholar Richard Gottheil remained academically cautious.[58] Personal interest and external reality dictated his decision not to place a Jewish stamp on the Semitics department. But many observers of citizen Richard Gottheil—committed Jewish and Zionist activist—misunderstood or purposefully failed to appreciate these efforts.

Early twentieth-century American academics adopted different rules for their public and classroom utterances. Within the classroom, professors were not to urge political positions on captive student audiences, but colleges and universities were supposed to tolerate political advocacy in a professor's public statements.[59] At Columbia, Richard Gottheil's scrupulous conformity to the scholarly role made academic and political sense. He took full advantage, however, of his freedom to advocate his commitment to Judaism and to Zionism outside ivy walls. Cognizant, as we have seen, that the formal rules were not fully applicable to Jews, especially Zionists, Gottheil used his personality and intellect to overcome hostility and misperception. His political enemies had to wait until his death before attempting to "capture" his chair.

Gottheil's continued, if diminished, participation in academic activities with a Jewish stamp partially explains the confusion. He edited the post-Biblical history and the post-Talmudic literature sections of the *Jewish Encyclopedia* (1901–1905), which organized scholarly knowledge concerning Jews and Judaism, and ran the Oriental department of the New York Public Library, which changed its name to the Judaica collection during his tenure from 1896 until his death. A member of the Jewish Historical Society of England, Gottheil became a vice-president of the American Jewish Historical Society in 1904. During the 1920s, he helped found, served as board chairman, and lectured at the Jewish Institute of Religion, a sectarian institution led by Stephen Wise.

Concerned with fraternity discrimination against Jews, Gottheil served as president and spiritual leader of the Zeta Beta Tau Fraternity.[60] The fraternity, according to its official history, aimed to foster contact with "non-Jewish comrades on the athletic field, in journalism, debate, dramatics, and in every field of campus activity which affords expression to that moral and physical courage, that capacity for sportsmanship, generosity, sociability and social conscience which form part and parcel of the Jewish racial heritage."[61] Cultivation of Jewish identity and the confrontation of Jewish problems, Gottheil believed, would overcome anti-Semitic stereotypes of bookishness and cowardice. Gottheil's ambitious goals for Zeta Beta Tau led him to counsel against accepting brothers desiring to join "simply for the sake of belonging to a Greek Letter Fraternity."[62] After the fraternity's annual convention, where the delegates heard Louis D. Brandeis, Israel Friedlander, Isaiah L. Sharfman, and Maurice Wertheim, Gottheil wrote, "The boys had more Jewish material shot into them in that one day than they usually get in a whole year."[63] Gottheil took pride in Zeta Beta Tau, but his continued insistence that the fraternity emphasize Jewish content suggests that reality fell short of expectations.[64]

Gottheil also worked for the Intercollegiate Menorah Association, founded in 1906 by Harvard student Henry Hurwitz. Menorah realized many of Gottheil's aspirations for Zeta Beta Tau by advancing and disseminating Jewish scholarship through student study groups.[65] Gottheil's work in Jewish education included Sunday school teaching early in his career, editing "Helpful Thoughts," a publication aimed at a Sunday school audience, and chairing the education committee of the Educational Alliance, which performed settlement work among newly arrived Jewish immigrants on Manhattan's Lower East Side.

But Gottheil's commitment to Zionism overshadowed these activities and led many observers to view his academic position as Columbia's Zionist chair. "It is sometimes held," he wrote in *Zionism*, "that an historian must be unbiased, and must stand vis-à-vis to his subject much as a physician does to his patient." Detachment would suffice for the antiquarian chronicler, "to whom dry dates and lifeless facts are all-important." Noting Henri Bergson's assertion that evolution is a creative process, Gottheil argued that "the attempt must be made to understand in what that creative spirit exists, and this can be attained only by active sympathy with the peculiar phase of the soul-life the historian has to depict."[66]

This embrace of "active sympathy" in his non-philological writings only hints at the depth of Gottheil's commitment. After attending the first World Zionist Congress in Basel in 1897, organized by his "long-time" friend Theodor Herzl, he established and chaired the Federation of American Zionists and became a prominent American speaker for the movement.[67] Gottheil kept a lower profile after 1910, not for lack of commitment, but because he considered himself a candidate for the ambassadorship to Constantinople, which had jurisdiction over Palestine. Gottheil described his fate to Horace Kallen:

Twice, already, I have had the Constantinople Ambassadorship within my reach. On the first occasion [Oscar] Straus came in and spoiled the combination. He wanted to be Ambassador, having previously been only Minister. I could not pull against him. This last time [1913, upon Woodrow Wilson's inauguration] it was [Henry] Morgenthau. M. did not want it. He told me in Paris last July that he had refused it and that he considered it an insult that the Turkish post was the only

one that a Jew could occupy. [Stephen] Wise forced him to take it; and Wilson—
who had to do something for Morgenthau and had nothing else, carried out his
original plan.[68]

Gottheil never obtained the ambassadorship. The onset of World War I made it
politically untenable for an American Zionist, who counted on an Anglo-French
victory, to be sent to the Ottoman Empire, aligned with the Central Powers.
Gottheil maintained contact with Allied diplomats during the war to lobby for a
Jewish homeland in Palestine in the peace settlement.[69]

Gottheil's commitment to Zionism led him to call the questions that heretofore preoccupied the American and European Jewish communities "minor
points connected with the synagogue service and with ritual observances." Compared to the Zionist question, "all others paled, so that many wondered how the
older questions could ever have called forth the feeling and the fire they did."
Zionism "set the Jews to thinking hard. . . . A question has been put that is one
of life and death. It has called into the firing-line of each of the two parties [Zion-
ists and anti-Zionists] the most experienced and best-tried warriors."[70]

American entry into the world war led Gottheil to redouble his Zionist activities. As early as 1898, his Columbia colleagues informally chided him for his outside activities.[71] During the war, Gottheil did little more than meet minimum
academic obligations.[72] He never forgot the distinction between advocacy and
objectivity, but he reduced the proportion of his time dominated by academic
norms. Gottheil witnessed the Balfour Declaration, the League of Nations mandate, and increased Jewish-Arab tension. He also observed the decline of university-based Semitic studies—he strongly supported Stephen Wise's Jewish
Institute of Religion—and the deteriorating status of Jews on American college
campuses. When Columbia authorities finally had to seek a replacement for Gottheil in 1936, they confused the political and academic roles that he attempted
to keep apart and initially identified as a replacement a "best-tried warrior" on
the anti-Zionist side.

Richard Gottheil died on May 22, 1936, after 49 years of service to Columbia. Stephen Wise and his circle had discussed possible successors for several
years, but no one could convince the aging professor to retire or at least to plan
for his department's future. "Our old friend, R. G. is, as you know, a very touchy
individual, and, like other people whom we know, it never occurs to him that he
ought to prepare for a successor," noted Wise. "The thing for us to do is to try
to make him see that his work should be continued by a first-rate Jew such
as L. F. [probably Louis Finkelstein]—or he will be succeeded by a third
rate *Goy*."[73] Early in 1936, President Butler tactfully broached the subject
of retirement, but at the time of his death, Gottheil remained in command
of his department.[74]

Shortly thereafter, Professor James G. Egbert of Columbia's Faculty of Philosophy asked Wise, Rabbi Louis Newman of the Jewish Institute of Religion,
and Emma Gottheil, Richard's wife, to suggest a future course for the Semitics

department. Wise and Newman urged that Columbia continue the chair and keep it within the graduate school, as opposed to transferring it to a seminary. Newman suggested William Popper, his former mentor and Gottheil's former student, as a possible successor. Emma Gottheil thought that Columbia might appoint a European scholar on a visiting basis for the following academic year. Wise concurred, adding that departmental assistants Abraham Halkin and Ralph Marcus could handle routine work while the university carefully searched for a successor.[75]

Barely three months later, President Nicholas Murray Butler invited George Antonius to succeed to Gottheil's chair. Gottheil's friends understood that appointment of a Jew to the Semitics chair in 1936 was unlikely, given Columbia's hostility towards Jews, the broad scope of the Semitics department, and the lack of provision for succession. Yet, none of these friends anticipated that Columbia would fill his chair with a man not only unqualified as a Semitist but also politically hostile to their former colleague. George Antonius served from 1921 to 1930 in the British civil service in Palestine, first as chief inspector in the Department of Education, and then, after a leave of absence, on the Chief Secretary's staff as Advisor on Arab Affairs. When the British questioned the impartiality of Antonius, a friend of the Mufti of Jerusalem, he was transferred back to the education department. Unwilling to return with a lower rank than he previously held, he resigned and joined the staff of the Institute of Current World Affairs, which monitored international politics for clients. Charles R. Crane, the institute's benefactor and director, nominated Antonious for the Columbia post.[76]

Crane, who made his fortune selling valves, fittings, and bathroom fixtures, had a long history of interest and travels in the Near East. A devotee of Arab cultural and political causes, he is mainly remembered for membership on the King-Crane Commission, which took a strong anti-Zionist stance in its 1919 report on the Near East to President Wilson.[77] Crane's anti-Zionism, some evidence suggests, may have arisen from anti-Semitism. William Howard Taft nominated Crane to the China ambassadorship in 1909 but recalled him shortly after Senate confirmation. Most accounts attribute the recall to Crane's "indiscreet" prediction of war between Japan and the United States.[78] But Rabbi David Philipson, who opposed the nomination, said that Taft acted upon learning that Crane had commented, "Well, now that Taft is President, I suppose that Jake Schiff and his Jew crowd will have a great deal to say in our national affairs."[79] Crane eventually served as minister to China during the waning days of the Wilson administration and devoted much of his later life to foreign affairs and to his institute.

Crane nominated Antonius to succeed Gottheil "in the chair of Arabic, so far as anyone can succeed him." Crane said he knew Gottheil well and that he "always thought of him more as a rabbi than as a professor, although he had the spirit of both in the highest possible degree." He stated that Antonius, a close associate residing in Jerusalem, knew classical Arabic "as well as any Arab" and also spoke some ten or twelve dialects. (Antonius was an interpreter as part of his duties for the British government.) Crane claimed that Antonius held "his doctor's degree both from Oxford and the Sorbonne," and reassured Butler that his nominee had the confidence of all Near Eastern leaders. Antonius, Crane added, being of Greek descent and thus neither Jew nor Arab, was "untouched by the deepest racial problems and carries very successfully an objective outlook."[80]

Crane's outline of the qualifications of Antonius was, to say the least, partial. Gottheil had held a chair in Semitics, not Arabic, and the ability of Antonius to speak modern Arabic dialects did not mean he could conduct philological research on the classical Semitic languages.[81] In fact, he wrote political essays, not articles on linguistics. Antonius held no doctor's degree—only the Bachelor of Arts (in mathematics), awarded by Cambridge in 1913. An avid anti-Zionist, Antonius in 1936 was conducting research on a book on the rise of Arab nationalism in the Near East. In *The Arab Awakening* (1938), he maintained that he "tried to discharge [his] task in a spirit of fairness and objectivity." Antonius added that he was "approaching the subject from an Arab angle"—he depicted Palestinian Arabs as helpless victims of Zionist and British machinations and omitted facts favorable to the Zionist cause—though he hoped that he arrived at his conclusions "without bias and partisanship."[82]

Butler appears to have consulted only Egbert, the dean of the graduate school, and perhaps Barnard dean Virginia Gildersleeve prior to making the Antonius appointment.[83] Butler suggested an initial one-year visiting appointment after which the university would decide on permanent retention.[84] Egbert concurred. "I am not sure that those who are interested in Professor Gottheil's connection with the University would necessarily favor Mr. Antonius," he wrote. But Egbert added that they would probably be happy to have the work of his chair carried on and to know that Columbia "would not interfere with the positions which are held at this time by the younger men who have been associated with Professor Gottheil."[85] Within hours of Egbert's agreement, Columbia offered an appointment to Antonius through Crane.

Why did Columbia act so quickly? Gottheil's sudden death left no senior professor in charge, and Butler felt the need for swift action in an area in which he claimed not to be knowledgeable.[86] Crane's recommendation and assurance of Antonius's scholarly competence were apparently persuasive. Butler's reliance on advice from a partisan on contemporary Near Eastern questions indicates that he too thought of Gottheil "more as a rabbi than as a professor." Indeed, no one correctly determined the educational background of George Antonius until the candidate himself set the record straight—after Columbia withdrew his appointment.[87] The need to preempt Jewish communal opposition to the appointment may also have dictated haste. Columbia authorities knew that Antonius would not sit well with Gottheil's associates. But they did not anticipate the strength of the opposition's case.

When Egbert informed Emma Gottheil of the appointment, almost a month after the decision, she immediately responded that Columbia had made an unacceptable choice. "George Antonius," she wrote, "is notoriously known as an anti-Semite, a great enemy of my people, as the one who, it is believed, has helped incite the present warfare in Palestine, where innocent men, women and children have been massacred."[88] Her private view of Antonius was even less restrained. "It will be a *Gesera* [punitive decree]," she wrote to Wise, "for the Jews in Palestine if this man George Antonius is permitted to lecture in my dear Richard's place at Columbia. It will be a victory for those who are murdering our brethren in Palestine. . . . A man like Antonius ought not to be allowed to land in America, he is an agitator who provoked civil warfare and that is what he did in Eretz [the land of] Israel."[89]

Wise needed no prompting. With the Arab pogroms against Jews at their height, the Palestinian situation appeared desperate. Saying it would dishonor Columbia and Gottheil's chair to permit Antonius to sit in it, even for an hour, Wise promised demonstrations. "We will make it impossible for Antonius to lecture at Columbia," he told Mrs. Gottheil. "He is a human skunk and everything he touches stinks with the foulness of his own empoisoning personality. There is no greater *sone Israel* [Jew hater], not even Hitler or Goebbels."[90]

Butler referred Emma Gottheil's letter to Crane. Walter Rogers, Crane's associate, replied that Antonius had many friends, including Jews and that contrary to the charge of fomenting civil war, "for years he has been aware that just such a situation as now exists in Palestine would arise unless some all-around acceptable solution to the problems should be found and put into effect. . . . I doubt whether there is any person who has struggled more to forestall the present crisis." Rogers, ignorant of Semitic scholarship and assuming that Antonius would lecture on contemporary subjects, added:

> But even if Mr. Antonius were distinctly anti-Semitic and pro-Arab—and he isn't either—I think that the pro-Zionist Jews would be well-advised if they listened to such a point of view, for it seems to me that the present crisis is in part due to a failure among Jewish leaders to learn the other sides of the Palestinian problem. In any event I see no reason why Americans generally should not have the opportunity to be informed regarding British, Arab and other aspirations as well as the pro-Zionist ones.
>
> If I have any reservations in regard to Mr. Antonious [sic] it goes to the likelihood that he will be so careful to balance his statements that it will be difficult to learn from him the precise views held by the various groups with whose ideas he is familiar, but which are not systematically presented to the American people.[91]

The lengthy letter reassured Columbia officials, though it should have alerted them to Antonius's lack of academic qualifications in Semitics. Frank Fackenthal, Butler's assistant, replied that "without knowing anything about it, I was sure that the situation was of the kind you describe," and added that he still looked forward to the arrival of Antonius.[92]

Basing his reply on the Rogers letter, Butler told Emma Gottheil that Antonius had "been recommended to us in the strongest terms by competent scholars and judges of scholarship in different parts of the world," that he stood "in friendliest possible relations with Jews, Moslems, Catholics, Protestants and others," that he is "deeply concerned to find a solution for the Palestinian problem," and that "the leading Jews, Moslems and Christians in that part of the world constantly meet for social and intellectual contact" at his home.[93]

Emma Gottheil immediately asked Wise to draft a letter for her signature reiterating that Antonius was "a deadly foe to everything that is Jewish." He "may not have the frankness of his anti-Jewish convictions," added the Gottheil–Wise reply, "but he is known in all Jewish circles to be a dangerous marplot against the security and well-being of Palestinian Jewry." Antonius, the letter added, lacked the necessary scholarly qualifications for the professorship: "Forgive me for saying that I have never heard him alluded to as a scholar in any sense of the term." Justice Louis Brandeis, Judge Julian Mack, Felix Frankfurter, and Stephen Wise, concluded the reply, would verify these statements.[94]

Wise, who had a poor personal relationship with Butler, assembled a Jewish delegation—including jurist Joseph Proskauer, businessman Sol M. Stroock, and Louis Newman—to meet with the Columbia president. The group, targeting Antonius's lack of scholarly credentials, elicited the testimony of William F. Albright: "George Antonius is a good propagandist and journalist with wide experience of political affairs in Palestine and Arabia, but is no scholar and hardly the man for a University." Cyrus Adler wrote: "Have talked the matter over with Professor James A. Montgomery, a leading Semitic scholar of the University of Pennsylvania, who has never heard of Antonius." He was also unknown to Dr. Frank Gavin of the General Theological Seminary. "Whether or not Dr. Antonius is a political propagandist for the Mufti," added the delegation, "our concern is that we believe it would be unfortunate from many viewpoints to accord an academic position to a man, whose chief claim to consideration is not as a scholar, but as a political propagandist in a highly tense situation."[95] Walter Rogers, presented with the academic testimonials, defended the abilities of Antonius in recent Near East history. But, he added, "so far as the enclosure concerns Mr. Antonius's competency in the field of Semitic languages and literature, there is nothing to be said, for the simple reason that, to the best of my knowledge, he himself has never set up a claim to special knowledge in that field."[96]

Within hours of the delegation's departure, Butler telegraphed Antonius to await an explanatory letter before accepting Columbia's offer of appointment.[97] The promised letter rehearsed the history of the appointment and added, "When it became known that you had been offered the appointment, attention was called to the fact that the highly technical courses hitherto given by Professor Gottheil were not in your field and that your special competence lay in the recent history and current affairs of the Near East." Butler used the passive voice to avoid revealing how he learned that Antonius was unqualified for a Semitics appointment. By concealing that this protest was of Jewish origin, he could place the Jewish role in a different light. "Later on," Butler continued, "certain Jews, under the misapprehension that you were being invited to offer courses in your proper field, questioned your competence to do so impartially."

The misapprehension was Butler's. By confusing Gottheil's political and scholarly roles, Butler made a serious mistake in academic policy, for which he tried to avoid responsibility by falsely blaming "certain Jews." Butler told Antonius that he wished to ponder whether to offer courses in current Near East affairs, that he would consider his candidacy should the university decide to go ahead, but that he wished to withdraw the outstanding offer.[98] Antonius acceded, but noted that he had not solicited the appointment and was trying to learn what the university expected him to teach when he received notice of the offer's recision. He worried that "the slanders to which you refer" might compromise his reputation for impartiality and asked Butler to do "whatever may be required to protect my good name."[99]

Butler subsequently asked two long-time acquaintances about Antonius—Bayard Dodge, president of the American University of Beirut, and Sir Herbert Samuel, former British commissioner to Palestine. Dodge and Samuel attested to Antonius's ability and his pleasant personality, but Dodge questioned his academic qualifications:

> I am not certain, but believe that Antonius has never done serious work in comparative Semitics. I question whether he knows Hebrew and feel sure that he does not know the other languages of ancient times. Furthermore, I believe that his knowledge of Arabic is that of a very well educated man, rather than a scholar. . . . From the scientific point of view he could hardly hope to measure up to scholars like Lippma, Gibbs, Sprengling and Hitti.[100]

Samuel replied that he knew nothing of Antonius's academic qualifications but that "he has always been regarded as a very strong partisan in the controversies which have been raging in Palestine. He is known as a very capable exponent of the Arab standpoint, and his house has always been regarded as a center of propaganda among visitors to Jerusalem."[101] He told Cyrus Adler of Butler's inquiry and commented: "Of course it would not be a bad thing if an appointment at Columbia were to remove him from Palestine! But my letter was not written with that in mind."[102]

These letters closed the Antonius dossier, and Columbia began a new search. Within two months, Arthur Jeffery, a professor in the School of Oriental Studies of the American University in Cairo and a Gentile, agreed to a visiting professorship in Semitics for the spring, 1937 semester. Egbert emphasized Jeffery's regard "by scholars in this country [Albright and Yale's Charles C. Torrey wrote laudatory letters] and also in Germany as an expert in the Semitic languages."[103] Jeffery impressed the Columbia community during his visit and received an offer to succeed permanently to Gottheil's chair.[104] He ably directed the Semitics department for a generation and followed Gottheil's precedent by giving equal access and encouragement to Jewish, Gentile, and Muslim students.[105]

Semitics: A Cup Half Full or Half Empty?

> The Professor is primarily a Jew. He has never disavowed his origins, yet the homes of the great of all peoples have always been open to

> him. He never bartered his tradition for social
> prestige. The strong convictions he holds are
> not theories of the academicians, untouched
> by the realities of life. Consider his work for
> Zionism: His book *Zionism* is a classic treating
> of the early stages of the movement. But he
> left his study and stood in the market-place in
> behalf of Zionism. He was one of the early
> leaders of the movement.[106]

By the end of the Hilprecht controversy, the intense competitiveness that typified the behavior of Semitists in the 1880s was exceptional. By the time of the Antonius controversy, the communal-academic-institutional reasons for Gottheil's 1886 appointment had supposedly given way to a *sine qua non* of specialized teaching and research, to which Richard Gottheil scrupulously adhered. Columbia, failing to distinguish Gottheil's academic and political life, resolved that his successor would be neither Jewish nor Zionist. But over 20 years of experience in combating campus anti-Semitism had taught Jewish community representatives to invoke academic norms against the overt and covert claims of other groups. That response to Columbia's actions assured that Richard Gottheil's academic precedents, though less visible than his communal activity, would endure. The chair was saved for Semitics, if not for Judaica—a not insubstantial achievement in a year when Columbia also sent a delegation to celebrate the 550th anniversary of the founding of the University of Heidelberg, by then Nazi-dominated.[107]

Neither Jastrow nor Gottheil perpetuated a role for Jewish learning within Semitics. John Peters's lengthy survey of achievements in American Oriental scholarship between 1888 and 1918 allotted precisely one sentence to Jewish scholarship, while Morris Jastrow's account listed no university-based achievements.[108] But what about the fate of Semitics, the parent field? Did low enrollments, communal indifference, and academic anti-Semitism seal its doom? John Peters viewed the first four decades as a time of progress:

> The student who would equip himself as a Semitic specialist does not now need
> to cross the ocean, but can obtain in general in every branch of Semitics, in a num-
> ber of institutions in this country, at least as good instruction as in any institution
> abroad. He may also find here libraries and museums containing not only mater-
> ial for practical training, but also material for original research, sufficient to de-
> mand the services of more men than are at present available for the work. In
> contrast with 1888, we have now in this country an abundance of Semitic schol-
> ars standing in the front rank in equipment and in achievement, equal to the best
> on the other side; and even in exploration and excavation our achievements in the
> Semitic field in the last thirty years have fallen little, if at all, below the best results
> achieved by others. In fact, the progress of the last thirty years in this country in
> all branches of Semitics, has been enormous.[109]

Morris Jastrow, in contrast, questioned the future of Semitics, not its progress. Bemoaning a lack of support—benefactorial, administrative, trustee, and public—for philological scholarship, especially Semitics, Jastrow reverted to his original pessimism:

> The preponderance of the natural sciences in this country at the present time, is such that even among educated persons those who devote their careers to the old "Humanities" are looked upon as "back numbers," left over from a passing generation, while those who choose such outlandish subjects as Assyrian or Arabic or Sanskrit or Persian are regarded in the light of intellectual freaks.

He chastised potential benefactors: "During . . . the past decade no *additional* chairs either for Semitics or for Sanskrit have been established at our Universities, and very few during the past two decades." Despite practitioner heroics, conditions bode ill for the field's ability to attract first-rate scholars. Students prepared in Oriental scholarship, Jastrow noted, often gave up their work to maintain a livelihood—a circumstance, chapter 5 shows, that strongly affected the outlook of Harvard's Harry Wolfson.[110]

Was the Semitics cup half full or half empty? Jastrow was the better prophet: Semitics was strongest at the outset when presidents, concerned community members, and practitioners perceived mutual benefits. The range of institutional attitudes towards Semitics gradually changed from encouragement and tolerance to indifference and hostility. Jewish Semitists had to deal early on with Jewish communal disappointment in their research topics, while their Gentile counterparts experienced indifference from a community whose interests turned away from Darwin and the higher criticism. Semitics—a field that observers found difficult to dissociate from Jews and Judaism, whatever the reality—then fell victim to changes in administrative attitudes toward its Jewish constituency.

To some extent, Semitics departments were also victims of their own success. American philologists helped to temper the higher criticism and the debates between science and religion, and Semitics programs helped to distinguish research-oriented universities from other institutions. A Jewish academic presence—a Jewish communal desideratum—was a fact, though increasingly regretted by many Gentile administrators. Attaining these goals, giving funding priority to the sciences, and permitting the elective system to determine curricular offerings more than counterbalanced claims to the field's intrinsic worth.

Several Semitics programs listed in William Rosenau's late nineteenth-century compendium completely terminated between the world wars. The programs at our six institutions barely persisted in the face of administrative indifference or hostility and reemerged only when nurtured more attentively after World War II. By that time, university-based Jewish learning had taken deeper root in other departments.

V

THE QUEST FOR RECOGNITION
AT HARVARD

My father writes that he has been asked to deliver the next Dudlean lecture at Harvard University in October. It is a religious foundation. The subject this year must be "Natural Religion." Father writes that in all probability he will choose as his special theme "Natural Religion as a factor in the development of the Religion of Israel." What pleases me the most is the official recognition this accords to the Jewish Church; next, of course, to a little justifiable pride in my Father being chosen to speak for our Church.

—Richard Gottheil, 1889[1]

I thank you heartily for your congratulations to the Harvard matter. It indeed looks like some recognition of Jewish learning on the part of a Christian university.

—Solomon Schechter, recipient of an honorary Harvard Ph.D., 1911[2]

It would mean a far-reaching service to the cause of education if Jews endowed chairs for the study of Jewish history and literature in American universities. First, it would mean a contribution to general enlightenment. Second, it would enhance respect for Judaism or Hebraism. And third, it would increase the self-respect of Jewish students at our universities, who, as things are now, often feel humiliated that their own tradition and heritage enjoy no academic recognition. Last, but not least, the academic study of Judaism would diminish, if not destroy the ignorance of Jewish experience and ideals, which so often is the source of suspicion and antagonism.

—Rabbi Hyman G. Enelow, 1925, before arranging the endowment of Harvard's Nathan Littauer Chair of Jewish Literature and Philosophy[3]

It has been the hope of many lovers of Jewish learning that by and by it might be recognized as a regular academic subject by the universities of the world.

—Rabbi Hyman G. Enelow, 1925, after the announcement of the endowment[4]

My conclusions have led me to establish this chair to stimulate research in Jewish thought and philosophy in the cause of higher education, not

from a religious but from a secular standpoint; that true enlightenment
may result from the contribution throughout the ages of the Jews to
the humanities; that they may become more fully and clearly understood; that truer evaluation of Jewish ideals may result and be widely
disseminated through instruction.

—Lucius Littauer, ca. 1925, explaining his gift[5]

Jewish learning entered American higher education at a time of optimism about
the future of the university, American Judaism, and the prospects for a successful encounter between the two. The Jewish community supported academic innovation and Jews contributed to the advancement of knowledge in the
emerging disciplines. In Semitics departments, Jews were expected to demonstrate the value of Jewish learning to a larger world that had heretofore rejected
or ignored it. In return, American Jews asked for recognition of their previous
and potential social contributions, their learning, and their scholars. Whether
scholarship could secure this recognition remained an open question. The failure of many Jewish philanthropists to support Jewish learning demonstrated that
not everyone believed that university-based research and instruction were ideal
meliorative agents. But proponents believed that support of Jewish learning was
a promising strategy for group betterment.

The emergence of American Jewry as a viable social and political force led
some Gentiles to identify a "Jewish problem." Some critics believed that Jewish
achievements came at a cost to other groups. Others felt that Jewish immigration had produced an unassimilable population with values and traditions alien
to American practice. A curious debate took place among university-associated
Gentiles, not over the existence of this problem—all participants agreed to that—
but over its origins. Columbia College dean Frederick P. Keppel (1910–1918)
postulated that the "problem" could be solved by distinguishing between "desirable" and "undesirable" Jews in student admission decisions and in faculty appointments. "Jews who have had the advantage of decent social surroundings for
a generation or two [usually German Jews] are entirely satisfactory companions,"
he wrote in 1915. The more recent arrivals (usually those from Eastern Europe)
who by hard work and sacrifice had academically prepared themselves might
create problems. Keppel stated publicly that universities must accord such
Jews access and help them overcome their "undesirable traits."[6] But privately,
Keppel and other Columbia authorities experimented with measures to limit
their numbers.[7]

Other Gentiles began with a different postulate: that Jews *as a group* posed a
"problem" apart from any Jew's individual characteristics. "Jews form a distinct
body, and cling, or are drawn, together," asserted Abbott Lawrence Lowell,
Charles Eliot's successor, who openly attempted to restrict the access of Jewish

students to Harvard. To Lowell, the recent growth in Harvard's Jewish constituency raised the fear that "where Jews become numerous they drive off other
people and then leave themselves."[8] He did not care whether Gentile prejudice,
Jewish "clannishness," or both factors caused this phenomenon, nor did he contemplate whether the group traits he perceived resulted from heredity or environment, whether Jews were a "race," and whether the passage of time could
eliminate "Jewish traits." These issues were too abstract for Lowell's world of
alumni, parent, student, and faculty concerns.[9] Jews as a group constituted a
"threat." If they ceased to do so, Harvard could reconsider its contemplated restrictions upon Jewish access.[10]

Such reasoning seriously challenged those Jews who insisted that the results
of Jewish scholarship would undermine the very prejudices, fears, and stereotypes that Lowell expressed and thereby improve the lot of American Jews. Indeed, strong reactions against the Jewish presence in higher education occurred
in some institutions that had heretofore welcomed them, such as Harvard, Columbia, and Johns Hopkins. Decades of attempts to explain Jews and Judaism
to the Gentile world appeared, for reasons not fully fathomed, to have gone for
naught. The universalism of American Reform Jews—a stance appropriate in the
late nineteenth-century era of liberal religion and social melioration—appeared
unreciprocated, even irrelevant, to post-World War I America.

Increased Gentile hostility led advocates of Jewish learning in American universities to replace their global aspirations with a more pragmatic outlook. Short
run increases in Jewish or Judaic representation appeared unlikely. At best, Jews
might maintain current levels of faculty representation and student attendance.
At Harvard, whose president viewed the "problem" in group terms, any member
of the "distinctive" group who aspired to scholarly or social recognition would
experience considerable difficulty. The encounters of Jewish philanthropist Jacob
H. Schiff and Judaica scholar Harry A. Wolfson with Harvard illustrate hard times
for university-based Jewish learning, the diminished expectations among Jews for
their position in American universities, and the problems encountered by the Reform Jewish vision of universalism, assimilation, and acceptance.

Confronted with the prospect of academic adversity, Jews placed a high priority upon retaining Jewish learning at Harvard—the prestigious and influential
institution that preceded the American republic by 150 years, and that James
Bryce called the most famous university on the North American continent.[11]
Harvard, whose roster of presidents included well-born, influential men—
Quincy, Sparks, Everett, Eliot, and Lowell—was a training ground for the elites
of New England and America. The institution retained a genteel, liberal culture
image while offering increasingly specialized courses of study.[12] Harvard be-
stowed instant and indisputable legitimacy on all associated with it—a fact well-
known to both Jacob Schiff and Harry Wolfson. And as a national institution,
with resources that permitted retention of marginal subjects, Harvard's be-
stowals could, indeed had to, depend on more than the prejudices of any one
man—even its president.

Harvard's image would not lead one to consider an immigrant with an accent,
even of financier Jacob Schiff's stature, a typical benefactor. But for Schiff, con-

scious that East European Jewish migrations between 1880 and 1920 could jeopardize his goal of Jewish assimilation into an American mainstream, Harvard could reduce Gentile antipathy and hostility by formally recognizing, through the curriculum, the importance of Jewish culture. Conversely, Schiff hoped that Gentile recognition and acceptance might induce Jewish Americans to participate more fully in American society.

Similarly, the image of a typical early twentieth-century Harvard faculty member brings to mind Bliss Perry, William James, George Santayana, or Barrett Wendell, not Harry Austryn Wolfson, student of medieval Jewish philosophy. Wolfson had little hope for his own future at Harvard. Yet, almost uncontrollably attracted to the institution, he believed that he could produce significant Jewish scholarship that, bearing the Harvard imprimatur, might foster Jewish recognition. Wolfson also hoped to show that "general" scholarship might strengthen the work of Judaica practitioners who worked in seminaries and *yeshivot*.

Schiff, the worldly scion of a wealthy New York German Jewish family, and Wolfson, the bookish resident of a cluttered basement office in Widener Library, thus viewed Harvard as a vehicle for recognition. They developed no close relationship, though their Harvard connections overlapped, perhaps because Wolfson's East European ancestry, his demeanor, intellectual interests, and accent rendered him an undesirable Jewish representative in Schiff's eyes. For years a marginal docent, only Lucius Littauer's endowment of the Nathan Littauer Chair in Jewish Literature and Philosophy in 1925 saved Wolfson from the academic oblivion to which Harvard had already consigned him. That both a major philanthropist and a promising young scholar experienced multiple difficulties at America's first institution of higher learning spoke volumes about the state of Jews and Jewish learning after World War I. These difficulties also reflected the plight of what had been one of Harvard's more important academic departments.

Fat Years and Lean: Jacob Schiff and the Harvard Semitics Department

> Indeed, the Jews, the modern representatives of the Semitic people, may well be proud of their origin and ancestry. Anti-Semitism in Europe, social prejudice and ostracism in free America may for a time be rampant; posterity will with shame and disgust repudiate these passions. To combat in the meantime these unsound currents in an efficient manner, opportunities should be created for a more thorough study and a better knowledge of Semitic history and civilization, so that the world shall better understand and acknowledge the debt it owes to the Semitic people.

—Jacob H. Schiff, at the opening of the Harvard Semitic Collection, 1891[13]

Jacob H. Schiff viewed his endowment of the Harvard Semitic Museum (opened 1903) as a good investment. The acceptance of Semitic culture, including ancient Hebrew culture, as a legitimate object of university investigation by the quintessential symbol of American intellectual life would be a major impetus towards full acceptance of the Jewish presence in America. Greek and Roman culture had long been viewed as ancestors of the American heritage; the scientific study of Semitic culture would prove that the ancient Hebrews belonged in the same pantheon, which would redound to the benefit of their descendants.

Born to a long line of rabbis and scholars, Schiff received his early religious and secular education in Frankfurt and then embarked upon a career in finance. At age 18, he emigrated to the United States and soon attained prominence by exploiting his family's financial connections in Germany. He joined the firm of Kuhn, Loeb and Co. in 1875 and became president in 1885 when Solomon Loeb, his father-in-law, retired. Schiff's philanthropic activities were legendary. His support of Harvard's Semitics Museum was only one of many gifts to American higher education,[14] and one of still many more gifts to causes with a Jewish cast.[15] The uniqueness of the gift lay in combining two favorite objects of philanthropy with the prospect of furthering the acceptance of American Jews by the dominant culture.

David Gordon Lyon and James Loeb, Schiff's brother-in-law and a Harvard undergraduate, first discussed the possibility of a museum endowment in 1888. Lyon and Schiff met soon thereafter, and the professor made a friend for himself and for Harvard's Semitics program.[16] In 1889, Schiff joined the Visiting Committee to the Semitics Department (he became its chair in 1893), thus beginning a 25-year relationship.[17] Schiff contributed $10,000 to acquire relevant material from European museums and antique dealers, promised subsequent contributions, and suggested that Lyon travel abroad to supervise the purchases and to establish his reputation.[18] The Peabody Museum offered its facilities to house the treasures, pending construction of a permanent home, but no one expected that "temporary" would mean 12 years.

Schiff could have donated the $50,000 necessary for construction of a Semitic Museum. Instead, he offered a $25,000 matching grant. Lyon attributed Schiff's preference for such contributions to his modesty—his refusal to have the museum considered his personal concern—but Schiff had other reasons. For his gifts to accomplish their purpose, Jews and broad-minded Gentiles had to become involved. Schiff objected in language "which bordered on the undiplomatic" to Lyon's suggestions that "we might hope for larger success by making the Museum a Jewish enterprise." Widespread participation, Schiff believed, would indicate Gentile recognition of Jewish culture; Jews could buy recognition no more easily than contemporary Gentile nouveaux riches could buy social acceptance.[19]

Schiff was frequently disappointed in pursuit of this goal. Initial attempts to match his gifts failed, but in 1899, six years after the original offer, a concerted effort resulted in over $19,000 in contributions. Apprised of the campaign's relative success, Schiff offered to subscribe the entire $50,000 if the other donors consented to have their gifts applied to the acquisitions fund. In the end, Schiff not only covered over $60,000 of actual construction costs, he added over $10,000 for furnishings.[20]

Schiff must have received satisfaction from the speeches at the museum's 1903 dedication, especially the addresses by Gentiles. Professor Charles Eliot Norton, representative of the Harvard Overseers, suggested that the museum was particularly appropriate for Harvard, "the first public institution of a Commonwealth which was founded on the rock of Semitic doctrine." Norton indicated that New England's Puritan founders derived from the Hebrew Scriptures "their spiritual nurture and their religious creed," their civil government, and their social institutions. Hebrew studies fell off at Harvard after the days of Judah Monis (described as a "Jewish teacher"), but, Norton concluded, "there has been a fuller and more general recognition of the immeasurable debt which our Western civilization owes to the Jewish race and to its sacred books, from the fact that they have contributed to it the law and doctrine of Righteousness."[21]

Museum curator David Gordon Lyon, aware that critics of unrestricted immigration often equated Nordicity with advanced civilization, noted: "In their somewhat restricted home in Southwest Asia, some of them [Semites] ran through the varied stages of civilized life before the art of writing in Europe had become known." Without the gifts the Semites offered humanity, "the Alphabet, and Monotheism, and the inspiring literature of the Bible, and the contagious example of Hebrew bards and seers, and the Church," he added, "there might have been a powerful Western civilization, but it could never have been the civilization which we know." Lyon said the museum would contribute to "a decrease of that prejudice, cruel and unjust, born of ignorance, which in the minds of some still attaches to the name Semitic."[22]

By then a close friend of Schiff through their mutual interest in the Semitics program, Charles Eliot stated on this occasion that modern man owed to the Semitic people "the greatest spiritual conceptions of all time."[23] Schiff himself invoked Goethe's "happy he who in gladness remembers those he sprang from." He implied that the museum would help answer the question, "Where did the history of my people begin?" To be investigated, he said, "lie centuries of Semitic history and development, to which the Hebrew has, however, by no means been the sole even if he has been the largest contributor."[24]

In the euphoria of the moment, Schiff may have temporarily forgotten the years it took for the museum's benefactors to match (almost) his contribution. Jewish philanthropy had not granted high priority to Jewish scholarship, and Gentiles remained reluctant to contribute to causes that appeared too Jewish. The financial burden implied in Lyon's future agenda largely fell to Schiff. "To mention the most obvious task that lies before us," said Lyon, "we should not longer delay, in emulation of the universities of Berlin, California, and Pennsylvania, to enter the field of exploration. . . . Never were the times more auspicious, never the revelations of discovery more wonderful, than at present."[25] Each visit to Europe in search of artifacts for the Semitic Museum aroused Lyon's interest in archaeology. Excavation, not antique dealers, would provide the real treasures.

Schiff initially told Lyon that in archaeology—as in business—only a consortium should undertake a major project since "much energy and considerable funds are spent in split efforts, where united efforts could accomplish so much more in every direction."[26] Unfortunately, Paul Haupt's exclusion from Pennsylvania's Babylonian expedition set a bad precedent, and universities that desired *firmans* viewed themselves as competitors. Apprised of this reality, Schiff joined Lyon in mounting a Harvard Near East expedition.

But at what site? Digging at a non-Egyptian site required an agreement with Turkey. Lyon urged that Harvard excavate in Egypt, where it was easier to obtain a *firman*, where excavators could remove a larger portion of the spoils from the country, and where George A. Reisner, the Harvard Egyptologist, could head the expedition. Turkish policy severely restricted the number of expeditions and formally required placement of unearthed treasures in the Constantinople museum.[27] But Schiff said that Egypt did not properly come under the heading of Semitic research and that Palestine, Babylonia, and Assyria were comparatively neglected.[28] Charles Eliot suggested Schiff's real motive: "He hoped very warmly that new excavations and researches would bring to light evidences that the Hebrew race developed before the Greeks and Romans a noble architecture and refined and beautiful plastic arts."[29]

In 1905 Schiff offered $10,000 annually for five years to support an expedition. Lyon acceded to Schiff's wishes and chose Samaria as an excavation site.[30] The Harvard Corporation appointed a committee on "Exploration in the Orient," and Lyon tried to obtain a *firman*.[31] This proved no simple task (Lyon blamed in part "the venal mind of Turkish officials in Beirut and Nablus"), and Schiff's impatience almost led to the withdrawal of his donation.[32] But perseverance led to the desired *firman* in late 1907, and a tactful reminder to Schiff of the Palestinian venture's origin may have convinced him to redeem his pledge.

Local interference, the weather and personal problems hampered digging, but Lyon said the results justified the excavation's tribulations. "On the summit [of the digging site]," he wrote, "we found a great stairway, with a large altar and the torso of a remarkable statue at its foot, all of which we believed to be of the Roman period, also the remains of a great building which we thought was probably the temple erected by Herod the Great [in honor of Augustus] on the site."[33] Further digging led to the discovery of the palace of Ahab, a Biblical Hebrew King, and of over a hundred ostraca (potsherds with inscriptions relating to wine and oil) that were the earliest specimens of Hebrew writing found to that point. George Reisner, who directed the expedition, Clarence Fischer, an architect affiliated with the expedition, and Lyon published the results in *Harvard Excavations in Samaria* (2 vols., 1924), subsidized by Schiff.[34]

By 1910, Harvard authorities looked with satisfaction upon two decades of remarkable growth in the Semitics program. A well-equipped Semitics museum, a fine faculty, and a successful expedition focused international attention on the Divinity Avenue center. Jacob Schiff was not the easiest benefactor to work with, but his genuine interest and his cordial friendships with Eliot, Lyon, and Toy allowed amicable resolution of disagreements. Schiff thought his benefactions produced mixed results but that the benefits outweighed the shortcomings. Most important, American Jews could view Harvard's sponsorship of these ventures (and especially Charles Eliot's personal support) as a sign of acceptance. Schiff would have preferred to share more of the financial burden, but he took satisfaction in the broad-based, successful fund-raising drives of 1899 and 1906.[35]

In 1906, Harvard expanded the Visiting Committee "to increase in Boston and its vicinity the number of those who take special interest in the further development and the increased usefulness of the Museum."[36] But the Samaria expedition's failure to yield evidence of Hebrew aesthetic accomplishment partly explains Eliot's remark that Schiff "was never fully content with the results of his large expenditures in this field."[37] Historians recall Ahab's reign as a period of idolatry and of the introduction of the Baal cult at the behest of Ahab's infamous Phoenician wife, Jezebel. Thus, the Samaria expedition did not place the Biblical Hebrews in the exclusive pantheon of the ancient high civilizations.

Would the relationship between Schiff and Harvard continue? The retirements of Eliot and Toy meant that the Harvard Semitics department, which was riding the crest of 20 fat years in 1910, was about to enter a transition period. But few observers would have predicted the leanness of the following two decades.[38] The loss of Toy's influence was a severe blow, but the loss of Eliot was an outright disaster. Presidents, despite the ongoing rationalization of university governance, could still influence divisional or departmental affairs.[39] Eliot's interest in the Semitics enterprise and his approval of its Judaic orientation enhanced the field's fortunes.[40] Lowell, in contrast, was irrepressibly hostile. If Eliot could sincerely state: "Some of my best friends are of Jewish descent," his successor had to dispel the belief that he was an anti-Semite.[41] Given Lowell's views on student admission to Harvard and on the general Jewish presence, his failure to do so was not surprising.[42]

The fate of another Schiff gift illustrates the change of attitude that resulted from Harvard's leadership change.[43] In 1905, Schiff contributed $50,000 to the Harvard Teachers' Endowment Fund with the proviso that "whatever its annual return may be, [up to, but] not exceeding $2,000 shall be applied to the salary of the Curator or professors connected with the Semitic Museum of [Harvard] College."[44] The purpose of the $2,000 limit is unclear, but Schiff expected his gift to yield a large sum for faculty salaries in the Semitics department. Between 1906 and 1910, Harvard complied with Schiff's wishes. But when Toy retired, the Harvard Corporation switched Lyon from the Hollis to the Hancock chair, and shifted both Schiff's endowment and the Hollis chair to the Divinity School to cover, ironically, the salary of New Testament scholar James H. Ropes.[45] Lyon called attention to the shift several years later, and the administration switched the money back, thereby freeing up other funds rather than augmenting the Semitics budget.[46] When Lyon retired in 1922, the university credited half the gift to Divinity School salaries and shifted considerable income from the Hancock endowment to the Divinity School.[47] Despite Lyon's persistent remonstrances, the administration continued the questionable diversion of Schiff's gift—and this at a time when Lowell refused to pay Harry Wolfson and other junior faculty in the Semitics department from university funds.

Lowell decided that the Semitics department had attained too much prominence, and exhibited no sympathy or support from the moment he took office. Schiff complained in 1910 that Semitic enrollments had significantly declined and that the appointment of a man to replace Toy might reverse the trend. Lowell replied that few students enrolled because "the demand for Semitic scholars in all our universities and other institutions is limited and uncertain." Harvard students, he noted, could enroll in William R. Arnold's courses at the now affiliated Andover Seminary. He also asserted that, aside from one course, relatively little fall-off had taken place.[48] He told Ropes that even after Toy's retirement, "we have professors enough on the subject, if they were doing just what is needed."[49] Harvard's subsequent appointment of James R. Jewett to an Arabic chair, shortly after rejecting Ropes's nomination of Yale's Torrey, can be explained partly by Jewett's willingness to subsidize his own salary.[50] Harvard appointed no other professors to the Semitics department until 1922, when Arnold replaced the retired Lyon as Hancock Professor.

Lowell's hostility towards the department's fund-raising initiatives matched his parsimony with university funds. Eliot recognized the importance of "numerous habitual givers to Harvard University" for the Semitics Museum fund drive of 1899, but Lowell refused Lyon access to that same group of benefactors.[51] Lowell remained intransigent between 1911, when Lyon asked to raise funds for further excavations in Samaria, and Lyon's retirement.[52] In 1921, for example, Lowell denied Lyon's request for permission to give fund-raising lectures: "We have just finished a very elaborate campaign for the Endowment Fund," Lowell wrote, "and there are other things now more pressing than that of endowment for the Semitic Museum."[53] "To state the case mildly," Lyon wrote after his retirement, "no favors may be expected from the present administration."[54]

These continual rebuffs deeply affected Schiff. Contributions, by then little more than tokens, came less frequently.[55] The inability of the Visiting Committee to attract Protestant Bostonians particularly discouraged him. "[Mr. Winslow and Mr. Stone] gave the matter considerable thought and each stated regretfully that he could not see his way clear to do it on account of the pressure of business," read one letter.[56] The department's decreased visibility, and the nation's increased anti-Semitism, took their toll, and Schiff decided that department and museum had to strike out on their own. In 1913, he resigned from the committee citing "the inability to get men of affairs in Boston to go on the Committee and to take an interest in its work."[57] A concerted effort by Lyon and Lowell led Schiff to delay his resignation for a year, but it took effect in 1914, after 25 years of service.[58] Schiff died on September 26, 1920, and Harvard subsequently learned that he had bequeathed $25,000 to the Semitics Museum, the income to be spent for the acquisition of artifacts.[59]

Within a few years, a once significant department found itself in a marginal position. "Secularization," the onset of World War I, the resultant New England economic dislocations, and the preeminence of other departments help to explain Semitics' loss of status. So does the department's Judaic emphasis and its strong identification with a man who, for all his prominence, was a first generation Jew. Schiff's association with the department did not appeal to Lowell, an immigration restrictionist.

Shortly after Schiff's death, Lyon suggested that the museum host a small ceremony for family and friends to honor his memory and to exhibit a portrait the benefactor reluctantly sat for almost 20 years earlier on the stipulation that it not be displayed in his lifetime.[60] Lowell tersely vetoed the suggestion: "In view of what was already done at the time the Semitic Museum was opened," he wrote, "the Corporation felt that another celebration in connection with the exhibition of the portrait of Mr. Schiff would not be appropriate. The portrait is not for the first time presented to us, but has been in our possession all along; only in accordance with the desires of Mr. Schiff has it not been publicly shown."[61] Seeking consolation, Lyon called upon Eliot. When he returned home, he wrote in his diary:

> Told E. about Lowell's opposition to any celebration in connection with placing of Schiff's portrait on exhibition and about his continued opposition to efforts to raise money for the Sem. Museum. He says both acts spring from Lowell's fear of the Jews and his hostility to them.[62]

A few months later, Lowell precipitated a major debate over Harvard's "Jewish Problem," and David Gordon Lyon led the opposition to restricted admission. Harry Wolfson's career did not go unaffected by these developments.

Enter Wolfson

> Things are happening to me as in a novel, and I see myself as a character in fiction. I am just watching the dénouement of the plot. Any thing may be the ending. If I ever happen to fly up through the flue in the fireplace in the Divinity Hall, you should not be surprised.
>
> —Harry A. Wolfson, 1924[63]

To a nineteenth-century Harvard undergraduate, Divinity Hall evoked all the remoteness and unworldliness inherent in its name. Physically segregated from the main campus by a quarter mile of wooded land, the building housed "divinity pills" and undergraduates attracted by its inexpensive quarters.[64] The seriousness of purpose that pervaded the structure was notably lacking in other student housing. "I take the purest and deepest pleasure in [study]," said a Divinity resident in an early college novel set at Harvard, "and I thought everyone else did, too; . . . I enjoy to the utmost every hour I can spend in this way; and I have worked hard, and given up a good deal, for the sake of it."[65] Most resi-

dents cooked their own meals in Divinity Hall's sparsely furnished rooms to save
the high cost of boarding. But, if Divinity's monetary cost was modest, its residents often paid an excessive emotional cost. Isolation, indifference, and os-
tracism resulted in loneliness, even desperation. "What I find it hardest to
accustom myself to," said the same student, "is the solitary life one leads: it was
almost unendurable at first, and this sitting down to a table alone and gobbling
something, I don't think I altogether enjoy even now."[66] Harvard's expansion
under Eliot and Lowell ended the physical isolation of Divinity residents, but the
hall had not dispelled its aura of remoteness when Harry Wolfson moved there
as an undergraduate in September, 1911. Divinity's atmosphere played havoc
with an insecure, first generation Jewish scholar.

Later in his career, Harry Wolfson recounted the story of a German Jewess
who, upon approaching a village one beautiful Sunday morning, became enrap-
tured by the town's church bells. She enviously watched the young, beautifully
attired women, nosegays and prayerbooks in hand, on their way to worship. She
compared their obvious joy with Jewish custom: "The happy Christians! Today
is Sunday!—how blissful it must be! A Jewish festival, spent by the men within
the damp walls of the synagogue and by the women in their kitchens, how close
and depressing that is!" Wolfson perceived that Christianity per se held no attraction for the Jewess. As a boy, he explained, he experienced similar feelings,
"far away from home in a strange city, weighed down with loneliness and home-
sickness, walking aimlessly the unfamiliar streets and looking with wistful eyes at
the shuttered doors and windows." The girl, like Wolfson, longed for "life, con-
tentment, friends and a desire to belong somewhere."[67]

The Harvard environment—though increasingly hostile to Jewish students
and faculty—would help to resolve Wolfson's sense of isolation. Wolfson's marginality derived from his longing to partake of Harvard culture and from his
knowledge that he could never fully participate. A meritocratic urge permitted
Wolfson and other marginal faculty members, including historian of science
George Sarton, to remain at Harvard.[68] But he lived at the periphery—working,
symbolically, in the library basement—for much of his academic career. Aspirations for inclusion did not lead him to deny his Jewishness. Instead he espoused
both academic and Jewish values in expanding the province of university-based
Jewish learning.[69] Unfortunately for Wolfson, President Lowell's ultra-assimila-
tionism prevailed at Harvard during his formative years, and we cannot say
whether a continuation of Charles Eliot's benign tenure would have heightened
Wolfson's sense of security. But Wolfson spent many potentially productive years
convinced that Lowell's Harvard would shortly cast him out.

Wolfson had not originally contemplated attending Harvard.[70] After extensive study in Russian *yeshivot*, he and his family migrated to America in 1903.
Wolfson studied at the Rabbi Isaac Elchanan Theological Seminary before it
became the core of Yeshiva College. Financially strapped, Wolfson accepted an
invitation to teach at a Hebrew school in Scranton, Pennsylvania. As a student
in the Scranton public schools, he distinguished himself academically while remaining socially aloof. Deciding to attend college, he narrowed his choices to

nearby Lafayette, his high school principal's alma mater, and the reputedly liberal University of Wisconsin.[71] One day, the principal called him to this office and suggested that he take the Harvard entrance examinations.[72] Wolfson, in contemplating college, probably had more in common with contemporary poor Gentile immigrants than with first generation Judaica scholars whose families already associated with nearby colleges. His reaction probably resembled immigrant Michael Pupin's when that Catholic Slavic youth first contemplated admission to the Columbia College of the 1880s:

> Columbia College, a daughter of great Trinity Church, an alma mater of men like Hamilton, Jay, Livingston, and of many other gentlemen and scholars who guided the destiny of these great United States—can that great American institution, I asked myself, afford to enroll a raw Serbian immigrant among its students; train me, an uncouth employee of a cracker factory, to become one of its alumni? . . . The college of Hamilton and of Jay expected certain other things which I knew I did not have and could not get from books. . . . "How shall I feel," I asked myself, "when I begin to associate with boys whose parents live on Madison and Fifth Avenues, and whose ancestors were friends of Hamilton and of Jay?"[73]

Encouraged by sympathetic representatives of the dominant culture, Pupin and Wolfson overcame their hesitations and passed their entrance examinations. Wolfson, recipient of a Price–Greenleaf scholarship, set out for Cambridge in 1908.[74]

Wolfson's experience at Harvard diverged sharply from Pupin's at Columbia. Pupin gradually ingratiated himself with his classmates through his strength and athletic prowess and secured a solid niche in the student culture. Wolfson, in contrast, found his greatest joy in scholarship and, like the fictional Divinity resident, was perceived as a "grind," not fit for proper social intercourse. His extracurricular activities focused around the Harvard Menorah Association, founded just two years before his entry. Menorah, which resembled a nineteenth-century collegiate literary society, had little appeal on a largely Gentile campus whose students worshipped football on Saturday and accepted as gospel the pronouncements of campus leaders. Football, clubs, and fraternities attained prestige *despite* the antipathy of nineteenth-century college officials, and Gentile students may have ignored Menorah both because of its Jewish orientation and its receipt of presidential and faculty support.

Wolfson's move into Divinity thus represented the culmination of marginalization abetted by an inadequate physique, a lack of social grace and financial means, and a strong East European Jewish accent. As an undergraduate, he contemplated a career in medicine and once resigned himself to Hebrew school teaching, perhaps in Palestine, but he ruled out a livelihood in writing because of financial insecurity. Events at Harvard led Wolfson to follow a different course.[75]

During Wolfson's undergraduate years, the Harvard Semitics department still evinced an aura of success. The Semitic Museum had amassed an important collection, the news from Samaria was favorable, and Jacob Schiff's munificence appeared boundless. No undergraduate could discern clouds on the horizon, such as Lowell's selection as president, and Schiff's gradual disaffection. Early in his undergraduate career, Wolfson met David Gordon Lyon, who was sufficiently impressed to arrange for Schiff to underwrite a scholarship.[76] Wolfson responded by writing a Menorah prize-winning essay that Cyrus Adler published in the *Jewish Quarterly Review*.[77] Convinced by Wolfson's response that he would go to Europe to study Crescas if awarded a travelling fellowship, Lyon decided to sponsor his candidacy. Crescas's *Or Adonai*—a critique of Maimonides and Aristotle—came within Lyon's province since continental and American Oriental studies departments often encompassed ancient through medieval studies.

Wolfson began his fellowship in Berlin. Finding the courses at the University of Berlin of limited value, Wolfson devoted most of his time to research. He told Lyon that his methodology involved

> a careful and painstaking study of the book, in ascribing the exact meaning of its contents, in closely following its arguments, in finding accurate English equivalents to the author's terminology and phraseology, to get ready for a translation of the text and an independent discussion of its subject matter.[78]

Wolfson's interests and methods progressed beyond the work of nineteenth-century philologists into the study of philosophy. He used texts as a means to an end. In his published *Crescas,* Wolfson termed his method the Talmudic hypothetico-deductive method of text interpretation. He contended that "any text that is deemed worthy of serious study must be assumed to have been written with such care and precision that every term, expression, generalization or exception is significant not so much for what it states as for what it implies." The scholar searches out an author's true intentions, underlying assumptions, qualifications, and reservations: "Statements apparently contradictory to each other will be reconciled by the discovery of some subtle distinction, and statements apparently irrelevant to each other will be subtly analyzed into their ultimate elements and shown to contain some common underlying principle." In short, "every phenomenon about the text becomes a matter of investigation."[79]

Wolfson tried to understand the philosophy of Crescas and the sources of his ideas. Within a few months, he had translated the first part of the manuscript and ventured away from his text to study the Hebrew translations of Aristotle's works, from which Crescas quoted extensively.[80] He explained to Lyon: "Already last winter, while comparing Crescas' reproduction of the Aristotelian arguments against the Infinite, the Vacuum, etc. I had noticed their radical disagreement with those already found in the Physics." Investigation in Paris led Wolfson to discover "beyond any doubt that Crescas quotes his arguments verbatim from Averroes' Middle Commentary on the Physics."[81] The identification of Crescas's sources was itself a major contribution to the history of philosophy. In 1915, Harvard awarded him the Ph.D. for this research.[82]

Lyon, satisfied with Wolfson's work, secured a renewal of his fellowship halfway through his graduate studies. Wolfson, whose doubts about the viability of an academic career tempered his intellectual satisfaction, expressed gratitude for "another year of peace and security."[83] Wolfson by this time had aspired to a scholarly career, despite its financial and professional insecurity, but opportunities in universities for Judaica practitioners were virtually non-existent. Wolfson therefore considered a lucrative offer to head the Semitic Division of the Library of Congress. Aware, by then, of Lowell's hostility to Semitics, Schiff's disenchantment, and stagnant enrollments, Wolfson leaned toward acceptance. The salary "is such that I have never expected even in thought," he wrote Lyon. The work, "though not inspiring, promises to be quite agreeable." Wolfson left unstated the position's strongest attraction—the security it provided.[84]

Sorely tempted "to accept the position in the hope that I may someday escape from it," Wolfson nevertheless turned down the offer. The fellowship provided an irresistible opportunity to accomplish what had become a "cherished" plan, collection of material for a more extensive study of Jewish philosophy. We do not know whether Lyon offered Wolfson further enticements, but a few months after Wolfson's return from Europe, prominent Jewish leaders with Harvard connections tried to find him a position. Federal Judge Julian Mack, a Harvard alumnus soon to become both a Harvard Overseer and chair of the Semitics Visiting Committee, headed the group.[85] Wolfson, back in Divinity Hall without financial support, remained in suspense for several seemingly endless months.[86] "For the present term I shall remain outside the University," he wrote in early 1915. "I wonder if they'll let me keep my room."[87]

Wolfson's patience was rewarded by a junior appointment at Harvard underwritten by "friends," not university funds.[88] In June, 1915, Lyon informed Lowell that Judge Irving Lehman of the New York State Court of Appeals "will bind himself to raise or give the sum of $1,000 a year for three years" upon Wolfson's appointment.[89] All parties agreed to a $1,500 salary and to the title of Instructor in Jewish Literature and Philosophy. The Harvard Corporation reserved the right to renew the appointment annually.[90]

Wolfson's erudition revealed itself, and initial renewals were almost automatic; in succeeding years, they were anything but routine.[91] Wolfson, sharing the Harvard mystique yet desiring security, had to jump many hurdles that exacted a mental toll—reappointments, military service, inability to see *Crescas* through publication, participation in solving Harvard's "Jewish Problem," and negotiations with the Jewish Institute of Religion and Hebrew Union College.

Prior to the expiration of Wolfson's third annual appointment, Judge Mack guaranteed a similar salary for a three-year period. This term initially gave Wolfson greater peace of mind while providing time to seek a permanent benefactor for Wolfson's position, or to convince the Harvard authorities to provide his salary from general funds.[92] The term also assured that Jewish literature and philosophy would continue to be taught at America's first college for another three years. Harvard agreed to this arrangement, at no advancement in rank, but Wolfson's fear of severance soon reemerged.[93] With Mack in Paris, Wolfson's salary fund was temporarily depleted. "But that did not matter much," he related, "as long as I had an anchorage in my room in Divinity Hall." Yet when he went to renew his room lease, "contrary to custom, the clerks, instead of acting upon it at once, began to hold counsel with each other. Then one of them came up and asked me whether I was still connected with the University, for he had not seen my name on the payroll." The bursar provisionally accepted the lease application, but the experience was traumatic. "I felt as if I were physically thrown out on the street. It was then that I realized the full meaning of that fear."[94]

Wolfson held out little hope for permanent tenure at Harvard. As the three-year term approached its end, his correspondence reflected an inability to control his fate, especially his fear of imminent consignment to academic oblivion. Mack, Lehman, and his other benefactors, Wolfson wrote, hoped that Harvard would absorb his salary, but those on the scene "have known all along that we could hope for nothing from the University." Wolfson wanted his benefactors to try to arrange a permanent endowment, but noting the diminished communal interest in university-based Jewish learning, he lamented: "If those contributors did for our Department half of what they did for other departments, we would not be now in our present plight."[95] Wolfson wondered whether his supporters would even continue their current provision. "What they intend to do now I do not know," he gloomily speculated. "I suppose they are going to throw up the game altogether right now."[96] He appeared ready to throw up the game just before his renewal came up for consideration before the Corporation in 1921.

Wolfson's difficulties in publishing *Crescas* did little to reduce this insecurity. No one doubted the book's scholarly value. "I do not know any work of comparable magnitude and difficulty," wrote George Foot Moore, "that has been undertaken of late years by one of our scholars, and carried through on so sound a method, and with such untiring persistence." Moore added, "the value of such a piece of work as Wolfson's lies, however, not solely in the light it throws on Crescas and on the thought of the period in which he lived, but in the exemplification of the way in which such an investigation should be conducted."[97] But Harvard University Press, though willing to publish the volume, required a considerable subvention—an estimated $5,500-$6,000 in 1920 for 750 copies—because of its length and the need for large amounts of Hebrew type.[98] Wolfson's friends failed to raise the money, and publication of *Crescas* awaited the beneficence of Lucius Littauer almost a decade later.[99]

Reassurances about job and publications abounded. "I have no doubt it will all come through satisfactorily," wrote Intercollegiate Menorah Association Chancellor and fellow Harvard alumnus Henry Hurwitz. "There'd be no question of continuing the contributions for your salary." This verbal support did not alleviate the young scholar's anxiety, but Hurwitz did provide an outlet for Wolfson to vent his feelings by publishing "The Needs of Jewish Scholarship in America" in the *Menorah Journal*.[100] Extrapolating from his personal history, Wolfson identified three primary needs: subsidies "to enable men of achievement, ability, and promise to carry on undisturbed work of research and investigation," provision of "the means whereby the result of intellectual labor can be conserved and made productive in published works," and unearthing buried Jewish treasures which "must be undertaken on a large scale, in a systematic manner, and with ample funds."[101] Jewish scholarship for Wolfson meant more than rabbinics, and he cited works of medieval Jewish philosophers as "the greatest and most important" treasures. This emphasis on the universality of medieval Jewish literature suggests Wolfson's reasons for specializing in that period. Next to the Bible, he wrote:

> medieval Jewish philosophy is the only branch of Jewish literature . . . which binds us to the rest of the literary world. . . . In it we meet on common ground with civilized Europe and with part of civilized Asia and civilized Africa. Medieval philosophy is one philosophy, written in three languages, Arabic, Hebrew, and Latin, and among these Hebrew holds the central and most important position. In it we have the full efflorescence of Arabic thought and the bud of much of scholasticism. It is in the interest of general culture and general scholarship that these hidden Hebrew treasures should be brought to light, carefully edited, properly indexed, equipped with the necessary glossaries, with a system of cross-references and with all other critical apparatus, so that the world may readily recognize their value for a reconstruction of the history of philosophy.[102]

Just as American Jews should desire to be of American society without escaping Judaism, and just as Wolfson wished to be of Harvard while retaining his identity, so should American Jewish scholarship concentrate on a historical era that itself featured Judaic participation in the intellectual life of the entire community. There being few George Foot Moores—sympathetic Gentile scholars devoted to the study of Judaism—skilled and interested Jewish scholars had to undertake the needed work. By moving back and forth among the Jewish, Christian, and Muslim medieval sages for whom Hebrew was an intermediary language—not propaedeutic, as it was for Semitists—these practitioners could participate in both universal and Jewish traditions. Attending to neglected medieval Hebrew texts would bring scholarly recognition, while underwriting "a veritable *Corpus Scriptorum Philosophicorum Hebraeorum*" would gain recognition for Jewish benefactors.[103] But the anti-Semitism at Harvard permitted Wolfson to go no farther: Scholarship would not necessarily dispel prejudice and gain acceptance for American Jews.

For the rest of his life, Wolfson created the *Corpus* he outlined in "The Needs of Jewish Scholarship in America." "He suspected, quite sensibly, what he was accomplishing, and he wanted more than parochial recognition for it," wrote Judah Goldin, professor of Oriental Studies at the University of Pennsylvania. "He wanted recognition from the larger world as well as from his own people, who were happier to be proud of him the more he won the admiration of the wide world of international scholarship. Wolfson certainly wanted this, but always at the highest cost of performance, not at reduced rates!"[104]

But would he write the *Corpus* at Harvard? In 1921, George Foot Moore persuaded Lowell that Wolfson's *Crescas* "will be of notable importance to philosophers, and worthy of the University," that Wolfson deserved reappointment and that, Wolfson's fears notwithstanding, Mack would guarantee his salary.[105] But Lowell, sharing Moore's vision that Wolfson would ultimately land in a Jewish institution, accepted his recommendation "that at the end of the time he will not be reappointed."[106] Wolfson was told that his three-year reappointment would be his last unless someone permanently endowed his position.[107]

Mack and Hurwitz faced the more immediate, difficult task of raising a significantly larger salary than necessary in the past. Judge Irving Lehman as usual promptly contributed; so did Sol Rosenbloom, a Pittsburgh-based, Russian-born philanthropist who helped to establish Jewish learning at the newly founded Hebrew University in Jerusalem, Mortimer Schiff, Jacob Schiff's son, and Felix Warburg (another Hebrew University supporter), members of "Our Crowd" of wealthy, assimilated New York Jews. All contributors were Jewish; many had Menorah or Harvard ties, and, except for Lehman, Rosenbloom, Schiff, and Warburg, all gave $100 or less.[108] Lowell, who discouraged Lyon and Schiff from tapping outside sources for aid to the Semitics department, made a successful solicitation a condition for Wolfson's reappointment. Why did he agree at all to retaining Wolfson? Perhaps prudence dictated that he tread lightly in the area of a Harvard overseer's pet project. He may have believed financial success impossible, or alternatively that the good will generated by Wolfson's retention would prompt his supporters to contribute for general university purposes. If, less charitably, Lowell hoped to defuse a confrontation over the growing "Jewish Problem," he failed in his purpose.

Julian Mack fought among the Overseers to thwart Lowell's infamous 1922 attempt to restrict access of Jewish students to Harvard College; David Gordon Lyon did the same among the faculty.[109] Lowell appointed the apolitical Wolfson to a committee to which the Overseers referred the proposed restrictions. Mack objected since his appointment came, in part, at the expense of the judge's candidate, law school professor Felix Frankfurter. "While Wolfson understands all classes of Jewish students," Mack wrote Lowell, "he is such a scholar pure and simple that I gravely doubt his availability to an inquiry such as is contemplated."[110] Mack counselled Wolfson to decline the appointment because of his cloistered existence, low academic rank, and temperament.[111] Yet Wolfson accepted, perhaps knowing that Lowell would not appoint Frankfurter if he declined, and hoping that he could render a unique perspective.[112] The committee recommended that "in the administration of rules for admission Harvard College maintain its traditional policy of freedom from discrimination on the grounds of race or religion." Harvard would covertly introduce restrictions on the admission of Jewish students in 1926; meanwhile, the controversy provided a graphic, public demonstration of tendencies the Semitics department experienced for more than a decade.[113]

The contingency placed upon the reappointment, the difficulty of fund raising, and the admissions controversy all prompted Wolfson to consider a 1923 offer to join the faculty of the Jewish Institute of Religion in New York City. Stephen Wise, involved in a factional dispute with the Reform supporters of Cincinnati's Hebrew Union College, founded the institute for rabbinical education—which Mack, Richard Gottheil and other influential Jews supported—as an alternative not only to Hebrew Union College, but also to New York's Conservative Jewish Theological Seminary.[114] Wise proffered a Jewish Institute of Religion professorship and a tender of Wolfson's services to Harvard, at no cost to the latter, for half of every academic year.[115] The controversial Wise had complex motives for proposing the arrangement. Wolfson already had a strong reputation among the few American Ph.D.'s with a Judaica specialty and was among the few potential faculty members "doing real research." He could help the Jewish Institute of Religion plan a viable course of rabbinical study.[116] Given the Institute's relatively small enrollment, Wolfson's half-time presence allowed for ample student exposure. Sharing Wolfson with Harvard automatically elevated the Institute's stature in the eyes of potential students and benefactors. Wise probably had no intention of terminating the relationship contrary to Wolfson's wishes, but he admitted that "we have considered that in time the burden of dividing your time between the two institutions might grow too heavy."[117] If this occurred, Wise hoped that Wolfson would opt for the Jewish Institute of Religion's relative security.[118]

Wolfson weighed professional and personal factors in his decision. Would he retain a professorial rank at Harvard? Would the arrangement be permanent or did Wise envision Wolfson's eventual full-time service at the Institute? Should he become involved with the controversial Wise? When a friend of Wolfson's suggested that Wise might raise funds for publication of *Crescas,* Henry Hurwitz had cautioned, "even granted Wise could do it (I'm not convinced of that), would you care to be beholden to him forever? Would you care to have him boast of carrying you, etc.?"[119] Should Wolfson affiliate with any religious seminary? Hurwitz reminded him: "You could always get a place in a Jewish seminary; the number of such men as you available in America is going to be limited for some time."[120] A status decline would inevitably accompany the appointment. Becoming a "professional Jew," Hurwitz warned, implied losing prestige. "The attitude towards you would change on all sides, even on the side of your new bosses. You would immediately contract. You *must* have the university world, I believe, in order to flourish."[121] But Hurwitz's reassurances concerning *Crescas* and endowments heretofore yielded no tangible results; could Menorah or anyone else suggest an alternative? Menorah's emphasis, Hurwitz stated, "is distinctly shifting from student societies to scholars, and creative workers in the arts." Hurwitz gave high priority to endowing Wolfson's position, but Wolfson chose not to rely upon the chancellor.

Wolfson accepted the Jewish Institute of Religion offer, contingent upon Harvard's concurrence. Wolfson's term had 18 months to go, but he was willing to begin at the Institute the following year if Harvard extended his current appointment. Harvard agreed to the proposal, "provided it is understood that this arrangement may be terminated at the end of any academic year."[122] Mack and Wolfson could not apparently negotiate better language, but the Corporation made an "informal record" of the agreement that the two found satisfactory. In 1924, Harvard again renewed Wolfson's appointment.[123]

Rumors circulated during Wolfson's second year at the Institute that the arrangement was temporary, and he warned Wise that he would tolerate no direct or indirect attempts to terminate his Harvard connection.[124] Yet, at just this time, Wolfson himself contemplated severing that connection. In late 1924, the Hebrew Union College offered him a permanent post in Cincinnati. Again, Wolfson carefully weighed the pluses and minuses. Hebrew Union College, in contrast to the Jewish Institute of Religion, had a well-balanced faculty with a clear-cut division of labor, a long history, and adequate financial support. The lucrative salary and publication fund more than met Wolfson's needs. On the other side were the Harvard connection and a feeling of greater personal freedom. Wolfson also felt inertia "which grows out of an uninterrupted course of regulated action" and "a natural disinclination to break away from a routine which has become part of one's life and which one has learned to enjoy immensely."[125]

Would "security" prompt Wolfson to overcome this inertia and give up Harvard and the Institute? "Every human being has his paramount fear as well as his paramount hope," Wolfson wrote Mack. "Mine has always been the fear arising from the uncertainty of my condition and my paramount hope has always been the getting away from the state of uncertainty." Relating nothing the judge had not known, Wolfson confessed:

> Ever since I came to Cambridge about sixteen and a half years ago I have been living in constant fear of the future. The more pleasant my condition became the greater grew that fear. Because of it I have never been able to do the things I should have liked to do,—I could never plan ahead. I have always had before my mind the fate of many men who had devoted their early years to Jewish learning. There was B., who had to become a poor library clerk, and S., who at the age of forty-five was compelled to begin the study of pharmacy, and L., who is now running a petty business for a living. All this has naturally made me look upon security as something to be valued above all other seeming advantages.[126]

The Jewish Institute of Religion, Mack reassured Wolfson, was a viable, going venture that filled a definite need. Wise's many supporters would continue the Institute as a memorial if he died. Nor would Hebrew Union College open a competing seminary that would threaten the Institute. Only the affiliation with the Institute, Mack added, allowed a continued relationship with Harvard. Wolfson's unique scholarly qualifications, Mack concluded, permitted him to virtually dictate the terms of a move to Hebrew Union College at any time.[127] "In the past," Wolfson wrote after declining Hebrew Union College's offer in early 1925, "I . . . organized my life on the basis of a fear that the worst was yet to come. I now realize that it was a mistake and that I should have taken a more cheerful view of the future."[128]

For almost 17 years, Harry Wolfson lived a marginal, insecure existence in Divinity Hall, yet at key moments he rejected the security he professed to crave. Inertia, though it weighed heavily in Wolfson's calculations, cannot entirely explain this behavior. "The continuance of my connection with Harvard was the decisive factor in making up my mind," he wrote after opting to remain at the Jewish Institute of Religion.[129] Wolfson could have written the same sentence many other times during his early career. Even a marginal existence at Harvard accorded Harry Wolfson a degree of recognition by the dominant culture about which others from similar backgrounds could only dream. The security of intellectual acceptance that Harvard offered led him to reject other lesser, more obvious forms of security. Wolfson would take as many "chances" as necessary to remain at Harvard. But, within six months, he would no longer have to do so.

A Deus ex Maecenas

> I do not think that Wolfson today would
> accept the Presidency of the Institute [Jewish
> Institute of Religion] if it were offered him,
> nor the Presidency of Yale. He is a Professor
> of Harvard,—that is the *ultima thule* of
> his desires.
>
> —Stephen Wise, 1929[130]

During the early twentieth century, Reform Jews, noting that practitioners gave priority to disciplinary over communal agendas, reduced presidential interest in Judaic Semitics, and heightened anti-Semitism, reduced their support of university-based Jewish learning.[131] Reform Judaism was also changing in response to changed conditions of American life and world Jewry—by the late 1930s, the moderate Columbus Platform replaced the strongly anti-Zionist Pittsburgh Platform—but Reform retained a more universalistic outlook than either Conservative or Orthodox Judaism. Postwar conditions complicated any contemplated reunification of academy and Jewish community. But if a communal initiative emerged, it would probably originate from the Reform camp, in particular from officials and congregants of New York City's Temple Emanu-El, the congregation of "Our Crowd," which had the most sustained association with university-based Jewish learning.

Felix Adler's short, unsuccessful tenure at Cornell launched the relationship between campus and congregation, and the appointment of Richard Gottheil, the Emanu-El rabbi's son, raised optimism about future connections. Jacob Schiff, a long-time Emanu-El member, did not join the Gottheil campaign, but the actions of his fellow congregants may have influenced his Judaica benefactions to Harvard. Other Emanu-El congregants made occasional gifts for Judaica, notably the Gustav Gottheil lectureship, and the temple donated its own valuable library to Columbia. Emanu-El's commitment to Jewish scholarship was an important symbol of turn of the century communal support. A generation later, Harry Wolfson benefited from the Emanu-El connection, but his benefactor was not an "Our Crowd" type. Instead, Emanu-El's marginal rabbi, Hyman G. Enelow, arranged for Wolfson, the marginal scholar, to receive permanent support from Lucius Littauer, a marginal congregant.

Enelow, born in Eastern Europe, migrated to the United States at age 16 to join his father, giving up a cherished dream of studying at the University of Heidelberg. His father continually discouraged his secular education as a threat to traditional piety. Enelow's parents divorced soon after his arrival in Chicago in 1893, and his mother encouraged him to train for the Reform rabbinate. He impressed Emil Hirsch, who had just assumed his duties at the University of Chicago, and Hirsch secured a scholarship for his pupil. Two years later, Enelow began rabbinical studies at Hebrew Union College and continued his secular education at the University of Cincinnati. After service as a rabbi in Paducah and Louisville, Kentucky, Enelow was appointed in 1912 to the Emanu-El pulpit, where he served, unhappily, for more than 20 years. Some congregants disliked his personality, others, his sermons. Some thought him too scholarly, others that he did not "look" like a rabbi. Always in the shadow of his senior colleague, Nathan Krass, Enelow looked for an opportunity to move on. A prolific writer, Enelow's scholarly credentials led some detractors to charge that self-interest motivated his campaign for university-based Judaica chairs.[132]

Enelow was indeed an active candidate for the Nathan Miller Chair of Jewish History, Literature and Institutions that Linda Miller, an Emanu-El congregant and close friend, endowed at Columbia in 1928. But he was motivated by more than self-interest. He often preached on the importance of education for Reform Judaism. "Reform Judaism cannot live by mere Rhetoric and Publicity," he wrote, "it must dedicate its own devotees anew to the Torah, to Jewish study and enlightenment; and our own organizations must work unceasingly toward that end."[133] His interest in Emanu-El's Sunday School and its adult education activities, his chairmanship of the Committee on Adult and University Education of the Union of American Hebrew Congregations, and his support of other Jewish scholars attest to his conviction that American Jewry required more Jewish education.[134]

The theme of recognition dominated Enelow's arguments for Judaica chairs. Jewish thought had "influenced all of Western civilization," he wrote, "not to mention Mahometan countries." Jewish contributions did not end with compilation of the Bible: "Even in the Middle Ages they produced a vast number of scientists, philosophers, and poets." But "our colleges offer courses on every conceivable subject, except the literature and history of the Jewish people. . . . How is it possible to ignore them at a university, the aim of which, in the words of Maimonides, should be to try to know all that is fit to know?" Endowed university chairs would insure the presentation of Judaism "to the larger world" so that it could take "its rightful place among the cultures of the past and present." But doesn't true recognition come when universities proceeded on their own instead of awaiting endowments? Non-Jewish scholars, Enelow answered, increasingly realized the importance of Jewish history, literature, and philosophy. Colleges would offer Judaica coursework if they "had the means to do so."[135]

Enelow took advantage of the opportunity to arrange "matches" between Emanu-El benefactors and institutions. He gave first priority to endowments at Harvard, Princeton, and Yale but seized upon Linda Miller's generosity to arrange the Columbia gift.[136] He expected initial success at Yale, where the two sons of Joseph Stroock, an Emanu-El congregant and New York lawyer, were undergraduates. Yale authorities were receptive to a chair in its divinity school or a Temple Emanu-El–Yale expedition to the Near East, but the Stroock family failed to subsidize either project.[137] Undeterred, Enelow enlisted the support of the Emanu-El Women's Auxiliary and participated in a conference on Jewish education held at Harvard in April, 1925.[138] Talk of chairs, benefactors, and endowments pervaded the Cambridge air that spring—talk that Harry Wolfson must have heard. Subsequent reports of Wolfson's surprise at his appointment to an endowed chair at Harvard are therefore exaggerated, but only somewhat, because whatever Wolfson heard, his nearly two decades at Harvard had given cause for skepticism. The appearance of a *deus ex machina* in the person of Lucius Littauer in Wolfson's Divinity Hall room on a June, 1925 morning "stunned" him with what seemed to him "a gift that was borne by a very messenger of God."[139]

Lucius Littauer, the son of a successful upstate New York Jewish merchant and an Emanu-El trustee, brought prosperity to the family glovemaking business while gradually being assimilated into a Gentile world.[140] He played on the Harvard football team and varsity crew and roomed with Theodore Roosevelt at a time when few Jewish undergraduates attended Harvard (he received his A.B. in 1880). Littauer maintained personal and political contact with the future president and served five terms in the House of Representatives as an upstate New York Republican. He retired in disillusionment after his involvement in "the gauntlet scandal" in which he was accused of illegally entering into a United States government contract while a Congressman.[141] His entrepreneurship in utilities, banking, textiles, and transportation hastened his assimilation into mainstream culture, and in 1913, he married Flora Crawford, a Gentile. The pair remained childless, and she died in 1924. When Littauer began to attend Emanu-El services, Enelow sensed that Flora Littauer's death had reawakened a dormant Jewish identity and that philanthropy might help to strengthen that identity. Littauer had no prior reputation as a philanthropist, although he had built the Nathan Littauer Hospital in Gloversville in 1894, shortly after his father's death. In 1923 and 1924 he funded an addition—including a home for nurses—named after his mother, and an annex named after his wife.[142] Enelow instructed his new protégé in Jewish ritual and practice, while stressing a central role for education in American Jewish life. Enelow felt that endowing a Judaica chair in his father's honor at Harvard, his alma mater, might well attract a man like Littauer.

If Wolfson depicted Littauer as God's messenger, then Enelow was the dispatching agent. He enlisted Mack, Hurwitz, and Moore to assure Littauer of Harvard's receptivity and of the presence of a highly qualified candidate for the post—the record contains no suggestion that Enelow sought the chair for himself. Moore wrote that the field "has not only a proper but an important place in university instruction and research," and could not be dealt with collaterally by scholars with other specializations because of its nature and its Hebrew sources. A chair, Moore added, had salutary implications for Jewish institutions of learning since "in this country they must come to depend more and more upon scholars who have been trained in this country, and here, as in Europe, however fundamental the old forms of rabbinical erudition may be thought, they must be enlarged and supplemented by the philological, historical, and philosophical training of the university." He stated that Harvard authorities would welcome endowment of a chair that promoted Jewish scholarship and that Wolfson was esteemed by all.[143]

A twenty-year friendship between two unlikely men began that June day in Divinity Hall. The friendship may be explained by their complementarity. Wolfson provided Littauer with rapid and convenient entry to a world of Jewish content, while Littauer ratified Wolfson's presence in a secular environment. Littauer left Wolfson's room resolved to endow a Nathan Littauer Chair in Jewish Literature and Philosophy. As Wolfson watched him leave, he realized that he had successfully completed his two decade quest for intellectual security.

Littauer agreed to provide a full professor's salary of $6,000 for three years, to be followed by a $150,000 endowment. Harvard would promote Wolfson to the rank of full professor in the Semitics and philosophy departments, beginning October 1, 1925.[144] Wishing to distinguish his chair from Harvard's long tradition in Christian Hebraica, Littauer twice stipulated that the incumbent be "well versed in Biblical and post-Biblical Hebrew, as well as in Jewish thought and philosophy."[145] "It is my conviction," he added, "that the proper fulfillment of [the chair's] purposes—the study and exposition of the character, influence, literature and philosophy of the Jewish religion—involve a profound knowledge of original Hebrew sources and materials that would require of its Professor a particularly authoritative knowledge of post-Biblical Hebrew and Hebrew Literature."[146] Littauer may not have read Ismar Elbogen's warnings about the fate of Jewish learning in disciplinary settings, but he took no chances.

Was Harry Wolfson's joint appointment with the philosophy department a milestone in the history of Jewish learning in American universities? The appointment did mark a move away from the dependence of Jewish learning on Semitics. Wolfson often argued that the congruence of Jewish and non-Jewish philosophy merited primacy for the subject among the humanities and among Judaica courses.[147] "Medieval philosophy is the history of the philosophy of Philo," he explained, and the succession of philosophers from Philo to Spinoza have only tried to expound, each in his own way, "the principles laid down by Philo."[148] Wolfson bracketed his *Corpus* by publishing major works on Spinoza (1934) and Philo (1947).[149] Subtitling his study of Philo *Foundations of Religious Philosophy in Judaism, Christianity, and Islam,* he later turned to the Church Fathers and Arab philosophers to fill the gaps between his major Jewish mileposts.[150]

Wolfson's long tenure and Littauer's stipulations assured a continued place for Jewish learning, but not for Jewish philosophy. A Judaic Semitics—not philosophical—tradition preceded Wolfson's appointment, and the young scholar was trained in—and remained primarily associated with—the Semitics department, despite the joint appointment. Philosophy students had to make an intellectual and physical trek for a course in Jewish philosophy. In the classroom, Wolfson was a Judaica generalist who devoted only part of his teaching to Jewish philosophy. When Wolfson retired, Isadore Twersky, his student and disciple, reoriented the chair to medieval Jewish history, emphasizing the intellectual biographies of rabbinic scholars.

Different patterns of Judaica growth help to explain why the Littauer chair remained Judaic, if not philosophical, while the parent field absorbed Richard Gottheil's chair. Richard Gottheil, the key agent in Columbia's Semitics department, decided to migrate from rabbinics to Semitic philology and points beyond. Wolfson, in contrast, had senior faculty support for the program he announced in "The Needs of Jewish Scholarship in America" and the methods he enunciated in his introduction to *Crescas*. Different academic and social positions within their respective universities reinforced initial tendencies. Gottheil not only originated the Columbia contact, he marshalled powerful communal support and rapidly gained institutional and social prominence. Wolfson remained a marginal faculty member for his first ten years, completely dependent on the good will of others. His appointment to the Littauer chair did not give him access to Harvard's inner sanctum. Gottheil's worldliness and intensity sharply contrasted with Wolfson's retiring, scholarly nature. Contemporaries could confuse Gottheil, the citizen, and Gottheil, the scholar, but no one similarly erred about Wolfson.

But precisely this prominence led to contention over Gottheil's succession, while Wolfson's marginality may have led to Harvard's indifference, despite general anti-Semitism. This indifference permitted Wolfson to pursue his scholarship, gain personal recognition, and assure a place for Jewish learning at Harvard.[151] Harvard, despite its anti-Semitism and Lowell's refusal to pay Wolfson's salary, gave Wolfson an affiliation and a title as long as his benefactors remained steadfast. Many observers believe that little innovation takes place at stodgy, tradition-encrusted universities, but these institutions, we will demonstrate in chapter 9, have the resources to house marginal scholars like Wolfson. For Harry Wolfson, Harvard was the worst possible environment, except for all the alternatives.

Conclusion

How does Harry Wolfson's encounter with Jewish learning at Harvard fit into the history of Jewish learning during the interwar years? At the end of the nineteenth century, about 15 American universities and several theological schools offered significant work in Semitics, and some institutions granted the Ph.D. The American Semitics professorate contained a goodly proportion of Jews who commanded sufficient resources to assure the subject's inclusion. Young Jewish scholars often saw philological work as the main entry route into university work in the humanities. Reform Jewish enthusiasm for American universities, and for Semitics, reflected satisfaction with American customs and institutions as well as the realization of the *Wissenschaft des Judentums* ideal. Speculation by Bernhard

Felsenthal and Emil Hirsch that universities might serve as Jewish theological seminaries demonstrated Reform's willingness to entrust important Jewish concerns to a non-Jewish American institution.

By 1920, few Jews shared this enthusiasm. "The influences about American universities does not seem somehow altogether favorable to the Jewish ministry," wrote one commentator; "experience would not warrant the Jewish people disbanding their special rabbinical courses in dependence upon Semitics departments of universities."[152] The anti-Semitism that replaced late nineteenth-century philo-Semitism also led Jews to doubt university support for one of the better Jewish access routes into the humanities. Presidents, perceiving less intellectual urgency for the subject as the departmental structure permitted the study of both science and religion, lacking their predecessors' concern for their Jewish constituency, and worrying more about budget-balancing than academic growth, offered little personal or financial support to Semitics—especially to any Jewish slant. The lack of presidential support was not in itself always fatal.[153] Lowell mobilized substantial resources in Harvard's battle over Jewish admissions, but Harry Wolfson's academic fate did not preoccupy him. Lowell probably assumed that Jewish learning would fade when Lyon and Moore retired, and if Wolfson had left Harvard, this erosion would have occurred. Program persistence generally depended upon the initiating party—in this case, the institution—but practitioners and community compensated for Lowell's hostility. Presented with the Littauer endowment, Lowell could do little but accept. Harry Wolfson's experience at Harvard was atypical—it illustrates a case in which a practitioner of Jewish learning *overcame* the difficulties the field usually encountered in attempting to gain access to interwar universities.

Reform's disenchantment with academic life, however, stemmed not only from institutional anti-Semitism. Some critics blamed the low quantity, if not quality, of scholarship on an "uncongenial" professional atmosphere in which "the rigid scrutiny of texts for the purpose of determining date and authorship and exact position, while of absolute necessity, is not calculated to interest or inspire more than an exceedingly limited number." University-based Jewish learning was too removed from the Jewish community, a critic concluded. "Unfortunately, there is tacked onto it [i.e., his professorship of Rabbinical Literature] a professorship of Semitic Languages," Richard Gottheil lamely explained to a communal audience in 1913, "and the exigencies of my service demand that I devote the greater part of my time to the latter."[154] Benefactors, never numerous and faced with conflicting demands, including needs arising from the East European migrations, gave low priority to the endowment of Semitics chairs, or to any chairs of Jewish learning, save for the Littauer and Miller endowments.

Perhaps American Jewish institutions will yet arouse "that stormy enthusiasm for 'Halaha' that shall have its fruitage in works of high scholarship," one observer wrote, "and yet abounding in that marked characteristic of usefulness, usefulness for life, for higher ideals for a larger and higher view of law and right."[155] Whether scholarship could accomplish salutary results for the American Jewish community remained doubtful; but these results, if at all attainable, would arise from an "inner spirit" that American universities seemed less able to provide as communal support waned and as the humanistic disciplines became less hospitable to Jews and Jewish learning.[156] To echo Ismar Elbogen: generating an "inner spirit" in scholars and potential scholars that made the Judaic whole greater than the sum of the disciplinary parts would have to occur elsewhere.

VI

FROM UNIVERSALISM
TO PLURALISM

> I am reminded of the Talmudic story of the Four that entered
> the Garden [of esoteric philosophy]. One died, one lost his
> mind, one became a heretic and only one entered in peace and de-
> parted again in peace. The same general proposition obtains today
> among *bechurim* [young men] who gain admittance to American
> graduate schools.
>
> —Nathan Isaacs[1]

During the first third of the twentieth century, American Jewry became increasingly pessimistic about university hospitality to Jews and Judaism. Campus discrimination and intergroup conflict had increased along with the Jewish
presence. Native Protestants had the ability to set the rules of the academic
game—and to change them when they did not produce a desired outcome. The
Jewish response to the Harvard controversy over admissions restrictions included
sorrow—that a great house of intellect should succumb to irrational prejudice.

Practitioners of Jewish learning shared in the disillusion. Late nineteenth-century American Jews, knowing that *Wissenschaft des Judentums* failed to attain university acceptance in Germany, had optimistically emphasized the differences
between the German and American situations—including the appearance of Jewish learning and Jewish instructors at American universities.[2] But increased hostility—and the pulls exerted by the parent discipline as identified by Ismar
Elbogen—led one observer to suggest that Jewish scholarship ran the danger of
remaining no more than "a minor section of Semitic linguistics" or a "pre-Christian culture, interesting in the Biblical aspects and Christian relations, confined
to Palestine; post-Biblical developments ignored."[3]

The patient was ill, but diagnoses and prognoses varied. Harry Wolfson traced
contemporary Christian antipathy toward the Jewish intellectual enterprise to
medieval origins:

> Throughout the history of religious controversies between Christians and Jews in the Middle Ages, Christianity was on the defensive. The Christians considered themselves called upon to prove the claims they made on behalf of Jesus by endeavoring to show that the vague prophetic promises were all fulfilled in Christ. The Jews had no counterclaims to make; they simply refused to be impressed. As the historical custodians of the Bible texts as well as of its manifold interpretations, the Jews were rather amazed and at times even amused by the confidence with which the erstwhile heathen interpreted at their own pleasure the mistaken Scriptures quoted from the Vulgate. This attitude of aloofness and incredulity was sufficient to enrage even saints among Christians, for it gave them an uneasiness of feeling, deepening into fear and and doubt and a general sense of discomfort, which explains much of the Christian intolerance of the Jews.[4]

Conscious of the deteriorating contemporary situation, Wolfson urged a burying of the hatchet, not the debate. But Wolfson's own story suggests that American universities would hire few partisans of a Judaic point of view.

Other scholars, less interested in dialogue with hostile academic colleagues and the Christian community, suggested major changes in the rationale for university inclusion of the field. Representatives of Jewish seminaries had pointed the way. Israel Friedlander, a professor at the Jewish Theological Seminary, noted the potentially salutary effects of Jewish learning on issues confronting American Jews and Judaism, especially questions that arose as a result of mass Jewish migration to America. Friedlander quoted Rabbi Hillel's famous dictum: "If I am not for myself, who is for myself?" He continued: "If not now, when then?"

Friedlander emphasized the particular as a corrective to a perceived overemphasis on the universal by university-affiliated Jewish Semitists and the Jewish community. But he, and contemporary university-based Judaica scholars who echoed this rationale, were actually centrists, or pluralists who reconciled the one and the many, the desirable and the possible. American Jewry, Friedlander suggested, should strive to attain an outlook possessed by the Spanish Jewish community of the previous millennium, "its close and intimate association with the general culture of the age on the one hand and, on the other, its ability to preserve and develop its distinct Jewish character and to sink deeply into the hearts and the minds of the Jewish people." The intellectual preoccupations of a culture, Friendlander argued, ultimately arose out of its immediate concerns. Intellectuals will seek answers outside the context of Judaism if necessary, but given the traditional importance of scholarship in Jewish life, Jewish scholars could participate in the general discourse and offer solutions compatible with Judaism's essential tenets.[5]

Advocates of university-based Jewish learning who questioned the universalism of the previous scholarly generation offered similar pluralist rationales for university inclusion; particularist rationales were still beyond the pale. New York University, for example, offered *modern* Hebrew language and literature during the 1930s—a subject of limited interest outside the Jewish community. But Abraham I. Katsh, the subject's chief advocate at N.Y.U., listed among its ad-

vantages "the great contribution of Judaism to Western civilization and American democracy."⁶ The academic study of Jewish history served many communal
needs, wrote Cecil Roth, a British historian of Jewry and a frequent visitor to
American universities. "It is for [the Jew] not merely a record: it is at once an inspiration and an apologia," he insisted. "It is only from an appreciation of his past
that he can be imbued with self-respect and hope for his future." But his conclusion resembled Friedlander's: "It will not only reëstablish decent Jewish
pride and inspire the world at last with true respect, but will be a significant
and absorbing contribution to universal history, an intellectual achievement of
vast importance."⁷

Interwar commentaries on Jewish learning emphasized Jewish distinctiveness
within a pluralist framework. The universal orientation of Semitic philology,
observers noted, had failed to forestall enmity, much less gain academic or communal "recognition." The field's supporters—including professors and representatives of the Intercollegiate Menorah Association—turned their attention to
gaining curricular footholds for modern Hebrew and Jewish history, identifiably
Jewish subjects that appealed to Jewish undergraduates. Hostile professors opposed what they called these "narrow" subjects, but academic anti-Semitism led
advocates to consider this characterization disingenuous.

The ability of students of Jewish history to analyze the "peoplehood" as well
as the philological and religious aspects of Judaism, Cecil Roth added, made this
subject attractive to traditional Jews. Historians of Jewry could observe institutional norms while emphasizing Jewish concerns. Finally, the subject facilitated
the expansion of Jewish learning from elite institutions with the resources necessary for ornamental fields to institutions dependent on enrollment, because
nearly all colleges by then had history departments.

Representatives of the Intercollegiate Menorah Association initially believed
that consumer demand—not presidential, scholarly, or communal initiatives—
would convince academic officials to add courses in Jewish learning. Jewish students at colleges and universities with relatively large Jewish undergraduate
populations would petition for and enroll in, say, a course in modern Hebrew,
and the success of this course would generate student demand for courses in Jewish history, literature, and religion. These courses might not reflect the cutting
edge of research, but broadening the field's disciplinary base would lead to the
recruitment of more faculty members and eventually to an identifiably Jewish,
university-based scholarship. Early issues of the *Menorah Journal* chronicled the
brief appearance of courses in Jewish learning mainly at comprehensive, urban
universities with sizeable Jewish constituencies.⁸

World War I, however, terminated most initiatives, and during the 1920s, restrictions on Jewish enrollment, and other manifestations of administrative hostility, reduced the viability of the consumerism strategy. Many Jewish students
adopted the norms of the dominant student culture to cope with peer hostility.
Jewish fraternities and sororities, for example, replaced the study-oriented
Menorah associations as the foci of Jewish student life.⁹ University-based Jewish
scholarship, some observers added, stood on thin ice when administrators hired

part-time teachers, perhaps even the local rabbi, to offer courses entitled "History and Literature of the Jewish People: 70 C.E. to the Present."[10] Further attempts to base Jewish learning on undergraduate enrollments awaited the next decade.

Menorah and other advocates of university-based Jewish scholarship then turned to philanthropic and communal initiatives to spur the field's growth. Donor disillusion, these supporters reasoned, previously resulted from practitioner indifference. Administrators could encourage practitioners to emphasize identifiably Jewish aspects of a broader span of parent disciplines. Anti-Semitism further undermined communal faith in universalist approaches, so appointment of pluralist scholars might lead not only to a merger of academic and communal agendas, but also to greater support from non-Reform Jewish benefactors.

But what should be the proper relationship between this newer breed of scholar and the Jewish community upon which advocates of university-based Jewish learning, lacking viable alternatives, placed great hopes? Should quid pro quos accompany communal benefactions? Did the envisioned Judaica scholars actually exist? Would scholarly enthusiasm actually result in communal munificence?

The first question elicited no definitive answer. Practitioner responses to perceived communal expectations still varied from immersion in communal concerns, through a balancing of communal and scholarly interests—sometimes mixing norms, sometimes compartmentalizing—to an exclusively academic outlook. But many scholars experienced strong communal pressure for active participation.[11] Even Harry Wolfson, never known for his communal activity, briefly instituted a religious service for Jewish students at Harvard. Designed to attract both orthodox and Reform students, it appealed to neither group and failed.[12] Jewish communities sought both a scholar's tangible service and the prestige of an academic association. Richard Gottheil, one historian hypothesized, achieved his stature in the Zionist movement "because of his academic standing and his fluency in the 'King's English,'" a verdict that suggests two conditions that members of the Jewish community considered desirable, if not sufficient.[13]

Communal service—here explicitly meaning "rabbinical"—and prestige elements surfaced in 1942 when the Durham, North Carolina, Jewish community raised money for a professorship of Jewish learning at Duke. The Jewish community and Gentile administrators who accepted the gift expected the appointee to introduce Jewish and Christian students to Judaism and Judaica through teaching, scholarship, *and* personal example: "someone thoroughly representative of the religious spirit of Judaism."[14]

Stephen Wise, still head of the Jewish Institute of Religion, nominated Theodore Gaster for the post. Wise said Gaster "would bring the best of Jewish learning and Jewish thought to students and at the same time could adequately represent everything Jewish throughout the University, and indeed the State."[15] The son of Moses Gaster, the chief rabbi of the Portuguese Jewish community of England, Theodore graduated from—and subsequently lectured at—the University of London. Gaster's search for an academic position led to his migration to the United States during the 1930s,[16] but he could only find unsatisfying communal work. "I cannot," he wrote, "but feel more acutely from day to day the absence of any real outlet for scholarship, which I know to be my real métier and the field in which I can make my most useful contribution."[17] Gaster's early scholarship focused on the Canaanite Ras Shamra texts, which shed light on the origins of Jewish religious practice and upon the Pentateuch.

Gaster thwarted his own candidacy for the Duke position by telling university authorities that he was an agnostic. Chancellor Harvie Branscomb denied that rabbinical ordination was required for the post, but, he added, "we would be wrong in securing someone whose knowledge of Jewish religion was solely objective and speculative."[18] The university eventually appointed Judah Goldin, whose communal work included the Hillel directorship at the University of Illinois.

Some observers believed that communal commitments of professors of Jewish learning benefited no one. Israel Friedlander, commented Eli Ginzberg, the son of Jewish Theological Seminary colleague Louis Ginzberg, "had largely squandered his very substantial talent by his determination to play an activist role in Zionist and other communal activities which had little use and less respect for the contributions of a scholar."[19]

Between the wars, Jewish philanthropists and aspiring Judaica scholars observed the fate of Richard Gottheil's chair and the continued isolation of communally prominent rabbis with academic appointments (Temple Sinai rabbi Louis Mann replaced Emil Hirsch at the University of Chicago, for example) from their university colleagues. The success of Jewish scholarship in American universities required a primary devotion to the life of the mind—in reality and appearance. Public service might be extolled at commencement orations, but colleagues valued scholarly productivity, and administrators often eschewed close identification with the Jewish community. Benefactors could not expect immediate, "practical" communal gain from their support of Jewish scholarship. Inquiry itself, they were told, was a salutary end in the long run. And quid pro quos were a thing of the past. Columbia accorded the backers of Richard Gottheil's position the right of "nomination." But the university controlled—to its benefit—the appointment to the communally endowed Nathan Miller Chair of Jewish History, Literature, and Institutions, and—to its harm—the appointment of Gottheil's successor.[20]

Benefactions to Jewish scholarship thus required donor comprehension of—even commitment to—academic norms. Anti-Semitism had led members of the Jewish community to ask about the consequences of disinterested scholarship. What if a study of Jewish history revealed a less than benign portrait of a Jewish individual or a group of Jews? "What will the Gentiles say?" Will Jewish learning give anti-Semites yet more ammunition? Cecil Roth argued for candor: "If our ancestors were as human as we are ourselves, it makes their steadfastness all the more glorious, and enhances by the contrast their heroism at the hour of crisis. . . . Indeed, by suppression we play into the hand of the anti-Semite, who may one day make capital out of the innocent humanity we have chosen to ignore."

But what if Jewish scholarship led to demonstrably harmful communal consequences? Roth answered: "But, above all, by repression we are faithless to the most sacred charge of history, which is the pursuit of truth."[21] "First truth, then peace," echoed Cyrus Adler, commenting on Zachariah's dictum, "Love ye truth and peace."[22] But neither benefactions nor comprehension of these norms came as often as advocates of growth through philanthropy would have liked.

Successful benefactions also required the existence of qualified scholars. "A chair is a man," wrote Menorah's Elliot Cohen. The first generation of Semitists educated protégés whose work was only marginally Judaic. After World War I, relatively few Americans traveled to Europe for their graduate education, and few scholars migrated from Europe until the 1930s. American seminaries did not award the doctorate. "I cannot think of any Jewish scholar worthy to occupy a chair," Cohen wrote just at a time when Menorah publicly advocated their creation, "the local rabbi or the Christian professor of Old Testament will not do."[23]

Menorah Chancellor Henry Hurwitz himself proved Cohen's point in his negotiations with Chicago philanthropist Albert Lasker. Lasker appeared willing to donate one million dollars for "a modern man's history and interpretation of the Jew in the modern world, past and present," but he insisted that the University of Chicago sponsor the project. Association with that university, Lasker reasoned, would assure scholarly quality, non-sectarianism, and successful administration of a substantial collaborative effort.[24] Lasker's ardor therefore cooled when Hurwitz, who lacked historical training and a defined approach to historical analysis, proposed to direct the project himself.[25] That neither Lasker nor the University of Chicago would have accepted the weak academic credentials of this major advocate of university-based Jewish learning spoke volumes about changes in the field.

Prospective donors awaited assurance of good results, but aspiring scholars viewed endowments as indicators of communal support and became discouraged when they failed to materialize. "We Jews are now lost, after a year or two of struggle, to learning," wrote Cohen.[26] Wolfson, Albright, and Salo Baron—all in secure posts by the early 1930s—began to educate a new generation of graduate students. But graduate education took time, and each disciple confronted a marginal field. The Depression and competition from European refugees further dimmed their prospects. Theodore Gaster spent more than a decade in marginal positions at Dropsie College, Hebrew Union College, the University of Chicago, the Library of Congress, Johns Hopkins, and New York University, and his despair resembled Wolfson's.[27] "There is so much I still want to do," he wrote, "and have actively planned and prepared, that I am getting more and more depressed at the thought that it will probably never get done, and I shall have to spend the rest of my life completely unfulfilled and frustrated, churning out articles for *Commentary* and the like."[28] Gaster achieved greater academic security after World War II, but other colleagues were less fortunate.

Thus, as the delicate knit between institution, practitioner, and community unravelled, Jewish scholarship attracted fewer donors. Assertions of "long-run benefits" did not sit well with philanthropists who constantly had to separate the urgent from the marginal. "There is another investigation I am thinking of proposing," wrote Menorah's Henry Hurwitz, "the amount of money American Jewry is spending for what might be called 'higher Jewish education' in comparison with what is spent for charities, 'communal life,' etc." Hurwitz, like his friend Harry Wolfson, expected Jewish scholarship to fare poorly even compared to general Jewish financial support to universities.[29]

A few philanthropists provided for Jewish scholarship: Felix Warburg and Sol Rosenbloom at Hebrew University and Linda Miller at Columbia joined Jacob Schiff and Lucius Littauer. But these exceptions, contemporaries argued, proved the rule, and the philanthropists associated with "Our Crowd" had become especially apathetic. Some scholars downplayed philanthropic indifference. If Jewish learning merited university recognition, they asked, why did presidents and trustees await endowments instead of committing unrestricted resources as they would for English or political science? Other practitioners replied that academic institutions tried to attract money in all fields, including Jewish learning. Would historians or chemists question institutional motives if a university tried to attract endowment of a chair in their disciplines?

Changing definitions of the American Jewish community and of university-based Jewish scholarship thus did not bring about enrollment growth or donor enthusiasm.[30] Some observers accepted this reality and awaited better times. Others pondered whether American Jewish scholarship might fare better in another setting.

Neutral Ground

If American university conditions retarded the production of identifiably Jewish scholarship, did alternatives exist? Independent lay and rabbinical scholarship were two possibilities. Independent scholars produced the bulk of nineteenth-century American Jewish scholarship. Isaac Leeser's 1853 Bible translation was a substantial accomplishment whose faults arose from the absence of colleagues and resources. Marcus Jastrow completed his *Talmudic Dictionary* late in life when illness prevented him from undertaking a full array of rabbinical tasks. But sustained scholarly production could not rely upon the ability of a few educated, interested scholars to divert attention from other pressing tasks.

Cyrus Adler recognized the need for full-time scholars and foresaw diminished university recognition of and receptivity to Jews, Judaism, and Jewish learning. A Conservative Jew, Adler's deep involvement with defense agencies, including the American Jewish Committee, led him to conclude that American Judaism needed to define itself with respect to the Jewish tradition, and not primarily by its relationship with American Protestantism. His migration from Johns Hopkins, whose broad Semitic orientation appeared increasingly inadequate for the nurture of Jewish scholarship, to the Smithsonian Institution, allowed him to organize, facilitate, and even legitimate ad hoc Jewish scholarly projects.[31] He initially served as a lieutenant on projects that others initiated but soon became the leading scholarly entrepreneur of his generation. He helped to revitalize the Jewish Theological Seminary of America by revamping its governing board and recruiting Cambridge University scholar Solomon Schechter to the Seminary presidency in 1902. Adler helped create—and became the first president of—Dropsie College, founded upon the bequest of Moses Aaron Dropsie as a "secular" institution (no rabbinical training) for the study of Hebrew and cognate learning (1906). He became acting president of Jewish Theological Seminary upon Schechter's death in 1915 (and president eight years later), while retaining his Dropsie post. Adler's access to patrons, his academic pedigree, his interest in identifiably Jewish scholarship, and his entrepreneurial and administrative abilities helped create permanent institutions and sustain the field in their absence. Adler's positions, power, and accomplishments brought him the admiration of some colleagues, the disdain of others, and the recognition of all.[32]

Between 1888 and 1916, Cyrus Adler participated in four major activities—in addition to his leadership of the Jewish Theological Seminary and Dropsie College—that advanced American Jewish scholarship. The Jewish Publication Society and the American Jewish Historical Society needed regular but modest attention. The *Jewish Encyclopedia* and the Jewish Publication Society Bible required intense but finite commitments. American universities, too closely tied to Reform Jewry, were inappropriate for endeavors that required the broad participation of American Jewry, but too-close association with a seminary, he believed, would also damage the non-partisanship vital to the success of these projects. The answer, Adler concluded, was independence from both university and seminary.

The Jewish Publication Society (founded 1888) aimed at dissemination—not creation—of knowledge.[33] Organizers debated whether Jewish individuals or a coalition of congregations might best sponsor a society dedicated to doctrinal neutrality, but no one argued for university affiliation.[34] Inspired by Reform Rabbi Joseph Krauskopf of Philadelphia's Keneseth Israel Congregation, the Society gave high priority to strengthening Jewish identity. Its book list stressed popularized, rather than original, research. The society occasionally ventured into fiction and children's books. Lay trustees and a publication committee that included rabbinical and lay representatives governed the Society—rabbis played only supporting roles in all Adler-connected projects. But only three members of the original publication committee had university affiliations: Cyrus Adler, Harvard historian Charles Gross, and Rabbi Abram S. Isaacs.[35]

Debate on publishing a contemplated American translation of Heinrich Graetz's *History of the Jews* soon resolved the questions of orientation and audience. A minority on the publication committee argued that Graetz's multi-volume, heavily footnoted work "is not of a nature to appeal to the public taste," that is, the non-scholarly Jewish constituency upon which the Society depended. This minority also objected to allocating the bulk of the Society's resources to a single project. Board chair Mayer Sulzberger led a majority that desired an abridged edition containing an extensive index but no footnotes, a source of continual scholarly complaint after publication.[36] At first glance, the books should have had limited appeal, but Sulzberger's majority proved correct: Graetz remained the society's most consistent seller for many years.

The decision to publish the Graetz history, the debaters understood, "related in a measure to the future policy of the Society for some years to come."[37] The Jewish Publication Society relied on foreign authors until a talented domestic crop ripened. The Society emulated neither a commercial nor a university press, and it rarely published the work of university-affiliated scholars. The few exceptions were non-scientific works—Richard Gottheil's *Zionism*, for example.[38] Instead, it attempted to convince recognized Jewish scholars "that to popularize Jews and Judaism is not unworthy even of the greatest of them."[39]

The Society's popular orientation argued against university affiliation, although Adler envisioned a future role for J. P. S. as publisher of Jewish scholarship, which often went unpublished because of high printing costs.[40] But the nonpartisanship that came to govern the American Oriental Society found analogous expression in the Jewish Publication Society's neutrality between religious and political factions—specifically between Reform, Orthodox, and Conservative Judaism. Adler acquired a Hebrew printing press, a scarce commodity at the turn of the century, for the nonpartisan Society, rather than for Dropsie College or for the Jewish Theological Seminary.[41] Scholarly cooperation, Adler believed, could offset lapses in communal commitment to American Jewish scholarship, and it became integral to his other projects.

Lack of interest—not a lack of scholarly orientation—helped keep the American Jewish Historical Society and its subject outside the university.[42] "No university or college has established a chair of American Jewish history, nor even a regular or systematic course of lectures on the subject," conceded Adler, "and in all probability these institutions were right because after all our fragment of history in this country is too small."[43] The founders defined American Jewish Historical Society membership by subject matter. Instead of inviting American Jews with an interest in history, or Americans with an interest in Jewish history in any part of the world, the Society limited its mission to the collection and publication of "material bearing upon the history of *our* country."[44]

The time had come, the Historical Society's founders believed, for a scientific rendition of the Jewish role in America's founding and growth. This role was underestimated, concealed, or ignored "because the early chronicles relating to America have been imbued with a strong religious bias" and because "the spirit of intolerance was such that the Jews who participated in these early colonizations, and who were refugees, concealed their race and religion in many instances, from motives of self-preservation."[45] Correcting these accounts required research by scholars who knew "what is understood by the term 'objectivgeschichtsschreiben.' "[46] This research emphasis probably resulted from the perceived inadequacy of eulogistic and journalistic Jewish responses to the disparaging historical statements about American Jews then appearing in respected American periodicals—statements probably occasioned by the mass migration of Russian Jews.[47] Scientific evidence, the society's founders believed, supported a sympathetic view of American Jewry. Academic recognition of this view was closely interconnected with broader social acceptance.

The society's stress on American Jewish history made the field too "narrow" for university inclusion at a time when American history had not yet gained full academic acceptance. The society courted all scholars with an interest in the subject. "With reference to the American Jewish Historical Association," Adler wrote to Bernhard Felsenthal in 1890, ". . . I fully agree with you that it should not be sectarian."[48] Here, "not be sectarian" meant not only neutrality between Jewish factions; the Historical Society welcomed Jews and non-Jews who believed in objectives "not *sectarian*, but *American*—to throw an additional ray of light upon the discovery, colonization, and history of our country."[49] The society courted Jewish Semitists with a personal interest in American Jewish history, such as Gottheil and Jastrow, as well as non-Jews such as Herbert Baxter Adams of Johns Hopkins and John Bache McMaster of the University of Pennsylvania.

The organizers initially obtained significant academic participation. Richard Gottheil, Charles Gross, Morris Jastrow, Max Margolis, and Columbia economist E. R. A. Seligman were early officers, and Gottheil, Gross, and Jastrow contributed to the Society's proceedings.[50] But no university-based scholar devoted primary attention to American Jewish history, and the contributions of these scholars diminished as their research took them in other directions. Jastrow, for example, published an article and a document in volume one of the Society's journal, an article in volume five, and another in volume ten. No more articles followed.[51]

The Society had less interest in, and consequently less success with, the American rabbinate. As professional Jewish advocates who usually lacked scientific historical training, rabbi-historians incurred the suspicion of the non-Jewish world and of Jewish scholars associated with other factions. Several rabbis had helped to organize the Society. Abram Isaacs editorialized on the need for a history of American Jewry in 1886. Bernhard Felsenthal is widely credited with suggesting the idea of a society to Adler in 1888.[52] Yet at the Society's organizational meeting in 1892, the committee on nominations failed to recommend a rabbi for any important office. Adler, a committee member, denied that the slight was intentional, but the attenders probably remembered a similar occurrence at the organizational meeting of Jewish Publication Society several years earlier.

An expanded executive council with rabbinical representation placated the rabbis, who threatened to withhold support, but control of the American Jewish Historical Society continued to reside in lay hands.[53] Lacking a critical mass of centrally concerned university (or seminary)-affiliated scholars, and remaining aloof from the rabbinate, the Historical Society relied on articles by stalwarts and on occasional pieces by others to fill its proceedings. A 1908 decision to broaden its scope beyond American Jewry failed to attract a larger membership, and its role increased only when Jewish history—especially American Jewish history—became more prominent in mid-century universities and seminaries.[54]

Mission and scope, respectively, thwarted significant university links with the Jewish Publication Society and the American Jewish Historical Society. On the other hand, both organizations adopted nonpartisanship and other norms and practices associated with American universities to offset potentially conflicting communal agendas. After initial birth pangs, both organizations and their small, well-defined constituencies settled into their respective niches. Their modest scale, de facto regionalism, professed neutrality between communal factions, and reliance on individuals for most projects all helped minimize conflict.[55]

The same factors argued against a university base when Cyrus Adler and his colleagues examined the feasibility of editing a Jewish encyclopedia in America. The venture's success depended upon the collective efforts of all American Judaica scholars—rabbis and laymen in secular and sectarian institutions—whose conceptions of Jewish knowledge might significantly diverge. No one wanted a single university or seminary to receive the accolades that would greet publication.

Successful completion of the encyclopedia would bring fame and recognition to its editors by displaying the vigor and fruits of American Jewish scholarship. An encyclopedia would inevitably draw resources, including scholars such as Joseph Jacobs, to America. Jacobs, an English Jew, believed that it would bring about no less than "a revolution of the world's attitude with regard to the Jews," and added that scientific knowledge would gradually and cumulatively dispel ignorance and the anti-Semitism that appeared to arise from it.[56] As with the American Jewish Historical Society, but on a larger scale, a scholarly Jewish encyclopedia would allow non-Jews to appreciate Jewish affinities and understand dissimilarities.

But the corresponding price of failure—not unlikely given the fissures and diverging research agendas among Jewish scholars—argued for caution. Much depended upon Isidor Singer, the encyclopedia's editor-in-chief. Singer, an Austrian, held a doctorate from Berlin but had pursued a literary and journalistic career after graduation.[57] The idea for a Jewish encyclopedia came to him, he recalled, when, glancing at a reference shelf at the Bibliothèque Nationale in Paris, he noted the absence of a Jewish counterpart to *L'Encyclopédie de la Théologie Protestante* and the *Katholische Encyclopedie*. Having failed to fund the project in Germany and France, Singer came to America in 1895 to secure a publisher. He spent his first years teaching French and learning English. Mayer Sulzberger told him that the Jewish Publication Society, still righting its bearings after accepting the more modest Graetz endeavor, could not handle such a large-scale project. Singer then secured the cooperation of Funk and Wagnalls, which published religious books under the direction of Rev. Isaac Funk, and which had recently published a large standard dictionary. In late 1898, Singer invited a cross-section of American Jewish scholars and one non-Jew—Harvard's Crawford Toy—to serve on an editorial board and to assume responsibility for a section of the encyclopedia.

The offer of an editorship tempted a jobless Louis Ginzberg, who had come to America expecting a post at Hebrew Union College. But Ginzberg had some doubts. "His [Singer's] idea was to incorporate in his encyclopedia the biographies of Jewish prize fighters and big businessmen," he wrote. "He thought that if businessmen were approached and the proposal put to them and that if they contributed five hundred dollars they would have half a page in the encyclopedia, and if they contributed one thousand dollars they would have a full page, the result would be a small fortune for himself."[58] Singer's proposed title, *The Encyclopedia of the History and Mental Evolution of the Jewish Race,* also confounded his credibility. But Singer's meetings with Funk and the proposed editors went well, and a favorable consensus emerged over his reputability.[59] The scholars also knew that once launched, "it is much better that we attempt to make it fairly respectable, because if it is produced, no other of the same kind will be undertaken for years to come." Adler, once convinced of the project's viability, sought to "know everything that is going on" by becoming the encyclopedia's literary editor since the quality of the encyclopedia would reflect upon all of American Jewish scholarship. Several potential editors doubted the scholarly merits of some colleagues, but Singer had an editorial board in place by March, 1899.[60]

The original board reflected the major groupings of Jewish scholars: Conservative and Reform Jewry, seminaries and university faculties. University-affiliated Semitists who served on the original editorial board included Toy—Hebrew philology and Hellenistic literature; Richard Gottheil—history from Ezra to 1492; and Morris Jastrow—Bible. Emil Hirsch replaced Jastrow after completion of two volumes, and William Popper (not yet at Berkeley) assumed responsibility for the bureau of translation after the third volume was finished. The *Encyclopedia* received subsidies and guarantees at critical junctures from Jacob Schiff, Leonard Lewissohn, Isidor Straus, and Cyrus L. Sulzberger.[61] The heterogeneous, often unwieldy, editorial board agreed that the *Jewish Encyclopedia* should be an objective, not a partisan vehicle. Board members reviewed all contributions with an eye toward removing bias. Editors referred controversial or questionable points to the entire board, which resolved questions by majority vote or referred them to a consulting board likewise empowered to resolve by majority vote. Articles written by one editor had to be reviewed by another editor of the author's choosing.[62]

Sensitive issues surrounded entries in the Bible section. Most Jewish and Gentile Biblical scholars conceded the validity of at least some tenets of the higher criticism, but some powerful members of the Jewish scholarly community demurred. Isaac Mayer Wise, still president of Hebrew Union College, forbade the teaching of Biblical criticism within the institution.[63] Solomon Schechter, still at Cambridge, expressed willingness to lend his expertise and prestige to the project if the Biblical department took a traditional approach.[64] Morris Jastrow agreed to a non-partisan *Encyclopedia,*[65] but his sympathy for Biblical criticism led to his replacement after publication of the second volume. The *Encyclopedia*'s preface, published in the first volume, contained Jastrow's suggested procedure: "in the more important Biblical articles to distinguish sharply between these two points of view, and to give in separate paragraphs the actual data of the Masoretic text and the critical views regarding them."[66] Kaufmann Kohler later recounted that since Jastrow had, under this policy, "allowed Christian scholars to furnish articles which rather militated against the spirit of positive Judaism, [Emil] Hirsch was appointed Department Editor at my suggestion."[67] Hirsch's editorship and contributions alleviated much concern since he believed in both the higher criticism and "the spirit of positive Judaism." And the articles on Deuteronomy, Exodus, and Genesis contained an elaborate "anti-criticism" by German Rabbi Benno Jacob.[68]

A sympathetic Christian reviewer remarked: "Toleration and comprehension may be of more importance than a strict adherence to tradition."[69] Jewish scholars cooperated and compromised because a successful encyclopedia would bear "impressive testimony to the growing importance of the Jewish community in the United States, and to the interest of American Jews in their own religion and history."[70] These scholars also knew that the enterprise provided encouragement and some financial recompense to scholars who often received little of either.

The fourth project—publication of a new Bible translation—also required participation of scholars from differing perspectives. Its organizers created a "neutral," ad hoc setting under Jewish Publication Society auspices in 1892. But, the final product, unlike the *Encyclopedia,* failed to include the names of Hirsch, Jastrow, or any other university-affiliated Judaica scholar. The reasons for this change illustrate the field's shift in orientation.[71]

By century's end, scholarship had rendered obsolete Isaac Leeser's Bible translation.[72] English Protestant scholars revised the King James version in 1885 to make it more accurate and comprehensible, and an American revised version appeared in 1901. Jewish leaders, too, wanted to showcase the fruits of Jewish Biblical scholarship.[73] Mindful of Leeser's warning that enemies utilized Christian misinterpretations "to assail Israel's hope and faith," these leaders also desired a "safe" translation that omitted Christological references. The editorial board for the Jewish Publication Society Bible originally included three rabbis and two laymen and was led by Marcus Jastrow. The proposed translator list—dominated by American scholars—aimed at making "an earnest effort to unite Jewry of every shade of opinion in the English speaking world."[74] University-affiliated Jewish Semitists on the list included Gottheil, Hirsch, Isaacs, Morris Jastrow, Rosenau, Voorsanger, and Max Margolis, still in his first Cincinnati tenure. Cyrus Adler, who resigned from Johns Hopkins just as the editorial board made its assignments, began his intimate involvement with the project as secretary of the Bible's editorial committee.

Despite the stellar array of scholars recruited for the project, the work failed to make headway. Some authors never submitted draft translations of their assigned books.[75] Cumbersome procedures—several committees were involved and the editors conducted most work by correspondence—also hindered progress, as did changes in the board's composition. Jewish Theological Seminary president Solomon Schechter replaced the deceased Marcus Jastrow 16 months after Jastrow's death in 1903. Simultaneous efforts on behalf of the *Jewish Encyclopedia* diminished the time scholars could devote to the Bible.

The fate of the Bible section of the *Jewish Encyclopedia* raised questions about broad-based participation on the Bible translation. A Bible that involved university-affiliated Judaic scholars inevitably confronted the higher criticism. If European scholars were the Bible's primary audience, the editors might have tried to prepare a Bible that reconciled the higher criticism and "the spirit of positive

Judaism" and that united "Jewry of every shade of opinion." But in 1908, Adler and his colleagues ratified the conclusion of the original editorial board that the edition should be "a translation destined for the people," that is, American Jews, not a Jewish Polychrome Bible. That Bible, the editors reaffirmed, "can follow only one text, and that must be the traditional."[76]

In 1908, organized Reform Jewry, frustrated at the 16-year delay in the Jewish Publication Society effort, and perhaps uneasy with the Conservative majority on the Bible's editorial board, began discussions with Oxford University Press for its own Bible. Cyrus Adler, concerned that the Reform translation would rely too heavily on the Protestant Revised Version and that communal fragmentation would increase if Jewish factions published competing editions, negotiated with Hebrew Union College trustee David Philipson, his friend and former Hopkins classmate.[77] Their compromise established a new board of editors composed equally of Central Conference of American Rabbis and Jewish Publication Society members. The board also represented the three extant Jewish colleges.[78]

Adler suggested that Max Margolis serve as editor-in-chief, even though Margolis had recently resigned from Hebrew Union College after battling with Philipson and Kohler over Zionism and other issues.[79] Philipson agreed, perhaps recalling that Hebrew Union had placed great stock in Margolis's academic credentials only a few years earlier. The memoirs of Adler and Philipson agree that the strain apparent at early board meetings gradually diminished.[80] Margolis prepared a new translation based on the Revised Version but also taking into account the Leeser Bible, the earlier Jewish Publication Society drafts, and other Christian versions. The board decided disputed points by majority vote, and each editor considered it "his duty to take full responsibility for the whole result, even for the passages to which he may not have given assent."[81]

The Jewish Publication Society published the final product in 1917. Later generations gave the edition high marks, but critics noted the infatuation of the editors with Elizabethan English, their questionable adoption of some Protestant renderings at the expense of Jewish scholarship, and their perhaps too frequent modifications of translations that Margolis suggested.[82] In the 1890s, a "neutral" translation of the Bible implied working with university-affiliated Judaic scholars, but by 1910 the strengthening of American seminaries permitted a more limited definition: a cooperative venture by organized Americanized Jewry.

The Jewish Publication Society Bible pointed toward a more distinctly American and distinctly Jewish conception of American Jewish scholarship. The 1782 publication of a Bible in Philadelphia, the Society's board noted, was America's "Biblical declaration of independence." The Society's Bible would provide American Jews with a similar sense of ownership.[83] The Society also felt justified in offering an American edition of Graetz's history despite the existence of a British edition.[84] Adler justified importing a Hebrew printing press from Europe as "necessary for the independence of Jewish scholarship and for the sake of the community here . . . [since] it seemed to me that Jewish scholarship would be provincial in America until we had our own press." Adler also hoped that the

American Jewish Historical Society would focus the attention of American Jewry on its substantial role among fellow Americans—and fellow Jews.

Adler's domestic goal was to increase American Jewish "self-awareness" through non-partisan, representative scholarship. The relative freedom America accorded to Jews made the congregation rather than the "community" the focus of Jewish life, and pulpit partisanship had become the rule. But American Jewish scholarship could not afford fragmentation. The Jewish Publication Society and other Adler-associated innovations evolved de facto ties with the Conservative movement, but these activities also needed support from rival communal factions. No modern Isaac Leeser nor any one group—even Adler's Conservatives—could produce a Bible for contemporary American Jewry.[85] Adler therefore insisted on unanimous editorial support for the entire Bible.

Adler refused to neglect the international scholarly community: "less universal" did not imply American communal or scholarly isolationism. Upon importing the prestigious but financially weak *Jewish Quarterly Review* from England to Dropsie College in 1910, Adler announced: "America is fast becoming the center of Jewry and, in all likelihood, will also become the center of Jewish learning in the English world." Guarantees of nonpartisanship and representativeness facilitated the *Review*'s transfer from Reform British to Conservative American hands, forestalling efforts by American Reform Jews to cosponsor the journal.[86] Adler also knew that attaining the stature of the *Monatsschrift für die Wissenschaft des Judentums* or the *Revue des Études Juives* required broad American acceptance of the *Review* as a scholarly medium.[87]

Adler advocated domestic control and domestic subject matter, non-partisanship, and representativeness, but he did not intend to exclude non-American scholars from participation in American endeavors. Adler witnessed how Paul Haupt's arrival from Germany enhanced the stature of American Oriental scholarship, and many European contributors appeared on the Jewish Publication Society booklists and early rosters of Bible translators. The permanent migrations to America of Louis Ginzberg, Joseph Jacobs, and Solomon Schechter resulted from their involvement in Adler-affiliated projects.

Adler was ever vigilant against projects that claimed to represent American Jewish scholarship but that violated the principles of domesticity, non-partisanship, and representativeness. He opposed, for example, the attempt of Yeshiva College president Bernard Revel to form a national organization for the promotion of Jewish scholarship composed of younger scholars (1916). The absence of American scholars of stature, he concluded, made the enterprise vulnerable to European disdain.[88] Several years later, Adler accepted honorary membership in the American Academy for Jewish Research, composed of "recognized" scholars and designed to "stimulate Jewish learning by helpful cooperation and mutual encouragement . . . as well as to formulate standards of Jewish scholarship."[89] Adler believed himself uniquely able to steer a straight course for American Jewish scholarship when many American Jews gave it low priority and many scholars abroad thought it inconsequential.

"American Jewish scholarship," Adler also believed, had to be Jewish. Recognizing that Jewish aspects were not at the cutting edge of Semitic philology, Adler opted for the former, with an emphasis on history and *kulturgeschichte* to complement traditional Jewish textual criticism.[90] In any case, scholars committed to expanding and refining the field in Jewish—not Semitic—directions would define the field. The American Academy for Jewish Research did not invite Gottheil, Jastrow, or Popper to become members, though these scholars had helped to compile the *Jewish Encyclopedia*.[91] The appearance of the word "Jewish" in three of the four Adler-initiated projects (as well as in the American Academy for Jewish Research) is no coincidence, nor is its absence in the Bible project. There might be *a* Jewish Publication Society, *a Jewish Encyclopedia, an* American Jewish Historical Society, but there was only *the* Bible—a Jewish statement best rendered to the world by Jewish commentators and translators.[92]

Adler wanted American *Jewish* scholarship to focus on issues of interest for Jews and Judaism, not on how Jewish perspectives illuminated universal questions. The life of the mind, Adler suggested, would remain a significant part of modern Judaism. Adler participated in many events that affected Jewish learning in American universities, but he concluded that the faulty, universalistic premise of university-based Jewish scholarship made successful pursuit of Jewish learning possible only in Jewish institutions such as the Jewish Theological Seminary and Dropsie. Adler tried to increase communal awareness and support, offer newer conceptions of the Jewish scholarly mission without abandoning the older ones, and facilitate scholarship in a period of minimal academic or communal support. But would cooperation between Jewish institutions in producing the Jewish Publication Society Bible presage a healthy alternative to the universities for Jewish scholarship? Others thought not.

Why Not the Seminaries?

Ad hoc settings could nurture unique scholarly projects—the *Jewish Encyclopedia* and the Bible—and modest undertakings—the American Jewish Historical Society and the Jewish Publication Society—but continued production of Jewish scholarship required a permanent setting. Emil G. Hirsch and Bernhard Felsenthal accorded primacy to late nineteenth-century universities as scholarly centers—perhaps even as educators of American rabbis. Other observers, who might not have shared Hirsch's and Felsenthal's unfettered enthusiasm, still believed that universities could help Reform and Conservative seminaries improve the education of rabbinical students. American rabbis, critics charged, beleaguered by constant demands, lacked the time to acquire the erudition of their European predecessors—even though rabbis required more, not less, scholarly and practical knowledge. Universities could instruct students in secular subjects, thus leaving the seminaries free to offer Judaica. Emil Hirsch's list of desiderata in a learned rabbi, for example, included philosophy, psychology, ethics and social relations, the literature and history of Judaism, and relevant languages. Undergraduate university education, followed by seminary work, would remedy these academic deficiencies: "We need a dozen or two young Rabbis who will not 'grab' for the first position they can obtain after leaving school," stated one late nineteenth-century editorial, "but who, for dear love of the cause, will give a few more years to purely professional training first in academic knowledge to be gained under great Semitic professors, afterwards in some old-fashioned *Jeshiba [yeshivah]*, where facility and practice go hand in hand." These rabbis would become leaders, "not merely ministers who can glibly discourse on superficial themes."[93]

Physical proximity facilitated the proposed academic division of labor. Philadelphia's short-lived Maimonides College (1867–1873), America's first Jewish seminary, aspired to close relationships with the University of Pennsylvania, and faculty members even helped Maimonides students prepare for the university's entrance requirements in the classical languages.[94] Hebrew Union College students took secular courses at the nearby University of Cincinnati. New York's Jewish Theological Seminary (1886) developed a close relationship with Columbia and moved to Morningside Heights in 1903, a few years after Columbia itself moved from midtown to the Upper West Side.

The nearness of the Jewish Theological Seminary to Columbia may have facilitated the education of rabbis, but it also enabled Richard Gottheil to reduce the proportion of Judaic instruction in his teaching load. "With the moving to Morningside Heights of the Jewish Theological Seminary in 1903 and of the Union Theological Seminary in 1910," wrote Columbia's Arthur Jeffery, "there was no further need for this Department [Semitics] to carry the burden of instruction in Rabbinic or in Biblical Hebrew, which were adequately cared for in the seminaries."[95] The Jewish community sometimes encouraged seminary proximity to redress their disappointed hopes for university-based Semitics. The reconstituted Jewish Theological Seminary board (1902) included Temple Emanu-El congregants who had previously promoted university-based Jewish learning.[96]

As Jewish and Judaic access to America's universities decreased during the twentieth century, seminaries came to view universities as competing, not complementary, institutions. University of Cincinnati–Hebrew Union College relations worsened after the turn of the century. Hebrew Union authorities also rejected a proposal made by Emil G. Hirsch and Jacob Voorsanger to move the seminary from Cincinnati to the vicinity of a more developed university. Morris Jastrow strongly urged Dropsie College trustees to locate the new college near the University of Pennsylvania, but the trustees built on land bequeathed for the purpose at a distance from the university.[97] Seminaries provided an alternative to intellectual exclusion from universities, just as Jewish students organized alternatives to Gentile social activities.[98] The decline of Judaic Semitics in universities probably increased communal support not only for Hebrew Union College and the Jewish Theological Seminary but also for Dropsie College, Graetz College, the Jewish Institute of Religion, Yeshiva College, the Chicago College of Jewish Studies—now Spertus Institute of Jewish Studies—and other identifiably

Jewish institutions.[99] By the 1910s, most observers considered seminaries the most promising setting for American Jewish scholarship. "It bodes well for the future of American Judaism," Solomon Schechter wrote in 1903, "when Rabbis begin to write the books which were til now the exclusive monopoly of University Professors."[100]

Greater seminary viability led to increased scrutiny. Some critics, finding seminaries wanting as sanctuaries of Jewish learning, urged continued support of university-based Jewish learning despite poor short-run prospects for growth. The multi-count indictment of the seminaries began with a denunciation of low intellectual standards. Elliot Cohen, one of the Menorah group that persisted in giving the nod to universities, considered seminary faculties:

> cliques of monopolistic Jewish scholars, who take in each others' intellectual washing, play the pettiest brand of academic politics and consider criticism lese majesté. . . . These perpetuate a low standard of learning, since they protect each other's mistakes, use the fear of the 'goy' to preserve their academic honor (criticize us and you'll cause anti-Semitism), and produce work almost entirely useless for humanistic studies.[101]

Hebrew Union College professor Jacob Mann privately agreed that academic standards were lower at seminaries than at the universities:

> It is unfortunate that the situation should be so that reviews of books have deteriorated into mere singing of praises. Immediately, if a review seriously discusses the contents of a work and offers some contribution to the understanding of the subject matter, with all due respect for the author, it must be the result of some imaginary grudge on the part of the reviewer—such has become, alas, the reasoning in our age of Kritikloskeit.[102]

Mann eventually resigned the editorship of the *Hebrew Union College Annual*, claiming his colleagues favored "a sort of enlarged edition of the B'nai B'rith magazine" over a high quality scholarly journal. The fate of the *Annual*, he believed, reflected Hebrew Union's indifference to scholarship.[103]

Cecil Roth echoed the Cohen–Mann critique. Jewish Theological Seminary professor Alexander Marx, Roth reported, broke off contact after receiving his corrections to *A History of the Jews* coauthored by Marx and Max Margolis. "I had hoped that he would have welcomed them (my first letter from him, berating me severely for certain blunders in my own published work had made me imagine that he at least was not a member of the Mutual Admiration Society which has been the bane of Jewish scholarship in our own days).''[104] Communal considerations, critics added, could even require the sacrifice of these already low seminary standards.

Seminaries, the indictment continued, rewarded scholarship that was incongruent with humanistic study, when they encouraged scholarship at all. Seminary faculty members taught Talmud traditionally, other fields superficially. Gentiles considered Talmudic study "narrow," a vague term that often masked hostility toward all Jewish learning but that at least suggested the incongruence between Talmud and the agenda of interwar universities. Jewish critics argued that an emphasis on traditional Talmud study helped exclude from seminary and university both modern Hebrew and Jewish history, subjects that, as chapter 8 shows, derived legitimacy from association with parent disciplines found in universities.

Some Jews and Gentiles disagreed. Harry Wolfson argued that Talmud study was a necessary prerequisite for all Jewish scholarship, an attitude that Jewish Theological Seminary professor and Reconstructionist movement founder Mordecai Kaplan attributed to "his early yeshiva training and probably also a sentimental temperament."[105] George Foot Moore, whose *Judaism in the First Centuries of the Christian Era—The Age of the Tannaim* depicted Jewish thought and civilization during the period of the Talmud's composition as more than an antiquarian "pre-Christian culture," also viewed Talmudic study as an asset. "I am well aware," he wrote, "how many pitfalls there are in the path of one who, without the advantage of a professional Talmudic training, ventures himself into this subject."[106]

Many Judaica scholars, however, considered the field stigmatized. Arthur Jeffery described his encounter with Samuel Feigin, a Yale Ph.D., who held Judaica posts at the University of Chicago's Oriental Institute and other Chicago institutions. "Why yes! I remember your name; you are a Talmudist," Jeffery recounted. Feigin looked indignant and asked Jeffery to explain his remark. Jeffery replied that he had read some of Feigin's articles on Talmudic matters and concluded that Talmud was his special interest. Feigin rejoined, "Oh! I thought you might have meant something else." Jeffery subsequently asked a Jewish colleague: "Is it considered derogatory to refer to a person as a Talmudist? It occurred to me that perhaps some Jews take that term as derogatory in the sense in which we refer to a Christian as a Fundamentalist, though I had not been conscious of that."[107] Sympathetic Protestants notwithstanding, most Gentiles, perhaps disingenuously, and many Jews concurred that the centrality of Talmud inhibited other forms of Jewish scholarship. Universities, the Menorah group argued, should not mimic the curricular timidity of the seminaries by emphasizing Talmud.

Critics might have cited the experience of Ralph Marcus to illustrate the charge of curricular superficiality, the next count in the seminary indictment. Marcus, the son of a rabbi who taught at the Jewish Institute of Religion, graduated from Columbia College in 1921, shortly after introduction of the contemporary civilization sequence that surveyed the development of western institutions. Rejected for a Rhodes scholarship, discouraged by the *Nation*'s Carl Van Doren from a career in journalism, and himself declining the rabbinical option, Marcus decided instead on graduate study.[108] He enrolled at Harvard where Harry Wolfson, his dissertation adviser, and George Foot Moore encouraged his interest in the relationship between Hellenistic culture and ancient Judaism: specifically whether the Jewish role assigned to wisdom in *Midrash Rabbah* on *Bereshit* (Genesis) implied direct or indirect acquaintance with Philo. Moore suggested that Marcus investigate the channels through which authorities for this

Midrashic view of wisdom may have become acquainted with Philo's work—a question that became the springboard for further investigations.[109]

Marcus was offered a position at the Jewish Institute of Religion as he neared completion of his doctoral work. Hoping to teach primarily in his specialty, he learned from Stephen Wise that resources precluded a separate department of Hellenistic Jewish history and literature. Wise expected Marcus to teach Bible and elementary Hebrew grammar and to tutor students, though he did not rule out occasional specialized courses.[110] The scarcity of academic positions—many colleagues worked in Sunday schools or communal posts—prompted Marcus to accept, and he grew to enjoy his teaching. Richard Gottheil's offer of a supplementary Gustav Gottheil Fellowship at Columbia improved his economic status and permitted him to work on his edition of Josephus.[111]

Marcus felt great rapport with Wise, who had known him since childhood, and with his seminary students. His rapidly increasing distaste for Columbia,"where Jews are barely tolerated," and his deteriorating relationship with Gottheil during the 1930s made him even more comfortable at the Institute.[112] Marcus told Wise that if the Institute offered him a promotion, a full-time professorship, and commensurate remuneration, he would gladly accept. Wise, however, did not have the resources to meet these conditions. When Gottheil died in 1936, Marcus signaled his candidacy for the Columbia chair "for the purely practical reason that a permanent appointment at Columbia would mean economic security."[113] The world soon learned of Arthur Jeffery's appointment—"Better that than an Arab," consoled Wise—and Marcus continued fractionally at Columbia and the Institute until 1943.[114]

All this time, Richard McKeon, dean of the humanities division of the University of Chicago and a former member of the Columbia philosophy department, tried to bring Marcus to the Midway. Initially thwarted by Chicago faculty members who suspected that the metaphysical hand of Robert Maynard Hutchins lay behind his every move, McKeon renewed his efforts in 1943. He offered Marcus an associate professorship in Hellenistic culture, jointly sponsored by the department of Oriental languages and literatures, the department of Greek, and the divinity school.[115]

Marcus finally realized a 20-year ambition to teach and conduct full-time research in his specialty, but campus and community often viewed him as a generalist—the common view of seminary faculty members—a tendency compounded by the historic identification of Jewish learning at Chicago with rabbis, including Emil G. Hirsch and Louis Mann. "I will merely repeat with as much dignity and detachment as I can shakily muster in this moment of demoralization," he protested to the editor of the *Encyclopaedia Britannica*, "That I did not critically read the article on the Jews, chiefly although not solely because I am not an authority on the history of the Jews. My field is Hellenistic Culture and ancient Judaism."[116] Marcus died prematurely in 1956, and we do not know how campus and community would have seen him after publication of the texts he edited at Chicago. He clearly would have continued to rely upon his strong ego and intellect to guide him through ambiguity.[117] Critics could cite the willingness of

Marcus to abandon the more congenial Jewish Institute environment for the university to show that seminaries favored the generalist over the specialist, save in traditional Judaica fields. Second generation scholars shared with their predecessors the need to reconcile self- and external perceptions about the nature of Jewish scholars and scholarship.

The last count in the indictment charged that the association of seminaries with contemporary partisan issues—especially Zionism—heightened communal tensions, thereby impairing teaching and scholarship. Cyrus Adler had consistently espoused the opposite vision—Jewish scholarship, he believed, must unify, not divide. "American Jewry has responded liberally and generously to the appeal made in behalf of the suffering Jews, and it is now high time that it becomes cognizant of [this] greater danger threatening Judaism," stated a draft memorandum of Adler's selective American Academy for Jewish Research. "Rent by dissension and split into parties, Jewish learning is the only bond of union that remains to Israel."[118] "If a more conservative type of Judaism is prevalent in the East than in the West," echoed David Philipson, "yet in the domain of literature, history and philanthropic work, all of us can be at one, no matter what the complexion of our religious or theological opinion."[119] To allay suspicions of partisanship, Adler avoided identifying his scholarly projects with Conservative Judaism, but ad hoc successes failed to translate into ongoing cooperation between seminaries.

An acrimonious debate over Zionism, seminary critics noted, accompanied intensifying theological schisms between seminaries.[120] The anti-Zionism that pervaded Kaufmann Kohler's Hebrew Union College helped to precipitate the 1907 resignations of Max Margolis—potentially one of Hebrew Union's most productive scholars—and two other faculty members. Was anti-Zionism, critics asked, an essential tenet of Reform Jewish doctrine that necessitated restrictions on the academic freedom of Zionists? Hebrew Union College remained identified with anti-Zionism for several decades, while Stephen Wise, the head of the Jewish Institute of Religion was a Zionist. The Nazi rise to power finally changed the terms of discourse, and the 1936 Columbus Platform adopted by Reform Judaism omitted the "America is our Zion" formulation of the 1885 Pittsburgh Platform. After World War II, most American Jews favored a Jewish state, as did most Judaica practitioners, and Reform Judaism overcame personality conflicts and the Zionist fissure to effect a merger between Hebrew Union College and the Jewish Institute of Religion in 1950.

Zionism also divided university-affiliated Jewish Semitists, but seminary critics noted that the often intense battles took place between individuals, not institutions. Two Reform Jews—anti-Zionist Emil Hirsch and Richard Gottheil, founder of the Federation of American Zionists—debated the issue after Gottheil espoused Zionism from the pulpit of Hirsch's Chicago Sinai Congregation. Little love was lost between the two antagonists, and Hirsch used the term "miserable imposters" to describe Gottheil and his Zionist "consorts."[121] The rivalry may have sharpened when the Temple Emanu-El trustees offered Gustav Gottheil's pulpit—to which Gustav expected Richard to accede—to Hirsch at century's end, an offer that Hirsch declined.[122]

Jewish Semitists in the Reform-dominated university movement often shared Reform's prevailing anti-Zionism. Zionism, wrote Abram Isaacs, "will have to detach itself from the fantasy of a *Judenstaat,* and devote itself wholly to practical and practicable colonization, if it hopes to secure a larger following in this country."[123] At one point, William Rosenau said, "I believe one can be a good reform Jew and be a Zionist," but he later changed his mind. "We look with disfavor," he stated at the time of the Balfour Declaration, "upon the new doctrine of political Jewish nationalism, which finds the criterion of Jewish loyalty in anything other than loyalty to Israel's God and Israel's religious mission."[124] Morris Jastrow, Richard Gottheil's friend and collaborator, opposed his colleague's Zionism. In a 1919 statement to the Paris Peace Conference, Jastrow challenged the creation of a Jewish state in Palestine—just as the Zionists attempted to realize the promises of the Balfour Declaration.[125]

The controversy spread when many Gentile Semitists sided with the Arab cause, out of conviction or out of fear that Zionist sympathies might threaten their research in the Near East. In 1942, the Harris Institute in Chicago invited a spectrum of academicians to a forum on the Near East. When the Palestine issue arose, Arthur Jeffery recounted, Columbia's Salo Baron "gave an excellent presentation of a difficult subject, historically defensible and academically respectable." Jeffery then described the ensuing acerbity between the Semitists:

> Then the fun began. First [Princeton Semitics Professor Philip] Hitti [a student of Richard Gottheil] for the Arabs and then [Samuel] Feigin for the Jews made impassioned speeches where emotion ran away with them, and Rabbi Fox (?) forgot himself, imagining he was in the pulpit, and preached us at great length a sermon. All three of them presented statements on the early history of Palestine that one would not accept in the paper of a sophomore.[126]

Interwar seminary critics did not envision that the founding of the state of Israel in 1948 would resolve the Zionism debate within the Jewish community while intensifying disputes among university-based Semitists who thenceforth depended on hostile protagonists, not on colonial powers, for access to archaeological sites, their colleagues, and, often, funding. These critics noted that partisanship notwithstanding, Richard Gottheil's Columbia students included Zionists and anti-Zionist Jews, Gentiles, and Muslims. In contrast, they added, by associating their *institutions* with a position on Zionism, the seminaries damaged the potential for Jewish scholarship to help unify the Jewish community.

Seminaries, critics concluded, were not conducive to high quality, disinterested, non-parochial, and non-partisan Jewish scholarship. A mid-1920s incident synthesizes their critique. In 1924 W. Mordechai Katz, a student in Richard Gottheil's department, requested permission to write a thesis based on the Talmud. Gottheil admitted that "it is on a subject about which I do not profess to know very much," though he originally held a chair of rabbinics. He asked

Jewish Theological Seminary professor Louis Ginzberg to see Katz and to decide "whether the subject is one which allows of treatment," whether "W. Katz
is able to treat it," and—when Katz finished his thesis—whether "it is a good
piece of work and worthy of being the foundation of Mr. Metz [sic] reception
of the Doctor's degree?" Ginzberg advised Katz, read the final draft, and wrote:
"I have read very carefully the thesis on the protection of the poor according to
Talmudic law and I find it to be quite satisfactory. Mr. Katz has contributed but
little," he continued, "to the history of the development of Talmudic law but his
work gives a fair view of what post-Biblical law has done for the protection of
the submerged classes and I am convinced that it will be welcomed by students
of Comparative Law."[127]

Columbia University Press published the defended dissertation as *Protection
of the Weak in the Talmud,* volume 24 of the *Columbia University Oriental Studies,* and Henry Hurwitz asked Nathan Isaacs, a Harvard Business School professor, and a long-time supporter of the Menorah movement, to review the book
for *Menorah Journal.* Isaacs, whose orthodoxy gave him a lay interest in the
subject, expressed disbelief at the book's poor quality, anger that Columbia
University Press accepted the manuscript, and sadness at the poor state of Jewish scholarship that the book reflected. The entire review read: "A liberal ignorance of the English language, of law, of Hebrew, of Hebrew law and of history,
combined with dogmatism, wild references, muddled thinking and general
slovenliness, result here—quite naturally—in a thoroughly worthless book on an
interesting subject."[128] Isaacs sent the draft to Gottheil and asked him to have the
book withdrawn.[129]

Gottheil accepted the blame for the book's publication, explaining that he relied on Ginzberg's judgment and that only when the book was set in page proofs
did he discover the manuscript corrections he requested—improving the poor
English and removing references to Greek and Roman matters about which Katz
knew nothing—were not made. The real fault, he wrote, lay with a Jewish
woman employed by the Columbia University Press. "She came to me and confessed her fault," Gottheil wrote; "I ought to have made a complaint to her man-
ager; but, then she would have lost her place at once. Out of *Rahamanuth*
[compassion] I did not do so."[130]

Gottheil asked Isaacs to withdraw the review and let the book go unnoticed,
citing potential damage to Ginzberg's reputation and to Columbia's relationship
to the Jewish Theological Seminary. "I was sorry that such an excellent scholar
as Professor Ginzberg is mixed up in this matter," he wrote. "I have tried to
bring the Jewish Theological Seminary into connection with the University. I
shall be forced to retire into my shell and eschew all such attempts." The review,
Gottheil added, "will do us a great deal of harm here, where the Jewish question
is one which I have been struggling through the thirty-nine or more years of my
professorship." Finally, Gottheil questioned the norms that guided Isaacs's review: "[The review] smacks of the yeshibah style and not of the University; . . .
it bears the marks and signs of one who is ridiculing. In fact, it reads as if it were
written by a German anti-Semite."[131]

Editors at the Menorah office had little love for Columbia, Gottheil, or Ginzberg, and reacted accordingly. "I'm itching to have your Katz review appear in the Journal," Hurwitz wrote. " 'Hail Columbia' or rather, 'Hail Jewish Columbia.' Another strike for the great Ginzberg!"[132] *Menorah Journal* editors urged Isaacs to ignore Gottheil's request. "Isaacs, by withdrawing the review," wrote a staff member, "makes himself almost as responsible for the book as Gottheil and Ginzberg; why go about a very simple matter in such an indirect, diplomatic manner. The book was rotten, Isaacs should say so in detail, anything else is the rankest politics."[133]

Nathan Isaacs's response to Gottheil illustrates the concerns—and fears—underlying the indictment against the seminaries. Isaacs respected Gottheil, and did not forget that Columbia once offered him a post. He disliked Gottheil's comparison of his review with that of an anti-Semite. "If I have written in the tone of a German anti-Semite," he wrote, "perhaps there is something in this whole performance that makes one feel like joining Hackenkreuiller." But he was more offended by Gottheil's suggestion that his review resembled the work of a *yeshivah* scholar. "But please do not group me with the Yeshiba," he wrote, "I mean the New York yeshiba. I have fled from that crowd, refused to speak at their Commencement or to accept an honorary degree at their hands, just because I have found their place overrun by 'scholars' of the Katz type."

Isaacs had made the difficult transition from seminary—in this case a *yeshivah*—to university, but that change may have led to some empathy with Katz. "You know as well as I do," he told Hurwitz in another context:

> what indelible scars the struggle of that transition has left on many of our contemporaries. They deserve our pity and have it, too, in spite of the awful things they perpetuate. I am reminded of the Talmudic story of the Four that entered the Garden [of esoteric philosophy]. One died, one lost his mind, one became a heretic and only one entered in peace and departed again in peace. The same general proposition obtains today among *bechurim* who gain admittance to American graduate schools.[134]

Katz had no future in university scholarship, and the world, after all, did not deeply care whether or not the review appeared. Perhaps a sense that "there but for the grace of God go I" prompted Isaacs to withhold the review.[135]

Conclusion

During the early twentieth century, practitioners of Jewish learning—whether located in university-based Semitic departments, special settings, or seminaries—had to achieve scholarly cooperation, define a relationship to the interested Jewish and Gentile communities, and attain domestic and international recognition. Cyrus Adler often served as an academic broker when a project required cooperation between seminaries. No one, not even William Rainey Harper, consistently performed a similar function for university-based Semitists. Instead, cooperation arose out of friendship or acquaintanceship, or on an ad hoc basis such as in the Hilprecht controversy.

Advocates of Jewish learning frequently employed a strategy of non-partisanship to allay communal suspicions about important projects, such as the *Jewish Encyclopedia* and the Jewish Publication Society Bible. Seminaries also excluded the higher criticism and other perceived threats to the essential tenets of Judaism, and often let their lay boards deal with the Jewish community. Universities permitted more controversial inquiries, but relied on sympathetic clergy and on Gentile scholars to fend off external attacks.

University and seminary devised similar strategies to achieve international recognition and scholarly parity with Europe—benefactions, cautious scholarship, importing European talent, and initiating visible, significant projects. University Semitists emphasized archaeological expeditions that promised long-term gains, while the fledgling seminaries emphasized imports that brought immediate recognition: scholars, including Solomon Schechter, Joseph Jacobs, and Louis Ginzberg, and apparatus, including a Hebrew printing press and the *Jewish Quarterly Review*.

University and seminary scholars confronted similar problems of domestic and foreign policy; their solutions sometimes coincided, more often they varied. Critics often denounced as inadequate the responses offered by seminaries, but they also fell back upon normative differences to explain why seminaries could not properly nurture the growth of Jewish learning. Universities, they suggested, embraced heterogeneity and the search for truth, while seminaries presupposed religious commonality and adherence to dogma. Off limits were the Pentateuch and other topics that might challenge basic religious tenets. University-based scholars could investigate any significant issue, view texts as data upon which to employ disciplinary techniques, and consider all disciplines of equal "worth." Seminaries—reflecting the traditional Jewish view that the key texts of Judaism contained all worthy knowledge—organized their structure and curricula around these texts. Universities thus had literature departments; seminaries had Talmud departments. Universities claimed to produce specialists who employed one or at most two disciplinary approaches to understand an aspect of the Jewish social or religious experience. Seminaries produced "jacks of all trades"—Elliot Cohen's derisive term—or Judaic generalists. Finally, universities claimed to embrace the creation of new knowledge, while seminaries emphasized transmission of extant knowledge. Seminaries, to use Florian Znaniecki's terminology, produced *sages* whose mastery of extant knowledge, no matter how esoteric, was insufficient for membership in the modern guild of scholars.[136] The problem resided in the approach rather than in the text itself—as George Foot Moore's scholarship demonstrated. But few contemporaries made the distinction, and before Jacob Neusner began his work in the 1960s, few university scholars devoted their energies to Talmud study.[137]

Critics attributed the occasional courtship of university scholars and the invocation of university norms and practices by seminaries to considerations of status, not true belief. "I believe it's of the utmost importance to keep one's academic skirts clear," wrote Menorah's Henry Hurwitz:

There will be more and more temptations—from sectarian institutions, organizations, etc. And, as you see, Reform, as well as Orthodoxy, is flirting with professors, scientists, etc. They won't respect them if they get them; and the force, dignity and function of the academic class in Jewry will be abraded, even destroyed, unless the academic men are like Caesar's wife (at least in one metaphorical respect!).[138]

Interwar seminaries might never have satisfied their critics, but financial constraints and the demand for clergy forced them to emphasize teaching at the expense of scholarship, thereby widening the chasm. After World War II, Jewish—and some non-Jewish—seminaries took the indictment to heart, recruited new faculty members from university doctoral programs, and emphasized scholarship in faculty promotion decisions. In the 1960s, Christopher Jencks and David Riesman criticized seminaries for conforming *too closely* to university norms. A research ethos might distract from an essential practitioner education in imparting basic doctrine and nurturing interpersonal skills. Early skeptics ridiculed university education of rabbis, but later critics cautioned against seminary education of scholars.[139]

Interwar seminaries, concluded proponents of university-based Jewish learning, could not compensate for the financial stringency, academic constraints, and anti-Semitism that hindered the growth of Jewish learning in universities. The 1928 endowment of a Judaica chair at Columbia was therefore a rare opportunity for proponents of Jewish learning to demonstrate the virtues of the university setting.

VII

"THE MOST AVAILABLE AND SUITABLE MAN": COLUMBIA'S MILLER CHAIR AND SALO BARON

> We have searched the heavens, the earth, and the waters under the earth, on three continents, and finally the unanimous judgment of our advisers rested upon Professor Baron as the most available and suitable man.
>
> —Nicholas Murray Butler[1]

In spring 1928, Linda Miller, a Temple Emanu-El congregant and recent widow of Nathan L. Miller, a prominent New York businessman, endowed a professorship of Jewish History, Literature, and Institutions at Columbia University in her husband's memory. President Nicholas Murray Butler thereupon appointed a committee to find the most suitable occupant. In the case of the Littauer endowment, Harvard chose a scholar already on the faculty. Columbia's 1928 roster yielded no candidate, and the committee looked outside the institution. The scarcity of positions in Jewish learning, especially at prestigious universities, and the number of potential candidates educated in American Semitics departments or abroad suggested that the committee would not conduct a lengthy or difficult search. But Columbia's optimism dissipated as interested parties exerted an array of communal and scholarly pressures concerning the appointment.

This chapter analyzes the diverse definitions of "suitability" that emerged during the committee's 15-month search—definitions offered by the donor, search committee members, and other practitioners. The eventual appointment of Salo Baron was an attempt to mediate between communal and institutional expectations for a position that could influence the growth of Jewish scholarship in universities for the rest of the century.

The committee confronted two difficult problems. What weight should it accord to a candidate's personality, religiosity, and denominational preference? Academic norms had supposedly made these factors irrelevant. Second, where did the chair best fit into the university? An earlier generation had favored inclusion of Jewish learning in Semitics departments. With the waning of interest in Semitics, would another discipline be more hospitable to—and profit more

150

from—the chair? Practitioners understood that in answering these questions the committee would consider the dearth of university-based Jewish scholarship, diminution of communal support, loss of presidential interest, and failure to achieve recognition.

Many observers noted that Jewish Semitists often strayed from the Jewish aspects of their discipline. They hoped that the Miller chairholder would focus primarily on Jewish topics and also speak to the general concerns of the parent discipline. No one argued that the chair should become the base of a separate department, the solution particularists later termed most conducive to retaining a Judaic scholarly focus. But which discipline would provide the most congenial environment?

Answers to these questions proved critical for the field's subsequent history. Indeed, Salo Baron, the most available and suitable man, permanently moved the university-based study of Judaism past Semitics and philology, opened the study of history in American universities to Judaic insight, placed his students in academic positions that advanced the study of Jewish history, and promoted the development of Jewish learning in universities.

The Endowment

By 1928, activity on behalf of Judaica chairs in major American universities again accelerated. Henry Hurwitz's Menorah Association shifted from nurturing student Menorah groups to advocating endowments for Jewish scholarship. In 1927, the B'nai B'rith announced that it too sought to endow Judaica chairs. But only Hyman Enelow, still the junior rabbi at Temple Emanu-El, actually succeeded in securing an endowment.[2]

Enelow's fortunes at Emanu-El worsened after he arranged the Littauer gift. Rival Nathan Krass held a commanding position, and Enelow was consigned to directing Emanu-El's Sunday School. In 1933, the temple would release him, and he died soon after, a broken man.[3] In the midst of his professional troubles, Enelow found refuge in the home of Nathan and Linda Miller. "There," wrote a friend of the Millers,

> he found true friendship, understanding, admiration, spiritual community. There he could expand, give full reign to his trenchant wit, pour out his versatile knowledge, lose the acerbity and harshness he seemed to present to an unsympathetic world, and express his true self in a native kindliness that answered spontaneously and joyously to the like quality in his hosts.[4]

The Millers had moved to New York City about a decade before the arrival of the young rabbi from Kentucky. Each spouse attained considerable stature, Nathan as a Wall Street businessman, Linda as a philanthropist and connoisseur of the arts. A deep, affectionate relationship developed between Enelow and the Millers. Shortly before his death, Nathan Miller wrote Enelow that he was "personally under many more obligations to you than I will ever be able to repay, even if I live to be as old as Methuselah."[5] Enelow's weekly Emanu-El sermons, his Monday morning lectures on Jewish topics, and his informal conversations intensified the Millers' interest in their Reform Jewish background. Enelow gradually impressed upon them the importance of Jewish scholarship, not as an end in itself, but as a method of deepening one's devotion to Judaism: "Jewish knowledge suffused with *kawanna,* soul," in the words of Linda Miller's biographer.[6]

Linda Miller's endowment was not her first gift to advance Jewish scholarship. At Enelow's suggestion, for instance, she subsidized Israel Davidson's *Ozar ha-Shirah ve-ha-Piyyut (Thesaurus of Medieval Hebrew Poetry)*. The thesaurus contained detailed information about 35,000 poems and prayers from post-Biblical times to the beginning of the *Haskalah* movement.[7] Enelow convinced Miller that an endowed chair—similar to the chair Lucius Littauer, her New Rochelle neighbor, gave to Harvard—would be the logical culmination of her philanthropy and an appropriate memorial to her husband. He then convinced Columbia authorities to accept the gift.

The endowment carried a stipulation: the chairholder should emphasize the "spiritual and intellectual aspects of Jewish life," not "the nationalist ideas which have recently become popular in some quarters." Sharing the anti-Zionism of Reform Judaism, and probably warned that Richard Gottheil would participate in the appointment process, Miller alerted Columbia to her wishes.[8]

The Littauer and Miller endowments occurred less than three years apart, but the difference in benefactorial expectations reflects the changes in communal thinking about university-based Jewish learning. Lucius Littauer endowed a research professorship, but Linda Miller was equally concerned with "spirituality," teaching, and scholarship. The Jewish undergraduate influx into American universities over the previous 20 years—Jews made up about 40 percent of the Columbia College student body just after World War I—turned communal interest toward maintaining or enhancing Jewish student identity. Linda Miller's concern led Columbia to consider the candidate's "personality" if not his "spirituality." So, too, the candidate's Jewish orientation. "There are, both within and without the Jewish group," Miller wrote Butler, "scholarly individuals who put an interpretation of Judaism that seems, to me, subversive of all that is finest in Jewish tradition. I feel that I might get a good measure of unhappiness out of certain conceivable appointments."[9] Miller knew of Enelow's unhappiness at Emanu-El and of his "spiritually" and "religiously" oriented scholarship. She assumed that a donor's wishes would have considerable weight and nominated her not unwilling mentor for the chair. She then listed his qualifications and inferred that she would supply the necessary funds "if I could put aside any uneasiness as to the personality of the professor in charge."[10]

Butler now understood that he was dealing with an earnest woman unwilling to settle for the mere honor of naming a professorship. American higher education had matured (and most faculties had been "professionalized") considerably since the days of Richard Gottheil's appointment. Columbia had accorded the benefactors of Gottheil's position the right of "presentation" but had reserved for itself the right of "acceptance." Butler now insisted that Columbia was responsible for its own appointments. "You will, I am sure," he replied to Miller, "see the embarrassment that would result from naming a professor at the insistence of a generous benefactor. No matter what the competence of such a man might be, his colleagues would regard him as one apart, and his power for the University service would be gravely diminished, if not destroyed."[11] Butler promised to send Enelow's credentials to the search committee but offered no assurances about the outcome of the committee's deliberations.

Miller accepted Butler's logic but added: "For me it reduces itself to the ever vexatious question of squaring practice with principle."[12] She asked to select the chairholder from a short list that Columbia provided. Butler only offered to submit the names of finalists "in confidence to you for your suggestions and criticism before any final steps were taken."[13] Miller thanked Butler for exhibiting "such a sympathetic understanding." She authorized her financial agent to transfer the necessary securities[14] and Columbia received the funds two months later.[15]

The Committee and Its Mandate

Butler then turned to recruitment. Perceiving the appointment's "vexatious" nature, he asked Graduate Faculties dean Frederick J. E. Woodbridge to chair the search committee and to choose "an outstanding scholar who will not be a factionalist but who will command respect both within and without the University."[16] Thinking that the chair might support growth in comparative history of religions, Butler suggested Joseph H. Hertz, London's Chief Rabbi. Hertz was a Columbia Ph.D. whose dissertation had analyzed the philosophy of James Martineau, a nineteenth-century English Unitarian clergyman and defender of theism against the challenges of the physical sciences.

Butler's suggestion, given Miller's strictures, reveals his paucity of information about Jews and Jewish scholarship. Hertz's writings, apart from his thesis, were popular, but not scholarly, and Hertz, an Orthodox Jew, battled Reform Judaism in England. He was also a Zionist who played a key role in the events that led to the 1917 Balfour Declaration. Miller would have identified him immediately as a "factionalist" who emphasized Judaism's "political" rather than "spiritual" or "intellectual" aspects.[17]

Fortunately for Butler, the composition of the committee precluded mistakes of the sort Columbia would make when replacing Richard Gottheil.[18] The presence of professors Gottheil, A. V. Williams Jackson (philology), James T. Shotwell (history), William Westerman (ancient history), and Herbert W. Schneider (philosophy) insured appointment of a recognized scholar. The presence of social science professor Robert M. MacIver (an authority on intergroup relations), university chaplain Raymond D. Knox, and Union Theological Seminary president Henry Sloane Coffin assured that the successful candidate would address issues that also interested non-Jews. Columbia College dean Herbert Hawkes, Barnard College dean Virginia Gildersleeve (an anti-Zionist), associate

Graduate Faculty dean Robert Fife, and Woodbridge represented divisions likely to work with the new appointee.[19] The committee contained two Jews, Gottheil and philosophy professor Irwin Edman, an associate of the Menorah movement. Edman conducted much of the committee's legwork despite his lack of knowledge of the field of Jewish learning and thereby gained considerable influence—especially during Gottheil's lengthy residence in France while on leave of absence.

Edman and Gottheil agreed on the importance of the appointee's personality. Gottheil believed that appointing someone with a difficult personality would exacerbate anti-Semitism at Columbia for many years. "So much—in the U.S. especially," he wrote, "depends upon a man's outward bearing that this has great influence upon the students and upon the community at large."[20] Edman sought a man with "culture," someone whose demeanor and scholarship reflected taste and refinement. Butler respected Linda Miller's wishes and sent Enelow's name and qualifications to the committee, but he reminded committee members that they, not the donor, would make a final recommendation to the president and trustees.[21]

Gottheil would naturally have an important say in the appointment, and viewed the endowment as a major addition to his severely understaffed department. Learning while in Paris that Butler had appointed a committee, he asked its members to delay their first meeting until he returned to campus. His wife's illness kept him in France for most of the 1928/29 academic year, but Gottheil's written suggestions served as the committee's initial agenda. His influence waned when these suggestions failed to bear fruit. The committee then set out on its own to define the chair's domain and to find an occupant.

Columbia could locate a chair of Jewish history, literature, and institutions in any of a half dozen departments. Gottheil assumed the chair would go to Semitics, but it could also go to Religion, English and Comparative Literature, History, or Philosophy, or become the basis for a new department. Should the committee seek out the scholar and then determine the location, or should it define the scope and then locate the scholar? The vested interests of possible consultants impeded the committee's ability to find answers and progress in filling the chair came slowly.[22]

In fall 1928, Gottheil's influence was at its peak. Enelow and Gottheil had known each other since Enelow's arrival in New York more than 15 years earlier. Gottheil wrote that Enelow had been "treated in our home—not only as a spiritual guide, but as a friend of the closest character."[23] In 1923, Gottheil suggested to Stephen Wise, then recruiting faculty members for the Jewish Institute of Religion, that Enelow would be an excellent professor of theology. He called Enelow "the best instructed of all the Rabbis here."[24] But Gottheil was cool to Enelow's candidacy for the Miller chair. Perhaps he objected to Enelow's intellectual orientation, which emphasized the study and criticism of texts and the suffusion of knowledge with "soul." Gottheil had waited too many years for the introduction of Jewish history and *kulturgeschichte* at Columbia to lose this opportunity, and he likely resented learning about the Miller chair from Butler rather than from Enelow.[25] Gottheil took serious offense at any slight to a family member, and he noted that "Enelow, who, certainly, must know about Mrs. Gottheil's illness, has not sent a word of spiritual encouragement."[26] Finally, Gottheil had settled upon another candidate—Michael Saul Ginsberg.

That Gottheil would sponsor a holder of the Doctor of Letters from the University of Paris came as no surprise to those who knew him. A long-time Francophile, and recipient of the Legion of Honor, Gottheil had married into a prominent French family and usually spent his summers in his wife's native land. Ginsberg was born in 1899 in Moscow, and after holding two minor university posts and a professorship at the Institute of Jewish Sciences in Petrograd, migrated to France. By the time of his nomination, he had received the *diplome* from the École du Louvre and the D. Litt. from the Sorbonne. Ginsberg applied for a professorship at the Jewish Institute of Religion, but Wise turned him down in 1927.[27] He renewed his application in August of 1928, stating that since his last letter he had received his doctorate and published a book on the history of political relations between Rome and Judea.[28] Wise took his candidacy somewhat more seriously this time, and his right-hand man at the institute, George A. Kohut, interviewed Ginsberg in Europe in late September.

Ginsberg convinced Kohut that his interest in the Institute stemmed from more than his poor prospects in Europe—his field and his Judaism worked against him—and from his family's desperate financial plight: he had applied to only one other American institution, apparently Jewish Theological Seminary. But President Cyrus Adler and trustee chairman Louis Marshall treated Ginsberg "cavalierly" (Kohut's word). His inability to speak Hebrew was a major liability since the Institute offered instruction in that language. "I think he knows a little Bible," wrote Kohut, "but nothing more, so that this constitutes a serious drawback to his efficiency as a teacher of Jewish history."[29] Gottheil, who chaired the Institute's board of trustees, heartily endorsed Ginsberg.[30] But Wise concluded that "it would be a great mistake to take a man in the History Department or in any other department who is not a good Hebrew scholar—and Ginsberg is not."[31] Wise expressed his regrets to Ginsberg and held out little hope for an appointment for some time to come.[32]

Gottheil then suggested Ginsberg to the Miller chair committee. With the venerable Semitics professor abroad, and with no other member familiar with Jewish scholarship, the committee tried to compile an acceptable short list. Enelow's name was ranked prominently. Other candidates included: Herbert Danby, an English Hebraist and canon of Jerusalem's Anglican Cathedral of St. George; Bernard Drachman, an orthodox rabbi in New York City and former instructor at Jewish Theological Seminary; Louis Ginzberg, a member of the Jewish Theological Seminary faculty, and Julian Obermann, then of the Jewish Institute of Religion and later of Yale University.[33] Relying heavily on Gottheil's recommendation, Woodbridge informed Butler that Michael Ginsberg "appears to me the most promising of the men suggested."[34]

Butler informed Linda Miller of the committee's first choice. Two months earlier, Stephen Wise had questioned Ginsberg's experience, but Butler told Miller

that the committee believed he was "the best living scholar for the newly endowed chair," that "there is no other scholar of his standing," and that "he
would be a great ornament to this new chair and to American scholarship in his
chosen field." Butler suggested an initial three-year appointment so that "he
might have the opportunity to display his qualities and his personality to his
American colleagues."[35]

Miller cast a skeptical eye on the proposed appointment. She asked three men,
"two of whom are amongst the most distinguished and learned professors at the
Jewish Theological Seminary . . . and all of them say they had never heard of the
man."[36] She reminded Butler of his promise and asked him to list the other candidates. Butler, easily deducing that Hyman Enelow was the "third man,"
elicited a memorandum from Woodbridge certifying Michael Ginsberg's competence. He forwarded the memorandum, over his signature, to Miller along
with the remainder of the committee's short list, adding Hertz's name, which
the committee had omitted.[37] This presentation did not heighten Miller's enthusiasm. "My impression [of Ginsberg]," she wrote, "is that of a promising
young man who is just beginning his career." She had added an extra $50,000
to her endowment "so as to enable Columbia to secure the service of the most
prominent scholar available," she reminded Butler.

She then criticized the other names on the short list—Hertz: "I am surprised that his name should be mentioned in this connection"; Drachman: "I
can't imagine how any responsible person should drag his name into such a
matter. . . . I don't see how anybody could ever dream of him as a University professor"; and Obermann: "I believe his specialty is in Semitic Languages or Comparative Religion rather than in Jewish History and Literature."

Louis Ginzberg met Miller's definition of prominence, but she understood
"that he is opposed to liberal Judaism, and I, for one, would rather see a man
appointed whose sympathies would embrace all types of Judaism." Henry Danby
was not Jewish, and while most academic searches at this time of heightened anti-
Semitism excluded Jewish candidates, the nature of the subject matter and
Miller's wishes here dictated the appointment of a Jew. That left Hyman Enelow,
about whom "your committee could easily find out . . . if they cared to consider
his name."[38]

Miller's letter, with its astute characterizations, stung Butler and the committee. Perhaps she went too far in suggesting that the appointee be a Reform Jew.
Reform Jews, she believed, were the only Jews that tolerated all major forms of
Judaism, since Orthodox and Conservative Jews as a class opposed major por-
tions of Reform doctrine. But, in truth, the committee could not justify a full
professorship at a premium salary to an unproven scholar like Ginsberg. Butler
sent Miller's letter to the committee and tried to disabuse Miller "as to the un-
desirability of choosing a young and promising scholar." Only a junior scholar
"has a real chance to succeed and distinguish himself and the chair," he wrote.
"Scholars of middle or mature age rarely bear transplanting without losing their
productivity."[39]

Without Richard Gottheil to maintain enthusiasm for Ginsberg,[40] the committee meanwhile convinced itself that Ginsberg "is not a Hebrew scholar, but

rather a classicist" and dropped his name.[41] Linda Miller had exercised a de facto veto, even if she did not have the right of "presentation," and Butler and the committee had learned the cost of bad homework. Butler lost the battle, but not his conviction that a young scholar might best fill the chair. Other confrontations lay ahead, and he invoked this belief again a year later.

Jockeying for Position

Richard Gottheil's frustration was no match for Hyman Enelow's. Most interested parties assumed that Columbia would soon appoint Enelow. "I earnestly hope," George Kohut wrote to Enelow, "that having inspired this gift, it may become your privilege to become the first occupant of the newly created Chair."[42] When rumors spread that Columbia would offer the position to someone else, many observers assumed that Enelow had removed himself from consideration. Dr. Wise "regretted to learn from me that you would not be available for appointment," Kohut told Enelow. "He agreed that your retirement from the ministry would mean a very great loss to the American Jewish pulpit."[43]

Others advanced claims—or enlisted friends to act on their behalf—upon learning that Enelow's appointment was not automatic. Felix Warburg, benefactor of the new Hebrew University in Jerusalem, wrote: "My brother in Hamburg has asked me to state that, as far as he can judge, Mr. Julian Obermann, who is in this country and is a man of high character, is well qualified for this field."[44] Kohut and Wise feared that Columbia would take this opportunity to replace the aging Gottheil with the new chair's occupant. Gottheil, however, reassured them that he had known of the endowment for months but that Butler had pledged him to secrecy. Feeling free to back a candidate, Wise and Kohut settled on Louis Ginzberg.[45]

Rumors abounded. "I hear all sorts of wild rumors as to who is to have it," Wise wrote Gottheil, "Enelow himself or Ginzberg of the Seminary, but those rumors mean nothing."[46] "Just at present," he wrote a few weeks later, "the rumor is that either Buttenweiser or Mann will be called."[47] (Moses Buttenweiser was professor of Biblical Exegesis at Hebrew Union College. Jacob Mann was Hebrew Union's professor of Jewish History and Talmud.) Speculation persisted, but most observers concluded that Columbia would turn to Hyman Enelow after a diligent search.

The Emanu-El rabbi was in an awkward position. He cherished hopes of receiving the call but confusion about his candidacy and Gottheil's hostility hampered his ability to mount an indirect campaign. Some influential Jews thought Enelow's personality a major hindrance. Kohut wished he might be "more of a *Mensch.*"[48] Wise thought him "a good student, but he is a sour, embittered truly cynical person, and the fact is that he has not the power of teaching and interesting young people."[49]

Learning that the committee was still considering his name, Enelow attempted to appear before it. He asked Julius A. Bewer, a professor at Union Theological Seminary, to arrange for a committee member (perhaps the Seminary's president, Henry Sloane Coffin) to hear his endorsement of Jacob Mann's candidacy. Bewer declined, noting that Miller had just urged Enelow's candidacy.[50] Enelow then enlisted Lucius Littauer. Still devoted to the rabbi who induced him to endow Harry Wolfson's position, Littauer was "prepared to do everything under heaven to get the place for [Enelow]."[51] His physician told Wise that Littauer wanted the Jewish Institute of Religion head to speak to the committee on Enelow's behalf. "The Institute," the emissary promised, "would be the beneficiary if I would do what I could." Wise said he declined the offer because Enelow "is not a great and outstanding scholar of Jewish civilization" and "lacks altogether the power of conveying, in an attractive way, the things he knows."[52]

Wise, and almost everyone else, still assumed that Enelow would ultimately receive the appointment. He asked Gottheil, as a last-ditch maneuver, whether he could approach Butler or Woodbridge "about some real and outstanding personality, such as [Ismar] Elbogen [of the *Hochschule für die Wissenschaft des Judentums* in Berlin] or, as I believe [Mordecai] Kaplan." Kaplan, founder of the Reconstructionist movement, taught at Jewish Theological Seminary. Wise twice entreated him to join the Jewish Institute of Religion faculty and actually succeeded on the second occasion only to learn that Kaplan had changed his mind. "Kaplan is not a Spinoza," Wise concluded, "but he is a Jewish teacher and a gentleman, and Enelow is one of these in a limited degree."[53] Gottheil authorized Wise to speak for him about Kaplan, but Wise hesitated, reasoning that since the chair appeared within Enelow's grasp, there was virtue in silence.[54]

When a Columbia delegation unexpectedly called upon Wise a few days later, he surveyed some possible candidates: Umberto Cassuto of Florence, "a fine representative of the Sephardic side of Jewish life"; Ismar Elbogen, "a good Hebrew scholar and a fine person"; Cecil Roth; and Mordecai Kaplan, "a sound scholar [with] a great gift for teaching and . . . a larger body of disciples than almost any Jew I know in this country." Wise, after learning that "the donor's wishes . . . were by no means binding," said about Enelow: "I merely raised the question that may be raised regarding him [presumably his personality]." Wise and other consultants apparently persuaded the committee to reject Enelow, but when committee members went further afield, they soon concluded that every name precipitated controversy.[55]

A Time of Assessment

Columbia's 1928/29 intersession came at an opportune moment. Needing to mount a full-scale search, committee members used the hiatus to evaluate potential candidates and to assess the academic and communal pressures facing them. Eliminating the Enelow and Ginsberg candidacies did little to define the scope of the chair—Jewish "history, literature, and institutions" encompassed an enormous amount of intellectual territory. From the academic sidelines, members of the Menorah movement, earnest if ineffective advocates of Jewish studies in universities, urged the committee to identify someone with the breadth that the chair's title suggested. Do not, urged Menorah's Herbert Solow, appoint a mere compiler and textual commentator. A century earlier, *Wissenschaft des Judentums* marked a significant intellectual milestone, but, Solow noted, by the 1920s, "the rationalistic, anti-medieval, assimilationist, reformist theological interests of [the] founders have become permanent restrictions on the thought of all their followers." A scholar in the *Wissenschaft* tradition might produce a catalogue or a compendium—never an intellectual synthesis—and would appeal to no one who defined history to include social and economic trends.[56]

Irwin Edman's presence on the committee assured the representation of this viewpoint. A frequent contributor to *Menorah Journal,* his emphasis on gentility and general education resonated with Menorah's stance. The committee concluded that the occupant should devote attention both to Jews and Judaism. This tendency, already present when the committee considered Michael Ginsberg's candidacy, came to the fore in the ensuing months. The sentiment arose from eclectic sources, including Gottheil's interest in *kulturgeschichte,* Menorah's ideology, and the presence on the committee of non-Jewish historians.

But would such an appointment please Linda Miller? Miller continued to express no interest in Jewish "peoplehood." Some, without citing Enelow by name, argued that Columbia must refrain from appointing a rabbi, since university scientific traditions placed a clergyman in an untenable situation. But Miller hoped the chair's occupant "would try to reach the student body along spiritual lines."[57] Some urged the committee to ignore the personal factional beliefs of any candidate, but Miller constantly pressed for a Reform Jew. "I personally prefer a scholar belonging to the liberal school," she frequently reminded Butler, since he "would be more likely to do justice to the various aspects of Jewish life." And while some urged that a young scholar receive the appointment since it would permit him to develop within a university environment, Miller had other ideas. At every turn, the committee confronted the desires of the benefactress. With no available member expert in Jewish history, literature, and institutions, and after the awkward encounter with Miller over Michael Ginsberg, the committee concluded that it must consider her wishes, but the effort failed.

During intensive deliberations in February of 1929, the committee concluded that Louis Ginzberg, professor of Talmud at Jewish Theological Seminary, merited the call. A preeminent Judaica scholar whose *Legends of the Jews* had received general acclaim, Ginzberg probably *believed* in little, save the importance of modern Jewish scholarship. However, he *observed* enough of Jewish tradition and felt enough empathy to work out his ambivalences within a Jewish framework.[58] He opposed Reform Judaism and Reconstructionism because he believed that significant changes in Jewish tradition would not lead to a major "return to religion" among American Jews and might further undermine Jewish religiosity. These views compounded the committee's difficulties.

Ginzberg, an established, imaginative scholar with an international reputation, was an excellent candidate, and Gottheil remained silent on the Katz incident. Knowing that Miller would object to a permanent appointment for Ginzberg, the committee recommended that Columbia use the endowment "to invite distinguished scholars here from time to time to lend their prestige to the enterprise and to devote a portion of the income from the fund to fellowships to encourage study and research on the part of younger men." It recommended Ginzberg's appointment as visiting lecturer for the 1929/30 academic year.

The committee recommended the religion department for the chair's home and the consideration of Ralph Marcus and Henry Rosenthal for fellowships.[59] Rosenthal, who had studied at Columbia, continued his education at Jewish Theological Seminary and became a rabbi, mainly because academic Judaica positions were scarce.[60] Butler sent the committee report to Miller, gave instructions to open negotiations with Ginzberg, and left for his annual vacation believing that he had solved a knotty problem.[61]

Dean Woodbridge had not contacted Ginzberg when Miller's reply arrived. While reiterating her preference for a Reform scholar, she took the university to task primarily for changing the endowment's terms unilaterally through the appointment of visiting professors. She reminded Butler about his promise "to secure the most eminent scholar available for this chair" and asked that their mutually agreed upon plan be executed.[62] Woodbridge, however, urged the Columbia president to move cautiously given the unprecedented nature of the appointment and "a difference of opinion regarding emphasis" among the interested parties. Universal recognition of Ginzberg's scholarship dictated his call, while its temporary nature indicated "that the University was not committed to an orthodox as over a liberal position." In fact, Woodbridge revealed, Miller's allegiance to the "liberal school" and the committee's desire not to prejudice its interests were strong reasons for its failure to recommend Ginzberg for permanent appointment.[63]

Several considerations prompted Butler to back his committee. First, the Columbia president had probably become exasperated with a benefactress who constantly refused attempts at accommodation. In addition, Butler evinced concern that considerations of scholarly competence had become entangled in sectarian rivalries within the Jewish community. Whereas Woodbridge viewed the endowment as "the really first great opportunity to give to Jewish studies the university significance they ought to have," Miller gave high priority to the spiritual inspiration of students. The result of Columbia's difficulty in "finding a man who will look at the development of the subject as a university enterprise as distinct from a sectarian one" was a resort to a solution all knew to be "makeshift."[64] Anticipating Ginzberg's unacceptability in Miller's eyes, the committee declined to recommend his permanent appointment.

To cover all bases, the committee sent Irwin Edman to interview Linda Miller's other Reform candidate, Jacob Mann of Hebrew Union College. Initially attracted by the prospect of moving to an institution where his scholarship would be appreciated, Mann's conversation with Edman rapidly disenchanted him. "Edman talked of a chair of Jewish culture," he recounted, "requiring the occupant to be a sort of jack of all trades who, in addition to advising graduate students on all sorts of Jewish culture (from Biblical times to 1929!) is also to give a three-hour per week course to undergraduates (Jewish and Gentile), which means a most elementary course on Judaism to people with no previous knowledge whatever of Jewish studies, not being even familiar with the Hebrew alphabet." Edman and Mann conceived of the chair in opposing terms: the former saw it as important for the propagation and advancement of culture, the latter for the advancement of scholarship. The interview did not change the committee's resolve.[65]

Butler approved negotiations for Ginzberg's temporary appointment, but a deal was never struck.[66] Indeed, there is no evidence that the committee contacted Ginzberg, who was on sabbatical in Palestine for the 1928/29 academic year. The committee probably failed to implement its earlier decision because just at this time its members became aware of a candidate who might merit permanent appointment. This candidate did not entail "local difficulties" and might prove more attractive to Linda Miller. The committee again turned to the European Jewish scholarly community.[67]

Ismar Elbogen

The *Hochschule für die Wissenschaft des Judentums* (opened in 1872) and located near the University of Berlin, was a response to, and benefitted from, the refusal of nineteenth-century German universities to welcome Jewish learning. In the summer of 1929, however, this major center for European Jewish scholarship faced an anxious future. One faculty member, Julius Guttmann, a historian of philosophy, accepted a visiting professorship at Hebrew Union College and eventually went to The Hebrew University in Jerusalem. Two colleagues departed soon after: Chanoch Albeck to Hebrew University in Jerusalem and Chaim Torczyner to the Jewish Institute of Religion, leaving Ismar Elbogen, professor of Jewish history and literature, among the small remaining senior staff.[68]

The appointment of Elbogen, a Reform Jew and a recognized senior scholar, Woodbridge and the committee concluded, "would be more agreeable to the donor than the appointment of anyone here with the exception of Rabbi Enelow whom the committee does not feel justified in recommending."[69] Elbogen, who had garnered considerable respect from his American colleagues while a visiting lecturer at the Jewish Institute of Religion, received strong testimonials from Wise and George Foot Moore.[70] Only Menorah members dissented from his candidacy. They acknowledged Elbogen's erudition but regarded him as "a typical product of the Germanic school of Jewish scholars, with no more of a humanistic approach, no more broadness of vision or depth of thought than any of a dozen competent textual scholars now professing in seminaries in Cincinnati, New York, London and Breslau." Calling Elbogen "an orthodox, theological-minded and dull scholar," the Menorah faction concluded that he would have few students and little general influence.[71]

The committee, decidedly rejecting these criticisms, recommended a permanent appointment at a premium salary, but Butler suggested an initial three-year term "with appropriate explanation that this is not an unusual method in the case of men from other institutions."[72] James Gutmann, a young Columbia philosophy professor, extended a "feeler" to Elbogen, and the committee asked Irwin Edman to conduct more extensive negotiations while in Europe for the summer.[73] Edman sent Columbia authorities guardedly optimistic reports. Elbogen found New York's research facilities tempting.[74] But he—like Paul Haupt 40 years earlier—emphasized salary and pension. Edman was authorized to offer a $7,500 salary, but when Elbogen requested $10,000 and a pension comparable to his German entitlement, Butler met the salary request and offered him a removal allowance.[75] He added: "It is the well-established tradition of Columbia University to permit none of its distinguished servants to suffer if old age or disability should overtake them."[76]

The detailed nature of the negotiations gave committee members cause for optimism. But on September 19, 1929, just before he received Butler's final offer, Elbogen cabled that he could not accept the call, and receipt of Butler's letter did not change his mind.[77] The Berlin Jewish community, students, and colleagues pressured Elbogen to remain at the *Hochschule*. Alluding to faculty attrition, he wrote, "the Trustees have urged me and placed the responsibility of the continuance of the college upon my shoulders."[78] Elbogen also declined offers of temporary appointments.[79] Contemporaries understood Elbogen's resolve to remain at the *Hochschule*.[80] No one envisioned that he would live out his years on Morningside Heights, a refugee from Nazism, with joint appointments at Hebrew Union College, the Jewish Institute of Religion, Jewish Theological Seminary, and Dropsie College.[81]

Butler thereafter communicated with Linda Miller on an *ex post facto* basis. Only after receiving Elbogen's cable declining the offer did he inform her that Columbia had embarked upon serious negotiations and that all hoped for a favorable reply. Miller responded that she had followed the negotiations through the newspapers and only regretted "that the committee seemed to find it impossible to find an American who, I think might have reached the student body in a spiritual way in addition to the pursuits of scholarly research." By the fall of 1929, Linda Miller was relegated to an insignificant role in the selection process. Her candidate out of the running, she merely acknowledged Butler's letters.[82]

While pondering the Columbia offer, Ismar Elbogen travelled to St. Moritz. There he encountered David S. Blondheim, professor of romance philology at Johns Hopkins. Elbogen said that he was still considering the offer but asked whether he could suggest Blondheim's name should he decline Columbia's invitation.[83] Blondheim, taken aback, replied in the affirmative, though he urged Elbogen to accept the call. A specialist in medieval Judeo-Romance dialects, Blondheim had studied at Johns Hopkins and later at the École des Hautes Études in Paris. He taught first at the University of Illinois and then at Johns Hopkins.

Blondheim's work differed from the research of most contemporaries. His research on the connections between certain Judeo-Romance texts and the earliest Latin Bible translation was reminiscent of Harry Wolfson's efforts to move between Jewish and non-Jewish scholarship, but his analyses of Old French glosses on Rashi's Talmudic commentaries were virtually unparalleled in secular institutions. Blondheim viewed an opportunity to teach a graduate course on French literary criticism at the University of Illinois as a burden, not an opportunity. The subject was "about as far from the one I am chiefly concerned with as anything could be." On the whole, however, the Illinois position initially satisfied him, and he turned down an assistant professorship at the University of California when Illinois met the California offer. Urbana was closer to the east, he noted, and Illinois had superior research facilities.[84] But Blondheim, unable to live comfortably as a Jew in Urbana, accepted a 1917 call from Johns Hopkins that brought him closer to the "Jewish center."[85] At Johns Hopkins, promotions and salary increases came more slowly than expected, and after a few research trips to Europe, Baltimore appeared to be "an abominable provincial town."[86] Europe's sophistication intoxicated other American scholars, but few colleagues readjusted so poorly to America.

Personal factors compounded matters. In the mid-1920s, Blondheim divorced his Orthodox wife and began an affair in Europe with Eleanor Dulles, sister of John Foster and Allen Dulles.[87] Conduct acceptable in Europe—Blondheim and his mistress lived together openly in Paris for a year—was condemned in America. The couple met covertly on weekends after their return to the U.S.[88]

Elbogen's proposition came as an attractive surprise to Blondheim. Blondheim believed that Edman was the committee's only Jewish member and was unsympathetic to his type of research.[89] George Kohut, an old acquaintance, told Blondheim that Gottheil sat on the committee. Kohut mounted an elaborate campaign on Blondheim's behalf and easily enlisted Wise.[90] Gottheil, finally back at his post, was more difficult—and not only because his relationship with Kohut had its testy side.[91] The Columbia professor thought of Blondheim as "an accomplished writer on subjects dealing with Jewish life in past and present," primarily from a linguistic point of view, not as a historian.[92] Blondheim's supporters never could overcome this crucial determination.

For Gottheil, and for the committee, the distinction between literary and historical approaches had become decisive. The heterogeneous composition of the committee—deans, theologians, Jewish faculty members, and disciplinary representatives—reflected the original, vague mandate to include Jewish history, literature, and institutions; but between the fall of 1928 and the fall of 1929, the committee made progress in defining the chair's scope, credentials suitable for its occupant, and its departmental location.

Committee members from the outset preferred a cultivated, engaging scholar who lacked strong feelings on Zionism. Michael Ginsberg's candidacy led them to comprehend the wishes of the chair's donor. Hyman Enelow's candidacy reinforced their caution on questions of personality and the eligibility of a rabbi, while Jacob Mann's candidacy prompted them to decide against a philologist or a textual critic. Consideration of Louis Ginzberg led committee members to prefer scholars who lacked strong ties to Orthodoxy or Conservatism. Ismar

Elbogen's candidacy—he would update Graetz's history of the Jews—heightened interest in historians, preferably with breadth. Along the way, the members came to prefer a European—to avoid domestic difficulties—with foreign training, though it is unclear whether committee members believed this education enhanced the candidate's scholarship or cultivation. The committee arrived at a consensus under the counsel of Gottheil—and of the historian Salo Baron from the Jewish Institute of Religion.

Baron on History

> Goddess, if I began at the beginning,
> If there were time to detail our tribulations,
> Evening would fall on Olympus before I had
> finished. . . .
>
> Achates, is there a place
> Left in the world not full of our miseries?[93]
>
> —Aeneas

Salo (Shalom) Wittmayer Baron was born in Tarnow, located in Galicia, in 1895, and came to Vienna during World War I. He earned doctorates in philosophy (1917), political science (1922), and law (1923) from the University of Vienna, and was ordained at the Jewish Theological Seminary of Vienna in 1920. Baron taught at the Jewish Teachers College (*Jüdisches Pädagogium*) in Vienna until 1926.[94] Stephen Wise took interest in Baron in 1925 and invited him to teach at the Jewish Institute of Religion on a "trial" basis.[95] The Institute's dean, Harry Slonimsky, did not at first favor Baron's retention since "he thinks we might get a bigger and stronger man," but Baron's teaching ability and personality impressed Wise. "He is not a genius," Wise noted, "but in some ways he is better than a genius, for he is solid, and substantial, and dependable, and, the Lord be praised, untemperamental."[96] Kohut shared Wise's enthusiasm and called Baron "a man of uncommon ability, not only in the field of learning, but in practical affairs as well." Baron, Kohut predicted, "will be heard of as a leader in many directions, and I am indeed proud of the fact of having persuaded our dear and lamented friend, Chajes, to release him for service in America."[97]

Baron came off probation within a year, and Kohut held out his productivity as a model for other J.I.R. faculty members: "[Baron] is writing many books and has nevertheless time to write minor articles of no mean importance, while all the others are conspicuous by their quiescence," he noted. "All of them have literary gifts, and if they cultivated the art of expression in public print it would go far toward stimulating interest in our work."[98] In 1928, Baron declined a call to the chair in modern history at the Breslau seminary, a chair that Heinrich Graetz once occupied.[99]

During the 1920s, Richard Gottheil secured inclusion of a course on Judaism among Columbia's offerings, to be taught in turn by scholars of different theological leanings. He retained Baron—then at J.I.R.—to teach the course, and the young historian established a reputation for excellent teaching. Baron's life's work was a multi-volume social and economic history of the Jews, but he also demonstrated knowledge of rabbinic literature and told the committee of his interest in the interaction between Persian and Hebrew culture.[100]

Baron apparently met with the committee to discuss Jewish history during the negotiations with Elbogen, a meeting that also permitted the committee to evaluate Baron if the Elbogen talks collapsed. We know little about the encounter save that Baron argued—apparently persuasively—that, with Wolfson at Harvard, university-based Jewish learning next needed a historian, located in a history department. But within weeks of this meeting, Baron published articles on "Research in Jewish History" and "The Study of Jewish History" that resembled criticisms offered by other contemporary Jewish historians and that suggest the tone and substance of his meeting with the committee. The articles examined American university precedents in the field of Jewish history, criticisms of scholarship in that field, and the congruence of university based Jewish history and the "New History," the predominant historical outlook in American universities.

In one sense, "Jewish history" was frequently taught in courses on ancient history or in connection with the Bible, but ancient history courses primarily surveyed the powerful neighbors of the Jews. Jewish history was a prolegomenon to the study of Christianity in university Bible courses, at least until publication of George Foot Moore's *Judaism*, and post-Biblical Jewish history remained largely unstudied even after the book's appearance. Semitists occasionally attempted to introduce Jewish history courses, just as some nineteenth-century classicists supplemented linguistic work with Greek and Roman history courses.[101] But university-based Jewish history courses required more resources and greater specialization than Semitists commanded. If history departments had been more hospitable to Jews—who were most likely to be interested and qualified to offer Jewish history—the appointees might have emulated the Jewish Semitists who neglected pertinent Jewish questions. Scholarly attention to Jewish history remained low, a condition the Miller endowment could redress.[102]

Including Jewish history in the university's subject pantheon, Baron probably told the committee, might reduce or eliminate partisanship, parochialism, pedantry, and preservationism or antiquarianism. Jewish interest in history arose in the nineteenth century, historiographies often noted, along with Jewish emancipation. Jews traditionally extolled their indifference to history and invidiously compared Gentile "activity" to their observance of timeless commandments. Jewish participation in general cultural life after emancipation awakened an interest in a more sophisticated understanding of the past. Practitioners of *Wissenschaft des Judentums,* such as Isaac Martin Jost and Leopold Zunz, were motivated by respect for a bygone era, while filiopietism inspired Heinrich Graetz.[103]

Subsequent generations of historians acknowledged the extraordinary grasp of disparate types of literature that Graetz displayed in his history of the Jews but criticized his subjectivity, especially his anti-Catholicism, ultra-rationalism, and bias against East European Jewry. "All persons who have favored the Jews inevitably figure as saints and heroes," Cecil Roth noted, "while whoever opposed or oppressed them automatically become ruffians and hypocrites."[104] Despite its faults and obsolescence, no one superseded the Graetz synthesis until Baron began publishing his opus. Graetz's partisanship probably appealed to assimilated German and American Jews who faced increased anti-Semitism and an influx of East European coreligionists.[105]

The American Jewish Historical Society spurred the study of American Jewish history—American Jews did not venture into other aspects of Jewish history for several decades—but critics charged that the Society, too, harbored partisanship. One detractor, for example, held the Society responsible for "a tendency to write American Jewish history in order to plead the Jews' case as citizens and human beings"—a tactic that failed to forestall the rise in anti-Semitism, or to improve the quality of scholarship.[106]

Parochialism, the second shortcoming of non-university based Jewish history, implied the sacrifice of contextual and comparative elements. "Our stock Histories are too much self-centered," a critic wrote. "We are not shown what our ancestors did learn from the rest of mankind, and what they did return, stamped with the genius of our race. For, unique as our History is, we are still a people made up of human beings, to whom nothing human is strange."[107] Some historians chastised Graetz's disciples for emphasizing minuscule events that pertained to German Jewry while ignoring important questions about other Jews that their master raised.[108] Methodologies, Baron and other advocates of university inclusion argued, also had to be universal, and categories that applied to other groups must explain Jewish motivations and actions. "God's will" was an unacceptable explanation for an event.[109] Within the university, Jewish scholarship suffered not from parochialism but from extreme universalism. Advocates of university-based Jewish scholarship believed universalism, in reasonable doses, was a salutary corrective to the writings of historians of the Jews who worked in other settings.

Baron disagreed with scholars who insisted that mastery of the Talmud was the inescapable prerequisite for all historical scholarship that involved Jews. Extant methodologies, not command of rabbinical texts, should determine the canons of historical Jewish scholarship.[110] Baron agreed with Jewish Theological Seminary bibliographer Alexander Marx that the Talmudic emphasis resulted from a need to insert a positive theme into the long, dreary period of Jewish history that began with the fall of the Second Temple. Historians could not employ Jewish political history as a viable organizational theme and the period was otherwise noted for the monotonous recitation of Jewish sufferings and martyrdoms. Marx employed the term "literary history" to denote the analysis of Jewish spiritual activity.[111] Cecil Roth termed it "the irreparable disaster of becoming almost a branch of theology."[112] Resulting historical scholarship neglected contextual elements and even neglected to ask the correct questions of the assembled data.

Critics suggested that socio-economic analysis replace the literary-theological emphasis. "The description of the ordinary life of the people, their legal status and their economic activities will not only relieve the dreary picture of the periodically recurring persecutions, but also help to explain the causes of these persecutions and contribute towards a better understanding of the course of events."[113] As long as aphorisms such as "history is past politics, and politics present history" determined scholarly agendas, the history of a people in diaspora was a poor candidate for university inclusion. But the eclipse of political history and a broadened conception of Jewish history facilitated entry. The committee had to identify an individual with a broad understanding of social and economic history, a command of Jewish source material—documenting the socio-economic history of a people required examination of more than the obvious sources—and the ability to employ the theoretical and methodological advances made since the emergence of *Wissenschaft des Judentums.*

Critics frequently denounced historians of the Jews for pedantry: finding a "broad" scholar would be difficult. Scholars, noted Cecil Roth, devoted "oceans of ink" to "the exact sequence and habitat of the various medieval German rabbis."[114] Historians of American Jewry were also charged with repetitiveness, pedantry, and myopia: "They were assiduous in the collection of such facts as would determine the first occurrence of this or that Jewish event or the initial appearance of a Jew in a certain locale, but they seemed incapable of doing more than that. They were interested in results, not causes or trends."[115] Historians, another critic wrote, "have now proceeded far enough in the prosecution of their researches to pause and objectively to contemplate the body of facts which they have accumulated thus far." Collection, preservation, and publication inadequately described the historian's domain. A "philosophy of Jewish history" giving due weight to material, as opposed to spiritual, motivation was within reach.[116]

Some observers questioned whether extant sources permitted the scholars to generalize. These observers called for examination of non-Jewish sources: documents and deeds, chronicles, letters, inscriptions, and references in non-Jewish literature and legislation. This necessary and painstaking process, Baron cautioned, was not an excuse to forego tentative scholarly syntheses.[117] Broader goals and strategies determine tactics, critics insisted, not the other way around. Jewish history, when studied at all, suffered from filiopietism, a tendency to chronicle rather than to interpret, lack of a political dimension, and a neglect of source material and methodology.[118] Its failure to conform to Christian or western periodization pointed to the subject's inability to draw upon general history or contribute to "general" historical scholarship.

Salo Baron indicted the prevalent lachrymose conception of Jewish history, that is, as "a history of scholars and persecutions (Gelehrten- und Leidensgeschichte)."[119] An emphasis upon great individuals, events, texts, and sufferings, and a myopic idealism flawed the historical study of Jews. Baron criticized the tendency in the *Wissenschaft des Judentums* movement to see "in Jewish history the gradual progression of the Jewish religious or national spirit in its various vicissitudes and adjustments to the changing environments," a secularized equivalent to the earlier theocratic attribution of the Jewish destiny to "God's will."[120] Lacking a university base, he asserted, the field still suffered from the dominance of theologians and philologists rather than trained historians.[121] The "official" historical outlook was a form of social control—a Jewish scholarly equivalent to the "bloody shirt" that traditional Jewish communal leadership tirelessly invoked. Academization of Jewish history would result in a new periodization scheme, based upon general history, to replace "the otherwise noteworthy Krochmal-Graetzian scheme of the successive cycles of growth and decay in Jewish history."[122] Locating the subject in a university would also allow for historical explanation based upon universal categories. "There is a growing feeling that the historical explanations of the Jewish past must not fundamentally deviate from the general patterns of history which we accept for mankind at large or for any other particular national group," Baron wrote.[123] University access, finally, would rectify the imbalance between sociological and religious emphases in historical analysis. "It is consequently but the unavoidable and intrinsically justified adaptation of the general method of sociological interpretation to the peculiar problems of Jewish history," Baron noted, "when the element of religious experience is given its due share within the totality of the social forces."[124] Baron thus emphasized general historical—rather than uniquely Jewish—methodologies.[125] He sought out Jewish topics with general implications—not issues deemed of intrinsic worth because they were "Jewish" or general issues that had possible Jewish implications.[126]

What did Columbia see, intellectually, in Jewish history? As Baron addressed the search committee, Carlton J. H. Hayes, chairman of the history department, also wrote about "landmarks" in the development of historical scholarship during the previous quarter century. Hayes cited the relative decline in the study of political history and the "rising vogue of *Kulturgeschichte*," the importance of archaeological excavations for understanding ancient history and ancient religion, and "the effort to reconcile the science of historical investigation with the art of presenting its results."[127] Hayes continued, "In the realm of material culture, economic factors in man's past provide nowadays the topics for innumerable monographs and the central theme for many a great coöperative publication."[128]

By 1928, "the New History," which accorded social, economic, and religious activities equal status with political behavior, stressed the contextual and expressed affinity with the social sciences, had been ascendant for almost two decades.[129] A stateless people that nonetheless had an important history in the Common Era, the Jews were now ripe for historical investigation. By applying new concepts and techniques to Jewish history, a broadly trained historian could reformulate old subjects for other historians while refuting the contention that mastery of the sacred corpus took precedence over methodological sophistication. When he assumed his Columbia post, Baron offered a lecture series on "the interrelation of social and religious forces, as exemplified in the long historic evolution of the Jewish people"—a Jewish topic with universal implications, not a general topic with Jewish implications, or a topic of supposedly intrinsic Jewish worth.[130] This outlook governed his next half century of scholarship.

Dénouement

Baron's ideas were sympathetically received by the committee's historians, especially Westerman, who needed a better knowledge of Jewish history to conduct his own research on the ancient world. With Elbogen out of the picture, the committee settled the question of scope and tried to answer a single question: was David Blondheim a historian? Kohut concluded that Gottheil knew nothing of Blondheim's works save for their titles, and slowly changed Gottheil's conviction that Blondheim was primarily a philologist.[131] Kohut then told Edman that American and foreign Judaica scholars preferred Blondheim's candidacy because of his distinguished scholarship (specifically the Rashi volume), his teaching experience, and his cultivation.[132] Blondheim's chances further improved when Elbogen informed Edman of his enthusiastic support.[133] Butler's request for immediate action once the Elbogen correspondence ended led the committee to send Edman and Herbert Schneider to Baltimore to interview Blondheim.[134]

The meeting went well, but Blondheim's referees destroyed his chances. The committee concluded that Blondheim's true expertise lay in medieval philology, although it recognized his interest in Jewish history. Whether the committee knew of Blondheim's divorce and love affair is not clear. But given the importance that key committee members attributed to personal traits, these "shortcomings" would have been fatal to his candidacy.[135] The news of the committee's decision shocked Blondheim, and the disappointment increased the frustrations in his tortured life—frustrations that culminated in his suicide in 1934.[136]

In retrospect, it appears that Salo Baron had always been the most available and suitable man for the Miller chair.[137] In fact, one not cognizant of the chair's history might assume that Linda Miller endowed it with him—not Enelow—in mind. The committee, after an exhaustive, two-continent search, reported that it chose Baron over Blondheim "because of his constant identification with Jewish studies and also because of his more historical and philosophical interests."[138]

Baron's youth was his major liability because Linda Miller still envisioned appointment of a mature scholar. Butler had conceded the point in the case of Michael Ginsberg but remained firm in Baron's case. Miller also asked about Baron's partisanship. "I do hope he will pay deference to my wishes on the subject of the so-called ethnic Jew," she wrote. "Of course Zionism is dead," she continued, but the "ethnic Jew" doctrine still endangered Judaism as a spiritual force.[139] Butler reassured her "that Dr. Baron is without any partisanship in reference to the matters which he will have to undertake to present" and that Baron impressed him academically and personally when they met.[140]

Baron has recounted his negotiations with Butler. Impressed that Butler had a feel for Jewish learning, Baron expressed two concerns—first that he have some graduate students, second, that Columbia assign the chair to the history department. He believed that Jewish history could not yet be taught on the graduate

level at a secular university since qualified students enrolled only in Jewish teachers colleges or in seminaries. The quality of students enrolled in his Columbia
extension course further discouraged him. Baron added that his students at the
Jewish Institute of Religion put his lectures to immediate use—often in their
next Friday night sermons.[141] Neither Butler nor the committee could assuage
him completely on this point. For these and financial reasons, Baron continued
to teach at the Institute for a number of years after his Columbia appointment.
But upon his arrival at Columbia, he found that his well-attended classes
included many students who took his courses for general, rather than specialized purposes.

Agreeing that the chair belonged in the history department, Butler and
Hayes secured the department's assent. Butler asked Baron to offer an undergraduate course, not for the spiritual edification of students as Linda Miller
would have wanted, but "with a view of interesting them in this general field of
study and so leading them forward, at least in some number, to become scholars in the branches of knowledge which will be under your direction."[142] Baron
received a $7,500 salary, not as much as Columbia offered Elbogen but more
than he received at the Jewish Institute of Religion.[143] George Kohut called the
appointment "providential."[144] Rabbi Arthur Hertzberg years later noted that
Baron was the first member of a history department at an American university
to teach Jewish history. He concluded that "the many such chairs that now
exist owe much to his example, and a substantial number of his former students
are among their occupants."[145] The true significance of the Nathan Miller chair
lies in Columbia's survey of the field of Jewish learning and its definition of
work of university quality and spirit. Jewish studies in secular universities could
thenceforth transcend philological and archaeological investigations and embark upon *kulturgeschichte*—to use Richard Gottheil's term. The endowment
breathed life into university-based Jewish learning at a time when universities
kept other chairs vacant after their occupants departed from the scene. Salo
Baron's appointment assured the survival of Jewish studies in universities and
opened new directions for research.

Conclusion

The history of Jewish scholarship in American colleges and universities mir-
rors thinking about modern Jewish history. Jewish history is often discussed in
dualistic terms—revolving around such dichotomies as universalism and particularism, tradition and modernity, the individual and the Jewish community, and
ethnicity and religion. Similar dichotomies characterize discussions of Jewish
learning: universal and particular, seminaries (including *yeshivot*) and university
(as centers of learning), piety and professionalization (as motivating forces), and
theological and "scientific" (as modes of interpreting the Jewish experience).
Jewish historical writing contains many titles that begin with the preposition
"from," suggesting a linear progression along an important axis, and progress to

a "to." Jewish emancipation, which brought rapid, visible changes to European Jewry, may explain the emphasis upon linear, dualistic analyses. The realities of Jewish life and the history of Jewish learning are more subtle. The creation of new institutions and norms did not immediately doom old structures, indeed, there were historical and scholarly Jewish counter-reformations. And individual Jews and Jewish scholars are subject to many "dualisms" at once, each demanding resolution, yet all interdependent.

Salo Baron's availability and suitability stemmed from his ability to straddle dualisms. Baron studied and taught in both universities and seminaries; communicated with academic and communal audiences; and successfully related Jewish history to general themes, while focusing on Jews and Judaism. Between 1930 and 1970—a period in which pluralism increasingly dominated American social thought—Jewish learning subfields and practitioners were most likely to gain access to universities when they displayed the ability to effect similar balances.

VIII

TRAGEDY, TRIUMPH, AND JEWISH SCHOLARSHIP: POST-WAR CURRICULAR DEVELOPMENTS

The preceding chapters examined the careers of individual scholars and the fate of Jewish learning at specific institutions—an appropriate strategy given the field's small size through the 1920s and the resonating significance of practitioners and institutions. Chapters 8 and 9, in contrast, examine the entire field of Jewish learning through the 1960s. Frozen in place for a generation, the field took on new life in post-World War II universities, then grew and flourished.[1] This chapter examines changes in the mosaic of courses that made up the Judaica curriculum from 1923 through 1968; chapter 9 examines the dimensions and direction of institutional growth and change.

"Heinrich Heine," wrote Ismar Elbogen after his migration to the United States, "aptly said that the Jew had a portable fatherland. Wherever the Jew migrated he carried with him his spiritual heritage."[2] Heine's aphorism is true, but when Jews carried their ancestral culture from one land of exile to the next, they took more than they actually used. Books praised by some Jews as works of piety, scholarship, and intellect might be forgotten by others, consulted infrequently by specialists, or forbidden by rabbinic authorities. Sheer volume and contradictions within the corpus conspired against making all past works obligatory.

What, then, were the principles of choice? What language ought to be taught? What texts—if any—would make up Jewish high culture and school culture? How much time and effort should Jews devote to Jewish subjects; how much to the vernacular culture of host populations? The traditional Jewish community debated the propriety of, and the relative emphasis to be given to, specific subjects—the relative importance of *Zohar*, philosophy, and Talmud, for example.[3] Advocates of Jewish emancipation proposed curricula that promoted social integration. Naphtali Herz Wessely's *Divrei Shalom v'Emet*, for example, distinguished between God's Law and *Torat haAdam* ("human knowledge" or secular studies) and argued that a knowledge of *Torah* required a strong general education.

Jews established priorities not only when addressing the education of their young but also when they encountered American higher education. The academic curriculum is rarely invented from a coherent, rational plan. Instead, it is usually a compromise among social and cultural notions of significance and value that compete for primacy in transmitting knowledge to the next generation. The result, especially in the humanities curriculum, is "one of those places where we have told ourselves who we are."[4]

The Judaica curriculum of American higher education *appeared* to emerge opportunistically. Serendipity often affected the order of subject entrance at a given institution, and entrance of one field did not imply automatic access for others. The local academic culture, the availability of departmental "lines," and the interests, capacities, and prejudices of current faculty members affected the evolution of Jewish learning on each campus, as did the concerns of donors, development officers, and university administrators. Salo Baron's and Harry Wolfson's appointments appeared to bring Jewish history and philosophy to Columbia and Harvard, respectively, not as responses to carefully laid plans, but almost as random events.

The appearance of randomness was equally characteristic of the charismatic and of many less momentous appointments. Before 1970, few institutions had more than one or two Judaica faculty members—and therefore more than one or two subjects—at a time. Growth might occur when a research specialist became a teaching generalist—a competent, interested American historian would initiate a course in American Jewish history, or an expert in a Hebrew-based subject might teach basic modern Hebrew. A department that lacked, but desired, a Judaic presence might invite a visiting senior faculty member—often an Israeli—to fill the vacuum temporarily. The pattern of subject diffusion varied considerably, though the typical curriculum broadened rather than deepened to include new subject areas.

But what appeared random at a specific time on a particular campus assumed a more systematic, orderly character—explained by ideological and contextual changes—in the aggregate. After 1920, Jewish learning, measured by changes in the number of courses in specific subjects across place and period, moved from Semitics toward historical and cultural studies, and from classical-rabbinical Hebrew to modern Hebrew. Preexisting intellectual traditions, or attractiveness to a growing undergraduate constituency on campuses with enrollment-driven curricula help to explain the growth of specific subjects.

To examine the field's postwar growth, we studied the sources of inception and patterns of diffusion of Judaica subjects. The time series in Table 1 gives the proportion of each subject area—Bible, Hebrew, history, philosophy, religion, social science, and Yiddish—in the Judaica curriculum for each decade from the 1920s through the 1960s.[5]

Jewish learning lacked independent program or department status until the 1960s, so advocates justified and gained inclusion in existing departments—philo-Semitic university presidents and the Jewish community played a reduced role—by demonstrating the salutary intersection of their subject and the relevant parent discipline. Bible study, Hebrew, history, religion, and Yiddish successfully identified the points of congruence. Jewish history positions, often filled by

TABLE 1

The Distribution of Judaica Courses by Field and Decade from the 1920s through the 1960s (Percent/Decade)

Subject	1920s	1930s	1940s	1950s	1960s
Hebrew*	63	60	68	61	66
Yiddish	0	0	3	6	6
Bible	0	3	5	8	11
Religion	13	1	1	6	8
Philosophy	13	4	1	2	2
Social Science	0	0	0	1	0
History	13	30	20	16	9
Total %	102**	98**	98**	100	102**
(N)	(40)	(76)	(202)	(686)	(990)

* = Classical and modern Hebrew, combined
** = Rounding error

Baron's students, emphasized Jews in the context of specific historical periods. Hebrew language and literature dominated the curriculum between the 1920s and the 1960s. The shift to modern Hebrew was initially justified by its affinity to other "modern languages," though its high school—not graduate school— roots attenuated these connections. The subject developed an independent rationale as particularistic approaches challenged pluralism. The study of Judaism as a "religion" grew as religion departments became part of university humanities divisions—especially at public universities that experienced the greatest post-World War II enrollment growth. Neither philosophy nor the social sciences went much beyond the chairs held by Harry Wolfson and Marshall Sklare, respectively, before 1970.[6]

   Curricular inclusion and expansion assumed greater urgency as world leadership in Jewish learning shifted to the two new centers of Jewish population and learning—the U.S. and Israel, a transition that began with the nineteenth-century migrations from Europe and intensified after the Holocaust and the creation of the State of Israel.[7] Observers asked how American scholars, institutions, and benefactors could advance the field, given the burden resulting from the destruction of European Jewry, the need for changes in the field's research agenda, and the importance of Jewish communal support.[8]

   The second and third generation of Judaica scholars—influenced by the events of the 1930s and 1940s—continued the migration toward a more pluralistic Jewish scholarship. But this migration, they argued, resulted from an *overemphasis* on the universal—not its irrelevance: "Universalism has been an essential content of Judaism for millennia, but I believe it is not that which has to be emphasized today," wrote philosopher Abraham Kaplan. " . . . I believe we must now reaffirm the literal significance of that great question of Hillel's, 'If I am not for myself, who will be?'" Kaplan added, "The more closely I look at the situation of the Jew in America and the world, . . . the more I feel that while there may be others who are for me, I am determined that first of all *I* will be for myself."[9] Israel Friedlander's earlier invocation of this aphorism signified that some scholars might supplement the quest for recognition with other goals. Kaplan's reiteration a half century later—there had been many in between— signified a shift in the field's academic center of gravity. New subjects could gain admittance, provided that advocates satisfied key academic constituencies.

The fields justified by pluralist considerations that entered the university Judaica curriculum in the middle third of the twentieth century matured in the 1960s—a time when particularists challenged the rationale for them, especially by raising issues of identity. Growth, fortunately, muted tension by permitting coexistent approaches. So too did the rise of Jewish studies departments that allowed some scholars to relate their findings to Jewish learning while paying less heed to the demands of parent subjects. If pluralists initially distinguished themselves from their universalist predecessors, by the 1960s, they dealt with particularists, often in Judaica departments, who, like Ismar Elbogen, questioned the implications of disciplinary context.

Jewish History

"Remember that you were slaves in Egypt," Jews are told each Passover, "remember Amalek," "remember the Exodus from Egypt." Jewish liturgy and Jewish consciousness are replete with references to past events, both tragic and triumphant. But academic history—the systematic ordering of events without reference to transcendent forces—came late to the Jews. Rabbinic tradition evinces profound ambivalence towards history. "There is neither former nor latter in Scripture," a *Talmud Yerushalmi* tractate states.[10] Scholars separated by centuries are portrayed as engaged in conversation and disputation with one another. Their link to the Absolute, insisted some Jewish metaphysicians, allowed Jews—but not Gentiles—to escape history.[11] This outlook, historians such as Cecil Roth charged, subordinated Jewish history to Jewish theology.[12] Jewish history is still absent from the *yeshivah*, and the German rabbinical seminary only taught the history of literature.[13]

This perspective, observers suggested, changed during the nineteenth and twentieth centuries. The modern Jewish historian, Yosef Haim Yerushalmi recently wrote, lives in a period of "ever-growing decay of Jewish group memory," in which "history becomes what it had never been before—the faith of fallen Jews." He added: "For the first time history, not a sacred text, becomes the arbiter of Judaism."[14] If Yerushalmi is correct, then the secularization of the Jews and other events—not the efforts of historians—made for the realization of Zunz's dream.[15]

Whether the "historic" books of the Bible—Samuel, Kings, Chronicles—Josephus, crusader period chronicles, or the *Sefer HaKabala* [Book of Tradition] should be subsumed under the rubric of "history" as defined by the academy is not the burden of this chapter. Academization of Jewish history, it is safe to say, took the field in new directions. The late entry of history into the academy—

Columbia did not establish a history department until 1897—further hindered a process already delayed by the traditional Jewish attitude toward history.[16] Only when the students of Salo Baron assumed university positions could American Jewish historians address both Jewish and general historiographic issues. During the decade prior to Baron's appointment, "history" courses comprised about an eighth of Judaica courses offered in secular institutions. But Semitics—not history—departments offered these "proto-history" melanges of history and literature. "Literary history," wrote Alexander Marx, "will have to be superseded by constitutional, social and economic history."[17]

Despite Baron's efforts, his Columbia colleagues included historians that still "thought that Jewish history and literature did not really belong in a history department but possibly in Semitics or maybe in a Department of Exotica."[18] The exclusion of Jewish history was at times deliberate, at other times an unthinking by-product of Protestant ethnocentrism. Jewish commentators often noted that for Christians, Jewish history ended with the birth of Jesus. Protestant historians neglected or stereotyped the role of Jews and Judaism in the medieval and modern world, just as histories of western civilization often omitted a balanced treatment of Catholics after the Reformation.[19]

These attitudes hindered the field's acceptance. Some of Baron's students found positions as professional historians during the 1930s, but most disciples labored in Jewish communal organizations and in congregations until they received academic appointments between the 1940s and the 1960s. In 1941, one in three contributors to *Jewish Social Studies,* founded and edited by Baron, held academic positions. By 1968, the proportion of academic contributors to *Jewish Social Studies* had doubled to two in three.[20]

Pre-Baron work in Jewish history reflected the predilection of Jewish scholars for Rankean scholarship—fact-obsessed, under-interpreted—that assured safety but trivialized their labors and the field.[21] Independent Jewish historians did amass much raw material and future generations of scholars used their research findings. But university inclusion implied less pedantry and less amateurish and apologetic justificatory literature, while demanding more breadth and durability, more context and conformity.[22]

Post-World War II university-based historians of the Jews took three directions beyond fact-collection. Some historians accepted Jewish history as an integrated subject and, like Graetz, subjected specific topics to an internal periodization. Historians of post-medieval Jewry, for example, based this periodization upon the rise and fall of the German and East European ghettoes.[23] American Jewish historians identified successive Sephardic, Ashkenazic, and East European periods.[24]

Internal periodization, critics of this approach noted, leads to a distinction between contemporary groups rather than a depiction of historical reality. These historians, agreeing with Baron's criticisms of partisanship, parochialism, pedantry, and preservationism, argued for harmony with general American or European history.[25] Baron, for example, noted parallels between Christian and Jewish humanism and rationalism while Gershom Scholem compared Christian and Jewish mysticism.[26] Other historians could compare environments for Jews, for example, medieval France and Germany, or modern Europe and America.[27] Americanists might, these historians added, examine variant responses to events affecting American society at large, such as war or depression, instead of analyzing successive waves of Jewish immigrants.[28] Accepting standard periodization and methodologies, proponents of congruence argued, facilitated synthesis of their work with the scholarship of university colleagues.

Israel's creation fueled a third, Zionist, approach popular among Israeli scholars, who employed statehood and exile as organizing categories. Zionist historiography, Baron feared, might resurrect the lachrymose conception by favorably contrasting the return to the Jewish homeland to diaspora life.[29] Baron, who had predicted the emergence of this perspective, wrote that Jewish historians had no more right to view the diaspora as foredoomed than Christian historians had to view Jews and Judaism as vestigial.[30] Historians, Baron reiterated, analyzed social and ideological conditions; they should not render heroic or tragic narratives.

Baron retained his basic historiographic outlook after World War II.[31] World Jewry, he maintained, benefited from historical understanding. Increased attention to African, Near Eastern, and American Jewry, he added, was an indisputable advance.[32] But he began to ask if university inclusion may have come at a price. Would increased congruence between general western and Jewish history suppress attention to unique aspects of Jewish life? Creating the Third Commonwealth did not imply that the categories historians traditionally applied to other national cultures automatically applied to Jewish history. The history of the Jewish people, the existence of a large diaspora, and even the circumstances of Israel's creation demonstrated uniqueness.[33]

During the 1940s, Baron thus reduced his rhetorical emphasis on congruence. Some newly hired Jewish historians, Baron noted, were unfamiliar with the source materials at the heart of Judaism. "Many of them," Baron wrote, "resemble . . . those numerous non-Jewish historians . . . who look at Jewish history from the outside, rather than (like most of their predecessors) as insiders with that unconscious 'feeling' for what was historically relevant to the past generations."[34] Emphasizing "external" factors, Baron suggested, distorted Jewish history.

But neither was 'feeling' sufficient for producing solid historical scholarship. Needed instead were histories that balanced external and internal forces. "One could indeed suggest," he wrote, "that all Jewish history, particularly during the last two millennia of the dispersion, was essentially the resultant of conflicting internal and external pressures."[35] The word "balance" and an appreciation of multiple perspectives appeared more frequently in Baron's historiographic writing. He did not automatically exclude Gentiles from writing acceptable historical scholarship on Jews, but his increased emphasis on empathy led some successors, writing in a more particularist age, to raise the question.

These historiographic perspectives partly reflected the need for congruence between history as a discipline in American universities and the agenda of "Jewish history." They also partly reflected the different circumstances of eastern and western European Jews. In the west, Jewish history became the history of "spiritual factors," especially in ancient times. In the east, Jewish history emphasized recent and present social and economic conditions.[36] America inherited both traditions through Baron and his students. Choosing between intellectual settings and between these traditions led historians to accentuate the Jewish aspects of a topic, or the overall scheme, perhaps at the sacrifice of the Jewish nuances.[37] The problem of synthesis—also confronted by professors of religion—was presumably more pressing for novices than for mature scholars.

Period specialists—an early modern European historian who emphasized Jewish topics, for example—would counter their "jack-of-all-trades" colleagues, assure a division of labor among Jewish historians, and guard against facile acceptance of assertions of the unity of Jewish history. One might attempt a history of *Judaism*, some scholars argued, but few common threads, save Judaism, united *Jews* over the centuries.[38] Period specialists added that mastery of the entirety was impractical—no scholar could master all the languages, literatures, and historiographies necessary to attempt a coherent, scholarly treatise.[39]

The appearance of Jewish histories, written by collaborating specialists, addressed the charge of impracticality and brought synthetic questions to the fore. These collaborators, while rejecting the concept of a "monolithic Hebrew mind that dominates the actions of Jews from Leviticus to the Likud," might still identify "constant themes . . . which have left their mark on Jewish consciousness." The possible themes—*exile, mistrust of political authority, intellectual poise and self-confidence,* and *the importance of communal organization* among them— admittedly might suffer from triteness and superficiality if treated by immature historians.[40] But some historians counselled period specialists against rejecting *a priori* the possibility of synthesis.[41]

Emphasizing context might permit historians to ask insightful questions, but perhaps these historians, like some university-based Judaica predecessors, might follow context away from specifically Jewish topics. Harvard historian and Americanist Oscar Handlin, attuned to university expectations and mores and especially to notions of congruence, first gravitated *to* American Jewish history. Responding to post-World War II social scientific criticism of American middle class life—some offered by Jews—Handlin studied Americans whose experience deviated from increasingly homogeneous, suburban-oriented norms.[42] "I would like to see general American history pay enough attention," Handlin wrote, "to those Americans who are Jews."[43] Insistence upon a separate Jewish culture in America, Handlin argued, distorted historical reality, but the Jewish experience—including values and actions—in America differed from the experience of other immigrant groups and of the Protestant majority.[44] Including American Jewish history in the more mature university in the late twentieth century, he concluded, required "an understanding both of the Jewish background and of the American context."[45]

Handlin, anticipating an Elbogen-like criticism for moving *away from* the field after 1955, said that his decision resulted "from efforts to deepen and broaden my research," not from the field's insignificance or exhaustion. "Long before the current wave of interest in ethnic antecedents," he later wrote, "I had attempted to treat the Jews as one of the constituent groups in American society. The same concern which had in the first place led me to study immigrants, Jews among them, later drew me off in search of the institutional factors in the development of American society that made free group life possible." Similar intellectual migrations, he suggested, were salutary for the field.[46]

Others disagreed. In the 1940s, Handlin and other younger "pluralist" historians criticized their seniors' concern with "Jewish contributions to and antiquity in the land" and attempted to balance context and intrinsic worth. But by the 1960s, some historians built upon Baron's misgivings about the triumph of context. Historiographic articles asked, "Does the Jewish Past Have a Future?"[47] The field's university inclusion more or less assured, particularist historians could de-emphasize the contextual in favor of the specifically Jewish.

The absolute growth in Jewish history within the Judaica curriculum between the 1920s and the 1950s permitted diverse practitioner outlooks. During the 1930s, history, along with classical and modern Hebrew language and text, dominated the interpretation of the Jewish experience. Growth continued between the 1930s and the late 1960s—a fourfold growth in our course sample—but all university-based Jewish learning simultaneously experienced a thirteenfold growth. By the 1960s, history shared its interpretive role with professors of religion, biblical scholars, and linguists, especially at institutions where historians did not shift their focus from premodern to modern times.

Language and Literature: The Core of the Curriculum

Modern Hebrew

> Language is the soil for the spiritual life of the nation. Just as all natural wealth comes from the earth and returns to the earth, so spiritual wealth comes from language and returns to language. Systems are born and pass away—their residues survive in language.
>
> —Chaim N. Bialik[48]

Traditional and university forms of higher Jewish learning, this book argues, differ in many respects. The *Rosh Yeshivah*, for example, dominated the lives and training of his students and assumed that all students shared his religious orientation. The professor of Jewish learning instructed—rather than inculcated—in courses that were small parts of the student's program. These professors could not even assume that all students were Jews. At first glance, there is a key exception to this emphasis on discontinuity. Texts and language dominated traditional Jewish learning, even as taught in European and American rabbinical seminaries. Text and language courses also comprised the vast majority of all American university Judaica courses—over three-fourths between 1923 and 1968.

The elective system, attacks on the concept of mental discipline, and increased interest in national traditions and languages led to an emphasis on modern language study at the expense of Greco-Roman, early Christian, and classical Jewish studies. The decline of Semitics departments after a generation of prosperity removed another place for textual study. Jews had two national languages to offer as replacements—Yiddish and modern Hebrew. But would American universities offer any instruction in the modern languages of the Jews? Post-World War I anti-Semitism could hinder inclusion of even one language. Curricular politics required concerned Jews to decide upon a primary candidate.

Emancipation in the west, proletarization in the east, the beginnings of acculturation in the east and west, and late nineteenth-century Jewish migrations to Palestine made language choice a socio-political statement as well as an instrumental decision. Were the Jews a proletarian mass, as Yiddishists suggested, struggling for their rights wherever they lived? Were they an ancient nation in exile, as the Hebraists believed, with the historic opportunity to return to their own land and language? Or were Jews a religious "persuasion," as assimilationist Jews contended, formerly a nation but now citizens of the lands in which they dwelt, a persuasion that rejected Yiddish and relegated Hebrew to ever less frequent cultic occasions?

The need for self definition resulted in a ferocious war of the languages among European and pre-independence Palestinian intellectuals, and communal, political, and cultural elites. Hebrew as a spoken language hardly existed in the late nineteenth century. Paul Haupt's arrival at Johns Hopkins occurred only two years after Eliezer Ben Yehuda, the codifier of the "revived" language, arrived in Palestine. Ben Yehuda expressed his commitment to a Jewish nation in Palestine and to Hebrew as its language by speaking and writing only Hebrew, editing a Hebrew newspaper and a dictionary, founding Hebrew-speaking societies, advocating Hebrew instruction in the schools, and creating a language council.[49] By 1913, Palestine contained 66 all-Hebrew educational institutions at every level below the university. Hebrew became the official language of the Technion in 1914, after an acrimonious debate, and was the language of the Hebrew University from its opening in 1925.[50] Eastern European Zionists adopted vernacular Hebrew in their schools for symbolic use and for the creation of a modern, secular Jewish literature.

The appearance of modern Hebrew—and of the Zionism associated with it—heightened the linguistic conflicts. Nineteenth and twentieth-century German Jewish enlighteners considered Yiddish a corrupt and degraded form of German.[51] Many non-Jewish contemporaries, these *maskilim* noted, construed Yiddish as a secret tongue that permitted Jews to cheat their non-Jewish neighbors. The local language became the vernacular of the Jews of central and western Europe, and ultimately, the United States.

Delegates to a 1907 Jewish language conference at Czernowitz called for Yiddish to become the language of the Jewish people. Yiddish became the language of the *Bund* (the General Jewish Workers Alliance), an anti-Zionist, left of center, political and social movement. Most Jewish migrants to the United States between 1880 and 1924 spoke Yiddish, and from 1899 to 1943, the American government categorized immigrants as Jews by their ability to speak Yiddish. But few American Jews were ideological Yiddishists. Yiddish, for most Jews, was their *"mame loshon"* or mother tongue. Hebrew newspapers never achieved the circulation of the Yiddish papers. Jews more often experienced literature, theater, and popular culture in Yiddish than in Hebrew. But when Jews prayed, Hebrew remained God's language. And Jews continued to study their sacred texts in the original Hebrew or Aramaic, though Yiddish was usually the language of instruction. Yiddish held numerical superiority, but Jewish mastery of English—to get along and perhaps to evince loyalty to their new homeland—came at the cost of Yiddish, not Hebrew. The American language war was less intense; the results were similar.

Pietists, radicals, and reformers were reluctant allies in the losing struggle of Yiddish against vernacular Hebrew. Some early twentieth-century Jewish schools used the *Ivrit b'Ivrit* (Hebrew in Hebrew) method—*Ivris b'Ivris* in the Ashkenazi pronunciation—to teach Hebrew text in the context of spoken Hebrew.[52] But some Orthodox Jews signified their aversion to vernacular Hebrew by shifting the vowels in the Ashkenazi pronunciation to obtain *Aveyres b'Aveyres*—sin through sin. Vernacular Hebrew was also anathema to socialists and many Reform Jews. President Kaufmann Kohler eliminated modern Hebrew from the Hebrew Union College curriculum. Modern Hebrew, he argued, "may be a necessity for Russian Jews who have no genuine national literature from which to derive culture and idealism. For us the English literature is a source of culture and enlightenment; wherefore Neo-Hebraic [modern Hebrew] Literature will be abolished here."[53]

Premodern Jews lived with both Hebrew and Yiddish, but for moderns, support for one language often meant denigrating the other. The normally prudent Harry Wolfson—a native Yiddish speaker—bitterly attacked Yiddish and Yiddishism in a 1918 pseudonymous article. Wolfson traced the problem "to the hoary past of the sixteenth century, when the Jews began to transliterate their wretched German in Hebrew letters." Recent Yiddish literature, he added, was "the dumping ground of whatever is filthy, pestilential and unwholesome in the subterranean sewerages of European letters." He denounced the political goals of the Yiddishists: "There is to be a Yiddish Empire, with its imperial seat in the Jewish quarters of Polish cities . . . [with] outlying colonies in the Whitechapel of London, in the Rue des Rosiers of Paris, in the East Side of New York." Wolfson termed "Yiddish Science," its scholarship, "the latest efflorescence of pedantry." Yiddish offered no true redemption and had neither past nor future. "The entire Jewish achievement in literature, in religion, and in the art of living, prior to [the sixteenth century]," he wrote, "stands to him [the Yiddishist] in the same relation as that of the Celtic Druids to modern England."[54] Many Jews shared Wolfson's sentiments: Hebrew, suggested some City College of New York students, would wean Jewish students away from Yiddish and the values for which it stands.[55]

Hebrew defeated Yiddish in America. But unlike the situation in Palestine and Israel, this triumph was only good enough for second place to the vernacular.[56] "Hebrew Schools" conducted an increasing proportion of Jewish religious education. Philadelphia's Gratz College (founded 1887) was the first Hebrew teachers college. Other communities established similar "Hebrew colleges"—including the Chicago College of Jewish Studies, Hebrew College in Boston, Baltimore Hebrew College, and the Cleveland College of Jewish Studies—in the 1920s, when the results of the language war had become clear.

American Jews began their campaign to include modern Hebrew in college curricula in the same decade, but the language faced severe handicaps—some idiosyncratic, some shared with other modern languages. Hebrew, an evolving language, lacked basic lexigraphical tools. The final volumes of Ben Yehuda's dictionary, for example, appeared only after World War II. American colleges usually taught the national languages of important European nations, but modern Hebrew was only recently recognized as one of three official languages of the Palestine mandate.

Developments in high schools and colleges slowed the growth of all modern language instruction, including Hebrew. Rapid American secondary school expansion between 1890 and 1930 initially facilitated undergraduate language instruction. Colleges accommodated high school growth by adding modern languages to the list of subjects acceptable for college entrance and by offering courses in these languages.[57] But when the proportion of college preparatory students in the high school population declined, high school educators eliminated languages and other "college-preparatory" subjects from the list of graduation requirements.[58] These educators cited the research by contemporary psychologists who challenged the traditional justification for language study: their strengthening of mental discipline. "The Seven Cardinal Principles of Education," a 1918 set of goals for secondary education promulgated by the National Education Association, gave no primacy to academic objectives but awarded equal weight to cognitive, mechanical, personal, and social skills. Two of these principles, at most, subsumed traditional secondary school subjects.[59] Secondary school foreign language enrollments peaked at 83.3 percent of all public high school students in 1910 and declined to 54.9 percent in 1922 and 20.6 percent in 1955. In 1955, nearly half of America's high schools offered no foreign language instruction.[60] This decline worked especially against a language that only slowly entered the consciousness of its principal constituency.

The decline of language study in college resembled the high school trend. A 1910s Menorah-sponsored movement to include modern Hebrew in the undergraduate curriculum came to naught. The changed preparation of college students, the loss of a key rationale for language study, and postwar academic retrenchment prompted administrators to echo Felix Frankfurter's conclusion that most colleges could not justify curricular inclusion. Coming at the height of campus-based anti-Semitism, this response may have been disingenuous at some colleges. But language offerings were generally unpopular, the elective system costly, and the number of actual matriculants questionable.[61]

Proponents of the curricular inclusion of modern Hebrew thus faced a formidable task. Semitics, Jewish history, and medieval Jewish philosophy—the fields of Jewish learning that had already gained academic acceptance—entered the university on the graduate level. But modern Hebrew, proponents argued, would enter as an upward extension of secondary school language instruction—via changes in college entrance requirements. Students who studied modern Hebrew in high school would ask colleges to accept it as meeting their entrance and graduation requirements in languages. Colleges that granted these requests would find it necessary, even desirable, to offer elementary instruction in modern Hebrew for students who could not or did not study the language in high school.

Urban, undergraduate-oriented, enrollment-driven colleges with large Jewish populations were the first targets—modern Hebrew lacked a rationale for graduate-level inclusion for another generation.[62] Hebrew's inclusion in contiguous secondary schools—advocates focused on New York City—would directly affect these colleges.[63] A 1909 editorial in *HaYom*, a Hebrew language newspaper, for example, advocated Hebrew instruction in the public schools as a secular exercise: "The study of Hebrew is not religious instruction which would be forbidden in public schools."[64] New York City public high schools offered their first Hebrew classes in 1930. The state syllabus construed instruction in Hebrew as a modern spoken language comparable to French and German. At the same time, the state adopted a version of Sephardic Hebrew "because it is the classic pronunciation of Hebrew . . . it is more in harmony with its cognate Semitic languages."[65] Sephardic Hebrew—actually a partial invention of modernists—became a marker for partisans, while some traditionalists pointedly continued to use Ashkenazic Hebrew. Less than a decade later, seven high schools offered instruction to over 2,000 students.

As predicted, students then presented modern Hebrew to colleges for foreign language entrance credit. Almost no colleges accepted Hebrew before 1930, but few needed to set a policy.[66] A 1938 study found 40 colleges ready to grant entrance credit for Hebrew.[67] A comprehensive 1940 survey identified 265 institutions willing to accept Hebrew as an entrance requirement; some, however, accepted it as an elective and not in lieu of other preparatory work in foreign languages.[68] Some colleges may have denied entrance credit for Hebrew to discriminate against Jewish applicants. But 84 percent of the 1,025 colleges in a 1950 survey accepted the language.[69] Colleges with a significant Jewish constituency that accepted modern Hebrew for entrance credit, Abraham Katsh of New York University argued, would soon include the subject in their own curricula.

The "congruence theory" resembled earlier attempts to make Jewish learning available and acceptable to a general audience. Proponents used generic justifications for Hebrew's inclusion: understanding the functions of language, practical worth—governmental, military, or business assignments that required use of a foreign tongue—and cultural values—international understanding and appreciation of another literary culture.[70] Equating Hebrew and other modern languages facilitated inclusion as the nation's mood changed from isolationism to internationalism, and colleges added distribution requirements that included foreign language study.

But the circumstances under which modern Hebrew appeared at Katsh's own New York University in the mid-1930s—Katsh is usually credited with introducing the subject to secular American higher education—suggest that modern Hebrew was not just another modern language.[71] The emerging Jewish middle class, wrote historian Deborah Dash Moore, presented itself to the outside world through Hebrew—mainly through the Bible. But the language also enabled Americans to identify with the new Hebrew citizen of Palestine and, later, with Israel. "Hebrew," Moore noted, "promised middle-class, second-generation Jews self-esteem and an assertive secular Jewish identity." Acceptance of modern Hebrew in the secondary school curriculum by The New York City Board of Education, Moore added, ratified a progressive, acculturationist, pluralism.[72] Public school attendance enabled Jews to participate in the general American culture. Hebrew's curricular inclusion symbolized reciprocal recognition of a Jewish component in common education.

Pluralist Gentiles—affected by neither Zionism nor the problematics of Judaism—facilitated curricular inclusion of modern Hebrew. George E. Payne, dean of the New York University School of Education, added modern Hebrew to the school's offerings. A sociology professor before assuming the deanship in 1939, Payne studied at the University of Chicago when its sociologists stressed ameliorationism. His scholarship focused on social problems that education might remedy, including health maintenance, accident prevention, drug abuse, and juvenile delinquency. Nazism's rise led Payne to ask if education might increase tolerance of minorities and improve intergroup relations. Viewing prejudice as part of America's European legacy, Payne concluded that education might accelerate the democratic impulse, thereby ridding the nation of inimical forces. "The fundamental condition of the democratic process," he wrote in 1939, "is heterogeneity as opposed to homogeneity of culture and practice." Prejudice hampered the creativity that yielded a salutary heterogeneity. Education would reduce prejudice, nurture creativity, and stimulate pluralism.[73] The study of modern Hebrew, Payne concluded, might increase Jewish self-esteem, enhance Gentile respect, reduce misunderstanding that resulted in prejudice, and permit expression of multiple religious viewpoints.[74]

Interwar proponents of modern Hebrew relied on multiple—and occasionally contradictory—rationales for courses mainly of interest to Jews: affinity with other languages, the need for understanding and tolerance, Hebraic—albeit Biblical not modern—influence upon American culture, religion, and national identification. One defender insisted that "inculcation of an allegiance to any particular nationalism . . . has no place in the modern language classroom." But he later commented, "The inclusion of Hebrew in the curriculum has impressed the student with a sense of the dignity of the culture from which he springs."[75] Many defenders considered these justifications mutually supportive. Hebrew courses benefited the general culture and the Jewish constituency.

Gradually, however, proponents increasingly emphasized internal agendas. The teaching of Hebrew, stated an early petition for Hebrew instruction in the New York City high schools, "will restore [the Jewish student's] self-respect and the respect for his past and his people."[76] Eliezer Rieger emphasized "emotional" objectives. "There is no more powerful factor in creating group unity than a common language," he wrote after Israel's founding. "In the case of Hebrew one can best identify himself with the Hebrew nation in the past and present through learning and using Hebrew."[77] Hebrew's popularity, David Rudavsky wrote in 1972, "is enhanced by an intensified ethnic consciousness and enthusiasm, its role in Judaism, and in the state of Israel."[78]

Advocates stressed the language's unique qualities, communal usefulness, and political connotations. "Jews of assimilationist tendencies" continued to oppose its inclusion since modern Hebrew literature was largely incongruent with their outlook. Students often read, for example, the work of Mordechai Feierberg, David Frischmann, and Isaac Loeb Peretz, who wrote about the Jewish confrontation with modernity and the relationship between spiritualism and nationalism.[79] Before 1950, writers and speakers made a conscious decision to use Hebrew and writers could make safe assumptions and presuppositions about their limited, defined audience.

After World War II, some proponents advocated the graduate-level study of Hebrew literature, but the inward orientation that facilitated undergraduate acceptance hindered graduate studies. Arnold Band, who later helped to legitimize this field, wrote that in the 1940s "modern Hebrew literature wallowed in dilettantism, and its normal genre of expression was the impressionistic essay."[80] The field, Band noted, remained the province of secular Zionists and others with non-academic agendas, save perhaps for Joseph Klausner, who held the world's only chair in modern Hebrew literature at The Hebrew University during the 1940s. Academization, Band argued, followed the standardization of Hebrew as the national language of Israel. Modern Hebrew literature, freed from having to serve nationalistic interests at the expense of all others, could then follow the critical styles applied to other literatures.

Band noted substantial progress between the 1940s and the 1960s. The appearance of journals and standard references, including dictionaries and basic literary histories, the offering of advanced instruction, and the emergence of a scholarly "tradition"—the field lacked a major intellectual force such as a Scholem, Baron, or Wolfson—all boded well for increases in the quality of scholarship and instruction. Band predicted a reaction against formalism and semiotic orientation—itself a reaction against the tendency toward allegory among members of the founding generation.[81] But he also noted that the concentration of modern literary Jewish studies upon Hebrew—at the unwarranted expense of Yiddish—made Israel the logical, perhaps inescapable, center of scholarship in this area. This focus, Band added, assured a particularistic emphasis. Scholars

H. N. Shapiro and Yisrael Tzinberg envisioned the study of a "world literature," but by the 1970s, Band concluded, this development had become unlikely.[82]

Modern Hebrew, despite the growth of graduate literary studies, remained mainly an undergraduate, linguistic field. Nine comprehensive, urban colleges and universities offered the subject in 1940; the number increased to 33 in 1950 and 38 in 1958. Brooklyn College appointed Columbia's Abraham Halkin in 1938; Hunter retained Israel Efros in 1940. City College followed suit under Halkin's direction in 1948, and Queens College began instruction in modern Hebrew soon after.[83] Some institutions offered concentrations in Hebrew—the New York colleges again led the way.

After World War II, registrations in modern Hebrew substantially increased, especially at New York City's municipal colleges, Philadelphia's Temple University, and Detroit's Wayne State University.[84] By 1950, the growing number of instructors employed by colleges, universities, seminaries, and teachers colleges warranted creation of the National Association of Professors of Hebrew, with Katsh as president. N.A.P.H. served as a clearinghouse for teaching materials, helped faculty members organize new courses, and worked with other associations of foreign language teachers.[85] David Rudavsky, professor of Hebraic studies at New York University, indicated that enrollments quadrupled nationally during the 1960s.

The growth patterns of modern Hebrew and other modern languages significantly diverged, especially late in the decade in institutions located in large Jewish population centers.[86] College enrollments increased 13 percent between 1968 and 1970, but aggregate language enrollments declined 1.4 percent as colleges reduced foreign language entrance and graduation requirements. Enrollments in modern Hebrew, by contrast, rose 70 percent.[87] By the early 1970s, the *Modern Language Journal* no longer included articles that invoked congruence to justify the inclusion of modern Hebrew.[88]

Hebrew language and literature comprised at least 60 percent of all Judaica courses in each decade between 1920 and 1970. Within this category, modern Hebrew grew at the expense of classical Hebrew. The sampled colleges only offered classical Hebrew in the 1920s. But the ratio of modern Hebrew to all Hebrew courses increased to one-third in the 1930s and to three-fourths by the 1950s. The proportion of modern Hebrew among all Judaica courses increased from one-fifth in the 1930s to one-third in the 1940s, 1950s, and 1960s. Institutional differences partly explain this shift. Membership in the Association of American Universities, which differentiated between Judaica and non-Judaica universities at the turn of the century, later distinguished between commitment to classical and modern Hebrew (Table 2). AAU institutions offered more classical and less modern Hebrew than non-AAU institutions in the 1930s and 1940s. The difference declined in the 1950s and 1960s, but AAU schools that *began* to offer Hebrew in the postwar period behaved like their peers.

At the outset, proponents of university-based modern Hebrew emphasized congruence with the modern language movement—though they occasionally re-

TABLE 2
Modern Hebrew Language and Literature by AAU Status

	Modern Hebrew Courses as a Percent of All Hebrew Courses	
	1930s through 1940s	1950s through 1960s
All Institutions	44 (190)	55 (1072)
AAU Institutions	20 (105)	36 (330)
Non-AAU Institutions	73 (85)	63 (742)

iterated nineteenth-century invocations of Hebrew as the key to the literature of antiquity.[89] But less than two generations after its first university appearance, the status and justifications for modern Hebrew greatly differed from those of most other languages. The role of modern Hebrew as the language of national rebirth heightened student interest.[90] Few students mastered Hebrew sufficiently to read modern literature, but many learned enough to become "members of the club." By 1970, observers accepted the strong association between modern Hebrew and nationalistic and religious ends. The debate then shifted to whether language study was the most expeditious means towards these ends.[91] Hebrew's inherent difficulties, some observers argued, hindered mastery. Enhanced identity might result from the study of Hebrew, but so might frustration and disaffection. But others noted that just as classical Hebrew was the propaedeutic course for Semitic studies, most current students in Jewish studies programs initially encountered modern Hebrew. If Judaica programs were to realize particularistic ends, modern Hebrew was inescapable.

Yiddish

Yiddish followed a different path into the university. Partisans of Yiddish in the war of languages ferociously defended Yiddish culture and scholarship and frequently denigrated the Hebrew renaissance.[92] But much of western Jewry—including the founders of *Wissenschaft des Judentums*—despised the language and its literature.[93] Indeed, Yiddish was of greater interest to nineteenth-century German Gentile scholars than to their Jewish colleagues.[94]

The linguistic wars also impeded the academization of Yiddish at The Hebrew University in Jerusalem. When a donor offered to endow a Yiddish chair within the University's Institute for Jewish Studies, two "western" Jews supported the proposal: Gershom (Gerhard) Scholem, who originated the academic study of Jewish mysticism, and Judah L. Magnes, president of Hebrew University and a Reform rabbi. Scholem and Magnes were maverick Zionists whose commitment to the Jewish cultural past overrode Hebrew absolutism. Scholem, who wrote trenchant, angry critiques of *Wissenschaft des Judentums,* saw Yiddish as part of the folk creativity of the Jewish people—a key component of the Jewish intellectual and moral tradition. Magnes became a partisan of East European Jewish culture, including Yiddish, while helping to create the New York *Kehillah,* or organized Jewish community.[95] But the remainder of the academic staff successfully opposed Magnes and Scholem and Hebrew University declined the gift. The Yiddish chair was not established until 1951. By then, the language was harmless.

Yiddish was a greater embarrassment for nineteenth-century German Jewish scholars than for twentieth-century American Jewish scholars.[96] Some first and second generation American anthropologists and linguists studied Yiddish—Leo Weiner at Harvard and Edward Sapir at Yale (appointed 1931), for example.[97] But the language remained outside the instructional program until the 1940 migration of Max Weinreich and his family to New York City.[98]

Weinreich was a founder of the Yiddish Scientific Institute—YIVO, the *Yidisher Visenschaftlikher Institut*—in Vilna in 1925. He and his family found themselves in Denmark at the outbreak of World War II and thereby avoided the fate of most European Jews. Upon migrating to New York, Weinreich transformed the New York YIVO branch into an autonomous research center on East European Jewry, its culture, language, literature, and folklore.[99] YIVO became a forum for Yiddish-speaking scholars and made scholarship published in other languages available to them. The City College, which offered Yiddish instruction by the late 1940s, strengthened its program immeasurably by appointing Weinreich to the faculty.[100] The City College rationale for conversational Yiddish stressed training social workers "who have some knowledge of Yiddish, a German tongue written in Hebrew characters."[101] The rationale sounds contrived, but the Chicago College of Jewish Studies—now Spertus Institute of Jewish Studies—used the same rationale when it added Yiddish to its curriculum in 1926.[102]

The Atran Foundation funded Columbia's appointment of Max's son, Uriel, to a Yiddish linguistics professorship in the 1950s. Frank Atran, an East European Jew who made his fortune in retailing in France and Belgium, supported hospitals and other medical institutions. Alternately described as a Menshevik, a Social Democrat, and a Bundist, Atran also funded left-of-center causes including the Jewish Labor Committee, the Bund Archives, and the Congress for Jewish Culture. The Columbia Yiddish chair, located in the linguistics department, was a natural outgrowth of Atran's interest in education and Yiddish culture.

By the time Yiddish appeared in American university curricula—The New School and Brooklyn College soon followed Columbia and City College—the Holocaust ended the language wars in Europe, and Israel was a Hebrew-speaking state. The American immigrant population was passing from the scene and native American Jews were increasingly monolingual in English, with a smattering of Yiddish and Hebrew, at most.[103] Yiddish and Hebrew textbooks reflected diminished linguistic antipathy. The reading exercises in Uriel Weinreich's *College Yiddish* and Reuben Wallenrod and Abraham Aharoni's *Modern Hebrew Reader and Grammar* show relatively small differences in cultural content. The Yiddish text is more oriented toward Europe and the Hebrew text toward Israel, but both texts maintain a positive attitude toward Jewish tradition.[104]

Yiddish is the only Judaica subject to enter the American university directly through European refugee scholars. Yiddish became a consistent offering in the late 1940s, but with only three percent of the total curriculum. Relatively few institutions offered Yiddish and relatively few scholars engaged in the academic study of Yiddish language and literature. Yiddish grew to six percent of Judaica courses offered in both the 1950s and the 1960s—still only one-tenth of Hebrew's proportion. But maintaining a constant proportion of a growing field meant that Yiddish held its own. In any case, American support to a subject that needed a home surpassed European and Israeli backing.

Religion and Bible

Religion: A Humanistic Field

> It seems to be one of the unavoid-
> able responsibilities of educated
> people to show by example that
> beliefs may be held and examined
> at the same time.
>
> —Northrop Frye[105]

Since World War II, the study of Judaism has been centered in religion departments located in college or university humanities divisions—not in divinity or theological schools. Other humanistic subjects offered religion departments little competition. Semitics departments, for example, failed to outlast their founder, relegated Jewish aspects to a supporting role, or failed to venture from a philological to a more broadly humanistic focus. But Semitics, if not a contemporary rival, provides historic landmarks later followed by religion departments in dealing with their Judaic subfield. At the outset, secularists and sectarians monitored both these fields to assess their effect on belief. Religion initially needed Judaism at least as much as Semitics needed Hebrew. But both religion and Semitics eventually faced definitional problems with a parent field that exerted pulls away from specifically Jewish aspects of the field.

"The medieval university had a principle of unity," wrote Robert Maynard Hutchins in his famous 1937 discussion of *The Higher Learning in America*, "it was theology." But a "faithless generation" in America that took "no stock in revelation" and that lacked "orthodoxy and an orthodox church" led Hutchins to conclude that "to look to theology to unify the modern university is futile and vain." Hutchins anointed metaphysics the "ordering and proportioning discipline" of the modern university.[106] But others did not "settle" for metaphysics—and for confining religion to theology schools. These advocates pressed for a "central" role for religious studies.

The collegiate study of religious dogma was as old as American higher education itself. Religion suffused the entire institution, including its course of study. Divinity schools were not created until the nineteenth century, a period of gradual curricular differentiation and of the professionalization of clerical training.

The study of religion as a generic human phenomenon—called comparative religion, history of religion, and *religionsgeschichte*—began in the latter part of the nineteenth century and aimed at systematic, comparative studies.[107] The field in part united the world of belief—lay and "professional"—against the world of unbelief. Lay leaders of the comparative religions movement helped to convene the World Parliament of Religions at the 1893 Columbian Exhibition in Chicago, which brought together representatives of the world's religions, including Judaism, in a common cause. In the academic world, the American Oriental Society established a section on the history of religions in 1897. Columbia, Johns Hopkins, and the University of Pennsylvania established the "American Lectures on the History of Religions" during the 1890s, and several universities introduced courses and departments of comparative religion. This movement offered an opportunity to introduce Judaism into the curriculum in a sympathetic environment. But actual inclusion of the study of Judaism within comparative religion at any specific university depended on the answers to three questions:

· Was the field part of normative theology useful in the teaching of missionaries, or was it a "value free" academic discipline?
· What were the methodological criteria for introducing specific religions into the arena of research? Would scholars emphasize primitive or sophisticated religions?
· Would philologically trained Judaica scholars apply their skills to the study of Judaism?

The answer to the first question was ambiguous. The curriculum pursued by doctoral candidates at the University of Chicago resembled requirements in other humanistic fields, but the department added that it "offers opportunities also to those who intend to enter foreign mission work." Divinity school students who invoked this option could substitute comparative religion for the divinity school course in practical theology. These students, followers of the long tradition noted in chapter 1, studied the religions of non-Christians to convert them to Christianity.[108]

In universities that emphasized the ecclesiastical over the academic mode, it was impossible to offer Judaism within the context of comparative religion without making the comparison invidious. N.Y.U. comparative religion professor Frank Ellinwood, for example, was a Christian supremacist: "I do not disguise the fact that I shall consider the subject from a Christian standpoint," stated Ellinwood, a Presbyterian minister; "I maintain that in discussion of this kind a perfectly colorless, opinionless attitude is impossible." Abram Isaacs later met a cool reception from N.Y.U. authorities when he proposed to teach "Hebrew as *literature,* not theology." The course, he admitted, would "frighten away all but a few," but it would attract communal support while fairly testing the popularity of Semitics, "which has been restricted, I fear, by young theologians." At N.Y.U., which charged little or no tuition to students studying for the ministry, comparative religion produced few Ph.D.'s and did not outlast Ellinwood.[109]

Comparative religion was divided into two related but distinct methodological subfields: archaic or primitive religion and sophisticated religion. Max Müller, "the father of comparative religion," studied archaic religion. "We shall learn," Müller wrote, "that religions in their most ancient form, or in the minds of their authors, are generally free from many of the blemishes that attach to them in later times."[110] To find *"echtreligion,"* or true religion, Müller turned not to sophisticated western religious systems but to ancient religions that reflected primal and pristine religious sensibilities. Modelling comparative religion on comparative philology, he studied the primary texts of ancient religious traditions, while some disciples studied "primitive" religion by using anthropological methods on pre-literate societies. Both Müller and his students, Wilfred Cantwell Smith notes, assumed "that the reality or truth of religion is to be found most purely or most surely in its earliest and simplest forms."[111]

The choice of method affected the proclivity of American scholars with the necessary linguistic, textual, and historical competence to study the history of Judaism. George Foot Moore and Morris Jastrow were early, enthusiastic supporters of *religionsgeschichte*. Jastrow initiated the American Oriental Society section on the historical study of religions and became its first leader. He also played a central role in the development of a popular lecture series in the history of religions.[112] At Pennsylvania, Jastrow designed courses—and later established and chaired a department—on the history of religions.[113] But, despite his interest in the subject and his competence in Jewish learning, Jastrow did not study, nor did he encourage others to study, post-Biblical Judaism. Reflecting on Jastrow's career post mortem, Richard Gottheil noted: "We have touched upon many religions [in the Committee on the History of Religions]; I could never get Jastrow to take up Judaism."[114]

At Harvard, history of religion found its initial home in the divinity school. The first divinity school course (1892/93), which drew enrollments largely from the college, focused on nonwestern, non-Judeo-Christian faiths. The course went unaccompanied until Moore's arrival in 1902. Moore thereupon brought together relevant courses from throughout the curriculum to form a department that he chaired and introduced new courses dealing with Judaism, Christianity, and Islam inter alia. In 1905, Moore, then beginning research for his magnum opus on rabbinic Judaism, introduced a course in the history of Judaism from 198 B.C. to modern times, the first university course to deal with Judaism as a living religious tradition, not only the matrix from which Christianity emerged.

The methodological starting points of Moore and Jastrow explain why the history of Judaism flourished at Moore's Harvard but did not exist at Jastrow's Pennsylvania. Jastrow, a loyal disciple of Müller, argued:

> Advanced religions like Christianity, Judaism, Islam, and Buddhism offer comparatively little opportunity for investigating the fundamental problems involved in religion viewed as a part of man's life. For understanding such problems we must turn to religions which are more naïve, which are less the result of conscious effort, in which speculation plays a minor part, which, in a word, are *direct* manifestations of man's emotional or religious nature. The religion of savages and of people living in a primitive condition of culture are the more special concern of the student of religions.[115]

Jastrow studied Assyro-Babylonian religion with some comparisons to the
Hebrew Bible and thus worked on "Hebrews" but not on Jews. Historian
Morton Smith appropriately termed Moore's contrasting approach "aristocratic
liberalism"—the study, Moore wrote, of "the religion of intelligent and religious men. . . ."[116] "Such men are always the minority," Moore wrote, "but they
are the true representatives of their religion in any age, teachers and examples to
their fellows."[117] The contemplative, elitist outlook of rabbinic Judaism aroused
Moore's interest, but not Jastrow's.

Harvard was committed to Moore, not to the history of Judaism. When
Moore left the scene, so did the subject. Arthur Darby Nock, Moore's successor
and a noted historian of religion, studied Christianity—not Judaism. Elsewhere,
neither the history of Judaism nor the history of religion developed strong
graduate programs. Karl Barth's theology, which became dominant among
Christian scholars, did not recognize religion per se but saw Christianity as
sui generis. Other "religions" were illegitimate—believing Christians need take
no cognizance.

The history of religions was in eclipse between the 1920s and the 1950s, as
was its Judaic subfield. The study of Judaism in the context of religion declined
from a substantial 13 percent of the Judaica curricular offerings in the 1920s to
but one percent in the 1930s and 1940s. The field re-emerged in the 1950s—6
percent—and grew to 8 percent by the 1960s. In relative terms, the 1920s exceeded the 1960s, but in sheer number of courses, the 1960s were friendlier to
the study of Judaism. Arnold Band identified 13 departments of religion that offered programs in the "study of Judaism" in 1966. Much of this growth reflected
the change in fortune of the parent field, the academic study of religion. As late
as 1959, Erwin Goodenough at Yale bemoaned the fate of "*religionswissenschaft*," but a few years later Willard Oxtoby saw the field flourishing.[118]

Motivations for inclusion of Judaism varied by institution. When the Iowa
School of Religion first opened, university authorities requested Protestant,
Catholic, and Jewish communal representatives to "furnish a high caliber man
to teach in our School of Religion."[119] Faculty members often came with rabbinical rather than academic backgrounds, and the community paid their
salaries.[120] But including Jewish faculty in religion departments served important
symbolic functions by deflecting charges of indoctrination and sectarianism
while permitting invocation of a "Judeo-Christian" tradition.[121] Ecumenism supplemented or replaced these motives during the 1960s when the theological climate underwent radical change. Among Christians on the campuses, Barthian
Christian triumphalism, which some blamed for the decline in the academic
study of religion, gave way to the more inviting neo-orthodoxy and Biblical faith
of Niebuhr and Tillich. Biblical, rather than philosophical, grounding became
the core of Protestant Christianity.[122] By the 1970s it became difficult to justify
the absence of a Jew on a religion faculty—even in religiously sponsored colleges.[123] Finally, Salo Baron and Jacob Neusner strongly led *religionswissenschaft*
advocates in the transformed, but continuing, debate with colleagues concerned
primarily with faith, rather than with its study.[124]

Advocates from public institutions contended with First Amendment restrictions. Public colleges first included the study of religion in the 1920s, when Yale professor Charles F. Kent offered financial incentives to several universities.[125] To assure the constitutionality of governance at the University of Iowa's School of Religion, academy and community shared the responsibility. Communal and foundation funds underwrote the academic posts—specifically allocated to Protestants, Catholics, and Jews.[126] Sixty of 100 state and land grant institutions, reported a 1944 survey, offered instruction in religion.[127] A 1960 study estimated that all church-related colleges, 60 percent of all colleges, and 45 percent of state colleges had religion departments or chairs.[128]

The Supreme Court's 1963 Schempp decision settled legal qualms when it sanctioned teaching *about* religion in public institutions while prohibiting devotional exercises. Justice Tom Clark's decision encouraged the field's proponents since most post-World War II enrollment growth occurred in public colleges. "Nothing we have said here," he wrote, "indicates that such study of the Bible or of religion, when presented objectively as part of a secular program of education, may not be effected consistently with the First Amendment."[129] Many social scientific and humanistic topics, Justice William Brennan concurred, required "some mention of religion." Justice Arthur Goldberg accepted "the teaching *about* religion, as distinguished from the teaching *of* religion. . . ."[130] But inadequate funding or denominational support—not legal prohibitions— had thwarted many plans.[131] The number of public institutions with religion programs or chairs doubled in the five years after the Schempp decision—also a prosperous decade for higher education. Religion course enrollments tripled at a group of 25 public institutions with pre-1964 religion programs.[132]

Schempp thus ratified, legitimated, and accelerated an ongoing movement. But neither legal qualms and academe's liberation from them nor "social understanding"—few other institutions cited this Iowa rationale—fully explains the field's emergence and growth pattern.[133] The justificatory literature is not illuminating. Clyde Holbrook's 1963 contention that "to attempt to understand man without reference to the systems of belief and insight within which he has attempted to understand himself is to reduce and distort his images of himself by which humanistic education at its best tries to direct its steps," could have been made at any time.[134]

Midcentury interest in the academic study of religion arose from the perceived need for academics who could mediate between secularism and orthodoxy, just as late nineteenth-century academics were expected to broker between higher critics, who accepted religion's collapse, and fundamentalists unwilling to adjust to modernity.[135] Liberal, secular, scientific culture, the field's advocates contended, failed to account for the entire human experience. The university-based study of religion, they added, offered an American answer to the seductiveness of totalitarian ideologies. A campus "return to religion" should stress—in contrast to progressive thought—the sinfulness of humankind, the inability to achieve salvation except through grace, and the importance of Biblical theology.[136]

Hutchins and other liberal educationists contemplated an increased role for religion in the undergraduate curriculum, noted advocates of the academic study of religion.[137] But the postwar general education movement, which grew in part as a response to both Nazism and Communism, was more concerned with the relationship between liberal education and political democracy.[138] *General Education in a Free Society,* the 1945 Harvard "Redbook," would not "exclude the religious idea" from general education. But partisans of the academic study of religion desired greater curricular centrality. The subject, they insisted, forced students to confront questions of authority and absolutes, and offered more satisfying answers to transcendent political dogmas than study of "the great tradition" (Hutchins) or "a heritage" (Harvard Redbook).[139] The existence of competing gods in religion, politics, and economics might lead the student away from monisms or reductionism.[140] The study of religion, more optimistic advocates suggested, might "provide a moral foundation for our political faith and practice." The American tradition had deep roots, noted philosopher Arthur E. Murphy: "Behind the twentieth century was the eighteenth and Thomas Jefferson, and behind the eighteenth the thirteenth and Saint Thomas Aquinas, and behind that Greek philosophy and, most fundamental of all, the abiding spiritual inspiration of the Judeo-Christian faith."[141] In any case, exposure to Barth's neo-Calvinism, to Niebuhr's view of the world's realities, or to Tillich's existentialism, might shore up the faith of students and make them wiser.[142]

Non-radical sociologists also emphasized the importance of religious thinking and attitudes for addressing problems "which *appear* in the time and culture, to be insoluble in terms of empirical knowledge and techniques." Religion arose, Talcott Parsons argued, following Durkheim, out of real, serious concerns. But Parsons considered "philosophy" to be the academic discipline that specialized in the solution of non-empirical cognitive problems. Others claimed the ground for the academic study of religion, noting that analytic philosophy abandoned classical philosophical questions.[143] Not all religious manifestations were theistic, an advocate argued, but all came under the rubric of religion, considered as a humanistic subject.[144]

The movement to incorporate the study of religion into the humanities fit a liberalism that saw religion as part of the cultural and humanistic endeavor to answer existential questions about the human experience.[145] But this liberalism denied the claim of religion over society, its political or economic institutions, or the academic disciplines that studied them. Defenders of denominational colleges and seminaries criticized academic religionists for eschewing advocacy when confronting the question of belief. The inclusion of religion as a "humanistic" study at public universities, these defenders argued, entailed substantial "costs," especially an inability to indoctrinate the laity and to educate the clergy. The field, moreover, dangerously subjected the basic assumptions of each religion to critical scrutiny and renounced not only a denominational—but also a Christian—focus.[146] Classifying religion as a humanistic field, critics argued, necessarily implied the formal equality of all religions.

"Secular" academics identified opposite dangers. Universities, these scholars claimed, created understanding, not converts. No one could object, wrote the philosopher Morton White, if *per accidens* students developed deep religious feelings while learning "what they should know about religious feeling, action, and belief." But, White concluded, anticipating the Schempp decree, conscious attempts to develop these feelings in students were inappropriate and doomed to failure.[147] White and his colleagues feared less the conscious subversion of an academic norm than the need for unceasing restraint by religious academics.

The secularist indictment continued: Religious studies curricula retained a de facto, if not de jure, Christian structure. Catholic and Protestant educators frequently asserted the truth of their religious teachings and the implications of those truths for college study.[148] Many academics exempted their own religion from comparative study on the grounds of uniqueness or superiority.[149] Non-Christian religions received short shrift in religion departments—measured by curricular and faculty representation. "The principle of *epoché*, the separation of a scholar's subjective commitments from the subject he is investigating, espoused by phenomenologists of religion," asserted a specialist in Islam, "has not always been observed by non-Muslim savants."[150]

Contemporary continental Biblical scholars, contended Charlotte Klein, still maintained "anti-Jewish" attitudes based upon Christian presuppositions. These scholars considered Christianity the true religion, questioned the continued existence of Judaism, asserted the inferiority of Jewish ethics and teachings, exhibited frequent, judgmental attitudes towards Judaism, and relied on Protestant interpretations—Strack and Billerbeck for Talmud, for example—rather than Jewish sources.[151] Scholarly emphasis on early—not modern—Judaism, critics added, suggests the continued Christological emphasis of religion departments.

What motivated academic religionists, secular critics asked? Should one accept the "vacuum" theories of Huston Smith and William Clebish? "The strongest force returning religion to the curriculum," Smith asserted, " . . . has been the pull of the vacuum created by its removal."[152] "This assumed monopoly (always shared by certain existential approaches to literature and philosophy) over The Big Issues," Clebish added, "came about more by others' temporary default than by some superiority of religious studies as to seriousness or comprehensiveness."[153] Talcott Parsons agreed, less approvingly, that a tendency exists "for religious thinking, backed by powerful sentiments, to fill all the principal 'interstices' left open by the state of scientific knowledge of a given time." Religion avoided confrontation with the natural and social sciences, Parsons noted. "But it does permeate into areas which are intrinsically accessible to science, and once having institutionalized religious doctrines in such areas they become difficult to change."[154]

The academic study of religion, despite sectarian and secular objections, expanded considerably during the 1960s as new rationales appeared. The "zoo" theory of religious representation—dominant at the first public experiments such as Iowa's School of Religion—fell into disrepute.[155] This theory asserted that religion "can be dealt with only by exhibiting representative members of the various species." Postwar rationales—curricular unity within general education, and transcendence within a democracy—also waned. But scholarship, growing enrollments, aid to other, recognized disciplines, and relevance to the ethical, moral, and transcendent issues of the 1960s strengthened the field's academic standing. By the late 1960s, research universities used customary academic criteria to evaluate religion professors and excluded external affiliations and recognition from the appointment calculus. Salo Baron's injunction that "a serious scholar of religion will not place the peculiarities of his discipline in a uniquely elevated position fenced off from normal approaches to it by spiritual presuppositions" finally became orthodoxy. Baron accepted this dictum because he viewed Judaism as a *historical* religion in which faith and history form "an association of two mutually complementary ingredients of the same outlook."[156] Christianity and Islam, he argued, could effect a similar reconciliation, but no practitioner was exempt from the university's charge to maintain objectivity and open-mindedness.

The field's growth led to changed relationships between universities and seminaries. As late as the 1950s, partisans of *religionswissenschaft* feared that theology might overwhelm their field since American universities still depended on seminaries to teach the relatively few students of religion. "Not by chance did anthropologists study religions avidly a century ago, and now study social structure," wrote E. R. Goodenough in 1959. "Religion was the burning issue then. Now social structure, by the rise of Communism, the threats of dictatorships, and the problems of industrial relations, stands at the forefront of all our minds." Goodenough added: "We must not fool ourselves: our scholarship reflects our own basic problems, and the modern intelligentsia feel these social problems much more intensely than the problem of the sacred and the profane."[157] Goodenough held out little hope for rapid growth of the academic study of religion.

But the field took only a decade to grow from Goodenough's beleaguered "remnant" to being on a par with—or surpassing—theology. Claude Welch, in his influential 1971 report on the graduate study of religion, ratified the changed order by applying the Schempp doctrine to seminaries. Seminaries, he argued, should offer academic instruction in religion only proximate to universities and only in conjunction with them.[158] By the late 1960s, the victory of *religionswissenschaft* prompted lay observers to ask if seminaries would henceforth produce scholars rather than pastors and rabbis.[159] The field parried external and internal attacks by relying upon the prestige and influence of universities.[160]

The debate continued into the early 1970s, when undergraduate enrollment growth led to a scarcity of university-trained instructors, forcing academic departments to recruit "religionists." These instructors often lacked lengthy scholarly apprenticeships, rebelled against the supposed constraints of *religionswissenschaft*—doubting the attainability or desirability of objectivity, and dissenting on issues of academic mission and classroom posture—and expressed a theological pessimism. Terminology changed: "Parahistory," "individualism" (Whitehead), and "essential" replaced "theology." "*Religions-*

wissenschaft" became "detachment," "objectivity," "collectivism" (Durkheim), and "manifestation."[161] As new challenges to the "about/of" dichotomy appeared, mature scholars urged caution, especially in dealings with students.[162] Some students entered the house of intellect under false pretenses, but others, upon entering, found their new accommodations were not as advertised.[163]

The Judaism subfield within religion departments itself grew to the point where some practitioners questioned the direction of their field, the meaning of academic norms, and the university's contemporary social role. "The major flaw in American education," argued an Orthodox observer, "is its sundering of learning from morality." *Wissenschaft des Judentums* contributed to the attenuation of Jewish beliefs and practices not in conformance with western notions. A fusion of critical method and traditional Jewish study, the critique concluded, would revive Judaism and strengthen the university and society.[164]

Another scholar argued for recognition of the subjective nature of knowledge—especially religious knowledge—the preoccupation with self as the proper subject matter of the study of religion, and the understanding of religion as a means toward self-transformation. Accepting these premises did not necessarily imply a return to tradition—or a fusion of traditional and western modes of thinking. Instead, it was thought they might result in new constructions of reality, including mysticism, that could lead a student to spontaneity, individualization, and self-actualization.[165] This discussion began and ended with Judaism in religion departments, but other post-1970 observers called for creation of separate Judaica departments that could directly address problems of student identity.[166]

Some *religionswissenschaft* practitioners, foreseeing potential conflicts between faith and scholarship, followed some early Semitists by compartmentalizing—worship on the weekend, scholarship during the week. But even those scholars who denied that a conflict existed, or who, like Northrup Frye, attempted a reconciliation, could more easily state the limits of the field than explain its dimensions.[167] University-based practitioners argued *against* religious scholarship, but they disagreed over whether they were studying *religion* or *religions*. The problem arose, Claude Welch argued, from the field's Protestant Christian origin, "which made fine distinctions within one tradition by subdividing the study of it into a battery of areas of investigation in Bible, history of Christianity, and theology (mainly Protestant, of course) and then throwing everything else into one bag called World Religions." The remedy, Welch insisted, was not

> giving more nearly 'equal time' to other religious traditions. . . . 'Judaic studies' and 'Buddhist studies' have their rationale mainly as temporary correctives to the traditional identification of religious studies with Christian studies. Or, I would add, they have a *raison d'être* simply as territories carved out for convenience and practicality in study.

Making Judaism a permanent subdivision of the study of religion militated against "mutual fructification"—Ismar Elbogen would have shuddered at the concept—and risked regression toward a confessional stance by emphasizing the unique, rather than the comparative. Instead, Welch prescribed cross-cultural scholarship that involved methodological pluralism, that interrelated with "cognate areas," and that built creatively upon the student's prior—usually liberal—studies.[168]

Welch's tactical tolerance of the study of Judaism elicited considerable debate. Everyone agreed on the desirability of comparative and historical studies; most on the advantages of methodological pluralism—though some asked how many methods one scholar could master. Excessive specialization came at the cost of interpretive breadth, some scholars added, not only in religion departments, but throughout graduate education in the humanities and the social sciences.[169]

But was Judaism to enter religion departments only to lose its internal integrity in the name of "mutual fructification?" Were Elbogen's qualms about the gravitation of scholars from Jewish learning to parent disciplines justified? Between 1965 and 1970, pragmatists noted, 3.2 percent of all Ph.D. dissertations in religion dealt with Judaism, and 3.5 percent of doctoral students in religion specialized in Judaic topics. In contrast, 10.4 percent of Ph.D. students specialized in theological studies, 18.9 percent in Biblical studies, and 18.8 percent in the history of Christianity. Welch's exemption would apply for some time to come.[170]

Some practitioners directly criticized Welch for rejecting the possibility of a mature, Judaic-oriented field. Welch's imprecise use of terminology—he confused, for example, the entirety of "Jewish studies" with "Judaism," the province of religion departments—showed a lack of understanding of the field.[171] Organizing religion departments on the basis of Christian or Jewish texts—especially Talmud—stated specialists in Judaism, was inappropriate, and university-based Jewish learning should liberate itself from insistence that mastery of the Babylonian Talmud must precede any useful contribution. But Welch tacitly sanctioned an equally threatening autodidacticism.[172] He should have considered, Jacob Neusner wrote, "the efforts of several universities to integrate the study of several religious traditions around a common theoretical or conceptual core, while attempting to achieve a measure of specialization on a given religious tradition."[173]

E. R. Goodenough, in 1959, hoped for university acceptance of a *religionswissenschaft* "which proposes minutely to examine the *homo religiosus*, including ourselves as *homines religiosi*, quite aware that over-all and hasty generalizations only curtain us off, again, from our subject."[174] By the 1970s, the study of Judaism within religion departments had found its niche, adopted the rhetoric and methodologies of secular critics, differentiated its domain from that of theology, claimed to illuminate general religious phenomena, and reserved to itself an internal integrity.

The academic study of religion survived where Semitics failed by enlisting an undergraduate base—in public institutions that accounted for three-fourths of higher education enrollments. But it remained necessary to remind some constituencies that Judaism, as well as Christianity, might exemplify general theories or problems.[175] Jewish practitioners, entering universities at the late 1960s turning point between pluralist and particularist rationales, were more successful than earlier Semitics colleagues in resisting the parent field's pulls, perhaps because they had a greater desire. Among themselves, practitioners expressed equal concern for Goodenough's primary desideratum: a mastery of the particular.

Bible

Biblical scholarship in the late nineteenth-century university was not sufficiently "shaken loose" from its churchly moorings—G. Ernest Wright's terms—for substantive Jewish participation, much less a distinctly Jewish approach to the study of the Bible. Scholars partly liberated the Hebrew Bible from its ascribed role as the fountain of the New Testament, but William R. Harper, criticized for the stance he took on "The Pentateuchical Question," remained vigilant lest churchly concerns undermine Biblical scholarship. Scriptural study posed even greater problems for Jewish scholars.

But it was not only a matter of the Bible's being too Christian (and Jews therefore feeling unwelcome). Traditional Jewish scholars neglected the study of Scripture for internal reasons. There were a number of noted scholars who bemoaned the state of Jewish biblical scholarship given the centrality of the Bible to the Jews and the study of Judaism. Naftali Herz Wessely's eighteenth-century call for greater emphasis on Biblical study—the literature that the Jews shared with Christendom—in *Divrey Shalom v'emet*, Samson Raphael Hirsch's nineteenth-century lament that "people studied Judaism but forgot to search for its principles in Scripture," and Solomon Schechter's later call for saving "the Bible from the *goyim*," were echoed in 1955 by a Jewish Bible scholar who wrote, "Bible studies have been notoriously neglected by Jewish scholarship."[176] Christian scholarly preemption and Jewish hesitation, chapters 2 and 3 show, precluded the linkage of Jewish scholarship to the universities, the western intellectual world, and to religious scholarship through the Bible. Instead, Semitics linked the first generation of university-based scholars; later, Harry Wolfson unsuccessfully (save for himself) urged that philosophy assume that role.

Advocates of *religionswissenschaft* reasserted the theological neutrality of university-based Bible study after World War II. "In its central part," Will Irwin asserted in his 1959 presidential address to the Society of Biblical Literature, " . . . there will be and can be no distinction between Jewish and Christian exegesis." Neutrality was now achievable, provided, of course, that all advocates of *religionswissenschaft* worked to keep theology at bay.[177] But many Jewish scholars redefined the issue: How could they develop methods and perspectives that enabled them to be both Jews and scientific scholars, thereby overcoming the Christian character of ostensibly neutral Biblical research? The answer included reviving the medieval Jewish tradition of biblical exegesis, learning Protestant biblical criticism—not dismissing it along with Solomon Schechter as "the higher anti-Semitism"—and creating a Jewish mode of criticism that differed from the work of Christians or post-Christian agnostics and atheists.

Bible scholar H. L. Ginsberg looked skeptically at professions of neutrality. Like Max Margolis, he asserted that scriptural interpretation required being "at one" with Judaism. Christians were intellectually disadvantaged, Ginsberg wrote, because "being Christians, they had begun to learn Hebrew as young men instead of as infants." He added: "It is difficult to conceive of anybody but a Jew acquiring the feeling for Hebrew which enabled him to make his particular observations on the subtleties of Hebrew idiom."[178]

Other scholars translated this quasi-mystical explanation into more rational terms. Yale's William Hallo identified methodological conservatism as the Jewish scholar's distinct contribution to the study of the Bible.[179] The Biblical text was an integral part of the "normative tradition" and had become central to Jewish liturgy. Jews, therefore, guarded the text and assimilated it to their religious outlook. Church scholars, in contrast, worked with the Biblical text in translation, thereby placing a veil between Scripture, the believer, and the scholar. Of the small proportion of Christian scholars who knew Biblical Hebrew, only the few that also knew rabbinic, medieval, and modern Hebrew could study Jewish commentators for their textual insights. Inadequate training, not Christianity per se, explained why a vast body of ancient and medieval scholarship remained terra incognita to most Christian scholars. Israelis, especially, were accepting the challenge laid down by Wessely, Hirsch, and Schechter, but the growing Israeli literature written in modern Hebrew remained literally a set of closed books to the Christians.

These inadequacies pointed to a distinctive Jewish response to Christian Biblicists, found in the Israeli literature.[180] Yehezkel Kaufmann's monumental eight-volume *History of Israelite Religion* (in Hebrew, 1937–1956)—an abridged English version became available only much later—mainly influenced Jewish Biblical scholars.[181] Kaufmann differed with Jewish traditionalists by accepting the notion of discrete documents edited into the Pentateuch. But he rejected the implicit theology and teleology in the Graf-Wellhausen documentary hypothesis that implied an inevitable Christian moral and religious triumph. Monotheism, Kaufmann asserted, was not a concept that the Israelites only dimly envisioned and that found its true expression in the religion of the Nazarene. Jewish monotheism and the Jewish people simultaneously emerged on the stage of history. The behavior of the ancient Israelites is comprehensible only by acknowledging their faith in a single God who transcended fate, the author of history and nature. Kaufmann thus gave his readers a scientific and intensely Jewish alternative to the higher criticism.

Our academic sample reflects evolutionary change. During the 1920s, we found no Biblical study within the Judaica curriculum. But the subject grew in each subsequent decade—absolutely (the number of courses offered) and relative to the rest of Jewish learning. By the 1960s, 11 percent of all Judaica courses were in Bible, a remarkable shift from the inhibition and reticence expressed by Gottheil and Popper. Subsequent university appointments in Bible suggested that Jewish scholars used Kaufmann's insights and a particular methodology to hold their own on a more level playing field. Universities and colleges finally permitted a non-Christian Biblical perspective as *religionswissenschaft* reemerged in the humanities curriculum.[182]

Outside the Gates: Philosophy and the Social Sciences

Lucius Littauer's endowment at Harvard ensured Harry Wolfson's scholarly success, but it did not lead to a major role for philosophy among the Judaica subjects taught in universities. Not all contemporary scholars shared Wolfson's vision of a unified philosophy. Isaac Husik, for one, considered Jewish philosophy to be an intellectual dead end. Religious doubts had led Husik, a Wolfson contemporary with Judaic training, to forego a rabbinical career. He instead studied rabbinics, Semitics, philosophy, and mathematics at the University of Pennsylvania. Husik wrote his doctoral dissertation on Messer Leon, a fifteenth-century Jewish physician, Hebrew grammarian, and philosopher, and published his *History of Medieval Jewish Philosophy* in 1916. He concluded that Jewish philosophy was only possible in the Middle Ages because of "an intellectual naïveté which we have lost for ever." The naivete resulted from an ahistoricism that read contemporary philosophy back into the Bible. Once critics questioned the Bible's authority as the word of God, investigators traced the Biblical text to the Jewish people rather than to First Causes.[183] Husik concluded: "There are Jews now and there are philosophers, but there are no Jewish philosophers and there is no Jewish philosophy."[184] The history of Jewish philosophy was possible, but creative philosophizing was not.[185] During the 1920s, when Wolfson was one of the few professors of Jewish learning, 13 percent of all sampled Judaica courses were in philosophy.[186] A decline to 4 percent in the 1930s and 3 percent in each of the ensuing three decades shows that most students agreed with Husik, not Wolfson. Philosophy failed to gain curricular inclusion, much less dominance.

Part of the problem, argued Brandeis philosopher Marvin Fox two academic generations later, was with the parent field. A half century earlier, Jewish learning appeared in American universities under the protective wing of Semitic philology. In contrast, Anglo-American—analytic—philosophy had little interest in applying the philosophical method to classical Jewish texts and to ancient and modern dilemmas, for example, the nature and assumptions of Jewish law and *aggadah*.[187] Jewish philosophers required difficult double training in mainstream philosophy and classical Jewish texts, but standing little chance of gaining collegial recognition for their efforts, few scholars accepted the challenge.[188] The paucity of academic posts, combined with skepticism about Wolfson's approach, meant that Wolfson would not attract large numbers of disciples. Wolfson's perspective does not dominate the current debate, though it remains a position to be reckoned with. These factors provide a straightforward explanation for philosophy's failure of inclusion. The story of the social sciences is more complex.

Few university-based Judaica scholars prior to World War II relied on the social sciences for methodologies and concepts, or saw modern Jewry as a source

of problematics. Instead, communal agencies and specialized institutions dominated the social scientific study of contemporary Jewry. The Bureau of Jewish
Social Research, a constituent part of the New York Kehilah, the American Jewish Committee, and the American Jewish Congress published the results of their
research in communal reports and in academic journals.[189] The Conference on
Jewish Relations (founded 1933), scholars who gathered around Salo Baron and
City College philosopher Morris R. Cohen, tried to improve Jewish action programs by generating adequate and accurate data on American Jews. Council
members often reported their findings in *Jewish Social Studies* (founded 1939).[190]
European Jews also conducted social research—YIVO in eastern Europe and the
Bureau für Statistik der Juden in Berlin (1904).[191] When Max Weinreich moved
YIVO from Vilna to New York City after 1940, the institute stressed the social
scientific understanding of Jews as individuals and as a group.[192]

The social scientists who worked for Jewish agencies dealt largely with communal issues—population size, immigrant living conditions, and child and female labor. How many Jews were there? Where did they live? How did they earn
a living? How many Jews intermarried and what became of the children? What
did Gentiles think of Jews? Was anti-Semitism growing or declining? Population
studies occupied center stage. But since the U.S. Census Bureau conducted only
one study that asked about religion—and that in 1957[193]—sociologists, demog-
raphers, and statisticians developed other methods to identify and count Jews.[194]
A sophisticated survey reported the first state-by-state estimates of Jewish population for 1877.[195] Educators, who estimated the potential clientele for Jewish
schooling, conducted some of the studies.[196]

In contrast to this communal research, less than 0.5 percent of the college and
university courses in our 45-year time period focused on the social, economic,
or political behavior of the Jews. Only one American social scientist of the postwar generation—Marshall Sklare—made a career as a university-based Jewish social researcher, and even Sklare first worked in a communal organization before
moving to Yeshiva and Brandeis.[197] Nor did the major American rabbinic seminaries—any more than their European counterparts—have social scientists on
their faculties.[198] No institution was designed to train Jewish social researchers,
though there was a school of Jewish communal service.[199]

"Assimilationism," which reflected both practitioner preference and the nature of the social sciences, hindered the prewar academization of Jewish social
research. This orientation characterized most of the sparse social scientific research on Jews conducted in universities between the wars, including *The Ghetto*,
by University of Chicago professor Louis Wirth. The first extensive interpretive,
monographic study of Jewish life by an American social scientist, *The Ghetto*,
Marshall Sklare contends, was ideologically motivated. Wirth's assimilationism
arose from his desire to be seen as an "American" not a "Jewish" intellectual.

But few "Jewish intellectuals" in any field received university appointments
during the interwar years, and Jewish learning for half a century had entered
American universities only when congruent with dominant disciplinary trends.
Wirth's field of study was dominated by assimilationism. "The concern to be
scientific," wrote a recent analyst of Wirth's work and career, "encouraged a dis-

tanced, analytical, comparative view of ethnic groups, which did not quite drain all the specifics of their culture but tended to stress both their common taxonomic traits and the large historic processes which they illustrated."[200]

To refrain from methodological assimilationism while continuing to be a rigorous, "scientific" sociologist required a substantial self-conscious effort. Most early Jewish social researchers desired inclusion, not exemption, and defined the field as the application—not the modification—of social scientific methods to the study of Jews. Jewish and non-Jewish social scientists showed that Jews exemplified generic social problems, that of Jews as immigrants, for example.[201] But social scientific conformance with academic norms gave communal agencies little reason to yield their own research to the universities prior to World War II. Lacking either practitioners or communal subvention, the field did not flourish.

After World War II, many educators explicitly called for a larger university role for the social sciences and for less assimilationism. Germany bequeathed to American Jewish learning a tendency toward detachment and abstraction, contended Rabbi Joshua Trachtenberg, a Columbia Ph.D. who held strong Zionist and Reform ties:

> Thus, along with German academic emphasis on philology, wide erudition and proficiency in classical and Semitic languages, American Jewish learning tended to be 'idealistic,' minimizing if not excluding altogether social and economic forces; it was also apologetic, with a strong assimilationist tinge, in the interests of emancipation and integration in western society, and respectably middle class in so far as it had any social orientation whatsoever.[202]

Trachtenberg was pessimistic about rapid change, given the paucity of academic posts. But the arrival of socially conscious East European refugees and the rise of a younger, native academic generation, he speculated, boded well for a future shift toward a social science orientation that would have a practical outcome for the American Jewish community.

Bernard D. Weinryb, an economic and social historian who taught in seminaries and universities, criticized practitioners of Jewish learning for occupying themselves "merely with spiritual factors and with the past." Failure to incorporate social scientific studies of the Jews into "official" Jewish learning had debilitating results: "The separation of [Jewish learning] from actualities and from the wider relations sometimes leads to idle speculations or to an exaggerated specialization which is not far from mere scholasticism."[203] Reform Rabbi Solomon Freehof of Pittsburgh's Rodef Shalom Congregation argued that a social imperative had accompanied Jewish scholarship since the nineteenth century. But the older impulse—justifying the rights of citizenship—had to yield to a newer mission: serving the "integrational" needs of the Jewish community—rebuilding Jewish life amidst the drastically altered conditions of the postwar world.[204]

The issue of the importance of social scientific methodology as a logical and necessary extension of Jewish learning and the responsibility of American Jewish scholars and scholarship for communal welfare dominated the postwar literature. In pinning their hopes for a better life in America on the results of social science research, these writers shared a consensus concerning the social power of the disciplines. Researchers who studied methods of reducing Gentile prejudice may have shared the goals of Joseph Jacobs, but they rejected his belief that presentation of facts would, by itself, dispel prejudice. Research would identify successful examples of intervention.

Given the interest in the social scientific study of the Jews, what accounts for the continued absence of an academic Jewish social research career line and of courses after World War II? Participants in a 1949 YIVO symposium on Jewish social research identified three inhibiting factors: American antagonism to social research, Jewish communal indifference, and practitioner scarcity. One participant criticized excessive American devotion to social research as a substitute for social action,[205] but most colleagues stressed that "Jewish attitudes toward Jewish sociological research have represented a rather exaggerated version of the common American attitude, which is strongly utilitarian and decidedly superficial."[206] "Social Studies on many a campus," noted a participant, "are looked upon as 'frosting,' nice if 'you can afford it,' a 'side show' that has little concern with what goes on in the main tent."[207] The perception that American optimism and self-assurance "retarded" the growth of Jewish social research reflected a belief that Jewish communal leaders had too readily assimilated stereotypically American values.[208]

Judaica practitioners might have facilitated the inclusion of Jewish social research as Richard Gottheil did for Jewish history at Columbia. But, Salo Baron exempted, most Judaica scholars also viewed social science as a sideshow—a too-relevant sideshow. Freehof and Weinryb were largely correct: mainstream Jewish scholarship in Germany and the United States never honored the call for the study of *statistik der juden* included in the founding documents of *Wissenschaft des Judentums*.[209] Most Judaica scholars mastered linguistic and literary skills and considered statistics—the language of the social scientist—a foreign, even vulgar, analytical tool. These scholars affirmed Arthur Schlesinger, Jr.'s assertion that "Almost all important questions are important precisely because they are *not* susceptible to quantitative answers."[210]

Judaica scholars held the substance of social scientific inquiry in equally low esteem. Zalman Shazar and his fellow students at the Academy of Jewish Studies in late nineteenth-century St. Petersburg wanted to study Jewish social and economic history. But Baron David Günzburg, the academy's benefactor, expressed hostility and derision: "It is as if a scholar had been asked to lecture to you on Kant," the Baron replied, "and then, instead of teaching you the *Critique of Pure Reason,* spent his time describing the restaurant Kant frequented and the kind of cutlets his wife gave him. And it is not Kant you are studying, but that sublime people God chose for His own!"[211] Social scientists, Günzburg and successor Judaica benefactors and scholars believed, wrote about "cutlets"— not philosophies and elites. Judaica scholars from fields already incorporated into universities (and seminaries) thus offered little internal aid to their social science colleagues.

The Jewish community inhibited academization of the field, YIVO symposium participants suggested, by inadequately funding the field and by refusing to yield control. Social research, like other Judaica research, required moral and tangible communal support. "It must be admitted," wrote Ralph Marcus, then at the University of Chicago, "that the number of institutional resources for the promotion of Jewish studies is not great in relation to the size and wealth of the American Jewish community."[212] Endowments were few, and the field had progressed to the point where significant research in Judaica required full-time practitioners.[213] Bluntness might deter potential benefactors, so critics wrote respectfully. But the message was clear: inadequate resources resulted from opposition by communal leaders who doubted the efficacy of academized social research. Jewish scholarship could benefit the Jewish community, but benefactions should correspond to the potential gain. Arguments that emphasized the importance of university subject acceptance apart from donor initiative rarely surfaced at a time when a shortage of resources existed in many areas of intellectual inquiry and when the support of the Jewish community appeared indispensable.[214]

The expensive data collection that social scientific research often required, whether conducted under communal or academic auspices, implied a greater level of support than needed for humanistic research. The Jewish community invested more in social research than in any other discipline, but in 1948, the combined budget for all projects to study American Jewry was smaller than the budget of projects on the causes and elimination of anti-Semitism. This research emphasized the social psychology of the anti-Semite, not the effects of anti-Semitism on Jews, but it was the first sustained American social scientific involvement in an issue of vital Jewish concern. If successful, optimists predicted, practitioners would perhaps conduct decision-oriented research on Jewish activities and resource allocations. These policy studies might in turn lead to research on long-term trends critical to the Jewish community's future.[215]

Investments in the social research capacity of communal agencies, critics added, diverted potential funding for academic research. Communal agencies preferred in-house research because of difficulties with university-based scholars. "Dealing with universities has not been easy," the American Jewish Committee reported:

> Much of the difficulty arose because the universities are used to dealing with foundations which make outright grants with a 'God-bless-you-my-children' benediction and then retire from the scene. Another difficulty arises out of the slow work-pace and lack of administrative skill often characteristic of many university research workers."[216]

But YIVO symposium participants charged that communal agencies often defined research narrowly and treated the findings as proprietary data, thereby discouraging interested university social scientists from further work.[217] Fear of facts ("What will the goyim say?"), they added, was a key reason for communal reliance on agency research.

Few social scientists with interests in topics with a Jewish bent, YIVO symposium participants agreed, adequately commanded both social scientific method and Jewish substance. Traditional Jewish learning was non- or anti-statistical, text-based, and temporally pre-modern. For both Orthodox Judaism and *Wissenschaft des Judentums,* which emphasized rabbinics and premodern Jewish history, greater prestige inhered in a study of Jews in sixteenth-century Rome than in twentieth-century Brooklyn.[218]

Social scientific literature on Jews often used general and communal surveys and other data sources to compare Jewish and general American norms. But gains in methodological rigor and comparative perspective often came at the price of deep, historic understanding of Jews and Judaism. "The Jewish intelligentsia that arose in America," wrote an educator, "lost Jewish knowledge at a greater rate than it gained general knowledge."[219] Commitment to quantitative methods or, among anthropologists, to participant observation, led social scientists to avoid textual and historical sources and to depend on secondary sources that they could not evaluate. The resultant shallowness, critics charged, in turn led to errors in method and substance. Humanists and social scientists, critics added, spoke different languages, metaphorically and literally. Inadequate command of Hebrew or Yiddish sources also compromised results.

As for volition, Sklare was not alone in blaming "second-generation assimilationism" among Jewish social scientists for inhibiting the field's growth. "Second generation Americans who are most qualified to do research in ethnic history, because of motivations which may be entirely subconscious," wrote Edward N. Saveth, "are inclined to write their doctoral dissertations on some aspect of American life that is unquestionably American: the frontier, tariff history, etc."[220] Sociologist Seymour Lipset agreed with the "escaping Jewishness" hypothesis, though he did not entirely relegate motivation to the subconscious realm. "All people and values are objects for study," Lipset noted, "rather than sources of personal identification." Sociology's universalism and egalitarianism implied avoidance of Jewish themes, lest practitioners be labeled "Jewish Jews."[221] What was true for scholarship on the Jewish aspects of Semitics also applied to social scientific research: Those who could, would not; those who would, could not.

YIVO symposium participants debated the issue of setting: was the university, with its methodological sophistication and constant concern for generalities and comparisons, more appropriate than an institute or center—YIVO, for example—where a scholar could work among colleagues better steeped in Jewish knowledge?

Advocates of university inclusion based their justifications on methodological assimilationism: Data collected on Jews could test many social hypotheses. "We have our theories of the development of Jewish life in this country, and our studies in social psychology," sociologist Nathan Glazer noted, "using more or less the same approach as other studies in American social psychology," all of which may be built upon.[222] "The study of Jewish socio-cultural evolution during the last hundred years," added sociologist Florian Znaniecki, a non-Jew, "is very instructive for a comparative theory of modern nationalities as complex societies united by common secular literary cultures, as distinct from religious societies."[223] In social science, as in the academic study of religion, Jewish topics were legitimate, often illuminating, and perhaps exemplary.[224] As Morris Jastrow might have said during an optimistic moment, all would come in time: Where demand existed, supply would soon appear. Lipset invoked the third-generation hypothesis of "the need for roots, for an identification with a group which is smaller than the total society" in predicting the growth of academic studies of American Jewry.[225]

Indeed, several social scientific approaches arose during the 1950s and 1960s. Functionalist sociologists and anthropologists focused on the consequences of religion, thereby eschewing judgmental questions. Many sociologists followed Durkheim, who argued that religion played a necessary role in the moral integration of every community. Indeed, functionalist discussions of religion's universal occurrence facilitated academic acceptance by placing the role of Christianity in western culture in a neutral context.[226]

A symbolist school, led by Clifford Geertz and Victor Turner, disputed key functionalist tenets. Religion, symbolists argued, "is not properly studied in abstract forms, but rather in terms of specific sets of symbols (and of the institutions related to them) which are 'believed in'—accepted and acted upon by groups of human beings who share them." Symbolists argued for religion's cultural specificity: "There is no religion 'in general' because there is no faith in general."[227] Neither Judaism nor any other religion could play an exemplary role since the relativism and particularism of the symbolist approach negated the concept of centrality and made comparison difficult at best.

Other social scientists saw Jews as part of the study of American minority groups. The genre, initially associated with University of Chicago sociologist Robert Park and his students, counteracted racial supremacists who made academic inroads earlier in the century. But Sklare dismissed advocates of this approach for their personal faith in—or their academic prediction of—minority assimilation. In any case, these social scientists legitimated the sociological study of ethnicity. Their students built upon their observations while rejecting their assimilationism for pluralism: an integrative impulse, a quest for unity based upon value judgment, and the belief that unity in a democracy required an acceptance of heterogeneity.[228] This generation emphasized prejudice reduction and intergroup (and interfaith) relations.[229] The content of minority cultures, they often noted, mirrored majority practice. Differences often were exaggerations of less desirable features of majority culture.[230] The pluralists who appeared during the 1950s and 1960s, noted historian John Higham, did not retain the normative orientation of these predecessors. The old pluralism was an unrealized ideal based upon a notion of national purpose, Higham added. The new pluralism was a condition; it "dissolved the 'ought' in the 'is.' "[231]

The distinction between sociologists of Judaism and of Jews as a minority group—exemplified, respectively, by Gerhardt Lenski's *The Religious Factor,* and Nathan Glazer and Daniel Patrick Moynihan's *Beyond the Melting Pot*—may have hindered access to social science departments in the 1960s. Attacks on functionalism and on methodological assimilationism did not help. But the symbolists did not drive out the functionalists, nor did the rise of a particularist sociology of the Jews in the 1960s signal the end of pluralist approaches. Particularists, who considered the pluralist "is" an inadequate description of reality, asked whether universities might offer more hospitable alternatives to social science departments for their work. Identifying, often strongly, with their subject of investigation, these scholars benefited from the rapidly growing ethnic studies movement. "What is needed is a synthesis of tools, knowledge and feelings," wrote one partisan, "for research in [Jewish] social science is not research in mathematics. It cannot be completely objective. It involves human emotions. As I see it, it should provide help in the adjustment of the Jewish group to survival and not to disappearance in America."[232] By 1970, some particularists argued that Jewish survival—the key problem that confronted sociologists of the Jews (not to mention Jewish sociologists)—was best addressed in separate Jewish studies departments or centers.

Marshall Sklare's commentaries provided ammunition for separatists. Sklare emphasized the importance of practitioner identity for the field's future. Sklare echoed Elbogen: A sociologist who lacked personal commitment to Jewish survival could follow disciplinary trends into and out of the field.[233] Sklare contrasted the survivalist orientation of his edited volume, *The Jews: Social Patterns of an American Group*,[234] with three earlier schools: assimilationist, including Wirth's *The Ghetto*;[235] anti-anti-Semitism, T. W. Adorno, *The Authoritarian Personality*,[236] for example; and alienationist, Judith Kramer and Seymour Leventman, *Children of the Gilded Ghetto*, for instance.[237] Sklare's belief in the ameliorationist value of the social sciences—his classification revolves around a communal, not a disciplinary orientation—and his frankness about his intellectual presuppositions made his views controversial. "If Jewish studies in the American university are to have a vital future," Sklare wrote, "it will be because they fulfill a need which the young Jew experiences":

> Thus, the push to the study of Judaica must originate in the desire to explore personal identity. It follows then that the future of Jewish studies in the American university will be abortive if they move too far in the direction of becoming a pure and impersonal science.[238]

Other late-1960s particularists emphasized failings that resulted from unfamiliarity with Jewish history, teachings, and institutions. Misinterpretations and factual errors accompanied facile assumptions that amounted to stereotyping—endurance of "respect for learning" as a Jewish value, for example. Some observers applauded the application of general social science research and concepts, social mobility, for example, as sources of hypotheses. But they also noted a tendency to emphasize these concepts at the cost of Jewish concerns. A reviewer of an ethnographic study of the American synagogue wrote:

> It is not a book about the religion of Orthodox Jews. . . . If the book succeeds in its purpose, the reader will finally know little if anything about the meaning that the Orthodox synagogue has for the faithful. . . . So while the manifest subject of this work remains the Orthodox synagogue . . . the study is more about behavior within a clearly defined setting which just happens to be an Orthodox synagogue.

The reviewer acknowledged the quality of the work, but added: "Those interested in the dynamics of contemporary Jewish life in general and Orthodox Judaism in particular, may find that they are given more information than they care to have on some subjects and much less on issues of significant concern to them."[239] Particularists also noted the lack of hypotheses based upon intimate knowledge of the Jewish community. Responding to charges of parochialism that arose from an over-emphasis on Jewish material, one practitioner insisted that excesses could "certainly be matched and outstripped by that sectarianism which is derived from an over-orientation on closed theoretical formulations from the 'outside.'"[240]

Post-Six Day War discussions continued to emphasize issues first raised at the YIVO symposium: practitioner education, relationships to parent disciplines and to other branches of Jewish learning, and communal support.[241] But by the late 1960s, most discussants resolved the academic locale question in favor of the university. Particularists urged creation of Jewish studies centers or departments, while colleagues who foresaw disciplinary receptivity considered the establishment of centers less urgent. But just as theoretical divisions may have impeded access, so may the administrative division: Divided efforts between social science departments and Jewish studies centers may have hindered scholarly communication, which impeded error reduction, which assured continued university neglect.

The particularism of "contemporary Jewish studies" programs that emerged after 1967—especially Sklare's notion of identity as a source of motivation—was indeed vigorously challenged. "But contemporary Jewish Studies that is modern and Jewish in that parochial context," two critics replied, "will not be social science scholarship and will have no place in the academy." The "theoretical and methodological underdevelopment" and "service course" orientation of many programs, as well as the lack of "systematic comparisons" in scholarship that emanated from them, these authors contended, demonstrated the drawbacks of particularism.[242]

The Institute of Contemporary Jewry at The Hebrew University in Jerusalem was a response to disciplinary indifference—and to the humanistic and historical dominance of Jewish studies departments. But the Institute, remarked director Moshe Davis, remained multidisciplinary rather than interdisciplinary: "We have not yet created that indispensable fusion which alone may interpret the many-faceted permutations of the contemporary Jewish experience."[243] If unity was difficult for a survivalist program housed within the friendly confines of an Israeli university, what were the prospects for American centers with particularist agendas?[244]

Focus on practitioner motivation and qualification for the conduct of social research on Jews raised thorny questions. Contra Sklare: Did not particularism virtually eliminate the potential contributions of sympathetic Gentiles who played important roles in other subfields of Jewish learning? Did his argument differ from that made by advocates of other ethnic and racial groups about the primacy of empathy? Might not such an emphasis alienate ambivalent intellectuals who might be attracted to the field? Finally, when does attention to credentials divert attention from scholarly product? Contra other particularists:

How was the litany of issues modified in light of the post-1967 influx into university positions of practitioners representing a broad range of American Jewry—including Orthodoxy?

Particularism came forth, ironically, just when Americans, or at least some vocal elements, questioned the meliorative ability of the social sciences. Early twentieth-century scholars, skeptics noted, disappointed communal representatives who expected university-based Jewish learning to result in recognition. If contemporary Jewish communal indifference ended and adequate resources appeared, could particularists produce scholarship and instruction that significantly enhanced prospects for Jewish survival in America?

Conclusion: Scholarship and Scholars, American and Jewish

Beginning in the late 1960s, the specter of particularism haunted American scholarship. Despairing of evolving predictive models for the relationship between the individual and society, sociologists, one critic noted, retreated into "particular and putatively empirical inquiries."[245] The popularity of ethnography symbolized the triumph of the particular: If one could say little about the broader questions that preoccupied the social sciences, one might at least study a single event exhaustively.

"The humanities," wrote an English professor, "are not merely entering, they are plunging into their worst state of crisis since the modern university was formed a century ago, in the 1880s." At that time, an extreme romanticism emphasizing the purely personal and idiosyncratic, and an academic specialization that rewarded methodological rigor and professional visibility set the tone for twentieth-century scholarship in English. Successive developments within the subject (philology and texts, New Criticism, structuralists, and deconstructionists), this critic continued, compounded the tendency toward fragmentation and particularism. Two late-1960s developments worsened conditions. "'Business English' courses (business schools have money; you can try for a job there teaching How to Write a Letter) exfoliated." A press for relevance accompanied heightened vocationalism: "The militant exclusiveness in focus of ethnic literatures is too well known to need comment, as is the sadness that excellent literature, among all minorities, should be treated in the isolation that liberal-minded people deplore." When English studies were taken seriously at all, "specialism deepened, and experiment in the medium . . . usurped . . . 'content as transmuted into expression.'"[246]

Historians who once pondered the American character and the "national purpose" now considered small subdivisions of American life as ends in themselves, not as data for comprehensive analyses. Avoid "larger social labels," one scholar advised, until exploration of particulars permitted their more sophisticated use. Historians "cannot claim to write about 'America' or 'American thought' on the basis of its ministers, novelists, or political pamphleteers," he added. "I hope we shall some day be able to return to a grander level of synthesis, . . . but such endeavors will be extremely difficult."[247] When the "new social history" failed to offer syntheses, some historians called for the "return of the narrative." Methodological sophistication—especially quantitative—overwhelmed and trivialized the historical imagination. Claims that results could be generalized were post hoc and undocumented. Whatever one thought of *Middletown,* Muncie, Indiana, was not New York City, or even Rochester, New York. Scholars, Jacques Barzun lamented, were learning more and more about less and less.[248]

Some observers attributed the particularist ethos to political provincialism: "We seem increasingly to have buried ourselves in our large continent; to have become so transfixed by the kaleidoscopic complexities immediately in front of us that we do not experience American life any longer as a unity but as a random aggregation," wrote historian Robert Kelley.[249] Revulsion against the excesses of American internationalism, and an inability to explain the extraordinary events of the 1960s using contemporary analytical models, conspired against academic venturesomeness. So did claims to university inclusion advanced by hitherto "neglected" groups. Group claims to monopoly over scholarship about that group also truncated the academic imagination. The "sympathetic Gentile," deemed crucial by another generation, seemed unnecessary, even counterproductive. Kelley's description of timidity also included the decline of area and comparative scholarship and the absence of speculative, integrative studies. By the late 1970s, the only universal left in academe was the omnipresence of particularism.

Particularists responded that less desirable tendencies—such as authoritarianism and the danger that "values related to our geographic area, our institutions, our time, would be imposed as universals, as eternal truth"—accompanied integrative scholarship. Nationalism, rather than internationalism, they added, actually inspired the arguments of their antagonists.[250] But Kelley was optimistic:

> Clearly, we must be more careful than our scholarly predecessors in making grand extrapolations outward from the sayings of the New England ministerial elite, and we are certainly a complex and many-sided country. We need go no further, however . . . than to read Alexis de Tocqueville or the hundreds of books written by British travelers in America . . . to learn that there is, in fact, a widely shared core culture in the United States, a dominant cluster of attitudes, beliefs, ways of living; a worldview. . . .
>
> The American way of living and thinking, after all, is no longer just the property of one ethnic community, but is increasingly shared and shaped by, and the property of, the many peoples of the United States.[251]

Renewed interest in undergraduate general education and in integrative graduate education foretold an attempted return swing of the pendulum in the 1980s. But heightened vocationalism accompanied the particularism of the 1970s: Many students found the debate irrelevant since they bypassed anything unrelated to their future occupation.

Increased interest in the history of the disciplines accompanied these debates. Earlier chronicles, critics charged, were often self-adulatory or represented attempts to claim intellectual turf.[252] Recent histories, in contrast, broadly challenged these "whig" renditions.[253] The progress of knowledge was not linear. Contemporaries often committed the sin of presentism by citing historical precedents for their own work, work often prompted by different motives, undertaken in various social contexts, and offering new meaning to the same terminologies employed by their academic forbearers.[254] The histories of many disciplines demonstrated discontinuity; more scholars invoked the memory and prestige of disciplinary giants than were actually justified in doing so.[255]

Concomitant with—related to, some argued—the rise of particularism was the perception that the academic profession had seen better days and that the status of individual academics had declined. Evidence of objective decline was mixed: Enrollments and other measures of growth increased during the 1960s. During the early 1960s, public authorities frequently consulted with academics on social and cultural issues. But by decade's end, conservatives "blamed" academics for advocating doctrines that led to failed social policies and to widespread campus disturbances. Research funds, plentiful at the height of the academic revolution, became scarce. Teaching loads increased, especially in service courses, and accountability replaced entrepreneurship as an academic desideratum.

The "new depression in higher education" (ca. 1970–1972) led to substantial budget cuts in the humanities as students migrated to vocational studies. American materialism—not the social or natural sciences—was the enemy, as it had been for Morris Jastrow a century earlier. This materialism led many to question the worth of a liberal education. Even during the 1960s, critics pondered whether "the inexorable substitution of an artificial environment and a materialistic outlook on life for the old natural environment and spiritual world view that linked us so irrevocably to the Recent and Distant Pasts" had created in Americans a "historical amnesia."[256] The growth of business schools and the scarcity of new positions in the social sciences and humanities appeared to reflect this attitude. Others blamed their colleagues: How many of the 600,000 American professors in the early 1970s really understood and practiced the academic morés developed over 800 years?[257]

Advocates of Jewish scholarship were opportunistic in obtaining subject inclusion throughout their century-long encounter with American higher education. During periods of possible inclusion, concerned scholars and laity undertook initiatives congruent with general developments in institutions with the resources to accommodate the field—most frequently research universities, then comprehensive institutions with large undergraduate enrollments, less frequently private four-year colleges. Advocates seized opportunities that appeared as the orientation of Jewish learning—reflected in scholarly agendas and curricular changes—shifted from the universalistic outlook of early practitioners to the particularistic outlook that held sway beginning in the late 1960s.

Lacking a base in the moral philosophy course that spawned many American academic disciplines or indeed in any part of the nineteenth-century classical curriculum, Jewish learning entered the late nineteenth-century university in Semitics departments, where it would facilitate American participation in Darwinian and Biblical controversies and earn recognition for American scholarship for its contributions to philology.

The rise in anti-Semitism after World War I and the Holocaust and the founding of the State of Israel bracketed a shift in rationale for the inclusion of Jewish learning in American universities—combining "contributions" and internal agendas. Subfields offered to enhance understanding of the western intellectual tradition, provide insights into social history when it claimed preeminence over political history, promote intercultural understanding and pluralism by offering a non-Protestant perspective on history and culture, deepen the understanding of the linguistic processes, or help reintroduce religion—or at least its study—into the university curriculum.

The fields of Jewish learning that entered American higher education in the 1960s and 1970s took on a more particularist case. Reflecting the general scholarly mood heightened the prospects of some subfields for disciplinary inclusion—thus continuing the century-long pattern. But beginning in the late 1960s, the "ethnic studies" movement opened a new avenue of university access through creation of separate departments. Advocates surmounted cross-campus resistance and difficult financial times to achieve a decade of unprecedented growth for the field (though some subfields still felt unrepresented).[258]

Changes in research topics illustrated this shift. An earlier generation might have sought out similarities between, say, modern Jewish literature and contemporary non-Jewish writings, but by the 1960s, scholars pointed to traditional themes in supposedly assimilated Jewish authors.[259] Attracting university-trained scholars to Jewish topics appeared of prime importance just after World War II. But concern later shifted to the inadequacy of Jewish knowledge among practitioners. A sociologist, for example, examined the *New York Times* for possible anti-Semitic bias in its wedding announcements. The scholar examined the listings for the spring season, apparently unaware that observant Jews only marry on one day between Passover and Shavuot, two spring holidays. Israel's emergence and the triumph of Zionist ideology abetted particularism by providing an alternate frame of reference. Comparisons, if attempted at all, were often between Jews in Israel and the diaspora, rather than between Jews and Gentiles in the same country.

Some observers, wary of particularism and relativism, asked whether one could specify *any* criteria for subject inclusion or whether "open admissions" applied to subjects and practitioners as well as to matriculants. Some scholars, such as historian Carl Bridenbaugh, supplied invidious criteria. Social origins, Bridenbaugh suggested, handicapped younger scholars:

> [They] are products of lower middle-class or foreign origins, and their emotions not infrequently get in the way of historical reconstructions. They find themselves in a very real sense outsiders in our past and feel themselves shut out. This is certainly not their fault, but it is true.[260]

These comments appeared as part of a general lament about the fragmentation of historical scholarship. Historians formerly shared a common culture and drew upon their world view to generalize upon central themes. Now, Bridenbaugh concluded, historians applied their admittedly well-developed technical skills to marginal problems.[261] The remark's significance derived not so much from its shrill, ad hominem tone as from the continued insistence of a white male Protestant on distinguishing center from periphery, a condition that advocates of Jewish learning still had to contend with in the 1960s.

Bridenbaugh's obtuseness facilitated refutation, but the underlying problem remained. Prior to 1970, practitioners of Jewish learning had to define a relationship to a parent discipline with its own history, and to the "field" of Jewish scholarship, whose existence facilitated their presence within higher education. Scholars who accepted this complex mission were often "assimilationist"—methodologically, if not ideologically. But as late as the 1960s, the Bridenbaughs, who still often dominated humanistic departments, tolerated only this type of scholar. By the end of that decade, Judaic scholars with a greater range of orientations applied for a growing number of academic positions, and Bridenbaughism faded from the scene. Advocates of Jewish learning turned from inclusion to self-regulation, partly to assure against a change in the then-hospitable academic climate, partly because the field's growth raised questions about the education and scholarship of some practitioners who obtained university posts.

The Association for Jewish Studies, founded in 1969, attempted to shore up this potentially vulnerable flank. A decade of informal conversations prompted Leon A. Jick of Brandeis University to summon a steering committee that included the prime discussants: Arnold Band, Charles Berlin, Gerson Cohen, Nahum Glatzer, Irving Greenberg, Baruch Levine, Michael A. Meyer, Yohanan Muffs, Nahum Sarna, and Frank Talmage. The field's postwar growth, the committee concluded, necessitated a new organization that would facilitate scholarly communication—informality would no longer suffice—and urge colleges and universities to appoint adequately educated scholars to contemplated posts in Jewish learning. The older American Academy for Jewish Research, founded in 1920, had similarly defined its objectives as "to stimulate Jewish learning by helpful cooperation and mutual encouragement as well as to formulate standards of Jewish scholarship." But the Academy, steering committee members concluded, could not meet these objectives. The Academy invited Fellows to membership; in contrast, A.J.S. opened membership to all dues-payers who agreed with the Association's goals. Historian Ira Robinson noted that the Academy had not responded to the field's expansion. As late as 1977, he noted, 62 percent of the Academy's 53 Fellows came from the small number of institutions represented at the time of the Association's founding.[262] In practice, the two organizations exhibited generational and intellectual differences, though one historian, writing in the mid-1980s, noted that the Association itself was dominated by "elder statesmen" who emphasized the premodern period, Europe and the Middle East (not North America), and philosophical, historical, and exegetical scholarship. "Younger scholars with their newer techniques and social-historical approaches and critical perspectives," this observer added, "are only gradually making their influence felt."[263]

In 1969 and 1970, the members of the Association resolved to convene annually, hold regional conferences, and publish a journal (*AJS Review,* 1976-

present). Association members also spelled out their "quality control" objectives: "setting advisory minimal standards for: a. survey courses in Jewish Studies b. undergraduate major programs; c. graduate programs; d. Jewish-studies elements in interdepartmental programs and . . . offering advisory services to colleges and universities beginning or expanding their programs in Jewish Studies."[264] Association newsletters chronicled battles against dilettantism, but scholarship about a people, their beliefs, and their practices, was not *inherently* questionable. A specific work of scholarship might justifiably be criticized as "narrow," but, as in Bridenbaugh's case, the criticism might also arise from suspect motives. Association founders reinforced this claim to legitimacy when they named the organization. Jewish Studies, wrote Arnold Band, was a "scholarly discipline which deals with the historical experience of the Jews in the religious, cultural, intellectual and social spheres, in all centuries and countries."[265]

The Association for Jewish Studies became a key arena for debate and for assuring the field's legitimacy. Internal controversies often resulted from the interaction of subfields with different dates of university admission, patterns of development, degrees of acceptance, and, sometimes, competing claims to subject matter. The location issue remained central. Jewish learning, some members suggested, might play a role in the renaissance of a liberal education that acknowledged a need to redefine the curricular "mainstream" in light of American absorption of minority groups. Jewish learning might also take advantage of calls for "integrated" graduate education that emphasized interdisciplinary connections as a corrective to overspecialization.[266]

Association particularists doubted that curricular reformers would incorporate Jewish scholarship into these broader contexts. Conscious exclusion, after all, was a major reason why practitioners of Jewish learning debated these questions at all. Why abandon an important new context for research and teaching in Jewish learning—the Jewish studies department or program—when this environment finally permitted the field to define its own agenda? Courtship by the disciplines resulted from scarcity of resources as well as from belated recognition of the field. Scholars who relied on the disciplines, particularists concluded, should stay on the alert.

IX

GROWTH AND SURVIVAL

Jewish learning found a long-term home in the Semitics departments of six American universities after 1880, but by 1920, Judaic Semitics was a spent field. Initiatives in Jewish history, modern Hebrew, religion, Bible, and Yiddish bore fruit during the 1930s and 1940s and dominated the Judaica curriculum through the late 1960s. The field then entered a new period characterized by rapid enrollment increases, subject expansion, and the emergence of separate Judaica departments.

Exogenous factors—external or institution-wide events—were more important in explaining changes *between* periods than *within* periods. The creation of universities—an exogenous event—gave Jewish learning its first six homes. But external events such as the founding of the Zionist movement in the 1890s did not affect the field until the curricular appearance of modern Hebrew decades later. Academic anti-Semitism, which reflected the resurgence of American nativism and xenophobia, then contributed to the field's decline. Jewish learning barely held on at Harvard and other formerly hospitable universities that imposed restrictions on the admission of Jewish students and on the hiring of Jewish faculty members. An influx of Jewish undergraduates into municipal and state colleges and universities led to the innovations of the 1930s, but the Holocaust and the creation of the State of Israel did not affect the growth of Jewish learning until the 1960s. A confluence of exogenous events in the late 1960s—especially the Six Day War and student unrest often related to ethnic and racial self-consciousness—marked the transition to a more inward-looking period.

Presidents, providers, and scholars determined the fate of the field within each period. Conditions at Johns Hopkins represented the typical pattern of first period growth and decline. The ratio of Semitics enrollments to total enrollments increased from 4.5 percent to 9.3 percent from 1883 through 1887 and from 1903 through 1907 but then declined to 1.3 percent in the period from 1918 through 1922. Even when the field showed absolute growth, its relative position declined. New institutions did not join the Judaica ranks, faculty members rarely migrated from their first institutions, and universities that accepted Judaica wavered in support. Most of the 15 to 20 university-based Judaica scholars, graduate fellows, and assistants were appointed by 1900. Practitioners attributed the decline in Semitics to the displacement of the humanities by the natural sciences in the university cur-

216

riculum.[1] The actual reasons, as we have seen, were more complicated, but academic anti-Semitism assured that the field would not overcome internal handicaps.

The six founding institutions provided more evidence of discontinuity. Salo Baron's appointment created new intellectual possibilities at Columbia at a time when only Richard Gottheil's longevity and academic neutrality perpetuated Semitics. Jewish learning atrophied at the University of Chicago, perhaps because of dependence on local rabbis. The 1944 appointment of Ralph Marcus raised as many questions as it answered, and during the 1960s and beyond, when several of the original six Judaica universities announced ambitious programs, Chicago was represented at most by a few scholars, for example Norman Golb. The University of California at Berkeley, like Columbia, based its program on history—and comparative literature—when it reentered the lists after World War II and not on William Popper's philological orientation. The founding institutions used their continued resource advantages to re-embark upon the field at propitious times.

The pessimism of the 1920s, bracketed by academic anti-Semitism and the emergence of a "mass" urban constituency, slowly eroded as Jewish learning expanded into new subject areas under the aegis of parent disciplines that had fewer restrictions than Semitics and into new types of colleges. "Pluralist" justifications for university inclusion that gave roughly equal billing to "Jewish contributions" and to internal integrity replaced the unqualified universalism of the preceding generation. The congruence of Jewish social and economic history with the "new social history," for example, permitted study of a people that went stateless for nearly 1,900 years. Religion departments that considered Judaism one of the "big three" permitted analysis on its own terms—not as a forerunner to Christianity. Modern Hebrew, by depicting itself as a "modern language," found a home in institutions that emphasized contemporary and conversational language instruction. Philosophy and literature departments that saw themselves as defenders of cultural tradition were unreceptive to Jews who studied Kant and Shakespeare, much less to Jewish learning "in translation." Jewish literature, when studied at all, was confined to colleges that offered Hebrew language instruction. Social scientific course work on the Jews awaited a third, post-1960s period and was often justified by particularist rationales.

By 1970, a new phase of rapid growth had set in. About 375 four-year colleges and universities—a sixth of the total—would offer Jewish learning after this date. The field continued to dwell within disciplines, but universities and colleges also established Jewish studies departments in response to exogenous events. Creation of the Association for Jewish Studies in 1969—and attendance by 58 scholars at the founding colloquium—marked practitioner recognition of this turning point.

Jewish learning—no longer restricted to philology and research institutions—thus made new curricular and institutional inroads and, eventually, permanent inclusion. But what was the growth pattern? What colleges and constituent units were most hospitable? Analysis of growth and location between 1920 and 1970 reveals a normalization process. Examination of academic and communal ideologies during the same period shows that pluralist rationales gave way to more particularist approaches. The field's size, content, and intellectual orientation changed, but the questions raised by Leopold Zunz and Ismar Elbogen endured.

Growth

Biographical and institutional analysis amply reveals practitioner concerns and development patterns before World War II. But quantitative analysis must replace case studies as the most efficient method of tracing the subsequent growth of Jewish learning. We have therefore traced the growth of Jewish learning by drawing a representative sample of 121 four-year American higher education institutions and examining the field's presence and content.[2] In 1968, 25 sampled institutions offered five or more Judaica courses—the equivalent of one full-time faculty member. We worked backward from 1968, the year of primary sampling, in three-year intervals and counted undergraduate Judaica courses at each of the 25-college subsample until 1923, when the study of samples becomes impossible.[3]

Between 1919/20 and 1965/66, the number of American colleges and universities granting the bachelor's degree more than doubled—from 1,041 to 2,230—and the number of bachelor's and first professional degrees conferred grew from 49,000 to 551,000—an elevenfold increase that was more a reflection of enrollment growth than of student retention. Master's degrees conferred grew by a factor of 35, doctoral degrees by a factor of 30. But the 90-fold enrollment increase in Jewish learning over 45 years strongly outpaced this overall growth. The field's growth resulted partly from the tide of enrollment that lifted all ships, partly from the much lower initial levels of Jewish learning that left room for the field to grow, and partly from developments at peer institutions, the same factor that explained growth in the previous period. By 1968, the 25 colleges averaged more than 11 courses—over twice the five-course minimum for admission to the sample.

Determining the pattern of growth helps to identify these growth determinants while eliminating others. The mathematical curve that describes Judaica growth is "logistic," an "s" that lies horizontally.[4] The logistic curve for Judaica grew slowly at its inception, shifted to a period of rapid growth, slowed down, and ultimately ground to a halt.[5] This is the theoretically expected pattern of growth in systems with finite resources, or alternatively, growth in a bounded system. For the first period of slow then rapid growth, the growth *rate* was constant. Just as a bank account grows from compound interest paid on increased amounts of capital, not from a change in interest rate, the growth in Jewish learning resulted from a change in the base number of courses offered. In other words, each moment of growth produced a multiple of itself in a subsequent period.[6] From 1923 through 1950, the number of undergraduate Judaica courses grew at a constant rate of about 70 percent per three-year period.

But constant growth cannot be sustained when resources are finite. If Jewish learning had begun in one institution, spread to a second college the following year, to another for each of the two in the following year, and so on for 11 years,

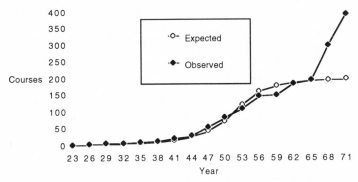

FIGURE 1: The Expected and Observed Number of Undergraduate Judaica Courses in a Sample of Colleges and Universities, 1923–1971.

the total number of institutions offering Judaica would approximate the total number of American BA-granting institutions and the Judaica faculty required would have far outstripped the available supply.[7] Between 1950 and 1965, the number of undergraduate Judaica courses continued to grow, but the volume of growth decreased—a mirror image of the earlier period. Contemporary complaints of stagnation actually reflected this decline in the growth rate. The field would have experienced stasis by the 1970s had the trend continued—the supply of imitator institutions, faculty members, and available students would have stopped growing.[8]

Actuality and theory coincide remarkably from 1923 to 1965 but then become discrepant. The growth rate rapidly increased between 1965 and 1968; the trend continued between 1968 and 1971. The curve, instead of continuing on its flattening trajectory, took a sharp turn upwards. By extending the time series to 1971, we determined that the upward turn represented a new growth spurt, not a statistical accident (a random event). Exogenous change is the most likely explanation for this phenomenon, which sometimes occurs toward the end of periods of logistic growth.[9] The chauvinism associated with the Six Day War propelled the field toward particularism just when American college and university students demanded curricular inclusion of the history and culture of theretofore excluded groups. Black students were most vociferous, but emulation by Jewish students in many types of institutions contributed to a revival of the Jewish learning growth curve. By 1970, slow or no growth no longer characterized the field; instead, practitioners began to address the opportunities and problems brought on by "an embarrassment of riches."[10] Figure 1 shows the actual pattern of growth and the theoretically derived logistic curve.

Several consequences follow if logistic growth best describes Judaica's pattern of development between 1920 and 1965. The field grew as a function of its present and ultimate size—responding to developments indigenous to the field—not as an expression of direct Jewish communal interest and concern. If growth had responded to external events, we would expect a change in the number of courses in the growth rate after these events. Events within the second period, such as the Holocaust and creation of the State of Israel, brought no drastic shifts in the growth curve, although they may have affected the nature and content of courses. This helps to explain persistent practitioner complaints of inadequate communal support—the Littauer and Miller endowments were exceptions that proved the rule. Changes in practitioner outlook from "universal" to "particular" did not result from direct communal interposition. A better explanation is that both scholars and community responded to gradual changes in objective conditions that affected the larger population. The economic improvement of the Jewish community increased the number of Jewish college students. This increase, in turn, permitted advocates of Jewish learning to propose curricular innovations. But this explanation turns on changes in another quantitative measure of growth: the ratio of undergraduate to total Judaica courses.

Graduates and Undergraduates

The conditions that promoted the early success of Jewish learning in American universities, first generation practitioners understood, could eventually lead to their exclusion. Judaica scholars were less sanguine than presidents or providers about the communal implications of their work. Fundamentalist invective aimed at William R. Harper during his Yale professorship showed that professors might bear the brunt of attack well after donors turned their attention to new projects and sympathetic presidents had left office. So Judaica practitioners accepted, worked within, and often internalized the norms of the parent field. Semitics, for example, implied a commitment to philology at the expense of literary or other cultural approaches and to the positivist scientific method, an emphasis on specialist training and on ancient over modern materials, and an aloofness from the liberal arts undergraduate curriculum. Subject specialization, university faculty members and administrators understood, facilitated scholarly productivity while shielding Jewish learning from potential religious controversy.

But the same commitments removed scholars from extra-mural constituencies and from large numbers of undergraduate students and thereby limited growth to institutions with a substantial graduate program and a graduate student constituency. Everyone understood the disadvantages, especially the financial implications.[11] Specialized graduate course offerings proliferated during the period of Judaic Semitics. Student/faculty ratios for graduate study were typically lower, and library, physical resource demands, and operating costs were higher. But tuition charges did not significantly differ on the two levels, and undergraduate courses typically subsidized graduate programs. Many institutions therefore pressured departments to overcome indifference and increase the proportion of undergraduate courses.

A committee of Harvard overseers, for example, noted a large discrepancy between graduate and undergraduate course enrollments in 1905/06. The overseers asked the faculty to "undertake a comprehensive revision of the present scheme of instruction with a view to securing more concentration of effort, increased educational efficiency, and if practicable, diminished expenditure."[12] Se-

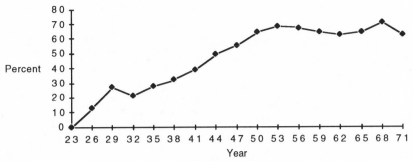

FIGURE 2: Percent of Judaica Courses Taught on Undergraduate
Level, 1923–1971.

mitics faculty members and departments jeopardized their budgets by concentrating their efforts and personnel on expensive specialized training. By failing to cultivate an undergraduate constituency, these scholars also failed to recruit a replacement generation. Paul Haupt and a few colleagues proposed to develop undergraduate Semitics curricula. But William Popper reflected the majority position when he reported that Berkeley's Semitics department addressed itself "largely to the use of advanced students."[13] Popper's course registrations fell to less than 20 percent of the students that Jacob Voorsanger had attracted to his nontechnical courses.[14]

The Semitists, by not responding, made themselves vulnerable to changed conditions. But future proponents of Judaica learned from experience. Philanthropic support remained minimal between the 1920s and the 1960s, so practitioners devoted increased attention to revenue-producing undergraduate courses. Judaica departments with an undergraduate following thrived, while other departments withered.

Jewish learning appeared exclusively at the graduate level in 1923, but the proportion of undergraduate courses steadily increased to two-thirds of all Judaica courses by the early 1950s (Figure 2). That proportion remained remarkably constant from 1950 to 1971, save for a minor aberration in 1968. The mature field had a stable balance of undergraduate liberal arts and graduate specialized offerings. Some undergraduates went on to graduate school, but the majority remained "consumers" of Judaica.

The shift from graduate to undergraduate courses reflected curricular changes that supplanted the field's preoccupation with ancient text and philological method. The shift also reflected the field's access to a new class of institutions.

Institutional Setting

From the 1880s through the early 1930s, save for episodic offerings, Jewish learning found a home at only six universities. The leaders of these six institutions had an intrinsic interest in the subject, believed that it addressed key issues of the day, or saw it as a route to academic recognition. Emulating the curriculum of continental universities, publishing critical editions of ancient Semitic texts, and composing arcane monographs would demonstrate intellectual cosmopolitanism. Semitics, including Judaica, became a marker of research institutions—part of coming of age in American higher education. The twentieth century witnessed changes in the field's intellectual center of gravity and growth in the number of courses and institutions offering Judaica. Did these changes result in a new institutional locale for Jewish learning? Or would the field remain associated with research universities?

Jewish learning remained associated—though more loosely—with research universities possessing substantial resources. All six originating Judaica universities were present at the founding of the Association of American Universities, the core of the research guild. AAU membership still characterized Judaica institutions in 1968, but the fit was less tight. Almost two-thirds of the 25 sampled institutions with at least the equivalent of one Judaica faculty member—five or more courses—were *current* AAU members. Since only ten percent of the non-Judaica institutions belonged to AAU, membership continued to distinguish Judaica and non-Judaica institutions.

Only institutions that offer advanced degrees may join AAU. We therefore compared other characteristics of Judaica and non-Judaica schools, including enrollments, the number of library volumes, faculty size, and student-faculty ratio at late nineteenth-century institutions that offered Judaica, Semitics, but no Judaica, and neither Semitics nor Judaica. Judaica institutions, Table 3 shows, were more likely to have superior scholarly resources—measured by total enrollments, undergraduate enrollments, the proportion of the student body matriculated on the graduate level, the size of the library, the number of faculty members, and the student-faculty ratio—in both 1896 and 1968, though these relationships were weaker in 1968. These characteristics bespeak an academic culture amenable to specialized and advanced subjects. Thus, while all institutions would be expected to include American history in their curriculum, the history of particular religio-ethnic groups, including Jews, requires greater faculty and student specialization, reflected in larger library holdings, lower student-faculty ratios, and a sizable graduate student population. In contrast, the institutions with no Semitics or Judaica had the smallest graduate enrollments and faculties, the largest student-faculty ratio, and the smallest libraries. Save for total enrollments, colleges and universities that offered Semitics, but no Judaica, fell in between.[15]

Institutional size usually compensated for research orientation in accounting for the 1968 distribution of Jewish learning. Many scholars identify a significant positive relationship between institutional size and innovation. Size implies a larger pool of talent that, on a random basis, is more likely to come up with more new ideas. Size permits combinations of faculty talents that create hybrid fields. Larger institutions need to divert a smaller proportion of their resources to support an innovation and are therefore less likely to face opposition. Size also permits an institution to offer basic courses while maintaining a "reserve" of faculty time and labor for new curricular enterprises. A large faculty, wrote sociologist Joseph Ben-David, "made possible the growth of the department, and within the

TABLE 3
Comparison of Judaica and Non-Judaica Institutions: 1896 and 1968
A. Characteristics

	1896			1968	
	No Semitics	Semitics without Judaica	Judaica	No Judaica	Judaica
Undergraduate enrollment	165	908	791	6,138	16,157
Total enrollment	389	1,709	2,034	7,766	23,650
Percent graduate students	1.5	7.0	18.4	11.4	35.9
Number of library books	11,315	108,918	176,805	442,396	2,000,400
Number of faculty	33	158	224	552	1,989
Student-faculty ratio	11.8	11.1	8.8	14.1	11.9
(N)	(25)	(11)	(4)	(96)	(25)

B. Ratios of Characteristics

	Ratio: Judaica/ No Semitics (1896)	Ratio: Judaica/ No Judaica (1968)
Undergraduate enrollment	4.8	2.6
Total enrollment	5.2	3.0
Percent graduate students	8.0	3.1
Number of library books	12.3	4.5
Number of faculty	6.8	3.6
Student-faculty ratio	0.75	0.84

department . . . the introduction of relatively independent sub-specialties," including Judaica. Some larger institutions even had the resources to create entire Jewish studies departments.[16]

The growth of American higher education meant that more institutions had a large enough student body and library to facilitate curricular differentiation and innovation. A "small" late nineteenth-century college enrolled perhaps 100 undergraduates. In the mid-twentieth century, "small" could mean several thousand students. Graduate enrollments and library size show similar absolute increases. By the 1960s, schools further toward the back of the academic procession surpassed the resource levels of front-end late nineteenth-century universities. The Judaica curriculum, as we have seen, changed so as to give itself a home in a somewhat broader range of institutions, while changes at these institutions benefited Judaica. Specifically, between 1950 and 1970, the pool of likely Judaica institutions expanded to include public "flagship" and regional universities.

Early twentieth century public normal schools that faced competition from the growing high school system, Christopher Jencks and David Riesman have noted, began to require a high school diploma for admission and four years of study for graduation. These colleges changed their names from "state normal school" to "state teachers college" and soon felt obliged to hire more university-educated Ed.D.'s, who "knew what constituted respectability in the academic world." Expansion into secondary school teacher preparation prompted the teachers colleges to recruit faculty members with Ph.D.'s in high school academic subjects.

The colleges then added programs for the non-professional students attracted by the presence of liberal arts faculty members and renamed themselves state colleges or state universities.[17] Much post-World War II four-year college enrollment growth occurred in these regional public institutions. The 1963 Schempp decision removed the constitutional barrier to eligibility of these institutions—and of flagship state universities—for Jewish learning. Among the regional public universities, Judaica institutions more closely resembled research universities.[18]

During the late 1960s and early 1970s, community colleges grew at least as rapidly as these public four year colleges—for a few years they opened at the rate of two or three per week. But community colleges were unlikely to offer Jewish learning. Two-year schools had no graduate enrollments and lacked most other predictors of Jewish learning. Increasing numbers of students enrolled in terminal vocational education, not graduate school.[19] Independent, four-year liberal arts colleges fell between these classes of institutions. Liberal arts colleges that offered Jewish learning had large Jewish constituencies, ample resources, and students oriented toward graduate education.[20] If Jewish learning was "contagious" between the 1920s and the 1960s, the institutions most prone to acquire a "case" of it were institutions with mass enrollments *and* research ambitions. The location of many of these institutions in or near large Jewish population centers—a characteristic historically associated with the field's university presence and still characteristic of the field in 1968—facilitated student enrollments and communal support.

Did renewed growth between 1965 and 1968 lead to the introduction of Jewish learning into a new class of institutions? We analyzed a 1970 survey of religious studies in American colleges and universities that asked religion department chairs for their plans for new faculty appointments. Almost ten percent of the responding chairs said they were seriously considering a Judaica appointment during the next three years.[21] These chairs represented institutions with larger enrollments and larger libraries. Their religion faculty members were more likely to hold the Ph.D. The expansion of Jewish learning followed its historic course. Serendipity and idiosyncrasy played their roles, but the field generally moved from larger research universities to institutions that realistically aspired to university status.

Is Jewish learning paradigmatic for academic innovation? No single model can account for all curricular innovation; different subject matters produce different patterns.[22] There are enormous differences in the academic cultures that would produce new courses in, say, accounting, but not scientific logic. Sinology, the study of Chinese culture, is a case in point. Sinology and Judaica faced similar problems of self-definition and often appeared together in early "Oriental Studies" departments. Neither subject directly emerged from the classical curriculum; both were exotic, had few adepts, and experienced relatively low student demand. We examined the distribution of undergraduate courses in Chinese language, history, literature, and culture in our 1968 sample of institutions to learn if a comparable field shows a similar distribution pattern.[23] The same institutional attributes predicted and facilitated the emergence of Sinology and Judaica, and both subjects tend to be found on the same campuses.[24]

Scholars have formed no consensus on where innovations begin in the "academic procession." Research universities, "trickle-down" advocates insist, have the resources, the intellectual talent, and the will to innovate.[25] Other scholars find no relationship between innovation and status, or argue that innovations begin in less-prestigious schools and "trickle-up."[26] Our data are consistent with the views of trickle-down scholars, perhaps because of the nature of the innovation. Jewish learning entered at the procession's head and still finds a home on campuses that resemble the elite character of its origins. All knew the requirements for attaining proper credentials among the elite. In contrast, we would not expect to find much "trickle-up" in the history of "low-prestige" applied fields that entered non-elite institutions. We would instead expect to find that these fields remained in non-elite settings at maturity. There are few innovations that resemble the now ubiquitous elective system, which was characteristic of all early Judaica institutions but found only in a fraction of the others. The patterns for Jewish learning and Sinology suggest that the "academic procession" may actually be segmented, with each segment having an independent sense of what should be academized.

Survival

Growth provided university-based Jewish learning with opportunities and problems. Many observers attributed the problems and malaise apparent throughout academe in the 1970s to rapid institutional and enrollment growth or, in Joseph Ben-David's words, "the difficulties of systems of higher education to accommodate within their existing structures their new and extended functions."[27] Growth appeared to upset existing equilibria—between the number of graduates and positions in appropriate occupations, between supply and demand for instructors, and between investment in research and the resultant growth of knowledge.[28] "To find the means required to be able to admit up to half of the relevant age group and to train people and forge ideas and tools for the research requirements of a society in which decisions in every walk of life are increasingly based on research," wrote Ben-David, "is the challenge faced by higher education today."[29]

After World War II, Jewish learning enrollments grew and scholarly production increased as its university base became increasingly hospitable and secure. The exogenous factors that resulted in the field's post-1965 growth rate—student demand for Jewish studies, the Six Day War and subsequent developments in Israel, and communal grants and endowments—may have strengthened practitioner confidence at a time when many colleagues in other subjects expressed increased pessimism—recall, for example, that modern Hebrew distanced itself from other modern languages at this time.

But these same exogenous factors brought an imbalance to the production of Judaica doctorates and the demand for instructors. The resultant faculty shortage exacerbated the tendency among academic officials to appoint Jewish "representatives"—especially rabbis—to Judaica posts.[30] So did calls from the field's large undergraduate contingent for greater attention to issues of religious and personal identity. Rapid growth based on exogenous factors, and the resultant heterogeneity of backgrounds in Judaica practitioners, renewed the debate about the field's aims within American universities. The debate became more pointed when an academic recession in the early 1970s led practitioners to fear that rapid contraction might follow rapid growth. Judaica enrollments and resources actually increased during the "new depression in higher education" (1970–1972), but left and right wing attacks on research universities that nurtured the field made practitioners feel vulnerable.[31] And just as higher education emerged from the recession of the early 1970s, the malaise of the Yom Kippur War replaced the exuberance of the Six Day War.

The communal agenda for university-based Jewish learning, practitioners understood, had substantially changed. "Survival"—the shorthand term for the social agenda of university-based Jewish learning in the late twentieth century—replaced "recognition." But communal concern for the survival of Jewish learning in universities was no more an end in itself than was academic recognition a century earlier. Anxiety over the future of Judaism replaced the desire for social and religious recognition. What did modern Jewish existence mean in a benign environment? The threat to Jewish survival in late twentieth-century America, thought some, increased along with social assimilation. Why should individuals continue to identify themselves as Jews?

The increasingly heterogeneous professorate included more practitioners who shared this concern. How would Judaism fare, pondered Cornell's Milton I. Konvitz in 1964, if secular, homogenized American institutions served heretofore distinctive cultural and spiritual needs? "Cultural cannibalism," he wrote, "is a practice not unknown in the history of civilization; and it is a practice which can be more easily pursued in a free than in an autocratic society, for the latter may lead to the voluntary or coerced erection of ghetto walls; but in a free society ghettoes sooner or later give way." Jewish survival, Konvitz concluded, required spiritual and cultural *separation*.[32] "The Jewish community (as all communities in America—only more so)," concurred Irving Greenberg, then at Yeshiva University, "is now open to positive assimilation (in both biological and cultural senses) as it has never been. Even its Jewishly committed components are more influenced by the general culture than ever before. . . . Thus the question of its survival becomes more of a question."[33]

The American Jewish infrastructure—synagogues, educational and charitable institutions, and community centers—earlier sustained Jews who were excluded from broader social participation. But these institutions, critics charged, now failed to insure communal survival through value and identity retention. An alarming increase in the Jewish intermarriage rate and in other indicators of communal instability appeared to accompany social inclusion. Indifference reduced parental ability and desire to teach their children about Judaism.

Could universities pick up the slack? By the 1960s, universities and colleges were perhaps the only institutions with a captive audience of most Jewish adolescents. The Jewish student influx would have delighted Emil Hirsch, who believed that academic culture could help nurture modern Judaism. But universities, Greenberg worried, might now actually destroy Judaism. "Here," wrote Greenberg, "the new universal culture is at its peak of influence, saturation and reality correspondence." Nineteenth-century denominationalists counseled student avoidance of universities that eschewed pietism. But concerned Jews, who could not now offer a similar prescription, hoped instead that university-based Judaica programs would nurture identity and religiosity. Judaica's growth would come "from the Jewish community's hope and desire to assure Jewish continuity, to hold or win the respect of its young by being present on the college campus in intellectually respectable and socially accepted ways."[34]

Some survivalists echoed Ismar Elbogen's hope that Jewish learning programs would more resemble a profession than a discipline, others urged that practitioners act more as rabbis than as professors. By countering the assimilationism of higher education from within, Jewish studies programs and professors might play a more important communal role than the congregational rabbi. Survivalists, including communal representatives and faculty members from the expanded teaching force, usually subordinated the research function of university-based Jewish learning to undergraduate teaching. The vitality of university-based Jewish studies, agreed Marshall Sklare, still at Yeshiva, depended upon fulfilling the need of Jewish students to explore personal identity. Sklare pinned his hopes upon identified "survivalist" faculty, willing to legitimate and introduce *contemporary* Jewish studies into the curriculum and their research. These studies, he argued, having arisen from Zionist and nationalist concerns, naturally address "the identity problem, and by extension . . . the welfare of the Jewish community." Confining Jewish interests to research allowed a scholar "to present a universalistic face to the 'academic-world-at-large,'" while denying students their best opportunity to confront issues of identity.[35]

Some colleagues disputed the potential efficacy, not the legitimacy, of this imputed function. Any salutary effect of Jewish learning upon Jewishness had to offset the general decline in student religious affiliation, behavior, and values that several generations of researchers identified between the freshman and senior years, especially among Jews.[36] Even a strongly identified Judaica professor who viewed proselytization as a key mission could experience success only among the self-selected student group that enrolled in the appropriate courses. "We should not exaggerate the potential effect of Judaics programs upon American Jews," wrote Arnold Band in 1966. "Nevertheless, they are a significant though small force in the slow, silent struggle to give institutional embodiment and communal identification to the essentials of Judaism (a minority tradition) for a meaningful identity within a leveling, permissive society."[37]

Survivalists often emphasized the importance of a separate location of Judaica offerings *within* a college or university. Sklare, for example, called for the extrication of Jewish learning from parent departments. The universal norms that governed research and teaching within a discipline-based department, he suggested, might discourage courses for and about Jews and Judaism. Within the social sciences, he added, Elbogen's fears had come true: Departmental organization hindered systematic scholarship on contemporary Jewry and advanced disciplinary interests over Jewish learning. The sociological literature on the "prioritization" of values, a literature to which Sklare contributed, suggested that a majority of Jewish academics identified with their discipline more strongly than with Judaism and that this majority resolved conflicts—does one teach on *Rosh Hashana?*—in favor of scholarship.[38]

Leon Jick, the first president of the Association for Jewish Studies, argued for the reconcilability of communal and academic agendas. Association members, he wrote, are devoted to their own pursuits, the totality of Jewish knowledge, *and* the community:

> Rejecting the *kapdanut*—the partisanship—of some and the *baishanut*—the detachment—of others, let us constitute ourselves a group which aspires to fulfill scholarly tasks; which employs scientific methodology (insofar as this can be applied to humanistic, historical, and social-scientific materials); which abjures apologetics, but recognizes its relationship to the totality of a culture; which is zealous for enhancing the understanding of this culture as well as for its continuation.[39]

Scholars must broaden their view of Judaism if they are to model it and demonstrate its vitality and value to their students. But broadening did not imply a diminution of quality. The Association would help, wrote another scholar, to assure against "the intervention of well-meaning but uninformed lay individuals and organizations" that "would reduce Jewish Studies from a rigorous academic discipline with a distinguished history to yet another Jewish fundraising, defense, or Zionist program."[40]

Gerson D. Cohen, then at Columbia, offered an academic rationale for a programmatic, rather than a disciplinary, orientation for Jewish learning. Intellectual fragmentation, which affected many institutions and departments over the preceding decades, abetted by administrative fragmentation of Jewish studies, threatened "to absolve us of responsibility or perhaps inhibit our coverage of material that we know to be essential to a basic and well-rounded program."[41] The reintegration of Jewish learning is necessary now that the concept of "Jewish tradition" has fallen before newer manifestations of Jewish intellectual and artistic creativity.[42]

> We can no longer dismiss Biblical criticism and its results as higher anti-Semitism; nor can we ignore the implications of the Dead Sea Scrolls, apocalyptic literature, Jewish gnostic and magical texts, Judeo-Christianity, Karaism, Jewish philosophy from Philo to the Jewish Averroists, kabbalah, Sabbatianism, hasidism and so on and on, as ephemeral or insignificant deviations of fringe groups that had no serious impact on the Jewish mainstream.[43]

Scholars of Jewish learning must transcend their own research and reformulate the Jewish center and periphery. Increasingly fragmented, discipline-based departments were poor environments for creating or teaching a new synthesis. But Cohen, writing in 1969, doubted that any major institution would soon adequately support a programmatic alternative.[44]

University-based Jewish learning, Cohen told the survivalists, could not compensate for the failure of other agencies to cultivate identity. But progress towards this communal goal was a feasible *by-product* of teaching and scholarship:[45] "Sheer cultivation of interest in their own past, to deeper and more discriminating attachment to their historic heritage" was perhaps the most efficacious method of reaching Jewish youth.[46] Adequate financial support, he added, might yield a bountiful harvest of this by-product.

Baruch Levine, who teaches at New York University, expressed concern with the structure of the disciplines. New programs must be built on existing institutional structures but offerings should become more comprehensive. Knowledge of Hebrew, though necessary in a first-rate program, is not sufficient. Nor, Levine added, is an understanding of

> historical method, the contribution of the social sciences, [and] the nexus of Judaic studies and other disciplines. . . . The best program is an integrated one, which brings together students whose original interests in Judaic studies were diverse, but who grow in their appreciation of the inter-relatedness of language and theory, text and method.[47]

Levine and other Association members echoed Elbogen's belief that Jewish learning was more than the sum of its disciplinary components. The disciplines constrained—even when they accommodated—Jewish learning by relegating the Jewish aspects of their subject from center to periphery. This tendency was especially threatening because advocates of Jewish learning based their strongest claims for university inclusion on subject domain, not specifically Jewish "techniques and procedures."[48] The absence of a separate Jewish studies program, past history showed, did not assure the presence of Judaica specialists in existing departments.[49] Nor was a scholar's location within an academic institution, program defenders insisted, the basis on which to judge scholarship or teaching ability. Some practitioners went beyond the moderates to challenge the purported salutary association between the disciplines and Jewish learning. Jewish learning, these scholars claimed, was itself a "discipline."

Other practitioners strongly resisted a shift from parent departments to Judaica programs. Jacob Neusner's strong belief in a structure for Jewish learning based on the academic disciplines arose from his insistence that universities should not succor self-validating theological systems, that comparative or morphological perspectives are intrinsic to a university's mission, and that parochialism is intellectually debilitating.[50] Neusner admitted the possibility of variant academic settings for Jewish learning, but he excluded departments of Jewish or Judaic studies, "for departments normally take shape around particular disciplines or approaches to data." He recognized the problems involved in the study of Judaism through the disciplines and the apparent breakdown of disciplinary lines that occurred in the 1960s and 1970s. But Neusner made a virtue out of what for a century had been a necessity. Jewish learning, he argued, could gain much from—and had much to offer to—well-developed disciplinary techniques.[51]

Judaica departments, Neusner added, would inevitably emphasize breadth, not depth, of coverage. The resultant loss of a comparative dimension made scholarship and teaching susceptible to extreme particularism. Neusner's methodological and disciplinary stance resembled mid-century formulations, but he rejected legitimations of Jewish learning by virtue of its contributions to matters of common concern, defined by others "with no regard whatever for the particular morphology of Judaism itself."[52] He argued instead for a straightforward acceptance criterion: the possibility of applying "university methods" to a particular subject matter.[53] Judaism as a religious study met this criterion, and might provide the paradigm for the reintegration of Jewish learning that Gerson Cohen desired. But Jewish history, as a field, did not make the grade; too many discontinuities existed for any scholar or group of scholars to draw a single line that traced all Jews. Scholars who ventured into Jewish history, he added, confronted insurmountable technical difficulties, especially that of language mastery.[54] Scholars should not characterize themselves as "generalist" Jewish historians, nor should institutions accept such characterizations. A specialist in medieval or modern European history, in contrast, might concentrate "mainly, but not exclusively, on Jewish sources."[55]

Neusner's key contribution to the debate came in the area of communal implications. Adhering to academic norms, he argued, was not a problem but an opportunity for the Jewish community to reencounter Jewish theology, neglected because of overriding concern with peoplehood issues in this century. A reencounter, based on prioritization of academic values, might transform a troubled American Jewish community. "People who lavish their best energies, their money, and their time upon Jewish activities," Neusner asserted, "also live lives remote from distinctive and particular Jewish meanings."[56] Preoccupation with externalities and with status attainment through wealth, especially through philanthropy, could change if a community based upon learning emerged and gained renewed access to its own intellect.[57] Study itself is an important Jewish act, Neusner reminded the Jewish community.

Many studies of higher education, going back to Thorstein Veblen's *The Higher Learning in America,* examined the consequences of the "invasion" of communal and business norms and practices into the academy.[58] Neusner, conversely, believed that "academization," the infusion of academic values, could change the Jewish community. Observers of other fields and disciplines shared this outlook. A university's activities and products should expand to enrich the lives of individuals by transforming the culture of the communities in which the university is a part, wrote philosopher Charles Wegener.[59] But neither Neusner nor Wegener advocated direct university intervention in communal affairs. Direct interventions produced transient change, at best, and diverted scholars from pursuits for which they were more suited.

Neusner's belief that Jewish scholarship is a possession not only of academics but of all American Jews led him to concur with colleagues who emphasized engagement with students. "You are our reason for being," he noted. "What happens in the class-room is not the delivery of facts to whom it may concern, but the analysis of possibilities and probabilities by concerned people, teachers and students alike."[60] He did not advocate indoctrination, or absorption of specific dogmas. Professors, presumably personally committed to Judaism, face a difficult burden: They must advocate "ultimate seriousness about the problematic of Judaism"—not specific dogmas, or even the entirety of Judaism. "Our task indeed is to teach, which means, not to indoctrinate; to educate, never to train."[61] Study, Neusner echoed Cyrus Adler, Morris R. Cohen, and others, is a characteristically Jewish act—one of the few unifiers of factionalized American Jewry.[62]

Discipline-based study of Judaism, Neusner added, was also salutary for the university, for the questions historically confronted by the Jews "face the generality of humanity." Torah, Neusner concluded, "shapes the condition of Israel into a paradigm of the human condition."[63] He reversed the earlier rationale for academic—and perhaps social—recognition: that Jewish scholarship would show that Jewish belief and practice resembled the Gentile world. Neusner hoped to convince the Gentiles that they resembled the Jews. Jacob Neusner's writings thus brought the justification for Jewish learning in American universities full circle. Instead of taking a communal agenda to the academy, Neusner brought a salutary academic agenda to the Jewish community and claimed academic legitimacy for Jewish learning on the basis of intellectual and constituent centrality.

The location debate was thus a surrogate for a more difficult issue raised by Ismar Elbogen a half century earlier: Was Jewish learning a "purpose-directed science" aimed at improving the condition of contemporary Judaism and Jewry or a disinterested academic field? Some university-based scholars believed that Jewish learning could reinvigorate, improve, even transform the American Jewish community. Some practitioners, believing other institutions inadequate to the task, emphasized the role of higher education in the intergenerational transfer of Jewish knowledge and values. Still others considered the act of study a Jewish affirmation, a *mitzvah* in itself. A final group tried to approach Judaica as their university colleagues approached other disciplines. Vigorous, dispassionate scholarship, they insisted, produced studies and students of Jews and Judaism. Scholarship did not and should not "produce Jews," they added. While not excluding salutary indirect effects, these scholars believed that Jewish learning could no more transform the Jewish community than universities could directly transform society. If Jewish survival depended upon university-based Jewish learning, these scholars added, American Jewry was a vulnerable group.

From the outset, university-based Judaica scholars had to orient themselves to the Jewish community. But an orientation, as we have seen, did not imply communal involvement, and both participation and aloofness entailed problems. Richard Gottheil's communal activism raised questions about his position within the university, while Morris Jastrow's detachment left him without communal support in his fight with Herman Hilprecht. The research and graduate origins of Jewish learning—modern Hebrew excepted—placed scholars with a "communal" agenda on the defensive, beginning with Emil Hirsch. Both Jews and Gentiles often confused academic and rabbinical province at "secularizing" universities—a confusion compounded by the appearance of rabbis in academic posts and the prior rabbinical aspirations (and even ordination) of several academically-oriented practitioners.

Gentiles, who conferred—and withdrew—academic status and subject recognition, changed their own relationship to the Jews and Judaism after World War I. Abbott Lawrence Lowell, for example, looked askance on initiatives that appeared "too Jewish." Judaica scholars, indeed many Jewish scholars, thereupon suffered exclusion or had to battle to retain inclusion within a generation of attaining access—just when universities had consolidated their gains and when government, business, and philanthropic foundations began to court American professors.[64] University-based Jewish learning, if it survived at all, could not rely exclusively upon scholarly productivity in recondite fields. After World War II, less esoteric, undergraduate-oriented, and potentially meliorative fields of Jewish learning entered the university, thereby focusing communal attention not only on research but on the effects of teaching on student identity.

The perception of Judaica's communal relevance *increased* as members of the Jewish community shifted concern to the implications of acculturation. The meliorative potential that 1960s observers imputed to religious studies, for example, at least equalled the expectations of their nineteenth-century counterparts for philology.[65] Changes in academic setting and in intellectual orientation, many Jewish community members believed, might convince university-based Judaica scholars to overcome communal aloofness. Communal organizations that invested resources only for visible communal gains implicitly—and the Marshall Sklares explicitly—challenged academics who conferred upon Jewish learning at best an indirect salutary effect on the Jewish community.

The field's growth facilitated a *modus vivendi* between academy and community. Before World War II—perhaps even before 1960—the small presence of university-based Jewish learning did not permit functional differentiation between "scholars" and "practitioners." Academic and communal norms might coexist and occasionally might reinforce each other, but when conflict arose, adherence to one set of norms led to diminished support from the other constituency. Gentiles might have been able to reconcile normative dissonance; Jews could not.

After 1965, practitioners began to sort themselves out. Few participants in the location debate explored the implications of multiple locations within and across institutions, though the option gained increased viability during the rapid growth of the late 1960s. Coexistence of Judaica programs and departments with discipline-based academic departments with Judaica specialists permitted an array of subject and communal orientations. Late 1960s meliorationist social scientists—whose communal orientation may have earlier kept their field out of American higher education—might have felt more at home in Judaica programs and departments than in either traditional departments or seminaries. Continued accommodation of departmentally based Judaica scholars after 1970 may have led to creative resolutions of tensions brought on by competing visions. Proliferation of programs and appointments permitted the Jewish community to tap selectively the strengths and interests of practitioners. The Association for

Jewish Studies also helped by providing conferences, publications, and networks for Judaica practitioners from different institutions.

No practitioner suggested Claude Welch–like sacrifices of the field's integrity on the altar of "mutual fructification." Some practitioners might once have applauded inclusion of Jewish learning, perhaps the writings of Maimonides, in the undergraduate western civilization programs formulated between the world wars. But Judaica practitioners did not contemplate trading the growing undergraduate component of their field for inclusion in the western civilization pantheon. This stance paid off when no side in the 1980s debates over canons, curricular relevance, and relativism accorded Judaica more than a marginal role.

Practitioner viewpoints on the communal implications of university-based Jewish scholarship mirrored the general discourse. By the 1960s, changed conditions heightened social expectations for American higher education. Clark Kerr accepted the existence of the multiversity as an established fact in his 1963 Godkin lectures. For Kerr, the question was not whether the multiversity *ought* to address the multiple demands of governments, corporations, the military, labor, and other clients, but rather to identify the consequences of this involvement.[66] Academic growth, Kerr noted, permitted functional differentiation; little cement held universities together, save for a universal concern about parking. If Kerr was correct, growth, which to some late 1960s observers appeared to increase tensions, may in the long run have reduced tensions not only within the field of Jewish learning, but also within universities that accommodated the field.

A Glimpse Ahead: Religiosity and Scholarship in the 1970s

Practitioner availability, Jewish communal interest, institutional aspiration to graduate status, and presidential support presaged the initial inclusion of Jewish learning in American universities. Undergraduate enrollment rates—determined by attractiveness of courses and quality of teaching—and location near a Jewish population center became keys to maintaining Jewish learning in American universities beginning in the 1930s. The growth of higher education during the postwar decades boded well for Jewish learning. The parent disciplines of Judaica—save for Semitics after World War I and the rapidly maturing field of "religion" before the Schempp decision—were strong. Course proliferation, electives, specialization, and depth facilitated curricular parity for Jewish learning. The debates over disciplinary or departmental organization, quality of graduate education in Jewish learning, and practitioner instruction and scholarship reflected the rapid founding and expansion of graduate programs to meet undergraduate enrollment growth.[67]

By the late 1970s, existential questions concerning the place of Jewish learning in American universities appeared solved.[68] A 1978 Association for Jewish Studies membership survey identified 124 tenured and 196 non-tenured college and university faculty members among the 371 respondents who indicated their rank—the remaining 51 respondents did not hold regular academic positions.

Practitioner age—45 percent of respondents were under 35—reflected recent and rapid growth. Receipt of the Ph.D. by 273 members between 1974 and 1978 explains in large part the shift in Association concern from undersupply to oversupply.[69]

Association faculty membership included 48 women. The one female full professor had 101 male peers. Traditional scholars considered women distractions or at best auxiliaries. Contentions that graduate education in Judaica required extensive Talmudic background effectively excluded women who had less access than men to extensive elementary and secondary Jewish education. Beginning in the 1960s, women actively pushed for inclusion as Judaica scholars. They argued that preparation for all is inadequate and that intensive text study may create a debilitating rigidity, especially if pursued at the expense of disciplinary knowledge and method. Academic specialization, these women added, had for a century implied reduced Judaic preparation.

Even without the Talmudic problem, there would still have been contextual questions. Professors of Jewish learning taught a clientele whom prejudiced Gentiles blamed for many of the world's ills and a subject that many observers regarded as obsolete and as having been replaced by a "higher" knowledge about which Jews remained ignorant and could not teach. Moreover, until recently, only fears of an institution's feminization exceeded fears of its Judaization. The academic marginality of Jewish learning thus dictated caution in admitting women students. In any case, until the 1960s, women with doctorates in Jewish learning would have been denied access to most university humanities departments. These complications do not, however, exculpate all practitioners: Few made special efforts to attract women to Jewish learning and failure to take gender bias into account neglects an important dynamic in the field.[70]

Jewish learning, the Association for Jewish Studies survey revealed, remained concentrated in northeast Jewish population centers. The secular centers of Jewish learning in 1897 and 1968 educated most of the 1978 Association membership—only Johns Hopkins fell from the list of 16 top doctorate-granting institutions.[71] Practitioner specialties reflected the field's diversity: 30 percent of the respondents specialized in Jewish history. Representation of other specialties ranged from 13 percent for rabbinics and Biblical studies to 4 percent for Yiddish studies.[72] Professors of Hebrew often belonged to the National Association of Professors of Hebrew.

What about the question of identity? Under what circumstances would university-based Judaica scholars compartmentalize or work to integrate their Judaic and academic orientation? Would a belief in Jewish learning as a "purpose-oriented science" affect identity?[73] Motives for a career in university-based Jewish learning were as complex for contemporary practitioners as for the field's university founders. For many practitioners of Jewish learning, the subject to which academic norms dictated that they unflinchingly apply critical scrutiny was also part of their innermost essence. Jewish learning offered twentieth-century university-based American professors what it earlier offered *Verein* members: escape, recognition, integration, or a *modus vivendi*. Harry Wolfson,

Mordecai Kaplan related, once said that "sometime ago he went into an orthodox schul on the first day of Rosh Hashannah and was so disgusted that he has
not gone into a synagogue since."[74] For Wolfson, who characterized himself as
"unobservant orthodox," and for others, study had replaced ritual as a mode of
worship and identification.[75] For other scholars, scholarship replaced the "God
idea" itself. Referring to another contemporary Judaica scholar, Kaplan wrote:

> Having long ago given up the traditional conception of God, he has not been able
> to achieve any other conception. His observance of religious customs and atten-
> dance at synagogue are basically part of his self-expression as a Jewish nationalist
> and are prompted by a vague sentimental attachment which he is unable and does
> not care to intellectualize.[76]

Scholarship permitted some practitioners to profess Judaism when other modes
failed.[77] For others, scholarship was compatible with other means of Jewish expression. For them, Judaism was less problematic, while the resolution of conflicting communal and academic pulls may have been more so. This much is
certain: With a large proportion of practitioners having been exposed to seminaries, and perhaps having considered the rabbinate, many must have opted for
universities after a confrontation with their Jewishness. For some, opting for the
professorate over the pulpit was probably as painful as it was for Morris Jastrow.
For others, the broadened scope of university-based Jewish learning facilitated
the transition.

"Identity" thus continued to play an important part in practitioner decisions
to enter the field. Indeed, this book ends where it began. University-based Jewish learning enabled American practitioners to broaden the Biblical injunction to
study Torah to include most components of *Wissenschaft des Judentums*. Many
other religions ascribe less importance to study, Judaism accords it a central place
among its tenets. This tenet may help explain the faith of some academic practitioners in the salutary results of university-based Jewish scholarship.[78]

By the early 1970s, Jewish learning found sanctuary in an environment more
secular than Protestant and practitioners could not only articulate the dilemmas confronted by the field, but could produce scholarship that addressed these
issues. Jewish learning in American universities even became a model for other
nations. In 1950, observers asked whether American Jewish scholarship could
assume the role tragically relinquished by European Jewry. A generation later,
Moshe Davis wrote: "The dominant patterns of programs in the United States
influence developments in other countries."[79]

On the tenth anniversary of the Association for Jewish Studies, President
Michael A. Meyer, a historian of *Wissenschaft des Judentums,* delineated a familiar problem—the existence of elements that unified Jewish learning—in the
midst of enumerating the field's many accomplishments:[80]

> As one cannot explain the dynamics of Jewish historical development—whether
> the functioning of a community or its literary creativity—apart from the pressures
> and influences of the environment, so one cannot hope to understand it indepen-

dently of the internal dynamics which makes every new movement or ideal a link in an unbroken dialectical process. The dialectic may be weightily affected by external factors, but it is never wholly determined by them.

The history of Jewish learning in American universities, Meyer's comments suggest, recapitulates the problems historically confronted by Jewry. Meyer's notion that Jewish history was an unbroken dialectical process—in part a response to Neusner—carried weight at a time when many practitioners questioned the structure of the disciplines.[81] His message was clear: The Association had to help to assure that Jewish learning remained primarily Jewish. But the field's main American legacy—its university inclusion—helped to protect Jewish learning from insularity.

NOTES

Preface

1. See, for example, Thomas W. Goodspeed, *A History of The University of Chicago: The First Quarter Century* (Chicago: University of Chicago Press, 1916), 87, and Richard J. Storr, *Harper's University: The Beginnings* (Chicago: University of Chicago Press, 1966), 39–40.

2. "We recognize in every religion an attempt to grasp the Infinite One, and in every mode, source or book of revelation held sacred in any religious system the consciousness of the indwelling of God in man. We hold that Judaism presents the highest conception of the God-idea as taught in our holy Scriptures and developed and spiritualized by the Jewish teachers in accordance with the moral and philosophical progress of their respective ages. We maintain that Judaism preserved and defended amid continual struggles and trials and under enforced isolation this God-idea as the central religious truth for the human race" (Central Conference of American Rabbis, *Yearbook* 45 [1935], 198). On universalism in Reform Judaism, see Joseph L. Blau, "Problems of Modern Jewish Thought: Tensions between Particularism and Universalism," *Journal of Reform Judaism* 25 (Fall, 1978), 47–62. On Felix Adler's extreme universalism, see Benny Kraut, *From Reform Judaism to Ethical Culture: The Religious Evolution of Felix Adler* (Cincinnati: Hebrew Union College Press, 1979), and chapter 3, below.

3. On the Hebrew language, see William Chomsky, *Hebrew—The Eternal Language* (Philadelphia: Jewish Publication Society of America, 1957).

4. Some of these chairs had Rabbinics components, Talmud-based, traditional Jewish learning that never became a significant part of the agenda of most practitioners.

5. At least 16 Jews offered instruction in Jewish learning in late nineteenth and early twentieth-century American universities. These scholars included Max Margolis, James M. Philips, William Popper, and Jacob Voorsanger at the University of California; Emil G. Hirsch at the University of Chicago; Felix Adler (briefly) at Cornell; Richard Gottheil at Columbia; Cyrus Adler, Immanuel Moses Casanowicz, Caspar Levias, and William Rosenau at Johns Hopkins; Abram S. Isaacs at New York University; Isaac Husik and Morris Jastrow at the University of Pennsylvania; Joseph Levy (briefly) at Temple; and Max Heller at Tulane.

6. See Ludwig Lewisohn, *Up-Stream: An American Chronicle* (New York: Boni and Liveright, 1922), and Susanne Klingenstein, *Jews in the American Academy 1900–1940: The Dynamics of Intellectual Assimilation* (New Haven: Yale University Press, 1991).

7. Records indicate sporadic, earlier offerings, notably Aaron Ember's courses at Johns Hopkins during the first quarter of the century.

8. Two contrasting views of Jewish learning may concretize the shift in justificatory rhetoric. Morton Smith, who taught ancient history at Columbia, defined Hebrew studies as "a branch of philology or of linguistics, the study of a particular language, of the words in which it has found expression, of the thoughts which it has expressed, of the societies in which it has lived and which it has enlivened during the past roughly three thousand years." Hebrew studies, Smith added, mainly provided windows through which to view other cultures, such as classical Greece. Smith distinguished sharply between Hebrew studies and Jewish studies: "Judaism is a religion, and Jewish studies, therefore are properly a branch of the study of religion." (See Morton Smith, "Hebrew Studies within the Study of History," *Judaism* 11 [Fall, 1962], 332, 344).

In contrast, in 1966 Arnold Band, professor of Near East languages at the University of California, Los Angeles, characterized Jewish learning as "the discipline which deals with the historical experiences, in the intellectual, religious, and social spheres, of the Jewish people in all centuries and countries." Band emphasized a people who happened, through part of its history, to speak, write, or pray in a specific language. Smith emphasized the language, which happened to be employed (though not exclusively) by a people. "Every culture has its own structure," wrote Band, "and the accusation of parochialism leveled at the intrinsic approach is therefore unwarranted." Band urged the primacy of Jews and Judaism over Hebrew; his attitude now dominates the field. (See Arnold J. Band, "Jewish Studies in American Liberal-Arts Colleges and Universities," *American Jewish Yearbook* 67 [1966], 5).

Moshe Davis, an Israeli historian of American Jewry, offered a compromise, "Jewish studies," he wrote, "should encompass the historic continuity and destiny of the Jewish people and Tradition the world over, in Eretz Yisrael and in the Diaspora from ancient times to the present. The pedagogy of Jewish studies should be *interdisciplinary* and designed to engage the serious student of world civilization as well as the specialist in Jewish history, culture and thought." Others criticize this formulation of the field's province, and its implications for individual scholars. (See Moshe Davis, "Jewish Studies in Universities: Alternate Approaches in Different Parts of the World," *Publication Series: Allan Lazaroff Chair of Jewish Education in the Diaspora* [Jerusalem: Institute of Contemporary Jewry, Hebrew University, 1974], 9).

9. We were not granted access to Harry Wolfson's papers, for example, though we worked around that obstacle.

10. Jacob Neusner, "Modes of Jewish Studies in the University," in Jacob Neusner, *The Academic Study of Judaism,* 2 vols. (New York: KTAV, 1975, 1977), 1:94–95. We avoid the term "Jewish studies," except for direct quotations, to minimize confusion. The term was employed as early as 1906 when the Menorah movement began to promote Jewish learning on American college campuses. Nineteenth-century scholars frequently used the term "Semitic studies" to describe scholarship within, rather than across, the discipline.

11. " 'Jewish Studies' had come into being," wrote Daniel Jeremy Silver, referring to current conditions, "but it was rarely, and never easily, defined. To some it meant the classic disciplines of *Tanakh,* Hellenistic literature and rabbinics, Hebrew, and Jewish theology. Others were interested in Yiddish literature, *kahal* structures, Ladino, the demography of the modern community, and the like. The term was as broad as the historic Jewish experience, and definition was pleasantly complicated as a number of scholars in various disciplines (by this time Jews provided a significant proportion of the faculty of many universities) found that they were moved by emotions that they had only partially acknowledged, particularly deriving from the Holocaust and the establishment of the State of Israel, and were eager to explore the Jewish component in their studies of Persian literature or the Gregorian chant or Renaissance art." (See Daniel Jeremy Silver, "Higher Jewish Learning," in Bernard Martin, ed., *Movements and Issues in American Judaism: An Analysis and Sourcebook of Developments since 1945* [Westport, Conn.: Greenwood Press, 1978], 206–16, quotation from 212).

12. Peter Novick, *That Noble Dream: The "Objectivity Question" and the American Historical Profession* (Cambridge: Cambridge University Press, 1988).

13. See Nathan S. Isaacs, "Study as a Mode of Worship," in Leo Jung, ed., *The Jewish Library: First Series* (New York: Bloch Publishing, 1943 [1928]), 57–77, and Nahum S. Glatzer, "Challenge to the Scholar: A Judaic View," *Judaism* 11 (Summer, 1962), 210–20.

1. European Background and the American Setting

1. Leopold Zunz, "On Rabbinic Literature," in Alfred Jospe, ed., *Studies in Jewish Thought: An Anthology of German Jewish Scholarship* (Detroit: Wayne State University Press, 1981), 21.

2. *Ethics of the Fathers,* 2:5.

3. Ismar Elbogen, "A Century of Wissenschaft des Judentums," in Jospe, ed., *Studies in Jewish Thought,* 26–37, quotation from 27.

4. Zunz, "On Rabbinic Literature," 23.

5. Ibid.

6. Ibid., 22.

7. Historians dispute the extent of Jewish-Muslim cordiality during these centuries but appear to agree that relationships deteriorated during the thirteenth century. See Norman A. Stillman, *The Jews of Arab Lands: A History and Source Book* (Philadelphia: Jewish Publication Society of America, 1979); Mark Cohen, "Neo-Lacrymose Conception of Jewish-Arab History," *Tikkun* 6 (May/June, 1991), 55–60; and Norman Stillman, "Myth, Countermyth, and Distortion," Ibid., 60–64.

8. "Condemnation of the Talmud Renewed, 1244," in Lynn Thorndike, ed. and tr., *University Records and Life in the Middle Ages* (New York: Columbia University Press, 1944), 48–50; "Statute of the Council of Vienne, 1312," ibid., 149; "Study of the Oriental Languages, 1256," ibid., 68–70; and "Raymond Lull Urges the Study of Oriental Languages, 1298–1299," ibid., 125–27. The suppression also covered Jews in other fields: "We doctors teaching in the medical faculty at Paris," stated a 1271 document, " . . . wishing to check so many errors, perils and scandals, confirm a statute of ours made long since . . . that no Jew or Jewess presume to operate surgically or medically on any person of catholic faith" ("Medical Restrictions Upon Jews, Surgeons and Pharmacists, Paris, 1271," ibid., 83). "No one of an alien sect, such as a Jew or a Saracen," stated the Perpignan charter (ca. 1389), may " . . . be given instruction by any doctor, master, licentiate, bachelor, scholar, publicly or privately in grammar, logic, philosophy, medicine or law, or other science" ("Only Christians Admitted, Perpignan, c. 1389," ibid., 257). See also Max Margolis and Alexander Marx, *A History of the Jewish People* (Philadelphia: Jewish Publication Society of America, 1927), 378, 454–56, 483–85, and M. A. Screech, "Two Attitudes to Hebrew Studies: Erasmus and Rabelais," in James M. Kittelson and Pamela J. Transue, eds., *Rebirth, Reform and Resilience: Universities in Transition 1300–1700* (Columbus: Ohio State University Press, 1984), 293–323.

9. Apart from Judaic investigations, Jews continued to teach on the Salerno medical faculty and at Padua under community protection, despite increased restrictions on university access and on university-controlled professional practice. See Nathan Schachner, *The Medieval Universities* (New York: A. S. Barnes, 1962 [1938]), 283. See also Guido Kisch, *Die Prager Universität und Juden 1348–1848* (Amsterdam: B. R. Gruner, 1969); Jacob R. Marcus, *The Jew in the Medieval World* (Cincinnati: Sinai Press, 1938), 381–88; Cecil Roth, *The Jews in the Renaissance* (Philadelphia: Jewish Publication Society of America, 1959); David A. Ruderman, *The World of a Renaissance Jew: The Life and Thought of Abraham Ben Mordechai Farissol* (New York: KTAV, 1981); and Moses A. Shulvass, *The Jews in the World of the Renaissance,* Elvin I. Kose, tr. (Leiden: Brill, 1973 [1955]).

10. See Simha Asaf, ed., *Mekorot le-Toledot ha-Hinukh be-Yisrael (Sources for the History of Education)* 4 vols. (Tel Aviv: Dvir, 1925–1948), 1:15, 2:115–120. Fifteenth-century Sicilian Jews had made a similar proposal. See Moritz Güdemann, *Geschichte des Erziehungswesens und der Kultur der Abendländischen Juden während des Mittelalters und der neueren Zeit,* 2 vols. (Vienna: Alfred Hölder, 1880–1884), vol. 2, chapter 9.

11. See, for example, Gustav Karples, "The Jew in the History of Civilization," in *Jewish Literature and Other Essays* (Philadelphia: Jewish Publication Society of America, 1895), 71–105.

12. Jerome Friedman, *The Most Ancient Testimony: Sixteenth-Century Christian Hebraica in the Age of Renaissance Nostalgia* (Athens: Ohio University Press, 1983), chapter 1. See also E. Harris Harbison, *The Christian Scholar in the Age of the Reformation* (New York: Charles Scribner's Sons, 1956), and C. E. Schertz, "Christian Hebraism in 17th Century England as Reflected in the Works of John Lightfoot" (Ph.D. diss., New York University, 1977).

13. See *Encyclopaedia Britannica,* 11th ed., s.v. "Reuchlin, Johann"; Ludwig Geiger, *Johannes Reuchlin, Sein Leben und Seine Werke* (Nieuwkoop: B. De Graaf, 1964 [1871]); and James H. Overfield, "A New Look at the Reuchlin Affair," in Howard L. Adelson, ed., *Studies in Medieval and Renaissance History,* vol. 8 (Lincoln: University of Nebraska Press, 1981), 165–207.

14. Levita was invited to teach in Paris but declined because Jews were not permitted to reside in the city. See Alfred Jospe, "The Study of Judaism in German Universities Before 1933," Leo Baeck Institute, *Yearbook* 27 (1982), 296 n. 6.

15. See Jacob Katz, *From Prejudice to Destruction: Anti-Semitism 1700–1933* (Cambridge: Harvard University Press, 1980), passim.

16. The quotation is from Joseph Blau, *Judaism in America: From Curiosity to Third Faith* (Chicago: University of Chicago Press, 1976), 36.

17. "The quip of the famous Orientalist Chwolsohn—that he was converted out of conviction, the conviction that it was better to be a professor in Petersburg than a *melamed* in Shnipishok—is only one of a long line of cynical anecdotes (going back at least as far as Heine), which illustrate the psychology of many such conversions" (Ben Halpern, "America is Different," in Marshall Sklare, ed., *The Jews: Social Patterns of an American Group* [Glencoe, Il.: Free Press, 1958], 630 n. 4). Adalbut von Ladenburg, the Prussian minister of education, claimed that such a chair would offer support to Jewish customs and laws and thereby violate academic norms. See Jospe, "Study of Judaism," 305–6.

18. Ibid. The literature on *Wissenschaft des Judentums* is vast. See especially Salo Baron, "Jewish Studies in Universities: An Early Project," *Hebrew Union College Annual* 46 (1975), 357–76; Jacob Katz, "Emancipation and Jewish Studies," *Commentary* 57 (April, 1974), 60–65; Michael A. Meyer, "Jewish Religious Reform and Wissenschaft des Judentums: The Positions of Zunz, Geiger and Frankel," in Leo Baeck Institute, *Yearbook* 16 (1971), 19–41; Ismar Schorsch, "Breakthrough into the Past: The Verein für Kultur und Wissenschaft der Juden," in Leo Baeck Institute, *Yearbook* 33 (1988), 3–28; and Gershom Sholem, "The Science of Judaism—Then and Now," in *The Messianic Idea in Judaism and Other Essays on Jewish Spirituality* (New York: Schocken Books, 1971), 304–13.

19. See Michael A. Meyer, *The Origins of the Modern Jew: Jewish Identity and European Culture in Germany, 1749–1824* (Detroit: Wayne State University Press, 1967), 181.

20. See Nathan Glazer, *American Judaism* (Chicago: University of Chicago Press, 1957), 33–34, and Michael A. Meyer, *Response to Modernity: A History of the Reform Movement in Judaism* (New York: Oxford University Press, 1988), 75–77.

21. See Katz, *From Prejudice to Destruction,* passim.

22. George L. Mosse, *Germans and Jews: The Right, the Left and the Search for a "Third Force" in Pre-Nazi Germany* (Detroit: Wayne State University Press, 1987 [1970]), esp. chapter 1.

23. Carl Diehl, *Americans and German Scholarship 1770–1870* (New Haven: Yale University Press, 1978). Renan experienced a personal religious crisis shortly before publication of his monograph on Semitics; indeed, the field included scholars who doubted, but could not ignore, traditional religion.

24. As quoted in S. L., "Book Reviews: The Spirit of Renan," *Liberal Judaism* 11 (November, 1943), 58. See also Edward W. Said, *Orientalism* (New York: Vintage, 1979), 132–48; Katz, *From Prejudice to Destruction,* 133–38; A. A. Roback, "Renan's Contribution to Jewish History and Semitic Philology," *The Jewish Forum* 6 (May, 1924), 302–6, 335; Harold W. Wardman, *Ernest Renan: A Critical Biography* (London: Athlone Press, 1964); and idem, *Renan, Historien Philosophe* (Paris: Editions C.D.U.–Sedes, 1979).

25. See Uriel Tal, *Christians and Jews in Germany: Religion, Politics, and Ideology in the Second Reich, 1870–1914* (Ithaca: Cornell University Press, 1975), 279–89; Abraham J. Peck, *Radicals and Reactionaries: The Crisis of Conservatism in Wilhelmine Germany* (Washington, D.C.: University Press of America, 1978); and Geoffrey G. Field, *Evangelist of Race: The Germanic Vision of Houston Stuart Chamberlain* (New York: Columbia University Press, 1981).

26. Ismar Schorsch, *Jewish Reactions to German Anti-Semitism, 1870–1914* (New York: Columbia University Press, 1972), 170.

27. On Lagarde, see Katz, *From Prejudice to Destruction*, 305–6; Robert W. Lougee, *Paul de Lagarde 1827–1891: A Study of Radical Conservatism in Germany* (Cambridge: Harvard University Press, 1962); Fritz Stern, *The Politics of Cultural Despair: A Study in the Rise of the Germanic Ideology* (Berkeley: University of Califronia Press, 1961), 3–44; and Tal, *Christians and Jews in Germany*, 271–73.

28. See Schorsch, *Jewish Reactions to German Anti-Semitism*, 170–71, and Naomi W. Cohen, "The Challenges of Darwinism and Biblical Criticism to American Judaism," *Modern Judaism* 4 (May, 1984), 121–57.

29. As quoted in Jospe, "Study of Judaism," 302.

30. Elbogen, "A Century of Wissenschaft des Judentums," 33–34.

31. Ibid., 36.

32. Ibid., 34.

33. Schorsch, *Jewish Reactions to German Anti-Semitism*, 11, 45.

34. Elbogen, "A Century of Wissenschaft des Judentums," 35.

35. On Jewish access to German universities, see Ismar Schorsch, "The Parameters of Wissenschaft: Jewish Academics at Prussian Universities," in Leo Baeck Institute, *Yearbook* 25 (1980), 3–19. See also Guido Kisch, "The Founders of *Wissenschaft des Judentums* and America," in *Essays in American Jewish History To Commemorate the Tenth Anniversary of the Founding of the American Jewish Archives under the Direction of Jacob Rader Marcus* (Cincinnati: American Jewish Archives, 1958), 147–70.

36. Arnold Band's 1966 essay, "Jewish Studies in American Liberal-Arts Colleges and Universities," includes an early criticism of this outlook. Band did not question the standard periodization, but he asked whether the history of American higher education was the proper context for understanding the field's development. The self-serving motives of the Puritan Hebraists, Band noted, differed considerably from the forces that led to the incorporation of Semitics into the late nineteenth-century curriculum, such as *Wissenschaft des Judentums* in Europe, and a general interest in philology. He traced a line of development from the European Jewish seminaries and university seminars through the late nineteenth-century American university Semitics appointments—he used the term "Judaic or closely related subjects"—to the second half of the twentieth century.

37. See Arthur A. Chiel, "Ezra Stiles and the Jews: A Study in Ambivalence," in Bertram W. Korn, ed., *A Bicentennial Festschrift for Jacob Rader Marcus* (Waltham, Mass.: American Jewish Historical Society and KTAV, 1976), 63–76; idem, "Ezra Stiles: The Education of a 'Hebraician'," *American Jewish Historical Quarterly* 60 (March, 1971), 235–41; George A. Kohut, "Ezra Stiles and His Friends," *Menorah Journal* 3 (February, 1917), 37–46; and idem, "Hebraic Learning in Puritan New England," *Menorah Journal* 2 (October, 1916), 206–19.

38. William Rosenau, "Semitic Studies in American Colleges," *Central Conference of American Rabbis Yearbook* 6 (1896), 99–113.

39. Cyrus Adler, "Hebrew and Cognate Learning in America," in *Lectures, Selected Papers, Addresses* (Philadelphia: privately printed, 1933), 278. See also idem, "The Beginnings of Semitic Studies in America," in Cyrus Adler and Aaron Ember, eds., *Oriental Studies Published in Commemoration of the Fortieth Anniversary (1883–1923) of Paul Haupt as Director of the Oriental Seminary of the Johns Hopkins University, Baltimore, Maryland* (Baltimore: Johns Hopkins University Press, 1926), 317–28.

40. See for example Abraham I. Katsh, "The Teaching of Hebrew in American Universities," *Modern Language Journal* 30 (December, 1946), 575–86. Hebrew instruction in colonial colleges was more sporadic than implied by most authors. See Shalom Goldman, "Hebrew at Early Colleges: Orations at Harvard, Dartmouth, and Columbia," *American Jewish Archives* 42 (Spring/Summer, 1990), 23–26.

41. See, for example, David Rudavsky, "Hebraic Studies in American Colleges and Universities with Special Reference to New York University," in Israel T. Naamani, David

Rudavsky, and Carl F. Ehle, Jr., eds., *Doron-Hebraic Studies* (New York: National Association of Professors of Hebrew in American Institutions of Higher Learning, 1965), 3–25; David Rudavsky, "Hebrew and Judaic Studies in American Higher Education," *Congress Bi-Weekly* 41 (October 25, 1974), 8–10; and David Rudavsky, "Hebraic and Judaic Studies in American Higher Education," *C.S.R. Bulletin* 6 (April, 1975), 3–5.

42. See "Jewish Studies at Columbia: A Brilliant Past . . . A Glowing Present . . . A Brighter Future," *Columbia Today* (December, 1976), 32–34.

43. Salo W. Baron, "From Colonial Mansion to Skyscraper: An Emerging Pattern of Hebraic Studies," in *Steeled by Adversity: Essays and Addresses on American Jewish Life* (Philadelphia: Jewish Publication Society of America, 1971), 106–26.

44. A historiography that emphasizes gradualism and complexity is currently challenging the prior belief that nineteenth-century American higher education retrogressed from its pre-revolution achievements until the universities righted the course. Studies in this genre question notions of intellectual sterility and deadening pedagogy in antebellum colleges, emphasize their positive role in the community, and argue against equating change with progress. See, for example, Lawrence A. Cremin, *American Education: The National Experience 1783–1876* (New York: Harper and Row, 1980), 400–409; James McLachlan, "The American College in the Nineteenth Century: Toward a Reappraisal," *Teachers College Record* 80 (December, 1978), 287–306; David B. Potts, "'College Enthusiasm' as Public Response: 1800–1860," *Harvard Educational Review* 47 (February, 1977), 28–42; and Wilson Smith "Apologia pro Alma Matre: The College and Community in Ante Bellum America," in Stanley Elkins and Eric McKitrick, eds., *The Hofstadter Aegis: A Memorial* (New York: Alfred A. Knopf, 1974), 125–53. See also Thomas C. Hunt and James C. Carper, *Religious Colleges and Universities in America: A Selected Bibliography* (New York: Garland Publishing, 1988). Richard Hofstadter was the key proponent of the older thesis. See Richard Hofstadter, *Academic Freedom in the Age of the College* (New York: Columbia University Press, 1961), chapter 5. An even earlier generation of "progressives" suggested that the eventual triumph of a diversified curriculum over the old-time college's uniformity reflected the triumph of democratic over aristocratic education. See, for example, R. Freeman Butts, *The College Charts its Course: Historical Conceptions and Current Proposals* (New York: Arno Press, 1971 [1939]).

45. See Samuel Eliot Morison, *Three Centuries of Harvard 1636–1936* (Cambridge: Harvard University Press, 1936), 3–31, and idem, *The Founding of Harvard College* (Cambridge: Harvard University Press, 1935), 200–207. Morison noted that the Jesuit *Ratio Studorium* of 1599 had the same requirements.

46. Morison, *Three Centuries,* 30.

47. Edmund Morgan, ed., *The Diary of Michael Wigglesworth, 1653–1657: The Conscience of a Puritan* (New York: Harper and Row, 1965 [1946]), 41. Baron listed other instances of discontent in "From Colonial Mansion," 111–12. See also Derek de Sola Pool, "Hebrew Learning Among the Puritans of New England Prior to 1700," *Publications of the American Jewish Historical Society* 20 (1911), 31–83.

48. Harvard professor Harry A. Wolfson, himself subject to frequent reappointments during his first decade at Harvard, noted Harvard's practice in his portrait of Monis published in the *Dictionary of American Biography.*

49. Morison, *Three Centuries,* 58. See also Harry A. Wolfson, "Hebrew Books at Harvard," *Harvard Alumni Bulletin* (April 29, 1932), and Isidore Meyer, "Hebrew at Harvard (1636–1760)," *Publications of the American Jewish Historical Society* 35 (1939), 145–70.

50. See, for example, Maurice Samuel, *The Professor and the Fossil: Some Observations on Arnold J. Toynbee's A Study of History* (New York: Alfred A. Knopf, 1956).

51. On Monis, see bibliographies in the biographical articles in the *Jewish Encyclopedia* and the *Dictionary of American Biography* (*DAB,* s.v. "Monis, Judah"). See also Arthur A. Chiel, "Judah Monis, The Harvard Convert," *Judaism* 23 (Spring, 1974), 223–32;

M. Klein, "A Jew at Harvard in the 18th Century," *Proceedings of the Massachusetts Historical Society* 97 (1985), 135–45; and Morison, *Three Centuries,* 57–58. Harry Wolfson stated in his *DAB* article that Monis derived his fame from several firsts: "The first Jew to receive a degree [A. M. in 1720] from Harvard, the first teacher at Harvard to bear the title of instructor, and the author of the first Hebrew grammar published in America."

52. Arthur Jeffery, appointed chair of Columbia's Semitics department in 1937, speculated that the reasons for the early prominence of Hebrew included its "extraordinary flexibility" and its position as key to Biblical history and therefore to divine truth (Arthur Jeffery, "The Department of Semitic Languages," in Jacques Barzun, ed., *A History of the Faculty of Philosophy Columbia University* [New York: Columbia University Press, 1954], 184).

53. See Shalom Goldman, "Isaac Nordheimer (1809–1842): 'An Israelite Truly in Whom There Was No Guile,'" *American Jewish History* 80 (Winter, 1990/91), 213–29, and Edward Robinson, ed., *Bibliotheca Sacra; or, Tracts and Essays Connected with Biblical Literature and Theology* (New York: Wiley and Putnam, 1843), 379–90. One dubious reminiscence claims that Nordheimer abandoned Judaism at the end of his life. See "Reminiscences of Dr. Isaac Nordheimer," *The New Englander* 33 (July, 1874), 506–12. Richard Gottheil ("Gli Studi Ebraici in America," *Rivista Israelitica* 6 [1909], 147), uses the word "conversione" but cites no source. An English version of Gottheil's work appeared in the *Jewish Exponent* (March 16, 1906, and March 23, 1906), a Philadelphia newspaper.

54. The University of the City of New York apparently cornered the market on Hebrew instruction in New York. Turner wrote: "When Nordheimer became known as a good Hebrew teacher, I felt it less incumbent on me to devote my time to this object. Since then I have never been required to give lessons in Hebrew, so that the professorship has become a sinecure" (quoted in Richard Gottheil, "Semitic Languages at Columbia," *Columbia University Bulletin* 19 [March, 1898], 94). Bush, not Nordheimer, taught Hebrew at the new institution.

55. See Louis Franklin Snow, *The College Curriculum in the United States* (New York: Teachers College, Columbia University, 1907), 49–50n, 54, and Frederick Rudolph, *Curriculum: A History of the American Undergraduate Course of Study Since 1636* (San Francisco: Jossey-Bass, 1978), 38.

56. On mental discipline, see "The Yale Report of 1828," in Richard Hofstadter and Wilson Smith, eds., *American Higher Education: A Documentary History,* vol. 1 (Chicago: University of Chicago Press, 1961), 275–91. On Hebrew's literary worth, see B. B. Edwards, "Reasons for the Study of the Hebrew Language," in Edwards A. Park, ed., *Writings of Professor B. B. Edwards,* vol. 2 (Boston: John P. Jewett, 1853), 206–33, quotation from 212. "The great problem for the friends of civilization and Christianity to solve," wrote Edwards, "is the conversion of the millions who use the Chinese and the Arabic languages. . . . A thorough knowledge of Hebrew will remove at least one half the difficulty of acquiring the Arabic" (ibid., 229, 232). Compare: "We, having learned the languages of the adversaries of God and ourselves, by preaching to and teaching them may overcome their errors in the sword of truth and render the people acceptable unto God and convert enemies into friends" (Thorndike, *University Records,* 127).

57. Chomsky indicated that Harvard employed Hebrew through the early nineteenth century. His questionable surmise that at least some in the audience understood these speeches is itself evidence of the language's curricular weakness. See William Chomsky, *Hebrew,* 248, and Goldman, "Hebrew at Early Colleges," passim.

58. Judah Monis published the first American Hebrew grammar. Nineteenth-century Americans extensively used the grammars of the philologist Gesenius, especially the English translations by Andover Seminary's Moses Stuart (1826) and by Conant (1839).

59. See Chomsky, *Hebrew,* chapter 13.

60. Isaac Nordheimer's grammar synthesized European scholarship, especially the work of Gesenius and philologist Heinrich Ewald. See Jack Fellman, "Notes Concerning Two Nineteenth-Century Hebrew Textbooks," *American Jewish Archives* 32 (April, 1980),

244 *Notes for Pages 14–15*

73–77, and Isaac Nordheimer, *A Critical Grammar of the Hebrew Language* (New York: Wiley and Putnam, 1838–1841). Emanuel Nuñes Carvalho's chrestomathy—a collection of literary passages—and grammar included Talmudic and modern constructions as well as Biblical references (see Carvalho, *Mafteah Leshon Ibrit, A Key to the Hebrew Tongue* [Philadelphia: Fry, 1815]). Carvalho, a Sephardic Jew, was a rabbi and educator who lived in New York, Charleston, and Philadelphia after arriving from England in 1806. See Moshe Davis, *The Emergence of Conservative Judaism: The Historical School in 19th Century America* (Philadelphia: Jewish Publication Society of America, 1963), 47–48. A generation later, Joseph Aaron published another grammar, and M. Henry's dictionary of Hebrew and Aramaic followed shortly. See Joseph Aaron, *Sefer Mafteah el lashon Ibri we-Hakhmat he Dikduk Meforash im Nekudot, A Key to the Hebrew Language and the Science of Grammar Explained, with Vowels, First Part* (New York: 1834); M. Henry, *Imrai Shaipher, Goodly Words* (New York: M. Jackson, 1838); and Bernhard Felsenthal, *A Practical Grammar of the Hebrew Language for Schools and Colleges* (New York: L. H. Frank, 1868).

61. See Jerry Wayne Brown, *The Rise of Biblical Criticism in America: 1800–1870—The New England Scholars* (Middletown, Conn.: Wesleyan University Press, 1969); Daniel Walker Howe, *The Unitarian Conscience: Harvard Moral Philosophy, 1805–1861* (Cambridge: Harvard University Press, 1970); Morison, *Three Centuries,* 241–43; Charles C. Torrey, "The Beginnings of Oriental Study at Andover," *American Journal of Semitic Languages and Literatures* 13 (July, 1897), 249–66; and George Hunston Williams, ed., *The Harvard Divinity School: Its Place in Harvard University and in American Culture* (Boston: Beacon, 1954).

62. On the history of American theological education, see John S. Brubacher and S. Willis Rudy, *Higher Education in Transition,* 3rd ed. (New York: Harper and Row, 1976), 3–23, 42–45, 198–203; James W. Fraser, *Schooling the Preachers: The Development of Protestant Theological Education in the United States, 1740–1875* (Lanham, Md.: University Press of America, 1988); Thomas C. Hunt and James C. Carper, *Religious Seminaries in America: A Selected Bibliography* (New York: Garland Publishing, 1989); Martin E. Marty, "Clergy," in N. O. Hatch, ed., *The Professions in American History* (Notre Dame: University of Notre Dame Press, 1988); Frank Dixon McCloy, "The History of Theological Education in America," *Church History* 31 (December, 1962), 449–53; Natalie A. Naylor, "The Theological Seminary in the Configuration of American Higher Education: The Ante-Bellum Years," *History of Education Quarterly* 17 (Spring, 1977), 17–30; and J. M. White, *The Diocesan Seminary in the United States: A History from the 1780s to the Present* (Notre Dame: University of Notre Dame Press, 1989).

63. Brown, *Rise of Biblical Criticism,* 180. The movement produced an internationally respected scholar, Edward Robinson, in addition to Moses Stuart. George P. Fisher, a New Haven scholar (see below), was a student of Stuart and later became dean of Yale's theology department (ibid., 45–59, 111–24).

64. See Louise L. Stevenson, "Between the Old-Time College and the Modern University: Noah Porter and the New Haven Scholars," *History of Higher Education Annual* 3 (1983), 39–57, quotation from 42. See also idem, *Scholarly Means to Evangelical Ends: The New Haven Scholars and the Transformation of Higher Learning in America* (Baltimore: Johns Hopkins University Press, 1986).

65. William Dwight Whitney, *Language and the Study of Language: Twelve Lectures on the Principles of Linguistic Science* (New York: Charles Scribner's Sons, 1867). On Whitney in Germany, see Diehl, *Americans and German Scholarship,* 120–30.

66. Chinese, Japanese, and other far eastern language studies had to wait until the twentieth century in most universities.

67. See Holger Pedersen, *The Discovery of Language: Linguistic Science in the Nineteenth Century,* John W. Spargo, tr. (Bloomington: Indiana University Press, 1962 [1931]), 116–20; 176–88. On Assyriology in America, see E. A. Wallis Budge, *The Rise and Progress of Assyriology* (London: Martin Hopkinson, 1925), 244–60.

68. Some Jews might have known of *The New Englander,* the journal of the New Haven scholars. The journal published a reminiscence of Isaac Nordheimer in 1874. See n. 53, above.

69. We adopted the broadest definition of philology, which originally included historical, literary, and linguistic studies (see chapter 2). Recall that advocates of *Wissenschaft des Judentums* offered equally broad definitions. We excluded Union Theological Seminary (Episcopal) from our sample. Francis Brown offered Assyrian at Union Theological as early as 1880.

70. Chapter 2 contrasts Daniel C. Gilman's experiences as president of California and of Johns Hopkins. See Geraldine Jonçich Clifford, "No Shade in the Golden State: School and University in Nineteenth-Century California," *History of Higher Education Annual* 12 (1992), 35–68.

71. See, for example, Daniel C. Kevles, *The Physicists: The History of a Scientific Community in Modern America* (New York: Alfred A. Knopf, 1978), 11–15. Semitics diverged from physics, however, in its greater dependence on external munificence.

72. Bryn Mawr, a women's college with some university characteristics, was the only Semitics institution to decline AAU membership.

73. At Harvard's philosophy department in the late nineteenth century, practitioners produced "technical specialized research published for technically competent audiences in technical journals, with popularizations in all areas of specialization relegated to hacks, incompetents, and has-beens" (see Bruce Kuklick, *The Rise of American Philosophy: Cambridge, Massachusetts, 1860–1930* [New Haven: Yale University Press, 1977], 565).

74. Governing boards infrequently included Catholics or Jews. The few exceptions were usually perceived as communal representatives rather than as qualified individuals who happened to be Catholic or Jewish. The University of Chicago trustee Eli B. Felsenthal provides an example. A leader in a key fund raising campaign for the newly founded institution, his reward consisted of appointment to the original board. Richard Storr used the word *representing* to characterize his role: "Felsenthal was the only trustee representing a specific group of donors" (Richard J. Storr, *Harper's University: The Beginnings* [Chicago: University of Chicago Press, 1966], 42). Julian Mack, a noted attorney and judge, played a similar role on the Harvard Board of Overseers; see Harry S. Barnard, *The Forging of an American Jew: The Life and Times of Judge Julian W. Mack* (New York: Herzl Press, 1974). Columbia consciously excluded Jews until the late 1920s and then appointed Judge Benjamin Cardozo precisely to overcome 30 years of exclusion. See Harold S. Wechsler, *The Qualified Student: A History of Selective College Admission in America, 1870–1970* (New York: Wiley-Interscience, 1977), 136–40.

75. George Foot Moore to Arthur Hadley, November 7, 1899, Records of President Arthur Twining Hadley, Correspondence, Yale Archives, Yale University Library (hereafter Hadley Records), box 73, file 993.

76. See Dan A. Oren, *Joining the Club: A History of Jews and Yale* (New Haven: Yale University Press, 1985), appendix 9, for a chronology of Jewish learning at Yale.

77. Hadley to Torrey, December 31, 1900, Hadley Records, box 124, file 623. See also Torrey to Hadley, December 8, 1900, February 5 and 11, 1901, ibid., box 109, file 1609, and Hadley to Torrey, March 15, 1901, ibid., box 126, file 122.

78. See *DAB,* s.v. "Kent, Charles Foster."

79. Levering Reynolds, Jr., "The Later Years (1880–1953)," in Williams, ed., *Harvard Divinity School,* 165. At Chicago, even Jewish students received divinity school degrees.

80. Harvard University, *Annual Reports of the President and Treasurer of Harvard College* (1894/95), 25, and ibid. (1896/97), 24. Andover did not charge students for either instruction or accommodations. Its officials wished to facilitate full-time study by eliminating the need to earn a living. See Naylor, "Theological Seminary," 19.

81. University of Chicago, *Annual Register* (1892/93), 58.

82. University of Chicago, *Decennial Publications,* vol. 1: *The President's Report, 1892–1902* (Chicago: University of Chicago Press, 1903), lxxi.

83. Francis Greenwood Peabody, "1902–03 Report of the Dean of the Divinity School," in Harvard University, *Annual Reports of the President and Treasurer of Harvard College* (1902/03).

84. Francis Greenwood Peabody, "1892–93 Report of the Dean of the Divinity School," in Harvard University, *Annual Reports of the President and Treasurer of Harvard College* (1892/93).

85. "Report of George P. Fisher, Dean, Department of Theology," in *Report of the President of Yale University and of the Deans and Directors of the Several Departments for the Academic Year 1901–1902* (1902), 102.

86. "Report of Frank K. Sanders, Dean, Department of Theology," ibid., *1904–1905,* 135.

87. *Yale University Catalogue,* 1902/03, 437. Yale divinity school tuition in the mid-1960s was less than half the amount charged by the college and graduate school (*Bulletin of Yale University, 1968–1969,* 156, 164, 245). See also Claude Welch, *Graduate Education in Religion, A Critical Appraisal* (Missoula: University of Montana Press, 1971), 40–41.

88. "Report of Dr. Frank K. Sanders, Dean, The Department of Theology," in *Report . . . 1902–1903* (1903), 120, and "Report of Dr. George P. Fisher, Dean, Department of Theology," in *Report . . . 1900–1901,* 83, emphasis added.

89. See J. G. Johnson, "The Yale Divinity School, 1899–1928" (Ph.D. diss., Yale University, 1936); Gerald Everett Knoff, "The Yale Divinity School, 1858–1899" (Ph.D. diss., Yale University, 1936); and James T. Wayland, "The Theological Department in Yale College" (Ph.D. diss., Yale University, 1933).

90. Butler to James M. Green, December 20, 1900, Nicholas Murray Butler Papers (hereafter Butler Papers), Rare Book and Manuscript Library, Columbia University (hereafter CU-RBML), "NEA, James M. Green" file.

91. See Roland Bainton, *Yale and the Ministry: A History of Education for Christian Ministry at Yale from the Founding in 1701* (New York: Harper and Brothers, 1957), and Ralph H. Gabriel, *Religion and Learning at Yale: The Church of Christ in the College and University 1757–1957* (New Haven: Yale University Press, 1958). John Pierpont Morgan's 1910 endowment of the William M. Laffan Professorship of Assyriology further augmented the department's ranks. Morgan nominated Albert Tobias Clay of the University of Pennsylvania as the inaugural chairholder (see Morgan to Hadley, January 3, 1910, Hadley Records, box 73, file 101). Some scholars found Clay's scholarship suspect. At a 1920 meeting of the Palestine Oriental Society, "Clay gave the first paper, an absurd one on 'The Amorite Name of Jerusalem,' mispronouncing both German and English, showing how little Arabic and Hebrew he knew, and making American scholarship a laughing stock" (see Leona Glidden Running and David Noel Freedman, *William Foxwell Albright: A Twentieth Century Genius* [New York: Two Continents Publishing Group, 1975], 78–79).

92. Yale permanently introduced Judaica by recruiting, first, Semitist Julian Obermann (visiting, 1933; permanent, 1935–1956) from the Jewish Institute of Religion (1923–1931), and then rabbinics scholar Judah Goldin (1958). Obermann became editor of the *Yale Judaica Series* in 1944. Rabbi Hyman Enelow's 1925 effort to endow a chair of Jewish learning in the Yale divinity school failed. See chapter 5. When William Albright turned down a call to the Laffan professorship (1933), he recommended the appointment of Albrecht Goetze, a Gentile refugee from Hitler's Germany, who then held the chair for many years. See Running and Freedman, *William Foxwell Albright,* 185–86.

93. Laurence Veysey, "Stability and Experiment in the American Undergraduate Curriculum," in Carl Kaysen, ed., *Content and Context: Essays on College Education* (New York: McGraw-Hill, 1973), 1–63.

94. See Paul Ritterband and Harold S. Wechsler, "Jewish Learning in American Universities," *Encyclopaedia Judaica Yearbook* (1977–1978), 73–77.

95. Paul Monroe, ed., *A Cyclopedia of Education* (New York: Macmillan, 1913), s.v. "Oriental Studies," A. V. Williams Jackson and Louis H. Gray, 4:561–66, quotation from 566.

96. On entrance requirements and the secondary school curriculum, see Wechsler, *The Qualified Student*, 115–19. On Hebrew as a college entrance requirement, see chapter 8, below.

97. See Roger L. Geiger, *To Advance Knowledge: The Growth of American Research Universities: 1900–1940* (New York: Oxford University Press, 1986).

2. Reforming the Universities

1. William Hayes Ward, "Retrospect and Prospect," *Hebraica* 5 (October, 1888), 82.

2. By century's end, the study of Bible had effected a modest comeback as advocates of its inclusion differentiated between devotional study and "collegiate" (meaning modern) and "radical higher criticism." See "Bible Study in American Colleges," *Report of the Commissioner of Education for the Year 1897–98* (Washington, D.C.: Government Printing Office, 1899), 2:1536–38.

3. Emil G. Hirsch, "Ministerial Training," *The Reform Advocate* 7 (June 9, 1894), 293.

4. "Unfolding the plan of an immutable Creator," stated Daniel Gilman, "[Science] will yet be recognized as the handmaid of religion" (Daniel C. Gilman, "The University of California in its Infancy," in *University Problems in the United States* [New York: Century, 1898], 153–85, quotation from 169).

5. "[The sudden collapse of] that decaying mass of outworn thought which attaches the modern world to medieval conceptions of Christianity," wrote Andrew Dixon White, Gilman's close friend since their undergraduate days at Yale, "[would be] distressing and calamitous, sweeping before it not only outworn creeds and noxious dogmas, but cherished principles and ideals, and even wrenching out most precious and moral foundations of the whole social and political fabric" (Andrew Dixon White, *A History of the Warfare of Science with Theology in Christendom* vol. 1 [New York: D. Appleton, 1897], vi). White chronicled this warfare in his major scholarly work (see Glenn C. Altschuler, *Andrew Dixon White: Educator, Historian, Diplomat* [Ithaca: Cornell University Press, 1979], 202–16). White concluded: "My hope is to aid—even if it be but a little—in the gradual and healthful dissolving away of this mass of unreason, that the stream of 'religion pure and undefiled' may flow on broad and clear, a blessing to humanity" (White, *History*, 1: vi). See also Winton Solberg, "The Conflict Between Religion and Science at the University of Illinois, 1867–1894," *American Quarterly* 18 (Summer, 1966), 183–99.

6. J. H. Seelye to J. M. Tyler, July 29, 1878, quoted in Thomas Le Duc, *Piety and Intellect at Amherst College 1865–1912* (New York: Columbia University Press, 1946), 85. See also George E. Peterson, *The New England College in the Age of the University* (Amherst, Mass.: Amherst College Press, 1964); David Potts, "American Colleges in the Nineteenth Century: From Localism to Denominationalism," *History of Education Quarterly* 11 (Winter, 1971) 363–80; idem, "Baptist Colleges in the Development of American Society" (Ph.D. diss., Harvard University, 1967); and Marilyn Tobias, *Old Dartmouth on Trial: The Transformation of the Academic Community in Nineteenth Century America* (New York: New York University Press, 1982).

7. See James McCosh, *The Religious Aspects of Evolution* (New York: Putnam's Sons, 1888); Laurence R. Veysey, *The Emergence of the American University* (Chicago: University of Chicago Press, 1965), 48–50, and J. David Hoeveler, Jr., *James McCosh and the Scottish Intellectual Tradition: From Glasglow to Princeton* (Princeton: Princeton University Press, 1981).

8. William R. Harper, "The Purpose of *Hebraica*," *Hebraica* 1 (March, 1884), 4.

9. As quoted in Leroy Waterman, "A Half Century of Biblical and Semitic Investigation," *The American Journal of Semitic Languages and Literatures* 32 (July, 1916), 219. See also Marion Le Roy Burton, *Our Intellectual Attitude in an Age of Criticism* (Boston: Plimpton Press, 1913), chapter 3.

10. Paul K. Conkin, *Prophets of Prosperity: America's First Political Economists* (Bloomington: Indiana University Press, 1980); Steven J. Diner, *A City and its Universities: Public Policy in Chicago, 1892–1919* (Chapel Hill: University of North Carolina Press, 1980); Robert E. L. Faris, *Chicago Sociology: 1920–1932* (San Francisco: Chandler Publishing, 1967); Henrika Kuklick, "Boundary Maintenance in American Sociology: Limitations to Academic Professionalization," *Journal of the History of the Behavioral Sciences* 16 (1980), 201–19, and Edward A. Shils, "Tradition, Ecology, and Institution in the History of Sociology," *Daedalus* (Fall, 1970), 760–825.

11. See Michael Silverstein, ed., *Whitney on Language: Selected Writings of William Dwight Whitney* (Cambridge: MIT Press, 1971).

12. See Oscar Handlin, *Race and Nationality in American Life* (Garden City, N.Y.: Doubleday, 1957), chapter 4, and Glenn C. Altschuler, *Race, Ethnicity, and Class in American Social Thought, 1865–1919* (Arlington Heights, Il.: H. Davidson, 1982).

13. Clark Kerr, *The Uses of the University* (Cambridge: Harvard University Press, 1964), 36. Italics in original.

14. Ibid., 34.

15. Morris Jastrow to Harper, October, 1888, William Rainey Harper Papers (hereafter Harper Papers), University of Chicago Special Collections (hereafter UCSC), box 1, file 6.

16. Harper entitled his dissertation (1875) "A Comparative Study of the Prepositions in Latin, Greek, Sanskrit, and Gothic," a topic that reflected Whitney's interest in the Indo-European language family rather than Harper's interest in Semitics.

17. Only with publication of his Amos and Hosea commentary in 1905 did speculation on the quality of his mature scholarship cease. See George Adam Smith, "[William R. Harper] as an Old Testament Interpreter," *The Biblical World* 27 (March, 1906), 200, and William R. Harper, *A Critical and Exegetical Commentary on Amos and Hosea* (New York: Charles Scribner's Sons, 1905).

18. E. Benjamin Andrews, "The Granville Period," *The Biblical World* 27 (March, 1906), 169.

19. "So far as I can recall," he concluded, "he relished the classic tongues less because of the history and literature to be got at through them than as a field for the application of his grammatical knowledge in reading by himself and in drilling others" (ibid., 168).

20. Eri B. Hulbert, "The Morgan Park Period," *The Biblical World* 27 (March, 1906), 171–76.

21. See Joseph E. Gould, *The Chautauqua Movement: An Episode in the Continuing American Revolution* (New York: State University of New York, 1961), chapter 2, and Theodore Morrison, *Chautauqua: A Center for Education, Religion, and the Arts in America* (Chicago: University of Chicago Press, 1974), chapter 6. See also Jastrow to Harper, October 7, 1886, Harper Papers, UCSC, box 1, file 4.

22. See Potts, "American Colleges," passim.

23. William R. Harper, "The Religious Spirit," in *Religion and the Higher Life: Talks to Students* (Chicago: University of Chicago Press, 1904), 27. David B. Owen called this quotation to our attention.

24. William Rainey Harper, "The Pentateuchal Question: I. Genesis 1:1–12:5," *Hebraica* 5 (October, 1888), 18–73; "The Pentateuchal Question: II. Genesis 12:6–37:1," *Hebraica* 5 (July, 1889), 243–91; "The Pentateuchal Question: III. Genesis 37:2–Exodus 12:51," *Hebraica* 6 (October, 1889), 1–48; and "The Pentateuchal Question: IV. Exodus 13–Deuteronomy 34," *Hebraica* 6 (July, 1890), 241–95. At Morgan Park, related Milton Mayer, "discovering that his critical conclusions on a certain problem involved the denial of the Davidic authorship of one of the psalms quoted by Jesus, he struggled with himself for days. At the time he spoke to no one of his problem. In the end, the haggard truth-seeker emerged resolute and calm, ready for the storm his decision would bring down upon him. He had decided to follow his scholarly findings" (Milton Mayer, *Young Man in a Hurry: The Story of WILLIAM RAINEY HARPER, First*

President of the University of Chicago [Chicago: University of Chicago Alumni Association, 1957], 16–17). See also Robert Funk, "The Watershed of American Biblical Tradition: The Chicago School, First Phase: 1892–1920," *Journal of Biblical Literature* 95 (1976), 4–22, and James P. Wind, *The Bible and the University: The Messianic Vision of William Rainey Harper* (Atlanta: Scholars Press, 1987).

25. As quoted in Mayer, *Young Man in a Hurry,* 37.

26. As quoted in Gould, *Chautauqua Movement,* 35.

27. William Rainey Harper, "Editorial: The Old and New Testament Student," *The Biblical World* 10 (August, 1897), 89, 93.

28. See Thomas Goodspeed to Harper, June 1, 1890, Correspondence of the Founder [John D. Rockefeller] and His Associates (hereafter Rockefeller Correspondence), UCSC, box 1, file 10; Thomas W. Goodspeed, *A History of the University of Chicago* (Chicago: University of Chicago Press, 1916), 87, and Storr, *Harper's University,* 39–40 (source of the phrase: "reformed Judaism and reformed Protestantism"). Goodspeed wrote: "This generous co-operation was one of the essential factors in the final success achieved. The fact that the Standard Club and the Jews generally were making this volunteer contribution for the new institution did much to invite public attention and to interest all classes of citizens in the movement." See also *Jewish Encyclopedia,* s.v. "Chicago." Protestant identity replaced denominational affiliation as a prerequisite for trustee appointment, but the liberalization rarely went further.

29. Harper's Jewish faculty appointments included the physicist Albert Michelson, chemists Felix Langfeld and Julius Steiglitz, professor of jurisprudence Ernst Freund, professor of law Julian Mack (who reappears in this narrative as a Harvard Overseer in chapter 5), professor of elocution Solomon Henry Clark, as well as Hirsch.

30. See Wechsler, *The Qualified Student,* chapter 9. But see also Vincent Sheean, *Personal History* (Garden City, N.Y.: Doubleday, Doran, 1936), chapter 1.

31. Emil G. Hirsch, "[William R. Harper] in the Field of Semitic Scholarship," *The Biblical World* 27 (March, 1906), 197. See also Thomas W. Goodspeed, *William Rainey Harper: First President of the University of Chicago* (Chicago: University of Chicago Press, 1928), 218. Nathan Isaacs, an orthodox Jew who became a key member of the Menorah movement during the 1920s, expressed the general consensus on the importance of Harper's pedagogy for the recognition of Jewish learning. In applying his inductive method in exactly the same way to Xenophon's *Anabasis,* Ceasar's *Gallic Wars,* and to Genesis, Harper reached "the point of convergence with other streams of thought: the point at which Jewish culture takes its place in the University curriculum and in the equipment of the educated man, alongside of Greek and Latin—perhaps alongside of even more modern contributions to civilization" (Nathan Isaacs, "Introduction of Dr. Ginzberg," attached to Isaacs to Henry Hurwitz, December 30, 1920, Henry Hurwitz Menorah Association Memorial Collection [hereafter Menorah Collection], American Jewish Archives [hereafter AJA], microfilm 2082).

32. S. H. Lee to Harper, September 5, 1887, as quoted in Gould, *Chautauqua Movement,* 33, 104. For Harper's views on the higher criticism, see Charles Farace, "The History of Old Testament Higher Criticism in the United States" (Ph.D. diss., University of Chicago, 1939), 96–100. See also Grant Wacker, "The Demise of Biblical Criticism," in Nathan O. Hatch and Mark A. Noll, eds., *The Bible in America: Essays in Cultural History* (New York: Oxford University Press, 1982), 121–38. On conditions in England, see Barbara Zink MacHaffie, " 'Monument Facts and Higher Critical Fancies,' Archaeology and the Popularization of Old Testament Criticism in Nineteenth Century Britain," *Church History* 50 (September, 1981), 316–28.

33. Haupt to Cyrus Adler, September 4, 1890, Seminary Autograph Collection (hereafter "Seminary Autograph"), Library of the Jewish Theological Seminary of America (hereafter JTS), Haupt-Adler Correspondence.

34. In 1890/91 Harper had at least 48 graduate students and about 150 theological students at Yale (Harper to Benjamin I. Wheeler, February 6, 1891, Benjamin I. Wheeler

Papers [C-B 104], The Bancroft Library, University of California, Berkeley [hereafter UCB], "William Rainey Harper, 1856–1906" file).

35. On Gilman, see *DAB.,* s.v. "Gilman, Daniel Coit"; Abraham Flexner, *Daniel Coit Gilman: Creator of the American Type of University* (New York: Harcourt Brace, 1910); Hugh Hawkins, *Pioneer: A History of the Johns Hopkins University 1874–1889* (Ithaca: Cornell University Press, 1960); and John C. French, *A History of the University Founded by Johns Hopkins* (Baltimore: Johns Hopkins Press, 1946), 26–32.

36. Flexner, *Daniel Coit Gilman,* 4.

37. Emil G. Hirsch made the quoted statement in reference to a famous lecture on "The New Knowledge and the Old Faith" offered by his predecessor at Sinai (and his brother-in-law) Kaufmann Kohler. See Max C. Currick, "Recalling Kaufmann Kohler," *Liberal Judaism* 11 (May, 1943), 17.

38. Hawkins, *Pioneer,* 17. "Let me say," wrote Gilman, "with the solemnity of deep conviction, that dearer than the fellowship of brethren, deeper than the love of knowledge, too precious to be ever given up, too sacred for careless speech, is the invigorating and inspiring belief that science in its ultimate assertions echoes the voice of the living God" ("The Sheffield Scientific School of Yale University, New Haven," in Gilman, *University Problems,* 148). See also Stevenson, *Scholarly Means to Evangelical Ends,* passim.

39. Quoted in Rudolf Glanz, *The Jews of California from the Discovery of Gold until 1880* (New York: Waldon Press, 1960), 99–100, quotation from 100.

40. Gilman, "The University of California in its Infancy," 176.

41. Ibid., 168–77, quotation from 174.

42. Minutes of the Regents of the University of California, July 16, 1872, and July 23, 1872; Martin Kellogg to A. J. Moulder, July 19, 1872, Records of the Regents of the University of California (CU-1, UCB). J. R. K. Kantor, former University Archivist at Berkeley, provided this information. See also articles by "Maftir" in *The American Israelite,* March 4, 1887, 9, and June 15, 1888, 8, and an article in *The Occident,* May 25, 1888, 162. Lynn D. Gordon brought the *Occident* article to our attention. "There is but little Orientalism over there [at the University] and the students in that branch are as rare as those who want to learn Chinese" ("Maftir," June 15, 1888, 8).

43. See Hawkins, *Pioneer,* 34–35, 215.

44. The other Jewish faculty members were Maurice Bloomfield, Sanskritist; Abraham Cohen; Simon Flexner; mathematician Fabian Franklin, who edited Gilman's biography; and political scientist J. H. Hollander.

45. "A visitor would note there Jewish rabbis, Catholic priests and students, and Protestant ministers of various denominations, all intent on one object and all, apparently, harmoniously pursuing it," wrote a Christian graduate of the Seminary. "And truly we were, for no incident, I can say, ever occurred to put the slightest strain upon the cordial and pleasant relations that existed among members of the seminary" (John F. Fenlon, "Theology and the Semitic Sciences," *Johns Hopkins University Circular* 28, no. 214 [1909], 270).

46. Hawkins, *Pioneer,* 158.

47. Murray to Gilman, March 1, 1876, and April 11, 1876, Daniel G. Gilman Papers (hereafter Gilman Papers), ms. 1, Special Collections, Milton S. Eisenhower Library, The Johns Hopkins University (hereafter MSEL-SC), "Thomas Murray" file.

48. Recall that Gilman was a librarian at Yale. Jastrow would hold the Pennsylvania librarianship beginning in 1888, while Richard Gottheil headed the New York Public Library's Oriental Division. A librarianship occasionally offered remuneration to a faculty member whose course enrollments might not by themselves justify a full salary.

49. Harvard had likewise failed to attract him in 1869. See Stevenson, *Scholarly Means to Evangelical Ends,* 41.

50. Whitney's influence is perceptible in nearly all Oriental language personnel decisions made at Hopkins. He vouched for Murray, Lanman, and Bloomfield, counselled

Lanman to accept the Harvard position, and advised Gilman to allow Bloomfield ample time to conduct original investigations (Hawkins, *Pioneer,* 86, 156, 157, 158). Gilman's memorial address for Whitney reflects affection and esteem. Not uncharacteristically, he made special mention of Whitney's devotion to Sheffield's use of "modern methods and of modern subjects in the courses of a liberal education" (Daniel C. Gilman, "Concluding Address," *Journal of the American Oriental Society* 19 [1897], 60). On Wiener, see Klingenstein, *Jews in the American Academy,* chapter 2.

51. See Brown, *Rise of Biblical Criticism,* chapter 5. See also Marcia Graham Synnott, "A Social History of Admissions Policies at Harvard, Yale and Princeton, 1900–1930" (Ph.D. diss., University of Massachusetts, 1974), 178–81.

52. Hugh Hawkins, *Between Harvard and America: The Educational Leadership of Charles W. Eliot* (New York: Oxford University Press, 1972), 128, 181.

53. Charles W. Eliot, "Address at a Meeting of the Harvard Menorah Society, December 20, 1907," in Henry Hurwitz and I. Leo Sharfman, *The Menorah Movement for the Study and Advancement of Jewish Culture and Ideals: History, Purposes, Activities* (Ann Arbor: Intercollegiate Menorah Association, 1914), 32. For additional discussion of Eliot's philo-Semitism, see chapter 5 below, and Marcia Synnott, *The Half-Opened Door: Discrimination and Admissions at Harvard, Yale and Princeton, 1900–1970* (Westport, Conn.: Greenwood Press, 1979), chapter 2.

54. The 1868/69 catalogue uninvitingly announced: "The Hebrew Language is taught to those [seniors] who desire to learn it." See David G. Lyon, "Semitic 1880–1929," in Samuel Eliot Morison, ed., *The Development of Harvard University since the Inauguration of President Eliot 1869–1929* (Cambridge: Harvard University Press, 1930), 232.

55. Eliot's faculty choices after the opening of Johns Hopkins became increasingly research-oriented. See Robert A. McCaughey, "The Transformation of Academic Life: Harvard University 1821–1892," *Perspectives in American History* 8 (1974), 239–332.

56. See Hawkins, *Pioneer,* 156.

57. He also published a widely used "Sanskrit Reader." See Charles Lanman, "Autobiographical Note," *Harvard Crimson* (February 24, 1925).

58. Ward, "Retrospect and Prospect," 81.

59. See *DAB,* s.v. "Ward, William Hayes." For a less sympathetic view, see Cyrus Adler to Solomon Schechter, July 21, 1911, Cyrus Adler Papers (hereafter Adler Papers), JTS, "Solomon Schechter" file.

60. The resignation was prompted by his contention that the "servant" in Isaiah 53 was the ideal Israel. See Farace, "History of Old Testament Higher Criticism," 66–67.

61. Morison, *Three Centuries of Harvard,* 336. See chapter 5 for extended discussion.

62. William C. Jones, *Illustrated History of the University of California* (San Francisco: Frederick H. Dukesmith, 1895), 3. See also Verne A. Stadtman, *The University of California 1868–1968* (New York: McGraw-Hill, 1970), 116–20, 179–80. Louis Sloss served as University Treasurer after 1885 and was succeeded by Lewis Gerstle, another Jew.

63. Jewish faculty members who received appointments before Voorsanger and Max Margolis included Albin Putzker and Joachim Henry Senger in German, Meyer Jaffa in agriculture, and Arnold Abraham D'Ancona and Charles Gabriel Levison in medicine. Putzker, a Gilman appointee, advocated "the scientific study of language." Jones notes that he employed "a rational, inductive method long before the idea became popularized in the country by men of great prominence" (Jones, *Illustrated History,* 118–19).

64. *DAB,* s.v. "Kellogg, Martin" and "Wheeler, Benjamin Ide."

65. John Fulton, *Memoirs of Frederick A. P. Barnard: Tenth President of Columbia College in the City of New York* (New York: Macmillan, 1896), 141–42. See also William J. Chute, *Damn Yankee! The First Career of Frederick A. P. Barnard: Educator, Scientist, Idealist* (Port Washington, N.Y.: Kennikat Press, 1978), 65–67.

66. Fulton, *Memoirs,* 346.

67. Ibid., 392.

68. See Columbia College, *Minutes of the Trustees,* May 2, 1887; Barnard to Hamilton Fish, April 9, 1887, Fish to Barnard, April 11, 1887, Hamilton Fish Papers (hereafter Fish Papers), CU-RBML, "January–April, 1887" file; Seth Low to Fish, June 8, 1887, ibid., "May–December, 1887" file. See also Columbia College, *Annual Report of the President, 1887* (New York: Columbia College, 1887), 49.

69. Low to Committee on Education, Trustees of Columbia University, January 31, 1911, Columbia University Files (408 Low Memorial Library, hereafter CUF), "Seth Low, 1910–1918" file. Low appointed four Jewish professors during his tenure. He resigned his university trusteeship in a dispute over Jewish access to the Columbia campus. See Low to Jacob Schiff, December 26, 1900, CUF, "Jacob Schiff" file, and Wechsler, *The Qualified Student,* 140–41.

70. See Francis N. Thorpe, *The Life of William Pepper, M.D., L.L.D. (1843–1896)* (Philadelphia: J. B. Lippincott, 1904), passim.

71. Cyrus Adler, *I Have Considered the Days* (Philadelphia: Jewish Publication Society of America, 1945), 61–62.

72. Edwards Potts Cheyney, *History of the University of Pennsylvania, 1749–1940* (Philadelphia: University of Pennyslvania Press, 1940), 350.

73. John P. Peters, "Thirty Years' Progress in Semitics," in Roland G. Kent, ed., *Thirty Years of Oriental Studies Issued in Commemoration of Thirty Years of Activity of the Oriental Club of Philadelphia* (Philadelphia: Intelligencer Printing, 1918), 25.

74. Levy served as a trustee until his death in 1826. He was also Recorder of Philadelphia (1802–1822), Presiding Judge of the District Court (1822–1825), and a member of the Pennsylvania legislature.

75. See Henry Samuel Morais, *The Jews of Philadelphia: Their History from the Earliest Settlements to the Present Time* (Philadelphia: Levytype, 1894), 431–42. "Some of the early college graduates in Pennsylvania became leaders in the profession of law, and it is notable that Pennsylvania was one of three states (together with Georgia and South Carolina) where there was any significant number of Jewish lawyers before the 19th cent." (*Universal Jewish Encyclopedia,* s.v. "Pennsylvania" [New York: Universal Jewish Encyclopedia, 1942], 8:428).

76. Jewish faculty appointments contemporaneous with the 1886 appointment of Morris Jastrow to a lectureship in Semitic languages included Lee K. Frankel (B.S. 1887, Ph.D. 1890), instructor in analytical chemistry; Leo Stanton Rowe, lecturer on municipal government in the new Wharton School of Finance and Economy; and Isaac Joachim Schwatt, who remained on the Pennsylvania faculty after receiving his Ph.D. in mathematics.

77. "Declaration of Principles Adopted by a Group of Reform Rabbis at Pittsburgh, 1885" (The "Pittsburgh Platform"), fifth paragraph, in *Yearbook of the Central Conference of American Rabbis* 45 (1935), 198–200, reprinted in Glazer, *American Judaism,* 151–52.

78. See Herbert Wallace Schneider, *Religion in 20th Century America,* rev. ed. (New York: Atheneum, 1964 [1952]), 121–29, quotations from 125, 126. On the parallel movement in Catholicism, see Robert D. Cross, *The Emergence of Liberal Catholicism in America* (Chicago: Quadrangle Books, 1968 [1958]), chapter 8. The 1893 World Parliament of Religions, part of the Columbian Exposition in Chicago, showed American Jews that American Protestants displayed less condescension than their continental colleagues in their discussions of orientalism. See Rebecca Trachtenberg Alpert, "Jewish Participation at the World's Parliament of Religions, 1893," in Ronald A. Brauner, ed., *Jewish Civilization: Essays and Studies* (Philadelphia: Reconstructionist Rabbinical College, 1979), 1:111–21.

79. Quoted in Blau, *Judaism in America,* 40. See also Jacob Voorsanger, "Science and Religion as Coordinate Factors in Civilization," *The Jewish Progress* 18 (March, 1894), 1.

80. See Michael N. Dobkowski, *The Tarnished Dream: The Basis of American Anti-Semitism* (Westport, Conn.: Greenwood Press, 1979).

81. Joseph Jacobs, rev. ed., *The Jewish Encyclopedia: A Guide to Its Contents and An Aid to Its Use* (New York: Funk and Wagnalls, 1910), 139.

82. Abraham Geiger, *Über die Errichtung einer jüdisch—theologischen Fakultät* (Wiesbaden, 1838), 9, quoted in Jospe, "Study of Judaism," 301.

83. Levy's contemporary, Mordechai Noah echoed this suggestion. See Davis, *Emergence of Conservative Judaism*, 54. See also Jonathan D. Sarna, *Jacksonian Jew: The Two Worlds of Mordechai Noah* (New York: Holmes and Meier, 1981), 127–28, and Publio, "About Men and Things," *The Jewish Exponent* (August 4, 1905).

84. Davis, *Emergence of Conservative Judaism*, 53–59. Chapter 6, below, discusses Maimonides College.

85. In 1908, the students of New York's Rabbi Isaac Elchanan Theological Seminary (RIETS—soon renamed Yeshiva College) went on strike to protest the exclusion of secular studies. President Bernard Revel's 1915 incorporation of secular subjects into the RIETS curriculum demonstrated a partial surmounting of this fear of the Enlightenment. On RIETS, which under Revel evolved into Yeshiva University, see Gilbert Klapperman, *The Story of Yeshiva University: The First Jewish University in America* (New York: Macmillan, 1969), and Jeffrey S. Gurock, *The Men and Women of Yeshiva: Higher Education, Orthodoxy, and American Judaism* (New York: Columbia University Press, 1988). On Revel, see Aaron Rothkoff, *Bernard Revel: Builder of American Jewish Orthodoxy* (Philadelphia: Jewish Publication Society of America, 1972).

86. Davis, *Emergence of Conservative Judaism*, 249–51.

87. See David Philipson, *The Reform Movement in Judaism* (New York: Macmillan, 1931), 377–99; Michael A. Meyer, "A Centennial History," in Samuel Karff, ed., *The Hebrew Union College—Jewish Institute of Religion at 100 Years* (Cincinnati: Hebrew Union College Press, 1976), 7–47; James G. Heller, *Isaac Mayer Wise: His Life, Work and Thought* (New York: Union of American Hebrew Congregations, 1965); Andrew F. Key, *The Theology of Isaac Mayer Wise* (Cincinnati: American Jewish Archives, 1962); Israel Knox, *Rabbi in America: The Story of Isaac M. Wise* (Boston: Little, Brown, 1957); Max Benjamin May, *Isaac Mayer Wise: The Founder of American Judaism* (New York: G. P. Putnam's Sons, 1916); and Sefton D. Temkin, *Isaac Mayer Wise: Shaping American Judaism* (New York: Oxford University Press, 1992).

88. See Davis, *Emergence of Conservative Judaism*, 179–80, and Hirsch, "Ministerial Training," 293.

89. "Hebrew Grammar, Reading of the O.T. and philological comments upon it, Introduction in the books of the O.T., and c., also Semitic languages and literatures in a wider sense, these and other branches the Jewish students might study under you and other non-Jewish Professors" (Felsenthal to Harper, February 25, 1892 [Presidents' Papers], UCSC, box 65, file 5). Felsenthal added a disclaimer that "this is only a thought hastily thrown out," but he may have had the name of Max L. Margolis in mind. Margolis had just completed his doctoral studies under Columbia Semitics professor Richard Gottheil. Gottheil had recently communicated to Felsenthal on his behalf.

90. See Philipson, *Reform Movement in Judaism*, 262.

91. The time devoted to Talmud in the rabbinical seminaries varied according to the degree of traditionalism. The orthodox Hildesheimer seminary devoted 60 percent of classwork to Talmud, conservative (historical) Breslau devoted 56 percent, while liberal (Reform) Hochschule allotted only 40 percent to Talmud. But the German rabbinical student emphasized the tractates most relevant for the practicing community rabbi (marriage, divorce, and personal status). The *yeshivah* was devoted primarily to the eduation of learned Jews, the seminary to the education of communal functionaries. See Baruch A. Levine, "On the Teaching of Talmud in the American University," in Leon A. Jick, ed., *The Teaching of Judaica in American Universities: The Proceedings of a Colloquium* (Waltham, Mass.: Association for Jewish Studies, 1970 [1969]), 47–53, and Bernard D. Perlow, "Institutions for the Education of the Modern Rabbi in Germany" (Ph.D. diss., Dropsie College, 1954), 63, 91, 118. Perlow discusses the revised Breslau curriculum on page 64.

92. Marcus Brann, *Geschichte des Jüdisch-Theologischen Seminars in Breslau* (Breslau: T. Schatzky, 1904), 71.

93. In each instance, the course offered was in *Pirke Avot (The Ethics of the Fathers)*, a collection of aphoristic statements contemporaneous with the *Mishna* and in no way representative of the vast bulk of Talmudic literature. The courses were offered in the theological faculty rather than in Semitics and were thus totally inaccessible to Jewish students. See Ira M. Price, "Notes from Abroad," *Old Testament Student* 4 (1885), 364–67. The editor of the *Old Testament Student* commented, "This list is an interesting one and full of suggestions"—another example of using German scholarship as a frame of reference.

94. The Jewish texts studied were listed in the catalogue under the term "Rabbinical Hebrew" or alternatively "Post-Biblical Hebrew." Zunz may have coined the term "rabbinical literature" when he entitled his 1818 formulation of *Wissenschaft des Judentums: "Etwas über die rabbinische Litteratur"* ("Concerning Rabbinic Literature"). By 1845, Zunz rejected "rabbinical literature," which included only religious texts, for *neuhebräische* or *jüdische Literatur*, which also included secular literature. We do not know who studied rabbinical Hebrew in American universities, but the choice of term was not accidental. The late nineteenth-century American university largely ignored the secular literature produced by premodern Hebraists, and students were instructed in the texts of the rabbinic religious tradition, even if the soteric value of that tradition was in doubt. See Michael A. Meyer, "Jewish Religious Reform and *Wissenschaft des Judentums*," in Leo Baeck Institute, *Yearbook* 16 (1971), 19–41, quotation from 26, and Ismar Schorsch, "From Wolfenbüttel to Wissenschaft: The Divergent Paths of Isaac Marcus Jost and Leopold Zunz," Leo Baeck Institute, *Yearbook* 22 (1977), 109–28.

95. The Johns Hopkins Semitics Seminary, when it offered *Baba Batra* in *Seder Nezikin*, a tractate from the Order of Torts, did so with "special reference to its bearing on the Canon of the Old Testament" (Johns Hopkins University, *Annual Report of the President of The Johns Hopkins University* 19 [1894], 59). American Semitics students, insofar as they learned Talmud, worked on tractates chosen and edited by Hermann L. Strack, a member of the (Protestant) theological faculty of the University of Berlin. Strack, the one German professor who offered Talmudic studies, also founded the *Institutum Judaicum*, part of the movement to evangelize the Jews, while serving on the Foreign Board of Consulting Editors for the *Jewish Encyclopedia*.

96. Johns Hopkins University, *Annual Report of the President of The Johns Hopkins University*, 20 (1895), 37.

97. Isaac Husik, "The Unity of Human Learning," in *Philosophical Essays: Ancient, Medieval and Modern*, Milton C. Nahm and Leo Strauss, eds. (Oxford: Basil Blackwell, 1952), 15–26, quotation from 21.

98. See Julius H. Greenstone, "The Pilpul System in the Talmud," *Jewish Theological Seminary of America Student's Annual 1914* (New York: Isaac Goldman, 1914), 152–62. The evolution of Talmudic scholarship in the twentieth century is discussed in David Weiss Halivni, "Contemporary Methods of the Study of Talmud," *Journal of Jewish Studies* 30 (Autumn, 1979), 192–201, and Baruch Micah Bokser, "Talmudic Form Criticism," *Journal of Jewish Studies* 31 (Spring, 1980), 46–60. Twentieth-century Jewish Theological Seminary Talmudists Louis Ginzberg and Saul Lieberman studied the *Talmud of the Land of Israel* (the *Yerushalmi*), which intersected with the world of Greece and Hellenistic culture. Scholarship on the *Yerushalmi* permitted a Talmudist to meet the demands of traditional Jewish scholarship and to participate in the world of classical learning. See Louis Ginzberg, "Introduction to the Yerushalmi," in *Talmud Yerushalmi* (Jerusalem: Makor, 1968); Saul Lieberman, *Greek in Jewish Palestine* (New York: P. Feldheim, 1965); and idem, *Hellenism in Jewish Palestine*, 2nd ed. (New York: Jewish Theological Seminary of America, 1962).

99. George Ernest Wright, "The Study of the Old Testament," in Arnold S. Nash, ed., *Protestant Thought in the Twentieth Century: Whence and Whither?* (New York: Macmillan, 1951), 17–44, quotation from 17.

100. For Semitist Paul Haupt, an early Johns Hopkins report noted, "the center of [his] work was the Old Testament" (Johns Hopkins University, *Annual Report of the President of The Johns Hopkins University* 9 [1884], 27). Haupt used an Arabic translation of the Book of Genesis as his text for part of his Arabic offerings.

101. Scholars differ on the precise dating of the fortunes and misfortunes of Jewish Biblical scholarship, but there is a consensus on the broad outlines. See, for example, Harold Louis Ginsberg, *New Trends in the Study of the Bible, Essays in Judaism* Series, no. 4 (New York: Jewish Theological Seminary of America, 1968). See also Moshe Goshen-Gottstein, "Modern Jewish Bible Research: Aspects of Integration," in *Proceedings of the Eighth World Congress of Jewish Studies* (Jerusalem: World Union of Jewish Studies, 1984), 1–18.

102. See Goshen-Gottstein, "Modern Jewish Bible Research," 2.

103. Summary articles on trends in Biblical scholarship include: J. F. McCurdy, "Oriental Research and the Bible," in Herman V. Hilprecht, ed., *Recent Research in Bible Lands* (Philadelphia: John D. Wattles, 1896), 3–28; Max L. Margolis, "The Scope and Methodology of Biblical Philology," *The Jewish Quarterly Review*, n.s., 1 (1910–1911), 5–41; Frederick A. Vanderburgh, "Excavations In the Orient and Bible Study," *The Jewish Forum* 5 (February, 1922), 73–80; James Barr, *Comparative Philology and the Text of the Old Testament* (Oxford: Clarendon Press, 1968); Steven Shaw, "Orthodox Reactions to the Challenge of Biblical Criticism," *Tradition: A Journal of Orthodox Thought* 10 (Spring, 1969), 61–85; David Lieber, "Modern Trends in the Study of the Bible," *Conservative Judaism* 20 (Winter, 1966), 37–46; and Baruch A. Levine, "Major Directions in Contemporary Biblical Research," address at Hebrew College, Boston, Massachusetts, April 25, 1977. An important synthesis of historical trends is S. David Sperling, with contributions by Baruch A. Levine and B. Barey Levy, *Students of the Covenant: A History of Jewish Biblical Scholarship in North America* (Atlanta: Scholars Press, 1992).

104. Schechter to Sulzberger, April 5, 1899, Solomon Schechter Papers, JTS, "Sulzberger" file.

105. Rabbi Samson Raphael Hirsch, the creator of nineteenth-century neo-orthodoxy, noted that "people studied Judaism but forgot to search for its principles in the pages of Scripture" (Samson Raphael Hirsch, *The Nineteen Letters on Judaism,* prepared by Jacob Breuer in a new edition based on the translation by Rabbi Dr. Bernard Drachman [New York: Feldheim Publishers, 1969 (1836)], 99). On Bible and *Wissenschaft des Judentums,* see Nahum Sarna, "Abraham Geiger and Biblical Scholarship," in Jacob J. Petuchowski, ed., *New Perspectives on Abraham Geiger* (Cincinnati: Hebrew Union College–Jewish Institute of Religion, 1975), 17–30, and Nahum Glatzer, "The Beginnings of Modern Jewish Studies," in Alexander Altmann, ed., *Studies in Nineteenth Century Jewish Intellectual History* (Cambridge: Harvard University Press, 1964).

106. Meyer, "Jewish Religious Reform," passim. Scholarly work published by Breslau alumni included very little in Bible. See Adolf Kober, "The Jewish Theological Seminary of Breslau and 'Wissenschaft des Judentums,'" *Historia Judaica* 16 (October, 1954), 85–122; idem, "The Breslaw [sic] Rabbinical Seminary," in Samuel Kalman Mirsky, ed., *Jewish Institutions of Higher Learning in Europe: Their Development and Destruction* [in Hebrew] (New York: Ogen, 1956), 5; and Max Gruenewald, "The Modern Rabbi," Leo Baeck Institute, *Yearbook* 2 (1957), 85–97. On Biblical criticism at Hebrew Union, see Meyer, "Centennial History," 44. Solomon Schechter, president of the Jewish Theological Seminary of America, "at first suspected [Israel] Friedlander of being an adept at Protestant Higher Criticism, but it soon became evident that his [i.e., Friedlander's] piety and loyalty were impeccable. To be sure, Friedlander was inhibited in biblical research and specialized instead in Arabic lore" (Elbogen, "A Century of Wissenschaft des Judentums," 56). Schechter briefly headed a project to translate the traditional text of the Bible for an American Jewish audience.

107. Arnold Ehrlich, an early twentieth-century Bible scholar, became persona non grata to Jewish and Christian institutions when he converted to Christianity and then recanted his conversion.

108. Margolis, "Scope and Methodology of Biblical Philology," 32.

109. The course descriptions stressed rapid reading and philological analysis of Biblical books rather than historic, literary, or religious approaches. See, for example, *Columbia University Catalogue* (1898/99), 141; ibid., (1900/01), 165; *Johns Hopkins University Circular*, 25, no. 7 (1906), 33.

110. See John Higham, "The Matrix of Specialization" in Alexandra Oleson and John Voss, eds., *The Organization of Knowledge in Modern America, 1860–1920* (Baltimore: Johns Hopkins University Press, 1979), 6–7.

111. Walter Metzger distinguishes between two types of growth in American higher education: subject matter growth that changes the curriculum, and student influx into a more or less preset curriculum. Institutions that initiated Jewish learning had no assurance that students would appear. Metzger notes that student/faculty ratios in the major private universities fell sharply from 1880 to 1900, the period of greatest innovation. At the same time, student/faculty ratios in public institutions increased since enrollments grew without a commensurate increase in faculty size. But from 1900 to 1910, student/faculty ratios in "major private institutions" increased while the same ratios in public institutions fell. The two ratios eventually converged. See Walter P. Metzger, "The Academic Profession in the United States," in Burton R. Clark, ed., *The Academic Profession: National, Disciplinary, and Institutional Settings* (Berkeley: University of California Press, 1987), 123–208.

112. Between 1873 and 1898, about half of all doctorates were awarded in the humanities, and about one-third of all doctorates earned were in one or another branch of philology. There were as many doctorates in Semitics as in Germanic or Romance philology. See U.S. Commissioner of Education, *Report of the Commissioner of Education, 1897–1898* (Washington, D.C.: U.S. Bureau of Education, 1899), 1803. At the University of Chicago, ten percent of the doctorates in the humanities and social sciences from 1892 to 1902 were awarded in Semitics. Only history granted more doctorates. See University of Chicago, *Decennial Publications*, vol. 1: *The President's Report, 1892–1902*, 29.

113. Rudolph, *Curriculum*, 51–52.

114. Pedersen, *Discovery of Language*, 79.

115. The historian was Barthold Georg Niebuhr, who taught the history of Rome at the universities of Bonn and Berlin. The quotation is from the preface to the second edition of Niebuhr's *History of Rome* (1827–1832) in Fritz Stern, ed., *The Varieties of History: From Voltaire to the Present* (New York: Meridian Books, 1957 [1956]), 52. On philology and history in the late eighteenth and early nineteenth centuries, see Stern's introduction, ibid., 17.

116. Carl Diehl, who analyzed the transfer of academic culture from Germany to the United States, argued that "by the time Americans were ready to absorb the German form of scholarship *wie es eigentlich gewesen,* that scholarship had changed. It had become less visionary and far more specialized. And this very change made it much easier for the Americans to assimilate" (Diehl, *Americans and German Scholarship,* 140). Some observers who noted the change in *Wissenschaft des Judentums* at the end of the nineteenth century expressed a similar sense of disappointment. Caesar Seligman commented in 1894: "Wissenschaft des Judentums, the spoilt darling of the fathers of the Jewish renaissance, has not turned out to be the Messiah one saw in it. That is because the highly praised Wissenschaft is merely philology, archaeology. A sad testimony. As if Judaism were only ancient and not new" (Caesar Seligman, *Die Deborah* [July 5, 1894], 4, cited in Meyer, "Jewish Religious Reform," 41).

117. Basil L. Gildersleeve, "Oscillations and Mutations of Philological Studies," *Johns Hopkins University Circular* 20, no. 151 (April, 1901), 45–50, quotation from 46.

118. See Stevenson, "Between Old-Time College and Modern University," 50. Stevenson adds: "He did however, use his knowledge of philology to argue in support of beliefs consistent with religiously-based New Haven values. For example, he said that philology proved that human beings had a social nature. This fact, he stated, refuted so-

cial contract theory because it proved that the state of nature upon which the theory rested was merely a man-made myth."

119. August Boeckh, *Die Staatshaushaltung der Athener,* 2nd ed. (Berlin, 1851), 1:2, cited in Meyer, "Jewish Religious Reform," 23. Meyer persuasively argues that this vision of philology was particularly attractive to a people and its scholars whose claim to significance lay in literary productivity, not political achievements. See also Anthony Grafton and Lisa Jardine, *From Humanism to the Humanities: Education and the Liberal Arts in Fifteenth and Sixteenth Century Europe* (Cambridge: Harvard University Press, 1986).

120. Elbogen, "A Century of Wissenschaft des Judentums," 35.

121. Ibid. A contemporary American Semitist similarly attempted "to develop the Arabic side of [his department's] activities, and to give Arabic a place of at least equal importance with Hebrew" by noting "the intrinsic value of Arabic philology and Arabic literature, by the fact that it is still the spoken language of millions more, and by the fact that Mohammedanism is a decisive factor in many of the world's political problems of today" (University of California, *Biennial Report of the President of the University 1904–1906,* 26–27). A decade later the same scholar wrote: "While most students of Semitics in America are primarily interested in theology, it should be noted that there is a large body of Semitic literature, especially Arabic, that makes its appeals to other students as well" (University of California, *Biennial Report of the President of the University 1915–1916,* 173). A 1902 University of Chicago document stated: "While the majority of students doubtless study Arabic for the light which it throws upon Hebrew grammar, it is believed that the field of Arabic literature is one which is more deserving of the attention of American students" (University of Chicago, *Annual Register* [July, 1903], 250).

122. *Johns Hopkins University Circular* 13, no. 113 (June, 1894), 96.

123. Hamilton Wright Mabie, "The University and Literature," *Johns Hopkins University Circular* 11, no. 96 (March, 1892), 53.

124. The English department sponsored a dissertation entitled: "The Present and Past Periphrastic Tenses in Anglo-Saxon: Secondary Accent in Modern English Verse (Chaucer to Dryden)" (see "List of Dissertations, 1878–1919," *Johns Hopkins University Circular,* 39, no. 321, n.s., no. 1 [1920]).

125. I. M. Casanowicz, "Notes on Paranomasia in the Old Testament," *Johns Hopkins University Circular* 11, no. 98 (May, 1892), 96.

126. René Wellek, "Literary Scholarship," in Merle Curti, ed., *American Scholarship in the Twentieth Century* (Cambridge: Harvard University Press, 1953), 117.

127. See Seth Low, "A City University," *Johns Hopkins University Circular* 14, no. 118 (April, 1895), 53–57, quotation from 54.

128. "Report of the Faculty of Philosophy," *Columbia University Bulletin* 11 (July, 1895), 19–20.

129. See *Johns Hopkins University Circular* 5 (1886), 40–43.

130. "Memorandum as to a College Professorship of the English Bible," University of Pennsylvania Archives, ca. 1890–1895, typescript.

131. See Gottheil "Semitic Languages at Columbia," 97–98.

132. Lowell to Jacob Schiff, December 1, 1910, A. L. Lowell Papers (hereafter Lowell Papers), Harvard University Archives (hereafter HUA), (1909–1914), file 1222: "Museums: Semitic—Dept. of . . . General Correspondence."

133. Student registrations under Popper declined to less than a fifth of enrollments during the department's formative years. Popper's Semitics department registered fewer students than any other department.

134. The exact percentages were: 57 percent in Greek, 70 percent in Latin, 64 percent in Germanic Languages, and 66 percent in Romance Languages. See *University of Chicago Quarterly Calendar* 4, no. 3 (whole number 16) (February, 1896), 66–74. Undergraduate proportions at Columbia in 1902/03 were: Semitic Languages, 34 percent; Indo-Iranian, 42 percent; Greek, 56 percent; Latin, 80 percent; Germanic languages, 81 percent; Romance languages, 76 percent.

135. Harvard University, *Reports of the President and the Treasurer of Harvard College* (1905/06), 10, 11, 14.

136. University of Chicago, *The President's Report, 1920–1921*, 26.

137. Harvard University, *Annual Reports of the President and Treasurer of Harvard College* (1901/02), 23–24.

138. Arthur Hadley, "Two Sides of University Life," *Johns Hopkins University Circular* 28, no. 214, n.s., no. 3 (March, 1909), 4–5.

139. Haupt to Cyrus Adler, September 4, 1890, Haupt-Adler Correspondence, JTS.

140. *University of Pennsylvania Catalogue* (1893/94), 49.

141. "Constitution of the American Oriental Society, Adopted April 7, 1843," *Journal of the American Oriental Society* 1 (1849), vi.

142. John Pickering, "Address," *Journal of the American Oriental Society* 1 (1849), 51–52. Edward Robinson was author (along with Eli Smith) of *Biblical Researches in Palestine, Mount Sinai and Arabia Petraea: A Journal of Travels in the Year 1838*, 3 vols. (Boston: Crocker & Brewster, 1841).

143. Paul Haupt's 1883 arrival turned the tide from Whitney's emphasis on Sanskrit to Semitics, testified John Peters. By 1886, "the bulk of these communications had become so considerable that I remember hearing complaints from some of my Indo-European colleagues, who had heretofore had everything their own way in the Society, that all the papers read nowadays dealt with Semitic topics" (Peters, "Thirty Years' Progress in Semitics," 28). See also Rosane Rocher, *The Crisis of 1890 and the Coming of Age of the A.O.S., 1890–1891* (Philadelphia: South Asia Regional Studies, University of Pennsylvania, 1971), 77–78. The American Oriental Society recognized the primacy of the American Philological Association in classics by abolishing its classical section in 1891.

144. See Harvard University, *Annual Reports of the President and Treasurer of Harvard College* (1897/98), 28.

3. Scholars

1. Felix Adler, "The Judaism of the Future," quoted in Kraut, *From Reform Judaism to Ethical Culture*, 78.

2. Ibid., 81.

3. As quoted in Morris Bishop, *A History of Cornell* (Ithaca: Cornell University Press, 1962), 165.

4. Kraut, *From Reform Judaism to Ethical Culture*, 95–96. See also Horace L. Friess, *Felix Adler and Ethical Culture: Memories and Studies,* Fannia Weingartner, ed. (New York: Columbia University Press, 1981), chapter 4. "No sectarian or political test shall be imposed," stated the Cornell Charter, and "persons of every religious sect or of no religious sect shall be equally eligible to all offices and appointments" ("An Open Letter from President White," May 4, 1877, Felix Adler Papers, CU-RBML, 3).

5. "The expectation of systematic instruction in the Semitic languages was not realized, as Dr. Adler's lectures were devoted rather to the origin and history of the various religions of the East, to modern philosophy in its relation to religion, and to Hebrew religion and literature from a critical standpoint," wrote Waterman T. Hewett, author of an early, massive history of Cornell. Hewett was professor of German language and literature and an enemy of Adler at Ithaca. See Waterman T. Hewett, *Cornell University—A History*, 2 vols. (New York: University Publishing Society, 1905), 2:3.

6. White, "An Open Letter," 7.

7. Kraut, *From Reform Judaism to Ethical Culture*, 102–3; Altschuler, *Andrew Dixon White*, 97–99. Adler's partial silence helped to stir the controversy over his removal. The accounts of Hewett and Walter T. Rogers take no position on the responsibility for his departure. See Hewett, *Cornell University*, 2:3, and Walter T. Rogers, *Andrew Dixon White and The Modern University* (Ithaca: Cornell University Press, 1942). After 1877,

Cornell's Semitics offerings fell mainly to Frederick Roehrig, whose facility in language acquisition enabled him to offer instruction in Romance as well as Semitic languages. A German by birth, Roehrig published a Turkish grammar and conducted language classes in Paris before coming to America, but he had no special philological training. The Cornell *Register* announced courses in Chinese, Japanese, Malayan, Arabic, Turkish, the Tartar languages, and Turanian philology, but Roehrig's offerings appealed to a very limited clientele. In 1885 the trustees disbanded his department. When Henry W. Sage, a major Cornell benefactor, underwrote a chair of Semitic Languages and Literature in 1896, Nathaniel Schmidt, a Baptist minister, assumed the chair. He had previously taught at Hamilton Theological Seminary and Colgate University. See Hewett, *Cornell University*, 2:1–6, and Bishop, *History of Cornell*, 109–10, 165, 274.

8. Philip's little-noted appointment at California preceded Adler's by about a year. See chapter 2.

9. Adler, *I Have Considered*, 54.

10. See Dobkowski, *Tarnished Dream*, passim.

11. Florian Znaniecki, *The Social Role of the Man of Knowledge* (New York: Columbia University Press, 1940), 116.

12. Rev. S. M. Isaacs in *The Jewish Messenger* (April 17, 1874), quoted in Kraut, *From Reform Judaism to Ethical Culture*, 97. Abram Isaacs, Samuel's son, later assumed a similar post at New York University. See nn. 13, 17, 31, and 128, below.

13. Emil Hirsch, Abram Isaacs, Joseph Levy, William Rosenau, Jacob Voorsanger, and Max Heller at Tulane in 1912.

14. See Will Herberg, *Protestant, Catholic, Jew: An Essay on American Religious Sociology* (Garden City, N.Y.: Doubleday, 1955).

15. Rosenau, "Semitic Studies," 110. Rosenau argued that when Semitics becomes an undergraduate study, thus freeing up graduate departments for advanced work, "the American college cannot help but be a fit rival, if not the superior, of the European University in Semitic studies" (ibid., 113).

16. Cyrus Adler, "The Semitic Seminary of Johns Hopkins University," in Cyrus Adler, *Lectures, Selected Papers, Addresses* (Philadelphia: privately printed, 1933), 171.

17. In 1882, several years before he began to teach Semitics at the University of the City of New York, Abram Isaacs wrote: "It strikes me that Judaism throughout the world needs a war-cry, a mission, a purpose—otherwise it is superfluous. The cry of despair of Landau, Gudemann, and the rest you mention is repeated in nearly every letter I receive from younger rabbis abroad who find their consolation in deciphering mss. and publishing books, when it is impossible to decipher the faith and convictions of their people. I call them cowards, because they work among the libraries rather than among the ignorant and superstitious. But they are partly justified—in view of the immensity of the task" (Issacs to Henrietta Szold, August 23, 1882, Letters to and from Henrietta Szold 1864–1944, AJA, microfilm 386D).

18. Jastrow to Szold, October 30, 1883, ibid. See also *DAB*, s.v. "Jastrow, Morris"; Morais, *Jews of Philadelphia*, 435–36; biography of Morris Jastrow in UPA, memorial essays in the *Journal of the American Oriental Society* 41 (December, 1921), 322–44; and Harold S. Wechsler, "Pulpit or Professoriate: The Case of Morris Jastrow," *American Jewish History* 74 (June, 1985), 538–55.

19. Felix Adler, "Address at the Meeting in Memory of Professor Morris Jastrow, Jr.," Felix Adler Papers, CU-RBML, box: "Ethical Culture and Ethical Movement," file: "Funeral Addresses, etc."

20. Laurence Veysey, "Intellectual History and the New Social History," in John Higham and Paul K. Conkin, eds., *New Directions in American Intellectual History* (Baltimore: Johns Hopkins University Press, 1979), 3–26.

21. Oren, *Joining the Club*, 114.

22. "As a language Hebrew is not of central and primary interest," wrote Union Theological Seminary president Francis Brown, one of the first men to teach Assyriology in

America. "Its vocabulary is not the most ample. Its structure has suffered from the wear and tear of use. Truth requires that we find its place among others of its group by comparing its qualities with theirs, and without the glamour of its association. When we have disposed of it philologically, as the facts require, we shall be all the freer to respect its contents and interpret its messages" (Francis Brown, "Semitic Studies in America," *Johns Hopkins University Circular* 28, no. 214 [1909], 242–43). George Foot Moore, while still at Andover Seminary, distinguished between exegesis and philology in referring to the place of Hebrew in the *Journal of the American Oriental Society:* "Exegetical papers, in the ordinary sense, esp. where the interest is predominantly theological should be printed elsewhere. But philology is philology, even if it is Hebrew, and we have no organ . . . for such investigations, which reaches the eyes of scholars, except for the proceedings of the Oriental Society" (Moore to Charles R. Lanman, April 14, 1892, Charles R. Lanman Papers, Harvard University Archives, HUG 4510.51, box "Ho-O," "George Foot Moore" file.

23. Gottheil, "Semitic Languages at Columbia," 89. This reversal helps to explain *Hebraica's* 1895 name change to *The American Journal of Semitic Languages and Literatures.* "The old name," wrote a subsequent editor, had "proven too narrow in scope from the very beginning" (see: "A Quarter-Centennial Issue," *The American Journal of Semitic Languages and Literatures* 32 [July, 1916], 218).

24. Leon A. Jick, "Judaica in American Universities," *Encyclopaedia Judaica Year Book 1975–1976* (Jerusalem: Keter Publishing House, 1976), 194: "There is little evidence of academic concern with the total Jewish experience, especially with the content of Jewish culture and history in the centuries following the separation of Christianity from its Jewish source."

25. Jastrow to Lyon, September 27, 1885, and August 12, 1886, David Gordon Lyon Letters, ca. 1881–1913 (hereafter Lyon Letters), HUA, HUG 1541.

26. On Pennsylvania, see Cheyney, *History of the University of Pennsylvania,* and Martin Meyerson and Dilys Pegler Winegrad, *Gladly Learn and Gladly Teach: Franklin and His Heirs at the University of Pennsylvania* (Philadelphia: University of Pennsylvania Press, 1978).

27. Two practitioners argued that only vocabulary presented difficulties; the grammars were comparatively easy, and dictionaries and grammars existed for most languages. See *Cyclopedia of Education,* s.v. "Oriental Studies."

28. *Wissenschaft des Judentums* also failed to obtain a state subsidy similar to that received by Christian theological schools.

29. Lee M. Friedman, *Jewish Pioneers and Patriots* (Philadelphia: Jewish Publication Society of America, 1942), 273.

30. E. D. Morris, brother of Cornell faculty member John Morris, as quoted in Kraut, *From Reform Judaism to Ethical Culture,* 101, emphasis in original. Kraut concluded: "The existence of such a debate even before the delivery of his controversial lectures suggests that Adler's Jewish origin was a significant factor contributing to the animosity which he experienced after his appointment" (ibid., 102).

31. Abram S. Isaacs shifted from Semitics to German at New York University; E. D. Perry changed from Sanskrit to Greek at Columbia. One study of changing morés surrounding appointments in the nineteenth century is Robert McCaughey, "Transformation," 232–332. See also Walter P. Metzger, *Academic Freedom in the Age of the University* (New York: Columbia University Press, 1961), and Richard H. Shyrock, "The Academic Profession in the United States," *A.A.U.P. Bulletin* 38 (1952), 32–73.

32. W. C. Cattell to William Pepper, September 28, 1886, University of Pennsylvania Archives (hereafter UPA), "Archives General—1886: Applications for Positions" file.

33. Gustav Gottheil began as an assistant rabbi at Emanu-El in 1873. See Richard Gottheil, *The Life of Gustav Gottheil—Memoir of a Priest in Israel* (Williamsport, Pa.: Bayard

Press, 1936). Richard Gottheil studied at Berlin, Tübingen, and Leipzig. On Richard's plans, see Gustav Gottheil to Bernhard Felsenthal, December 22, 1888, Bernhard Felsenthal Papers (hereafter Felsenthal Papers), AJA, box 2156.

34. Columbia College, *Minutes of the Trustees* (November 1, 1886), 9256–57.

35. Ibid. (May 2, 1887), 9412.

36. Much relevant correspondence is reprinted in Richard Gottheil, *Life of Gustav Gottheil.* See also Columbia College, *Minutes of the Trustees* (May 2, 1887), 9409–13 and (June 6, 1887), 9436–37.

37. Columbia College, *Minutes of the Trustees* (October 3, 1887), 9449. The university raised only a technical objection: Since the proposed endowment would not provide for a professor's salary, the chair's occupant would acquire full professorial rights only when "the founders shall have made the salary attached to it equal to that of existing first class Professorships or shall have paid to the College the amount prescribed by the Statutes for founding a Professorship."

38. See Morais, *Jews of Philadelphia*, 77–78, *DAB*, s.v. "Jastrow, Marcus" and *Encyclopaedia Judaica*, s.v. "Jastrow."

39. Morris Jastrow, ed., *The Weak and Germinative Verbs in Hebrew by Abu Zakariyya Yahya ibn Dawud of Fez* (1897).

40. Jastrow recounted his academic training in considerable detail in Jastrow to Lyon, Sepember 7, 1886. Lyon Letters, HUA, HUG 1541. See also Guido Kisch, ed., *Das Breslauer Seminar: Jüdisch Theologisches Seminar (Fraenkelscher Stiftung) in Breslau 1854–1938* (Tübingen: Mohr, 1963). On the significance of Leipzig and Franz Delitsch, see editorial in *The American Israelite* (December 10, 1888), 4.

41. Jastrow to Lyon, September 7, 1886, Lyon Papers, HUA, HUG 1541; Morris Jastrow Jr., *Jews and Judaism: An Address by Morris Jastrow Jr., Ph.D. Before the Congregation Rodef Shalom, December 9, 1886* (Philadelphia: Edward Stein, 1886), 17.

42. Peck also offered instruction in Hamitic languages. See Gottheil, "Semitic Languages," 95. Several years later, Sanskrit instructor E. D. Perry accepted the Jay professorship of Greek.

43. Endowed in 1903 by a group of Temple Emanu-El benefactors in memory of Richard's father.

44. Prince continued some instruction in Akkadian and Coptic. See Jeffery, "Department of Semitic Languages," 187.

45. During his first year, Jastrow canvassed possibilities for an academic post (see *Minutes of the Board of Directors of Congregation Rodef Shalom*, AJA, 213). Jastrow speculated that the vacancy caused by Roehrig's departure from Cornell might be filled by "one of the 'new school.'" Instead, the institution dispensed with Semitic instruction until 1896 (see n. 7, above). He inquired about the prospects for Semitics at the University of Michigan, but President James B. Angell replied that the university was not yet in a position to provide offerings in that field. See Jastrow to Lyon, November 26, 1886, Lyon Letters, HUA, HUG 1541.

46. See University of Pennsylvania, *Trustees' Minutes* 13 (July 6, 1886), 269; (September 7, 1886), 272; (October 5, 1886), 278; and (November 2, 1886), 282. See also Jastrow to Lyon, September 7, 1886, Lyon Letters, HUA, HUG 1541. On Hilprecht, see *DAB*, s.v. "Hilprecht, Herman Volrath."

47. Jastrow to Lyon, November 26, 1886, Lyon Letters, HUA, HUG 1541: "I do not wish to come in conflict with Hilprecht—in whose interest this step is being contemplated—but so long as I have accepted the position of lecturer for one year, I think it decidedly unjust for the trustees to establish a chair meanwhile and put somebody else in."

48. Jastrow to Pepper, November 3, 1886, and December 1, 1886, UPA, "Archives General, 1886: Applications for Positions" file.

49. University of Pennsylvania, *Trustees' Minutes* 13 (December 7, 1886), 285, and (January 4, 1887), 290. The university was rewarded when significant numbers of stu-

dents appeared for the courses. See *Annual Report of the Provost of the University of Pennsylvania including Reports of Departments and Abstract of the Treasurer's Report for the Year ending October 1, 1887* (Philadelphia: Printed for the University, 1888), 16–17.

50. Cheyney, *History of the University of Pennsylvania*, 323–24.

51. Schechter at that time tutored Claude Montifiore, a wealthy London Jew, and spent the rest of his time conducting manuscript research (see Norman Bentwich, *Solomon Schechter: A Biography* [Philadelphia: Jewish Publication Society of America, 1938], 83–115).

52. Richard Gottheil to Solomon Schechter, undated, Seminary Autograph, JTS, "To S. S. from Richard Gottheil" file. His mentor did not share Gottheil's view of the situation. Schechter wrote Gottheil at about the same time: "Indeed, I have the impression as if European Judaism was a big financial concern governed by its shareholders. You and I are poor people, and we had better hold our peace. . . . At bottom, we are both more believers than all the officials who denounced us as heretics" (Bentwich, *Solomon Schechter,* 73).

53. Gottheil to Schechter, August 17, 1889, Seminary Autograph, JTS, "To S. S. from Richard Gottheil" file.

54. Gottheil, "Semitic Languages at Columbia," 97.

55. Ibid., 98. Topics for the 1897/98 Semitic seminar included: the Semitic dual, the Semitic plural, inflection in the Semitic languages, Semitic nominal and verbal formations, and sounds peculiar to Semitic speech.

56. Columbia established agreements with Jewish Theological Seminary and with Union Theological Seminary, which would likewise move to Morningside in 1912, permitting student cross-registration.

57. Low to Fish, October 8, 1890, CUF, "Hamilton Fish" file.

58. This situation was not peculiar to New York philanthropists. At precisely this time, the University of Chicago made its initial appointments including that of Rabbi Hirsch. Rabbi Bernhard Felsenthal, a venerated rabbi also of Chicago, wrote that another appointment for the purpose of advancing Jewish scholarship was out of the question for the present: "It could only be realized if some rich Jews here or elsewhere would endow such a chair sufficiently. I cannot discover any trace of willingness to do so among my wealthy fellow-Israelites in this city. And if there should be such well-disposed, science loving, rich Israelites here, men like Jacob Schiff, J. Seligman, Oscar Straus,—however, I am afraid there is none of that color in Chicago,—their [sic] forthcoming with their financial support in the tragic times in special requisition by the Russian Refugees Aid Societies &c." (Felsenthal to Richard Gottheil, April 7, 1892, Felsenthal Papers, AJA, box 2156).

59. The Emanu-El trustees donated the temple's valuable library to Columbia. The library became the backbone of Columbia's Semitics collection. See Columbia College, *Minutes of the Trustees* (March 7, 1892), 109, 128; Columbia University, *Charter and Official Records,* vol. 1 (New York: Columbia University, 1920), 566–68.

60. See Morris Jastrow, *Religion of Babylonia and Assyria* (Boston: Ginn and Company, 1898), *Die Religion Babyloniens und Assyriens* (Giessen: J. Ricker, 1905–1912), and *The Civilization of Babylonia and Assyria. Its Remains, Language, History, Religion, Commerce, Law, Art and Literature* (Philadelphia: J. B. Lippincott, 1915).

61. George A. Barton, "The Contributions of Morris Jastrow, Jr., to the History of Religion," *Journal of the American Oriental Society* 41, pt. 5 (December, 1921), 327. See also Morris Jastrow, Jr., "The Historical Study of Religions at the University of Pennsylvania," *Old Penn* 9 (March 11, 1911), 645–47 and 9 (March 18, 1911), 713–15. On the history of religion as a scholarly field, see chapter 8.

62. W. F. Albright to J. S. Ames, June 13, 1927, Records of the Office of the President, the Ferdinand Hamburger, Jr. Archives of The Johns Hopkins University (hereafter MSEL-FHA), Record Group 02.001, series 1, box 50, file 52.

63. Richard Gottheil to Hubert Banning, November 27, 1906, Letter-Book of Richard J. H. Gottheil, 1906–1908 (hereafter Gottheil Letter-Book), Columbiana ms. 59, CU-RBML.

64. Morris Jastrow, Jr., "The Present Status of Semitic Studies in this Country," *Hebraica* 5 (October, 1888), 77–91, quotations from 77, 79.

65. William Popper tribute in "Berkeley Honors Memory of Jacob Voorsanger," *Emanu-El* (August 28, 1908), 2. See also Marc Lee Raphael, "Rabbi Jacob Voorsanger of San Francisco on Jews and Judaism: The Implications of the Pittsburgh Platform," *American Jewish Historical Quarterly* 63 (December, 1973), 185–203, and Kenneth C. Zwerin and Norton B. Stern, "Jacob Voorsanger: From Cantor to Rabbi," *Western States Jewish Historical Quarterly* 15 (April, 1983), 195–202.

66. "It was always a cause of regret to Dr. Voorsanger," wrote William Popper, "that his busy life left him no time for extended literary productions of a scholarly kind; but his lectures, his sermons, and his editorials bore sufficient evidence of his learning, as also of his breadth of view" (William Popper tribute, 3). Voorsanger wrote a biography of Moses Mendelsohn while in Houston.

67. *Report of the Secretary To Board of Regents at the University of California for the Year ending June 30, 1894* (Sacramento, 1894), 38.

68. *Emanu-El* 4 (May 28, 1897), 5.

69. See Jones, *Illustrated History of the University of California*, chapter 4, and *Emanu-El* 3 (February 26, 1897). Enrollment grew to 114 in 1902/03, but it consisted almost exclusively of students in Old Testament and ancient Near East lecture courses. The department granted only four advanced degrees before 1950. See William Brimmer, "Near Eastern Languages," *The Centennial Record of the University of California* (Berkeley: University of California, 1968), 94.

70. *Report of the Secretary to Board of Regents*, 1897, 26; ibid. (1898), 33–34; and *Emanu-El* 3 (February 26, 1897). "We can dispense with salaries and labor—with enthusiastic devotion for the cause—but we cannot do without books. We need the books first," Voorsanger had written earlier (see "Editorial," *The Jewish Progress* [November 2, 1894]).

71. Wheeler to Voorsanger, February 6, 1901, Records of the President of the University of California [hereafter Presidents' Papers] (CU-5), UCB, "Voorsanger, Dr. Jacob, 1901" file. See also Voorsanger to Wheeler, May 7, 1903, ibid. Voorsanger wrote in the same tone: "We are earnest in this matter, believing that the Jewish cause of religion, humanity and the spread of useful knowledge would derive much strength from the growing influence of the University of California" (*Emanu-El* 3 [January 15, 1897], 5).

72. *Report of the Secretary to Board of Regents*, 1897, 28.

73. Margolis received an A.M. in 1890 and a Ph.D. in 1891—the first doctorate awarded by Columbia's Oriental department.

74. As quoted in Alexander Marx, "Max Leopold Margolis," in *Essays in Jewish Biography* (Philadelphia: Jewish Publication Society of America, 1947), 269.

75. While studying at Columbia, Margolis served as Felix Adler's secretary and taught a course on *Tannaim* (scholars of the *Mishneh*, ca. 1–200 CE) and *Amoriam* (scholars of the *Gemmorah*, ca. 200–500 CE) in Adler's summer school at Plymouth, Massachusetts. At Columbia, he was also exposed to Zionism. After receiving his Ph.D., Margolis became University Fellow in Semitic Languages at Columbia (1891/92) and Lecturer on Jewish Literature at the Glenmore School for Culture Sciences, Keene, New York. (See Seth Low to Alexander Kohut, April 13, 1891, Seminary Autograph, JTS, "Seth Low" file.) Gottheil, attempting to place his student, inquired of Bernhard Felsenthal, rabbi of Chicago's Zion Congregation, whether the University of Chicago might have some interest. For Felsenthal's reply, see nn. 33 and 58, above. The call to Cincinnati came shortly thereafter.

76. *University of California Register*, 1895/96, 81–82; 1896/97, 95–96, 165–66; 1897/98, 140–44. "The greater part of this important work," wrote Voorsanger, "falls necessarily on Dr. Margolis, who is an adept in all these tongues and has the thorough academic and scientific training required for their thorough presentation" (*Report of the Secretary to Board of Regents*, 1898, 33–34).

77. See *Emanu-El* 4 (May, 28, 1897), 14; 4 (July 30, 1897), 5 (source of quotation); and 4 (August 6, 1897), 3, 5; see also Margolis to W. W. McKowen, June 7, 1897, UCB, "Max Margolis" file.

78. Central Conference of American Rabbis, *Yearbook* 13 (1903), 185–308, and "Professor Max Margolis a Zionist," *The Maccabaean* 14 (March, 1907), 98: "Towards the end of 1903, a young friend presented me with the first volume of *Al-Parashat Derakim* which at once exerted a powerful influence on my thinking." *Al-Parashat Derakim* [*At the Crossroads*], by Ahad Ha'am, was an important essay in the intellectual history of Zionism. See also Max Margolis, "The Mendelssohnian Programme," *The Jewish Quarterly Review* 17 (April, 1905), 531–44.

79. *Emanu-El* 20 (September 22, 1905), 5.

80. "[A] very marked advance in salary (from $2400 to $3600)," wrote Wheeler to Harper, "made it so attractive to him that he was probably justified in accepting" (Wheeler to Harper, August 1, 1905, Presidents' Papers, UCB, "President William R. Harper" file. See also Wheeler to Margolis, May 23, 1905, and Margolis to Wheeler, July 6, July 21 and November 1, 1905, ibid., "Max Margolis" file).

81. Salary was important at several other stages of his career. His promotion to associate professor in 1898 may have resulted from an attempt by Hebrew Union College to lure him back to Cincinnati. In any case, Hebrew Union officials decided they could not meet his financial conditions at that time. When Margolis finally left California for Cincinnati in 1905, his salary surpassed that of all but one of his colleagues (see Meyer, "Centennial History," 66, 258n). Financial arrangements later affected Margolis' discussions with officials of the new Jewish Institute of Religion: "The determinant factors are many and they might be made lighter to render what must be a wrench under the most favorable conditions less acute." The negotiations collapsed when the Institute's board informed him that "it is impossible now to meet the conditions which you have set" (see Margolis to Stephen S. Wise, May 30, 1922, and Julian Mack to Margolis, June 20, 1922, Jewish Institute of Religion Papers (hereafter JIR Papers), AJA, no. 19, 26/6, "Max Margolis" file.

82. Cyrus Adler, "Max Leopold Margolis," *American Jewish Yearbook* 35 (1933–1934), 144. Margolis taught at Dropsie from 1909 until his death in 1922. On his career, see also Richard Gottheil, A. V. Williams Jackson, and Ludlow S. Bill, "The Life and Work of Max Leopold Margolis," *Journal of the American Oriental Society* 52 (1932), 106–9; Robert Gordis, "The Life of Professor Max Leopold Margolis: An Appreciation," in Dropsie College for Hebrew and Cognate Learning Alumni Association, *Max Leopold Margolis: Scholar and Teacher* (Philadelphia: Dropsie College, 1952), chapter 1; and Leonard J. Greenspoon, *Max Leopold Margolis: A Scholar's Scholar* (Atlanta: Scholars Press, 1987).

83. Margolis to Joseph Stolz, January 2, 1905, Max Margolis Collection, AJA.

84. "It was not given to me to pursue an even road; mine was a zig zagging line," Margolis wrote years later, referring to his theological thought. The same may be said of his pre-Dropsie career. See Margolis to Nathan Isaacs, December 17, 1922, "Letters to Professor Isaacs, 1910–1945" AJA, microfilm 674.

85. *Report of the Secretary to Board of Regents*, 1901, 22.

86. Voorsanger to Joseph C. Rowell, November 3, 1904, Joseph C. Rowell Papers (C-B 417), UCB, "Jacob Voorsanger, 1852–1908" file.

87. The controversy turned on whether a profession of Zionism rendered Margolis ineligible to teach certain aspects of Reform Jewish dogma. Underlying this dispute may have been a personality conflict between Margolis and Kaufmann Kohler, Hebrew Union's president. See Meyer, "Centennial History," 62–67.

88. See Margolis to Wheeler, July 6, 1905, Presidents' Papers, UCB, "Max Margolis" file and Wheeler to Harper, August 1, 1905, Presidents' Papers, UCB, "President William R. Harper" file.

89. Popper to Wheeler, June 20, 1905 and Wheeler to Popper, August 8, 1905, Presidents' Papers, UCB, "W. Popper" file.

90. Popper later recalled that this financial agreement allowed Wheeler to hire a Sanskritist for the extra $1,000 previously paid to Margolis. He noted that his move significantly reduced his income but that Voorsanger, just through with the Margolis negotiations, told him "California is a wonderful place; you don't need to worry about money." Popper recounted: "So I telephoned home and asked my family to send me my books and clothes, as I was staying in California." See William Popper, Interviews, 1956, Records of the Centennial History Office (CU-5.92), Interview 1, June 21, 1956, UCB. See also Harper to Wheeler, August 17, 1905, and Wheeler to Harper, August 22, 1905, Presidents' Papers, UCB, "President William R. Harper" file.

91. On Popper, see Monroe Deutsch, "Foreword" in Walter J. Fischel, ed., *Semitic and Oriental Studies: A Volume Presented to William Popper* (Berkeley: University of California Press, 1951), vii–x; Walter J. Fischel, P. A. Boodberg, and W. M. Brimmer, "William Popper, 1874–1963," *In Memoriam* (Berkeley: University of California, 1965), 63–67; and Walter J. Fischel, "William Popper (1874–1963) and his Contribution to Islamic Scholarship, In Memoriam," *Journal of the American Oriental Society* 84 (July-September, 1964), 213–20. See also the two part oral history, William Popper, Interviews, 1956 (June 21 and June 22, 1956) in UCB.

92. William Popper, Interviews, 1956, Interview 1, June 21, 1956, UCB.

93. See Fischel et al., "William Popper," 66–67, 214f. William Brimmer attributed Popper's cooler relationship with the Jewish community in part to its poor reception of his first, and last, talk at Emanu-El and to his refusal to teach there (as had Margolis) as being beneath the dignity of a university faculty member (Interview, September 12, 1977).

94. William Popper, Interviews, 1956, Interview 1, June 21, 1956, UCB.

95. Ibid., and "Semitics Department" report in University of California, *Biennial Report of the President of the University in Behalf of the Regents to His Excellency the Governor of the State: 1926–1927 and 1927–1928*, 66. See also "Semitic Languages" attached to Popper to Robert G. Sproul, June 27, 1931, Presidents' Papers, UCB, "Semitic Languages" file, box 1, CU 5.1.

96. William Popper Interviews, 1956, Interview 1, June 21, 1956, UCB.

97. See "Semitics Department" report in University of California, *Biennial Report . . . 1910–1912*, 45, and Martin Meyer to Alfred L. Kroeber, January 17, 1912, Alfred L. Kroeber Papers (C-B 927), UCB, "Martin A. Meyer" file.

98. See "Semitics Department" report in University of California, *Biennial Report . . . 1921–1922*, 59: William Popper Interviews, 1956, Interview 2, June 22, 1956, 1, and David Barrows to F. H. Lutz, May 12, 1921 and Lutz to Barrows, May 14, May 18, May 21, and May 26, 1921, Presidents' Papers, UCB, file 1164.

99. "I believe the gulf between your position and mine is neither wide nor deep," Hirsch wrote Adler. "Sometime[s] I regret that I did not take the step which you have. At other times I feel that you ought to have staid [sic] with us" (Hirsch to Adler, June 6, 1918, as quoted in Kraut, *From Reform Judaism to Ethical Culture*, 225; emphasis in original). See also Bernard Martin, "The Religious Philosophy of Emil G. Hirsch," *American Jewish Archives* 4 (June, 1954), 66–82, and idem, "The Social Philosophy of Emil G. Hirsch," ibid. 6 (June, 1954), 151–65.

100. Stephen S. Wise, "Memorial Address," in David Einhorn Hirsch, *Rabbi Emil G. Hirsch—The Reform Advocate* (Chicago: Whitehall, 1968), 183. Wise wrote: "Liberal Judaism in its beginnings . . . was for the most part . . . a rationalistic movement. That movement I do not disparage when I say that it was hyper-intellectualized and perhaps under-ethicized, so that the Ethical Culture movement grew therefrom as an explicable and yet not inevitable sequence thereto."

101. The Sinai Executive Board had advertised for "Jewish theologians of modern reform principles and of good repute who have graduated at a German university, with honor, are excellent also in all those branches of study which characterize the learned rabbis of our day, and who are good orators, able to preach in the German and English vernacular." This was quite a tall order. See Louis Wirth, *The Ghetto* (Chicago:

University of Chicago Press, 1928), 175, and Morris A. Gutstein, *A Priceless Heritage: The Epic Growth of Nineteenth Century Chicago Jewry* (New York: Bloch Publishing, 1953), 116–17.

102. These activities included a directorship of the Chicago Public Library and presidency of the library board (1888–1897), commissionership of public charities of Illinois (1897, 1906–1920), organizer of the Civic Federation, work on many non-sectarian charities, and membership on Chicago's Commission of Morals and on the Peace Council of Churches. He participated in the World's Parliament of Religions at the 1893 World's Fair and was Republican presidential elector-at-large for Illinois (1896). Notable Jewish activities included editorship of the *Reform Advocate*, founder of the Jewish Manual Training School, and organizer of the Associated Jewish Charities. See David E. Hirsch, *Rabbi Emil G. Hirsch*, passim; *The National Cyclopedia of American Biography*, s.v. "Hirsch, Emil G."; Gerson B. Levi, introduction in Emil G. Hirsch, *My Religion* (New York: Macmillan, 1925), 11–23; Ira Maurice Price, "Emil Gustav Hirsch," *The University [of Chicago] Record* 9 (April, 1923), 117–20; and *The Jewish Encyclopedia*, s.v. "Hirsch, Emil Gustav." On reformism at the University of Chicago, see Diner, *A City and its Universities*, passim.

103. Emil G. Hirsch, "Ministerial Training," 293.

104. "Nickerdown," in *Chicago Israelite* reprinted in *The Jewish Progress* (May 5, 1894), 5 and (June 1, 1894), 6. The latter issue contains an evaluation by Jacob Voorsanger.

105. John A. Wilson, "James Henry Breasted—The Idea of an Oriental Institute," in James A. Sanders, ed., *Near Eastern Archaeology in the Twentieth Century: Essays in Honor of Nelson Glueck* (Garden City: Doubleday, 1970).

106. William R. Harper, "The Statement of the President of the University," *Quarterly Calendar* 4 (3) (February, 1896), 12–24, quotation from 12.

107. University of Chicago, *The President's Report, 1905–1906*, 59; ibid., *1910–1911*; ibid., *1914–1915*.

108. See, for example, Harper to Hirsch, October 20, 1896, Harper Papers, UCSC, box 3, file 5, in which Harper invokes his "parental duty regarding your health," and Hirsch to Harper, February 20, 1905, ibid., box 7, file 21, upon learning of Harper's final illness.

109. Price, "Emil Gustav Hirsch," 117–18.

110. On the Semitic library, see correspondence in Chicago Sinai Papers, AJA. On Hirsch-Birnays, see Harper to Julius Rosenwald, November 29, 1904, and Harper to Hirsch, December 1, 1904, Harper Papers UCSC, box 7, file 16, and Rosenwald to Harper, December 5, 1891, Chicago Presidents' Papers, 1889–1925, UCSC, box 21, file 8. On Mandel Hall and Rosenwald Hall, see Harper to Hirsch, May 13, 1899, Harper Papers UCSC, box 4, file 28.

111. Price, "Emil Gustav Hirsch," passim, and Storr, *Harper's University*, 234.

112. Hirsch to Harper, July 21, 1892, Chicago Presidents' Papers, 1889–1925, UCSC, box 38, file 16.

113. Hirsch to Goodspeed, June 11, 1895, Board of Trustees Correspondence, 1890–1913, UCSC, box 2, file 2.

114. Harper to Hirsch, June 20, 1895, Harper Papers, UCSC, box 2, file 14. Harper wrote: "I do not think there is a man in the University who has been more loyal to it and there is no man whose departure I should mourn more greatly."

115. As related in Eli B. Felsenthal to T. W. Goodspeed, December 10, 1895, Chicago Presidents' Papers, 1889–1925, UCSC, box 65, file 5.

116. Hirsch to Harper, July 21, 1892, Chicago Presidents' Papers, 1889–1925, UCSC, box 38, file 16.

117. See Charles Breasted, *Pioneer to the Past: The Story of James Henry Breasted, Archaeologist* (Chicago: University of Chicago Press, 1977 [1943]), 28–29, 121–22, 131–33 and 212–14; Storr, *Harper's University*, 334; Harper to Arthur Hadley, February 1, 1900, Harper Papers, UCSC, box 5, file 12; Harper to Benjamin I. Wheeler, Au-

gust 17, 1905, Presidents' Papers, UCB, "President William R. Harper" file, and Timothy Dwight to Harper, July 22, 1889, Harper Papers, UCSC, box 12, file 16.

118. Goodspeed to Harper, June 1, 1890, Rockefeller Correspondence, UCSC, box 1, file 10.

119. *DAB*, s.v. "Hirsch, Emil Gustav," 68.

120. Gutstein, *Priceless Heritage*, 117; Wirth, *The Ghetto*, 186; Breasted, *Pioneer to the Past*, 95; James Jewett to Harper, April 11, 1902, Harper Papers, UCSC, box 6, file 13.

121. Emil G. Hirsch, "The Doctrine of Evolution and Judaism," *My Religion*, 262.

122. Emil G. Hirsch, "Judaism and the Higher Criticism," ibid., 237.

123. Ibid., 238.

124. Emil G. Hirsch, "From the Rising to the Setting Sun," *The Biblical World* 8 (August, 1896), 116. At Chicago, Hirsch offered a wide range of Judaica courses, including Talmud and related literatures. While in Chicago in 1915, the Romance philologist and Talmudist David Blondheim, who had been trained at Johns Hopkins, checked the university's holdings in rabbinics and commented that "Hirsch as a professor of Rabbinics hasn't bothered to have a Wilna [Talmud] put into the Chicago library and has only the Vienna and Warsaw editions himself!" Serious Talmud scholars prefer the Wilna edition above all other printed editions. These omissions raised questions about Hirsch's competence in Talmud. See Blondheim to Alexander Marx, April 17, 1915, Alexander Marx Papers, JTS, "David S. Blondheim" file.

125. Adler to Solomon Schechter, August 3, 1909, in Ira Robinson, ed., *Cyrus Adler: Selected Letters*, 2 vols. (Philadelphia: Jewish Publication Society of America and Jewish Theological Seminary, 1985), 1:168. Adler added: "His name was regularly put down for courses which he never gave and I have it on authority that he never even appeared at the University for several years at a time. You can imagine therefore his scholarly interest."

126. Hirsch to Wise, October 7, 1901, Stephen S. Wise Papers (hereafter Wise Papers), American Jewish Historical Society (hereafter AJHS), box 45, file 7, "Emil Hirsch." See also Hirsch to Solomon Schechter, November 11, 1915, Seminary Autograph, JTS, "To S. S. from Emil Hirsch" file. Rabbi Louis Mann, in his portrait of Hirsch in the *Dictionary of American Biography* (9:67), called him "one of the learned group of research scholars that William Rainey Harper, the first president of the University gathered around him."

127. Louis Mann succeeded to Hirsch's academic position in 1923 with the title "professorial lecturer in Rabbinics." Gerson B. Levi was the runner-up candidate. Levi was rabbi (along with Joseph Stolz) of Isaiah Israel Congregation, son-in-law of Emil G. Hirsch, and father of a future University of Chicago president. See James M. P. Smith to E. D. Burton, October 24, 1924, and Burton to Smith, November 3, 1924, Chicago Presidents' Papers, 1889–1925, UCSC, box 106, file 8. For subsequent events at Chicago, see material in the Ralph Marcus Papers, AJA.

128. Born in New York City in 1853, Isaacs obtained his bachelor's and master's degrees at the University of the City of New York and then embarked upon rabbinical studies at the Jewish Theological Seminary at Breslau and Semitic studies at the University of Breslau (1874–1877). Upon his return, his alma mater granted him the Ph.D. honorus causa; in the same year, he assumed editorship of the *Jewish Messenger*, a position he would relinquish 25 years later upon the merger of that publication with the *American Hebrew*. He served as preacher to the East 86th Street Synagogue (1886–1887), and as rabbi of the Miriam Barnert Temple, Patterson, New Jersey (1896–1905). Whereas Richard Gottheil's early publications consisted largely of Syriac texts, Isaacs' consisted of *Jewish Messenger* editorials, popular articles—"Religion in the Public Schools," "Current American Judaism," "Stories from the Rabbis," for example—and juvenile books. Isaacs received a nominal salary when he was transferred to the German chair in 1889 upon the death of the incumbent. He continued to teach German until 1906 when he became head of the Semitics Department. (On Isaacs, see Joshua Bloch, "Professor Abraham Samuel Isaacs, A.B., '71, A.M., '74, Ph.D., '78," *New York University Alumnus* 1 (October, 1920),

11–13; Abram Isaacs, *School Days in Home Town* (Philadelphia: Jewish Publication Society of America, 1928); Lewis M. Isaacs, "Abram S. Isaacs," *American Jewish Yearbook, 5682,* 23 (1921–1922), 80–83; and *Biographical Catalogue of the Chancellors, Professors and Graduates of the Department of Arts and Sciences of the University of the City of New York* (New York: published by the Alumni Association, 1894), 270.

129. University of the City of New York, *Council Minutes 12 January, 1877–4th October, 1896* (November 2, 1885), 190; ibid., November 1, 1886–May 27, 1892 (January 13, 1887), 11 and (May 2, 1887). In 1893, the university appointed John D. Prince, a Paul Haupt student, to a chair of Semitic languages and comparative philology. Prince had just returned from the Pennsylvania Babylonian expedition. (See University of the City of New York, *Chancellor's Report,* 1893, 4–5.) Throughout these years, the department geared its courses primarily toward theology students "who are desirous of obtaining an accurate acquaintance with the languages of the Old Testament in order that they may be able to understand and appreciate the many questions arising from the study of the Scriptures and connected with the comparative history of religion" (University of the City of New York, *Catalogue and Announcements for 1897–1898,* 127). The department's faculty published few major scholarly works and educated few early Semitists. Prince soon left to assume a Columbia professorship. The university gained visibility in Judaica only in the 1930s when it offered courses in modern Hebrew (see chapter 8).

130. Born in England in 1865, Levy came to America in 1889 after obtaining rabbinical ordination in England and receiving the A.B. from the University of London. After four years in a Sacramento pulpit, he was called to Philadelphia's Keneseth Israel Congregation in 1893. The characteristics of his professorship are familiar: lack of published scholarship, heavy communal involvement on Levy's part including some secular activities, and editorship of *Lyceum Weekly,* a publication associated with Keneseth Israel's youth group called "Lyceum," which met to discuss educational and literary topics. (See Morais, *Jews of Philadelphia,* 96–97.) The lack of either institutional resources or significant communal backing accounts for the relative obscurity and marginality of this post.

131. On Heller at Tulane, see file in Tulane University Archives. There is also some routine correspondence in the Max W. Heller Papers, AJA.

132. By mid-century, over 50 theological schools had been established, mostly based on Andover. Most schools required a bachelor's degree for admission and an extended course of study for graduation. See Naylor, "Theological Seminary," 17–30.

133. Francis Greenwood Peabody, "1891–92 Report of the Dean of the Divinity School," in Harvard University, *Annual Reports of the President and Treasurer of Harvard College* (1891/92), 109–10.

134. He added: "It enlarges the curriculum of the Faculty of Arts and Sciences by about thirty courses; and draws to the service of the College and the Graduate School as teachers, administrators and members of committees, colleagues whose predecessors passed their days in a corner of University Life" (Francis Greenwood Peabody, "1902–03 Report of the Dean of the Divinity School," in *Annual Reports of the President and Treasurer of Harvard College* [1902/03], 154–63, quotation from 155).

135. Financial considerations plagued both chairs. When the Hollis endowment grew inadequate to meet a professor's salary, the authorities permitted the chair to remain vacant from 1840 to 1882. To maintain the Hancock professorship, Harvard combined the income from the Hancock endowment with the incomes from the Dexter professorship endowment and from an 1891 bequest of Charles L. Hancock, a descendent of the chair's founder. See Lyon, "Semitic 1880–1929," 232, 234n.

136. Ibid., 232–33.

137. David Gordon Lyon, "A Half Century of Assyriology," *The Biblical World* 8 (August, 1898), 142. Lyon was a Baptist, as was Hollis. Hollis had stipulated that "none be refused on account of his belief and practice of adult baptism," but he also stated that he preferred a man "of sound and orthodox principles." Morison commented: "What Hollis meant by orthodoxy is questionable, but there can be no doubt that the Overseers, in altering [this] recommendation to a positive qualification, meant 'orthodox' to be taken

in the strict New England Congregational sense, and to exclude a member of any other denomination from the chair." He added: "Let us hope that Thomas Hollis was gratified at last to have a Baptist on his foundation, even though his job was to teach Semitic Languages and not Divinity!" (Morison, *Three Centuries*, 67, 68n).

138. In 1891, Lyon asked William Rainey Harper about his chances for appointment at Chicago (Lyon to Harper, January 30, 1891, Harper Papers, UCSC, box 1, file 17).

139. Toy and Lyon trained Reisner, who then completed his doctoral studies in Berlin as a Rogers and John Harvard fellow. Reisner himself trained one specialist during the 1890s, Albert Lythgoe, who occasionally offered an elementary course. With Reisner and Lythgoe usually in Egypt on excavations sponsored by the University of California, Harvard, and the Boston Museum of Fine Arts, the university offered little formal instruction in Egyptology. In urging that Harvard establish a separate Egyptology department, Reisner indicated that many European universities recognized the subject "although it can never play any great part in education." He thought Egyptology especially useful for comparative purposes. See Morison, *Three Centuries*, 241–47, and Reisner to Abbott L. Lowell, March 4, 1910, Lowell Papers, HUA, file 428: "Egyptology–Dept. of."

140. Moore later became Frothingham Professor of the History of Religions. His erstwhile Andover colleague, Charles C. Torrey, had previously failed to induce the Yale administration to recruit Moore. See chapter 1.

141. The field was variously known at Harvard as the "Science of Religion," "Comparative Religion," or the "Comparative History of Religion." Moore expanded upon a discontinuous prehistory. James Freeman Clarke, the author of *Ten Great Religions: An Essay in Comparative Theology*, 2 vols. (Boston: Houghton, Mifflin, 1872–1886), held a marginal appointment in the Divinity School from 1867 to 1871. See Edward Everett Hale, ed., *James Freeman Clarke: Autobiography, Diary, and Correspondence* (Boston: Houghton, Mifflin, 1891). Toy later organized a history of religions club and taught a course entitled "History of the Religion of Israel." During the 1890s, Everett offered "Studies in the Comparative History of Religions, particularly the Vedic Religion, the Hindu Philosophies, Buddhism, Mazdaism, and the Chinese Religions."

142. See Morris Jastrow, *The Study of Religion* (New York: Charles Scribner's Sons, 1902).

143. Moore taught the course only once; Harry Wolfson taught Harvard's next Talmud course.

144. Moore wrote that the planning committee for a proposed international congress of orientalists in America "ought to see to it from the beginning that there is no possibility of perverting the meeting into a brass band competition in which the 'shofar' vies with the 'Posaune' or even that in less vulgar ways the attempt be made to *make something* out of the Congress" (Moore to Lanman, Lanman Papers, HUA, HUG 4510.51, box: "Ho-O," file: "George F. Moore"). On the congress, see chapter 4.

145. Lyon tactfully wrote: "There was intimate connection between certain courses of his [Moore] and some of those given by Toy (Lyon, "Semitic, 1880–1929," 234). After Toy's retirement, Moore continued to offer his history of religions course, but at the suggestion of the Harvard administration, he devoted the remainder of his time to his research and writing. The result was his three-volume *Judaism*. See Lowell to Dean W. W. Fenn, February 23, 1911, and Moore to Lowell, March 8, 1911, Lowell Papers, HUA, file 363: "Divinity School: George Foot Moore."

146. Jewett, like Reisner, was initially exposed to Semitics at Harvard in the 1880s. He served as instructor in Semitics for one year (1887/88) and then completed his doctoral training at Strasbourg. Upon his return to America, Jewett taught Arabic at Brown, Minnesota, and Chicago. Lyon urged Harvard to appoint Jewett as early as 1902. (See Lyon to Eliot, June 10, 1902, Charles W. Eliot Papers [hereafter Eliot Papers], HUA, Ua 1.5.150, box 114, file 209.) Jewett's independent wealth permitted him to subsidize his own salary and the salary of departmental assistants such as Martin Sprengling. See Lyon, "Semitic, 1880–1929," 234–35, and Lyon to Lowell, May 17, 1914, Lowell Papers, HUA, 1909–1914, file 1222: "Museums, Semitic: Department of . . . General Correspondence."

147. Lyon, "Semitic, 1880–1929," 234, and Lyon to Lowell, April 9, 1910, Lowell Papers, HUA, 1909–1914, file 1022: "David G. Lyon."

148. Hawkins, *Pioneer*, 206. Three of the six original professors at Johns Hopkins were Europeans. "Naturally, the Beiträge will principally contain studies of German Semitists, though other languages, especially English and French or Latin will by no means be excluded," wrote Haupt. "The editors would be most happy indeed to receive contributions from other countries such as France, England or the United States. I hope that above all in this country, where Semitic studies have in the last few years made such great strides, the younger workers in this field will always pay due attention to comparative grammar. It would give me special pleasure to publish in the organ of the new school a number of thorough studies from the pen of American Semitologists" (Paul Haupt, "On a new periodical devoted to Assyriology and comparative Semitic grammar," *Journal of the American Oriental Society* 13 [1889], cclxvi).

149. Hawkins, *Pioneer*, 133.

150. On Brown, see Union Theological Seminary, *Memorial Service in Honor of the Reverend Francis Brown, Ph.D., D.D., D.Litt., L.L.D.* (New York: Gilbert T. Washburn, 1917), and *DAB*, s.v. "Brown, Francis."

151. Haupt to Basil Gildersleeve, February 3, 1883, Gilman Papers, MSEL-SC, "Paul Haupt" file.

152. Gilman to Haupt, March 10, 1883, "Gilman Letters: September 1880–September, 1889," Gilman Papers, MSEL-SC, 169, and Haupt to Gilman, April 17, 1883, and July 4, 1883, Gilman Papers, MSEL-SC, "Paul Haupt" file. Haupt's negotiations with Gilman over working conditions shed light on the relative unattractiveness of American universities. Had he continued to work in Germany, Haupt would have been entitled to participate in a well-developed pension system. American universities in general, and Hopkins in particular, did not offer a similar benefit. Haupt also quickly learned that the cost of living in America was higher than in Germany and that he had accepted a decidedly low remuneration. During the years immediately after his arrival, years in which he formally retained his Göttingen professorship while teaching at Johns Hopkins, he repeatedly raised these issues with Hopkins authorities. Gilman received his requests sympathetically, knowing that his treatment of Haupt would affect the ability of Johns Hopkins to recruit faculty members from abroad. He also knew that Haupt incurred considerable expense upon his wife's sudden death. Finally, not only was the Johns Hopkins academic year much longer than Göttingen's, Haupt had to shoulder the entire work of the Johns Hopkins Semitics department for the whole year. At Göttingen, Haupt had five colleagues.

Haupt began work at Johns Hopkins in fall, 1883, but the financial issues remained unsettled until January, 1886, when Gilman agreed to indefinite tenure, a salary increase, and a teaching assistant. But the university, under greater financial duress than at the start of the decade, declined to offer a pension. The trustees continued to grant Haupt leave to perform his work at Göttingen until 1888, when they cancelled the privilege, citing financial reverses. The Carnegie Foundation began to offer pensions to American faculty members in 1905, but Haupt never benefited from Carnegie largesse since he remained at his post until his death in 1926. See Haupt to Gilman, November 1, 1884, July 25, 1885; Gilman to Haupt, December 1, 1885, January 12, 1886, Gilman Papers, MSEL-SC, "Paul Haupt" file; Gilman memorandum, November 7, 1884, Miscellaneous Collection, ms. 34, MSEL-SC, "Paul Haupt" file; and Hawkins, *Pioneer*, 158–59.

153. "Mrs. Haupt [Haupt had married his first wife's sister in 1886] sends her best regards," Haupt wrote Adler in 1888. "She says she would not allow me to go alone [to America] if she did not know that I should be under your care. This is about the highest praise you can ever expect to get from Mrs. Haupt. Well, I think she is right" (Haupt to Adler, April 25, 1888, Seminary Autograph, JTS, Haupt–Adler Correspondence).

154. On Adler, see Adler, *I Have Considered*, Abraham Newman, *Cyrus Adler: A Biographical Sketch* (New York: American Jewish Committee, 1942), and Robinson, ed., *Cyrus Adler: Selected Letters.*

155. Haupt to Gilman, March 31, 1887, Gilman Papers, MSEL-SC, "Paul Haupt" file. Haupt knew of Adler's connections. Mayer Sulzberger, for example, became President Judge of Pennsylvania's Court of Common Pleas.

156. Adler to Gilman, May 31, 1889, Gilman Papers, "Cyrus Adler" file.

157. Haupt to Adler, December 25, 1892, Seminary Autograph, JTS, Haupt–Adler Correspondence. Haupt could have offered a Talmud course himself had he wished, as evidenced by the paper on Talmudic he presented at a meeting of the American Oriental Society. See Johns Hopkins University, *Report of the President of The Johns Hopkins University* (1906), 44. Haupt's allusion to low enrollments does not bear up under scrutiny. Text and language courses generally had low enrollments, as few as one or two students. Talmud registrations ranged up to nine students with the latter number comparing favorably with other text courses. See, for example, Johns Hopkins University, *Report of the President of The Johns Hopkins University* (1904), 71–72.

158. Cyrus Adler, *I Have Considered*, 179–80; Newman, *Cyrus Adler*, 24; Louis Finkelstein, preface, in Robinson, ed., *Cyrus Adler: Personal Letters*, 1:xix. On Adler's role as facilitator and entrepreneur, see chapter 6.

159. Adler, *I Have Considered*, 181.

160. As to its fate, Adler wrote in his memoirs: "After several years' work, [W. Muss-] Arnolt [a Haupt student and later professor of Semitics at the University of Michigan] retained the cards to which we had all contributed and published the dictionary over his own name" (Adler, *I Have Considered*, 60). See Paul Haupt, "Prologomena to a Comparative Assyrian Grammar," *Journal of the American Oriental Society*, 13 (1889), ccxiv–ccxix; Haupt to Adler, July 28, 1890, Seminary Autograph, JTS, Haupt–Adler correspondence; and Haupt to Gilman, March 27, 1893, Gilman Papers, MSEL-SC, "Paul Haupt" file.

161. Haupt enlisted his fellow scholars to prepare the Bible, but the venture was only a partial success. The Johns Hopkins Press found it unprofitable and published only six English and 16 Hebrew volumes (see *DAB*, s.v. "Haupt, Paul," and French, *History of the University Founded by Johns Hopkins*, 223–24.

162. After failing to join forces with the proposed Pennsylvania expedition, Haupt tried another tack. He suggested that Mesopotamia serve as a refuge for Jewish refugees from East European oppression and that the Smithsonian organize a scientific expedition there as an initial step, its membership to include three Assyriologists. See Paul Haupt, *Über die Ansiedlung der russischen Juden im Euphrat- und Tigris-Gebiete* (Baltimore: Friedenwald, 1892), and Moshe Perlmann, "Paul Haupt and the Mesopotamian Project, 1892–1914," *Publications of the American Jewish Historical Society* 47 (1957–1958), 154–75. Perlmann wrote: "Cyrus Adler was then working for the Smithsonian Institute and, in 1891, was in the Near East. . . . It seems plausible, in view of Adler's connection with Haupt and Adler's later role in the story of the Mesopotamia project, that the project was originally, a joint one, to say the least" (156, n. 3). For corroborating evidence, see Adler, *I Have Considered*, 92. See also Marnin Feinstein, *American Zionism 1884–1904* (New York: Herzl Press, 1965), 161–63.

163. Charles Farace viewed Haupt as a "very radical literary and textual critic" (see "History of Old Testament Higher Criticism in the United States" [Ph.D. diss., University of Chicago, 1939], 130). George Barton wrote: "He could not discriminate between what his fertile imagination suggested as possible and what sound critical principles allowed one to accept as probable. He was of the opinion, too, that the Hebrew poets always wrote in rigid metrical forms, which later editors spoiled by insertions, but which he was able to restore; hence, instead of interpreting an Old Testament text he usually rewrote it. This habit, together with the notion that much Old Testament literature originated in the Maccabean period, vitiated all his critical work. If his literary and historical judgment had been as good as his philological judgment, he would have been a great Biblical scholar. As it was, however, his works are not safe guides in this field" (*DAB*, s.v. "Haupt, Paul," 402. See also Hawkins, *Pioneer*, 159). For a more sympathetic critique,

see William Foxwell Albright, "Paul Haupt as a Scholar and Teacher," in Adler and Ember, eds., *Oriental Studies*, xxi–xxxii.

164. At Hopkins, William Foxwell Albright, then a graduate student and eventually Haupt's successor "found himself with many Jews and was learning to speak Modern Hebrew with one of his teachers, Dr. Aaron Ember. A second professor, Dr. William Rosenau, was the rabbi of the nearby Oheb Shalom synagogue. William joked to his mother that he did not expect to become Judaized." See Running and Freedman, *William Foxwell Albright*, 28.

165. Isaac M. Fein, *The Making of an American Jewish Community. The History of Baltimore Jewry from 1773 to 1920* (Philadelphia: Jewish Publication Society of America, 1971), 200.

166. See Running and Freedman, *William Foxwell Albright*, 23. F. R. Blake's presence may have served a similar function for Gentile students.

167. Gilman to Haupt, October 27, 1884, Gilman Papers, MSEL-SC, "Paul Haupt" file. But the Semitic Seminary attracted many aspiring or practicing ministers: "In my own day here," wrote a graduate, "every student in the Semitic Seminary was a minister of religion with the exception of two or three, including myself, and we soon followed the good example of the rest" (Fenlon, "Theology and the Semitic Sciences," 270).

168. See Meyer, "Centennial History," 86–88. When he turned Rosenau down, Ira Remsen, Gilman's successor, knew that Hebrew Union College had offered a professorship to Aaron Ember, a full-time junior member of the Semitics department. Ember specialized in Semito-Egyptian affinities and offered instruction in modern Hebrew, a rarity at the time. Haupt told Remsen that Ember's popularity and academic success made it "far more important that Dr. Ember receive an increase of $200 than that Dr. Rosenau, whose income is more than $8,000, be paid $500." Ember also remained at Hopkins. See Rosenau to Remsen, January 4, 1909, and Remsen to Rosenau, May 13, 1909, Records of the Office of the President, MSEL-FHA, Record Group 02.001, series 1, box 50, file 52.

169. Rosenau to President Frank J. Goodnow, February 19 and March 16, 1918; Goodnow to Rosenau, March 5, 1918, Records of the Office of the President, MSEL-FHA, Record Group 02.001, series 1, box 50, file 52. "In 1904 in addition to teaching Bible classes, supervising the congregational school, and attending to other routine duties, Rabbi Rosenau delivered 56 sermons, gave 20 talks in and out of town, performed one conversion and 34 marriages, attended 35 funerals, and made 637 calls with Mrs. Rosenau and 1127 calls by himself" (Fein, *The Making*, 185).

170. Running and Freedman, *William Foxwell Albright*, passim; "William Foxwell Albright" in Louis Finkelstein, ed., *American Spiritual Autobiographies* (New York: Harper and Brothers, 1948); and David Noel Freedman, ed., *The Published Works of William Foxwell Albright: A Comprehensive Bibliography* (Cambridge: American Schools of Oriental Research, 1975).

171. Samuel Sandmel, "Scholar or Apologist?" in Jick, ed., *Teaching of Judaica in American Universities*, 107.

172. William R. Harper moved from Morgan Park to Yale and then to Chicago under exceptional circumstances.

173. Running and Freedman, *William Foxwell Albright*, 140–41; see also French, *History of the University Founded by Johns Hopkins*, 243–48.

174. See M. H. Goshen-Gottstein, "Comparative Semitics—A Premature Obituary," in Abraham I. Katsh and Leon Nemoy, eds., *Essays on the Occasion of the Seventieth Anniversary of The Dropsie University (1909–1979)* (Philadelphia: Dropsie University, 1979).

4. The Price of Admission

1. See, for example, James D. Watson, *The Double Helix: A Personal Account of the Discovery of the Structure of DNA* (New York: Atheneum, 1968).

2. The competition for appointment to the Miller Chair at Columbia is a case in point. See chapter 7.

3. Recall that Morris Jastrow served as university librarian.

4. "Proceedings of the American Oriental Society . . . 1890," *Journal of the American Oriental Society* 15 (1893), xxxvii–xxxviii.

5. "Proceedings of the American Oriental Society . . . 1891," *Journal of the American Oriental Society* 15 (1893), lxxxii–lxxxiii. See Adler to Haupt, May 22, 1889, in Robinson, ed., *Cyrus Adler: Selected Letters*, 1:14–15, for an account of an apparently typical meeting.

6. Robert Harper to W. R. Harper, June 11, 1892, Chicago Presidents' Papers, 1889–1925, UCSC, box 37, file 15.

7. Robert Harper to W. R. Harper, June 28 and April 15, 1902, Chicago Presidents' Papers, UCSC, 1889–1925, box 37, file 15. Italics in original.

8. Robert Harper to W. R. Harper, March 29, n.y., ibid.

9. Haupt to Adler, July 1, 1887, Seminary Autograph, JTS, Haupt-Adler Correspondence.

10. The *Journal of the American Oriental Society*, he added, "has already a vast amount of *intangible plant* (the expression is my own) required for such a journal—it has a name, dignity, and standing among the very best scholars all over the world. I am not personally interested, mind you,—and would be exceedingly glad to retire from any and every part in the administration this very day" (Lanman to Harper, June 12, 1891, Chicago Presidents' Papers, 1889–1925, UCSC, box 51, file 6).

11. Lanman was American Oriental Society corresponding secretary and a member of the journal's publication committee.

12. Lanman to Gottheil, December 26, 1889, Richard Gottheil Papers, Central Zionist Archives, Jerusalem (hereafter CZA), "Charles Lanman" file. Italics in original. "Now just look at Jackson straining every nerve and overwhelming himself as it is, in order to push ahead the completion of his *Avestan Reader*, sitting up till all hours of the night when he ought to be asleep," Lanman wrote (ibid.).

13. Quoted in Rocher, "Crisis of 1890," 74.

14. Robert Harper to W. R. Harper, April 15, 1902, Chicago Presidents' Papers, 1889–1925, UCSC, box 37, file 15. Robert Harper's loyalty might have wavered had he known that his brother attempted to find a post for him at several other institutions. See chapter 3, n. 117.

15. Haupt to Adler, April 28, 1888, Seminary Autograph, JTS, Haupt-Adler Correspondence.

16. Lanman to Gottheil, December 26, 1889, Richard Gottheil Papers, CZA, "Charles Lanman" file.

17. Joseph Ben-David, *Trends in American Higher Education* (Chicago: University of Chicago Press, 1981 [1972]), 101.

18. Haupt proposed to land the party in New York, hold the Congress in Washington, and then travel to Chicago—site of the 1893 World's Fair—via Baltimore (Haupt), Philadelphia (Jastrow), New York (Gottheil), and Niagara Falls, thus completely ignoring New England (Haupt to Adler, November 29, 1891, Seminary Autograph, JTS, Haupt–Adler Correspondence). "The American Congress is *sure* to be a failure," wrote Robert Harper to his brother from England. "It seems that Haupt, Gottheil, and Jastrow are the chief men—as at least Hilprecht writes to Bezold. They would kill anything. I won't join til later, if ever. *None* of the Assyriologists will have anything to do with it and very few of the other Semitic men. They don't take it seriously here. I am sorry that you did not see your way to take hold of it" (Harper to W. R. Harper, June 11, 1892, Chicago Presidents' Papers, 1889–1925, USCS, box 37, file 15). Haupt wrote Richard Gottheil: "I quite agree with you in thinking that Lanman's conduct in the whole affair has been most curious. I never believed that he was heartily in favor of having a congress in the U.S.—at any rate, Whitney never approved of the idea, in fact all Sanskritists were opposed to it. This is quite natural as there would have been about four times as many Semitic scholars than Sanskritists. A Congress in the U.S. would have

clearly shown that Semitic studies are more flourishing in the U.S. than Sanskrit and Indo European research" (Haupt to Gottheil, June 19, 1892, Richard Gottheil Papers, CZA, "Paul Haupt" file).

19. John P. Peters, *Nippur or Explorations and Adventures on the Euphrates: The Narrative of the University of Pennsylvania Expedition to Babylonia in the Years 1888 to 1890*, 2 vols. (New York: G. P. Putnam's Sons, 1897), 1:1.

20. "The romantic story of the discovery and excavation of Ninevah so graphically told by Layard, and the immediate bearing of his magnificent results upon the interpretation of the Old Testament and upon the history of art and human civilization in general, appealed at once to the religious sentiment and to the general intelligence of the people" (Herman V. Hilprecht, *The Babylonian Expedition of the University of Pennsylvania*, Series D: *Researches and Treatises*, vol. 1 [Philadelphia: Department of Archaeology, University of Pennsylvania, 1904], 289–90).

21. Peters to J. Randolph Tucker, February 16, 1888, Tucker Family Papers, University of North Carolina, copy in John Peters Collection, Museum Archives, University of Pennsylvania, document 3.

22. See correspondence in the Gilman Papers, JHU, and Adler to Sulzberger, March 8, 1888, in Robinson, ed., *Cyrus Adler: Selected Letters*, 1:11.

23. Herman V. Hilprecht, *Explorations in Bible Lands During the Nineteenth Century* (Philadelphia: A. J. Holman, 1903).

24. Such a library would contain "astronomical, mathematical and religious texts (hymns, prayers, etc), letters, Temple accounts in large numbers (*grosse menge*), whereby the character of a Temple Library is fixed and assured" (Herman V. Hilprecht, *The So-Called Peters–Hilprecht Controversy* [Philadelphia: A. J. Holman, 1908], 112–13).

25. Gottheil to Jastrow, January 2, 1908, Gottheil Letter-Book, CU-RBML.

26. Jastrow to Lyon, April 2, 1906, Lyon Letters, HUA, HUG 1541.

27. Gottheil to Jastrow, May 7, 1907, Gottheil Letter-Book, CU-RBML.

28. *Hilprecht Anniversary Volume: Studies in Assyriology and Archaeology Dedicated to Hermann V. Hilprecht upon the Twenty-fifth Anniversary of his Doctorate and his Fiftieth Birthday (July 28) by his Colleagues, Friends and Admirers* (Chicago: Open Court Publishing Co., 1909).

29. Lanman to Hilprecht, March 5, 1908, and March 21, 1908, copies in Hilprecht, ed., *The So-Called Peters–Hilprecht Controversy*, 330, 331.

30. *In Re Resignation of Dr. Herman V. Hilprecht: Copies of Letters Addressed, at the Direction of the Trustees of the University of Pennsylvania, by the Provost of the University to Various Correspondents and Inquirers* (Philadelphia: University of Pennsylvania, 1911), 2.

31. The Hilprecht controversy is discussed in Paul Ritterband and Harold S. Wechsler, "A Message to Lushtamar: The Hilprecht Controversy and Semitic Scholarship in America," *History of Higher Education Annual* 1 (1981), 5–41.

32. E. Washburn Hopkins, "Thirty Years of Indo-European Studies," in Kent, ed., *Thirty Years of Oriental Studies*, 77.

33. John D. Prince and Frederick A. Vanderburgh, "The New Hilprecht Deluge Tablet," *The American Journal of Semitic Languages and Literatures* 26 (July, 1910), 304.

34. See Jastrow to Lyon, April 10, 1906, Lyon Letters, HUA, HUG 1541 and Jastrow to George McClellan, July 7, 1908, Museum Archives, University of Pennsylvania, 671/3.

35. Gottheil to Jastrow, January 2, 1908, Gottheil Letter-Book, CU-RBML. But compare Gottheil's attitude in this dispute with his invocation of *Rahmanuth* (compassion) a generation later in allowing the circulation of an extremely weak published dissertation. See chapter 6.

36. Peters, "Thirty Years' Progress in Semitics," 32. "Semitic scholars," he continued,

as we know them are not quite so wild and lawless as they were before 1888, and partly, I think, that is due to the increasing part which we have taken in training scholars in that field. While myself a student of two German universities, Berlin and Leipzig, and an admirer of the great scientific achievements of German scholarship, I must own that in my own department I found in the German system much that was unsound. Rewards seemed to go to the men who could put forth some new theory and defend it with the ingenuity and technical skill with which a lawyer prepares his brief. Young men were tempted and trained not to seek and find the truth, but to propound and defend a theorem. On that depended their advancement. The result was a lack of sincerity, which seriously affected the value of their work." (ibid., 47)

While probably not a conscious reference to Hilprecht, Peters' critique is congruent with Prince's analysis of the Deluge tablet.

37. Hopkins, "Thirty Years," 79.

38. Recent scholarship on the role gender played in obtaining advanced education, faculty positions, and scholarly legitimacy demonstrates institutional readiness to compromise professional norms. See Ellen F. Fitzpatrick, *Women Social Scientists and Progressive Reform* (New York: Oxford University Press, 1990); Rosalind Rosenberg, *Beyond Separate Spheres: Intellectual Roots of Modern Feminism* (New Haven: Yale University Press, 1982); and Margaret W. Rossiter, *Women Scientists in America: Struggles and Strategies to 1940* (Baltimore: Johns Hopkins University Press, 1982).

39. On admissions, see Synnott, *Half-Opened Door*, passim; Wechsler, *The Qualified Student*, passim; and David O. Levine, *The American College and the Culture of Aspiration, 1915–1940* (Ithaca: Cornell University Press, 1986), chapter 7. On campus life, see Harold S. Wechsler, "An Academic Gresham's Law: Group Repulsion in American Higher Education," *Teachers College Record* 88 (Summer, 1981), 567–88, and idem, "The Rationale for Restriction: Ethnicity and College Admission in America, 1910–1980," *American Quarterly* 36 (Winter, 1984), 643–67. On faculty members, see Lewis S. Feuer, "The Stages in the Social History of Jewish Professors in American Colleges and Universities," *American Jewish History* 71 (June, 1982), 432–65; Klingenstein, *Jews in the American Academy 1900–1940*; Oren, *Joining the Club*, chaps. 6 and 13; and Harold S. Wechsler, "The American Jewish Academic: Dilemmas of Exclusion and Inclusion," in Byron L. Sherwin ed., *The Solomon Goldman Lectures*, vol. 6 (Chicago: Spertus College of Judaica Press, 1993), 183–209.

40. Gottheil's inadequate salary forced him to undertake outside work, including Sunday school teaching, to supplement his income early in his career. This work did not help to create an image as a research scholar. See Gottheil to Seth Low, January 15, 1898; Low to Gottheil, January 22, 1898; Gottheil to Nicholas Murray Butler, December 27, 1901; Butler to Gottheil, December 28, 1901; Gottheil to Butler, January 6, 1909 (acknowledging his first salary increase in about 15 years), and March 4, 1917, CUF, "Richard Gottheil" file; and Gottheil to Butler, November 17, 1926, CUF, "G" file.

41. Jeffery, "Department of Semitic Languages," 186, and Gottheil to Butler, November 14, 1907, Gottheil Letter-Book, CU-RBML.

42. Columbia College, *Minutes of the Trustees* 23 (February 2, 1903), 65; Richard Gottheil to H. S. Davidson, February 11, 1907, Gottheil Letter-Book, CU-RBML; Jeffery, "Department of Semitic Languages," 186–87.

43. Columbia's 1896 move to its new, expensive Morningside Heights campus prompted President Low to ask the officers of Temple Emanu-El to resume their support. Gottheil told Low to emphasize that the work of the Semitics department "has been greatly broadened, so as to cover all of the Semitic Languages." But the Columbia president (though including this argument) emphasized the parochial side. "I have also thought," he wrote James Seligman, president of the Emanu-El Trustees, "that just as the German-Americans of the city have been interested in making some permanent provision for our German work in honor of Carl Schurz, so your Board might be pleased, in like fashion, to take an interest in placing the Department of Semitics on a similar footing." The Emanu-El trustees donated $500 for current expenses and promised to consider the matter again. The Gustav Gottheil lectureship was endowed three years later.

See Richard Gottheil to Low, February 8, 1899, Low to Gottheil, November 4, 1899, and December 5, 1899, CUF, "Richard Gottheil" file; Gottheil to Low, November, 1899, Low to Gustav Gottheil, March 8, 1899, CUF, "Go" file; and Low to James Seligman, March 22, 1899, CUF, "Se" file.

44. Richard Gottheil, "Semitic Languages at Columbia," 100–101; Gottheil to Low, May 22, 1893, May 9, 1895 (received), December 3, 1896, November 13, 1899; Low to Gottheil, May 10, 1895, December 4, 1896, and November 14, 1899; Gottheil to Butler, April 10, 1906, CUF, "Richard Gottheil" file.

45. Columbia augmented the Emanu-El library, which contained over 4,000 books and pamphlets, by drawing upon the Alexander I. Cotheal Fund for the Increase of the Library, an endowment established in 1896 by Cotheal's estate for the purchase of Oriental books and manuscripts (Columbia College, *Minutes of the Trustees* 16 [June 1, 1896], 182). Subsequent gifts from the same donors increased the fund to $17,024.87 by 1920.

46. Many of Popper's early works emphasized Judaic topics, but, as chapter 3 notes, Popper's major work was a critical edition of Abul Mahasin ibn Tagri Birdi's Arabic manuscript, "The History of Egypt under Mohammedan Rule." See Fischel, ed., *Semitic and Oriental Studies*, vii–viii.

47. Columbia officials were aware that the New York Jewish community might view hesitation on their part as a sign of anti-Semitism. These officials became concerned when "by some singular inattention" the trustee committee assigned to consider the matter failed to meet for two months (F. A. P. Barnard to Hamilton Fish, April 9, 1887, Hamilton Fish Papers, CU-RBML, "January–April 1887" file). The trustee's chairman, Hamilton Fish, said he regretted that the committee failed to meet and added, "I cannot imagine any hesitation as to the desirability of such a chair" (Fish to Barnard, April 11, 1887, ibid.). The formal agreement encountered a second delay over the issue of the chairholder's participation in faculty actions while his salary was below professorial level. See Seth Low to Fish, June 8, 1887 and June 20, 1887, ibid., "May–December, 1887" file.

48. Columbia College, *Minutes of the Trustees* 9 (May 2, 1887), 9410.

49. See Wechsler, *The Qualified Student*, chapter 7.

50. "Diary of Richard J. H. Gottheil," September 28, 1898, Richard J. H. Gottheil Collection, AJHS, 49.

51. Gottheil held a deep animus for Burgess. In 1917, just after American entry into World War I, he noted that Burgess, now retired, edited *The German-American Yearbook*. Calling the doctrines of this yearbook "seditious," Gottheil asked Butler "whether it is consistent with either the dignity of Columbia University or the standing which it takes in national affairs that Professor Burgess shall still be carried on the rolls of emeritus professors?" (Gottheil to Butler, May 28, 1917, CUF, "Richard Gottheil" file). For an example of the attitudes held by Burgess, see John W. Burgess, *Reminiscences of an American Scholar: The Beginnings of Columbia University* (New York: Columbia University Press, 1934), 241–42.

52. Gottheil to Horace Kallen, September 5, 1914, Horace M. Kallen Papers (hereafter Kallen Papers), AJA, "Richard Gottheil" file.

53. Several years earlier, Union Theological Seminary agreed to send Gottheil "all those students who desire to pursue Semitic studies other than purely Biblical ones." In exchange, Gottheil's students could register for Union Theological courses in Hebrew, Biblical Aramaic, and Biblical criticism. This agreement relieved Gottheil from entering a realm where his Jewishness, and even his "objectivity," might raise concerns. See Gottheil to Low, March 11, 1891, CUF, "Richard Gottheil" file. Columbia and the General Theological Seminary later concluded a similar agreement.

54. Gottheil to Low, January 21, 1896, ibid.

55. Low to Gottheil, February 1, 1896, ibid.

56. Gottheil to Robert Harper, January 14, 1907, Gottheil Letter-Book, CU-RBML. For Gottheil's desire that Oriental languages at Columbia take into account the Far East,

see Gottheil and A. V. Williams Jackson to Butler, March 28, 1902, CUF, "Richard Gottheil" file.

57. Gottheil to George H. Knox, October 27, 1906, and February 5, 1907, Gottheil Letter-Book, CU-RBML.

58. Perhaps if Gottheil had been a better campus politician he would have secured more perquisites for his department. He attended Columbia College at the same time as Nicholas Murray Butler and attained seniority over the other faculty members. However, he believed that American professors were "too much concerned with legislation." He wrote Butler: "That ought to be left to the authorities, assisted by a small committee of professors. In this manner, the authorities would keep in sufficient touch with University opinion. Professors should teach and lecture only. In such a manner, too, we should get rid of a great deal of University 'politics'—which are of advantage to no one" (Gottheil to Butler, March 14, 1911, Butler Papers, CU-RBML, "Richard Gottheil" file).

59. Max Weber, "Science as a Vocation," in Hans Gerth and C. W. Mills, *From Max Weber: Essays in Sociology* (New York: Galaxy, 1958), 129–56. Many classic academic freedom cases involved institutional restraint of public utterances. See Mary O. Furner, *Advocacy and Objectivity: A Crisis in the Professionalization of American Social Science, 1865–1905* (Lexington: University Press of Kentucky, 1975); Carol Gruber, *Mars and Minerva* (Baton Rouge: Louisiana State University Press, 1974); and Walter P. Metzger, *Academic Freedom*, passim.

60. For Gottheil's views on social anti-Semitism, see Gottheil to Daniel Guggenheim, February 9, 1907, Gottheil Letter-Book, CU-RBML.

61. Clarence K. Weil, ed., *ZBT 1898–1923: The First Twenty-Five Years* (New York: Zeta Beta Tau, 1923), 6–7.

62. As quoted in ibid., 59.

63. Gottheil to Horace Kallen, January 3, 1914, Kallen Papers, AJA, "Richard Gottheil" file.

64. Weil, ed., *ZBT*, 41.

65. See Elinor J. Grumet, "The Menorah Idea and the Apprenticeship of Lionel Trilling" (Ph.D. diss., University of Iowa, 1979); Jenna W. Joselit, "The Menorah Years: 1906–1930: A Collegiate Search for Jewish Identity" (unpublished masters essay, Columbia University, 1975); and idem, "Without Ghettoism: A History of the Inter-Collegiate Menorah Association 1906–1930," *American Jewish Archives* 30 (November, 1978), 113–54.

66. Henry Bergson, *Creative Evolution*, Arthur Mitchell, tr. (New York: Henry Holt, 1911), and Richard J. H. Gottheil, *Zionism* (Philadelphia: Jewish Publication Society of America, 1914), 14.

67. See Minutes of the Federation of American Zionists, Bernard C. Ehrenreich Papers, AJHS, December 15 and 25, 1897. Many early Federation members were Gottheil's students, such as Stephen Wise, or students at the Jewish Theological Seminary, such as Bernard C. Ehrenreich, the Federation's first recording secretary. See Harold S. Wechsler, "A Northern Progressive Goes South," in Samuel Proctor et al., eds., *Jews of the South* (Macon, Ga.: Mercer University Press, 1984), 45–63.

68. Gottheil to Horace Kallen, January 31 and March 6, 1914, Kallen Papers, AJA, "Richard Gottheil" file.

69. This work was important because of the initial pro-German sentiments of some notable German-Jews. See Gottheil to Kallen, November 2, 1914, ibid.: "It seems that the English, French and Russian Ambassadors at Washington have the idea that all the Jews are on the side of Germany because the International German-Jewish bankers are. It was necessary to dispel that illusion."

70. Gottheil, *Zionism*, 107.

71. "Unfortunately," he wrote to the prominent Chicago rabbi Bernhard Felsenthal, "I have allowed myself to be dragged into all sorts of things, Zionist Federation, Religious School Union, 'Helpful Thoughts,' and the like. My colleagues at the University have

justly blamed me for going out of my way in this manner, and I long heartily to get back again to my study table. It is true 'a man cannot serve two masters:' cannot serve the public and serve science at the same time. I hope, if possible to throw off a great many of these things next winter; but you know how difficult it is to do when one's heart is once engaged" (Gottheil to Felsenthal, May 27, 1898, Felsenthal Papers, AJA, box 2186, "Richard Gottheil" file).

72. "I do not wonder that your colleagues at the University are commencing to complain," Gottheil wrote to Kallen in 1915. "I took time by the forelock last September and told the President that my work this year would be worthless on account of the war. He evidently understood, for he answered me that his case was the same" (Gottheil to Kallen, January 29, 1915, Kallen Papers, AJA, "Richard Gottheil" file).

73. Stephen S. Wise to Sol (?) M. Stroock, October 17, 1931. Stephen Wise Papers, AJA, box 947, "Correspondence with Richard Gottheil, 1930–1936" file. Finkelstein subsequently became president of the Jewish Theological Seminary.

74. Butler to Gottheil, January 23, 1936, CUF, "G" file.

75. Louis Newman to Egbert, June 4, 1936, Wise to Egbert, June 5, 1936, Wise to Newman, June 5, 1936, Wise Papers, AJA, box 947, "Correspondence with Richard Gottheil, 1930–1936" file. Marcus aspired to Gottheil's chair but failed to receive serious consideration. See Wise to Marcus, June 2 and 5, 1936, Marcus to Wise, June 3 and 9, 1936, JIR Papers, AJA, box 26, file 4; "Ralph Marcus, 1930–1948." On Newman, see Alexander M. Shapiro and Burton I. Cohen, eds., *Studies in Jewish Education and Judaica in Honor of Louis Newman* (New York: KTAV, 1984).

76. On Antonius, see *London Times* (May 27, 1942), 7e, and *New Judea* 18 (May–June, 1942), 108–9.

77. See Stuart E. Knee, "The King-Crane Commission of 1919: The Articulation of Political Anti-Zionism," *American Jewish Archives* 29 (Spring, 1977), 33, and Harry N. Howard, *The King-Crane Commission: An American Inquiry in the Middle East* (Beirut: Khayat, 1963), which includes "The Recommendations of the King-Crane Commission" (345–61). The recommendations for Syria and Palestine are also reproduced in George Antonius, *The Arab Awakening* (London: Hamish Hamilton, 1938), 443–58. Crane was also trustee of the Constantinople College for Women and treasurer of the Armenian and Syrian Relief Committee, organized in the United States in 1915.

78. See Crane's obituary in *The New York Times* (February 16, 1939), 21:1.

79. As quoted in David Philipson, *My Life as an American Jew* (Cincinnati: John G. Kidd & Son, 1941), 173–74.

80. Charles R. Crane to Butler, June 12, 1936, CUF, "C" file.

81. Bayard Dodge to Butler, October 22, 1936, CUF, "D" file.

82. Antonius, *Arab Awakening*, x. Antonius dedicated the book to Crane. See also Hans Kohn's review in *Menorah Journal* 27 (Spring, 1939), 234–38. On "inconvenient" facts in scholarship, see Weber "Science as a Vocation," 147. Antonius de-emphasized the provocative role of Haj Amin el Husseni in Middle Eastern politics. In 1920, Husseni was sentenced in absentia to fifteen years in jail for instigating an Arab attack on unarmed Jewish worshippers in the Jewish Quarter of the Old City of Jerusalem. Shortly thereafter, Herbert Samuel, recently appointed to head a British civilian administration of Palestine, pardoned Husseni and named him President of the Supreme Moslem Council and Mufti of Jerusalem. In 1936, the Mufti organized a general strike and economic boycott of Jewish and British businesses to support Arab demands for a ban on land sales to Jews, a halt to Jewish immigration, and creation of an Arab national government. These actions rapidly devolved into violent, Mufti-supported, large-scale guerilla actions. The next year, he informed the Nazi government that he supported "the new Germany." *The Arab Awakening* recounts none of these events. Antonius had close personal and political connections to the Mufti, and his enemies charged that he helped foment the 1936 riots. See Bernard Postel and Henry W. Levy, *And the Hills Shouted for Joy: The Day Israel Was Born* (New York: David McKay, 1973), 55, 62–63, 72–73, 78.

83. Crane suggested that Butler might derive some impression of Antonius's personality from Gildersleeve, whom Crane had introduced to Near Eastern politics and to Antonius years earlier. Gildersleeve's 1954 memoirs recounted that although Antonius died during World War II, "his name is still an open sesame to friendship with any Arab you may meet." Her exposure to Crane and Antonius led her to blame "International Zionism" for plunging much of the region into war, sowing long-lasting hatred, and changing the Arab attitude toward America from trusting to hostile. Butler would likely have accepted Crane's suggestion—eight years earlier Gildersleeve served on the committee that searched for the first occupant of the Nathan Miller Chair of Jewish History at Columbia. Gildersleeve, knowing that the appointment of Antonius would deal American Zionism a symbolic blow, would have taken the initiative if Butler had not. See Virginia Gildersleeve, *Many a Good Crusade* (New York: Macmillan, 1954), 171–72, 174–77, 182. On Gildersleeve, see Lynn D. Gordon, "Annie Nathan Meyer and Barnard College: Mission and Identity in Women's Higher Education," *History of Education Quarterly* 26 (Winter, 1986), 503–22. See also Frank Fackenthal to James C. Egbert, July 1, 1936, CUF, "James C. Egbert" file, and Louis I. Newman, "George Antonius," memo attached to Newman to Felix Warburg, September 28, 1936, Felix W. Warburg Papers (hereafter Warburg Papers), AJA, box 353, file: "1936." Stephan Brumberg brought relevant materials in the Warburg Papers to our attention.

84. Butler to Fackenthal, August 11, 1936, CUF, "Nicholas Murray Butler" file.

85. Egbert to Fackenthal, July 28, 1936, CUF, "James C. Egbert" file.

86. "Personally, I have no present knowledge of conditions and personalities of the Near East," stated Butler, perhaps disingenuously. See Butler to Herbert Samuel, October 2, 1936, CUF, "S" file.

87. Antonius to Fackenthal, October 2, 1936, CUF, "A" file.

88. Emma Gottheil to Butler, August 29, 1936, CUF, "Richard Gottheil" file.

89. Emma Gottheil to Stephen Wise, August 31, 1936, Wise Papers, AJA, box 947, file: "Correspondence with Richard Gottheil, 1930–1936."

90. Wise to Emma Gottheil, September 2, 1936, ibid.

91. Rogers to Fackenthal, September 7, 1936, CUF, "R" file.

92. Fackenthal to Rogers, September 9, 1936, ibid.

93. Butler to Emma Gottheil, September 12, 1936, CUF, "Richard Gottheil" file. Butler deceived Mrs. Gottheil on the progress of the appointment. He said Antonius was under favorable consideration but implied that he had not yet been invited—all this six weeks after he reached his decision.

94. Wise to Emma Gottheil, September 16, 1936, and Emma Gottheil to Butler, September 18, 1936, Wise Papers, AJA, box 947, file: "Correspondence with Richard Gottheil, 1930–1936." Wise caught Butler's intimation that the appointment was not a fait accompli (see n. 93). He wrote as a part of the letter for Mrs. Gottheil's signature: "Most solemnly do I beg you, in my husband's name and spirit, to reconsider the invitation. It ought never have been extended to him. He deserved it neither as scholar nor as man, and I have no doubt that his name was suggested by one who is not interested in Semitic learning but in anti-Semitic good will."

95. Joseph M. Proskauer, Sol M. Stroock, and Louis F. Newman to Butler, October 2, 1936, CUF, "P" file. The letter said that other journalists told the *New York Times* correspondent "that Antonius was the man with whom all Mufti contacts had to be established, that he was in effect the publicity counsel for the Mufti, and the directing spirit of Arab propaganda." Louis I. Newman to Felix Warburg, September 28, 1936, Warburg Papers, AJA, box 353, "1936" file, details the preparations for the meeting.

96. Rogers to Fackenthal, October 2, 1936, CUF, "R" file.

97. Telegram, Rogers to Antonius, October 1, 1936, ibid.

98. Butler to Antonius, October 6, 1936, CUF, "A" file.

99. Antonius to Butler, November 12, 1936, ibid.

100. Dodge to Butler, October 22, 1936, CUF, "D" file.

101. Herbert Samuel to Butler, October 16, 1936, CUF, "S" file. See also Felix M. Warburg to Samuel, Warburg Papers, AJA, box 353, "1936" file. The house to which Sir Herbert Samuel referred was located at Karm Al-Mufti, Jerusalem. Judge Proskauer mistakenly referred to his address as "Haram al Mufti," the house of the Mufti. Rogers wrote that Karm Al-Mufti was the proper address and that it was the name of a hill: "How it received its name I don't know, but I have a vague recollection of having been told that the family of the Grand Mufti has owned most of it for many years." Rogers added that the father-in-law of Antonius paid for the house. See Rogers to Fackenthal, October 22, 1936, CUF, "R" file.

102. As quoted in Felix Warburg to James N. Rosenberg, Esq., November 12, 1936, Warburg Papers, AJA. Cyrus Adler kept close tabs on these events. See Adler to Julian Morgenstern, October 23, 1936, in Robinson, ed., *Cyrus Adler: Selected Letters*, 2:320–21.

103. Egbert to Butler, December 14, 1936, CUF, "James C. Egbert" file. See also Henry S. Coffin to John J. Coss, October 13, 1936, excerpt in CUF, "Arthur Jeffery" file.

104. Egbert to Butler, April 2 and 20, 1937, Butler to Egbert, April 5, 1937, and Fackenthal to Egbert, April 7, 1937, CUF, "James C. Egbert" file. After Jeffery's appointment as visiting professor, Salo W. Baron, Nathan Miller Professor of Jewish History, Literature and Institutions, sent Butler an unsolicited statement concerning the future of Semitics at Columbia that included detailed analyses of the sub-disciplines. Columbia had no such document the previous summer, although Baron apologized for writing at such length "largely relating facts familiar to you." See Baron to Butler, January 29, 1937, CUF, "B" file.

105. Ralph Marcus and Abraham Halkin remained on the staff for eight and two years respectively before they obtained professorships elsewhere, Marcus at the University of Chicago, Halkin at Brooklyn College.

106. Baruch Braunstein, "Professor Gottheil at Seventy," Jewish Telegraphic Agency Release, November 4, 1932, copy in Zionist Archives, New York City.

107. "The appointment of Antonius would degrade the Semitic Department of Columbia from a department of scholarship to a department of political propaganda," James Rosenberg told Cyrus Adler. "It would be tragic if a great university, on top of its acceptance of the invitation to the Heidelberg party which all the European universities refused, were now, to appoint a mufti propagandist" (Rosenberg to Adler, September 29, 1936, Warburg Papers, AJA).

108. Peters, "Thirty Years' Progress in Semitics," 46, and Morris Jastrow, Jr., "Supplementary Account of Thirty Years' Progress in Semitic Studies, and Discussion of Dr. Peters' Paper," in Kent, ed., *Thirty Years of Oriental Studies*, 58–60.

109. Peters, "Thirty Years' Progress in Semitics," 30–31.

110. Morris Jastrow, "Supplementary Account," 64–72, quotations from 67, 69.

5. The Quest for Recognition at Harvard

1. Gottheil to Solomon Schechter, August 17, 1889, Seminary Autograph, JTS, "To S. S. from Richard Gottheil" file.

2. Solomon Schechter to "Rabbi," May 23, 1911, Solomon Schechter Archives, JTS, "?" file.

3. Hyman G. Enelow, "On Chairs of Judaism at American Universities," attached to Enelow to E. N. Williamson, May 8, 1925, Hyman Enelow Papers (hereafter Enelow Papers), AJA, General Correspondence, 1924–1925, box 573, "E" file.

4. Hyman G. Enelow to Jacob Landau, December 29, 1925, Enelow Papers, AJA, General Correspondence, box 575, "J" file.

5. Lucius Littauer, undated memorandum, ca. 1925, Lucius Littauer Foundation Files, New York City.

6. Frederick Paul Keppel, *Columbia* (New York: Oxford University Press, American Branch, 1914), 179–80, and idem, *The Undergraduate and His College* (Boston: Houghton Mifflin, 1917), 81–84.

7. See Wechsler, *The Qualified Student*, chapter 7.

8. Lowell to W. E. Hocking, May 19, 1922, Lowell Papers, HUA, file 1056, "Jews," and Henry Aaron Yeomans, *Abbott Lawrence Lowell, 1856–1943* (Cambridge: Harvard University Press, 1948), 210–12. See also Wechsler, "An Academic Gresham's Law," 567–88.

9. The literature on Jews as a race was voluminous at the time. See especially Irwin Edman, "Race and Culture," *The Menorah Journal* 10 (November, 1924), 421–27; Charles W. Eliot, "The Potency of the Jewish Race," ibid. 1 (June, 1915), 141–44; Alexander A Goldenweiser, "Concerning 'Racial Differences,' " ibid. 9 (October, 1922), 309–16; and Alfred L. Kroeber, "Are the Jews a Race?" ibid. 3 (December, 1917), 290–94.

10. In line with this reasoning, Lowell proposed restrictions upon the total number of Jews admitted to Harvard (called, wrote his biographer, "by Jewish writers a numerus clausus" or quota) irrespective of the individual qualities of those admitted. See Yeomans, *Abbott Lawrence Lowell*, 209–17, quotation from 212.

11. James Bryce, *The American Commonwealth*, Louis M. Hacker, ed., 2 vols. (New York: G. P. Putnam's Sons, 1959), 2:461.

12. See Peter D. Hall, *The Organization of American Culture, 1700–1900: Private Institutions, Elites, and the Origins of American Nationality* (New York: New York University Press, 1982), and Ronald Story, *The Forging of an Aristocracy: Harvard and the Boston Upper Class, 1800–1870* (Middletown, Conn.: Wesleyan University Press, 1980).

13. As quoted in Cyrus Adler, *Jacob H. Schiff: His Life and Letters*, 2 vols. (Garden City, N.Y.: Doubleday, Doran, 1929), 2:21.

14. Historians Merle Curti and Roderick Nash would have termed Schiff a "friend"—someone "who had never developed collegiate loyalty in ivy-clad halls" but in whom an appeal struck "a responsive and lucrative chord" (Merle E. Curti and Roderick Nash, *Philanthropy in the Shaping of American Higher Education* [New Brunswick, N.J.: Rutgers University Press, 1965], 136). The care with which Lyon nurtured his relationship to Schiff qualifies Curti and Nash's assertion that friends were not cultivated by organized efforts but "on whatever influence general statements about needs, by educational leaders together with trustees and alumni, might happen to have on people of wealth who themselves had no collegiate background" (ibid., 164–65). Schiff also helped to meet the expenses incurred by Columbia University during its move to Morningside Heights and to endow chairs and fellowships at Columbia. He endowed Barnard Hall (1915), the student activities center of Barnard College (Schiff was Barnard's first treasurer), a Department of Public Affairs at New York University's School of Commerce, and a fund for the "Promotion of Studies in German Culture" at Cornell. He also established a loan fund at Amherst, the college attended by his son, and contributed to Cooper Union in New York. See Adler, *Jacob H. Schiff*, 2:6–18, 37–38.

15. Adler, *Jacob H. Schiff*, vol. 2, summarizes Schiff's gifts to sectarian education. His contributions to the Jewish Theological Seminary illustrated his interest in Jewish acculturation. Schiff purchased the land and built a home for the Seminary in Manhattan's Morningside Heights, the location of Columbia University. He offered to establish a teacher-training department, provided that it too be located at the Morningside site, despite the difficulty its many part-time students would have commuting from New York's predominantly Jewish Lower East Side to the predominantly non-Jewish Upper West Side. "Apparently," sociologist Marshall Sklare wrote of Schiff and his fellow Seminary trustees, "they felt that establishing the school in a highly Jewish neighborhood would impede the Americanization of the student body and hence vitiate institutional purposes. The atmosphere of Morningside Heights, however, would be conducive to the proper kind of acculturation." Schiff accepted a compromise to the teacher-training institute question. See Marshall Sklare, *Conservative Judaism: An American Religious Movement*, new, augmented edition (New York: Schocken Books, 1972 [1955]), 191–95, quotation from 192.

16. See David Gordon Lyon, "Relations of Jacob H. Schiff to Harvard University," Lyon Papers, HUA, HUG 1541.30, 1. Cyrus Adler based his discussion of the Semitics Museum in his biography of Schiff on this unpublished essay. See Adler, *Jacob H. Schiff*, 2:18–33.

17. Lyon, "Relations," 2; Charles F. Adams to Schiff, November 12, 1889, A. O. Peabody to Schiff, November 23, 1889, and Lyon to Schiff, November 24, 1889, "Letters about Harvard Semitic Museum" (hereafter Museum Letters), AJA, box 2541. The year 1889 proved interminable for Lyon, who viewed the future of Semitics at Harvard as dependent upon Schiff's munificence. A poem that Toy sent to his protégé just before summer recess included this verse:

> May some mighty cathreal surge
> Schiff's eyes from film pecuniar purge
> And soon before your gladdened eye
> A fair Museum quickly rise
> Well stocked with tablets, seals and gems
> Manuscripts and books of stems
> And all material archaeologic
> To suit the student Semitologic!

("A Wish" by C. H. Toy to Lyon, May 24, 1889, David Gordon Lyon Journals, HUA, May 24, 1889).

18. Lyon, "Relations," 2–5, Eliot to Schiff, December 23, 1889, W. H. Hooper to Schiff, December 30, 1891, Charles F. Adams to Schiff, January 11, 1890, and Lyon to Schiff, May 16, 1891, Museum Letters, AJA, box 2541.

19. Lyon, "Relations," 4. "I think it is a great advantage," Schiff wrote, "to have awakened the interest of a larger circle, for the subscribers will all feel that this is to be more or less *their* museum, and they will in turn interest others. It was probably for this reason why I thought it best to wait before I came forward with the entire sum, so as not to have it the movement of one individual, which, as a rule, is not desirable" (ibid., 13). Ultimately, 98 contributors donated amounts ranging from $5.00 to $1,500.

20. Ibid., 13; Eliot to Schiff, December 15, 1889, Museum Letters, AJA, box 2541.

21. *Addresses Delivered at the Formal Opening of the Semitic Museum of Harvard University on Thursday, February 5, 1903* (Cambridge: Published by the University, 1903), 12–13.

22. Ibid., 3, 4, 5–6. See also David Gordon Lyon, "Contributions of Judaism to the Growth of Civilization of the World," *The American Jews' Annual* (1894–1895), 40–49.

23. *Addresses Delivered at the Formal Opening*, 27–28. See also Thomas Wentworth Higgenson to Eliot, February 8, 1903, and Eliot to Schiff, February 10, 1903, Museum Letters, AJA, box 2541.

24. *Addresses Delivered at the Formal Opening*, 21–22. Schiff cited "a deep attachment to my race, proud of its past achievements, sensible of its continuing responsibilities," as his motives for his interest in Jewish history (ibid., 21). Eliot wrote that Schiff "was moved by a strong attachment to his race, by a profound faith in the historical convictions of the Hebrew race that there is one God, and that righteousness is the foundation of his character and of Man's progress, and by pride in the Semitic origin of three great religions, the Hebrew, Christian, and Mohammedan. He believed that the history and literature of the Semitic race ought to furnish one of the great fields for study and research by scholars of all races all down the centuries" (Charles W. Eliot, "Jacob H. Schiff," *Menorah Journal* 7 [February, 1921], 17).

25. *Addresses Delivered at the Formal Opening*, 11.

26. Schiff to Lyon, December 24, 1901, Lyon Letters, HUA, Special Folders, ca. 1882–1935, HUG 1541.5.5, "Jacob H. Schiff" file. Schiff, Lyon wrote, thus showed himself "at least two decades ahead of the experts in this kind of research. . . . Only in the present year, 1925, has this correct view met a partial fulfillment in the appointment of Dr. Clarence S. Fischer as Professor of Archaeology in the American oriental school at Jerusalem, with the express intention of trying to co-ordinate the various American archaeological undertakings in Western Asia." See Lyon, "Relations," 16.

27. Ibid., 15.

28. Schiff to Lyon, March 15, 1904, Lyon Letters, HUA, Special Folders, ca. 1882–1935, HUG 1541.5.5, "Jacob H. Schiff" file.

29. Eliot, "Jacob H. Schiff," 17.

30. "I believe that important results affecting Jewish and Biblical history may be expected at Samaria," he wrote Schiff in 1906. See Lyon to Schiff October 29, 1906, Lyon Letters, HUA, Special Folders, ca. 1882–1935, HUG 1541.5.5, "Jacob H. Schiff" file.

31. The committee's membership included Toy, Moore, and Lyon (chair).

32. Lyon, "Relations," 33. Schiff reasoned: "If the Turks, as is apparent, are so unwilling to permit foreigners to dig, it is very likely that even with a firman in hand progress would be impeded in every possible manner, and that the results to science in general and to the Harvard Museum in particular would not be worth the proposed expenditure" (ibid., 37).

33. Ibid., 37–43.

34. The volumes were published in Cambridge by Harvard University Press. According to Lyon, delays in the preparation of the manuscript and the onset of World War I prevented prompt publication. Schiff's family met the increased publishing costs characteristic of the 1920s and provided for the gratis distribution of over half the volumes to major libraries. (See Lyon, "Relations," 47–48.) Many secondary sources contain accounts of the site. See, for example, William F. Albright, *The Archaeology of Palestine and the Bible* (New York: Fleming H. Revell, 1932), 31–33. Harvard and four other sponsors resumed exploration on the site from 1931 to 1935.

35. See Lyon, "Relations," 32. Isidore Strauss, who served on the Visiting Committee for about 15 years, occasionally donated sums for specific purposes. See, for example, Strauss to Eliot, February 14, 1908, Lyon Letters, HUA, Special Folders, ca. 1882–1935, HUG 1541.5.5, "Semitic Museum, Harvard University" file, in which Strauss offered $1,000 to defray Lyon's expenses in supervising the Samarian excavations.

36. Lyon, "Relations," 32. Each new member resided in or near Boston and none, apparently, was Jewish.

37. Eliot, "Jacob H. Schiff," 18.

38. After Toy's retirement, his colleagues presented him with a festschrift subsidized by Schiff: David Gordon Lyon and George Foot Moore, eds., *Studies in the History of Religions* (New York: Macmillan, 1912). The friendship between Toy and Schiff, Charles Eliot wrote, "was based on an appreciation of Dr. Toy's extraordinary learning, devout liberalism, and simple-hearted love towards God and Man. The friendship grew with the years and was expressed in numberless acts of kindliness and affection through all Dr. Toy's life" (Eliot, "Jacob H. Schiff," 17).

39. Compare Veysey, *Emergence of the American University*, 302–17, to Michael D. Cohen and James G. March, *Leadership and Ambiguity: The American College President* (New York: McGraw-Hill, 1974). See also the classic Thorstein Veblen, *The Higher Learning in America: A Memorandum on the Conduct of Universities by Business Men* (New York: B. W. Huebsch, 1918), and Walter Metzger's critique in *Academic Freedom*, 177–93.

40. When Schiff retired from the Visiting Committee in 1914, Eliot assumed its chairmanship. "While I was President of Harvard University (1869–1909)," Eliot wrote Julius Rosenwald, "my interest was strong in building up the Division of Semitic Languages and History in the University." The same letter, written to solicit Rosenwald's membership on the Visiting Committee, noted the department's Judaic orientation: "This committee is composed partly of Harvard Alumni of New England birth, and partly of eminent Jews the majority of whom reside in other parts of the country. [It] takes an active interest in all matters relating to the development of the Department, and the progress of knowledge concerning the history and records of the Jewish race" (Eliot to Rosenwald, September 15, 1915, Lyon Letters, HUA, Special Folders, ca. 1882–1935, "President Charles W. Eliot" file).

41. See Charles W. Eliot, "Address at a Meeting of the Harvard Menorah Society," in Hurwitz and Sharfman, eds., *Menorah Movement*, 32. For conflicting views concerning

Lowell's anti-Semitism, see Synnott, *Half-Opened Door*, passim, and Yeomans, *Abbott Lawrence Lowell*, 209–12.

42. The contrast between Eliot's and Lowell's attitude towards American Jews resembles the contrast between contemporary and successive Columbia presidents Seth Low (1889–1901) and Nicholas Murray Butler (1901–1945). See Wechsler, *The Qualified Student*, chapter 7, esp. 140–41.

43. Schiff's other gifts to the Semitic Museum included funds for its library and scholarships, loans, and prizes for the department's students.

44. Schiff to H. McK. Twombley, Esq., February 3, 1905, and Twombley and Robert Bacon to Schiff, February 9, 1905, attached to Mortimer Schiff to Lyon, November 11, 1925, Lyon letters, HUA Special Folders, ca. 1882–1935, HUG 1541.5.5, "Jacob H. Schiff" file. See also Lyon, "Relations," 25–27.

45. Recall that a sizable contribution had replenished the Hancock endowment in 1891. See Lyon, "Semitic 1880–1929," 234.

46. C. F. Adams to F. W. Hunnewell, December 2, 1914, Lowell Papers, HUA (1914–1917), file 320: "Semitics Department: Budget 1914–1915." Adams wrote, "I think it would be better to pay $2000 a year directly to the Semitic Museum account, in order that it may be clear to Mr. Schiff or anyone else interested in the department, that we were carrying out our promise to him, as well as to keep alive in our own minds this promise which we seem to have forgotten."

47. Lyon, "Relations," 28.

48. Schiff to Lowell, November 25, 1910, and Lowell to Schiff, December 1, 1910, Lowell Papers, HUA (1909–1914), file 1222: "Museums: Semitic—Dept. of . . . General Correspondence." The course was "The History of Israel," which Lowell considered too easy. Schiff replied that Lowell's own statistics showed a 12 percent decline from 1898/99 and a 35 percent decline from 1904/05. He professed it discouraging "to find that the time, thought and money . . . expended for the advancement of the Department has apparently been for naught, as far as increasing interest is concerned" (Schiff to Lowell, December 5, 1910, ibid.). Lyon pointed out that the decline in Semitics enrollments most probably resulted from the trend among theological schools to make Hebrew an elective, instead of a required entrance subject. See Lyon to Schiff, November 11, 1913, Lyon Letters, HUA, Special Folders, ca. 1882–1935, HUG 1541.5.5, "President A. Lawrence Lowell" file.

49. Ropes to Lowell, February 7, 1910, Lowell Papers, HUA, 1909–1914, file 1222: "Museums, Semitic: Dept. of . . . General Correspondence."

50. Ibid. Schiff suggested "Professor Horowitz of the Indian Government University at Bombay"—probably Josef Horovitz (1874–1931), who taught Arabic at the Muhammedan Anglo-Oriental College of Aligarh in India between 1907 and 1914, simultaneously serving as curator of Islamic inscriptions for the Indian government, and who then taught Semitic languages at the University of Frankfurt—but his Jewish name did little to promote his chances.

51. *Addresses Delivered at the Formal Opening*, 26.

52. Lyon to Lowell, April 18, 1912, Lyon Letters, HUA, Special Folders, ca. 1882–1935, HUG 1541.5.5, "President A. Lawrence Lowell" file.

53. Lyon to Lowell, February 5, 1921 and Lowell to Lyon, February 15, 1921, Lowell Papers, HUA, 1919–1922, file 847: "Semitics Dept.: Lyon, David G."

54. Lyon, "Relations," 28.

55. See Gorman Brooks to Schiff, July 6, 1915, Jacob H. Schiff Correspondence, 1914–1920, AJA, box 443, "Education" file, acknowledging Schiff's contribution of $1,000 for the Semitic Museum, and Lyon to Schiff, May 28, 1916, Lyon Letters, HUA, Special Folders, ca. 1882–1935, HUG 1541.5.5, "Jacob H. Schiff" file, discussing Schiff's contribution for 1916.

56. D. A. Ellis to Lyon, September 24, 1913, Jacob H. Schiff Correspondence, 1914–1920, AJA, box 443, "Semitic Museum, Harvard University" file.

57. Schiff to Lowell, November 14, 1913, Lowell Papers, HUA, 1909–1914, file 1222: "Museums, Semitic, Dept. of . . . General Correspondence."

58. Lyon to Schiff, November 11, 1913, Lyon Letters, HUA, Special Folders, ca. 1882–1935, "President A. Lawrence Lowell" file, and Lowell to Schiff, November 13, 1913, Lowell Papers, HUA, 1909–1914, file 1222: "Museums, Semitic, Dept. of . . . General Correspondence." Lowell told Lyon, "I should think there would be no great difficulty in getting men here interested in the Semitic Committee if they were not expected to raise or give money." Lyon replied, "I am quite sure that such additions to the Committee would not satisfy Mr. Schiff. He wants men who will show their interest by their gifts or by their power to make others give. Therein lies the difficulty of the situation." See Lyon, "Relations," 59.

59. F. W. Hunnewell to C. F. Adams, October 29, 1902, Lowell Papers, HUA, 1919–1922, file 741: "Jacob H. Schiff."

60. Lyon, "Relations," 23–24. Lyon to Lowell, November 4, 1921, and December 1, 1921, Lowell Papers, HUA, 1919–1922, file 847: "Semitics Dept., Lyon, David G."

61. Lowell to Lyon, December 1, 1921, ibid. Lowell also vetoed Lyon's request to embark on a fund-raising drive on this occasion. On the recent status of the Semitic Museum, see Janet Tassel, "The Semitic Museum Rises Again," *Harvard Magazine* 84 (March/April, 1982), 40–46.

62. David G. Lyon Journals, January 8, 1922, HUA, HUG 1541.10.

63. Wolfson to Nathan Isaacs, December 21, 1924, Letters to Professor Isaacs, AJA, microfilm 674.

64. See Morison, *Three Centuries*, 243.

65. [George Henry Tripp], *Student-Life at Harvard* (Boston: Lockwood, Brooks, and Co., 1876), 324.

66. Ibid., 319.

67. Harry A. Wolfson, "Escaping Judaism," *The Menorah Journal* 7 (August, 1921), 157–58.

68. See Arnold Thackray and Robert Merton, "On Discipline Building: The Paradoxes of George Sarton," *Isis* 63 (December, 1972), 473–95.

69. See especially Horace M. Kallen, *Culture and Democracy in the United States: Studies in the Group Psychology of the American Peoples* (New York: Boni and Liveright, 1924).

70. Many details related here are found in Lewis Feuer, "Recollections of Harry Austryn Wolfson," *American Jewish Archives* 28 (April, 1976), 25–50, and in Leo W. Schwarz, *Wolfson of Harvard: Portrait of a Scholar* (Philadelphia: Jewish Publication Society of America, 1978), chapter 1.

71. Feuer related that during Wolfson's studies at the Elchanan Seminary, the director, cognizant of his academic prowess and social and physical limitations, told him, "Wolfson, you will never be a good rabbi, you don't mix with people. You're a yeshivah bucher" (Feuer, "Recollections," 26). *Yeshivah bucher*, meaning *yeshivah* student, connotes unworldliness among those who devote themselves to traditional Jewish learning.

72. The principal, Schwarz noted, referred Wolfson to a local Harvard alumnus, who informed him that Harvard gave scholarships to students who performed well in the examinations. See Schwarz, *Wolfson of Harvard*, 20.

73. Michael I. Pupin, *From Immigrant to Inventor* (New York: Charles Scribner's Sons, 1929 [1922]), 103–4.

74. For a discussion of stated and unstated entrance requirements at this time, see Wechsler, *The Qualified Student*, especially pt. II.

75. Leo Schwarz related that Wolfson dissuaded his fellow Harvard student Isidor Rabinovitz from a career in Jewish scholarship. He cited Reuben Brainin, a Russian Hebrew and Yiddish author, who had settled in America in 1909 as a disillusioning example of an impoverished Jewish scholar: "[Wolfson] wondered whether he ought not to give up his own studies and try his luck in New York on Grub Street or perhaps to become a doctor. Mostly, he kept hammering away at Rab [Rabinowitz], showing how he could carve a niche for himself in the sciences rather than the humanities, above all in chemistry which, he felt held out undreamed-of possibilities" (Schwarz, *Wolfson of Harvard*, 32). Rabinovitz ultimately became a chemist. The Brainin example is doubly instructive since his

work, like Wolfson's, emphasized Hebrew literature in the context of world literature. See *Encyclopaedia Judaica*, s.v. "Brainin, Reuben."

76. Schiff to Lyon, May 2, 1910, Lyon Letters, HUA, Special Folders, ca. 1882–1935, HUG 1541.5.5. See also Schwarz, *Wolfson of Harvard*, 25. Schiff asked Lyon to dissuade Wolfson from a teaching career in Palestine, stating "right in our midst it is so important that we get good teachers, who will understand and undertake the Americanizing of the enormous numbers of Eastern Jews, whose children, to a very large number, grow up without the religious and sometimes other education adopted to American conditions and surroundings." The next year, Schiff proffered a second fund for Wolfson, this time at the behest of Horace Kallen. See Schiff to Kallen, March 30, 1911, and April 3, 1911, Kallen Papers, AJA, box 27, file 5: "Schiff, Jacob H., 1911–1919."

77. Harry A. Wolfson, "Maimonides and Halevi: A Study in Typical Attitudes Towards Greek Philosophy in the Middle Ages," *Jewish Quarterly Review*, n.s., 2 (1912), 297–339. Lyon did not know that Jewish Theological Seminary president Solomon Schechter read the paper and commented that the author should be encouraged for he "seems a very brilliant man, and might do good work one day." See Schechter to Adler, October 5, 1911, Solomon Schechter Archives, JTS, "Cyrus Adler" file.

78. Wolfson to Lyon, September 20, 1912, Lyon Letters, HUA, Letters ca. 1884–1913, HUG 1541.

79. Harry A. Wolfson, *Crescas' Critique of Aristotle: Problems of Aristotle's Physics in Jewish and Arabic Philosophy* (Cambridge: Harvard University Press, 1971 [1929]), 25–26. Wolfson commented: "Now, this method of text interpretation is sometimes derogatorily referred to as Talmudic quibbling or pilpul. In truth it is nothing but the application of the scientific method to the study of texts" (ibid., 27).

80. Wolfson to Lyon, February 14, 1913, Lyon Letters, HUA, Letters ca. 1884–1913, HUG 1541.

81. Wolfson to Lyon, April 27, 1913, ibid.

82. See Harry A. Wolfson, "Crescas on the Problems of Infinity and Divine Attributes" (Ph.D. diss., Harvard University, 1915). See also Wolfson to Lyon, July 11, 1913, Lyon Letters ca. 1884–1913, HUA, HUG 1541, and Schwarz, *Wolfson of Harvard*, chapter 3.

83. Wolfson to Lyon, April 27, 1913, Lyon Letters, HUA, ca. 1884–1913, HUG 1541.

84. Wolfson to Lyon, July 11, 1913, ibid.

85. For Mack's role, see Harry Barnard, *The Forging of an American Jew: The Life and Times of Judge Julian W. Mack* (New York: Herzl Press, 1974).

86. During this time Wolfson completed his thesis. His supporters included Harvard Law School professor Felix Frankfurter. (See Wolfson to Frankfurter, March 9, 1915, The Papers of Felix Frankfurter, Library of Congress, box 109: "W" miscellany, "Wof-Wol" file).

87. Wolfson to Kallen, February 23, 1915, Kallen Papers, AJA, "Harry Wolfson, 1915–1920, 1948–1972" file.

88. Cyrus Adler, then President of Dropsie College and editor of the *Jewish Quarterly Review*, which published Wolfson's first article, claimed to have been instrumental in arranging Wolfson's appointment: "When Judge Mack, Felix Frankfurter and Judge Lehman interested themselves in Wolfson, it was at their request that I took up the matter with the Harvard authorities through Prof. Moore, and he was good enough to consult Professors Lyons [sic] and Jewett of the Semitic Department and Perry of the Philosophical Department and President Lowell himself. It was as a result of these steps that Wolfson received his appointment at Harvard" (Adler to Jacob Billekopf, September 7, 1920, copy in Menorah Collection, AJA, microfilm 1099. See also Lyon to Lowell, June 19, 1915, Lowell Papers, HUA, 1914–1917, file 528: "Semitic Dept., Budget 1915–16").

89. Lyon to Lowell, June 19, 1915, ibid. The apparent financial dependence of his parents on Wolfson further complicated matters. See Lyon to Lowell, September 2, 1918, Lowell Papers, HUA, 1917–1919, file 92: "Semitics Department: Budget 1918–1919."

90. F. W. Hunnewell to Charles F. Adams, June 21, 1915, Lyon to Lowell, June 22, 1915, and Roger Pierce to C. F. Mason, July 6, 1915, Lowell Papers, HUA, 1914–1917

file 528: "Semitics Dept.: Budget 1915–16"; Lyon to Lehman, June 25, 1915, and Lehman to Lyon, July 1, 1915, Lyon Letters, HUA, Special Folders ca. 1882–1935, HUG 1541.5.5, "Semitic Museum, Harvard University" file; Lowell to Lehman, October 4, 1915, Lowell Papers, HUA, 1914–1917, file 338: "Semitics Museum."

91. Lyon to Lowell, March 31, 1916, Hunnewell to Lyon, August 23, 1916, and Lyon to Hunnewell, August 25, 1916, Lowell Papers, HUA, 1914–1916, file 1032: "Semitic Budget 1916–1917"; Lowell to Lyon, April 1, 1916, and Hunnewell to Lyon, April 3, 1916, ibid., 1914–1917, file 1055: "Semitics Dept.: Chairman."

92. When Horace Kallen assured Wolfson of a three-year term, Wolfson cynically replied: "Your reference to reappointment is news to me. Personally I don't care if not. Suppose I don't get it,—all that I am short of is a yearly income. I think I can always make my living, at least for one day. And what difference is there between a daily uncertainty and an annual uncertainty." When Lyon verified Kallen's report, Wolfson's tone changed radically: "Three years seems almost a lifetime. When I see you next time I'll tell you of some of the things I plan to do within the next three years." See Kallen to Wolfson, January 26, 1918, and Wolfson to Kallen, January 31, 1918 and February 1, 1918, Kallen Papers, AJA, box 32/4, "Harry Wolfson, 1915–1920, 1948–1972" file. See also Kallen to Mack, January 11, 1918, and Mack to Kallen, January 18, 1918, ibid., box 20, file 10.

93. Lyon to Lowell, February 13, 1918, Lowell Papers, HUA, 1917–1919, file 92: "Semitic Department: Budget 1918–1919." Considerable correspondence ensued over technicalities that were resolved in Wolfson's favor, but only after periods of uncertainty. Would Wolfson's friends make up the salary cut Wolfson suffered when drafted into the army in 1918? See Lyon to Lowell, September 2, 1918, ibid.; Hunnewell to Mack, February 25, 1919, Lowell Papers, HUA, 1917–1919, file 647; J. W. Mack to C. F. Adams, December 10, 1919, Adams to Hunnewell, December 11, 1919, and Hunnewell to J. L. Taylor, December 15, 1919, ibid., file 749: "Semitics Department: Budget 1919–1920." Would he share in general salary increases awarded to faculty shortly after the war? See Mack to Adams, February 14, 1920, and Hunnewell to Mack, February 17, 1920, ibid., 1919–1922, file 341: "Semitics Department: Budget 1919–1920"; Hunnewell to Lyon, March 6, 1920, and Lyon to Hunnewell, March 9, 1920, Lowell Papers, HUA, 1919–1922, file 534: "Semitics Department: Budget 1920–1921." Lyon suggested that Harvard avoid asking Wolfson's sponsors for the additional sum because some benefactors actively participated in the university's general endowment drive. He added: "Next spring (1921) when the question of providing for Wolfson comes up again the time may seem opportune to ask these friends if they will not endow the position which Wolfson now holds."

94. Wolfson to Mack, January 18, 1925, JIR Papers, AJA, "Prof. Harry A. Wolfson" file.

95. What was Jacob Schiff's attitude toward Wolfson? Shortly after Schiff's death, Henry Hurwitz sarcastically remarked that he took a "loving personal interest in Wolfson's progress." Schiff's concern with Americanization makes it hard to believe that Wolfson would have been his first choice for a Judaica chair at Harvard. (See Hurwitz to Mack, May 2, 1921, Menorah Collection, AJA, "Julian Mack" file.) Louis Kirsten, a successful Jewish merchant from Boston, allowed "how mean it was of Schiff not to have done it [endow a chair for Wolfson]," and agreed that "American Jews were not doing nearly enough to promote Jewish learning in our universities." Wolfson aside, Schiff's munificence was the exception that proved the rule. See Hurwitz to Wolfson, February 23, 1921, Menorah Collection, AJA, microfilm 2099.

96. Wolfson to Hurwitz, February 20, 1921, ibid.

97. Moore to Hurwitz, May 27, 1920, ibid.

98. Ibid., and Harvard University Press to Hurwitz, July 12, 1920, ibid., microfilm 2103.

99. See Hurwitz to Moore, May 13, 1920, ibid., microfilm 2099; Frank Stein to Hurwitz, June 8, 1920, and Hurwitz to Stein, June 24, 1920; Lyon to Hurwitz June 11,

1920, and Hurwitz to David A. Ellis, August 30, 1920, ibid., microfilm 2103. Cyrus Adler stated that he had Wolfson under contract to prepare a text and translation of *Or Adonai* for the Jewish Classics Series of the Jewish Publication Society. Wolfson did not publish that edition because he desired to publish a definitive volume with the Harvard Press and because Hurwitz virtually promised to secure the necessary funds. See Adler to Billekopf, May 4, 1921, ibid., microfilm 2099. See also Schwarz, *Wolfson of Harvard*, 49–50.

100. Hurwitz to Wolfson, April 11, 1920, and February 23, 1921, and Wolfson to Hurwitz, December 17, 1920, Menorah Collection, AJA, microfilm 2099. Wolfson wrote: "It is written in the grand style, full of oratorical flights, and exhortations and perorations, not without, however, some practical suggestions." Hurwitz replied: "Your 'oration' is fine stuff. It has the double virtue of giving vent to your feelings and of providing us with necessary grapeshot for our cannonading. It is a big battle we have to fight, and give 'em all that's coming to 'em. I promise you we'll make headway, if you will continue to provide ammunition" (Hurwitz to Wolfson, December 21, 1920, ibid.).

101. Harry A. Wolfson, "The Needs of Jewish Scholarship in America," *Menorah Journal* 7 (February, 1921), 28–32. Norman Roth updated Wolfson's essay in "The Needs of Jewish Scholarship in America," *Judaism* 27 (Winter, 1978), 72–79.

102. Wolfson, "Needs of Jewish Scholarship in America," 32–33.

103. Ibid., 34–35.

104. Judah Goldin, "On the Sleuth of Slobodka and the Cortez of Kabbalah," *The American Scholar* 49 (Summer, 1980), 398, 400.

105. "For Corporation Meeting," memorandum by A. L. Lowell, March 29, 1921, Lowell Papers, HUA, 1919–1922, file 823: "Semitics Department: Budget 1921–22." Mack did not state a precise figure but guaranteed a minimum of $2,500. Ordinarily assistant professors received $3,500. Wolfson received $2,200, including $700 from the Corporation, at that time. See Hunnewell to Lyon, January 11 and 28, 1921, and Mack to Lowell, April 7, 1921, ibid.

106. "For Corporation Meeting," memorandum by A. L. Lowell, March 29, 1921, Lowell Papers, HUA, 1919–1922, file 823.

107. Wolfson to Hurwitz, November 8, 1922, Menorah Collection, microfilm 2099.

108. Mack to Hurwitz, April 14 and 18, 1921, May 3, 1921, July 18, 1921, and September 1, 1921; Hurwitz to Mack, April 15, 1921, May 2 and May 3, 1921, and July 13, 1921, ibid., "Julian Mack" file. For a typical solicitation, see Hurwitz to Samuel Strauss, October 10, 1921, Menorah Collection, AJA, microfilm 2103.

109. Many writers have discussed this incident. Detailed accounts that rely on archival material are: Synnott, "A Social History," passim, and idem, *Half-Opened Door*. See also Henry L. Feingold, "Investing in Themselves: The Harvard Case and the Origins of the Third American–Jewish Commercial Elite," *American Jewish History* 77 (June, 1988), 530–53, and Harold S. Wechsler, "The Discriminating Ivy League," *History of Education Quarterly* 22 (Spring, 1982), 103–10.

110. Mack to Lowell, June 6, 1922, Lowell Papers, HUA, 1919–1922, file 1056: "Jews."

111. Mack to Lowell (telegram), June 15, 1922, ibid.

112. See Hurwitz to Wolfson, June 15, 1922, Menorah Collection, AJA, microfilm 2099. Frankfurter wrote Lowell about Wolfson: "Prof. Wolfsohn [sic], whatever his views may be, is a naive, bookish man, without talent or training, which would enable him to share effectively in the direction of such an inquiry as is called for by the Overseers' vote. Doubtless your own estimate of Dr. Wolfsohn [sic] is not very different" (Frankfurter to Lowell, June 29, 1922, Lowell Papers, HUA, 1919–1922, file 1056a: "Jews").

113. Synnott, "A Social History," 402.

114. Meyer, "Centennial History," 137–70.

115. Wolfson to Hurwitz, November 8, 1922, Menorah Collection, AJA, microfilm 2099.

116. Unsigned memorandum to Wise, April 24, 1924, JIR Papers, AJA, box 1511, "Prof. Harry A. Wolfson" file.

117. Wise to Wolfson, February 3, 1925, ibid.

118. Initially apprehensive about his post at the Institute, Wolfson gave Wise hope after completing his first half year: "My teaching at the Institute last year turned out to be one of the most pleasant experiences in my life and I am looking forward to it with the keenest expectation" (Wolfson to Wise, December 7, 1924, ibid.).

119. Hurwitz to Wolfson, May 26, 1921, Menorah Collection, AJA, microfilm 2099. An embarrassing example of how far Hurwitz's reach could exceed his grasp occurred at the 1922 Menorah dinner at Harvard shortly before the debate over Jewish students became public knowledge. Lyon, completing his 40th and final year as a faculty member, was the guest of honor. Hurwitz proposed that Harvard establish a chair of Jewish learning and name it after the retiring professor. Unfortunately, Hurwitz had not secured a check in advance to implement the proposal. Lyon cordially wrote that the proposal "was an inspiration and the suggestion to have the professorship bear my name was more than generous," but he suggested that Harvard call the chair the Menorah professorship (Lyon to Hurwitz, May 2, 1922, ibid.). Wolfson, not a disinterested party, chastised Hurwitz for the empty declaration. "Do you really think that a 'drive' is the proper method of raising funds for the endowment of a chair at Harvard?" he wrote. "Has it ever occurred to you that it would be necessary to consult the University authorities before starting a 'drive' of that kind? In my opinion, you had better drop the subject right now. Don't mention it in public. Don't refer to it in the [Menorah] Bulletin" (Wolfson to Hurwitz, May 6, 1922, and Hurwitz to Wolfson, May 8, 1922, ibid.). Hurwitz did not abandon his campaign, but he proceeded, with Wolfson's concurrence, far more discreetly. See Wolfson to Hurwitz, June 19, 1922, Menorah Collection, AJA, box 61, file 1.

120. Hurwitz to Wolfson, November 9, 1922, ibid.

121. Ibid.

122. Wise to Henry Epstein, January 16, 1923, and Mack to Moore, January 12, 1923, JIR Papers, AJA, box 1511, "Prof. Harry A. Wolfson" file. Wise to "The President and Fellows of Harvard College, April 7, 1923," Lowell Papers, HUA, 1922–1925, file 429, "Semitics Department: Harry A. Wolfson."

123. Mack to Hunnewell, November 26, 1923, ibid. The documents do not state whether, in case of Harvard's abrogation, Wolfson could have returned to Harvard full time or if that action would have consigned him permanently to the Jewish Institute of Religion. See also Hurwitz to Wolfson, January 18 and 22, 1924, Wolfson to Hurwitz, January 20, 1924, Menorah Collection, AJA, microfilm 2099.

124. Unsigned memorandum to Wise, April 24, 1924, and Wolfson to Wise, January 31, 1925, JIR Papers, AJA, box 1511, "Prof. Harry A. Wolfson" file.

125. Wolfson to Wise, December 7, 1924, ibid.; Wise to Gottheil, January 22, 1925, February 9, 1925, JIR Papers, AJA, file 16/18, "Richard Gottheil"; Gottheil to Wise, March 8, 1925, Wise Papers, AJA, box 947, "Correspondence with Richard J. H. Gottheil, 1923–1929" file. "Any new experience," Wolfson continued, "looms up like an adventure which, to be sure, becomes pleasurable, once embarked upon, but looked at in anticipation, is frightening by its novelty." This consideration, he added, made him hesitant to accept an offer to teach for a year at the Hebrew University in Jerusalem, which was about to open. Compare with Wolfson to Wise, October 28, 1924, JIR Papers, AJA, box 1511, "Prof. Harry A. Wolfson" file.

126. Wolfson to Mack, January 16, 1925, ibid.

127. Mack to Wolfson, January 30, 1925, ibid.

128. Wolfson to Wise, January 31, 1925, ibid.

129. Ibid.

130. Wise to George A. Kohut, April 4, 1929, George Kohut–S. S. Wise Correspondence (hereafter Kohut–Wise), AJA, box 2308, "1928–1929" file.

131. Stephen Wise told his wife about another near-miss during his years in Oregon at the turn of the century. Solomon Hirsch, president of Portland's Temple Beth Israel and minister to Turkey under Benjamin Harrison, told him that he could "for the raising of his hand, induce the State Regents, all of whom are his friends, to offer me a professor-

ship of Semitics at the University. [Wise was then a student of Columbia's Richard Gott-heil.] He will not do so and he is right. He says, 'The President, Dr. Strong, and the Regents must come and beg you of their own will to help them in the work.'" Wise never received an invitation. See Justine Wise Polier and James Waterman Wise, eds., *The Personal Letters of Stephen Wise* (Boston: Beacon Press, 1956), 73.

132. Biographical details for Enelow may be found in "Hyman Gerson Enelow—A Biographical Sketch" in Felix A. Levy, ed., *Selected Works of Hyman G. Enelow*, vol. 1: *Memoir and Sermons* (Kingsport, Tenn.: Kingsport Press, 1935); David Philipson, "Hyman Gerson Enelow," *American Jewish Yearbook* 36 (1934–35), 23–53; and the Hyman G. Enelow "Miscellaneous file," AJA. Lucius Littauer subsidized the publication of the four volumes of selected works. Best known for his *A Jewish View of Jesus* (New York: Macmillan, 1920), Enelow also published an edition of Israel Al-Nakawa's *Menorah ha-Ma'or*, 4 vols. (New York: Bloch Publishng, 1929–1932) and an edition of *The Mishnah of Rabbi Eliezer* (New York: Bloch Publishing, 1933). His private library numbered over 20,000 books.

133. Levy, ed., *Selected Works of Hyman G. Enelow*, 1:20.

134. Ibid., 1:19–21.

135. Hyman G. Enelow, "On Chairs of Judaism at American Universities," attached to Enelow to E. N. Williamson, May 12, 1925, Enelow Papers, AJA, General Correspondence 1924–1925, box 573, "E" file; Levy, ed., *Selected Works of Hyman G. Enelow*, 1:20.

136. See Hurwitz to Leo Wormser, March 29, 1924, Menorah Collection, AJA, box 267, "Leo F. Wormser" file.

137. There is material relating to Yale in the Enelow Papers, AJA, 1924–25 correspondence, and the papers of the Babylonian Library, Sterling Memorial Library, Yale University. See especially Enelow to A. T. Clay, October 17, 1924, March 3 and 25, 1925, and Clay to Enelow, October 28, 1924, November 4, 1924; March 20, 1925, and May 5, 1925, Yale Babylonian Collection; and Enelow to Joseph Stroock, October 31, 1924, Enelow Papers, AJA, 1925 correspondence, box 572, "S" file.

138. See for example, Mrs. B. Sessler to Hurwitz, March 16, 1925, Menorah Collection, AJA, microfilm 2099, announcing a publicity campaign.

139. See Feuer, "Recollections," 32.

140. On Littauer, see Burton A. Boxerman, "Lucius Nathan Littauer," *American Jewish Historical Quarterly* 66 (June, 1977), 498–512; Herbert M. Engel, *Shtetl in the Adirondacks: The Story of Gloversville and its Jews* (Fleischmanns, N.Y.: Purple Mountain Press, 1991); Paul Ritterband interview with Harry Starr, January 22, 1970, and *Encyclopaedia Judaica*, s.v. "Littauer, Lucius Nathan."

141. See Boxerman, "Lucius Nathan Littauer," 506–7. Secretary of War Elihu Root found that at least on one account a prima facie case existed, but Attorney General Philander C. Knox concluded that Littauer violated neither the letter nor the spirit of the law and dropped further litigation.

142. Ibid., 508.

143. Moore to Enelow, June 11, 1925, Enelow Papers, AJA, box 573, 1925–1926, General Correspondence, "M" file.

144. Littauer to Lowell, June 25, 1925, Lowell Papers, HUA, 1925–1928, file 43: "Littauer Professorship of Jewish Literature." This file contains routine correspondence concerning the establishment of the chair and the public announcement.

145. Littauer to Lowell, October 2, 1925, ibid.

146. Littauer to Lowell, January 18, 1933, Lowell Papers, HUA, 1930–1933, file 309: "Fellowships: Littauer." Lowell's retirement and Littauer's desire that "this memorandum of these qualifications will at all times be given primary consideration in the selection of future encumbants of this Chair" occasioned this letter.

147. See Leo W. Schwarz's bibliographical essay (in American Academy for Jewish Research, *Harry Austryn Wolfson Jubilee Volume on the Occasion of His Seventy-Fifth Birthday, English Section*, 2 vols. [Jerusalem, AAJR, 1965], 1: 1-38), for a detailed survey of

Wolfson's scholarly career. Wolfson implicitly likened his scholarly mission to the desperate need for the physical restoration of Jewish scholarly works. When in a major library Wolfson once found long rows of bookshelves containing the works of the church writers, "the choicest products of the printer's art of Venice, Basel, Leipzig, Paris and Rome, bound in pigskin and in morocco leather, with gilded backs and bronzed corners," he mentally contrasted that array of treasures with "those shabby tomes which incarnate the spirit of Saadia, Halevi and Maimonides, of those unpublished works of Gersonides, Narboni, and the Shem-tobs, scattered all over the world and rotting in the holds of libraries." A feeling of sadness and sorrow overtook Wolfson, a feeling "which to our forefathers was ever present throughout their exiled life amid the foreign splendor of European cities" (Wolfson, "Needs of Jewish Scholarship," 33).

148. Harry A. Wolfson, *Philo: Foundations of Religious Philosophy in Judaism, Christianity, and Islam*, 2 vols. (Cambridge: Harvard University Press, 1947), 2:459–60.

149. Harry A. Wolfson, *The Philosophy of Spinoza: Unfolding the Latent Processes of His Reasoning*, 2 vols. (Cambridge: Harvard University Press, 1934), and Wolfson, *Philo*. After Littauer subsidized publication of Crescas, Wolfson successfully secured subventions for future books from the General Education Board, the Lucius Littauer Foundation, and other sources.

150. Harry A. Wolfson, *The Philosophy of the Church Fathers*, vol. 1: *Faith, Trinity, Incarnation* (Cambridge: Harvard University Press, 1956). Between Philo and the medieval philosophers, Wolfson wrote, "there lay a long stretch of eight centuries covered by the work of the Church Fathers. It occurred to me to find out whether the philosophy of the Church Fathers could be treated according to the same plan and whether it could be fitted into the same historical framework" ("Reply by Professor Harry A. Wolfson" [to an address by professor George H. Williams on "The Place of Professor Wolfson's Philosophy of the Fathers"], *Harvard Divinity School Bulletin* 21 [1955–1956], 95).

151. Existence on a cultural periphery, Thorstein Veblen argued, gives rise to the skepticism required for intellectual preeminence. See Thorstein Veblen, "The Intellectual Pre-eminence of the Jews in Modern Europe," in Max Lerner, ed., *The Portable Veblen* (New York: Viking Press, 1948), 467–79. Wolfson's marginality may have helped him to identify an intellectual agenda, even if it was not the spur for his intellectual preeminence. In any case, Wolfson's friends perceived that marginality had taken its toll. To Lewis Feuer, for example, he questioned his wisdom in not marrying. Feuer told Horace Kallen, another long-term Wolfson friend, that his many accolades offered him little satisfaction and that illness left him concerned that he might not finish his work. See Feuer to Kallen, August 1, 1973, Kallen Papers, AJA, box 9, file 15: "Feuer, Lewis M., 1953–1975."

152. Publius [pseud.], "Development and Influence of Jewish Jurisprudence," *The Jewish Exponent* (January 19, 1906).

153. See Publius [pseud.], "Locating a Rabbinical Institute," ibid. (January 5, 1906).

154. Richard Gottheil, "Rabbinical Literature," in Hurwitz and Sharfman, eds., *Menorah Movement*, 74.

155. Publius [pseud.], "Development and Influence of Jewish Jurisprudence."

156. Publius [pseud.], "Locating a Rabbinical Institute," passim.

6. From Universalism to Pluralism

1. Nathan Isaacs to Hurwitz, February 6, 1929, Menorah Collection, AJA, box 2722, "1927–1932" file.

2. Enemies even used the movement's findings as weapons against European Judaism and Jewry. See Schorsch, *Jewish Reactions*, passim.

3. Elliot Cohen, undated memorandum, attached to Henry Hurwitz to Nathan Isaacs, May 26, 1926, Menorah Collection, AJA, microfilm 2083. Cohen partially blamed the Reform rabbinate for the field's truncation even in Semitics departments that tran-

scended philology: "Judaism considered—thanks to these reform rabbis—as a religion entirely and to be studied only for its religious implication."

4. As quoted in Isadore Twersky, "Harry Austryn Wolfson, in Appreciation," in Schwarz, *Wolfson of Harvard,* xxv.

5. Israel Friedlander, "The Function of Jewish Learning in America," *Jewish Theological Seminary Association of America Student's Annual, 1914* (New York: Isaac Goldmann, 1914), 124–37, quotations from 137, 128.

6. Abraham I. Katsh, "The Teaching of Hebrew in American Universities," *The Modern Language Journal* 30 (December, 1946), 586. See also idem, *Hebrew in American Higher Education* (New York: New York University Bookstore, 1941); idem, "Modern Hebrew in American Colleges and Universities," *The Modern Language Journal* 35 (January, 1951), 3–6; and idem, "Hebraic Studies in American Higher Education: An Evaluation of Current Trends," *Jewish Social Studies* 21 (January, 1959), 15–21.

7. Cecil Roth, "Jewish History for Our Own Needs," *The Menorah Journal* 14 (May, 1928), 419, 434. Jewish proprietorship over Jewish history, many commentators argued, prevented the subject from falling into alien hands, as occurred in Germany in the late nineteenth and mid-twentieth centuries (see Friedlander, "The Function," 137). For contemporary views on Jewish history, see Harold Jonas, "Writing American Jewish History," *Contemporary Jewish Record* 6 (April, 1943), 144; H. Schmidt, "A Broader Approach to Jewish History," *Commentary* 8 (1949), 588–93, and Bernard D. Weinryb, "American Jewish Historiography: Facts and Problems," *Hebrew Union College Annual* 23 (pt. 2), (1950–1951), 221–44. See also chapters 7 and 8, below.

8. See Charles K. Feinberg, "Jewish Studies in American Universities," *Menorah Journal* 2 (December, 1916), 319–21, and "Intercollegiate Menorah News," ibid., 3 (April, 1917), 115–22 for early student initiatives.

9. See Paula Fass, *The Damned and the Beautiful: American Youth in the 1920s* (New York: Oxford University Press, 1977), esp. chapters 3 and 4, and Joselit, "Without Ghettoism," passim.

10. Yale briefly employed a doctoral candidate, Eugene H. Lehman, who offered a course with this title between 1910 and 1913. See Oren, *Joining the Club,* 116–17.

11. "The questions of Jewish learning," stated an American Academy of Jewish Research manifesto, "is, however, not a matter of effecting [sic] the intellectual life only of the Jew. It is an undisputed fact of history that knowledge always brings the great center of attraction towards which the entire spiritual life of the Jew gravitates. . . . Modern developments of life make it unavoidable that the number of those who can give their time and abilities to Jewish learning is very limited. Not only is the learned 'Balaboos' a thing of the past but also the Rabbi is no longer the Jewish scholar as the Rabbi of old was, whether we regret or are pleased with it." (See American Academy of Jewish Research, undated, copy in Ginzberg Archives, JTS, "Cyrus Adler" file).

12. Mordecai Kaplan Diary, JTS, September 20 and 23, 1928.

13. Feinstein, *American Zionism,* 226. One writer states that at the turn of the century, the Federation of American Zionists "was in the hands of Semitic or Hebrew scholars." See Eisig Silberschlag, "Zionism and Hebraism in America (1897–1921)," in Isidore S. Meyer, ed., *Early History of Zionism in America* (New York: Arno Press, 1977 [1958]), 333.

14. Harvie Branscomb to Abram Sachar, September, 8, 1942, copy in Wise Papers, AJHS, "Abram Sachar" file. The funds were channeled through the local Hillel foundation.

15. Sachar to Wise, March 31, 1942 and Wise to Sachar, April 16, 1942, ibid. Wise further wrote that Gaster was "a man of intellectual distinction who will render fine service as an interpreter of Hebraism and as a medium of better understanding between Christian and Jewish men and scholars" (Wise to Robert L. Flowers, June 5, 1942, JIR Papers, AJA, no. 19 9/4 "Faculty—Candidates for" file). Sachar's position as national Hillel director led him to take an active role in this search. (See Abram Sachar, "B'nai B'rith Hillel Foundations in American Universities," *American Jewish Yearbook* 47

[1945–1946], 141.) For Sachar's influence at the School of Religion at the University of Iowa, see chapter 8.

16. In 1936, Gaster had applied to Wise for a post at the Jewish Institute of Religion, but the institute's financial condition prevented the otherwise impressed Wise from retaining Gaster until 1940, when he offered him a lectureship: "If there were room in an almost too full faculty, I would want him to come to us at the Institute at once" (Gaster to Wise, May 8, 1936, and Wise to Paul Klapper, December 14, 1940 [source of quotation], JIR Papers, AJA, no. 19, 9/3 and 9/4, respectively, "Faculty—Candidates for" file).

17. Gaster to Wise, September 30, 1940, ibid, 9/4. Gaster worked for both the American Jewish Congress and the American Jewish Committee. He obtained a doctorate from Columbia in 1943.

18. Branscomb to Sachar, September 8, 1942, copy in Wise Papers, AJHS, "Abram Sachar" file. Of the same opinion as Branscomb, Sachar wrote Gaster discouragingly and shifted his support to John Tepfer of the Jewish Institute of Religion faculty "because he has such a superb rabbinical background and he is such a thoroughly assimilated American." Wise held fast to Gaster's candidacy, but Gaster suspected treason in that quarter. Gaster's recriminations ended any chance he had of obtaining a full-time Institute post. See Sachar to Gaster, June 25, 1942, and Sachar to Wise, July 10, 1942, Wise Papers, AJHS, "Abram Sachar" file; Gaster to Wise, May 28, 1943, and June 6, 1943, and Wise to Gaster, June 2, 1943, Shalom Spiegel to Wise, February 24, 1943, Wise to Spiegel, July 29, 1943, and Ralph Marcus to Wise, July 6, 1943, JIR Papers, AJA, no. 19, 9/4 "Faculty—Candidates for" file. See also Gaster to Marcus, August 4, 1942, and August 7, 1942, Ralph Marcus Papers (hereafter Marcus Papers), AJA, box 945, "Theodore Gaster" file.

19. See Eli Ginzberg, *Keeper of the Law: Louis Ginzberg* (Philadelphia: Jewish Publication Society of America, 1966), 150–51. Many observers blamed Gottheil for indirectly causing Friedlander's death. Gottheil was said to have informed the British government of Friedlander's German sympathies, thus denying him access to Palestine in 1920. Instead, Friedlander went to Poland on a dangerous relief mission and was killed. See ibid., and Gottheil to Wise, October 5, 1922, JIR Papers, AJA, no. 19, 16/18, "Richard Gottheil" file.

20. Indeed, attempted communal interventions could meet with substantial protest. Judah Magnes, for example, sanctioned a governing board of businessmen for an Institute for Jewish Studies at the new Hebrew University in Jerusalem. The board ratified a program of study drafted by Rabbi Joseph Hertz of London. Louis Ginzberg found the program "amateurish." It stamped "its author or authors as being entirely unfit for work of this kind." The board eventually enlisted the aid of "representative scholars," but Ginzberg complained that Magnes found fault with Hertz's committee, its curriculum, and its questionable nominations for academic appointments "only on account of its making appointments without furnishing 'the cash.' In other words, he accepts the principle that if you pay the piper, you may choose the music." Ginzberg foreshadowed his own deep involvement with Hebrew University when he wrote: "If this principle should prevail at the proposed Jewish University, its doom is decreed before its birth. Only then may we hope to see such an institution develop to a center of Jewish learning if its policy is to be guided by Jewish scholars" (Ginzberg to Cyrus Adler, October 31, 1923, and October 16, 1924, Ginzberg Archives, JTS, "Cyrus Adler–L.G." file). For subsequent developments, see Herbert Parzen, *The Hebrew University: 1925–1935* (New York: KTAV, 1974), and Yaacov Iram, "Vision and Fulfillment: The Evolution of the Hebrew University, 1901–1950," *History of Higher Education Annual* 3 (1983), 123–43.

21. Roth, "Jewish History," 423.

22. *Zechariah* 8:19. See Louis Finkelstein, preface, in Robinson, ed., *Cyrus Adler: Selected Letters,* 1:xxiv.

23. Elliot Cohen, undated memorandum, attached to Henry Hurwitz to Nathan Isaacs, May 26, 1926, Menorah Collection, AJA, microfilm 2083.

24. Hurwitz to Leo Wormser, June 17, 1926, ibid., microfilm 2083. "Laskar is a tough customer," Hurwitz wrote. "He knows what he wants and is accustomed to having things his own way" (Hurwitz to Isaacs, July 2, 1926, ibid.). Individual benefactors and Jewish federations were often frustrated by the small-scale, multiple requests that scholars made for research support. "Our Budget Committee [of the Greater Miami Jewish Federation]," wrote its chairman to Saul Lieberman, President of the American Academy for Jewish Research in 1953, "felt that although the work of the Academy has scholarly recognition it does not merit general community support because of the size of its operations. Therefore, its operations should be combined with those of other organizations whose operations and programs are of wider scope" (Sidney D. Ansen to Lieberman, March 24, 1953, American Academy for Jewish Research Papers [hereafter AAJR Papers], JTS, unfiled). Creation of specific foundations for the support of research, such as the Littauer Foundation, the Memorial Foundation for Jewish Culture, and the National Foundation for Jewish Culture (particularly for dissertation research support) helped to solve this problem.

25. Menorah stalwarts admitted to themselves that the association lacked a philosophically defensible definition of its principles. "A preliminary work of the [Menorah] foundation would be," wrote Elliot Cohen, "to discover and establish its own philosophy. Otherwise, we go off half-cocked and go off to discover something without knowing what we want to discover, or what use we may put it to. Since Menorah is still in embryo, it should be developed in womb of mother and not put out, a five months baby, to shift for itself in the world" (Elliot Cohen, undated memorandum, attached to Henry Hurwitz to Nathan Isaacs, May 26, 1926, Menorah Collection, AJA, microfilm 2083). Hurwitz himself wrote: "I think we shall have to make clear what we mean by Jewish scholarship, or what kind of Jewish scholarship the Menorah is particularly interested in. I wish I were competent to write on it—or at least to feed me" (Hurwitz to Isaacs, February 13, 1929, ibid., box 2722, "1927–1932" file).

26. Ibid. Two members of the Kansas City Jewish community, saying that the local Jewish studies instructor was incompetent, asked Salo Baron to suggest a replacement. Baron could recommend no one and said that more scholars had to be trained. As a result, the visitors eventually endowed two fellowships. Salo Baron interview, New Canaan, Conn., August 30, 1978.

27. Part of Gaster's difficulty resulted from an inability to categorize his work. He believed himself sui generis. "In general," he wrote, "I am moving away from the Oriental field and concentrating more on Comparative Religion, Folklore and Literature. In fact, I am thinking of resigning from the AOS and SBL ['who, for my money, are a bunch of cut-throat mediocrities' and who are 'primitive, obscurationist and boring'], and going into an entirely different world" (Gaster to Marcus, March 29, 1953, Marcus Papers, AJA, box 945, "Theodore Gaster" file). "My approach to the history of Religion," he wrote earlier, "is not the usual *schmoos* [informal discourse] but an approach through study of documents, and . . . no one is doing this for the newly recovered Ancient Near East Material" (Gaster to Marcus, July 4, 1946, ibid.).

28. Gaster to Marcus, August 30, 1952, ibid.: "The encouraging reception which my work received in Europe has led me to think that, despite what the Cyruses [Gordon] and H. L. Ginsbergs and the American Orientalists in general may think (and I am no fool about it), I really may have something to offer and contribute, and this only makes me more mad at the absence of any opportunity to do so." On another occasion, Gaster wrote, "My little book on PASSOVER will be out on April 1. I don't know how the Jews will take it. The Seminary will say it is superficial and the Yeshiva boys that it is *epikourosy* [heretical]. But I don't give a goddam. It wasn't written for them, and I believe that the kind of people I had in mind will like it" (Gaster to Marcus, August 30, 1952, and undated, late 1940s, Marcus Papers, ibid.).

29. Hurwitz to Nathan Isaacs, June 21, 1920, Menorah Collection, AJA, microfilm 2082.

30. Ismar Elbogen devoted one paragraph to university-based research in "American Jewish Scholarship: A Survey in Honor of the Centenary of Kaufmann Kohler," *American Jewish Yearbook* 45 (1944), 47–65; see 52.

31. "Jewish religious objects (like the Sulzberger family shofar) in the Smithsonian, a Judaica collection in the Library of Congress, and the inclusion of ancient Jewish history in graduate Semitics courses of American universities," wrote Naomi W. Cohen, "could do at least as much to validate the presence of Jews in the United States as the filiopietistic studies of Jewish colonists by the American Jewish Historical Society." (See Naomi W. Cohen, Introduction, in Robinson, ed., *Cyrus Adler: Selected Letters,* 1:xxviii.) Adler's mother was a Sulzberger.

32. See eulogistic pieces by George A. Kohut, "The Contributions of Cyrus Adler to American Jewish History," *Publications of the American Jewish Historical Society* 33 (1934), 17–42, and Abraham A. Neumann, *Cyrus Adler: A Biographical Sketch* (New York: American Jewish Committee, 1942). But, see also Ginzberg, *Keeper of the Law,* 135–37; Ira Robinson, "Cyrus Adler and the Jewish Theological Seminary of America: Image and Reality," *American Jewish History* 78 (March, 1989), 363–81; and Jonathan D. Sarna, "Cyrus Adler and the Development of American Jewish Culture: The 'Scholar-Doer' as a Jewish Communal Leader," *American Jewish History* 78 (March, 1989), 382–98. In 1928, Wise, then president of the Jewish Institute of Religion, complained to Max Margolis about the omission of any mention of the Institute in the latter's one-volume history of the Jews. Wise deemed Margolis's reply unsatisfactory and wrote, but did not send the following message: "I exonerate you in the matter of the omission of the name of the Jewish Institute of Religion in your volume of the so-called 'History of the Jewish People.' I have reason to know, for a number of years, that they who serve the Chairman of the Jewish Publication Society or the President of Dropsie College must do his bidding, whether voiced or unvoiced" (Wise to Margolis, undated, unsent, JIR Papers, AJA, no. 19, 26/6, "Max Margolis" file).

33. The Society had two previous, brief incarnations. Isaac Leeser established the first in 1845 and promised to give American Jews "a knowledge of the faith and proper weapons to defend it against the assaults of proselyte-makers on the one side and of infidels on the other." This Jewish Publication Society issued pamphlets that consisted largely of didactic fiction or Biblical popularizations. Leeser's brief *The Jews and Their Religion* was the only American contribution to the series. After five years, the Society ceased its publication program largely due to American indifference. A fire in the area where the Society stored its property sealed its fate. See *Jewish Encyclopedia,* s.v. "American Jewish Publication Society"; Solomon Grayzel, "The First American Jewish Publication Society," *Jewish Book Annual* 3 (5705 = 1944–1945), 42–44; Ephraim Lederer, "The Origin and Growth of the Society," *American Jewish Yearbook, 5674* (1913–1914), 59–61, and Lewis C. Littman, "Stages in the Development of a Jewish Publication Society" (unpublished masters essay, Hebrew Union College-Jewish Institute of Religion, 1967).

A group of Jews, predominantly from New York City, made a second attempt in 1873. This Jewish Publication Society published three volumes of works translated from German practitioners of *Wissenschaft des Judentums,* including Graetz, Hertzberg, Perles, and Zunz. Memory of this three-year failed effort gave the founders of the third, successful movement pause about focusing on scholarship. See *Jewish Encyclopedia,* s.v. "American Jewish Publication Society."

34. Jonathan D. Sarna, *JPS: The Americanization of Jewish Culture, 1888–1988—A Centennial History of the Jewish Publication Society* (Philadelphia: Jewish Publication Society, 1989) surpasses all previous histories of the Society.

35. Max Margolis was the next committee member whose career included a university affiliation. Margolis joined in 1916, a decade after he left the University of California for Hebrew Union College and then Dropsie College. Second generation Jewish scholars participated more frequently. Salo Baron, David S. Blondheim, Isaac Husik, Louis Mann,

Abram Sachar, and Harry Wolfson accepted publication committee seats before World War II. Husik was editor, a part-time position, between 1924 and 1939.

36. Henrietta Szold compiled the index. On the absence of apparatus, see Elbogen, "American Jewish Scholarship," 53, and Solomon Grayzel, "Graetz's *History* in America," *Historia Judaica* 3 (October, 1941), 63–64. Grayzel, who succeeded Husik as JPS editor, attributes omission of the footnotes to financial exigency.

37. Lederer, "The Origin," 68.

38. Max Margolis's Bible-related publications, Isaac Husik's *A History of Medieval Jewish Philosophy* (New York: Macmillan, 1916), Husik's edition of Joseph Albo's *Sefer ha'ikkarim* [*The Book of Principles*] (Philadelphia: Jewish Publication Society of America, 1929–1930), and volumes in the Schiff Classics series are some exceptions to this generalization.

39. Joshua Bloch, *Of Making Many Books: An Annotated List of the Books Issued by the Jewish Publication Society of America, 1890–1952* (Philadelphia: Jewish Publication Society of America, 1952), 32. See also Charles A. Madison, *Jewish Publishing in America: The Impact of Jewish Writing on American Culture* (New York: Sanhedrin Press, 1976), chapter 2, and articles published in the *American Jewish Yearbook* (a Society publication conceived by Cyrus Adler) for 5674 (1913–1914), 19–187.

40. See Adler to Schiff, September 26, 1916, and Adler to Warburg, February 8, 1929, in Robinson, ed., *Cyrus Adler: Selected Letters,* 1:322, 2:165.

41. Kohut, "Contributions," 25.

42. "With the fullest sympathy for the general dissemination of knowledge, and an entire understanding of the responsibility which any body of scholars has towards the public," wrote Cyrus Adler, "this Society at the outset did not endeavor to become a popular organization. It was conceived to be our function to learn the truth and to state it, whether it were entertaining or not. . . . We have left it to our sister society, the Jewish Publication Society of America, to disseminate knowledge" (Cyrus Adler, "Address of the President," *Publications of the American Jewish Historical Society* 9 [1901], 3–4). The Jewish Publication Society would popularize existing knowledge concerning Jews and Judaism, Adler had earlier written, but American Jewish Historical Society members would issue "dry-as-dust-material" primarily for the benefit of their colleagues. Quoted in John J. Appel, "Hansen's Third-Generation 'Law' and the Origins of the American Jewish Historical Society," *Jewish Social Studies* 23 (January, 1961), 3–20, quotation from 14.

43. Cyrus Adler, "Address of Dr. Cyrus Adler, President of the American Jewish Historical Society," *Publications of the American Jewish Historical Society* 17 (1909), 5.

44. "Objects," *Publications of the American Jewish Historical Society* 1 (1893), iii. Italics ours.

45. Oscar S. Straus, "Address of the President," *Publications of the American Jewish Historical Society* 1 (1893), 3.

46. Adler, "Address of Dr. Cyrus Adler," 2.

47. John J. Appel attributes the society's very establishment to German-Jewish status anxieties rather than to filiopietism or other motives. See Appel, "Hansen's Third-Generation 'Law'," passim.

48. As quoted in Isidore S. Meyer, "The American Jewish Historical Society," *The Journal of Jewish Bibliography* 4 (January–April, 1943), 9.

49. Straus, "Address of the President," 1.

50. See the extensive correspondence concerning the American Jewish Historical Society between Adler and Gottheil in the Cyrus Adler Papers (hereafter Adler Papers), JTS.

51. "In the busy life that Professor Jastrow led, as professor at the University of Pennsylvania, as the librarian of that university, as lecturer, writer, and as *homme du monde*," apologized Richard Gottheil, "it is natural that his contributions to the *Publications* of our Society cannot have been many" (Richard J. H. Gottheil, "Morris Jastrow, Jr.," *Publications of the American Jewish Historical Society* 29 [1925], 170–73, quotation from 172).

52. Abram Isaacs, "America's Discovery," *The Jewish Messenger* 60 (November 12, 1886), 4. Despite his New York University connection, Isaacs viewed the writing of this

history as a sectarian venture: "It is fortunate that there are several rabbinical organizations to take the subject in hand and their effective co-operation would lead to happy results." Meyer's essay on the Society describes its prehistory (6–10).

53. Appel recounted that Kaufmann Kohler left the meeting exclaiming that "if the 'Jewish laymen connected with this society,' wished to 'put down Jewish ministers,' the rabbis would have 'nothing to do with the society,' would 'cry them down' from their pulpits, and pay no further attention to 'their scribbling.' " Marcus Jastrow, perhaps recalling the slight at the Jewish Publication Society's meeting, commented that Jews had been accustomed to " 'look on their pastors as good for many affairs' but wished to exclude them from all 'public matters'" (quoted in Appel, "Hansen's Third-Generation 'Law'," 13; Lederer, "The Origin," 64, and *New York Times* (June 7, 1892), 2.

54. The Society changed its objective to read: "The object of this Society is to collect and publish material bearing upon the history of America, and to promote the study of Jewish history in general, preferably so far as the same is related to American Jewish history, or connected with the causes of emigration from various parts of the world to this continent." Adler succeeded in recruiting Alexander Marx, Jewish Theological Seminary librarian and professor of history, to Society membership after the change in objectives. See Adler to Schechter, December 21, 1908, in Robinson, ed., *Cyrus Adler: Selected Letters,* 1:150.

55. But see Henrietta Szold "How the Publication Committee Does Its Work," *American Jewish Yearbook* 5674 (1913–1914), 85.

56. Joseph Jacobs, rev. ed., *Jewish Encyclopedia,* 137; Adler to Gottheil, December 3, 1899, Adler Papers, JTS, "Letters: Cyrus Adler to Richard Gottheil" file.

57. He served in the press bureau of the French Foreign Service.

58. Ginzberg, *Keeper of the Law,* 66.

59. Adler to Gottheil, January 15, 1899, January 24, 1899, and March 8, 1899, Adler Papers, JTS, "Letters: Cyrus Adler to Richard Gottheil" file. But, Adler added, Singer was "lacking judgment and employing the persistent methods which most people employ when they have a pet project to put through."

60. Adler to Gottheil, February, 1899 and March 16, 1899, ibid., Israel Zangwill, the British author, declined to undertake several historical and literary articles because he lacked scholarly training. See Zangwill to Gottheil, May 30, 1900, Gottheil Papers, AJA, 1898–1919, "Zangwill–Gottheil" file.

61. On the encyclopedia, see Nancy L. Barth "History of the Publication of the Jewish Encyclopedia" (unpublished masters thesis, University of Chicago, 1969); Shimeon Brisman, *A History and Guide to Judaic Encyclopedias and Lexicons* (Hoboken: Hebrew Union College–KTAV, 1987); Joseph Jacobs, *The Jewish Encyclopedia; The Launching of a Great Work: The Jewish Encyclopedia–Publisher's Announcement Upon the Completion of the First Volume* (New York: Funk and Wagnalls, 1901), Madison, *Jewish Publishing,* 57–58, and Shuly Rubin Schwartz, *The Emergence of Jewish Scholarship in America: The Publication of the Jewish Encyclopedia* (Cincinnati: Hebrew Union College Press, 1991).

62. Barth, "History of the Publication," 10, 39.

63. See Blank, "Bible," and Meyer, "Centennial History," 288–91, 43–44.

64. Adler to Gottheil, March 16, 1899, Adler Papers, JTS, "Letters: Cyrus Adler to Richard Gottheil" file.

65. Adler to Gottheil, March 27, 1899, ibid.

66. Preface, *Jewish Encyclopedia,* 1:xii. The editors of the *Encyclopaedia Judaica* (1972) took a different tack. Desiring to please all readers, the editors included the traditional and the critical viewpoints, but not necessarily in the same article. "Inevitably," the editors wrote, "an individual entry may sometimes appear weighted in one direction or another, but a thorough reading of the entire Bible section will reveal the overall effort to present every aspect" (Introduction, *Encyclopaedia Judaica,* 1:9).

67. Kaufmann Kohler, "Emil G. Hirsch" in *Studies, Addresses and Personal Papers* (New York: Alumni Association of the Hebrew Union College, 1931), 550. Recall that Kohler and Hirsch were brothers-in-law.

68. See Jacobs, *Jewish Encyclopedia,* 4–8.

69. Henry Preserved Smith, "The Jewish Encyclopedia," *The American Journal of Theology* 11 (October, 1907), 655.

70. Ibid., 653.

71. The following account draws heavily upon Sarna, *JPS,* 95–116.

72. See Matitiahu Tsevat, "A Retrospective View of Isaac Leeser's Biblical Work," in American Jewish Archives, *Essays in American Jewish History, to Commemorate the Tenth Anniversary of the Founding of the American Jewish Archives Under the Direction of Jacob Rader Marcus* (Cincinnati: Hebrew Union College Press, 1958), 295–313.

73. Leeser had similarly relied upon medieval Hebrew exegetes and upon German scholarship. See Bernard J. Bamberger, "American Jewish Translations of the Bible," *Jewish Book Annual* 15 (5718 = 1957–1958), 33–40, esp. 33–35, and Max L. Margolis, *The Story of Bible Translations* (Philadelphia: Jewish Publication Society of America, 1917), 94.

74. Cyrus Adler, "The Bible Translation," *The American Jewish Yearbook* (5674 = 1913–1914), 105, 113.

75. Only Margolis, Rosenau, and Voorsanger among the Semitists completed their assignments.

76. [Max L. Margolis, ed.], *The Holy Scriptures According to the Masoretic Text* (Philadelphia: Jewish Publication Society of America, 1955 [1917]), v. See also Max L. Margolis, *The Hebrew Scriptures in the Making* (Philadelphia: Jewish Publication Society of America, 1922).

77. Adler to Sulzberger, October 18, 1909, in Robinson, ed., *Cyrus Adler: Selected Letters,* 1:172.

78. Schechter and Joseph Jacobs of the Jewish Theological Seminary, Philipson and Kohler from Hebrew Union College, and Adler and Margolis from Dropsie. New York Rabbi Samuel Schulman, president of the Central Conference of American Rabbis, rounded out the membership. Adler appointed Margolis to the Dropsie College faculty in 1909. Scholars were in the majority on this board and in the prior effort at reorganization (1905) headed by Solomon Schecter.

79. The incident is recounted in Meyer, "Centennial History." Adler confronted a similar situation in 1922 when members of New York City's Orthodox Jewish community demanded that Jewish Theological Seminary dismiss Mordecai Kaplan, whose views they found heretical. Adler refused the demand, though he disagreed with Kaplan's outlook. See Finkelstein, preface, in Robinson, ed., *Cyrus Adler: Selected Letters,* 1:22.

80. Adler, *I Have Considered,* 287–91, and Philipson, *My Life as an American Jew,* 197.

81. Solomon Schechter, "The Bible," *The American Jewish Yearbook* (5674 = 1913–1914), 173; [Max Margolis], "The New English Translation of the Bible," ibid. (5678 = 1917–1918), 161–93; Harry M. Orlinsky, *Essays in Biblical Culture and Bible Translation* (New York: KTAV, 1974); and idem, "Jewish Biblical Scholarship in America," *The Jewish Quarterly Review* 45 (April, 1955), 397–98.

82. See Greenspoon, *Max Leopold Margolis,* passim; Madison, *Jewish Publishing,* 33–35; Alexander Marx, "Max Leopold Margolis," in *Essays in Jewish Biography* (Philadelphia: Jewish Publication Society in America, 1947), 271–72; and F. Zimmerman, "The Contributions of M. L. Margolis to the Fields of Bible and Rabbinics," in Dropsie College, *Max Leopold Margolis,* 17–26. "No translation in the English tongue . . . can be anything but a revision, a revision of the English Bible of 1611," wrote Margolis. "All attempts at modernizing the Bible English must necessarily fail. Once and for all time the revisers of 1611 fixed the model for all future undertakings" (Margolis, *The Story,* 104–5).

83. Samuel Straus, "The Diffusion of the Bible," *American Jewish Yearbook* (5678 = 1917–1918), 523.

84. Society head Mayer Sulzberger repudiated the agreement Charles A. Gross had negotiated to purchase the preprinted sheets of the British edition. He purchased instead only the North American rights. See Sarna, *JPS,* 35.

85. Benisch and Friedlander had produced Bibles in nineteenth-century England.

86. Adler to Sulzberger, October 18, 1909, in Robinson, ed., *Cyrus Adler: Selected Letters,* 1:171–73.

87. Solomon Zeitlin, "Seventy-Five Years of the *Jewish Quarterly Review*," in Abraham A. Neuman and Solomon Zeitlin, eds., *The Seventy-Fifth Anniversary Volume of the Jewish Quarterly Review* (Philadelphia: Jewish Quarterly Review, 1967), 62–63.

88. Ira Robinson, "Bernard Revel, Cyrus Adler and American Jewish Scholarship," *American Jewish History* 69 (September, 1979), 497–505.

89. American Academy for Jewish Research, September, 1919 meeting, copy in Ginzberg Archives, JTS, "American Academy for Jewish Research" file.

90. A sense that the world had changed, at least in its receptivity to assimilated Jews, may also have influenced his choice.

91. American Academy for Jewish Research, September, 1919 meeting, copy in Ginzberg Archives, JTS, "American Academy for Jewish Research" file.

92. "The Jew, to whom the Scriptures were given, who treasured the sacred writings in the synagogues of dispersion, in whose memory the meaning of the original largely, if not wholly, persisted, who, though at times he swerved into far-off fields of mental activity, was again and again recalled to the Book, may be trusted to have a truer and more adequate knowledge of it," wrote Adler's colleague, Max Margolis. See Margolis, *The Story,* 105.

93. *The Jewish Progress* (November 3, 1893), 4, (December 15, 1894), 4 (source of Hirsch statement), and (May 4, 1894) 4 (source of quotation).

94. Bertram Wallace Korn, *Eventful Years and Experiences: Studies in Nineteenth Century American Jewish History* (Cincinnati: American Jewish Archives, 1954), 181.

95. Jeffery, "Semitic Languages," 187.

96. Jacob Schiff, an Emanu-El congregant, sat on the Seminary's board. Schiff contributed heavily to Columbia and Barnard during the 1890s but reserved his Semitics gifts for Harvard, perhaps because he and Richard Gottheil disliked each other and disagreed over Zionism. Columbia's repeated refusal to appoint a Jewish trustee led him to discontinue these gifts. This refusal may also have intensified his support for the Seminary as a more secure vehicle for Jewish learning. See Wechsler, *The Qualified Student,* 136–40.

97. Meir Ben-Horin, "Scholars' 'Opinions': Documents in the History of Dropsie University," in *Salo Wittmayer Baron Jubilee Volume on the Occasion of His Eightieth Birthday, English Section* (Jerusalem: American Academy for Jewish Research, 1974), 1:195–96, and Herbert Parzen, "New Data on the Formation of Dropsie College," *Jewish Social Studies* 28 (1966), 131–47. Dropsie is located near Temple University, which at the time was not a major research institution.

98. "One of the offices of a rabbinical institution," wrote Jewish Institute of Religion founder Stephen S. Wise, "is to help men to pursue the richly rewarding career of learning and research in *Juedische Wissenschaft*" (Stephen S. Wise, *Challenging Years* [New York: G. P. Putnam's Sons, 1848], 133). The elevation of seminary entrance requirements to include a baccalaureate degree from a four-year college, reflecting a trend among American professional schools during the early twentieth century, made a disengagement of seminary from university feasible. By certifying liberal education, the degree requirement freed the seminaries from the need to adjust their curricula to a neighboring university or to offer secular studies.

99. On the history of these institutions, see Morris Jacob Loren, "Hebrew Higher Educational Institutions in the United States" (Ph.D. diss., Wayne State University, 1976), and Jacob Mann, "Modern Rabbinical Seminaries," *Yearbook of the Central Conference of American Rabbis* 35 (1925), 295–310. On the Jewish Institute of Religion, see Hyman J. Fligel, "The Creation of the Jewish Institute of Religion," *American Jewish Historical Quarterly* 58 (December, 1968), 260–70.

100. Schechter to William Rosenau, March 16, 1903, William Rosenau Papers, AJA, no. 41, 2/2, "S. General."

101. Elliot Cohen, undated memorandum, attached to Henry Hurwitz to Nathan Isaacs, May 26, 1926, Menorah Collection, AJA, microfilm 2083.

102. Mann to George A. Kohut, August 14, 1930, Ginzberg Archives, JTS, "Mann–L. G." file.

103. A productive faculty would have avoided contention with the editor, said Mann. But instead Mann's Hebrew Union colleagues resorted to "the usual strategies of vilification and attack" to neutralize his editorial demands. Mann to Hyman Enelow, March 18, 1927, Enelow Papers, AJA, box 15, file 13: "Mann, Jacob, 1922–1932."

104. Roth to Israel Davidson, February 15, 1928, Israel Davidson Archives (hereafter Davidson Archives), JTS, "Cecil Roth" file. Some accused the *Menorah Journal* of going to the opposite extreme. Nathan Isaacs, long identified with Menorah, took Henry Hurwitz to task for selecting antagonists as reviewers. "I suspect that you get a certain intellectual pleasure in seeing what a Carver will say about a book on Jewish self-identification. It's fun. But is it fair? And isn't the fun dulled by the monotony of the scheme? And can you continue to say, 'Utter honesty in the reviewer is taken for granted'?" (Isaacs to Hurwitz, February 26, 1929, Menorah Collection, AJA, "Nathan Isaacs" file). Similarly, Alexander Marx criticized Hurwitz's choice of anthropologist Paul Radin as a reviewer of Louis Ginzberg's *Legends of the Jews,* stating that Radin blamed Ginzberg for thwarting his participation in an expedition to Abyssinia. See Marx to Hurwitz, March 25, 1926, ibid., microfilm 2083.

105. Mordecai Kaplan Diary, JTS, September 20 and 23, 1928. Isadore Twersky, Wolfson's successor at Harvard, attributed his predecessor's stance to the subject's propaedeutic and screening functions: "He was uncomfortable with academic upstarts and 'nouveaux riches' who lacked such Jewish education and pretended to be authorities in Judaica" (Twersky, "Harry Austryn Wolfson, In Appreciation," xxiii).

106. Moore to Alexander Marx, July 23, 1922, Alexander Marx Archives (hereafter Marx Archives), JTS, "George F. Moore" file.

107. Jeffery to Ralph Marcus, July 30, 1942, Marcus Papers, AJA, "Arthur Jeffery" file.

108. Few if any Jews won Rhodes scholarships at that time. The Columbia nominating committee rejected Marcus's application, it stated, because of insufficient qualifications in the areas of "physical rigor and extra curricular activities of an athletic nature." (See Hawkes to Marcus, October 27, 1921, Marcus Papers, AJA, "Columbia University" file, and Frank Aydelotte, *The American Rhodes Scholarships: A Review of the First Forty Years* [Princeton: Princeton University Press, 1946], chapter 2). On journalism, see Carl Van Doren to Marcus, July 14, 1922, Marcus Papers, AJA, box 945, "Various Magazines and Publications" file, and John Hayes Holmes to Marcus, May 1, 1923, ibid., "Miscellaneous" file. "You say that you are not going to be a Rabbi," Holmes wrote, "—that is rather a pity for you have convictions and you are not afraid to stand up and speak them out, and this means qualities which are greatly needed in the ministers both of Jewish and Christian churches."

109. Moore to Marcus, May 12, 1925, Marcus Papers, AJA, box 945, "George F. Moore" file. Moore wrote, "The investigation would then widen out into a search for other indications of acquaintance with Hellenistic philosophy and would lead you to go over the discussion of the question by [David] Neumark [of Hebrew Union College]. It would be most to your profit, after a general survey of the material, to plan out your own method and follow it. You would doubtless find that a more detailed study of the evidence would require a modification of the original plan—that is the way all scientific investigation is conducted."

110. "Much as I want you to come," wrote Wise, "I feel that, if you desire merely to give some course in the Hellenistic field, it will not be possible to have you with us. As a younger man, I feel you ought to be ready to do teaching in the fields in which your teaching is most immediately necessary, reserving a goodly part of your time for your particular field, and giving some courses in that field until, in time, it may be possible to establish a Department in that field" (Wise to Marcus, February 1, 1927, Marcus Papers, AJA, box 945, "JIR–Wise" file).

111. Gottheil even wrote Wise on behalf of Marcus's financial situation. See Gottheil to Wise, November 7, 1931, and Wise to Gottheil, November 13, 1931, JIR Papers, AJA, box 26, file 4: "Ralph Marcus, 1939–1948."

112. The immediate cause of the breach was the "Braunstein affair." Baruch Braunstein came to Columbia from the Jewish Institute of Religion, where he was completing his rabbinical studies, as an adviser to Jewish students. "It has been no easy matter to openly and avowedly espouse Judaism on a campus like that of Columbia, where most Jewish students have not been significantly motivated in their early youth by the nobility of the Jewish faith and tradition," he wrote (Braunstein to Wise, February 25, 1931, JIR Papers, AJA, no. 19, 5/8, "Columbia University" file. See also his article "Religion at Columbia University," *Religious Education* 25 [September, 1930], 669–73). Gottheil, "the one man at Columbia most interested in spiritual and social work among Jewish students of the University," took an immediate professional and personal interest. (See Wise to W. E. Weld, January 23, 1929, JIR Papers, AJA, no. 19, 5/8, "Columbia University" file.) Braunstein reciprocated—he later wrote a laudatory piece, "Professor Gottheil at Seventy," copy in "Richard Gottheil Scrapbook," Zionist Archives, New York City—and enrolled for graduate work in the Columbia Semitics department. At his defense, Gottheil and Marcus disagreed over the quality of the dissertation, and Gottheil passed it over Marcus's protest. Gottheil then informed Marcus that, because of adverse economic conditions, Columbia would not require his services "next year or thereafter." "I am fairly certain it's more his dislike of me as a result of the Braunstein thesis affair than economy," Marcus wrote Wise. "Well, if I had it to do over again I would. But isn't it a shame that people like that should be allowed to occupy responsible positions?" (Marcus to Wise, October 17, 1933, JIR Papers, AJA, box 26, file 4: "Ralph Marcus, 1930–1948." See also Marcus to Wise, June 9, 1936, ibid.). Gottheil relented and kept Marcus on the payroll, but their relations remained cool until Gottheil's death in 1936. See Wise to Gottheil, November 13, 1931, ibid.

113. Marcus to Wise, November 19, 1936, and Wise to Marcus, June 2, 1936, ibid. But, he added, that was the only reason; "I've seen too many academic awards and high positions go to mediocrities to have any illusions about the necessary connexion between academic position and scholarly or pedagogical distinction" (Marcus to Wise, June 3, 1936, November 19, 1936, ibid.). Compare Max Weber's dictum that only those who "can stand seeing mediocrity, year after year, climb beyond you, without becoming embittered and without coming to grief" should aspire to habilitation. See Weber, "Science as a Vocation," 134.

114. Wise to Marcus, November 20, 1936, Marcus Papers, AJA, "Jewish Institute of Religion" file; Marcus to Wise, April 21, 1937, May 18, 1937, JIR Papers, AJA, box 26, file 4: "Ralph Marcus, 1930–1948." In a letter not sent but dated June 5, 1936 (ibid.), Wise actually offered Marcus a professorship ("not of Bible, even though you teach it, but of Semitic Languages. After all, Hellenistics and Semitics are your forte; so you ought really to have the title of Professor of Hellenistic Literature or Professor of Semitic Languages. Name your choice"). But he offered no concomitant salary increase. Wise probably thought better of such action since it would leave him open to the charge of unreasonableness and double standards. "From what certain interested friends have said I gather that you have no objection to promoting me to a full Professorship," Marcus wrote Wise. "If that is true, the question remains whether the Institute budget can afford a corresponding increase in salary" (Marcus to Wise, May 18, 1937, ibid.). It couldn't and Marcus did not get his promotion.

115. McKeon to Marcus, November 21, 1936, and May 22, 1943, Marcus Papers, AJA, box 945, "Correspondence–University of Chicago" file. McKeon also asked his former colleagues to regularize Marcus's position at Columbia. On McKeon, see George Kimball Ploughman, *Richard McKeon: A Study* (Chicago: University of Chicago Press, 1990).

116. Marcus to Walter Yost, September 16, 1946, Marcus Papers, AJA, box 945, "Correspondence—University of Chicago" file.

117. Some University of Chicago faculty members questioned the worth of Marcus's forte, his textual editing of Philo and Josephus, an acceptable *form* of scholarship within the seminary. "When I came to the University," he wrote, "I had committed myself to producing a volume of Philo and two volumes of Josephus for the Loeb Library. These particular three volumes might reasonably be expected to take nine years to finish. But apparently, this kind of scholarship is not regarded by my administrative heads as of the first importance. I disagree, but even if I agreed, I should feel myself bound to continue the work." Marcus argued that internal critics could not judge his specialized work: "My work is done in three departments and three fields. There is hardly anyone in these three departments who has the particular competence necessary for a fair appraisal of the quality of my work under these peculiar circumstances." External critics, he added, praised his scholarship (Marcus to Hutchins, July 29, 1947, Marcus Papers, AJA, box 945, "Correspondence—Carbon Copies" file). This issue had financial implications, for Marcus felt economic discomfort during his Chicago tenure. See Marcus to Bernard Loomer, October 6, 1951, ibid.

118. "The American Academy of Jewish Research," undated memorandum, Ginzberg Archives, JTS, "Cyrus Adler" file.

119. "Dr. Philipson's Plea for National Interest," *Jewish Exponent* (May 26, 1905), 10.

120. A nasty schism between early twentieth-century Hebraists and Yiddishists affected the Alexander Kohut Publication Fund, which subsidized the publication of Jewish scholarship. The publication committee received a request for support for Alfred Landau's Yiddish dictionary, a work that Ismar Elbogen called "epoch-making." George A. Kohut, Alexander's son and the fund's administrator, admitted to "a violent prejudice against Yiddish," but he attempted to retain an air of neutrality within the committee. Alexander Marx counselled Kohut that his "personal prejudice ought not to be overruled by the Committee, however good the book may be. There is no reason why your Foundation should sponsor a publication which will not give you real satisfaction." (See Kohut to Marx, October 31, 1928, and Marx to Kohut, November 7, 1928, Marx Papers, JTS, "G. A. Kohut, 1928" file.)

121. Hirsch to Bernhard Felsenthal, October 11, 1898, Felsenthal Papers, AJA, "Emil Hirsch" file; Feinstein, *American Zionism 1894–1904,* 177–81.

122. See David E. Hirsch, *Emil G. Hirsch,* chapter 5.

123. Abram Isaacs, "The Jews of the United States," *American Jewish Yearbook* 1 (1899–1900), 14–19, quotation from 17.

124. As quoted in Fein, *The Making,* 198–99.

125. Morris Jastrow, Jr., *Zionism and the Future of Palestine: The Fallacies and Dangers of Political Zionism* (New York: Macmillan, 1919), 151–59. Jastrow's pre-war pro-German attitude similarly stood in sharp contrast to Gottheil's support of the Triple Alliance. Though he came to abhor "Germany's shameful conduct of the war—so bitterly disappointing to those who, like myself, felt deeply attached to the country, and still feel an intellectual bond," that very opposition may have *increased* his opposition to Zionism. "The trying position in which hundreds of thousands of loyal American citizens were placed," he wrote, "because in days of peace and in an unsuspecting manner they permitted their feelings for Germany, due to sentimental or personal attachment, unbound sway, should serve as a warning now that peace has come again, to avoid a repetition of such a condition" (Jastrow to Gottheil, January 12, 1915, March 24, 1915, and December 15, 1917, Gottheil Papers, Correspondence 1898–1919, AJA, "M. Jastrow to R. Gottheil" file [quotation from December 15, 1917 letter], and Jastrow, *Zionism,* 121).

126. Jeffery to Marcus, July 30, 1942, Marcus Papers, AJA, box 945, "Arthur Jeffery" file. Could anti-Zionist Semitists routinely be deemed anti-Semitic? Most agreed that the answer, at least in Hitti's case, was no. The Jewish organizers of a proposed Richard Gottheil *festschrift* had seriously considered Hitti as an editor, and several years later, when the precise question was raised, Ralph Marcus stated that he was "not so sure that Hitti is

anti-Jewish at least not openly. He mentions the cultural contributions of the Jews favorably in his new History of the Arabs, and he maintains perfectly correct relations with Jewish scholars. He has always been courteous to [Abraham] Halkin and me, and always spoke respectfully to his teacher Gottheil" (Marcus to Wise, January 31, 1938, JIR Papers, AJA, box 26, file 4: "Ralph Marcus, 1930–1948"). Similarly, when Richard Gottheil opposed the election of Yale's A. T. Clay as president of the American Institute of Archaeology in 1921 on the grounds of anti-Semitism, Cyrus Adler told Louis Ginzberg that he had known Clay "a good many years and do not consider him an anti-Semite. He is an anti-Zionist" (Adler to Ginzberg, December 4, 1921, Adler Papers, JTS, "Louis Ginzberg" file).

127. Gottheil to Ginzberg, March 22, 1924, and September 30, 1925; Ginzberg to Gottheil, October 6, 1925, Ginzberg Archives, JTS, "Gottheil, Richard–L. G." file.

128. "Book Review," undated, Menorah Collection, AJA, microfilm, 2083.

129. Isaacs to Gottheil, undated, attached to Isaacs to Hurwitz, March 16, 1926, ibid.

130. Gottheil to Isaacs, March 22, 1926, attached to Isaacs to Hurwitz, undated (received March ?, 1926), ibid. This story reveals more than a university–seminary fissure, for Richard Gottheil himself was caught between compassion for the press employee and accepted academic norms.

131. Gottheil to Isaacs, March 27, 1926, attached to Isaacs to Hurwitz, undated (received March ?, 1926), ibid.

132. Hurwitz to Isaacs, March (?), 1926, ibid.

133. Handwritten note, unsigned, undated, ibid. Hurwitz told Isaacs: "The question then is (I put it bluntly): may it not conceivably be murmured that we connive in the monstrosity if we are silent. I don't know—but it remains that this stuff is being spread abroad without protest from Jewish scholars or Jewish critical writers (unless someone else should have it)" (Hurwitz to Isaacs, April 9, 1926, ibid.).

134. Isaacs to Hurwitz, February 6, 1929, Menorah Collection, AJA, box 2722, "1927–1932" file. For a vivid fictional account of this transition, see Chaim Potok, *The Chosen* (New York: Simon and Schuster, 1967).

135. Isaacs to Gottheil, April 23, 1926, Menorah Collection, AJA, box 2722, "1927–1932" file.

136. Samuel C. Heilman's *The People of the Book: Drama, Fellowship, and Religion* (Chicago: University of Chicago Press, 1983) is instructive on the norms associated with Talmudic scholarship in traditional settings. (See esp. 15–16.)

137. David S. Blondheim, about whom more in the next chapter, was the major prewar Jewish exception.

138. Hurwitz wrote to congratulate Nathan Isaacs for declining the chair of the academic department of Yeshiva College, an honorific position that would not have interfered with his Harvard duties. See Isaacs to Hurwitz, June 24, 1926, and Hurwitz to Isaacs, July 2, 1926, Menorah Collection, AJA, "Nathan Isaacs" file.

139. Christopher Jencks and David Riesman, *The Academic Revolution* (Garden City, N.Y.: Doubleday, 1968). See also David Kornfield, "Socialization for Professional Competency of Protestant Seminarians in Latin America" (Ph.D. diss., University of Chicago, 1980).

7. "The Most Available and Suitable Man"

1. Butler to Julian Mack, December 21, 1929, CUF, "N" file.

2. On Menorah, see Joselit, "Without Ghettoism," 133–54. On B'nai B'rith, see "Plan Chairs of Hebrew," *New York Times* (January 21, 1927), 17:1.

3. See the protest against his dismissal offered by several key members of the Jewish Theological Seminary faculty in the Marx Papers, JTS, "Hyman Enelow" file.

4. See Ruth S. Hurwitz, "Linda R. Miller: A Memoir," *Menorah Journal* 25 (October–December, 1937), 360.

5. Miller to Enelow, March 20, 1925, Enelow Papers, AJA, box 573, "General Correspondence 1924–1925" file.

6. Hurwitz, "Linda R. Miller," 361.

7. Davidson to Enelow, August 7, 1925, and Enelow to Davidson, September 15, 1925, Enelow Papers, AJA, General Correspondence, box 574, "D-E" file.

8. Miller to Butler, May 9, 1928, CUF, "Mi-My" file.

9. Miller to Butler, June 2, 1928, ibid.

10. Miller to Butler, May 15, 1928, ibid.

11. Butler to Miller, May 28, 1928, ibid. Compare Butler's reasoning with that of Max Weber in "The Bernhard Affair," in Edward Shils, ed. and tr., *Max Weber on Universities: The Power of the State and the Dignity of the Academic Calling in Imperial Germany* (Chicago: University of Chicago Press, 1974).

12. Miller to Butler, June 2, 1928, CUF, "Mi-My" file.

13. Butler to Miller, June 4, 1928, ibid.

14. Miller to Butler, June 6, 1928, ibid. Enelow envisioned a $200,000 endowment that would provide for a $9,000 to $10,000 salary at prevailing interest rates. Butler suggested $250,000, arguing that "it is very desirable in order to make the work of such a chair as useful as possible that the incumbent have at his disposal a small fund for those forms of assistance and items of equipment which make his work so much more productive. He frequently needs scholarly assistance for a longer or shorter time and various illustrative material, books and other, which are always available for his service" (Butler to Miller, May 11, 1928, ibid.). Mrs. Miller concurred, contingent upon a satisfactory agreement concerning the chair's occupant.

15. The trustees accepted the gift at the beginning of the 1928–29 academic year. See Frederick A. Goetze to Butler, August 28, 1928, CUF, "Frederick Goetze" file; Columbia University, *Trustees' Minutes* 49: 26–27, and Columbia University, *Charters, Acts of the Legislature and Official Documents and Records* (New York: Printed for the University, 1933), 319–20.

16. Butler to Woodbridge, June 7, 1928, CUF, "Frederick Woodbridge" file.

17. See *Encyclopaedia Judaica*, s.v. "Joseph Herman Hertz."

18. In fact, one might speculate that Butler took precipitous action in 1936 to avoid the morass in which the Miller committee soon found itself.

19. Butler to Woodbridge, June 20, 1928, CUG, "Frederick Woodbridge" file.

20. Gottheil to Wise, June 29, 1925, JIR Papers, AJA, no. 19, 16/18, "Richard Gottheil" file.

21. Butler to Woodbridge, September 27, 1928, CUF, "Frederick Woodbridge" file. Mrs. Miller, in acknowledging receipt of a list of committee members, called the list "impressive," but added: "The fact that no final selection can be made without the sanction of the President, etc., is nevertheless an especial source of satisfaction" (Linda Miller to Butler, September 28, 1928, CUF, "Mrs. Nathan Miller" file).

22. Gottheil to Butler, July 9, 1928, CUG, "Gi-Gu" file. "Of course," he wrote, "the Chair will be in the Department of Oriental languages and literatures."

23. Gottheil to Wise, October 24, 1928, Wise Papers, AJA, box 947, "Correspondence with Richard J. H. Gottheil, 1923–1929" file. For one example of their relationship, see James F. Carr to Gottheil, October 2, 1915, Gottheil Papers, AJA, Correspondence 2, 1898–1919, "Misc. and unidentified" file.

24. "R. G." memo, attached to Gottheil to Wise, November 2, 1923, Wise Papers, AJA, box 947, "Correspondence with Richard Gottheil, 1923–1929" file.

25. In an interview, Salo Baron commented that Gottheil had desired a philologist, but the latter's avid backing of historian Michael Ginsberg indicates otherwise (Baron interview, New Canaan, Conn., August 30, 1978). "What has become of the matter about which you and I spoke when we last met?" Gottheil wrote Enelow. "Do you not think that it is proper and fitting that I should know? On your account, I am ashamed to ask at

this end of the line" (Gottheil to Enelow, May 30, 1928, Enelow Papers, AJA, box 8, file 7: "Gottheil, Richard J. H., 1913–1932").

26. Gottheil to Wise, October 24, 1928, and November 11, 1928, Wise Papers, AJA, box 947, "Correspondence with Richard J. H. Gottheil, 1923–1929" file. Gottheil demonstrated his sensitivity on family matters when he reproached Stephen Wise for failing to include his father in the pantheon of American Reform Jewish leaders in an article; see Gottheil to Wise, April 13, 1927, ibid.

27. Wise to Ginsberg, September 20, 1927, JIR Papers, AJA, no. 19, 9/3, "Faculty—Candidates for" file.

28. Ginsberg to Wise, August 9, 1928, ibid.

29. Kohut to Wise, October 3, 1928, George Kohut–Stephen S. Wise Correspondence (hereafter Kohut-Wise), AJA, box 2308.

30. Gottheil to Wise, September 27, 1928, JIR Papers, AJA, no. 19, 9/3, "Faculty—Candidates for" file.

31. Wise to Kohut, October 10, 1928, ibid.

32. Ibid. See also Wise to Salo Baron, August 27, 1928, and October 8, 1928, and Ginsberg to Wise, October 2, 1928, ibid.

33. Woodbridge to Butler, November 28, 1928, CUF, "Frederick J. Woodbridge" file. Danby translated the Mishnah and Tosefta of the tractate *Sanhedrin* (1919) and Joseph Klausner's *Jesus of Nazareth: His Life, Times, and Teaching* (New York: Macmillan, 1925) and published *The Jew and Christianity* (1927). One of the first Christian Hebraists to see modern Hebrew as a serious academic medium, Danby would accept an appointment as professor of Hebrew at Oxford in 1936 (*Encyclopaedia Judaica*, s.v. "Danby, Herbert"). Drachman severed his Seminary connection when it began to deviate from Orthodoxy; he later taught at Yeshiva College. Best known for his autobiography, *The Unfailing Light: Memoirs of an American Rabbi* (New York: Rabbinical Council of America, 1948), Drachman was not a prolific scholar. (See *Encyclopaedia Judaica*, s.v. "Drachman, Bernard," and Jeffrey S. Gurock, "From Exception to Role Model: Bernard Drachman and the Evolution of Jewish Religious Life in America, 1880–1920," *American Jewish History* 76 (1987), 166–81.) Obermann taught Semitic languages at Hamburg and came to the Jewish Institute of Religion shortly after publishing his study of Al-Ghazali's philosophy (*Der philosophische und religiöse Subjektivismus Ghazalis*). At Yale, he edited the Yale Judaica Series (*Encyclopaedia Judaica*, s.v. "Obermann, Julian Joel"). Louis Ginzberg is discussed below.

34. Woodbridge to Butler, November 21, 1928, CUF, "Frederick J. Woodbridge" file.

35. Butler to Miller, November 22, 1928, CUF, "Mrs. Nathan J. Miller" file.

36. Israel Davidson almost certainly was one consultant. The other consultant may have been Alexander Marx (Miller to Butler, November 25, 1928, ibid.). Columbia's looser formal relations with the Jewish Theological Seminary help explain why the search committee had a Union Theological but not a Jewish Theological Seminary representative.

37. Butler to Woodbridge, November 26, 1928, CUF, "Frederick J. Woodbridge" file; Woodbridge to Butler, November 2, 1928, ibid., and Butler to Miller, December 3, 1928, CUF, "Mrs. Nathan J. Miller" file.

38. Miller to Butler, December 5, 1928, ibid.

39. Butler to Miller, December 7, 1928, ibid. See also Butler to Woodbridge, December 7, 1928, CUF, "F. Woodbridge" file.

40. "About the professorship at Columbia, I can know little at this distance," a frustrated Gottheil wrote Wise. He later lamented: "It is most unfortunate that I cannot be at my post at so important a moment" (Gottheil to Wise, November 25, 1928, ibid., and Gottheil to Wise, February 9, 1929, JIR Papers, AJA, no. 19, 16/19, "Richard Gottheil" file). "I was told," Wise wrote Gottheil a month after Miller's final letter, "that your own candidate, the young French Jew, was not in the running" (Wise to Gottheil, January 10, 1929, Wise Papers, AJA, box 947, "Correspondence with Richard J. H. Gottheil,

1923–1929" file). A year later, Gottheil renewed his suggestion that Wise call Ginsberg to the Jewish Institute of Religion. Wise again declined. See Gottheil to Wise, August 22, 1930, and Wise to Gottheil, September 2, 1930, JIR Papers, AJA, no. 19, 16/19, "Richard Gottheil" file.

41. Wise to Gottheil, February 1, 1929, Wise Papers, AJA, box 947, "Correspondence with Richard J. H. Gottheil, 1923–1929" file. Wise privately agreed with the committee but did not wish to offend his mentor. He wrote: "I don't know how they got that information, but in any event the opinion does obtain that he is not a [Judaica] text man at all."

42. Kohut to Enelow, October 18, 1928, Enelow Papers, AJA, box 582, "K" file.

43. Kohut to Enelow, November 7, 1928. Kohut apparently misinterpreted a sentence that Enelow wrote in reply to his earlier letter. Enelow had stated: "As to who will be appointed to the chair endowed by Mrs. Miller, I really haven't the least notion, and I am quite sure that no outsider will be allowed to say anything about it" (Enelow to Kohut, October 23, 1928, ibid.). Kohut assumed that Miller did not proffer a nomination because Enelow preferred to remain at Emanu-El. See Kohut to Wise, October 26, 1928, Kohut-Wise, AJA, box 2308, "1928–1929" file.

44. Warburg to Butler, December 3, 1928, CUF, "Wa-Wh" file.

45. Kohut to Wise, October 26, 1928, Wise to Kohut, October 31, 1928, JIR Papers, AJA, no. 19, 16/19, "Richard Gottheil" file, and Gottheil to Wise, October 24, 1928 and November 11, 1928, Wise Papers, AJA, box 947, "Correspondence with Richard J. H. Gottheil, 1923–1929" file.

46. Wise to Gottheil, November 12, 1928, ibid.

47. Wise to Gottheil, December 7, 1928, ibid.

48. Kohut to Wise, October 22, 1928, Kohut–Wise, AJA, box 2308, "1928–1929" file.

49. Wise to Gottheil, March 18, 1929, Wise Papers, AJA, box 947, "Correspondence with Richard J. H. Gottheil, 1923–1929" file.

50. Bewer to Enelow, December 4, 1928, and Enelow to Bewer, December 6, 1928, Enelow Papers, AJA, General Correspondence 1928–1929, box 582, "S" file. Mann had experienced increased dissatisfaction with Hebrew Union following his arrival from Baltimore several years earlier. "Our Rabbinical Schools are turning out Rabbis, but not scholars," he wrote Enelow. "How often at our own faculty meetings, when I insist on raising the standard, is this Pontifical argument hurled at me:—'But we need Rabbis and not specialists!' Whatever hopes I may have had when I came here, of raising some disciples, they are now gone. I have to find some consolation in my own research work. Our 'Nachwuchs' will not come from the Rabbinical schools in America, and certainly not from the HUC with all its millions, buildings, largest Faculty and student body, etc., etc." (See Mann to Enelow, March 26, 1929, ibid., box 583, "M" file).

51. Wise to Gottheil, February 7, 1929, Wise Papers, AJA, box 947, "Correspondence with Richard J. H. Gottheil, 1923–1929" file.

52. Wise to Julian Mack, January 29, 1929, Wise Papers, AJHS, box 119, "Julian Mack" file.

53. Wise to Gottheil, January 10, 1929, Wise Papers, AJA, box 947, "Correspondence with Richard J. H. Gottheil, 1923–1929" file. Linda Miller endorsed Enelow's anti-Zionism, but Wise considered these beliefs another liability. Referring to Enelow's allusion to the serious situation the Jewish Agency for Palestine faced that year, Wise wrote: "It is terrible for a Russian Jew, such as he is, to deal in that bitterly hostile way with what he sneeringly and contemptuously calls 'the Palestinian Movement' " (Wise to Gottheil, July 1, 1929, ibid.).

54. Gottheil to Wise (telegram), January 21, 1929, JIR Papers, AJA no. 19, 16/19, "Richard Gottheil" file. Gottheil considered Kaplan's personality a greater selling point than his erudition. "Religion and life to him are identical," he told Wise in another context, "and his influence upon the students will be tremendous. They are attracted by his personality; they are charmed by his depth of thought and of feeling; they are ready to go

through fire and flame in order to carry out the ideals that he implants in them" (Gottheil to Wise, July 14, 1923, Wise Papers, AJA, box 947, "Correspondence with Richard Gottheil, 1923–1929" file).

55. Ralph Marcus apparently arranged the meeting. See Wise to Gottheil, February 1, 1929, ibid. Littauer, perhaps realizing that his indirect tactics failed, telephoned Butler on February 19, ostensibly to register his disappointment that Columbia had yet to make an appointment. (See Butler to Miller, February 19, 1929, CUF, "Mrs. Nathan Miller" file.) A rumor subsequently circulated that Enelow met with search committee members including Woodbridge and that "he had made himself utterly impossible at and for Columbia by reason of his arrogance and the acrimonious way in which he had talked" (Wise to Gottheil, July 1, 1929, Wise Papers, AJA, box 947, "Correspondence with Richard J. H. Gottheil, 1923–1929" file). For a sympathetic description of Enelow, see Davidson to Miller, April 24, 1929, Davidson Archives, JTS, "Mrs. N. Miller" file.

56. Herbert Solow to Irwin Edman, June 15, 1929, Menorah Collection, AJA, box 9, file 15.

57. Miller to Butler, March 4, 1929, CUF, "Mrs. Nathan J. Miller" file.

58. See Ginzberg, *Keeper of the Law,* 82.

59. Woodbridge to Butler, February 28, 1929, CUF, "Frederick Woodbridge" file.

60. The committee subsequently reaffirmed its fellowship recommendations. "Dr. Ralph Marcus of the Semitics Department, and of the Jewish Institute of Religion," it reported, "should be encouraged to intensify his researches in the field of Hellenistic Judaism. He is unusually competent in the field and promises soon to become an authority on Philo." The committee called Rosenthal "the most promising young man in New York for the kind of work we need." His publications portended "significant contributions to the field of Talmudic scholarship." Rosenthal planned to resume the history of the Talmud where George Foot Moore had left off. See "Memorandum to the Committee on the Appointment of Professor of Jewish Institutions, Dean Woodbridge, Chairman," undated (accepted as a report of the Committee, May 29, 1929), William L. Westerman Papers (hereafter Westerman Papers), CU-RBML, "W" file.

61. Butler to Woodbridge, March 1, 1929, CUF, "Frederick Woodbridge" file; Butler to Miller, March 1, 1929, CUF, "Mrs. Nathan J. Miller" file; and Philip Hayden to Woodbridge, March 22, 1929, CUF, "Frederick Woodbridge" file.

62. Miller to Butler, March 4, 1929, CUF, "Mrs. Nathan J. Miller" file.

63. Woodbridge to Butler, March 25, 1929, CUF, "Frederick Woodbridge" file.

64. Woodbridge to Butler, April 11, 1929, ibid.; "Memorandum to the Committee."

65. Mann was also indignant at Edman's discussion of salary. He told Edman that the committee should decide on the chair's scope and then consider likely candidates. He concluded that a call from Columbia would be unlikely (Mann to Enelow, April 11, 1929, Enelow Papers, AJA, General Correspondence 1928–1929, box 583, "M" file). Enelow concurred: "I can see now that if that is what the committee wants, you are out of the question. There is no sense in jumping from the frying pan into the fire, however disagreeable the former might be" (Enelow to Mann, April 17, 1929, ibid.). Enelow did not encourage Mann's aspirations. Edman may have eliminated Mann on the grounds of personality: "He is no gentleman; a horrible person," Israel Abrahams once said of him. "He is a great scholar, but I understand, not a gentleman," wrote George Kohut. Stephen Wise concurred. In 1926 Wise offered a position at the Jewish Institute of Religion to Salo Baron instead of to Mann. See Wise to Kohut, October 24, 1928, and Kohut to Wise, October 26, 1928, Kohut–Wise, AJA, box 2308, "1928–1929" file.

66. Butler to Woodbridge, April 13, 1929, CUF, "Frederick Woodbridge" file.

67. Woodbridge to Butler, June 1, 1929, ibid.

68. Salo Baron to Wise, July 23, 1929, JIR Papers, AJA, box 1467, "Dr. Salo W. Baron" file. See Richard Fuchs, "The Hochschule für die Wissenschaft des Judentums in the Period of Nazi Rule," Leo Baeck Institute, *Yearbook* 12 (1967), 3–31, and Isi Jacob Eisner, "Reminiscences of the Berlin Rabbinical Seminary," ibid., 32–52. Elbogen sub-

sequently co-edited the *Encyclopaedia Judaica* (10 vols., 1928–1934), and wrote *A Century of Jewish Life* (Philadelphia: Jewish Publication Society of America, 1944) to update Graetz.

69. The committee ascertained that Elbogen could perform his work effectively in English. See Woodbridge to Butler, June 1, 1929, CUF, "Frederick J. Woodbridge" file.

70. Wise told Julian Mack, whom the committee also consulted, that "Columbia could not find a better person in all the world than Elbogen, and that Elbogen is not only a great Jewish scholar but a rare teacher; that he knows how to deal with non-Jews as well as with Jews and that he is the embodiment of Jewish culture" (quoted in Wise to Kohut, June 6, 1929, Kohut–Wise, AJA, box 2308, "1928–1929" file).

71. Herbert Solow to Irwin Edman, June 5, 1929, Menorah Collection, AJA, box 9, file 15: "Irwin Edman."

72. Butler to Woodbridge, June 4, 1929, CUF, "Frederick J. Woodbridge" file.

73. The committee reaffirmed its fellowship suggestions and added Beryl Levy's name to its list. Levy, an academically distinguished Columbia College senior, planned graduate work in Jewish learning at Columbia ("Memorandum to the Committee"). The report stated: "On the basis of our own experience in this matter, that finding an effective personnel to supplement the individual work of the occupant of the chair, involves considerable familiarity with the student body, with local conditions, with other departments of the University, and with the general mode of procedure here; that therefore it would be an almost impossible task for an outsider (like Dr. Elbogen) to face such a problem immediately; and that therefore this Committee ought to assume some responsibility in this matter, in order to prevent further delay or rasher decisions."

74. Elbogen's interest in New York's manuscripts suggests the field's maturation. Forty years earlier, Richard Gottheil spent much time and effort acquiring the first such manuscripts, and most American Semitists were still obliged to cross the Atlantic to visit European archives.

75. Edman to Woodbridge, July 11, 1929, attached to Fackenthal to Edman, July 25, 1929, CUF, "E" file.

76. Butler to Elbogen, September 12, 1929, ibid. Elbogen would have begun service at Columbia at a relatively advanced age, and the statutory pension was admittedly inadequate; hence Butler's reassurance. See Fackenthal to Elbogen, September 19, 1929, ibid.

77. Elbogen to Butler, September 19, 1929; Fackenthal to Butler, September 23, 1929; and Edman to Elbogen, September 19, 1929, ibid.

78. Elbogen to Butler, September 28, 1929, ibid.

79. Butler to Elbogen, October 24, 1929, and November 15, 1929; Elbogen to Butler, October 28, 1929, and November 13, 1929, ibid. We do not know whether Butler's failure to spell his first name correctly in any of his correspondence affected Elbogen.

80. See for example Wise to William Rosenau, September 20, 1929, JIR Papers, AJA, no. 19, 9/3, "Faculty—Candidates for" file.

81. See Adler to Warburg, June 24, 1937, in Robinson, ed., *Cyrus Adler: Selected Letters*, 2:331–32.

82. Butler to Miller, September 30, 1929, and Miller to Butler, October 2, 1929, CUF, "Mrs. Nathan J. Miller" file.

83. Blondheim to Alexander Marx, September 8, 1929, Marx Papers, JTS, "D. S. Blondheim, 1925–1930" file.

84. See *Encyclopaedia Judaica*, s.v. "Blondheim, David Simon." "You seem to be the only man in the country really interested in the Jewish side of what I have tried to do," he wrote Marx in 1913 (Blondheim to Marx, March 21, 1913, Marx Papers, JTS, "David S. Blondheim" file). He favorably compared the Illinois facilities to those at the University of Wisconsin. Wisconsin, he noted, had a Semitics department and Illinois had none. But "we are much better off for Judaica and Hebraica than they are" (Blondheim to Marx, April 26, 1916, ibid.).

85. Blondheim to Marx, March 18, 1917, ibid.

86. Kohut to Enelow, October 18, 1928, Enelow Papers, AJA, box 582, "K" file; Blondheim to Marx, April 14, 1923, and September 8, 1929, Marx Papers, JTS, "D. S. Blondheim" file.

87. Blondheim to Marx, March 29, 1923, ibid. See also Mordecai Kaplan Diary, JTS, August 11, 1929.

88. On the Blondheim–Dulles relationship, see Leonard O. Mosley, *Dulles* (New York: Dial, 1978), and Eleanor Lansing Dulles, *Eleanor Lansing Dulles, Chances of a Lifetime: A Memoir* (Englewood Cliffs: Prentice-Hall, 1980).

89. Mordecai Kaplan shared Blondheim's uneasiness about Edman: "Edman, like Morris R. Cohen, is or had been poisoning the minds of the Jewish boys against Judaism. Again I am basing my inference in the case of Edman not upon direct but only upon circumstantial evidence" (Mordecai Kaplan Diary, JTS, September 18, 1929).

90. See Blondheim to Wise, October 12, 1929, and Wise to Blondheim, October 16, 1929, JIR Papers, AJA, no. 19, 5/8, "Columbia University" file.

91. "[Kohut] is a man without any backbone whatever. . . . I have no use for the whole K. family. . . . I am extremely surprised to see that this particular member of it is so closely connected with your Institute," Gottheil told Wise (Gottheil to Wise, January 20, 1923, Wise Papers, AJA, box 947, "Correspondence with Richard J. H. Gottheil, 1923–1929" file). For Kohut's attitude, see Kohut to Marx, October 30, 1929, Marx Papers, JTS, "George A. Kohut, June–December, 1929" file.

92. Kohut to Marx, October, 19, 1929, ibid.

93. Vergil, *The Aeneid,* Patric Dickinson, tr. (New York: New American Library, 1961), 17, 19.

94. *Encyclopaedia Judaica,* s.v. "Baron, Salo (Shalom) Wittmayer."

95. Gottheil to Wise, July 29, 1925, JIR Papers, AJA, no. 19, 16/18, "Richard Gottheil" file; Wise to Elbogen, June 2, 1926, Wise Papers, AJHS, box 35, "I. Elbogen" file.

96. Wise to Kohut, December 1, 1926, JIR Papers, AJA, "Salo Baron" file; Wise to Elbogen, June 2, 1926, Wise Papers, AJHS, box 35, "I. Elbogen" file.

97. Kohut to Marx, January 7, 1928, Marx Papers, JTS, "G. A. Kohut, January–March, 1929" file.

98. Kohut to Wise, October 29, 1928, Kohut–Wise, AJA, box 2308, "1928–29" file; Wise to Gottheil, September 22, 1929, JIR Papers, AJA, no. 19, 16/19, "Richard Gottheil" file.

99. Wise to Kohut, April 18, 1928, and Baron to Wise, April 20, 1928, JIR Papers, AJA, box 1467, "Dr. Salo W. Baron" file.

100. Irwin Edman and Herbert W. Schneider, "Report to the Chairman of the Committee on the Appointment of a Professor of Jewish Institutions," December 6, 1929, attached to Woodbridge to Butler, December 12, 1929, CUF, "Frederick Woodbridge" file.

101. See, for example, Herbert Weir Smyth, "The Classics, 1867–1929" in Morison, *Development of Harvard University,* 60–61. By the end of the nineteenth century, many classicists had shifted their arguments for curricular predominance from the ability to train the mental faculties to an emphasis on Greek and Roman culture as antecedents to modern Western civilization (see Rudolph, *Curriculum,* 183. Cf. Daniel Bell, *The Reforming of General Education: The Columbia College Experience in the National Setting* [Garden City, N.Y.: Anchor Books, 1966], 223–24). Just as Tenny Frank and William L. Westerman undertook research on ancient history after advanced study of Latin literature, James H. Breasted and other scholars who wrote the history of the ancient Near East were trained in Semitics. See John Higham with Leonard Krieger and Felix Gilbert, *History: Professional Scholarship in America* (New York: Harper, 1973 [1965]), 37–38.

102. Charles Gross, a Jewish professor of history at Harvard, specialized in medieval history and the British constitution. Gross, an exceptional case, published several articles with Jewish themes, notably in the *Publications of the American Jewish Historical Society.* See Morison, *Three Centuries,* 375–76; Feuer, "Stages in the Social History of Jewish Professors"; and Novick, *That Noble Dream,* 172.

103. See Heinrich Hirsch Graetz, *The Structure of Jewish History and Other Essays,* Ismar Schorsch, tr. and ed. (New York: Jewish Theological Seminary of America, 1975).

104. Roth, "Jewish History," 422–23.

105. Sarna, *J.P.S.,* 34–39.

106. Jonas, "Writing American Jewish History," 142.

107. George Jeshurun, "Wanted—A Modern Reader's Jewish History," *The Jewish Forum* 4 (January, 1921), 681.

108. "A man may busy himself with every country on the surface of the globe," Cecil Roth wrote, "but until he touch upon the Jews of Germany he is regarded as a pure antiquarian. On the other hand, the young native who presents his doctorate thesis on the vicissitudes of the community of his township is reckoned at once a universal authority" (see Roth, "Jewish History," 424).

109. If a scholar "declares that the Jews came here and prospered in America because God, blessed be He, willed they should," wrote a critic, "his crusading piety and energy are scarcely likely to convince a critic who has drunk deep at the materialistic spring." See Albert M. Friedenberg, "Thoughts on the Philosophy of American Jewish History," *Publications of the American Jewish Historical Society* 28 (1922), 234.

110. "The professional world looks down with scorn upon any neophyte who has not served his apprenticeship over the folios of the Talmud," wrote Cecil Roth. "Now a profound knowledge of the Talmud is a useful adjunct to any student of Jewish history. But it is by no means indispensable. The only indispensable requirement for research in Jewish history or any period or from any angle—as for any branch of scholarship—is a knowledge of the principles and methods of research. . . . Jewish history is written and taught today by persons whose education may qualify them to deal with Rabbinical texts, but who have not mastered even the elements of the historian's craft." Roth urged scholars to view the Talmud as "a highly interesting theological and psychological phenomenon" not as "the substance of Jewish history" (Roth, "Jewish History," 426, 428).

111. Alexander Marx, "Aims and Tasks of Jewish Historiography," *Publications of the American Jewish Historical Society* 26 (1918), 14–15.

112. Roth, "Jewish History," 426.

113. Alexander Marx, "Aims and Tasks," 15. See also Roth, "Jewish History," 428.

114. Roth, "Jewish History," 428.

115. Jonas, "Writing American Jewish History," 143, 147, quotation from 147.

116. Friedenberg, "Thoughts," 234, 236.

117. See Marx, "Aims and Tasks," 29; Wolfson, "The Needs of Jewish Scholarship," 28–32; and Salo Baron, "Research in Jewish History," *The Jewish Institute Quarterly* 4 (May, 1928), 1–8.

118. "We see God in each ethical action, but not in the finished whole, in history; for why would we need a God, if history were divine?" wrote Franz Rosenzweig in a modern restatement of the antihistorical position. Quoted in Lionel Kochan, *The Jew and His History* (New York: Macmillan Press, 1977), 99.

119. Salo W. Baron, "The Study of Jewish History," *The Jewish Institute Quarterly* 4 (January 1928), 9. This denunciation became closely identified with Baron. See Arthur Hertzberg and Leon A. Feldman, "Foreword" in Salo W. Baron, *History and Jewish Historians: Essays and Addresses by Salo W. Baron,* Arthur Hertzberg and Leon A. Feldman, comps. (Philadelphia: Jewish Publication Society of America, 1964), ix, and Jeanette Meisel Baron, "A Bibliography of the Printed Writings of Salo Wittmayer Baron" in *Salo Wittmayer Baron Jubilee Volume on the Occasion of His Eightieth Birthday* (Jerusalem: American Academy of Jewish Research and Columbia University Press, 1975), 3.

120. Baron, "Emphases in Jewish History" in Baron, *History and Jewish Historians,* 76.

121. Baron, "Study of Jewish History," 8.

122. Baron, "Emphases in Jewish History," 69. "Not accepting the periodization of post-exilic Jewish history by Zunz and his 19th century successors into literary epochs with its implication that literature was the be-all of Jewish history," wrote Lloyd P. Gart-

ner, a Baron student, "Baron orients it to the dynamic of general history." (See Lloyd P. Gartner, "A Successor to Graetz," *Midstream* 16 [November, 1970], 71).

123. Baron, "Emphases in Jewish History," 77–78.

124. Ibid., 86.

125. "Some Talmudists have cavilled at alleged inadequacies of Baron's rabbinic learning," wrote Gartner, "but no Talmudist has yet attempted these fundamental topics—a social history of Talmudic times and the analytic, unhomiletic study of the social teachings of Talmudic Judaism" (Gartner, "Successor," 69).

126. Baron echoed Cyrus Adler's contention that Jewish scholarship, properly undertaken, might also help to unify a Jewish community that fragmented during emancipation. See Baron, "Emphases in Jewish History," 89.

127. Carleton J. H. Hayes, "History" in Dixon Ryan Fox, ed., *A Quarter Century of Learning 1904–1929* (New York: Columbia University Press, 1931), 19, 25.

128. Ibid., 19.

129. See James Harvey Robinson, *The New History: Essays Illustrating the Modern Historical Outlook* (New York: Macmillan, 1912), and Higham, *History*, 104–16. "How silly it is," Hayes quotes Robinson, his mentor, and the movement's ideologue as saying, "for historians to waste time in determining 'whether Charles the Fat was in Ingelheim or Lustnau on July 1, 887,' when they should be contemplating the jaw of the Heidelberg Man." See Hayes, "History," 11.

130. See Salo W. Baron, "Preface," *A Social and Religious History of the Jews* (New York: Columbia University Press, 1937), 1:v, and Gartner, "Successor," 68.

131. Kohut to Marx, October 8, October 9, October 30, and November 11, 1929; Marx to Kohut, October 11, 1929, Marx Papers, JTS, "George A. Kohut, June–December, 1929" file; Marx to Blondheim, October 13, 1929; Blondheim to Marx, October 27, 1929, Marx Papers, JTS, "D. S. Blondheim, 1925–1930" file.

132. Kohut to Edman, October 11, 1929, Marx Papers, JTS, "George A. Kohut, June–December, 1929" file.

133. Kohut to Marx, October 9, 1929, ibid., Blondheim to Marx, October 11 and October 14, 1929; Marx to Blondheim, October 13, 1929, Marx Papers, JTS, "D. S. Blondheim" file. Elbogen also mentioned Jacob R. Marcus of Hebrew Union College, Julian Obermann of the Jewish Institute of Religion, and Cecil Roth. Kohut dismissed Marcus as too young, Obermann as not a historian, and Roth as unavailable. When Elbogen subsequently endorsed Fritz Baer's candidacy, Kohut expressed little surprise since he knew of prior judgment reversals and attributed them "to [Elbogen's] anxiety to be kind to everyone." Kohut added that Elbogen "overplays his generosity and gives the impression that he is all things to all men," thus reducing the importance of his endorsement. See Kohut to Blondheim, November 11, 1929, Marx Papers, JTS, "George A. Kohut, June–December 1929" file.

134. Fackenthal to Woodbridge, November 15, 1929, CUF, "Frederick J. E. Woodbridge" file.

135. Blondheim to Marx, November 19, 1929, Marx Papers, JTS, "D. S. Blondheim" file. Harry Wolfson and Cyrus Adler endorsed him "with [unspecified] reservations," and Kohut concluded that Wolfson's "interference . . . completely nullified Blondheim's chances" (Kohut to Marx, December 17, 1929, Marx Papers, JTS, "George A. Kohut, July–December, 1929" file). See also Edman and Schneider, "Report. . . ." Ironically, about 15 years later, Schneider, a professor of religion, was forced to resign from Columbia when the university administration learned of his recent divorce. Blondheim's subsequent marriage to Dulles led to demands for his resignation from Jewish scholarly organizations, including the JPS and the American Academy of Jewish Research. Louis Ginzberg spearheaded the drive against Blondheim, according to his son. See Eli Ginzberg, *My Brother's Keeper* (New Brunswick, N.J.: Transaction Publishers, 1989), 25.

136. Kohut to Marx, December 27, 1929, and January 6, 1930; Marx to Kohut, January 3, 1930, Marx Papers, JTS, "George A. Kohut, July–December, 1929" file; Kohut

to Blondheim, February 3, 1930, Marx Papers, JTS, "G. A. Kohut, January–March, 1930" file; Marx to Blondheim, February 17, 1930, Marx Papers, JTS," D. S. Blondheim, 1925–1930" file.

137. The committee also considered Isaac Husik, professor of philosophy at the University of Pennsylvania, and Louis I. Finkelstein, professor of theology at the Jewish Theological Seminary. Husik received warm recommendations, but the committee desired a historian, not a medieval Jewish philosopher. It eliminated Finkelstein because of his sectarianism and his domestic training. See Woodbridge to Butler, December 12, 1929, CUF, "Frederick J. Woodbridge" file. Finkelstein's prior scholarship included studies of Jewish self-government in the Middle Ages and of the conflict between the Sadducees and Pharisees. He succeeded Alder as president of the Jewish Theological Seminary.

138. Woodbridge to Butler, December 12, 1929, CUF, "Frederick J. Woodbridge" file. Elbogen, Wolfson, Wise, and Ralph Marcus would enthusiastically endorse Baron's candidacy for the Miller chair.

139. Miller to Butler, December 20, 1929, CUF, "Mrs. Nathan Miller" file.

140. Butler to Miller, December 16, December 19 and December 23, 1929, ibid.

141. When he expressed these concerns at a meeting with committee members, Herbert Schneider replied that he should then go home and write books. Baron replied that he wasn't ready to retire.

142. The university also retained Baron's assistant and promised to build up its library collection (Butler to Baron, December 14 and December 19, 1929; Baron to Butler, December 16 and 21, 1929, CUF, "Ba" file).

143. "It will be a great loss to the Institute, as there is no one, so far as I know who can adequately replace him," Kohut told Marx. "Baron covers such a wide field and his range of knowledge is so remarkable that we would have to get three or four people to take over the subjects which he has been teaching, quite apart from his directorship of the School of Advanced Studies and his Librarianship, which was by no means a negligible part of his activities." (See Kohut to Marx, December 17, 1929, Marx Papers, JTS, "George A. Kohut, July–December, 1929" file.)

144. Kohut to Marx, January 6, 1920, ibid., "January–March, 1930" file.

145. *Encyclopaedia Judaica,* s.v. "Baron, Salo (Shalom) Wittmayer."

8. Tragedy, Triumph, and Jewish Scholarship

1. Compare Katsh, "Teaching of Hebrew," 582, and "Modern Hebrew," 3. The number of theological schools that offered Hebrew—mostly classical—also increased.

2. Elbogen, "American Jewish Scholarship," 47.

3. *Mishna Avot* V:2, for instance, identified the canonical texts and the age for, and sequence of, study.

4. Rudolph, *Curriculum,* 1.

5. The sample is described in chapter 9, notes 2 and 3.

6. See 201–210, below.

7. Indigenous scholars would have to supply this leadership. Continental universities had few specialists who could strengthen American Jewish scholarship, as did the refugee intellectuals in the social and physical sciences. On Jewish studies in pre-war Hebrew University, see Parzen, *Hebrew University, 1925–1935,* passim.

8. Moses Hadas's 1939 comment upon reviewing Louis Ginzberg's *Legends of the Jews* is typical: "The book is printed in English in the United States. The center of Jewish studies has shifted to English speaking countries and in particular to the United States" ("Legends and Learning," *Menorah Journal* 27 [Winter, 1939], 108).

9. Abraham Kaplan, "The Problems We Face" in *When Yesterday Becomes Tomorrow: 125th Anniversary Celebration, Congregation Emanu-El of the City of New York 1845–1970* (New York: Congregation Emanu-El of the City of New York, 1971), 80–103, quotation from 102. The aphorism was invoked repeatedly between Friedland-

er's and Kaplan's enunciations. See, for example, Emanuel Gamoran, "A Challenging First Step," *Liberal Judaism* 11 (November, 1943), 21. Gamoran spoke under Reform auspices at the establishment of the American Institute for Jewish Studies in 1943.

10. Orthodox reading of *Pesahim* 6b.

11. Franz Rosenzweig shared this perspective. See *Star of Redemption: Translated from the German of the 2nd Edition of 1930 by William W. Hallo* (New York: Holt, Rinehart and Winston, 1971), pt. 3, bk. 1, and Alexander Altmann, "Franz Rosenzweig on History," in *Studies in Religious Philosophy and Mysticism* (London: Routledge & Kegan Paul, 1969), 275–91. See also Lucy Dawidowicz, "What Is the Use of Jewish History," in her book *What Is the Use of Jewish History,* Neal Kozodoy, ed. (New York: Schocken Books, 1992), 3–19.

12. Roth, "Jewish History," 426.

13. Max Gruenwald, "The Jewish Teacher," in Leo Baeck Institute, *Yearbook* 19 (1974), 63–69, quotation from 65, and Bernard D. Perlow, "Institutions for the Education of the Modern Rabbi in Germany," 63–64. Perlow reports that history made up less than two percent of the semester hours in the Breslau Seminary in the mid-1880s. Marcus Brann's history of Breslau reports four percent of the course hours in history. Only pedagogy received less attention than history. Graetz taught more Bible and texts than history. See Marcus Brann, *Geschichte des Jüdisch-Theoligischen Seminars in Breslau* (Breslau: W. Koebner, 1904), 68:xix–xxiv.

14. Yosef Hayim Yerushalmi, *Zakhor: Jewish History and Jewish Memory* (Seattle: University of Washington Press, 1982), 86.

15. See Ismar Schorsch, "From Wolfenbüttel to Wissenschaft," 35.

16. Only 11 history professorships existed in 1880, and the majority of the founders of the American Historical Association (1884) did not earn a living as historical scholars in academic institutions. Sherman B. Barnes, "The Entry of Science and History in the College Curriculum," *History of Education Quarterly* 4 (1964), 44–58; David D. Van Tassel, *Recording America's Past: An Interpretation of the Development of Historical Studies in America, 1607–1884* (Chicago: University of Chicago Press, 1960), 175. When Columbia established the Seth Low chair of history in 1897, the president's report noted: "Up to this time the University has had no separate Department of History." (See Columbia College, *President's Annual Report* [1897], 9–10.)

17. Marx, "Aims and Tasks," 15. This placement resembles the earlier assignment of ancient Greek and Roman history to classics departments. See Sherman Barnes, "Entry of Science and History," 49, and Higham with Krieger and Gilbert, *History: Professional Scholarship,* 37–38.

18. See Henry F. Graff, "His America," *Jewish Heritage* 11 (Summer, 1969), 46.

19. Gavin I. Langmuir, "Majority History and Post-Biblical Jews," *Journal of the History of Ideas* 27 (July, 1966), 343–64, and idem, "Tradition, History, and Prejudice," *Jewish Social Studies* 30 (July, 1968), 157–68.

20. The relative proportion of historical writing on Jews provides another indicator of the field's growth. Among books on modern European history published between 1968 and 1978, 49 were on Jews, 17 on historical demography, 34 on urban history, and 77 on churches and religion. See William H. McNeill, "Modern European History," in Michael G. Kammen, ed., *The Past Before Us: Contemporary Historical Writing in the United States* (Ithaca, N.Y.: Cornell University Press, 1980), 95–112.

21. Guido Kisch, "The Founders of Wissenschaft des Judentums and America," in Jacob R. Marcus, ed., *Essays in Jewish History* (Cincinnati: American Jewish Archives, 1958), 147–70. "To the Greeks Clio was a muse: our compatriots have turned her into a scavenger," wrote Cecil Roth. See Roth, "Jewish History," 431. On Roth, see Irene Roth, *Cecil Roth: Historian without Tears* (New York: Sepher-Hermon Press, 1982).

22. Oscar Handlin, "A Twenty Year Retrospect of American Jewish Historiography," *American Jewish Historical Quarterly* 65 (June, 1976), 296, 297. See also idem, "Our Unknown Jewish Ancestors," *Commentary* 5 (February, 1948), 104–10. The dominant

political emphasis continued to impede the writing of academically rigorous, interpretive social and religious history.

23. See Ben Halpern, "Modern Jews and Their History," *Commentary* 56 (August, 1973), 72–74.

24. "By the third quarter of the last century, students of American Jewish life were fully aware that there had been three 'waves' of migration to this country: the Spanish-Portugese, the German, and the East European. What is more, they were conscious of the fact that these 'waves' represented different cultures. . . . In my opinion, this division of the material of American Jewish history is natural and correct, and should be definitively adopted" (Jacob Rader Marcus, "The Periodization of American Jewish History," *Publications of the American Jewish Historical Society* 14 [1957/1958], 125).

25. "Among Jews, the tripartite division into Spanish, German and East European periods had [distinguished] the established from the newly arrived families. That framework which reflected the attitudes of the 1890's survived a long time. Few traces of it survive now" (Handlin, "A Twenty Year Retrospect," 297). Hasia Diner's *A Time for Gathering: The Second Migration 1820–1880* (Baltimore: Johns Hopkins University Press, 1992) directly challenges the tripartite periodization. Historian Lloyd P. Gartner noted another problem with internal periodization: the readiness of some Jewish historians to assign "transcendental meanings" to historical periods. See Lloyd P. Gartner, "Ideas of Jewish History," *The Jewish Journal of Sociology* 18 (June, 1976), 64.

26. See Gerson Cohen, "A Global Approach to Jewish History," *Jewish Heritage* 11 (Summer, 1969), 47–50.

27. On comparative environments, see, for example, Jonathan D. Sarna, "Anti-Semitism and American History," *Commentary* 71 (March, 1981), 42–47, which argues against the contemporary tendency to equate European and American anti-Semitism.

28. Marcus Hansen's contemporary investigations of American immigration led historians to ask antecedent and derivative questions about identifiable immigrant groups.

29. See Salo W. Baron, "New Horizons in Jewish History," in Salo W. Baron, Ernest Nagel, and Koppel S. Pinson, eds., *Freedom and Reason: Studies in Jewish Philosophy and Culture in Memory of Morris Raphael Cohen* (Glencoe, Il.: Free Press, 1951), 340–44. Baron also termed a post-Holocaust emphasis on Jewish heroism an understandable counteractant to concentration on passive martyrdom. But this trend, he added, might result in the questioning of traditional Jewish values.

30. Ibid., 342–44, 350–53; Halpern, "Modern Jews," 73; Marc E. Kellner, "E. J. on Contemporary Jewry," *Association for Jewish Studies Newsletter,* n.v. (February, 1973), 7; and Chaim Raphael, "The Texture of Jewish History," *Commentary* 63 (January, 1977), 64–65.

31. On Baron's scholarship, see the articles in the special issue of *Jewish Heritage* 11 (Summer, 1969). His stance was not above criticism. Baron's work, some scholars argued, reflected a contemporary Jewish communal agenda. See Langmuir, "Tradition, History, and Prejudice," 163–65, and Irving Agus, "Preconceptions and Stereotypes in Jewish Historiography," *Jewish Quarterly Review,* n.s., 51 (January, 1961), 242–63.

32. Salo W. Baron, "American Jewish History: Problems and Methods," *Publications of the American Jewish Historical Society* 39 (March, 1950), 207–66.

33. Baron, "New Horizons in Jewish History," 344–53.

34. Baron, "Newer Emphases in Jewish History" in Baron, *History and Jewish Historians,* 101.

35. Ibid., 102. See also Baron, "World Dimensions of Jewish History," ibid., 23–42.

36. See Bernard D. Weinryb, "Jewish Research and Its Tasks," *The Jewish Review* 1 (May, 1943), 13–27.

37. Martin A. Cohen, "Structuring American Jewish History," *American Jewish Historical Quarterly* 57 (December, 1967), 137–50, cogently states the generalist position.

38. Solomon Zeitlin, "The Need for a Systematic Jewish History," *Jewish Quarterly Review,* n.s., 58 (April, 1968), 261–73, and Handlin, "A Twenty Year Retrospect," 296–97.

39. Neusner, "The Problematic of 'Jewish History,' " in *Academic Study of Judaism*, 2:106–28.

40. See, for example, H. H. Ben-Sasson, ed., *A History of the Jewish People* (Cambridge: Harvard University Press, 1976 [1969]), and Elie Kedouri, ed., *The Jewish World: History and Culture of the Jewish People* (New York: H.N. Abrams, 1979). The "monolithic Hebrew" quotation is from Robert Alter, "A New Theory of Kashrut," *Commentary* 68 (August, 1979), 52. The "constant themes" quotation is from Chaim Raphael, "Inside Jewish History," *Commentary* 69 (February, 1980), 62–63.

41. "One looks long (and as a rule in vain, however)," wrote historian Lloyd Gartner, "for significant statements at the level between heaven-storming teleological chronologies and the books and articles published all the time on the most specialized and arcane subjects" (Gartner, "Ideas," 64). Gartner's lament is reminiscent of sociologist Robert Merton's call for an emphasis on "middle range generalizations"; see Robert K. Merton, "Of Sociological Theories of the Middle Range," in *Social Theory and Social Structure*, 3rd ed. (New York: Free Press, 1968), 39–72.

42. See, for example, David Riesman, Nathan Glazer, and Reuel Denny, *The Lonely Crowd: A Study of the Changing American Character* (New Haven: Yale University Press, 1950).

43. Oscar Handlin, ed., *Report on a Conference of the Jewish Experience in America Held at Hotel Warwick, NYC, NY, May 22–23, 1948* (New York: n.p., 1948), pt. 2, 65. See also idem, "New Paths in American Jewish History: Afterthoughts on a Conference," *Commentary* 7 (April, 1949), 388–94.

44. Compare: "Surely it does not follow either morally or logically that a Jewish historian trained in the scientific technique of modern historiography must needs surrender the unique function of his tradition to evaluate the history of his people and its future from the viewpoint of its own self-conceived ideal experience and purpose" (Abraham A. Neuman, "Visions and Visionaries in Jewish History," *Publications of the American Jewish Historical Society* 47 [1957/1958], 136). Compare also: "To overlook the distinctions in favor of the supposed similarities and identities of the Jewish and the American historical experiences is to destroy the peculiar qualifications of Jews as pupils, critics, and mentors. This is, of course, not to say that American Jews are any the less Americans because they are Jews, but that if they would accept their double inheritance they must also accept the burden of an inner tension. In America of all places they cannot refuse to be Double-men culturally" (in Daniel J. Boorstin, "A Dialogue of Two Histories: 'Jewish Contributions to America' in a New Light," *Commentary* 8 [October, 1949], 316).

45. Handlin, "A Twenty Year Retrospect," 309. Compare: "Historians of American women ignore Jews just as scholars of American Jews overlook women. The irony is compounded by the fact that many of the women's history scholars are Jewish by birth while the specialists in American Jewry include a significant minority of women" (see Deborah Dash Moore, "Studying the Public and Private Selves of American Jewish Women," *Lilith* 10 [Winter, 1982–1983], 28).

46. Handlin, "A Twenty Year Retrospect," 295.

47. Sholome Michael Gelber, "Does the Jewish Past Have a Future?" in Joseph Blau, Philip Friedman, Arthur Hertzberg, and Isaac Mendelsohn, eds., *Essays in Jewish Life and Thought Presented in Honor of Dr. Salo Wittmayer Baron* (New York: Columbia University Press, 1959), 251–64.

48. Chaim N. Bialik, "Machsorey Leshonenu Ve-Tihuna," *Dvarim Shebeal Pe* (Tel Aviv: Dvir, 1935), 136.

49. See G. R. Driver, "The Modern Study of the Hebrew Language," in Arthur S. Peake, *The People and the Book* (Oxford: Clarendon Press, 1925), 73–120. Michael Berkowitz (*Zionist Culture and West European Jewry Before the First World War* [Cambridge: Cambridge University Press, 1993], 40–76) discusses the place of revived Hebrew in the Zionist program.

50. See Avraham Arnon, "The History of Modern Hebrew Education in Israel," *Ha-Enziglopedia Ha-Ivrit* 6 (1956), 996; Roberto Bachi, "A Statistical Analysis of the Revival of Hebrew in Israel," *Scripta Hierosolymitana* 3 (1956), 179–247; Jack Fellman, *The Revival of a Classical Tongue: Eliezar Ben Yehuda and the Modern Hebrew Language* (The Hague: Mouton, 1973); Chaim Rabin, "The Revival of the Hebrew Language," *Ariel* 25 (Winter, 1969), 25–34; and Reuven Swan, "Ben-Yehuda and the Revival of the Hebrew Speech," ibid., 35–39.

51. Sander L. Gilman (*Jewish Self-Hatred: Anti-Semitism and the Hidden Language of the Jews* [Baltimore: Johns Hopkins University Press, 1986]) discusses Jewish language use and its meaning for self-identification and self-hatred.

52. As early as 1905, the *Ivrit b'Ivrit* method was proposed for advanced students at the Uptown Talmud Torah in Harlem, a new and growing Jewish neighborhood in Manhattan. See Jeffrey S. Gurock, *When Harlem was Jewish, 1870–1930* (New York: Columbia University Press, 1979), 100.

53. Cited in Meyer, "Centennial History," 59.

54. El. Lycidas [Harry A. Wolfson], "Pomegranates," *Menorah Journal* 4 (1) (February, 1918), 16–26, quotations from 19, 20. Horace Kallen, a proponent of cultural pluralism, shared Wolfson's anti-Yiddish sentiment but disagreed with his intemperate tone: "I was pleased with the stuff in 'Pomegranates' but the manner is too irritating for those who do not agree with you" (see Horace Kallen to Harry Wolfson, February 19, 1918, Horace Kallen Papers, AJA, box 32/4. See also Kallen to Wolfson, March 5, 1918 and Wolfson to Kallen, March 17, 1918, ibid.).

55. Letter to Felix Frankfurther in Menorah Collection, AJA. Recall George Kohut's "violent prejudice" against Yiddish when he was asked to consider subvention of a Yiddish dictionary. See chapter 6, n. 120.

56. Compare Arnold Marsh, "Eire: The Revival of the Irish Language," Eliezer Rieger, "Palestine: The Revival of Hebrew," and Suniti Kumar Chatterji, "India: Language Problems," in *The Year-Book of Education* (1949), 157–66, 471–79, and 483–501. When the Irish prime minister, who wished to revive Erse, asked why partisans succeeded in reviving Hebrew in Israel, Elihau Elath responded that whereas Erse had one formidable challenger—English—Hebrew had many challengers: "If Israel were not to become a second Tower of Babel," Elath added, "Hebrew would have to be the country's language, and all our newcomers would have to learn to use it in their daily lives" (Elihau Elath, *Hebrew and the Jewish Renaissance* [Leeds: Leeds University Press, 1961], 13–14).

57. See Theodore Sizer, *Secondary Schools at the Turn of the Century* (New Haven: Yale University Press, 1964); Hawkins, *Between Harvard and America,* passim, and Wechsler, *The Qualified Student,* chapter 4.

58. Some colleges even accepted vocational courses for admission. See Edward A. Krug, *The Shaping of the American High School,* vol. 2: 1920–1940 (Madison: University of Wisconsin Press, 1972), 62; Harry C. McKown, *The Trend of College-Entrance Requirements, 1913–1922* (Washington, D.C.: U.S. Bureau of Education, 1924), bulletin 35, 92; and Wechsler, *The Qualified Student,* chapter 10.

59. See Lawrence Cremin, "The Revolution in American Secondary Education," *Teachers College Record* 56 (March, 1955), 295–308; idem, *The Transformation of the School: Progressivism in American Education 1876–1957* (New York: Knopf, 1961); and Edward A. Krug, *The Shaping of the American High School,* vol. 1: 1880–1920 (Madison: University of Wisconsin Press, 1964).

60. See Edward S. Krug, *The Secondary School Curriculum* (New York: Harper and Row, 1960), 258–59.

61. See Floyd Reeves et al., *The Liberal Arts College* (Chicago: University of Chicago Press, 1932), 194–201.

62. There was one significant exception: Many linguists realized in modern Hebrew an excellent subject for analysis either because as a "revived language" one could observe the methods by which languages grow and change, or because it well illustrated the princi-

ples of transformational grammar, a new area of linguistics. See Noam Chomsky, *Morphophonetics of Modern Hebrew* (New York: Garland Press, 1979); Eliezer Rieger, *Modern Hebrew* (New York: Philosophical Library, 1953); idem, "Palestine," 471–79; Haiim B. Rosen, *Contemporary Hebrew* (The Hague: Mouton, 1977), esp. 53–54; Scott B. Saulson, *Institutionalized Language Planning: Documents and Analyses of the Revival of Hebrew* (The Hague: Mouton, 1979); Edward Ullendorff, "Modern Hebrew as a Subject of Linguistic Investigation," in his volume *Is Biblical Hebrew a Language? Studies in Semitic Languages and Civilizations* (Wiesbaden: Otto Harrassowitz, 1977), 68–80; Ralph W. Weiman, *Native and Foreign Elements in a Language: A Study in General Linguistics Applied to Modern Hebrew* (Philadelphia: Russell Press, 1950); and idem, "The Re-Creation of Hebrew: A 'Dead Language' Lives Again," *Commentary* 7 (June, 1949), 559–65.

63. Several other school systems—Chelsea, Massachusetts, Chicago, Illinois, St. Louis, Missouri, and Schenectady, New York—experimented with the language before World War II. See Mordecai H. Lewittes, "Hebrew Enters New York High Schools," *The Menorah Journal* 26 (Spring, 1938), 238.

64. Zvulun Ravid, "When Was Hebrew Language Instruction Initiated in Community Schools in America?" (in Hebrew), *Shviley Hinukh* 40 (December, 1980), 69–81. Israel Friedlander, a convinced Hebraist, noted: "There is naturally no intention whatsoever to make Hebrew a spoken language in this country—such a task would be impossible, and if possible, scarcely desirable" (Israel Friedlander, "The Problem of Jewish Education in America and the Bureau of Education of the Jewish Community of New York City," in *Report of the Commissioner of Education for the Year Ended June 30, 1913* (Washington, D.C.: Government Printing Office, 1914), 389.

65. The state declined to view Hebrew as an ancient language such as Latin. See Bureau of Curriculum Development, New York State Education Department, *Syllabus in Modern Hebrew* (Albany: University of the State of New York, 1949), 7.

66. See Wechsler, *The Qualified Student*, 65.

67. See Lewittes, "Hebrew," 236.

68. Katsh, *Hebrew in American Higher Education*, passim, and Katsh, "The Teaching of Hebrew," 580–81.

69. Katsh, "Hebraic Studies," 20. See also Judah Lapson, *Hebrew for College Entrance: A Directory of Colleges and Universities Accrediting Hebrew for Admission* (New York: Hebrew Culture Service Committee for American High Schools and Colleges, 1953).

70. See Krug, *Secondary School Curriculum*, 260–70, and William R. Packer, "Why a Foreign Language Requirement?" *The Modern Language Journal* 42 (December, 1958), 370–78.

71. Aaron Ember taught modern Hebrew at Johns Hopkins until his tragic death in 1925, and Max Radin taught the subject during the Columbia University summer session. The Katsh offerings—if not unprecedented—were pivotal since earlier attempts did not outlast the instructor. Columbia provided an exception to the pattern of undergraduate entrance—modern Hebrew joined pre-modern Hebrew on the graduate level. Abraham Halkin and Ralph Marcus, the two instructors during the 1930s, specialized in Judeo-Arabic and in Hellenistic Judaism, respectively, though both were competent Hebraists. Halkin left Columbia in 1938, Marcus in 1943. Columbia and the University of Pennsylvania were among the universities that borrowed young Jewish instructors from other disciplines to teach modern Hebrew through 1968 and beyond.

72. Deborah Dash Moore, *At Home in America: Second Generation New York Jews* (New York: Columbia University Press, 1981), 110. Israel Friedlander and Mordecai Kaplan evolved—and Isaac Berkson, Alexander Dushkin, and Leo Honor propagated—this ideology.

73. E. George Payne, "Personal Versus Social Control," *The Journal of Educational Sociology* 13 (November, 1939), 139. Payne imported the subject from New York University's Extension Division. It subsequently migrated into the College of Arts and Science.

N.Y.U. placed Katsh on annual contract; he was supported by extra-mural contributions. See May 23, 1944, and June 28, 1945 memos, Abraham Katsh Papers, New York University Archives, box 1, file 1.

74. Payne, "Personal Versus Social Control," 139. See also David Rudavsky, "Current Trends in Hebraic Studies in American Colleges and Universities," *Bulletin of the Association of Departments of Foreign Languages* 3 (March, 1972), 36, and Abraham I. Katsh, "Education and Racial Prejudice," *Jewish Social Studies* 6 (July, 1944), 227–32.

75. Lewittes, "Hebrew," 239, 243.

76. Samson Benderly and Stephen Wise signed the petition. See Nathan Winter, *Jewish Education in a Pluralist Society* (New York: New York University Press, 1966), 127. A prominent Reform layman expressed the opposite viewpoint: "The value of Hebrew to the scholar, and to the man who has to be grounded in it so as to equip him for the ministry, whether Jewish or Christian is apparent. But the little you can give to the children who go to the Sabbath school can serve no purpose . . . It is not going to do as so many have argued to wit, draw closer the relationship existing between parent and child" (see Lee Kohns to Israel Friedlander, June 4, 1914, Israel Friedlander Papers, JTS).

77. Rieger, *Modern Hebrew,* 10.

78. Rudavsky, "Current Trends," 40.

79. Harry Blumberg, "Increasing Reading Experience in Hebrew," *The Modern Language Journal* 26 (March, 1942), 199–204, contains a revealing list of books in modern Hebrew read by students in his classes.

80. Joshua Trachtenberg similarly wrote in the early 1950s: "Modern Hebrew literature has received a good deal of attention, but works of sound scholarship and esthetic judgment are few indeed in this field" (see Trachtenberg, "American Jewish Scholarship," 435).

81. Arnold Band, "Modern Hebrew Literature" (paper delivered at Hebrew College Conference, Brookline, Mass., April 25, 1977). Band, who created a preeminent center for the study of modern Hebrew literature at the University of California, Los Angeles, obtained his doctorate in Greek and Latin. The *literary* student of Hebrew was, until the 1960s, at a loss for a place to study. See also Robert Alter, "The Kidnapping of Bialik and Tchernichovsky," in *After the Tradition: Essays on Modern Jewish Writing* (New York: E. P. Dutton, 1971 [1969]), 226–40, an earlier assessment.

82. See Eisig Silberschlag, "The Thrust of Hebrew Letters in America," *Jewish Social Studies* 38 (Summer–Fall, 1976), 277–88.

83. The City College of New York faculty curriculum committee would not initially count Hebrew towards the foreign language requirement and accepted the language only as an elective. Dean Morton Gottschall—following Jacob Voorsanger—later alluded to Brooklyn College and N.Y.U., City College's reference institutions, to justify adding Hebrew to the list of acceptable languages. The relevant documents do not refer to Columbia's modern Hebrew offerings. See City College Dean's file, City College Archives, New York.

84. Contemporaries had difficulty determining enrollment levels since many colleges did not distinguish between classical and modern Hebrew. But Abraham Katsh estimated 3,500 enrollments in modern Hebrew in 1950 and inferred that the number doubled by 1958. (See Abraham I. Katsh, "Current Trends in the Study of Hebrew in Colleges and Universities," *Modern Language Journal* 44 [February, 1960], 66.) David Rudavsky believed these figures high, but he considered a 1960 Modern Language Association estimate of 3,874 students conservative. (See Rudavsky, "Current Trends," 37.) Not all growth resulted from the addition of regular faculty members. Several institutions recognized courses offered by the local Hillel director or rabbi, a practice that raised questions about the academic legitimacy of the subject.

85. Louis Schoffman, "National Association of Professors of Hebrew," *The Modern Language Journal* 35 (May, 1951), 298. *Iggeret,* the association's newsletter, included articles about the growth of Hebrew departments. See, for example "Hebrew in Non-Jewish Institutions of Higher Learning," *Iggeret* (November, 1977) for the growth of the

Department of Hebrew and Semitic Studies at the University of Wisconsin, chaired for many years by Menaham Mansoor.

86. Rudavsky, "Current Trends," 39. See also idem, "Hebraic and Judaic Studies in American Higher Education," *CSR Bulletin* 6 (April, 1975), 3–5.

87. Rudavsky, "Current Trends," 38. See also Richard I. Brod, "Foreign Language Enrollments in U.S. Colleges," *Bulletin of the Association of Departments of Foreign Languages* 3 (December, 1971), 46–50.

88. See Blumberg, "Increasing Reading Experience in Hebrew"; Max Zeldner, "You Too Can Learn Hebrew," *The Modern Language Journal* 35 (February, 1951), 124–34; idem, "And It's All in Hebrew," *The Modern Language Journal* 40 (February, 1956), 71–75; and idem, "Patrick Sullivan Learns Hebrew," *The Modern Language Journal* 42 (December, 1958), 404.

89. Arnold Band lists (in temporal order) seven types of Hebrew that Jewish and non-Jewish Americans employed: (1) Puritan, Old Testament Hebrew, (2) Semitic Philology Hebrew (the Hebrew of Gottheil and Jastrow), (3) American Wissenschaft Hebrew (as exemplified in the American Academy of Jewish Research and the 1905 *Jewish Encyclopedia*), (4) Americanized Tarbut Hebrew (modern in its orientation and the province of the American Jewish immigrant *maskilim*; loosely linked to cultural Zionism), (5) Area Studies Hebrew (which emphasized language rather than literature and culture), (6) Jewish Studies Hebrew (which took all forms of Hebrew and its cultures as its domain), and (7) Israeli Hebrew (the language of a nation state). See Arnold Band, "From Sacred Tongue to Foreign Language: The Case of Hebrew in the American University" (paper delivered at "Hebrew in America: Perspectives and Prospects" conference, March 26, 1990, University of Maryland).

90. See Rosen, *Contemporary Hebrew*, chapters 1 and 2. "The uniqueness of Israeli Hebrew is adequately described by characterizing it as a language the very existence of which is part of the national self-identification of the community that uses it; a language created by intended rebirth; a language whose creation as a vehicle of communication was an ideological act and also the result, at least in part, of scholarly research; a language scientifically studied and analyzed within some seventy years following its emergence, but given a name of its own in scholarship only as a result of recognition, by virtue of that same scholarly study, of its historical autonomy" (ibid., 15).

91. See, for example, Michael Landmann, *Reform of the Hebrew Alphabet* (Ann Arbor: University Microfilms International, 1976), esp. 302–09.

92. Chaim Zhitlovsky referred to Hebrew as "philologically a cemetery. Life may no longer be expected of it" (in Emanuel S. Goldsmith, *Architects of Yiddishism at the Beginning of the Twentieth Century: A Study in Jewish Cultural History* [Rutherford, N.J.: Fairleigh Dickinson University Press, 1976], 247).

93. German missionaries began to compose Yiddish grammars in the eighteenth century, and German university students defended many dissertations on Yiddish during the early nineteenth century. See Peter Hans Althauser, "Yiddish," in Thomas Sebeok, ed., *Current Trends in Linguistics,* IX: *Linguistics in Western Europe* (The Hague: Mouton, 1972), 1347–82, esp. 1353, 1355.

94. See Jerold Frakes, *The Politics of Interpretation* (Albany: State University of New York Press, 1989).

95. Gershom Scholem reported that Magnes signed his name with his Yiddish middle name, Leibusch, rather than with Leon, as he was known in American circles. See Gershom Scholem, *From Berlin to Jerusalem* (New York: Schocken Books, 1980), 171.

96. Heinrich Graetz refused to allow a Yiddish translation of his history of the Jews. See Zosa Szajkowski, "The Struggle for Yiddish During World War I: The Attitude of German Jewry," in Joshua Fishman, ed., *Never Say Die* (The Hague: Mouton, 1981), 565–89.

97. See, for example, Leo Weiner, *The History of Yiddish Literature in the Nineteenth Century* (New York: Charles Scribner's Sons, 1899), and Edward Sapir, "Notes on Judeo-

German Phonology," *Jewish Quarterly Review*, n.s., 6 (1915), 231–64. Max Weinreich participated in Sapir's seminar on the impact of culture on personality at Yale. See also Emanuel S. Goldsmith, "Yiddishism and Judaism," *Judaism* 38 (Fall, 1989), 527–36; idem, *Modern Yiddish Culture: The Story of the Yiddish Language Movement* (New York: Shapolsky Publishers and the Workmen's Circle Education Department, 1987); and Leonard Prager, "Yiddish in the University," *Jewish Quarterly* 22 (Spring/Summer, 1974), 31–40. The 1917–1918 *American Jewish Yearbook* stated that Yale offered instruction in Yiddish, but Dan Oren could not confirm the statement. Oren suggests that Max Mandell, an instructor in Russian (1907–1924) might have informally offered Yiddish instruction. See *American Jewish Yearbook* (1917–1918), 406, and Oren, *Joining the Club*, 356.

98. Weinreich, a native German speaker, came to Yiddish scholarship through the political attractiveness of the *Bund*. See Lucy Dawidowicz, "Max Weinreich (1894–1969): The Scholarship of Yiddish," *American Jewish Yearbook* (1969), 60.

99. The Vilna branch of YIVO, founded in 1925, was equally interested in contemporary Jewish society and Yiddish language and linguistics. In New York, YIVO would become more historical and linguistic—a living memorial to the Jews and the communities destroyed during the Holocaust.

100. See Ascher Penn, *Yiddishkeit in America* (in Yiddish) (New York: n.p., 1958), 539–47. Max Weinreich had already taught Yiddish in the UCLA summer school, but the language only became part of the regular course of study years later.

101. Sol Liptzin to Morton Gottschall, November 19, 1946, City College Dean's file, City College Archives.

102. See Byron Sherwin, *Contexts and Content: Higher Jewish Education in the United States, Spertus College of Judaica—A Case Study* (Chicago: Spertus College of Judaica Press, 1987), 235.

103. On the number of Yiddish language "knowers" in the U.S. in 1970, see Frances Kobrin, "National Data on American Jewry: A Comparative Evaluation of the Census Mother Tongue Subpopulation and the National Jewish Population Survey," in U. O. Schmelz et al., *Papers in Jewish Demography, 1981* (Jerusalem: Institute of Contemporary Jewry, 1983), 129–43.

104. Uriel Weinreich, *College Yiddish* (New York: Yiddish Scientific Institute, 1949), and Reuben Wallenrod and Abraham Aaroni, *Modern Hebrew Reader and Grammar* (New York: Shiloh, 1949).

105. Northrop Frye, "The Critical Path: An Essay on the Social Context of Literary Criticism," *Daedalus* 99 (Spring, 1970), 299.

106. Robert M. Hutchins, *The Higher Learning in America* (New Haven: Yale University Press, 1936), 96, 97.

107. See Robert S. Shepard, *God's People in the Ivory Tower: Religion in the Early American University* (Brooklyn: Carlson Publishing, 1991), and idem, "The Science of Religion in American Universities: 1880–1930, A Comparison of Six Institutions" (Ph.D. diss., University of Chicago, 1988).

108. University of Chicago, *The President's Report, 1896–1897*, 209; ibid., *1911–1912*, 52.

109. Shepard, *God's People in the Ivory Tower*, 22–31, quotations from 25, 26.

110. Friedrich Max Müller, *Chips from a German Workshop* (New York: Charles Scribner's Sons, 1869), 1:48, cited in Philip H. Ashby, "The History of Religions," in Paul Ramsey, ed., *Religion* (Englewood Cliffs: Prentice-Hall, 1965), 1–49, quotation from 14.

111. See Wilfred Cantwell Smith, "Comparative Religion: Whither and Why?" in Mircea Eliade and Joseph M. Kitagawa, eds., *The History of Religions: Essays in Methodology* (Chicago: University of Chicago Press, 1959), 37. Durkheim and Freud also suggested that to know origins is to understand current functions. Rudolf Otto was reportedly inspired to write his classic *The Idea of the Holy* by his experience in a traditional synagogue in North Africa. See Isaak Heinemann, *Taamey HaMitzvot b'Sifrut Yisrael*, 2nd ed. (Jerusalem: Histadrut HaTsiyonut, The Religious Section, 1956), 185.

112. Peters, "Thirty Years' Progress in Semitics," 43.

113. University of Pennsylvania, *Catalogue*, 1911/12:298–301.

114. Gottheil to Wise, July 19, 1927, JIR Papers, AJA, no. 19, 16/19, "Richard Gottheil" file.

115. Morris Jastrow, Jr., "The Historical Study of Religions in Universities and Colleges," *Journal of the American Oriental Society* 20, second part (July–December, 1899), 317–25, quotation from 318.

116. Morton Smith, "The Work of George Foot Moore," *Harvard Library Bulletin* 15 (April, 1967), 169–79, quotation from 175.

117. George Foot Moore, *History of Religions* (New York: Charles Scribner's Sons, 1928), 2:xi.

118. E. R. Goodenough, "Religionswissenschaft," *A.C.L.S. Newsletter* 10 (June, 1959), 8–9, and Willard Gurdon Oxtoby, *"Religionswissenschaft* Revisited," in Jacob Neusner, ed., *Religions in Antiquity, Studies in Memory of Erwin Ramsdell Goodenough* (Studies in the History of Religions, Supplements to *Numen* 14) (Leiden: Brill, 1968), 590. On Goodenough, see Robert S. Eccles, *Erwin Ramsdell Goodenough: A Personal Pilgrimage* (Encino, Calif.: Scholars Press, 1985).

119. George F. Kay to Rabbi Eugene Mannheimer, August 3, 1926, as quoted in Marcus Bach, *Of Faith and Learning: The Story of the School of Religion at the State University of Iowa* (Iowa City: School of Religion, State University of Iowa, 1952), 115. See Foster to Enelow, October 2, 1924, and October 27, 1924, Enelow Papers, AJA, General Correspondence 1924–1925, box 573, "F" file.

120. Maurice H. Farbridge, formerly associate professor of Semitic studies at Victoria University, Manchester, England, was the first Jewish faculty member at the Iowa School of Religion (1928–29). His three successors had worked for the Hillel Foundation at the University of Illinois: Rabbi Moses Jung (1929–1939), former Hillel director at the University of Illinois, who later worked for the B'nai B'rith's Anti-Defamation League; Rabbi Morris N. Kertzer, who came to Iowa from the University of Alabama after Hillel work at Illinois; and Judah Goldin (1945–1952), formerly at Duke and Illinois. Hillel Extension Service assumed sponsorship of the School's Jewish interests upon Kertzer's appointment.

121. For other prewar communal initiatives and responses, see "Professorship for Rabbi: Tulane's Chair of Hebrew to be Filled by Dr. Heller," *The American Citizen* 2 (January, 1913), 23; William T. Amiger to Jacob Schiff, October 28, 1915, Schiff Correspondence, AJA, box 442, "Education" file (concerning the University of Louisville); Abraham E. Pinanski to Nathan Isaacs, May 21 and November 28, 1936, and December 8, 1941 (includes Isaacs' handwritten reply), AJA, "Letters to Professor Isaacs" (microfilm 674) (concerning the Instructorship Fund in Jewish History and Philosophy at Boston University); H. J. Ettinger, professor of mathematics, University of Texas, to Wise, August 3 and September 8, 1938, Wise to Ettinger, September 1 and 13, 1938, Wise Papers, AJHS, box 43, file 1: "Education." See also the early volumes of the *Menorah Journal*.

122. Goodenough, "Religionswissenschaft," 8, and Philip Ashby, "History of Religions," 1–49.

123. See John F. Marley, "Jewish Studies at a Catholic University," *Jewish Spectator* (Spring, 1978), 46–49, on student motivation for enrollment.

124. But Neusner also argued against "positivist reductionism," the explanation of expressions of the Jewish spirit "in some terms other than those of which they speak—of the spirit or the soul." Judaism had, Neusner argued, a role in a religion department—all cannot be reduced to the secular. See Jacob Neusner, "Departments of Religious Studies and Contemporary Jewish Studies," *American Jewish Historical Quarterly* 63 (June, 1974), 356–60, quotation from 359.

125. See Harold Remus, "Origins," in Claude Welch, *Graduate Education in Religion: A Critical Appraisal* (Missoula: University of Montana Press, 1971), 124–27; Clyde A. Holbrook, *Religion: A Humanistic Field* (Englewood Cliffs: Prentice-Hall, Inc.,

1963), 57–58; O. D. Foster, "Denominational Cooperation in Religious Education at State Universities," *Christian Education* 5 (December, 1921), 12–20; idem, "Religion in American Universities," *Christian Education* 4 (June, 1921), 3–69; idem, "Schools of Religion at State Universities," *Christian Education* 5 (April, 1922), 183–93; and Charles F. Kent, "Can We Fill the Gap in Modern Education?" *Educational Record* 66 (December, 1923), 251–57.

126. See Bach, *Of Faith and Learning,* passim, and M. Willard Lampe, *The Story of an Idea: The History of the School of Religion at the University of Iowa* (Iowa City: State University of Iowa, 1963), bulletin 806.

127. C. P. Shedd, *Religion in the State University,* pamphlet 16 (New Haven: Edward M. Hazen Foundation, 1947), 20.

128. Huston Smith, "The Interdepartmental Approach to Religious Studies," *Journal of Higher Education* 31 (February, 1960), 62.

129. *Abington School District v. Schempp,* 374, *United States Reports,* 225 (October term, 1962).

130. Ibid., 300, 306.

131. See especially Milton D. McLean, ed., *Religious Studies in Public Universities* (Carbondale: Southern Illinois University, 1967); Robert Michaelsen, *The Study of Religion in American Universities: Ten Case Studies with Special Reference to State Universities* (New Haven: Society for Religion in Higher Education, 1965); and Erich A. Walter, *Religion and the State University* (Ann Arbor: University of Michigan Press, 1958).

132. Welch, *Graduate Education in Religion,* 178. The criteria for selecting these 25 institutions are not clear; they probably were the only colleges and universities with data available for 1964. Total enrollments at these institutions increased 55 percent.

133. "To have deep convictions and still be generous in understanding one's fellow-man was the desideratum in the quest for instructors," Bach wrote about the Iowa School. "An increasingly popular phrase defined it, 'We expect and respect differences' " (Bach, *Of Faith and Learning,* 132).

134. Holbrook, *Religion,* 53.

135. On the pre-World War II history of the study of religion, see Jacques Waardenburg, ed., *Classical Approaches to the Study of Religion: Aims, Methods, and Theories of Research,* 2 vols. (The Hague: Mouton, 1973).

136. See Winthrop S. Hudson, *Religion in America* (New York: Charles Scribner's Sons, 1965), 379–84.

137. "At times," Norman Birnbaum noted, "Hutchins' views have had a faint resemblance to the late Dwight Eisenhower's curious stand on religion: He felt that every American ought to have one, but he did not care which one anybody chose. Is it so with metaphysics for Hutchins? There has to be one—if not Aristotelian, then some other kind." Birnbaum added that for Huthcins, "the university has to educate a citizenry which is spiritually mature and sovereign in its judgment—above all, in its judgment of cultural and political issues which cannot be left to (often self-proclaimed) experts. Metaphysics, on this view, is a tool of judgment. Hutchins, again, was an exponent of an evaluative social science—one which would go beyond empiricism to make critical judgments of the polity." Birnbaum argued: "The erosion of the religious foundations of American liberalism deprived secularized liberalism of that kind of self-confidence, or élan, without which, no doctrine triumphs." (See Norman Birnbaum, "Students, Professors and Philosopher Kings," in Carl Kaysen, *Content and Context: Essays on College Education* [New York: McGraw Hill, 1973], 433–34.)

138. See David D. Henry, *Challenges Past, Challenges Present: An Analysis of American Higher Education Since 1930* (San Francisco: Jossey-Bass, 1975), chapters 3, 5, and 6; Rudolph, *Curriculum,* 264–65; and Wechsler, *The Qualified Student,* chapter 10.

139. Committee on Objectives of A General Education in a Free Society, Harvard University, *General Education in a Free Society: Report of the Harvard Committee* (Cambridge: Harvard University Press, 1945), 76.

140. "There is a world-wide challenge to the moral and spiritual values which have been the foundation of our western culture," stated a resolution of the National Education Association's Department of Higher Education,

> there is wide-spread evidence of moral and spiritual deterioration in our midst. Competence, in and of itself, has little meaning apart from the direction in which it is applied and this direction depends upon a reflective commitment to moral and spiritual values by which the individual is willing to work and live. Be it therefore resolved that institutions of higher learning accept their responsibilities in the area of values by: 1) clarifying their policies regarding the moral and spiritual aspects of education and, 2) by implementing these policies in administrative practice, in curriculum content, and in extra-curricular activities. (quoted in Bach, *Of Faith and Learning*, 258)

141. Arthur E. Murphy, "Philosophical Scholarship," in Merle Curti, ed., *American Scholarship in the Twentieth Century*, 200.

142. Sidney D. Ahlstrom, "Continental Influence on American Christian Thought Since World War I," *Church History* 27 (September, 1958), 256–72; Richard Fox, "Reinhold Niebuhr and the Emergence of the Liberal-Realist Faith, 1930–1945," *Review of Politics* 38 (April, 1976), 244–65.

143. Talcott Parsons, "The Institutionalization of Social Science and the Problems of the Conference," in Lyman Bryson, Louis Finkelstein, and R. M. MacIver, eds., *Perspectives on a Too Troubled Decade: Science, Philosophy, and Religion, 1939–1949* (New York: Harper and Brothers, 1950), 229–34, quotation from 230.

144. Holbrook, *Religion*, 35.

145. "The syncretism of our own time expresses the exhaustion of radical individualism," asserted sociologist Daniel Bell. "It shows us to be in search of community (*Gemeinschaft*) and primordial attachments. Hence the revival of certain cults from Eastern religions, hence the appeal of certain art-groups, meditation, mediating institutions, and so on. All these seek some assurance that coherent answers *are* available to what I would call the existential predicament that confronts every human being: how to face death; the nature of tragedy; the character of obligation; the encounter with love, etc. Modern liberalism has no answers to these questions." Advocates of religious study in the university argued that "the real problem of modernity is the problem of belief," but urged reflection about the problematic of belief as the proper realm of university inquiry. See George Urban, "A Conversation with Daniel Bell: On Religion and Ideology," *Encounter* 40 (February, 1983), 13.

146. "Social science is indeed a dangerous and socially, as well as intellectually, difficult enterprise," wrote Talcott Parsons, thinking especially of its relationship to religion (see Parsons, "Institutionalization," 241).

147. Morton White, "Religion, Politics and the Higher Learning," in his *Religion, Politics, and the Higher Learning* (Cambridge: Harvard University Press, 1959), 94–96, quotation from 96. By the time White wrote, the distinction had become well-ingrained. Judah Goldin, then teaching at Iowa's School of Religion, noted:

> In a certain sense, to say that the School of Religion *teaches* religion, would be the height of naïveté or presumption. The best teachers of religion are not teachers in the limited sense. The best teachers of religion are the saints of the different religions; and saints have not always been the best educated men, that is, formally educated, of their times. They have been more than that.

> What, then, is it that the School of Religion does, if it does not *teach* religion? It offers various opportunities, within the limits of the teachers' abilities and time, for the disciplined, critical and sympathetic study of different religious cultures, and, especially, of the religious traditions of the Western world. . . . Whatever the spec-

ified course, the principal concern is to present the material carefully to the student, so that he will arrive at a deeper understanding of the subject, and acquire what might be called a genuine knowledge, rather than a market-place notion, of it. (quoted in Bach, *Of Faith and Learning*, 235–36)

148. See Holbrook, *Religion*, 108–09.

149. See Joachim Wach, *The Comparative Study of Religions*, Joseph Kitagawa, ed. (New York: Columbia University Press, 1958), 28–30. But see also R. J. Zvi Werblowsky, "The Comparative Study of Religions—A Review Essay," *Judaism* (Fall, 1959), 356, and William A. Clebsch, "Apples, Oranges, and Manna: Comparative Religion Revisited," *The Journal of the American Academy of Religion* 49 (March, 1981), 13–14, which argued that Wach's scholarship employed a doctrine of Christian exceptionalism.

150. Richard C. Martin, "On the Teaching of Islam as Religion," *Bulletin of the Council on the Study of Religion* 6 (February, 1975), 3. Martin also writes: "Traces of prejudice arising out of a tradition of religious crusades and anti-Muslim polemic are still to be found in Western scholarship" (ibid., 3–4). See also R. C. Zaehner, "Why Not Islam?" *Religious Studies* 11 (June, 1975), 167–79.

151. Charlotte Klein, *Anti-Judaism in Christian Theology*, Edward Quinn, tr., (Philadelphia: Fortress Press, 1978). See also George Nickelsburg's review of Klein's book in *Religious Studies Review* 4 (July, 1978), 161–68, and George Foot Moore's much earlier discussion of the same theme, "Christian Writers on Judaism," *Harvard Theological Review* 14 (July, 1921), 197–254.

152. Smith, "Interdepartmental Approach to Religious Studies," 61.

153. William A. Clebsch, "Religious Studies Now: Not Why Not? But Why Not Not?" *Religious Education* 70 (May/June, 1975), 266.

154. Parsons, "Institutionalization," 238–39. See also Harry T. Gideonse, *The Higher Learning in a Democracy: A Reply to President Hutchins' Critique of the American University* (New York: Farrar and Rinehart, 1937). Compare the following: "I can think of no department from which the current of religion can be rightly separated. Art, education, literature and the various skills can all be brought into a central terminus where the student feels the pulse of religion and finds that faith is not something isolated and detached, but actually the central core of his educational training" (O. D. Foster as quoted in Bach, *Of Faith and Learning*, 68).

155. Welch, *Graduate Education in Religion*, 16. On the early practices at the University of Iowa's School of Religion, see the first part of Bach, *Of Faith and Learning*.

156. Salo W. Baron, "The Problem of Teaching Religion," *Columbia College Today* 10 (Spring/Summer, 1963), 25–27.

157. Goodenough, "Religionswissenschaft," 9.

158. Welch, *Graduate Education in Religion*, 34–47. See Samuel Sandmel's strong response, "The Welch Survey: One Man's Opinion," *Bulletin of the Council on the Study of Religions* 3 (April, 1972), 8–12, and Claude Welch, "Six Months Later: A Response," ibid., 21–23.

159. Jencks and Riesman, *Academic Revolution*, 207–12.

160. "As colleges have added to their religion departments, and as tax-supported schools in particular have established new programs, the religious traditions of the non-Western world have been a prime area for development," wrote Willard Gurdon Oxtoby in 1968. "American global involvements of recent decades have helped to pull interest in this direction, while at the same time the sensitivity of college administrators to avoid preferential treatment of Christian or even Judeo-Christian topics has often provided a helping push toward a broader range of comparison" (see Oxtoby, "*Religionswissenschaft* Revisited," 593). For a summary of the state of scholarship in religion up to the Schempp decision, see Paul Ramsey, ed., *Religion*.

161. See John F. Wilson and Thomas P. Slavens, *Research Guide to Religious Studies* (Chicago: American Library Association, 1982), 12–14.

162. Thus, Gerald S. Sloyan, speaking of Roman Catholic campuses, wrote; "There is to be found a kind of academic person, firm in a particular tradition and not in revolt against anything [written in 1969], who is withal a searcher in the best sense" (Gerald S. Sloyan, "The New Role of the Study of Religion in Higher Education: What Does it Mean?" *Journal of Ecumenical Studies* 6 [Winter, 1969], 1–17, quotation from 15). Or there is Raymond Abba: "Religion is essentially response to what is given: hence the necessity for the historical, factual, informative element in religious studies. But it is only as the historical and parahistorical become luminous in their fusion that the awareness, the sensitive understanding which is the essence of true religious thinking is evoked" (Raymond Abba, "Athens and Jerusalem: Religious Studies in the Secular University," *Religious Education* 70 [July/August, 1975], 355–74, quotation from 373). See also Langdon Gilkey: "Technology, the new religions, the omnipresence of ideology, and the encounter of cultures and religions involve, seemingly inescapably, deeper questions than we expected, not only questions of fact and the scholarly interpretation of facts but reflective questions calling for new self-understanding and so for philosophical and technological creativity" (Langdon Gilkey, "The AAR and the Anxiety of Nonbeing: An Analysis of Our Present Cultural Situation," *Journal of the American Academy of Religion* 48 [March, 1980], 5–18, quotation from 17). Robert Bellah wrote: "I am not afraid . . . of blurring the boundary line between religion and the teaching of religion, since the teaching of religion itself is a kind of religious discipline" (quoted in James E. Dittes, "Confessing Away the Soul with the Sins, or: The Risks of Uncle Tomism Among the Humanists. A Reply to Robert Bellah," *Bulletin of the Council on the Study of Religion* 2 [December, 1971], 23. Original in Robert Bellah, "Christianity and Symbolic Realism," *Journal for the Scientific Study of Religion* 9 [Summer, 1970], 89–115).

163. Facile statements also abounded. "A genuinely pluralistic society entails the educational need for the teaching of (or about) religions especially in institutions of higher learning," stated one scholar. "Incidentally," he wrote, "I'm not at all chary of using the proposition 'of' instead of 'about' since the pervasive tone of a genuine university requires more than description" (Anthony Nemitz, "The Study of Religion in a Pluralistic Society," in Milton D. McLean, ed., *Religious Studies in Public Universities* [Carbondale: Southern Illinois University Press, 1967], 23).

164. "For university teachers of Judaica to fail to inculcate in their students the notion of study as a mitzvah is to be as unfaithful to their discipline as for teachers of physics to fail to inculcate an acceptance of the scientific method" (Richard N. Levy, "The American University and Olam Ha-Ba," *Religious Education* 69 [Special Edition, May/June, 1974], 15, 22, 23).

165. Jeremy Zwelling, "Religion in the Department of Religion," ibid., 99–137.

166. For a personal statement in response to the same questioning of the nature of higher education, see Samuel Sandmel, "Antiquarianism and Contemporaneity: The Relevance of Studies in Religion," *Journal of the American Academy of Religion* 35 (December, 1967), 372–78. Gerson Cohen viewed such criticisms as part of a larger tendency for advocates of religion and of humanism perhaps to tolerate, perhaps to ignore each other, but in any case to avoid confrontation. See Gerson D. Cohen, "The Decline of the Confrontation Between Religion and Humanism in Higher Jewish Education," in Program of General Education in the Humanities, Columbia University, *Seminar Reports* 5 (Fall, 1976), 47–53.

167. On compartmentalization as a strategy for conflict resolution, see Veysey, "Intellectual History and the New Social History," 3–26.

168. Welch, *Graduate Education in Religion*, 18–29, quotations from 20, 21, 25. On religion in liberal education, see idem, *Religion in the Undergraduate Curriculum: An Analysis and Interpretation* (Washington, D.C.: Association of American Colleges, 1972). The *Bulletin of the Council on the Study of Religions* contains many relevant articles. See also Jacob Neusner, "Introducing Judaism in the University: The First Course and Its Problems," *Journal of Reform Judaism* 26 (Summer, 1979), 35–53.

169. See Bernard Berelson, *Graduate Education in the United States* (New York: Mc-Graw Hill, 1960), especially 60–61; Lewis G. Mayhew and Patrick J. Ford, *Reform in Graduate and Professional Education* (San Francisco: Jossey-Bass, 1974), chapter 5, and Commission on Graduate Education, University of Chicago, "Report," *University of Chicago Record* 16 (May 3, 1982), chapter 3. Welch specifically argued against the "jacks of all trades" notion; see Welch, *Graduate Education in Religion,* 19, n. 3.

170. Welch, *Graduate Education in Religion,* 246.

171. See Sandmel, "Welch Survey," passim, and Jacob Neusner, "Judaic/Jewish Studies in the Welch Report," *Bulletin of the Council on the Study of Religion* 3 (October, 1972), 3–5.

172. See Neusner, "Autodidacts in Graduate School," in *Academic Study,* 1:145–49, and Nachum M. Sarna, "Remarks on Graduate Jewish Studies in the University," *Association for Jewish Studies Newsletter* 8 (February, 1973), 5, 7.

173. Neusner, "Judaic/Jewish Studies," 5. See also Meyer, "Types of Graduate Programs in Judaic Studies," ibid., 3, 6.

174. Goodenough, "Religionswissenschaft," 19.

175. Jacob Neusner, "Judaism Within the Disciplines of Religious Studies: Perspectives on Graduate Education," in Jacob Neusner, ed., *New Humanities and Academic Disciplines: The Case of Jewish Studies* (Madison: University of Wisconsin Press, 1984). See also his introduction to his edited volume, *Take Judaism, For Example: Studies Toward the Comparison of Religions* (Chicago: University of Chicago Press, 1983).

176. Joshua Trachtenberg, "American Jewish Scholarship," in *The Jewish People: Past and Present* (New York: Jewish Encyclopedic Handbooks, 1955), 4:419. See also Glatzer, "Beginnings of Modern Jewish Studies," 33.

177. Cited in William Hallo, "Biblical Studies in Jewish Perspective," in Jick, ed., *Teaching of Judaica in American Universities,* 44.

178. Ginsberg, *New Trends in the Study of the Bible,* 11–12.

179. See Hallo, "Biblical Studies in Jewish Perspective" 44–45.

180. An important traditionalist, but far from fundamentalist critique of the use and misuse of the documentary hypothesis is Umberto Cassuto, *Torat Ha-Teudot Ve-Siduram Shel Sifre Ha-Torah* [The Documentary Hypothesis and the Composition of the Pentateuch] (Jerusalem: Magnes Press of Hebrew University, 1953).

181. Yehezkel Kaufmann, *The Religion of Israel,* Moshe Greenberg, tr. and ed. (New York: Schocken, 1972 [1960]). See also Moshe Greenberg, "Kaufmann on the Bible: An Appreciation," *Judaism* 13 (Winter, 1964), 77–89, and Shemaryahu Talmon, "Yehezkel Kaufmann's Approach to Biblical Research," *Conservative Judaism* 25 (Winter, 1971), 20–28.

182. Near Eastern or Middle Eastern language and literature departments abetted the change as they broke through the positivistic version of philology.

183. See Husik, *Philosophical Essays: Ancient, Mediaeval & Modern,* xxv.

184. Husik, *History of Medieval Jewish Philosophy,* 432. Husik remained interested in some classical Jewish philosophers but opted for law school and the philosophy of law.

185. "The systematic approach that is found in such social sciences as economics, politics, and sociology is lacking in Jewish learning which consists of a historical approach towards aspects of Jewish life," wrote Bernard D. Weinryb, a social scientist. "Even such a systematic branch of learning as philosophy has been transformed into a *history* of Jewish philosophy" (Weinryb, "Jewish Research and Its Tasks," 15–16). Chinese philosophy, when taught in Oriental studies or East Asian departments, has no impact on philosophy departments and—like Jewish philosophy, it was said—remains isolated from the mainstream of the philosophical canon (see George L. Anderson, "Oriental Languages and Literatures," in Victor Lange, ed., *Modern Literature* [Englewood Cliffs: Prentice-Hall, 1968], 3:223–77, esp. 234–38).

186. The category includes "Jewish thought" as well as philosophy.

187. See Marvin Fox, "The Role of Philosophy in Jewish Studies," in Rachel Jospe and Samuel Z. Fishman, eds., *Go and Study: Essays and Studies in Honor of Alfred Jospe* (Washington, D.C.: B'nai B'rith Hillel Foundations, 1980), 97.

188. "Altogether, while American scholars are doing quite a little to bring out the connections between medieval Jewish thought and the mainstream of Western culture, the general philosophical world has still to be persuaded that Medieval Jewish philosophy is of any interest to any but the specialist historian" (see John Passmore, "Philosophical Scholarship in the United States, 1930–1960," in Roderick M. Chisholm et al., *Philosophy* [Englewood Cliffs: Prentice-Hall, 1964], 64).

189. There were at least ten studies of New York City's Jewish population between the 1880s and the 1960s. An incomplete bibliography of Jewish social research for the period 1920–1970 lists 5,572 items. See U. O. Schmelz, ed., *Demography and Statistics of Diaspora Jewry, 1920–1970* (Jerusalem: Institute of Contemporary Jewry, Hebrew University of Jerusalem, 1976). A less comprehensive volume that covers 1969–1971 abstracts over 300 items. See U. O. Schmelz et al., eds., *Studies in Jewish Demography, Survey for 1969–1971* (Jerusalem: Institute of Contemporary Jewry, Hebrew University of Jerusalem, 1975).

190. On the Conference, see Salo W. Baron, "The Conference on Jewish Social Studies," in *Conference on Jewish Social Studies: Its Work and Program, 1933–1955* (New York: Conference on Jewish Social Studies, 1956), Morris Raphael Cohen, "Jewish Social Studies: A Contribution to American Democracy," in *A Dreamer's Journey: The Autobiography of Morris Raphael Cohen* (Boston: Beacon Press and The Free Press, 1949), 237–57, and "Conference on Jewish Social Studies (CJSS)," in Michael N. Dobkowski, ed., *Jewish–American Voluntary Organizations* (New York: Greenwood Press, 1986), 131–33. On *Jewish Social Studies*, its main publication, see Salo W. Baron, "Introduction: Reflections on the Achievements and Prospects of *Jewish Social Studies*," *Jewish Social Studies* 41 (Winter, 1979), 1–8, and idem, "The Journal and the Conference of Jewish Social Studies," in Abraham Duker and Meir Ben-Horin, eds., *Emancipation and Counter Emancipation* (New York: KTAV, 1974), 1–11.

191. See Bruno Blau, "Sociology and Statistics of the Jews," *Historia Judaica* 11 (1949), 145–62, and Fritz Bamberger, "Zunz's Conception of History," *Proceedings of the American Academy of Jewish Research* 11 (1941), 1–25.

192. On YIVO, see Dan Miron, "Between Science and Faith: Sixty Years of the YIVO Institute," *YIVO Annual of Jewish Social Science* 19 (1990), 1–15; Solomon Liptzin, *The Maturing of Yiddish Literature* (New York: Jonathan David, 1970), 218–24; idem, *YIVO in America* (New York: Yiddish Scientific Institute, 1945); idem, *YIVO's Way* (New York: Yiddish Scientific Institute, 1943); David Rosenthal, "In the Springtime of the Modern Jewish Spirit," *Jewish Frontier* 42 (December, 1975), 7–12; and Arnold Shankman, "YIVO Institute for Jewish Research (Yidisher Visnshaftlikher Institut)," in Dobkowski, ed., *Jewish–American Voluntary Organizations*, 502–05.

193. U.S. Bureau of the Census, *Religion Reported by the Civilian Population of the United States, March, 1957* in *Current Population Reports: Population Characteristics,* series P-20, no. 79 (Washington D.C.: U.S. Bureau of the Census, February 2, 1958).

194. Not all of these social scientists were Jews; a non-Jewish faculty member from Johns Hopkins conducted one pioneering study: see Henry Chalmers, "The Number of Jews in New York City," *Publications of the American Statistical Association* 14 (1914–1915), 68–75.

195. Board of Delegates of American Israelites and the Union of American Hebrew Congregations, *Statistics of the Jews of the United States* (Philadelphia, 1880).

196. See for example, Alexander M. Dushkin, "A Statistical Study of the Jewish Population of New York," in *The Jewish Communal Register of New York City, 1917–1918* (New York: Kehillah of New York City, 1918), 75–88.

197. Social scientists fared little better at Israeli universities. Arthur Ruppin, the chief Jewish social researcher in Germany, was appointed, on a part time basis, to the first fac-

ulty of the Institute for Jewish Studies of The Hebrew University. When he died, he was not replaced. Israel currently has only one tenured social scientist who takes as his principal mandate the social scientific study of the Jews.

198. The Cincinnati and New York campuses of Hebrew Union College–Jewish Institute of Religion and the main campus of the Jewish Theological Seminary intermittently appointed visiting social scientists to their academic staffs. H.U.C.–J.I.R. later appointed a sociologist at its Los Angeles branch campus whose main function was to work with social work students.

199. See Leslie B. Alexander and Milton D. Speizman, "The Graduate School for Jewish Social Work, 1924–40: Training for Social Work in an Ethnic Community," *Journal of Education for Social Work* 19 (Spring, 1983), 5–15.

200. Fred Matthews, "Louis Wirth and American Ethnic Studies: The Worldview of Enlightened Assimilationism, 1925–1950," in Moses Rischin, ed., *The Jews of North America* (Detroit: Wayne State University Press, 1987), 126.

201. In spite of a need for accurate social statistics, significant elements in the Jewish community objected to government studies that identified and studied the Jews as a nationality or ethnic group. The author of the Jewish population article in the first *American Jewish Year Book* described the enumeration of Jewish immigrants as "a discrimination which has been properly condemned, but is held by the officials to be expedient" (see Abram S. Isaacs, "The Jews of the United States," *American Jewish Year Book* 1 [1899–1900], 14–15).

202. Trachtenberg, "American Jewish Scholarship," 413. On Trachtenberg, see *Encyclopaedia Judaica*, s.v. "Trachtenberg, Joshua," and A. J. Zuckerman's obituary in *Central Conference of American Rabbis Yearbook* 70 (1961), 180–81.

203. Weinryb, "Jewish Research and Its Tasks," 16, 21. Jewish social studies, Weinryb added, suffered from methodological deficiencies because of a lack of Jewish knowledge. We will return to this theme. On Weinryb, see *Encyclopaedia Judaica*, s.v. "Weinryb, Bernard Dov Sucher."

204. Solomon B. Freehof, "Prospects for American Jewish Scholarship," *Judaism* 3 (Fall, 1954), 381–90. On Freehof, see Walter Jacob, Frederick C. Schwartz, and Vigdor W. Kavalev, eds., *Essays in Honor of Solomon B. Freehof* (Pittsburgh: Rodef Shalom Congregation, 1962), and *Encyclopaedia Judaica*, s.v. "Freehof, Solomon."

205. Selig Perlman statement in Harry L. Lurie and Max Weinreich, eds., "Jewish Social Research in America: Status and Prospects, A Symposium," *YIVO Annual of Jewish Social Science* 4 (1949), 172.

206. W. F. Albright statement in ibid., 177. See also Nathan Reich statement, ibid., 254.

207. S. Ralph Harlow statement, ibid., 213.

208. "If you have a feeling that you are a marked improvement on your predecessors, that you are stronger, healthier, more prosperous and have attained greater prestige than your parents or grandparents, you have little desire for spending time or money in finding out about your antecedents" (see Harry Lurie statement, ibid., 160–61).

209. See for example, Leopold Zunz, "Grundlinien zu einer künftigen Statistik der Juden" in *Zeitschrift für die Wissenschaft des Judentums* 1 (1823).

210. Taken from C. Van Woodward, "History and the Third Culture," *Journal of Contemporary History* 3 (April 1968), 29–30.

211. As quoted in Zalman Shazar, *Morning Stars,* Sulamith Schwartz Nardi, tr. (Philadelphia: Jewish Publication Society of America, 1967), 189–90.

212. Ralph Marcus, "American Jewish Scholarship Today," *Chicago Jewish Forum* 6 (Summer, 1948), 264–68, quotation from 265.

213. "There are only a handful of rabbis who manage to fight off the demands of daily duties to devote some hours to study and perhaps even to creative scholarship," wrote Solomon Freehof (see "Prospects," 384).

214. See Band, "Jewish Studies," 20. In 1966, Band noted, of more than 60 individuals holding full time university posts, perhaps ten held endowed chairs.

215. Harry L. Lurie statement in Lurie and Weinreich, eds., "Jewish Social Research," 154–58. See also Lurie, "Jewish Social Research," in Baron et al., eds., *Freedom and Reason*, 383–96.

216. Report of the Department of Scientific Research and Program Evaluation, American Jewish Committee, December 5, 1947, in Departments and Divisions Scientific Research Reports file, Ad, 45–58.

217. The communal agency as an operating entity frequently feels the need to maintain "authority over the data." Further, some non-profits [i.e. universities] refuse to take on projects where the confidentiality of results must be respected, although even the most strict will make some exceptions" (The American Jewish Committee, Division of Scientific Research, "Memorandum on Program Orientation of the Division of Scientific Research," October 7, 1963; Research, AJC Programs and Plans, Dom, 63–67).

218. Abraham G. Duker statement in Lurie and Weinreich, eds., "Jewish Social Research," 268. Duker argued that the rabbinate might serve "as a source for at least part-time social scientists."

219. Charles B. Sherman statement, ibid., 227. See also Mark Wischnitzer statement, ibid., 220–23.

220. Edward N. Saveth statement, ibid., 206.

221. Seymour Lipset, "Jewish Sociologists and Sociologists of the Jews," *Jewish Social Studies* 17 (July, 1955), 178.

222. Nathan Glazer statement in Lurie and Weinreich, eds., "Jewish Social Research," 193.

223. Florian Znaniecki statement, ibid., 252.

224. The YIVO symposium, of course, was not bereft of critiques of both contemporary American sociology and American society; see the Nathan Glazer statement, ibid., 192–98, and the Daniel Bell statement, ibid., 246–48.

225. Lipset, "Jewish Sociologists," 178.

226. See, for example, J. Milton Yinger, *The Scientific Study of Religion* (New York: Macmillan, 1970).

227. Allan W. Eister, introduction in idem, ed., *Changing Perspectives in the Scientific Study of Religion* (New York: Wiley-Interscience, 1974), 5.

228. See Znaniecki statement in Lurie and Weinreich, eds., "Jewish Social Research," 252. See also John Higham, "Ethnic Pluralism in Modern American Thought," in *Send These to Me: Jews and Other Immigrants in Urban America* (New York: Atheneum, 1975), 196–230, esp. 212–18; Robert E. Park, *Race and Culture* (Glencoe, Il.: Free Press, 1950); Everett V. Stonequist, *The Marginal Man: A Study in Personality and Culture Conflict* (New York: Charles Scribner's Sons, 1937); and Frederick Thrasher, *The Gang: A Study of 1,313 Gangs in Chicago* (Chicago: University of Chicago Press, 1927). Louis I. Wirth's *The Ghetto* was devoted to the Jewish ghettos of Europe and America. Sklare criticized its outlook: "The closing pages of *The Ghetto* make clear Wirth's belief that the Jewish community was an anachronism whose life had been artificially prolonged by Gentile prejudice, and he came to look upon the Jews as a dead—rather than a living people" (see the introduction in Marshall Sklare, ed., *The Jews: Social Patterns of an American Group* [New York: Free Press, 1958], 15).

229. See Gordon Allport, *The Nature of Prejudice* (Cambridge: Addison-Wellesley, 1954): Isaque Graber and Stuart H. Britt, eds., *Jews in a Gentile World* (New York: Macmillan, 1942); Higham, "Ethnic Pluralism," 218–23; and Kurt Lewin, "Self-Hatred Among Jews," *Contemporary Jewish Record* 4 (June, 1941), 219–32. For the comments of a "sympathetic Gentile" on "defense" research, see Robert M. MacIver, *As a Tale That Is Told: The Autobiography of R. M. MacIver* (Chicago: University of Chicago Press, 1968), 180–82.

230. Higham, "Ethnic Pluralism," 223–25; William L. Warner and Leo Srole, *The Social Systems of American Ethnic Groups* (New Haven: Yale University Press, 1945).

231. Higham, "Ethnic Pluralism," 226.

232. Abraham G. Duker, "Historical and Sociological Factors in Jewish Communal Leadership," *Jewish Social Studies* 17 (July, 1955), 190.

233. But even a strong communal commitment did not guarantee sustained scholarship. See the introduction in Sklare, *The Jews*, esp. 8–10, and idem, "Assimilation and the Sociologists," *Commentary* 39 (May, 1965), 63–67. "The balance between ethnocentrism on the one hand and self-hatred on the other remains a particularly delicate one for the social scientist of today who rejects assimilation and wishes in some way to reaffirm his Jewishness" (Sklare, *The Jews*, 19).

234. In 1974, Sklare published a new anthology, *The Jews in American Society* (New York: Behrman House, 1974).

235. Wirth, *The Ghetto*, passim.

236. T. W. Adorno et al., *The Authoritarian Personality* (New York: Harper, 1950). See also Melvin M. Tumin, *An Inventory and Appraisal of Research on American Anti-Semitism* (New York: Freedom Books, 1961).

237. Judith R. Kramer and Seymour Leventman, *Children of the Gilded Ghetto: Conflict Resolutions of Three Generations of American Jews* (New Haven: Yale University Press, 1961).

238. Marshall Sklare, "The Problem of Contemporary Jewish Studies," *Midstream* 16 (April, 1970), 35. See also idem, "Problems in the Teaching of Contemporary Jewish Studies," *American Jewish Historical Quarterly* 63 (June, 1974), 361–68. On Sklare's work, see "The Sociology of Marshall Sklare: Special Issue," *Contemporary Jewry* (Fall/Winter, 1978), 3–45.

239. Leon A. Jick review of Samuel C. Heilman, *Synagogue Life: A Study in Symbolic Interaction* (Chicago: University of Chicago Press, 1976) in *American Jewish History* 67 (June, 1978), 380–81.

240. Joshua Fishman, "American Jewry as a Field of Social Science Research," *YIVO Annual of Jewish Social Science* 12 (1958/1959), 92. Things will get worse, wrote Jewish Theological Seminary Chancellor Louis Finkelstein, "if these studies in modern Judaism are left to people who are entirely divorced from the past. . . . [We should], in cooperation with some social scientist, build up here a Research Department in present day conditions in Judaism" (see Finkelstein to Ginzberg [undated fragment, ca. 1945], Ginzberg Archives, JTS, "Finkelstein, Dr. L. G." file).

241. See Daniel J. Elazar, "The Place of Jewish Political Studies on the Campus," *American Jewish Historical Quarterly* 63 (June, 1974), 334–39. The article was part of a symposium on contemporary Jewish studies.

242. Calvin Goldscheider and Alan S. Zuckerman, "Contemporary Jewish Studies in the Social Sciences: Analytic Themes and Doctoral Studies," in Neusner, ed., *New Humanities and Academic Disciplines*.

243. Moshe Davis, "From the Vantage of Jerusalem," *American Jewish Historical Quarterly* 63 (June, 1974), 315.

244. "The subjects selected should be pulsed by the nerve-centers of community and society. . . . The study of contemporary Jewry is a bridge of relevance to the Jewish people and its tradition in their totality" (ibid., 316).

245. Geoffrey Hawthorn, *Enlightenment and Despair: A History of Sociology* (Cambridge: Cambridge University Press, 1976), 257.

246. Walter Jackson Bate, "The Crisis in English Studies," *Harvard Magazine* (September/October, 1982), 46, 49, 51, 49–50.

247. Veysey, "Intellectual History and the New Social History," 20, 22, 23.

248. Jacques Barzun, *Clio and the Doctors: Psycho-history, Quanto-history and History* (Chicago: University of Chicago Press, 1974).

249. Robert Kelley, "The History the Masses Learn, and Historians Ignore," *Reviews in American History* 8 (September, 1980), 301.

250. Merle Curti, "The Setting and the Problems," in his *American Scholarship*, 31.

251. Kelley, "History," 302.

252. Fox, ed., *A Quarter Century*, is of this genre.

253. Henrika Kuklick used the term in this connection in "Restructuring the Past: Toward an Appreciation of the Social Context of Social Science," *The Sociological Quarterly* 21 (Winter, 1980), 5–21.

254. Ibid., 8–9.

255. The issue of linearity in disciplinary progress related closely to the challenge to the distinction between the "context of discovery" and the "context of justification" that tried to resolve pulls between advocacy and objectivity. Some scholars argued that the scholarly obligation to employ universalistic criteria in the use of evidence did not extend to the choice of subject. But Thomas Kuhn, other historians of the disciplines, and New Left critics suggested that methods of validation might be subject to the same social pressures that motivated the choice of topic. See Robert S. Lynd, *Knowledge for What? The Place of Social Science in American Culture* (Princeton: Princeton Univeristy Press, 1939), 183–84.

256. Carl Bridenbaugh, "The Great Mutation," *American Historical Review* 68 (January, 1963), 316.

257. Robert Nisbet, *The Degradation of the Academic Dogma: The University in America 1945–1970* (New York: Basic Books, 1971), and Everett C. Ladd and Seymour Lipset, *The Divided Academy: Professors and Politics* (New York: McGraw Hill, 1975), esp. chapter 7.

258. Marvin Fox, "Philosophy and Contemporary Jewish Studies," *American Jewish Historical Quarterly* 63 (June, 1974), 350–55.

259. Howard Schwartz, "Modern Jewish Literature and the Ancient Models," *Midstream* 29 (January, 1983), 49–52.

260. Bridenbaugh, "The Great Mutation," 322–23.

261. "At our own Annual Meetings we make room on the program for railroad history—in a year or so I anticipate further fragmentation with a program on the history of the narrow gauge and then one on the air brake" (ibid., 325). Robert Fogel would soon publish his seminal work on railroads in American economic history (*Railroads and American Economic Growth: Essays in Econometric History* [Baltimore: Johns Hopkins University Press, 1964]).

262. Ira Robinson, "American Academy for Jewish Research (AAJR)," in Dobkowski, ed., *Jewish–American Voluntary Organizations*, 10. See also Salo W. Baron and Isaac E. Barzilay, eds., *American Academy for Jewish Research Jubilee Volume* (Jerusalem: American Academy for Jewish Research, 1980), esp. preface.

263. "Association for Jewish Studies (AJS)," in Dobkowski, ed., *Jewish–American Voluntary Organizations*, 75.

264. Joseph L. Blau, "A Proposal for a Professional Association," in Jick, ed., *Teaching of Judaica in American Universities*, 91.

265. Band then distinguished "Jewish" from "Judaic" studies, "which implied a reified entity . . . a structure of ideas and movements abstracted from the living experience of the people who embodied them" (*AJS Newsletter* 1 (1) [May, 1970], 1–2, quotation from 2).

266. See William A. Frankena, ed., *The Philosophy of Graduate Education* (Ann Arbor: University of Michigan Press, 1978).

9. Growth and Survival

1. Even in the "golden age," perceptions may have been deceiving. American Oriental Society membership grew by 129 percent between 1890 and 1920, for example, but Modern Language Association rolls grew by 423 percent, and American Historical Association membership grew by 232 percent. See Veysey, *Emergence of the American University*, 70–71.

2. This sample was drawn from a stratified random sample first employed in James A. Davis, *Great Aspirations: The Graduate School Plans of America's College Seniors*

(Chicago: Aldine, 1964), appendix 5. The Davis sample included 135 institutions that offered the bachelor's degree in 1961, but we excluded 14 institutions that did not offer a full liberal arts course—engineering schools, for example—or for which full information was unavailable. Student characteristics discussed later in this chapter were taken from the responses of individual students by institution, as recorded in the raw data of the Davis study. Institutional characteristics, also discussed below, were taken from Otis A. Single-tary, ed., *American Colleges and Universities,* 10th ed. (Washington, D.C.: American Council on Education, 1968).

3. The results: 1923, 0; 1926, 1; 1929, 3; 1932, 4. We also calculated the growth pattern for courses open to undergraduates, including graduate courses, and found the same growth pattern, explained below. The use of college catalogues assumes that discrepancies between catalogue announcements and reality of course offerings are random, that is, that universities and colleges were not significantly more likely to inflate (or deflate) the number of offerings in 1968 than in 1923 or 1938.

4. On logistic curves and their theoretical meaning, see Michael T. Hannan and John Freeman, *Organizational Ecology* (Cambridge: Harvard University Press, 1989), chapter 5, esp. 100. Logistic growth, Diana Crane notes, occurs in several stages:

(1) a preliminary period of growth in which the absolute increments are small although the rate of increase is large but steadily decreases; (2) a period of exponential growth when the number of publications in a field doubles at regular intervals as a result of a constant rate of growth that produces increasing amounts of absolute growth; (3) a period when the rate of growth declines but the annual increases remain approximately constant; and (4) a final period when both the rate of increase and the absolute increase decline and eventually approach zero.

Crane used the number of scholarly publications to measure logistic growth, but the pattern remained essentially the same when professional manpower or number of course offerings was substituted (see Diana Crane, *Invisible Colleges: Diffusion of Knowledge in Scientific Communities* [Chicago: University of Chicago Press, 1972], 2).

5. The mathematical form of logistic growth is represented by the equation:

$$\frac{dx}{dt} = kx(N\text{-}x)$$

where $\frac{dx}{dt}$ represents the change in x with respect to time (t), where k represents the growth constant, x the number of units that already exist, and N the maximum size.

6. *Exponential growth* best describes this pattern. Graphically, exponential growth is described by an arc whose increasing magnitude is a function of an exponent of the original number of institutions, not a function of the occurrence of external events. The curve shifts gradually from the horizontal axis toward the vertical axis but never arrives at that axis. Exponential growth represents a constant rate of growth. Logistic growth begins with an exponential phase but flattens out as the rate of growth declines.

7. Expressed mathematically, $2^0=1$, $2^1=2$, and $2^2=4$ institutions adopted Judaica after one, two, and three constant time intervals, and so on. For a description and analysis of this process, see Crane, *Invisible Colleges,* 22–84. Crane employs the term "contagion" to explain how early adopters of an innovation influence others to consider it.

8. The growth pattern was endogenous, but substantial university-based growth in Jewish learning occurred after the appearance and entrenchment of other fields. This "lag" led some practitioners to make ahistorical comparisons between other disciplines and Jewish learning, often to the detriment of the latter.

9. Derek J. de Solla Price, *Little Science, Big Science* (New York: Columbia University Press, 1963), 23–32. See also idem, *Science Since Babylon* (New Haven: Yale University Press, 1961).

10. Gerson Cohen, "An Embarrassment of Riches: Reflections on the Condition of American Jewish Scholarship in 1969," in Jick, ed., *Teaching of Judaica in American Universities.*

11. Harvard University, *Annual Reports of the President and Treasurer of Harvard College, 1897–1898,* 28.

12. Ibid., *1905–1906,* 10, 11.

13. University of California, *Biennial Report of the President of this University on Behalf of the Regents to His Excellency the Governor of the State, 1902–1904,* 45.

14. Ibid, *1898–1900,* 33; *1905–1906,* 210.

15. We have restricted our analysis to factors for which we have precise information for 1896 and 1968. We have accurate information on the number of Jewish students for each campus in 1968 that shows that the absolute number of Jewish students and enrollment rates are associated with the presence of Jewish learning on the campus. Interviews with Judaica professors suggest that at least three-fourths of their students, mainly undergraduates, were Jewish. We do not have unambiguous enrollment information for 1896, but for several years, Johns Hopkins published the names of students enrolled in each course. Using onomastic criteria, we estimate that less than half of the students registering in Judaica courses were Jewish. See, for example, *Johns Hopkins University Circulars* 8, no. 71 (March, 1889), 53, and ibid., 9, no. 83 (November, 1890), 18.

The "universalism" and classicism of the earlier period made Judaica attractive to a higher proportion of non-Jewish students. Enrollments became increasingly dependent on the presence of Jewish students as the growing field shifted to a more particularist orientation. Ross similarly found that the rate of non-white enrollment predicted the emergence of departments of ethnic and urban studies but did not predict other curricular innovations, e.g., biophysics, computer science, linguistics, and environmental studies. This finding is consistent with the explanation that non-white (presumably black) students were the major constituency for black studies courses. See R. Danforth Ross, "The Institutionalization of Academic Innovations: Two Models," *Sociology of Education* 49 (April, 1976), 146–55.

16. See Joseph Ben-David, "The University and the Growth of Science in Germany and the United States," *Minerva* 7 (1968–1969), 1–35, esp. 20–21 (source of quotation); Warren O. Hagstrom, "Inputs and Outputs and the Prestige of University Science Departments," *Sociology of Education* 44 (Fall, 1971), 375–97; idem, *The Scientific Community* (New York: Basic Books, 1965), 202; and Peter M. Blau, *The Organization of Academic Work* (New York: Wiley, 1973), 200.

17. Jencks and Riesman, *Academic Revolution,* 232–33.

18. "The weight of tradition in older universities dampens the innovative spirit," argues sociologist Peter Blau. But our data shows that institutional age facilitated, rather than inhibited, the introduction of Judaica. In 1898 and 1968, Judaica institutions were older than their non-Judaica counterparts. Newer institutions are more likely to emphasize applied subjects (see Blau, *Organization of Academic Work,* 206).

19. The vocationalization trend is controversial. See, for example Steven Brint and Jerome Karabel, *The Diverted Dream: Community Colleges and the Promise of Educational Opportunity in America, 1900–1985* (New York: Oxford University Press, 1989); Arthur Cohen and Florence B. Brawer, *The Collegiate Function of Community Colleges: Fostering Higher Learning Through Curriculum and Student Transfer* (San Francisco: Jossey-Bass, 1987); and L. Steven Zwerling, *Second Best: The Crisis of the Community College* (New York: McGraw–Hill Book Company, 1976). See also Harold S. Wechsler, *The Transfer Challenge: Removing Barriers; Maintaining Commitment: A Handbook for Four-Year Colleges* (Washington, D.C.: Association of American Colleges, 1989), and idem, review of *Diverted Dream* in *Science* 250 (December 21, 1990), 1755–56.

20. Spertus College of Judaica in Chicago served as the Jewish studies department for a consortium of about 20 local colleges including two- and four-year public colleges, church-related institutions, and small, private liberal arts institutions that probably would not otherwise have had access to this field. See Sherwin, *Contexts and Content,* passim.

21. The survey asked: "In what fields, in order of priority, would you consider it most desirable to make replacements or additional faculty appointments in the next three years?" Of the 39 "priority" respondents (out of 411 chairs), nine gave Judaica first priority, 14 gave it second priority, and 16 gave it third priority; 354 gave the subject no priority at all. See Welch, *Graduate Education in Religion*, and idem, *Religion in the Undergraduate Curriculum*, passim.

22. See Blau, *Organization of Academic Work*, 198, and Ross, "Institutionalization of Academic Innovations: Two Models," passim.

23. The distribution of Sinology courses is a positive function of the size of the undergraduate student body, the ratio of graduate students to total enrollment, and library size: $R = .33$; partial correlation controlling for rate of graduate enrollment = .14. Unlike Judaica, however, institutional age has no effect on Chinese studies.

24. See H. P. Judson to J. M. P. Smith, October 6, 1911, University Presidents' Papers, UCSC, and Richard Gottheil and A. V. W. Jackson to Nicholas Murray Butler, March 29, 1902, CUF, "Richard Gottheil" file. See also Anderson, "Oriental Languages and Literatures," 234–38.

25. Hagstrom, *Scientific Community*, 202.

26. Blau, *Organization of Academic Work*, 206.

27. Joseph Ben-David, *Centers of Learning: Britain, France, Germany, United States* (New York: McGraw-Hill, 1977), 180–81.

28. Ibid., passim, especially chapter 8.

29. Ibid., 182.

30. Indeed, the Association for Jewish Studies devoted considerable attention to the issue. Several newsletter articles questioned whether enough qualified instructors were available to fill an increasing demand; local rabbis with *smichot* (ordination degrees), but no advanced scholarly degrees, were the main target of such attacks. These rabbis would likely adopt an unabashedly communal posture while posing as "jacks-of-all-trades," thereby denying posts to university-educated specialists and assuring a diminution of the field's rate of scholarly productivity. By decade's end, the transitory nature of the supply shortage became apparent; with a slowdown in growth, the field again confronted a surplus of unemployed or underemployed practitioners. Increased supply did not universally force out the rabbinical contingent; indeed, the field continued to display a disproportionate number of part-time instructors. See Arnold J. Band, "AJS Survey of the Field of Jewish Studies," *Association for Jewish Studies Newsletter* 24 (March, 1979).

31. Ben-David, *Centers of Learning*, 174–75.

32. Milton R. Konvitz, *The Jewish Intellectual, The University and the Jewish Community* (Washington, D.C.: B'nai B'rith Hillel Foundations, 1964), 11.

33. Irving Greenberg, "Scholarship and Continuity: Dilemma and Dialectic," in Jick, ed., *Teaching of Judaica in American Universities*, 117.

34. Ibid., 117, 118.

35. Sklare, "The Problem of Contemporary Jewish Studies," in ibid., 68, 69, 65.

36. See Moshe Davis, *University Teaching of Jewish Civilization: Summary of a Policy Report* (Jerusalem: n.p., 1981), 9–10. See also Kenneth A. Feldman and Theodore M. Newcomb, *The Impact of College on Students: An Analysis of Four Decades of Research* (San Francisco: Jossey-Bass, 1973), 1:8–10, 23–28; Alexander W. Astin, *Four Critical Years: Effects of College on Beliefs, Attitudes, and Knowledge* (San Francisco: Jossey-Bass, 1977), 57–59, 67–71, 78–79, 219; and Howard W. Bowen, *Investment in Learning: The Individual and Social Value of American Higher Education* (San Francisco: Jossey-Bass, 1977), 125–31. Dissimilar institutions had different effects on religiosity, and large standard deviations could be associated with these trends (ibid., 251–52).

37. Band, "Jewish Studies," 27.

38. See David Singer, "Profile of the Jewish Academic: Some Recent Studies," *Midstream* 19 (June/July, 1973), 57–64, and Marshall Sklare, *America's Jews* (New York: Random House, 1971), 68.

39. Jick, "Tasks for a Community of Concern," in Jick, ed., *Teaching of Judaica in American Universities*, 84.

40. "Association for Jewish Studies (AJS)," in Dobkowski, ed., *Jewish-American Voluntary Organizations*, 74.

41. Cohen, "Embarrassment of Riches," 141.

42. Ibid., 146.

43. Ibid., 147.

44. Ibid., 145–46. Elbogen feared the positive attractions of parent disciplines, but Cohen saw departments as a refuge: "We have thus tacitly resigned ourselves to teaching those elements of Jewish history and expression that interest *us* as scholars rather than what we have, after careful and prolonged consideration, concluded is relevant to, and vital for, the needs of our student constituencies" (ibid., 146).

45. Ibid., 148. Nahum N. Glatzer, professor of Jewish history and social ethics at Brandeis, concurred but in even stronger terms. We discourage applicants, he wrote, "who state that they wish to find themselves or those who are in search of their identity. Though we sympathize with such objectives we are quite busy working with students who are ready to find other things than themselves" (see Nahum N. Glatzer, "Jewish Studies: Past and Present," in *Jewish Studies: History and Perspectives, A Colloquium Presented at the Dedication of the Philip W. Lown School For Near Eastern and Judaic Studies* (Waltham, Mass.: Brandeis University, 1972), 2.

46. Cohen, "Embarrassment of Riches," 149.

47. Baruch A. Levine, "Issues and Perspectives in Jewish Studies" in *Jewish Studies: History and Perspectives*, 4.

48. "Is Jewish studies a *Wissenschaft* in the sense of a particular discipline employing its own conceptual tools?" asked Michael Meyer. "A moment's reflection reveals that it is not. Ismar Elbogen recognized this clearly sixty years ago when he wrote, 'The peculiarity of our discipline lies only in its substance, not in the method or mode of thinking of the scholars.' Jewish studies is in fact a congeries of many disciplines: philosophy, history, literary analysis, sociology—to name only some. Its distinctiveness is not of form but of content. Formally it has no unity or integrity" (see Michael A. Meyer, "Toward a Definition of Jewish Studies," *Association for Jewish Studies Newsletter* 24 [March, 1979], 2).

49. This was a widespread concern. "Nor is it clear," stated a report on the future of the study of education at Harvard,

> that the departments would welcome the newer responsibilities that such an arrangement [departmental absorption of relevant educational topics] would envisage for them quite apart from the question whether they are equipped to discharge these responsibilities effectively. It is unlikely that even the natural applications of the scholarly and research disciplines to education would be adequately fostered by the departments alone, much less that methods courses for teachers would be seriously undertaken; it is, in our opinion, fantastic to imagine that abolition of the School would diffuse educational interest throughout the University.

(See Committee on the Graduate Study of Education, Harvard School of Education, *The Graduate Study of Education: Report of the Harvard Committee* [Cambridge: Harvard University Press, 1966], 9).

50. Neusner, "Modes of Jewish Studies in the University," 109–10.

51. Ibid., 97.

52. Neusner, "Jewish Studies in the University," in *Academic Study of Judaism*, 1:18–27, quotation from "Comment," 25. These theories included his own early formulations.

53. Neusner, "Modes of Jewish Studies in the University," 104.

54. Ibid., 99–100, and "Problematic of 'Jewish History' as an Academic Field," passim.

55. Neusner, "Modes of Jewish Studies in the University," 100.

56. Neusner, "The New Setting for Jewish Learning: Towards A Theory of University Studies in Judaism" in *Academic Study of Judaism*, 2:35–48, quotation from 46.

57. Neusner, "Two Settings for Jewish Studies," in *Academic Study of Judaism*, 1:49–68, esp. 52, and idem, "New Setting for Jewish Learning," 44. Recall Zunz's polemic against *rachmones* and *aufklärung* and *chilluk* quoted in chapter 1.

58. Thorstein Veblen, *The Higher Learning in America,* passim. In *The Academic Revolution*, David Riesman and Christopher Jencks posited and decried the opposite trend—the infusion of research norms in professional schools, small four-year colleges, and community colleges where other norms should dominate. On the link between Veblen and Riesman, see Harold S. Wechsler, "Robert Maynard Hutchins and David Riesman," in John McAloon, ed., *General Education and the Social Sciences: Centennial Reflections on the College of the University of Chicago* (Chicago: University of Chicago Press, 1992), 217–22.

59. Charles Wegener, *Liberal Education and the Modern University* (Chicago: University of Chicago Press, 1978), 69.

60. Jacob Neusner, "To the Class of 1976," in *Academic Study of Judaism*, 1:166–72, quotation from 171.

61. Neusner, "New Setting for Jewish Learning," 41.

62. See, for example, Nathan Glazer, *American Judaism*, 2nd ed. (Chicago: University of Chicago Press, 1972), 151–86.

63. Neusner, "New Setting for Jewish Learning," 48.

64. "In my four years as instructor and assistant professor [at Columbia]," wrote Alvin Johnson, "my two outstanding students were Carlton J. Hayes, Catholic, and Meyer Jacobstein, Jew. They promised great things in scholarship, equally. Carlton Hayes went straight up, to the rank of a foremost historian. Meyer Jacobstein, after threshing the country over, got a position as instructor in the remote University of North Dakota." (See Alvin S. Johnson, autobiography, in Finkelstein, ed., *American Spiritual Autobiographies*, 46).

65. The scholarship on the early history of the social sciences has increased rapidly in recent years. Much of it recounted, first, the replacement of amateur by professional scholars in various fields and then "professional" disengagement with associated constituencies. Some studies accepted the concept of "objectivity" more or less at face value, but other historians argued that it masked the substitution of a concern for preserving the status quo with a concern for social reform. See especially Furner, *Advocacy and Objectivity*, and Haskell, *Emergence*.

66. "The university's invisible product, knowledge, may be the most powerful single element in our culture, affecting the rise and fall of professions and even of social classes, of regions and even of nations" (see Clark Kerr, *The Uses of the University*, 3rd ed. [Cambridge: Harvard University Press, 1982], viii).

67. Modern Hebrew, having started as a high school, not a graduate level subject, always confronted questions of practitioner quality. These questions were exacerbated when colleges began to recruit Israelis to teach Hebrew because of their fluency.

68. "*The Encyclopedia of Religion* [Mircea Eliade, ed., 15 vols. (New York: Macmillan, 1987)] is resounding evidence that the field of Jewish studies is at last not only in the university but of it," wrote Jewish Theological Seminary Chancellor Ismar Schorsch in 1987. "The subject is no longer a structural appendage, the product of enlightened Jewish donors in an age of affluence and the insatiable academic need for fresh funds. It has finally been woven into the very fabric of American scholarship because of the inherent human value of the Jewish experience. Admission into the university has gradually culminated in scholarly acceptance" (Ismar Schorsch, "The Place of Jewish Studies in Contemporary Scholarship," in Shaye J. D. Cohen and Edward L. Greenstein, eds., *The State of Jewish Studies* [Detroit: Wayne State University Press, 1990], 16–20, quotation from 19).

69. Compare: "We do not have the trained academic personnel to fill all the positions which have been created. Concomitantly, since other academic fields are over-crowded and the daily chores of the rabbinate are often trying, we discover more and more candidates for positions whose qualifications are questionable" (editorial, "Who is a Judaics Scholar?" *Association for Jewish Studies Newsletter* 11 [June, 1974], 1–2); and "we must admit that our calls for curtailed production were issued too late to be useful, even if they were to be heeded. We should have limited admission to graduate programs drastically as early as 1969, when the first signs of a deteriorating academic market were becoming evident" (Band, "AJS Survey," 35).

70. See Dora Askowith, "The Role of Women in the Field of Higher Jewish Education, 1922–1956," *Judaism* 5 (1965), 167–72, and Shulamit Magnus, "'Out of the Ghetto': Integrating the Study of Jewish Women into the Study of the Jews," *Judaism* 39 (Winter, 1990), 28–36.

71. The AJS list of graduate schools attended by ten or more members included Columbia 91, Brandeis 88, Harvard 48, New York University 34, J.T.S. 32, H.U.C.–Cincinnati 30, Pennsylvania 24, UCLA 23, Dropsie 23, Yeshiva 18, Brown 17, Berkeley 16, Chicago 12, Temple 12, U.S.C. 12, and Ohio State University 11.

72. Jewish philosophy—11 percent, Jewish religion—10 percent, Hebrew literature—9 percent, Hebrew language—6 percent, and Jewish sociology—5 percent held the intermediate places. Subfield terminology is that of the survey. The reported specialization may differ from courses actually taught. Historians, Bible scholars, and others, for example, often taught Hebrew courses to undergraduates as a service obligation. See chapter 8, table 1.

73. The AJS survey showed that 37 percent of the respondents attended a rabbinical seminary and 17 percent attended a Hebrew college (some may have attended both).

74. Mordecai Kaplan Diary, JTS, September 20, 23, 1928.

75. See Nathan Isaacs, "Study as a Mode of Worship," in Leo Jung, ed., *The Jewish Library*, First Series (New York: Bloch, 1943 [1928]), 57–77.

76. Mordecai Kaplan Diary, JTS, June 23, 1936.

77. See also Ginzberg, *Keeper of the Law*, 82.

78. Historian Laurence Veysey, in contrast, viewed academic life as increasingly denoting "undesirable visions of technicality, routinization, and, above all, divorce of job from self." Thus viewing work for external agencies as deleterious, Veysey suggested that some academics did not "wish to offer themselves to particular clients (whether individuals or agencies)." See Laurence Veysey, "Who's a Professional? Who Cares?" *Reviews in American History* 3 (December, 1975), 420. Veysey viewed the university as a peripheral social institution and denounced the "academic imperialism of the early 1960s, which hailed the university as the central institution of the emerging society and trumpeted the dominance of the academically trained elite of professional experts in American life." See Laurence Veysey, "A Postmortum on Daniel Bell's Postindustrialism," *American Quarterly* 34 (Spring, 1982), 51 and Bell's reply, "Mr. Veysey's Strabismus," 82–87. Veysey's *The Emergence of the American University* did not systematically discuss the incorporation of professional education into the university, an area that might have provided important analogies.

79. Moshe Davis, "Jewish Studies in Universities: Alternate Approaches in Different Parts of the World," *Publication Series: Allan Lazaroff Chair of Jewish Education in the Diaspora* (Jerusalem: Institute of Contemporary Jewry, The Hebrew University, 1974), 8. Such progress posed problems for those writing from an Israeli perspective since Zionist thinking assigned to Israel cultural as well as political centrality for world Jewry. The resolutions offered—that Israeli-based Jewish learning serve as a repository (Israel holds considerable book and manuscript collections) or perform a propaedeutic and perhaps a spiritual function (providing commitment to the scholar who in America adheres to universalist norms)—all begged the central issue: that Israel could not exercise a monopoly,

indeed even dominance, over university-based Jewish learning. See Davis, *University Teaching,* 17–18; A. J. Band, "Editorial," *Association for Jewish Studies Newsletter* 25 (September, 1979), 1; William W. Orbach, "American Jewish Studies—Babylonia or Alexandria?" *Forum* 37 (Spring, 1980), 25–36, esp. 33–35; and Meyer, "Toward a Definition," 2–3.

80. See Meyer, *Response to Modernity,* 75–77. Other synthetic articles and books include: Cohen and Greenstein, eds., *State of Jewish Studies;* Davis, "Jewish Studies in Universities"; Robert Gordis, ed., "Jewish Studies in the University," *Judaism* 35 (Spring, 1986), 134–97; Orbach, "American Jewish Studies," passim; and Silver, "Higher Jewish Learning."

81. Meyer, "Toward a Definition of Jewish Studies," 2; Orbach, "American Jewish Studies," 27–29; Abba, "Athens and Jerusalem," 355–74; and Welch, *Graduate Education in Religion,* passim.

INDEX

Abbott, Ezra, 68
Adler, Cyrus: academic cooperation and, 147;
on alternatives to universities for Jewish
scholarship, 130–31, 144; and American
Jewish Historical Society, 133; and American
Oriental Society, 79; on Antonius, 94; appointment to assistantship at Johns Hopkins,
70–71; on communal and academic norms
of scholarship, 48; on continuity in Semitic
studies, 11; on Emil Hirsch, 67; and Jewish
Publication Society, 132, 137–39; on Margolis, 62; on presidential leadership and Semitic studies, 31–32; on J.P.S. translation of
Bible, 137–39; on study of Jewish history,
129; and Wolfson, 286n.88
Adler, Felix, 45–46, 47, 50, 52
Adler, Samuel, 45, 54
admissions, university: discrimination against
Jewish applicants, xi, 74, 99–100, 114,
281n.10
AJS Review, 214–15
Albeck, Chanoch, 161
Albright, William F., 59, 72, 94, 272n.164
Alexander Kohut Publication Fund, 302n.120
American Academy for Jewish Research, 138,
139, 144, 214, 292n.11, 294n.24
American Jewish Committee, 205
American Jewish Historical Society, 88,
132–34, 166, 296n.42, 297n.54
*American Journal of Semitic Languages and
Literatures, The,* 25, 65
American Oriental Society, 43, 78–79, 190,
258n.143
American Philological Association, 258n.143
Amherst College, 21
Andover Seminary, 13–14, 68, 69, 106
Andrews, E. Benjamin, 24
anti-Semitism: anti-Zionism and,
302–303n.126; Gottheil and, 87, 89;
growth of in universities in twentieth century, 75, 85–86; and Jewish scholarship in
prewar period, xi, 52; social research on,
205; and study of Jewish history, 128–29;
and Wolfson's scholarship at Harvard,
113, 121
Antonius, George, 91–95, 278n.82, 279n.95
Arabic language, study of, 40, 257n.121
archaeology, in Near East, 59, 81–85, 104
Aristotle, 110
assimilationism, x, 202–203, 206–207
Association of American Universities (AAU),
16, 186, 222

Association for Jewish Studies, 214–15,
232–33, 234, 334n.30
Assyriologische Bibliothek, 69–70
Atran, Frank, 188

Balfour Declaration, 90, 145
Band, Arnold, 185–86, 192, 215, 227,
238n.8, 241n.36, 318n.81, 319n.89
Barnard, Frederick A. P., 31
Baron, Salo, xiv, 11, 145, 164–71, 176–77,
196
Barth, Karl, 192
Barton, George, 271n.163
Barzun, Jacques, 211
*Beiträge zur Assyriologie und Semitischen
Sprachwissenschaft,* 69–70
Bell, Daniel, 323n.145
Ben-David, Joseph, 81, 222–23, 225
Ben Yehuda, Eliezer, 180
Bewer, Julius A., 157–58
Bezold, Carl, 83
Bible: publication of new translation by Jewish
Publication Society, 136–37, 298n.82;
scholarship in postwar period, 199–201;
study of Biblical criticism, 13–14, 38, 68,
255n.106
Birnbaum, Norman, 322n.137
Blondheim, David S., 162–63, 169, 267n.124
Boeckh, August, 40
Bomberg, Daniel, 3
Brainin, Reuben, 285–86n.75
Branscomb, Harvie, 128
Braunstein, Baruch, 301n.112
Brennan, William, 193
Breslau seminary, 36–37, 313n.13
Bridenbaugh, Carl, 213
Briggs, Charles Augustus, 21
Brown, Francis, 70, 259–60n.22
Brown, Jerry W., 14
Bryn Mawr College, 245n.72
Buber, Martin, 8
Burgess, John, 87
Bush, George, 13
Butler, Nicholas Murray, 18, 31, 87, 92,
93–94, 94–95, 152–53, 155–56, 162
Buxtorf, Johannes, 4

Cassuto, Umberto, 158
Cattell, James McKeen, 54
Chamberlain, Houston S., 7
Chauncey, Henry, 11
Choate, Joseph H., 29

PAUL RITTERBAND is Professor of Jewish Studies and Sociology at the City College and Graduate School, City University of New York. He is author of *Education, Employment, and Migration: Israel in Comparative Perspective*, the editor of books dealing with Jewish philanthropy and Jewish fertility, and has published numerous articles on the sociology of ethnicity and religion. He is currently engaged in a study of New York's Jewish population and geography, *People and Places*.

HAROLD S. WECHSLER is Associate Professor in the Margaret S. Warner Graduate School of Education and Human Development at the University of Rochester. The author of *The Qualified Student: A History of Selective College Admission in America* and coauthor of *The New Look: The Ford Foundation and the Revolution in Business Education*, he is currently studying the history of efforts to reduce prejudice against minority students on American college campuses. He serves on the Academic Council of the American Jewish Historical Society.